# Contemporary Issues
## in Higher Education Law

D0324855

**Editors**
Joseph Beckham
David Dagley

EDUCATION LAW ASSOCIATION
DAYTON, OHIO

# Disclaimer

The Education Law Association (ELA) is a private, nonadvocacy, nonprofit, international member association. The opinions expressed in this publication are those of the authors and do not represent official views of the Association.

# About the Editors

## *Joseph Beckham*

Joseph Beckham, co-editor, is Allan Tucker Professor of Educational Leadership and Policy Studies at Florida State University. He received his J.D. (1969) and Ph.D. (Educational Leadership 1977) from the University of Florida. He served as president of the National Organization on Legal Problems of Education in 1991 and was awarded the McGhehey Award for service to the fields of law and education by the Education Law Association in 1996. Dr. Beckham is currently a member of the editorial board of the Journal of Law and Education and the editorial advisory committee of West's Education Law Reporter. His vita lists over 100 publications, including books, monographs, refereed journal articles, book chapters, and invited articles dealing with higher education policy, law, finance, and administration.

## *David Dagley*

Dave Dagley is Professor of Education Law and a former department chair at the University of Alabama. He has been a classroom teacher, principal, assistant superintendent, and superintendent in the public schools. He received the Ph.D. degree from the University of Utah and the J.D. degree from the Cumberland School of Law at Samford University. He serves as legal counsel for several school districts in Alabama. He has contributed to the activities of the Education Law Association in various capacities over the years, including membership on its Board of Directors.

# Dedication

This book is dedicated to the memory of Albert S. Miles, J.D., Ph.D. Al came to the University of Alabama as Vice President for Student Affairs in 1976, after stints as Vice Chancellor at the University of California, Riverside, Vice President at Central Michigan University, and Dean of Students at Seton Hall University. Al began his teaching career in the Peace Corps, serving in Nigeria. He received his Ph.D. in Counseling and Personnel Administration from Cornell in 1969 and his law degree from the University of Alabama in 1985. He began teaching in the higher education administration program in 1984. He contributed to the activities of the Education Law Association for many years and was a friend to many of its members. He never lost the ability to be a counselor to colleagues and students, and will be greatly missed.

**Al Miles**
1940-2003

# About the Authors

*Joseph Beckham*, J.D., Ph.D., Allan Tucker Professor of Educational Leadership and Policy Studies, Department of Educational Leadership and Policy Studies, The Florida State University, Tallahassee, Florida.

*Carole de Casal*, Ed.D., Assistant Dean for Professional Education, and Professor, Department of Educational Leadership and Research, College of Education and Psychology, The University of Southern Mississippi, Hattiesburg, Mississippi.

*Brad Colwell*, J.D., Ph.D., Professor and Chairman, Department of Educational Administration and Higher Education, Southern Illinois University, Carbondale, Illinois.

*Luke Cornelius*, Ph.D., Assistant Professor of Educational Leadership and Professional Studies, Department of Educational Leadership and Professional Studies, The University of West Georgia, Carrollton, Georgia.

*David Dagley*, J.D., Ph.D., Professor of Education Law and a former department chair, The University of Alabama, Tuscaloosa, Alabama.

*Philip T.K. Daniel*, J.D., Ed.D., Professor, Educational Administration/ Higher Education, Adjunct Professor of Law, The Ohio State University, Columbus, Ohio.

*John Decman*, EdD., Assistant Professor of Educational Administration, School of Education, University of Houston - Clear Lake, Houston, Texas.

*Todd DeMitchell*, Ed.D., Professor, Department of Education and Justice Studies Program, University of New Hampshire, Durham, New Hampshire.

*Gus Douvanis*, J.D., Ed.D., Professor of Educational Leadership and Professional Studies, Department of Educational Leadership and Professional Studies, The University of West Georgia, Carrollton, Georgia.

*Suzanne Eckes*, J.D., Ph.D., Assistant Professor, Department of Educational Leadership and Policy Studies, Indiana University, Bloomington, Indiana.

*Richard Fossey*, J.D., Ed.D., Professor of Educational Leadership, Department of Educational Leadership and Cultural Studies, University of Houston, Houston, Texas.

*Ralph Mawdsley*, J.D., Ph.D., Professor of Educational Administration, Department of Counseling, Administration and Adult Learning, Cleveland State University, Cleveland, Ohio.

*Martha McCarthy*, Ph.D., Chancellor's Professor, Department of Educational Leadership and Policy Studies, Indiana University, Bloomington, Indiana.

*Kerry Brian Melear*, Ph.D., Assistant Professor of Higher Education, University of Mississippi, Oxford, Mississippi.

*Patrick Pauken*, J.D., Ph.D. Associate Professor of Educational Administration and Leadership Studies, School of Leadership and Policy Studies, Bowling Green State University, Bowling Green, Ohio.

*Nathan Roberts*, J.D., Ph.D., Mr. & Mrs. E. P. "Pat" Nalley/BORSF Endowed Professor in Education, Director of Graduate Studies in Education, The University of Louisiana at Lafayette, Lafayette, Louisiana.

*Charles Russo*, J.D., Ed.D., Panzer Chair in Education and Adjunct Professor of Law, University of Dayton, Dayton, OH.

*Stephen Thomas*, Professor and Coordinator, Educational Administration, Kent State University, Kent, Ohio.

*William Thro*, M.A., J.D., State Solicitor General of the Commonwealth of Virginia, Office of the Attorney General, Richmond, Virginia.

*R. Craig Wood*, Professor, Department of Educational Leadership, College of Education, University of Florida, Gainesville, Florida.

# Contents

## 1 Public Colleges and Universities

## 2 Private Colleges and Universities

# 3 Religious Colleges and Universities

# 4 Faculty

# 5 Non-Academic Personnel

# 6 Faculty Speech

# 7 Tort Liability

# 8 Contracts With Students

# 9 Student Speech

# 10 Student Equal Protection and Due Process

# 11 Sexual Harassment

# 12 Employment Discrimination Under Title VII

# 13 Disability Law

# 14 Intellectual Property

# 15 Business Management

# 16 Athletics

# 17 Town and Gown Issues

# Introduction

Colleges and universities remain vulnerable to lawsuits and face an increasingly litigious environment. To bolster their defenses, these institutions need the guidance of legal counsel and a comprehensive risk-management strategy that is known and understood by board members, administrators, faculty, and students. *Contemporary Issues in Higher Education Law* is intended to meet the needs of this varied constituency and to provide a basis for informed decision-making that will reduce the risk of liability through a preventive law approach.

As editors, our goal has been to provide a text that will place the emphasis on preventing crises rather than managing crises in higher education institutions. Chapter narratives integrate legal principles of contemporary relevance to college and university administrators and provide examples drawn from judicial decisions that inform the reader about the practical applications of those legal principles. The approach is intended to help college and university administrators reduce the risks of liability rather than simply resolve disputes as they arise. Chapter narratives survey the law in a particular domain, provide guidance on compliance with existing legal standards, and promote heightened sensitivity to the corporate responsibility that college and university leaders must have.

Institutional administrators will find this text to be a useful source that reflects long-standing trends in the law, details current case law on a particular subject, and provides guidance on institutional policy. However, this book is not intended to be a substitute for the informed guidance of legal counsel. Effective leadership requires a commitment to a team approach in which counsel is involved in a creative process that addresses institutional needs and strategic goals. *Contemporary Issues in Higher Education Law* should therefore be an invaluable resource for administrators and attorneys in understanding the legal risks to their offices and institutions and should also provide a source for informed collaboration on appropriate, risk-management strategies, institutional compliance audits, and policy development.

The mission of the Education Law Association is to remain "The Premier Source of Information on Education Law." *Contemporary Issues in Higher Education Law* is offered to students, scholars, and practitioners in the fields of education and law to help fulfill that promise.

# 1 Public Colleges and Universities

## Brad Colwell

## Introduction

Three distinguishable phases characterize the development of a unique relationship between higher education and state government in the United States. The first phase, extending from the colonial period through the American Revolution, may be said to have come to a close with the onset of the Civil War. This first phase in the development of American colleges and universities was marked by the creation of private, autonomous colleges, often organized by religious groups and chartered as private corporations under the laws of the state in which the institution was located.[1] A second phase began with the initiation of the Land-grant College and the evolution of state universities in the latter half of the nineteenth century. Exemplified by the development of constitutionally autonomous state universities in the Midwest and West, this second phase was characterized by the expansion of educational opportunity and the enunciation of broad, secular educational goals for public colleges and universities.[2] American higher education's third phase paralleled the expansion of state government and the trend toward centralization of state administrative functions that began in the latter half of the twentieth century. This third phase reflected the creation of state systems of public higher education; the expansion of access for minorities, women, and non-traditional students; increased dependence of public and private higher education upon state and federal financial resources; and a concomitant demand for greater accountability, particularly in the operation of newly created public higher education systems.[3]

In the modern era, each of the fifty states has a complex mix of public and private higher education institutions and a variety of governance systems. Colleges and universities may often be distinguished as public by examination of institutional mission, governance structure, and financing. Public institutions have missions that may be defined by state legislative statute or constitutional mandate, their governance is often overseen by a lay board appointed by a governor with the consent of the state legislature, and their finance system is typically more dependent on state-legislative, appropriation-funding operating expenses and capital projects. However, with fifty states and a variety of public higher education institutions within each state, diversity, rather than uniformity, characterizes public higher education in the United States.

## State Systems

State systems of higher education may be responsible for regulation of both the public and private sectors, but in most instances, these systems have either a governing or coordinating role relative to public sector institutions. These state systems may be characterized as segmented, unified, or federal.[4] Segmented systems are comprised of independent governing boards for each institution with no centralized control by a state governing board. In segmented systems, such as those found in Michigan and Delaware, institutional governing boards prevail, although voluntary associations between institutions may develop for the purpose of planning or coordination. Furthermore, there is no system-wide control applied beyond the power of the state legislature to appropriate funds for the institutions. Unified systems, such as Georgia, have a single, consolidated governing board that is responsible for the governance and control of all public higher education institutions within the state. Federal systems, such as Illinois, Texas, and Florida, include both individual institutional governing boards and a single, statewide board that provides for coordination of a variety of activities, which may include comprehensive planning, program approval, and the development of a single annual budget for the system.

## Constitutional Provisions

A constitution is the fundamental law of a country or state that establishes the character of the government and describes the function of its different departments and the rights of its citizens.[5] The United States Constitution does not specifically address education; and, consistent with the Tenth Amendment,[6] authority not expressly delegated to the federal government is reserved to the states. Consequently, states make provision for public higher education institutions either through a constitutional provision or legislative statute addressing higher education.

Some states have a constitutional provision that removes the public university or universities from legislative control and establishes a governing board as an independent body charged with the responsibility to manage and operate the higher education institution free from political influence and control.[7] For example, the state constitutions of Minnesota[8] and California[9] are among several state constitutions that confer constitutionally autonomous status on public universities, namely the University of Minnesota and the University of California. In states like California,

Georgia, Idaho, Michigan, Minnesota, Nebraska, Oklahoma, and Utah, constitutional status creates reasonable independence from state legislative, executive, or judicial interference.

As a Michigan justice stated the principle, "Regents and legislature derive their power from the same supreme authority ... a direct power conferred upon one necessarily excludes its existence in the other ..."[10] The Supreme Court of Oklahoma reinforced this legal principle when it ruled that its state's Merit Protection Commission (Commission) had no authority to hear a university employee's grievance. In holding that the legislature cannot delegate any constitutional control over higher education to any state agency or commission, the state court noted that the university's board of regents was a constitutional entity, enabled "to conduct the internal affairs of their subordinate institutions of higher learning free of any interference" by the Commission, a legislatively created agency.[11]

The authority enjoyed by Idaho's constitutionally mandated public higher education system extends to the exclusive power to employ faculty, administrators, and staff,[12] while Minnesota's governing board possesses unrestricted power over funds applied to the institution;[13] and California's university system enjoys exemption from local building and zoning codes.[14] However, even though a constitutionally autonomous university is intended to operate as independently of the state as possible, its operation is not completely free from legislative regulation,[15] particularly as to legislative appropriations and in areas of statewide concern that do not regulate matters of internal university affairs.[16] As the Supreme Court of Minnesota noted, "... At one extreme, the Legislature has no power to make effective, in the form of a law, a mere direction of academic policy or administration. At the other extreme, it has the undoubted right within reason to condition appropriations as it sees fit."[17] Yet, the Supreme Court of Nebraska cautioned against using appropriations to overtake the operation of a university when it held, "The Legislature can not use an appropriations bill to usurp the power or duties of the Board ... and to give directions to the employees of the University."[18]

## Legislative Delegation

It is the duty of the legislature to implement the constitutional provisions regarding public higher education in each state. One exercise of this legislative duty would be to enact statutes that vest the general government of the public colleges and universities in a governing body (board of trustees or board of regents).[19] Representative constitutional provisions may authorize the legislature to make provision for a governing board or boards,[20] establish board member qualifications,[21] and define the powers and duties of the board of trustees.[22]

However, while the state legislature establishes the basic organizational structure of public higher education, it is the responsibility of the designated governing board to provide for the management and administration of the institution or institutions under the board's control. For example, a New York court noted that its state's judiciary has consistently interpreted the legislature's grant of power over academic requirements and system governance as "exclusive" to the university.[23]

## Institutional Governing Boards

The power to act on behalf of the corporate status of the institution is generally vested in a governing board. Described as a "board of trustees," "board of regents," or "governing board," this corporate entity is vested with full or plenary power to govern within the scope of its constitutional or statutory powers.[24] Generally, governing boards are empowered to do everything necessary for the management, operation, and administration of the institution. This minimally includes the power to sue and be sued,[25] to contract,[26] to adopt an official seal,[27] and to make bylaws for the governance of the institution.[28]

As one federal appeals court stated, the legislative grant of general authority provides the board with "latitude and discretion in its formulation of rules and regulations and general standards of conduct."[29] However, some states restrict the power of the board and require an express delegation of legislative authority. For example, the Kansas Supreme Court emphasized that a public board receives its power from state statute and cannot act absent a delegation of express authority.[30] In another example, a Louisiana appellate court ruled that a board of trustees did not have the authority to change the name of a state college. The court reasoned, "Inasmuch as the Constitution has not given those powers … to the Board…, then those powers are vested in the Legislature."[31]

Duties of a governing board may stipulate the authority to hire and terminate employees,[32] award tenure,[33] fix the compensation of employees,[34] appoint the university president or chancellor,[35] establish rates of tuition and fees,[36] manage fiscal affairs,[37] acquire and control personal and real property of the university,[38] erect new facilities,[39] administer gifts and trusts for the institution,[40] determine courses of instruction,[41] establish admission standards,[42] set graduation requirements,[43] develop an institutional mission statement,[44] or confer academic (and honorary) degrees.[45]

In some instances, even in the absence of a governing board's express authority to act under constitutional or statutory mandate, a court will presume inherent authority in the board. Inherent authority applies when an institution has no express authority to act, but it would be illogical given the nature of the board's corporate authority for it to be powerless to act. Examples of inherent authority include a governing board's right to revoke a degree obtained by student fraud[46] and to maintain order and discipline students.[47] For instance, a Texas appellate court, while reviewing state law regarding a university's inherent authority, stated that the law implies the power to act "to maintain proper order and decorum on the premises."[48]

## Fiduciary Responsibility

To instill public confidence in the integrity of government, public officials are expected to be independent and impartial in their decision-making. Members of a governing board have a legal obligation to act in the best interest of the institution they represent. In meeting their fiduciary responsibility, a board member has to perform his or her duties in good faith; with the care an ordinarily prudent person in a like position would exercise under similar circumstances; and in a manner that is reasonably related to the best interests of the institution's mission and objectives. As one New York court suggested, a member of a governing board must act in a way that is consistent with the central goals of the university.[49] Failure to do so could result in legal consequences for the board member who fails to act in a manner consistent with their official obligations.[50] The consequences for a breach of fiduciary duty may include voiding the act that was associated with the breach, criminal or civil liability for the breach, and/or a member's removal from the board.

Part of a board member's fiduciary responsibility is to ensure he or she avoids a conflict of interest between private interests and public duties as a trustee.[51] A principal threat to a board member's fiduciary obligation is self-dealing.[52] For example, several states make it unlawful for a board member to have a financial interest in any contract or transaction affecting the interests of any institution governed by the board.[53] Prudent action would require a board member to make a full disclosure of a potential conflict of interest and abstain from discussion and a vote on that topic.

A board will often have express policies and procedures in place to minimize the potential for a conflict of interest. However, loyalty with respect to serving the institution may require additional steps. If the state has not already taken this initiative, the board should adopt a substantive conflict of interest policy that addresses direct and indirect related-party transactions with officers and/or board members, including those that occur with "close family members" of officers and/or board members. This same policy should also address perceived conflict of interest transactions and the approach that will be used to insure appropriate disclosure and avoid the appearance of impropriety. Board policies may also stipulate the proper procedures for decision-making on matters implicating the public trust. For example, if competitive bidding requirements are applicable to the purchase of goods or services, then the board should avoid any deviation from those requirements in contracting for goods and services.

To assist board members in adhering to their fiduciary responsibilities, institutions may take several steps; first, recruit knowledgeable board members with skills in financial, programmatic, and other substantive areas relevant to the higher education institution; second, educate board members regarding their duties and encourage them to actively question management and outside advisors on concerns they have relative to the management of the institution; third, establish written policies and procedures for the board that mirror the requirements of state law and institutional best practice; fourth, ensure that board members know and follow written policies and procedures of the institution and that they ensure that management complies with these requirements as well; fifth, develop internal controls that require management to report significant events to the board and that specify those transactions that require board approval; and finally, institute internal self-evaluation and external audit and review policies to ensure effective operation of the board and reduce potential conflicts of interest and self-dealing.[54]

## Appointment and Removal of Board Members

State statutes usually mandate the composition of the board as well as qualifications for board membership. For example, in the University of Massachusetts system, five of the seventeen appointed members must be alumni of the institution, and one member must be a representative of organized labor.[55] States often establish minimum qualifications in order to serve as a member of the board of trustees. Kansas mandates state residency to serve on the governing board.[56] Mississippi's constitution includes a residential qualification and a minimum-age requirement for board appointment.[57] California and Connecticut encourage board membership to be reflective of the economic, cultural, and social diversity of the state.[58]

Some states stipulate some form of student representation on the board. Minnesota statute requires student representation on the board of trustees,[59] while in Connecticut, students may be elected by the student body to serve on the governing board.[60] In Florida and Michigan, selection is based on serving as student body president.[61] In Ohio, the governor appoints the student representative.[62] However, Colorado does not afford the student member full-membership privileges and limits the position to an advisory role without the right to vote.[63] In Massachusetts, student representatives have full-voting membership, but only one student member is selected each year as the voting member (on a rotating basis, if multiple campuses), and any other student members serve in an advisory capacity.[64] Massachusetts also requires that student members maintain full-time student status and make satisfactory academic progress.[65]

Once seated on the board, members have a right to serve the length of their term,[66] unless their service is ended in accordance with statutory law. A vacancy may occur when a board member leaves office before the completion of the term, usually due to death, resignation, or the enforcement of a provision that restricts holding simultaneous public offices.[67] A trustee's service on the board may also end as a result of the expiration of his or her term or as a result of "for cause" removal. State statutory law will often define "for cause" removal from the board, which may include acts of misconduct, incapacity, or neglect of duty, such as a failure to attend a minimum number of annual board meetings. Most states also provide a mechanism for filling a vacancy prior to the end of a board member's term by appointment of the state's governor[68] or legislature[69] for the unexpired term.

## Board Officers

A board will often have designated officers whose duty is to provide formal leadership for the board. These positions may include a chairperson, vice-chairperson, and secretary.[70] Colorado and Florida specify that the duties of the board chairperson include presiding at all meetings of the board and calling special meetings, while the vice-chairperson's primary task is to serve as acting chair during the absence of the chairperson.[71] Typically, a board secretary maintains the board's records and ensures their accuracy, keeps minutes of meetings, and provides notice to the general public of upcoming meetings.[72] The terms of board officers are often specified in state statute.[73]

In some instances an executive committee of the board will be vested with the authority of the board during the interim between meetings, although this authority may be restricted, particularly when the action of the executive committee is manifestly inconsistent with actions taken by the board at a previous meeting. The executive committee may be required to report its actions to the board at regular board meetings and seek ratification for its actions by the full board.[74]

## Sunshine Laws

Every state has enacted sunshine laws to insure that, as a matter of public policy, citizens are entitled to complete information regarding the affairs of their government so that they may fully participate in the democratic process. State sunshine laws distinguish between "open meetings" and "open records." "Open meeting" provisions require public governing bodies, subject to express exceptions, to conduct their meetings in a manner open or accessible to the public.[75] "Open records" or "public records" provisions allow citizens and the press to inspect and/or obtain copies of specific government documents. These laws typically apply to the official meetings of public higher education governing boards;[76] however, some jurisdictions may extend beyond the activities of governing boards and cover meetings of college and university officials engaged in the conduct of institutional affairs.

Open meetings laws have the general purpose of insuring a right of access to the proceedings of a public board and may extend to any gathering of two or more members of the board who meet to discuss some matter that will foreseeably come before that board. These laws apply to more than just board meetings and include committee meetings of a public body that are organized to serve a public purpose.[77]

Most open meetings laws not only require access to the meeting, but also compel adequate notice to the public. To insure quality public participation, a board of trustees must not only list its meeting dates, but it must also post an agenda of business to be conducted. Further, an agenda must be worded with such clarity that the public will understand what the board proposes to accomplish. For example, a Nevada statute requires an agenda to consist of a "clear and complete statement of the topics scheduled to be considered during the meeting."[78]

Open meeting statutes may prohibit the members of institutional governing boards not just from conducting official meetings in secret, but also from conducting informal, out-of-session "meetings" as well. This feature of open meeting statutes leaves public officials, and ultimately state attorneys general and the courts, with the task of determining what types of informal communications among public officials constitute illegal "meetings" and which types of communications are outside the scope of an open meeting statute altogether. In essence, public officials, courts, and state attorneys general may be required to determine the legality of new and sophisticated methods of communication under statutes that were enacted before the public had ready access to personal computers or even telephones with conference call capabilities.[79] For example, Nevada Regents sought to conduct an informal "straw ballot" relating to the public comments of one of the members of the governing board. The Supreme Court of Nevada ruled that when a quorum of the governing board uses electronic media to communicate on a decision, the state's open meetings law must be invoked.[80]

Acknowledging that there are circumstances when a governing board must address confidential issues, most states' open meetings laws allow governing boards to discuss select topics in closed (or executive) session. Such sessions are generally limited to issues in which the public's interest would be clearly compromised or the privacy rights of individuals would be clearly in danger of unwarranted invasion. For instance, a governing board may conduct business in closed session when deliberating on topics that involve personnel issues, collective bargaining matters, purchase/lease of real estate, establishment of emergency security procedures, discussion of current or pending litigation, and deliberations as of a quasi-judicial body. Other exceptions may apply to discussions with staff members who are providing information and developing reports. Most states require that minutes of closed-session deliberations be released to the public after such time as the need for confidentially has passed.[81]

A particularly problematic area for the application of sunshine law has been executive searches. When governing boards initiate the search process for a new president or other executive leadership for the institution, the potential disclosure of the names of candidates and the deliberations of the search committee may discourage potential candidates from applying out of a fear that the disclosure of interest in the position may compromise their current position with another institution.[82] In most cases, the governing board will appoint a search committee that announces the search, screens applications, conducts interviews, and recommends finalists to the governing board, which makes the final selection.[83]

If the statute does not provide clear guidance on whether such searches are exempt from disclosure, state courts must resolve the issue. For example, in 1994, the Supreme Court of Michigan ruled that its state's Open Meetings Act did not apply to a presidential search committee because the meetings were not "formal" sessions of the governing board as defined by the Act.[84] In 2001, the Supreme Court of Nevada rejected an argument that the Open Meetings Act required candidate interviews for the position of college president be conducted in open session. The court ruled that the president was not a "public officer" since that position did not regularly exercise sovereign governmental functions set by law but, rather, implemented policies of the governing board.[85] However, the Arizona Supreme Court determined that the Arizona Board of Regents was required to release the names of those candidates interviewed on the campus but not the names of prospects. The court ruled that disclosure is favored but not absolute because of countervailing interests of confidentiality, privacy, or the best interests of the state.[86]

## President

The governing board is to set its broad educational policies and to monitor the general allocation of resources, while the institution's chief executive officer (president or chancellor) is to advise the board, execute and enlarge on those policies adopted by the board, and administer the educational programs and operations of the institution. The public college or university president serves as the chief executive officer and often corporate secretary to the board of trustees. In Florida, for example, university presidents are responsible to the institutional board of trustees for all operations of the institution.[87] While in some cases a president will receive authority to act from statutory or constitutional provision, it is more often the case that a board of trustees delegates its authority to undertake specific duties. For example, North Carolina and Massachusetts have enacted statutes giving a board of trustees broad authority to delegate authority over the administration of a university to the university president.[88]

Once the board has made a delegation to the president, the president may then re-delegate those duties to other senior-level administrators and staff, provided that statutory law or constitutional provision does not mandate that the board of trustees has sole responsibility. For instance, in 2001, the Supreme Court of Oregon rejected a faculty member's argument that he was improperly denied tenure because the president made an informal delegation of tenure-related decisions to the provost. The court held that state law specifically delegated to the president the decision to "award" tenure. Consequently, the Court determined the president could re-delegate any decision not to award tenure under the statutory authority to re-delegate "practical affairs of the university."[89]

The primary function most often delegated to a university president and other senior university administrators is the authority to make decisions regarding faculty reappointment. For example, in 2002, a North Carolina appeals court ruled that, according to the faculty handbook, senior university officials could overrule a dean's recommendation to reappoint a faculty member consistent with the senior officials' obligation to consider "institutional needs and resources" in making personnel decisions.[90]

## Agency

Most state laws provide that a public college or university be established as a corporation. A corporation is a legal entity, which can only act through its designated agents (trustees or employees) to pursue corporate purposes. There are three parties treated under agency law: the principal, which is typically the institution and/or its governing board; the agent, who is a representative of the institution; and the third party or parties with whom the agent interacts. The Restatement (Second) of Agency, the American Law Institute's last complete treatment of this subject, distinguishes over five-hundred defining aspects of the tripartite relationship.[91] For example, agents that exceed their corporate authority may be held to have acted *ultra vires*, or beyond delegated powers. When a third party has reasonably relied on the acts of an agent, the question of whether the third party may hold the institution liable for any loss attendant to that reliance will often come before a court. Therefore, it is essential for higher education institutions and their agents to understand the scope of an agent's power to execute duties, and for an institution and its agent to avoid concealing or misrepresenting the authority of an agent.

Agents of an institution may act under varying types of authority. Express authority occurs when a principal explicitly authorizes an agent to act on the principal's behalf.[92] Actions an agent undertakes on behalf of the institution are binding upon the institution when there is express authority to act.[93] Implied authority may arise as a necessary or reasonable action required to effectuate some other authority expressly conferred by the college or university on an agent.[94] Apparent authority may be inferred even when an institution's agent does not have express authority to act but it would work an undue hardship on a third party who entered into an agreement with the agent and the third party reasonably relied on the institutional agent's presumed authority to bind the institution. An agent's apparent authority is influenced by the acts of the institution and not solely the conduct of the agent.[95]

## Legal Counsel

Public institutions of higher education have increasingly come to the realization that the range of legal issues confronting modern institutions requires that the institutions rely on the services of attorneys. Particularly in universities, whose complex mission and large operations involve a range of legal services, the university counsel or general counsel should be a regular participant on the university's administrative team and a part of the policy-making process.[96]

In its infancy during the early 1960s, the role of counsel was limited to counsel on retainer from a law firm external to the institution that would occasionally review contracts and provide legal guidance as requested. Few universities employed a full-time attorney as in-house legal counsel.[97] While this arrangement may serve a small public college, in the university environment, the need for legal services has increased as a result of student activism, growing federal and state regulations over higher education, advances in technology, and the exponential growth of the university community. Today, institutional counsel has become a full-time practice providing guidance in a variety of circumstances, which include the civil rights of students and employees; workplace law; environmental regulations; copyright, trademark, and patent law; public records and meetings law; taxation; real estate law; trusts and deeds; and tort liability.[98] The involvement of institutional counsel may be critical at an early stage in the policy-making process in order to prevent legal problems that may arise in policy formulation or implementation.

Institutional counsel may play a role in policy decisions and should be consulted when drafting or reviewing contracts, catalogs, handbooks and codes. Educational leaders should not defer to counsel in making policy decisions but should rely on the attorney for guidance on the review of proposed policy in order to ensure it complies with statutory law, case law, and regulation.[99]

In today's legal climate, many public institutions not only have in-house legal counsel, but also rely on special counsel for specific topics or for handling specialized litigation. Special counsel is necessary because it is difficult for an in-house college or university attorney to retain expertise in all areas of law that affect college or university administration. Even when in-house counsel is available, the attorney is ethically bound to represent the interests of his or her client, often limited to the governing board and senior-level administrators who have direct access to the institution's counsel. In most cases, in-house counsel seeks a "balanced approach" to providing legal guidance, ensuring access to institutional counsel by deans and key administrators whose decisions relate to institutional concerns.[100] Consequently, the institution's counsel may be limited in the range of legal advice that can be provided to mid-level administrators, faculty, and staff. When in-house counsel advises these agents of the institution, there is an obligation to clarify whose interests are being represented.

## Endnotes

[1]   *See* J.S. BRUBACKER AND W. RUDY, HIGHER EDUCATION IN TRANSITION: A HISTORY OF AMERICAN COLLEGES AND UNIVERSITIES, 3-11 (3d ed. 1976).

[2]   *Id.* at 156-167.

[3]   *See generally*, J. R. THELIN, A HISTORY OF AMERICAN HIGHER EDUCATION, (2004).

[4]   *See* K. R. Bracco, R.C. Richardson, P. M. Callan, and J. E. Finney, *Policy environments and system design: understanding state governance structures*, THE REVIEW OF HIGHER EDUCATION, 23:1 (Fall 1999).

[5]   BLACK'S LAW DICTIONARY 282 (5th ed. 1979).

[6]   U. S. CONST. amend X

[7]   Board of Regents of Univ. of Neb. v. Exon, 256 N.W.2d 330, 332 (Neb. 1977) (The Supreme Court of Nebraska stated, "In prescribing the powers and duties of the [the Board] a legislative act must not be so detailed and specific in nature as to eliminate all discretion and authority on the part of the [Board] as to how a duty shall be performed."). *Id.* at 333.

[8]   MINN. CONST. art. VIII, § 3.

[9]   CAL. CONST. art. IX, § 9.

[10]  Sterling v. Bd. of Regents, Univ. of Mich., 68 N.W. 253, 261 (Mich. 1896).

[11]  Board. of Regents of Okla. State Univ. v. Okla. Merit Prot. Comm., 19 P.3d 865 [152 EDUC. L. REP. 295] (Okla. 2001).

[12]  Dreps v. Bd. of Regents, 139 P.2d. 467 (Idaho 1943).

[13]  State v. Chase, 220 N.W. 951 (Minn. 1928).

[14]  Regents of Univ. of Cal. v. City of Santa Monica, 143 Cal. Rptr. 276 (Cal. Ct. App. 1978).

[15]  Federated Publ'ns, Inc. v. Bd. of Trs. of Mich. State Univ., 594 N.W.2d 491, 497 [135 EDUC. L. REP. 242] (Mich. 1999); Kanaly v. State of S.D., 368 N.W.2d 819 [25 EDUC. L. REP. 558] (S.D. 1985), *cert. denied*, 484 U.S. 998 (1988), *reh'g denied* (1988).

[16]  Campbell v. Regents of Univ. of Cal., 106 P. 3d 976, [2005 WL 517295] (Cal. 2005). *See*, Regents of the Univ. of N.M. v. N.M. Fed. Of Teachers, 962 P.2d 1236 [129 EDUC. L. REP. 468] (N.M. 1998). *See also*, HAW. CONST. art. 10, § 6.

[17]  University of Minn. v. Chase, 220 N.W. 951, 955 (Minn. 1928).

[18]  *Exon*, 256 N.W.2d at 333. *See also*, Turkovich v. Bd. of Trs. of the Univ. of Ill., 143 N.E.2d 229 (Ill. 1957) (The Supreme Court of Illinois held, "The General Assembly cannot be expected to allocate funds to each of the myriad activities of the university and thereby practically substitute itself for the Board of Trustees in the management thereof."). *Id.* at 233.

[19]  *Exon*, 256 N.W.2d at 332-33.

[20]  ALA. CONST. art. XIV, § 264; ARIZ. CONST. art. 11, § 5; N.M. CONST. art. 12, § 13.

[21]  COLO. CONST. art. 9, § 12; CONN. CONST. art. 8, § 2; MICH. CONST. art. 8, § 5; NEB. CONST. art. VII, § 10.

[22]  ALASKA CONST. art. 7, § 3; GA. CONST. art. 8, § 4, par. 1.

[23]  Perez v. Giuliani, 697 N.Y.S.2d 470 [139 EDUC. L. REP. 582] (N.Y. App. Div. 1999).

[24]  *See, e.g.*, ARK. CODE § 6-64-202; FLA. STAT. § 1004.21; 110 ILCS 520/1; KY. REV. STAT. § 164-160; N.C. GEN STAT. § 116-3; S.C. CODE § 59-117-40.

25. *See, e.g.,* CONN. GEN. STAT. § 10a-109d(3); 110 ILCS 305/1; N.J. REV. STAT. § 18A:64E-18; S.C. CODE § 59-117-40. *See also,* Miller v. Chou, 257 N.W.2d 277 (Minn. 1977).

26. *See, e.g.,* COLO. REV. STAT. § 23-40-104; 110 ILCS 305/1; N.J. REV. STAT. § 18A:64E-18; S.C. CODE § 59-117-40; WASH. REV. CODE § 28B.35.120.

27. *See, e.g.,* COLO. REV. STAT. § 23-40-104; 110 ILCS 305/1; N.J. REV. STAT. § 18A:64E-18; S.C. CODE § 59-117-40.

28. *See, e.g.,* DEL. CODE ANN. tit 14, § 5106(a); IDAHO CODE § 33-3006; 110 ILCS 305/1; N.J. REV. STAT. § 18A: 64E-18; S.C. CODE § 59-117-40; TENN. CODE § 49-8-203(c); WASH. REV. CODE § 28B.35.120.

29. Esteban v. Cent. Mo. State Coll., 415 F.3d at 1088 (8th Cir. 1969), *reh'g denied* (1969), *cert. denied,* 398 U.S. 965 (1970).

30. Garrity v. State Bd. of Admin. of Educ. Insts., 162 P. 1167 (Kan. 1917).

31. Board. of Regents v. Bd. of Trs. for State Coll. and Univs., 491 So. 2d 399 [33 EDUC. L. REP. 968] (La. Ct. App. 1986), *writ denied* (1986).

32. N.J. REV. STAT. § 18A:64E-18; S.C. CODE § 59-117-40; TENN. CODE § 49-8-203(c); WASH. REV. CODE § 28B.35.120.

33. MASS. GEN. LAWS ch. 75, § 1A.

34. ALASKA STAT. § 14.40.170; DEL. CODE ANN. tit 14, § 5106(a); N.Y. EDUC. LAW § 6206; S.C. CODE § 59-117-40.

35. ALASKA STAT. § 14.40.170; IDAHO CODE § 33-3006; N.J. REV. STAT. § 18A:64E-18; N.Y. EDUC. LAW § 6206; S.C. CODE § 59-117-40; TENN. CODE § 49-8-203(c); WASH. REV. CODE § 28B.35.120.

36. ALA.CODE § 16-47-34; ALASKA STAT. § 14.40.170; 110 ILCS 520/8; IND. CODE § 20-12-1-2; MASS. GEN. LAWS ch. 75, § 1A; N.J. REV. STAT. § 18A:64E-18; N.Y. EDUC. LAW § 6206; S.C. CODE § 59-117-40.

37. LA. CONST. art. 8, § 5; DEL. CODE ANN. tit. 14, § 5106(b); IND. CODE § 20-12-1-2; KY. REV. STAT. § 164-160; MASS. GEN. LAWS ch. 75, § 1A; N.Y. EDUC. LAW § 6206; TENN. CODE § 49-8-203(c).

38. ALASKA STAT. § 14.40.170; COLO. REV. STAT. § 23-40-104; IDAHO CODE § 33-3006; IND. CODE § 20-12-1-2; MASS. GEN. LAWS ch. 75, § 1A; N.J. REV. STAT. § 18A:64E-18; N.Y. EDUC. LAW § 6206; S.C. CODE § 59-117-40; WASH. REV. CODE § 28B.35.120.

39. TENN. CODE § 49-8-203(c); WASH. REV. CODE § 28B.35.120.

40. 110 ILCS 520/8; N.J. REV. STAT. § 18A: 64E-18; N.Y. EDUC. LAW § 6206; N.C. STAT. sec. 116-3; S.C. CODE § 59-117-40; TENN. CODE § 49-8-203(c); WASH. REV. CODE § 28B.35.120.

41. ALA.CODE § 16-47-34; ALASKA STAT. § 14.40.170; IND. CODE § 20-12-1-2; N.Y. EDUC. LAW § 6206; TENN. CODE § 49-8-203(c); WASH. REV. CODE § 28B.35.120.

42. IDAHO CODE § 33-3006; IND. CODE § 20-12-1-2; MASS. GEN. LAWS ch. 75, § 1A.

43. IDAHO CODE § 33-3006.

44. MASS. GEN. LAWS ch. 75, § 1A.

45. ALASKA STAT. § 14.40.170; IDAHO CODE § 33-3006; MASS. GEN LAWS ch. 75, § 1A; N.J. REV. STAT. § 18A: 64E-18; N.Y. EDUC. LAW § 6206; S.C. CODE § 59-117-40.

46. Crook v. Baker, 813 F.2d 88 [38 EDUC. L. REP. 81] (6th Cir. 1987), *reh'g denied en banc* (1987); Waliga v. Bd. of Trs. of Kent State Univ., 488 N.E.2d 850 [30 EDUC. L. REP. 503] (Ohio 1986).

47. *Esteban,* 415 F.2d at1077

48. Morris v. Nowotny, 323 S.W.2d 301, 311(Tex. App. 1959), *reh'g denied* (1959), *cert. denied,* 361 U.S. 889 (1959).

49. Vacco v. Diamandopoulos, 715 N.Y.S.2d 269 [148 EDUC. L. REP. 1012] (N.Y. Sup. Ct. 1998).

50. *See, e.g.,* Stark v. Troy State Univ., 514 So. 2d 46 [42 EDUC. L. REP. 1010] (Ala. 1987) (The Alabama Supreme Court ruled, "If the individual defendants have not acted toward the plaintiff in accordance with the rules and regulations set by the university,

their acts are arbitrary and an action seeking to compel them to perform their legal duties will not be barred by the sovereign immunity clause...."). *Id.* at 50.

[51] BLACK'S LAW DICTIONARY 563 (5th ed. 1979). *See* Reed v. Bd. of Trs. for Ala. State Univ., 778 So. 2d 791 (Ala. 2000), *reh'g denied* (2000) (Supreme Court of Alabama determined that a trustee was not subject to removal from the board since she cured the conflict by terminating her relationship with the other college).

[52] Hinds Cmty. Coll. Dist. v. Muse, 725 So. 2d 207 [132 EDUC. L. REP. 584] (Miss. 1998), *reh'g denied* (1999).

[53] 110 ILCS 310/3. *See In re* Beychok, 495 So. 2d 1278 [35 EDUC. L. REP. 892] (La. 1986).

[54] E. W. McVeigh and E. R. Borenstein, *The Changing Accountability Climate and Resulting Demands for Improved Fiduciary Capacity: Affecting the World of Public Charities*, 31 WM. MITCHELL L. REV.119, 143-144 (2004).

[55] MASS. GEN. LAWS ch. 75, § 1A.

[56] 110 ILCS 310/.01; KAN. STAT. ANN. § 76-3a16. *But see* Florida, where state statute provides that there will be no state residency requirement, but that diversity and regional representation shall be considered (FLA. STAT. § 1001.71).

[57] MISS. CONST. art. 8, § 213-A.

[58] CAL. CONST. art. IX, § 9(d); CONN. GEN. STAT. § 10a-103.

[59] MINN. REV. STAT. § 137.023.

[60] CONN. GEN. STAT. § 10a-103; 110 ILCS 520/2.

[61] FLA. CONST. art. 9, § 7c; MICH. CONST. art. VII, §10; N.C. GEN. STAT. § 116-7(a).

[62] OHIO REV. CODE § 3335.02.

[63] COLO. REV. STAT. § 23-40-104; N.C. GEN. STAT. § 116-7(b).

[64] MASS. GEN. LAWS ch. 75, § 1A.

[65] MASS. GEN. LAWS ch. 75, § 1A.

[66] *See, e.g.*, Tully v. Edgar, 664 N.E.2d 43 [109 EDUC. L. REP. 315] (Ill. 1996) (The Illinois Supreme Court ruled that a new law changing trustees from an elected to an appointed position could only take effect after the terms of the trustees expired).

[67] *See, e.g.*, N.C. GEN. STAT. § 116-7(b).

[68] *See, e.g.*, CAL. CONST. art. IX, § 9(b); COLO. REV. STAT. § 23-40-104; DEL. CODE ANN. tit.14, § 5105; MISS. CODE ANN. § 37-101-3(2). *See also*, Denish v. Johnson, 910 P.2d 914 (N.M. 1996).

[69] *See, e.g.*, N.C. GEN. STAT. § 116-7.

[70] *See, e.g.*, 110 ILCS 520/5; IND. CODE § 20-12-56-4; N.C. GEN. STAT. § 116-80.

[71] COLO. CONST. art. 9, § 12; FLA. STAT. § 1001.71(3).

[72] *See* http://www.boardsource.org

[73] *See, e.g.*, IND. CODE § 20-12-56-4 (one year); FLA. STAT. § 1001.71(3); N.C. GEN. STAT. 116-8 (two years)

[74] *See, e.g.*, S. C. CODE § 59-117-40.

[75] 5 ILCS 120/1. *See* Jackson v. E. Mich. Univ. Found., 544 N.W.2d 737 [107 EDUC. L. REP. 1002] (Mich. Ct. App. 1996) (A Michigan Court of Appeals ruled that a university's foundation was a 'public body' for purposes of the Act); *See also*, Board of Regents of the Regency Univ. Sys. v. Reynard, 686 N.E.2d 1222 [122 EDUC. L. REP. 752] (Ill. App. Ct. 1997)(An Illinois appellate court ruled a university's 'athletic council' was a public body subject to the requirements of the Act).

[76] Del Papa v. Bd. of Regents of the Univ. and Cmty. Coll. Sys. of Nev., 956 P.2d 770 [126 EDUC. L. REP. 471] (Nev. 1998); Auburn Univ. v. Advertiser Co., 2003 WL 21205832 (Ala.) (Supreme Courts of Nevada and Alabama both noted that the Act only applies if a quorum of the public body is present).

[77] Associated Press v. Crofts, 89 P.3d 971 [187 EDUC. L. REP. 1064] (Mont. 2004). *But see* University Prof'ls of Ill. v. Stukel, 801 N.E.2d 1054 [184 EDUC. L. REP. 462] (Ill. App. Ct. 2003), where an Illinois appellate court ruled, "... the Meetings Act cannot be triggered every time public officials meet and converse." *Id.* at 1064.

[78] Nev. Rev. Stat. § 241.020(2)(c)(1). *See* Sandoval v. Bd. of Regents of the Univ. and Cmty. Coll. Sys. of Nev., 67 P.3d 902 [175 Educ. L. Rep. 779] (Nev. 2003).

[79] *See* J. F. O'Connor and M. J. Baratz, *Some Assembly Required: The Application Of State Open Meeting Laws To Email Correspondence*, 12 Geo. Mason L. Rev. 719 (Spring, 2004).

[80] Attorney Gen. v. Bd. of Regents, 956 P.2d 770 (Nev. 1998).

[81] *See, e.g.*, 5 ILCS 120/2.06(c).

[82] *See* N. Estes, *State University Presidential Searches: Law and Practice,* 26 J.C. & U.L. 485, 489 (2000); M. J. Sherman, *How Free is Free Enough? Public University Presidential Searches, University Autonomy, and State Open Meeting Acts,* 26 J.C. & U.L. 665 (2000); Charles N. Davis, *Scaling the Ivory Tower: State Public Records Laws and University Presidential Searches,* 21 J.C. & U.L. 353 (1994).

[83] *See* Star Tribune Co. v. Univ. of Minn. Bd. of Regents, 683 N.W.2d 274 [189 Educ. L. Rep. 867] (Minn. 2004) (The Supreme Court of Minnesota concluded that University Regents could not meet privately with candidates for president before it met publicly to discuss and select the finalists.). *Id.* at 278.

[84] Federated Pubs., Inc. v. Bd. of Trs. of Mich. State Univ., 594 N.W.2d 491 (Mich. 1999).

[85] University and Cmty. Coll. Sys. of Nev. v. Dr. Partners, 18 P.3d 1042 [151 Educ. L. Rep. 596] (Nev. 2001).

[86] Arizona Bd. of Regents v. Phoenix Newspapers, Inc., 806 P.2d 348 (Ariz. 1991) (citing Ariz. Rev. Stat. § 39-121).

[87] Fla. Stat. § 1001.71(4)

[88] N.C. Gen. Stat. § 116-3. *See* Board of Governors of the Univ. of N.C. v. U.S. Dep't of Labor, 917 F.2d 812 [63 Educ. L. Rep. 738](4th Cir. 1990), *cert. denied*, 500 U.S. 916 (1991). *See also*, Massachusetts' statute provides that the board of trustees may delegate to the university president any of the express powers and responsibilities listed in statute (Mass. Gen. Laws ch. 75, § 1A).

[89] Matthew v. Or. State Bd. of Higher Educ., 22 P.3d 754 (Or. 2001).

[90] Zimmerman v. Appalachian State Univ., 560 S.E.2d 374 (N.C. Ct. App. 2002).

[91] *See* Restatement (Third) of Agency, 1 (Tentative Draft No. 1, 2000).

[92] Huyett v. Idaho State Univ., 104 P.3d 946 [195 Educ. L. Rep. 319] (Idaho 2004).

[93] Drake v. Med. Coll. of Ohio, 698 N.E.2d 463 [128 Educ. L. Rep. 330] (Ohio Ct. App. 1997).

[94] State of Haw. v. Hoshijo, 76 P.3d 550, 561 [180 Educ. L. Rep. 900] (Haw. 2003).

[95] Faulkner v. Univ. of Tenn., 1994 WL 642765 (Tenn. Ct. App. 1994), *appeal denied* (1995).

[96] Robert D. Bickel, *A Revisitation of the Role of College and University Legal Counsel*, 85 Educ. L. Rep. 989, 990 (1993).

[97] Roderick Daane, *The Role of University Counsel*, 12 J.Coll & U.L. 399 (1985).

[98] Dennis E. Gregory, *The Role of College and University Legal Counsel with Regard to Operational or Policy Making Responsibilities for Student Issues on Campus*, 10 Coll. St. Aff. J. 26 (1991).

[99] Bickel, 85 Educ. L. Rep. at 995.

[100] *Id.* at 992-94.

# 2 Private Colleges and Universities

## Ralph Mawdsley

## Introduction

Some of the most prestigious private colleges and universities in the United States began in the seventeenth and early eighteenth centuries as religious institutions to prepare individuals for the ministry.[1] Throughout the nineteenth century, three phenomena occurred that affected the nature of colleges and universities. First, many of the religious institutions that continued to exist departed from their religious roots and became secular.[2] Second, a significant number of private colleges and universities were started without religious affiliation, reflecting the products of new-found industrial wealth and social consciousness.[3] Third, states founded their own universities[4] that began generally with the purpose of meeting vocational and agricultural needs not addressed in private institutions.[5] The creation of public universities was aided by Congress' enactment of the Morrill Acts.[6]

Private colleges and universities can be divided into sectarian and nonsectarian. For purposes of this chapter, since a separate chapter is devoted to sectarian institutions, the term "private" will be used to refer to those colleges and universities without religious affiliation.

The purpose of this chapter is to discuss legal issues that relate to the governance and management of private colleges and universities. Where appropriate, references will be made to statutes, regulations, and court decisions that apply to private institutions although many of these references will apply to both sectarian and nonsectarian colleges and universities.

## State-Action Doctrine

Like religious institutions, private colleges and universities are not subject to federal constitutional provisions unless it can be established that the private college or university was engaged in state action. Because the Fourteenth Amendment is a limitation on states,[7] the guarantees in the Constitution extend only where state government can be viewed as having acted. Similarly, injured plaintiffs cannot use section 1983 of the Civil Rights Act of 1871 to seek redress for alleged constitutional (or federal statutory) wrongs without satisfying the same state action concept.[8] A claim that a private college or university was engaged in state action will depend on the nature and degree of contacts between the private institution and state government.

Establishing that a private college or university was engaged in state action and, thus, liable for a violation of a constitutionally protected right is a difficult claim to prove. Plaintiffs have alleged a variety of state-institutional contacts in order to meet the threshold test for state action, but in most instances, the institution's receipt of funds, compliance with state requirements, or submission to state inspection has been insufficient to qualify as state action.[9] For example, students at Strayer College failed to meet their burden to prove a constitutional violation when the college obstructed the formation of student government on campus. The students' First Amendment claims were dismissed because they were unable to establish that the private college was engaged in state action.[10] In *Blackburn v. Fisk University*,[11] students alleged that they had been suspended without receiving the due process required under the Constitution. However, in upholding dismissal of the student's complaint, the court opined that the university's possession of eminent domain pursuant to state law, reception of substantial grants from the state, and exemption from state and local taxes were not sufficient contacts to invoke state action. Finally, in *Imperiale v. Hahneman University*,[12] a federal appeals court found no state action to support a resident physician's claim that his degree had been revoked in violation of his constitutional rights. The court acknowledged that the university received funds from the state and was subject to financial disclosure requirements, but these contacts were insufficient to meet the judicial standard for state action.[13]

In *Powe v. Miles*,[14] the Second Circuit applied state action in such a way that part of the university was subject to state action while another part was not. While seven suspended students in the College of Liberal Arts were not able to prove state action, three students within the College of Ceramics were able to do so. In reaching this Solomonic decision, the court found state action because the College of Ceramics was operated under contract with the state, the state provided a small amount of state aid, the state exercised some regulatory authority over educational standards, and the university's president and dean had made and enforced regulations regarding demonstrations involving students. *Powe*, however, has had only limited precedent value. It has been followed only in isolated, and rather obvious, fact situations such as where a private university has been merged into the state system[15] and where a private school enrolls state-funded, public-school students because there is an insufficient number of students to support a public school.[16]

## Organization and Management of Private Colleges and Universities

Private colleges and universities receive their authority to operate from state statutes. All states have nonprofit incorporation laws that cover colleges and universities as well as other organizations. Although private colleges and universities may be immune from constitutional liability because of the absence of state action, they are not immune from statutory requirements imposed by the state.

Like any corporation, nonprofit corporations generally fall within the authority of secretaries of state in the various states who are responsible for nonprofit corporations within the state. The authority of secretaries of state to act are set forth in state statutes and require that private colleges and universities, organized in the state, file articles of incorporation,[17] usually with the stipulation that the corporation be perpetual.[18] Some states have statutes particularly directed at educational nonprofit organizations[19] and give the directors or trustees of these corporations broad grants of authority to operate the educational institutions.[20]

State statutes regulate much of the manner in which private colleges and universities are organized, although in many cases, state requirements can be altered by the articles of incorporation. The law of the state may address voting rights of members,[21] election of directors,[22] maximum term of office of directors or trustees,[23] and notice of meetings.[24] Property of private institutions is tax exempt when used for an educational purpose,[25] and certain functions of the colleges and universities may be exempt from state taxes.[26]

Boards of directors of private colleges and universities have a fiduciary obligation in managing the corporation. The standard of care for management of charitable corporations for directors generally is one of gross negligence rather than the higher standard of simple negligence for trustees of charitable funds.[27] In *Corporation of Mercer University v. Smith*,[28] the Supreme Court of Georgia refused to hold board members to a higher fiduciary standard regarding its decisions following a merger of two colleges. The court opined that

> The formalities of trust law are inappropriate to the administration of colleges and universities which, in this era, operate as businesses. These institutions hold a variety of assets, and those persons responsible for the operation of the institutions need the administrative flexibility to make the many day-to-day decisions affecting the operation of the institutions, including those decisions involving the acquisition and sale of assets.[29]

However, because many private colleges and universities hire managers for the various endowment accounts, courts expect that the minimum responsibilities for board members would include (1) attending meetings of the board and assigned committees; (2) examining financial statements of the institution; (3) acquiring a working knowledge of institutional policies; (4) making appropriate inquiries; and (5) discharging responsibilities in a reasonable, prudent, and informed manner.[30]

In addition to their responsibilities to their institutions regarding board meetings, board members have a fiduciary duty in their financial dealings with their institutions. For example, board members who engage in business transactions with their own colleges or universities run the risk that their dealings may be voidable in a lawsuit by a corporation member or beneficiary. In *Gilbert v. McLeod Infirmary*,[31] a state supreme court scrutinized a board member's purchase of the private institution's property and his participation at the board meeting at which this transaction was approved. The court examined the profit to the member and loss to the institution, considered the relationship between the transaction and a fair market price, and adherence to notice requirements for the meeting in the institution's constitution. Even in the absence of evidence of actual fraud in the transaction the court set it aside because the board member's conduct failed "to measure up to the high standard required by the law of one in his fiduciary relationship."[32]

To whom board members owe a fiduciary duty is a difficult legal issue. The Supreme Court of New Hampshire, in *Brizica v. Trustees of Dartmouth College*,[33] had to determine whether the board owed a fiduciary duty to the college's alumni association. Three years after completing a $568 million fund-raising campaign from alumni, the institution's board decided to eliminate all single-sex fraternities and sororities. Plaintiff-alumni alleged that failure of the board to announce this change at the beginning of the fund-raising campaign was a breach of fiduciary duty to the alumni. The court refused to find a fiduciary duty owed to the alumni association because there was no evidence that "the alumni stood in such a submissive, inferior, or dependent position with respect to the college in the capital campaign so as to support the existence of a fiduciary relationship."[34]

Acceptance of funds for specific purposes carries special responsibilities for a private college where governing officials at a later date decide to make changes. The difficulty of such decisions is reflected in *Russell v. Yale University* (Russell).[35] In *Russell*, the trustees of a charitable trust bearing the donor's name voted in 1930 to donate funds for a quadrangle to be designated in the trust fund donor's name. However, in 1996 Yale approved changes that included demolishing large parts of the quadrangle. In dismissing the lawsuit by an heir of the settlor of the charitable trust, the court observed that no restrictions had been placed in the grant and no property reservations had been reserved. In addition, the court noted that the Attorney General of a state has a primary, although not exclusive,[36] responsibility to sue to preserve the assets of a charitable trust.[37] In the absence of a state statute permitting a university board member to bring a lawsuit against the rest of the board for an ultra virus action[38] or a special interest by a person in the administration of the university, claims against boards for their financial decisions will be left to Attorneys General.[39]

Many of the operations of a private college or university are realized through employee decisions outside the direct knowledge of board members. Yet the institution may face liability as a result of these day-by-day decisions. Whether colleges and universities will be vicariously liable for the actions of employees depends on the scope of the employees' responsibilities and the duty that higher officials had for supervising the employees. If those in leadership positions in a college or university have cloaked an employee with apparent authority to make decisions, they may find that persons relying on that authority may have a triable claim against the institution.[40] Like the board member who may face liability for breach of a fiduciary duty to participate in board meetings, supervisory officials of the institutions they represent may face liability for failure to adequately instruct or supervise.

## Regulation of Private Colleges and Universities

The ability of state governments to regulate private colleges and universities is not without limit. As Daniel Webster queried in his closing argument to the Supreme Court in the memorable Dartmouth College case,[41] "Shall our state legislature be allowed to take that which is not their own, to turn it from its original use, and apply it to such ends or purposes as they, in their discretion, shall see fit?"[42] In holding that the charter of Dartmouth College was a contract and the State of New Hampshire had abrogated that contract by bringing the College within state control, the decision clarified "the distinction between private and public institutions."[43] Although the distinction between private and public institutions has remained a legacy of the Dartmouth College case, private colleges and universities increasingly have come within the regulatory control of local, state, and federal governments to the extent that the regulation of private institutions is not markedly different from public ones.

Private colleges and universities, like their public counterparts, are subject to numerous local, state, and federal statutes and regulations. Federal regulation falls into three categories: those that apply to the institution as an employer, those that apply to the institution as a recipient of federal funds, and those that apply to the institution as a consequence of its research and teaching mission.

In the first category are Title VII,[44] the Age Discrimination in Employment Act of 1967,[45] the Equal Pay Act of 1963,[46] the Americans with Disabilities Act of 1990,[47] the Family Medical and Leave Act (FMLA),[48] and the Immigration and Reform and Control Act (IRCA).[49] The second category includes the Rehabilitation Act of 1973,[50] Titles VI[51] and IX,[52] the Age Discrimination Act of 1975,[53] and the Family Educational Rights and Privacy Act (FERPA).[54] The third category includes a potpourri of laws such as those governing research on human subjects,[55] treatment of animals used for research,[56] copyright,[57] trademark,[58] and environmental issues.[59]

To these statutes can be added local and state statutes regulating similar subjects.[60] However, some local and state regulations differ from their federal counterparts and include zoning requirements[61] and protected categories, such as marital status[62] and sexual orientation,[63] which are not covered at the national level.

Unlike religious colleges and universities,[64] private, nonsectarian colleges and universities are subject to the full force of federal and state nondiscrimination laws. In addition, private institutions are subject to collective bargaining under the National Labor Relations Act (NLRA);[65] however, religious colleges and universities are exempt from NLRA,[66] although they may be subject to state bargaining statutes.[67]

Within the penumbra of regulation falls state approval of programs to offer degrees and to permit state graduates to be licensed by the state. State licensing agencies generally establish requirements for state approval, thus entitling graduates to be eligible for a state license. Failure of a private institution to satisfy the licensing agency's requirements can lead to withdrawal of state approval.[68] As long as state licensing agencies' standards for private colleges or universities are reasonably related to state-legislative enabling provisions, enforcement will be upheld, even to the point of denying degree-granting status.[69] However, although state licensing agencies have broad authority to determine requirements, this authority is not unlimited. In *Indiaan v. Department of Professional Regulation*,[70] a Florida appeals court found that a state licensing board requirement for both professional and regional accreditation exceeded the legislative authority of the board. As a result, graduates from a private chiropractic college that was approved by the United States Department of Education were entitled to sit for the state exam.

## Colleges and Universities Doing Business in Other States

Many private colleges and universities have chosen to expand their offerings and have devised a variety of methods for enrolling students off campus without expending funds to build additional facilities. The earliest method was by mail, which permitted students to take correspondence courses without attending the campus,[71] but the results met with fragmented success because of student detachment from the instructor-student relationship. A subsequent alternative to correspondence was learning centers located at key locations, often in other states, where students could gather for classes and have access to nearby libraries. More recently, colleges and universities have turned to videotapes and web-based courses that can offer visual and real-time contact with instructors.[72] However, contrary to correspondence courses that involved relatively little preparation expense for the institution, production of videotapes and online web-based courses required an investment in technology, not only for the college or university, but for the student as well.[73]

Inhibiting the extensive use of various technological distance learning academic courses and programs have been two federal requirements regarding financial aid. Higher Education Act[74] regulations forbid institutions of higher education that offer more than 50 percent of their courses through correspondence, or enroll more than fifty percent of their students in correspondence courses, to offer student financial aid.[75] In 1998, Congress amended the Act to read that even telecommunications courses counted as correspondence courses.[76] A second regulation requires that, in order for students to be eligible for financial aid, higher education institutions must provide their students with twelve hours per week of professor-led instruction, exams, or preparation for examinations.[77] Although one can argue that online courses differ from correspondence courses because of student-professor interaction, the effect of these two regulations is to force online universities to restrict the type and number of Internet courses offered that are eligible for federal financial aid.

Most states have statutes regulating foreign corporations, including higher education institutions, doing business within their states.[78] Such statutes present a variety of legal issues under federal and state law. For example, in *City University v. Office of Educational Policy and Planning* (City University),[79] an Oregon appeals court held that a state statute regulating differently Oregon and out-of-state higher education institutions violated the interstate commerce clause of the Constitution.[80] An Oregon statute provided that Oregon colleges and universities could be exempt from certification requirements by the Office of Educational Policy and Planning (OEPP) if they were an Oregon institution accredited by the Northwest Association of Schools and Colleges (NASC) or were part of the state's public higher education system.[81] Academic programs of out-of-state higher education institutions were reviewed every three years by OEPP using a different set of accreditation requirements than those imposed on Oregon's own institutions by NASC, even though NASC accreditation occurred only every five years.[82] A private Washington State degree-granting higher education institution accredited by NASC challenged Oregon's differential accrediting standards under the interstate commerce clause. An Oregon appeals court applied the United States Supreme Court's test that state statutes regulating out-of-state entities violate the interstate commerce clause unless they "serve a legitimate purpose ... that ... could not be served as well by available nondiscriminatory means."[83] In finding the state statute facially unconstitutional under the interstate commerce clause, the appeals court observed that the state provided no evidence that its concerns about the five-year, NASC accreditation versus the three-year, state-certification requirement and the absence of visitation of out-of-state facilities could not be addressed by statutes or rules that were nondiscriminatory.[84]

In a later Oregon case involving a different state statute regulating career schools,[85] the Ninth Circuit Court of Appeals upheld regulation of an out-of-state career center offering paralegal courses in the State of Oregon.[86] The court found this statute facially nondiscriminatory against an alleged interstate commerce violation and, in the absence of evidence that the state did not enforce it against Oregon schools, ruled that the statute effected a valid state interest in exerting state authority over schools which confer only non-degree certificates in order to ensure that the certificate would not "mislead the student or the public to think it is a degree."[87]

Both Oregon cases suggest two different kinds of state regulation problems involving out-of-state higher education institutions and the Interstate Commerce Clause. First, a state whose statutes facially treats differently out-of-state institutions from similarly situated in-state ones (for example, both are accredited by the same regional/national accrediting body) will need to produce evidence that it cannot accomplish its purposes with less-restrictive requirements. Second, a statute that facially treats the same category of in-state and out-of-state institution the same is constitutional unless a claimant produces evidence of uneven treatment.

State efforts to regulate out-of-state higher education institutions can also encounter First Amendment objections. Two cases involving the same Florida-incorporated private university represent the issues. In *Nova University v. Educational Institution Licensure Commission* (Nova I),[88] the university challenged a D.C. statute requiring that private educational institutions seeking to operate in the District first obtain licensure from the Educational Institution Licensure Commission (Commission). The statute required that degree-conferring institutions incorporated outside the District obtain a license to operate in the District without regard to where the degree is conferred.[89] The university, which offered its programs at cluster sites with twenty to twenty-five students, used a combination of its own full-time faculty from Florida and part-time faculty from other traditional higher education institutions. When the university applied to the Commission to offer course sequences in the District of Columbia for its Doctor of Public Administration, the Commission denied the license on the grounds that the university had not complied with D.C.'s regulations "with respect to adequate full-time faculty and adequate library resources."[90]

In rejecting the university's claim that D.C.'s statute interfered with freedom of speech, the D.C. Court of Appeals reasoned that D.C. regulated the operation of out-of-district institutions within the District the same as it regulated in-district colleges and universities. Being engaged in a First Amendment activity of teaching did not immunize an institution from regulation. "Schools are not shielded from governmental regulation of business conduct deemed detrimental to the public merely because they are engaged in First Amendment activities ... [The court would not] accept a theory of the First Amendment that conditions its protection on *where* a school is incorporated."[91] Although educational institutions "have a First Amendment right to teach and to academic freedom,"[92] that right is not infringed by a statute that "ensure[s] that degree-conferring educational institutions incorporated or operating in the District [meet] minimal academic standards—*whatever* their message [is]."[93]

As *Nova I* indicates, the states are not prohibited by the First Amendment from protecting the interests of citizens regarding the operation of educational institutions. Clearly, states have the power to regulate degree conferral by their own institutions[94] and, while the District of Columbia has no authority to affect Nova's granting of degrees in Florida, it may choose "to impose the same regulations on Nova as it imposes upon its own degree-conferring schools."[95]

However, the power to regulate out-of-state colleges and universities must be consistent with state law. In *Nova University v. Board of Governors of University of North Carolina* (Nova II),[96] the Supreme Court of North Carolina struck down a state effort to deny a license to Nova University by the Board of Governors of the University of North Carolina. A state statute vesting the Board of Governors with authority to license degree conferral by North Carolina colleges and universities could not be applied to Nova's teaching its clusters in the state. Adopting a strict construction of the state statute, the supreme court reasoned that the power to license the conferring of degrees by state institutions did not extend to the control of teaching that leads to the conferring of a degree.

State regulatory efforts regarding colleges and universities can affect other areas common to both in-state and out-of-state institutions. In *Philip Crosby Associates, Inc. v. State Board of Independent Colleges*,[97] a state appeals court ruled that the State Board exceeded its authority when it ruled that a consulting firm could not use the term "college." Where state statute restricted the use of "college" or "university" to accredited degree-granting institutions, a Florida appeals court held that the statute did not apply to plaintiff because, as a management consulting firm offering seminars, it did not offer academic degrees or academic credit.[98] In a more mundane case, *Strang v. Satz*,[99] a Florida gerontologist brought suit against the State of Florida, claiming that a state statute prohibiting the use of "Ph.D." or "Dr.," unless the degree or title was conferred by an accredited institution or by an institution recognized by the U.S. Department of Education, violated free speech. In this case, the honorary degree had been conferred by Pacific Western University, an unaccredited institution. Although a federal district court agreed that the use of "Ph.D." or "Dr." is potentially misleading when it does not meet the statutory requirements, the terms were entitled to commercial speech protection. In finding for plaintiff, the state statute operated to prohibit all potentially misleading, but truthful, speech and "narrower limitations such as a disclosure requirement would allow for the speech and ensure that it is presented in a non-misleading manner."[100]

## Administration and Management

College and university constitutions and bylaws generally provide for the appointment and terms of officers.[101] Like any higher education institution though, officers in a private higher education institution have a fiduciary duty to lead and manage according to the direction of the governing board. In *Cahn v. Antioch University*,[102] law school co-deans at Antioch Law School were considered to have a fiduciary duty to the university with which the law school was affiliated. The court considered the legal relationship between a university and its administrators to be one of employer and employee, implying that the employer reposes some confidence in the employees and that the latter are bound to the exercise of the utmost good faith, loyalty, and honesty toward the employer.[103] When the deans in *Cahn* spent $8,000 of the university's money for an unauthorized expenditure, not only was the university's dismissal of the deans upheld, but the university was entitled to recover the $8,000. Whether the deans had acted in good faith was irrelevant where they had breached their fiduciary duty to the university.

The leadership of higher education administrators encompasses a wide range of activities, including selection of faculty and staff, publication of faculty and student handbooks, and oversight of curriculum. Not only are administrators, as in any college or university, likely to be replaced when they do not perform these functions according to the expectations of the board, but they face the added responsibility that they must perform their duties according to the religious requirements of the board.

## Faculty in Private Colleges and Universities

Like their counterparts in religious colleges and universities, faculty rights in private institutions are almost solely dependent on statutory and contractual authority. Absent state action, faculty in private institutions normally would have no constitutional rights associated with their employ-ment. Private colleges and universities can have numerous contacts with state governments without subjecting themselves to constitutional liability under a state action theory. Thus, state action could not be established by a showing that a private institution receives funding from the state,[104] is granted a state charter,[105] is tax exempt,[106] engages in delivering educa-tion that is considered a state function,[107] establishes policies required by government,[108] is subject to state inspection and regulation,[109] and includes public officials on the governing board.[110]

However, a private university could choose to confer on their faculty the same rights that their colleagues have in public institutions under the federal Constitution. Although such an occurrence would seem highly improbable, it can occur. In *Franklin v. Leland Stanford, Jr. University*,[111] a California appeals court reviewed a private university's dismissal of a faculty member using free speech analysis under *Pickering v. Board of Education*[112] and *Mt. Healthy City Board of Education v. Doyle*.[113] In *Franklin*, the court analyzed the faculty member's breach of contract claim using due process analysis solely because the university had gratuitously declared the result would have been the same whether the university was considered public or private. However, even in the absence of the university's concession to due process in *Franklin*, courts would still expect treatment of faculty that demonstrates "color of due process."[114]

Given the very limited situations in which constitutional standards are relevant to private colleges and universities, the rights and responsibilities of faculty in these institutions will be determined by contract. Courts will scrutinize whether the institution has complied with contractual language in fulfilling its obligations to its faculty in order to evaluate a legal claim. Religious colleges and universities are immune from this scrutiny under statutory[115] or constitutional[116] theories to the extent that faculty responsibilities involve religious functions. However, private nonsectarian institutions do not enjoy such immunity and, indeed, cannot fabricate a constitutional theory to prevent scrutiny of employment decisions. In a novel case, *Kyriakopoulos v. George Washington University*,[117] the university sought to block judicial scrutiny of its promotion process, claiming that academic freedom,[118] a hybrid free speech right, protected it from such scrutiny. The court refused to provide this private university the measure of immunity that it requested, citing to an earlier private university case, *McConnell v. Howard University*,[119] for the principle that "we do not understand why university affairs are more deserving of judicial deference than the affairs of any other business or profession.... [E]ven if there are issues on which courts are ill equipped to rule, the interpretation of a contract is not one of them."[120]

In terms of contract issues for private colleges and universities, both sectarian and nonsectarian institutions are equally affected. Except where faculty contracts at religious institutions involve religious functions or impose religious requirements on faculty,[121] faculty in all nonpublic higher education institutions are similarly situated.

Contract issues involving college and university faculty fall into three categories: (1) whether allegedly improper faculty conduct is covered by published contract language; (2) whether the institution has complied with its own contractual requirements in dealing with faculty; and (3) whether the college or university's interpretation or enforcement of contract terms exhibited good faith and fairness.

### Faculty Conduct and Published Contract Language

Employers can influence faculty contracts a great many ways, but termination of a person's employment is probably the most traumatizing for the employee and the most contentious for both employee and employer. In any contract termination, a threshold question always concerns the nature of the contract that an employee has.

Every faculty contract essentially falls into one of three categories: employment-at-will, fixed term, or continuing. Generally, absent contract language to the contrary, employment-at-will contracts can be terminated at any time by either the faculty member or the institution. Indeed, in some states, contracts for an indefinite period of time are considered to be employment-at-will.[122] Unless the contract states otherwise, an employment-at-will contract can usually be terminated without providing cause for termination.[123] Employment-at-will contracts can even be withdrawn before a prospective employee begins working.[124] However, some states have modified the at-will doctrine to limit dismissal or discipline in situations involving public policy, implied contracts, and covenants of fair dealing.[125]

Contracts for a fixed term generally expire at the end of the term with no official action necessary to be taken, but the terms of the faculty contract will govern. The ultimate measure is whether a faculty member can entertain a successful breach of contract lawsuit when a term contract is not renewed. Generally, nontenured, tenure-track faculty members are probationary employees and have contracts for a fixed number of years.[126] Apart from an expectation of employment during the term of a probationary contract a tenure track faculty usually cannot expect employment beyond that term. In *Stanton v. Tulane University*, a state appeals court upheld a university decision to nonrenew a tenure-track faculty member after the fourth year of his probationary contract because he had not met the requirements set down by the faculty review committee.[127] In dismissing one tenure-track faculty member's action for negligent misrepresentation following nonrenewal of his contract after his first year, an Oregon appeals court observed that a university owes no duty "to further the economic interests of the employee in the negotiation of the employment contract."[128] In *DeSimone v. Sienna College*,[129] a probationary faculty member with a contract that stated it was for one year and nonrenewable had no breach of contract even though he received notice of nonrenewal two days late according to the faculty handbook. However, faculty handbooks that create rights prior to termination of term contracts can present a triable issue for the faculty member.[130]

Since faculty members in private colleges and universities lack the protection of the Fourteenth Amendment because of the absence of state action, continuing or tenure contract rights are determined by the contract terms between the faculty member and the university. Tenure-track faculty, absent contract language to the contrary, with a contract specifying "teaching and/or service" permits reassignment of a faculty member to a service responsibility without violating the terms of the contract as long as the agreed-to compensation is not changed.[131] Although a continuing contract creates an expectation of employment from one year to the next, it does not assure that a faculty member's status cannot be changed for violations of the contract. In *Klinge v. Ithaca College*,[132] a tenured faculty member could be demoted in rank and issued a one-year terminal contract for plagiarism.[133]

### Compliance with Contract Language

The threshold issue in deciding whether a private college or university has complied with an employee's contract is determining what constitutes the employment contract. Although most colleges and universities probably consider the faculty handbooks to be part of the contract, there is by no means agreement among institutions.[134]

Colleges and universities may have faculty handbooks that they reserve the right to modify at any time. Normally this right of unilateral change will not affect the contractual nature of handbook provisions, but not every court may agree. In an unusual case, *Dunfey v. Roger Williams University*,[135] a discharged admissions officer sought to enforce a personnel policy provision that an involuntarily discharged administrator was entitled to one month's salary for every six months of service. However, the manual provided that "Additional policies and practices or changes may evolve and the Personnel Policy Manual may be amended, modified, or superseded at any time. Written notice of such changes will be distributed as soon as possible." In rejecting the former employee's claim, the court held that under Rhode Island law, "the Manual does not create any contractual rights between [the university] and [plaintiff] ... because an employee cannot rely on statements in a manual if the manual can be altered or revoked at any time and for any reason...."[136]

The *Dunfey* court chose not to treat provisions in the handbook as enforceable up to the point of change, a position that seems as easily compatible with a contract theory as that of *Dunfey*. In *Fairbanks v. Tulane University*,[137] the university was required to provide a tuition benefit in place when a faculty member died and before the handbook was changed eliminating the benefit. *Dunfey* presents an interesting anomaly because presumably the university would expect employees to adhere to handbook provisions relating to conduct even though those provisions, like the rest of the handbook, could be changed at will.[138]

Employment standards are created by faculty handbooks, not by external provisions, unless those provisions are expressly incorporated into the handbook. In *Waring v. Fordham University*,[139] the American

Association of University Professor's (AAUP's) position against tenure quotas could not form the basis of a breach of contract claim where the university had chosen to set tenure quotas. In *Hill v. Talladega College*,[140] an AAUP guideline that the tenure track "probationary period should not exceed seven years" did not confer tenure on a faculty member who had taught at the College for ten years. Finally, in *Krasek v. Duquesne University*,[141] employment standards in a law school were determined by the faculty handbook, not by the standards of the accrediting bodies, the American Bar Association (ABA), or the American Association of Law Schools (AALS).

## Good Faith and Fairness in Contract Enforcement

Generally, a covenant of good faith and fair dealing is implied in every contract, although this covenant cannot be used to obliterate express contract language. "Good faith is the faithfulness of an agreed purpose between two parties, a purpose which is consistent with justified expectations of the other party. The breach of good faith is bad faith characterized by some conduct that violates standards of decency, fairness, or reasonableness."[142] Thus, a faculty member cannot claim a lack of good faith or fair dealing in nonrenewal of his contract where the contract explicitly contains a "no tenure" provision.[143] Similarly, nonrenewal of a one-year contract will not require notification where the faculty handbook only suggests but does not require notification,[144] nor will courts require that an objective standard, requiring an objective and justifiable cause for nonrenewal before a year-by-year contract, can be nonrenewed.[145]

In *Logan v. Bennington College*,[146] a tenured faculty member terminated for sexual harassment lost in his claim that his allegedly flawed hearing demonstrated lack of good faith and fair dealing. The burden of proof to demonstrate lack of good faith and fair dealing is on the faculty member, and in *Logan,* he had failed to prove how alleged bias against him by two of the hearing committee members and how knowledge among some of the members of his past reputation for similar conduct and his drinking violated his handbook rights to a fair hearing.

However, lack of good faith and fair dealing can be demonstrated where a college or university acts capriciously or arbitrarily. Thus, where a higher education institution refuses to permit a faculty member to continue teaching after a court has determined that he acquired tenure by default, the faculty member is entitled to recover his salary until he retires, minus anticipated earnings of the faculty member through his good-faith efforts to find employment.[147] Likewise, when a university fails to follow the procedures found in its own faculty handbook involving discipline of a faculty member, such failure can demonstrate breach of good faith and fair dealing implied in every employment contract.[148]

## Students in Private Colleges and Universities

Student rights in private colleges and universities parallel those of faculty. Because of the absence of state action, students do not enjoy constitutional rights. Like their faculty counterparts, students have contract rights framed by an institution's student handbook. Although contractual handbook rights do not have to be the same as the constitutional rights that students might enjoy in public colleges and universities, courts can compare contract rights with the requirements of due process.[149]

At the heart of due process is the expectation that students will be treated fairly and will be subject to fair rules. While, in the public sector, this expectation has the constitutional appellation of substantive or procedural due process rights; in the nonpublic sector, the expectation is for clearly stated rules and a review process that is neither arbitrary nor capricious. The influence of due process on private colleges and universities is reflected in *Fellheimer v. Middlebury College*[150] where a student found guilty of "disrespect of persons," mirroring student handbook language, "to respect the dignity, freedom, and rights of others," was entitled to another hearing because he had been charged, and found not guilty, of another provision (rape) and had not been charged with the "disrespect of persons" language prior to his hearing. Observing that the college's contractual responsibility was "to state the nature of the charges with sufficient particularity to permit the student to defend himself,"[151] the court reasoned that the two charges—rape and disrespect of persons—were different enough that the student should have been notified that he would be expected to defend himself against both conduct standards.

Courts appear to grant considerable discretion to private colleges and universities to define their codes of conduct and will permit discipline for violations of quite general language.[152] Generally, the only due process to which a student is entitled is the institution's conformity to its own disciplinary procedures.[153] Even omissions in procedures required in the student handbook may be overlooked as long as the university's overall conduct of a student disciplinary proceeding is not considered to be arbitrary and capricious.[154]

Student contractual rights are similar to faculty and involve the same three issues: (1) whether allegedly improper student conduct is covered by published contract language; (2) whether the institution has complied with its own contractual requirements in dealing with students; and (3) whether the college or university's interpretation or enforcement of contract terms exhibited good faith and fairness.

### Student Conduct and Published Contract Language

As suggested above, private colleges and universities can discipline students pursuant to general language in student handbooks. Thus, in

*Aronson v. North Park College*,[155] a student's dismissal was upheld under a college catalog provision allowing the college "to dismiss any time a student who in its judgment is undesirable and whose continuation in the school is detrimental to himself or his fellow students."[156] In a tragic case, *Harwood v. Johns Hopkins University*,[157] a state appeals court upheld the university's refusal to award a diploma to a student during the annual spring commencement even though he had finished his academic program at the end of fall semester. During the spring semester while the student was not enrolled in any courses, he killed another student on campus, plead guilty, and was sentenced to thirty-five years in prison. The university's student handbook provided that a student would not receive a diploma solely on the basis of completing course work and that to receive a diploma, a student must resolve all charges of misconduct before being approved for graduation. The Dean of Students, following appropriate notification to the student, found him guilty of misconduct under the handbook, expelled him, and denied him his diploma. In dismissing the student's claim that the university no longer had jurisdiction because he had completed his academic program prior to the murder, the court reasoned that the relationship between the student and the private university was governed by contract and because he had not yet been awarded his diploma "he remained subject to the policies and procedures enumerated in the [Student] Handbook."[158] The fact that the student would have received his diploma if the university had a commencement at the end of fall semester did not detract from the authority of a private university to determine compliance with published student conduct requirements.

A similar result was reached in *Dinu v. President and Fellows of Harvard University*[159] where students were ordered to withdraw from the university for one year and not participate in commencement because of past misconduct with the finding of guilty occurring after completion of courses at the end of spring semester and prior to spring commencement. The students lost in their breach of contract claim because the student handbook required that graduating students be "in good standing."

Private higher education institutions can also withhold diplomas and transcripts for outstanding financial obligations pursuant to language in the student handbook.[160] However, federal law can override the student-university contract and a private university cannot refuse to send a transcript if the student has filed for bankruptcy under the Bankruptcy Code and listed the university obligation as one of the debts.[161]

## Compliance with Contract Language

Unlike faculty handbooks, parties do not challenge that student handbooks are part of the contract between a private college and university and students. What is contested is not only whether the parties have complied with handbook provisions, but the extent to which the contract with students includes other college and university publications.

Grade disputes are subjects of higher education litigation where courts defer to the judgment of college and university faculty as long as handbook procedures are followed. In *Lyon College v. Gray*,[162] a state appeals court reversed a breach of contract award for a student who had been found guilty of an honor code violation, suspended for the balance of the year, and awarded an "F" in a course. In holding that the trial court should have granted a directed verdict for the college, the appeals court observed that "once it was shown that [the college] followed its own procedural guidelines and based its disciplinary decision on substantial evidence, judicial review of [the college's] actions should have ceased."[163]

More troublesome are student-breach-of-contract or misrepresentation lawsuits involving a college or university's performance of statements regarding academic programs, courses, and financial obligations. At issue is a concept of an institutional contract that goes beyond student handbooks and includes official publications describing programs, courses, and financial obligations.

In *Idress v. American University of the Caribbean*,[164] a prospective medical student successfully sued on the theory of fraudulent misrepresentation where a university brochure described equipment and facilities that were not available when the student arrived for classes. In *Reynolds v. Sterling College, Inc.*,[165] a student had breach of contract and consumer fraud claims when the college refused to refund an amount of money, following the student's withdrawal, consistent with catalog language in effect when the student enrolled. Finally, a student had a breach of contract action when life-experience credits awarded the student upon enrollment were later revoked.[166] The court's comments concerning commitments to nontraditional students in colleges and universities are worth reflecting upon:

> The economic reality is that colleges and universities are competing to attract nontraditional age students and many of these institutions have designed programs to cater to them. Through advertising and recruitment campaigns, an increasing number of colleges and universities are promising students who wish to return to school, flexible schedules, evening and weekend classes, and academic credit for life experiences. Students, in turn, attracted by these options, may seek to apply to a particular institution and inquire as to the requirements they will have to meet in order to achieve their degrees. When an individual is induced to enroll in a university or college based upon the award of certain life credits, the institution cannot then, after the student's enrollment, revoke those credits.[167]

## Good Faith and Fairness in Contract Enforcement

Covenants of good faith and fair dealing are implied in contracts between students and colleges or universities. However, educational institutions normally have broad discretion in interpreting rules, policies, or handbooks, and, especially when academic standards are concerned, courts will not intervene in the absence of bad faith.

In *Shields v. School of Law, Hofstra University*,[168] a state court rejected a student's claim that the law school's continuing to count a failing grade in her GPA, after she had retaken and passed the course, represented bad faith. Because the law school had acted pursuant to its published policy of counting failing grades, the court found the matter of a grading policy to be within the law school's sound discretion "unfettered by contract and unreviewable by courts."[169] Similarly, in *Napolitano v. Princeton University*,[170] a state court upheld the university's postponement of a student's degree for one year after a finding of plagiarism. The court observed that it was not its function "to second-guess academic decisions and judgments in colleges and universities," and, as long as the faculty decision had a rational basis, the court would not find the decision to be arbitrary and capricious.[171] The reluctance of courts, in the absence of evidence of bad faith, to intervene in grade disputes reflects not only the court's lack of expertise in the subject matter, but a deference for academic decision-making and a concern about promoting litigation by countless, dissatisfied students.[172]

However, courts will not hesitate to declare a justiciable claim where a student appears to have proof of bad faith. Thus, a student who could prove bad faith in receiving a failing grade in his final medical school course that resulted in his not being awarded a degree was entitled to damages concerning the loss of his earning capacity without the medical degree.[173] A student stated a claim for breach of contract where, following a fight with an Asian-American student, he was expelled for a violation of the college's race discrimination policy.[174] In ordering the case to trial, a federal judge found that the college had breached its contract with the expelled student by not providing "fundamental fairness" in judicial procedures as provided in the student handbook. In effect, by promising "fundamental fairness," the court was relieved of having to limit itself to only bad faith conduct by the college.

# Conclusion

The legal status of private colleges and universities is midway between public universities and religious ones. Like their religious counterparts, private higher education institutions enjoy a certain amount of freedom from legal liability in terms of the absence of state action. Neither faculty nor students have constitutional rights in private colleges and universities. However, unlike religious colleges and universities, private institutions do not enjoy the protection of the First Amendment religion clauses and various statutory religious exemptions.

Nonetheless, despite an increasing regulation by local, state, and federal governments, private colleges and universities, the first higher education institutions in the United States, continue to thrive. The challenge for such institutions is to chart a course that maintains their competitiveness with the less-expensive, public counterparts and, at the same time, ensures the distinctiveness of their private roots.

# Endnotes

[1] *See* JOHN S. BRUBACHER, HIGHER EDUCATION IN TRANSITION 7 (1976) (all pre-revolutionary colleges, except the College of Philadelphia, had as their purpose the training of students for Christian ministry); WILLIAM KAPLIN AND BARBARA LEE, THE LAW OF HIGHER EDUCATION 45 (1995) (For example, Yale began as a Christian seminary, and Dartmouth began as a school to teach Christianity to the American Indians).

[2] For example, Antioch College was begun in 1852 under the auspices of the Christian Church with Horace Mann as its first president but was then reorganized as an independent nonsectarian college. *See* www.antioch-college.edu/aboutantioch.html.

[3] *See generally*, FERDERICK RUDOLPH, THE AMERICAN COLLEGE AND UNIVERSITY 244-47 (1962) Among the prominent private colleges and universities founded with post-Civil War industrial money were Cornell, Vassar, MIT, Johns Hopkins, and Lehigh. Carnegie Mellon University was founded in 1900 by industrialist Andrew Carnegie as a vocational training school for the sons and daughters of working-class Pittsburghers. *See* www.cmu.edu/home/about/about.html; Johns Hopkins University began in 1876 as a private research institution. *See* http://webapps.jhu.edu/jhuniverse/information_about_hopkins/about_jhu/a_brief_history_of_jhu/index.cfm; Oberlin College (the college founded in 1833 had evangelical religious roots but has become independent and was the first higher education institution in America to grant baccalaureate degrees to women, and by 1900 one-third of all African Americans who had graduated from predominantly white colleges had graduated from Oberlin). *See* www.oberlin.edu/coladm.

[4] The first state American university was the University of Virginia founded in 1818 by Thomas Jefferson that included professorships in ancient languages, modern languages, mathematics, natural philosophy, natural history, anatomy and medicine, moral philosophy, and law, but not theology.

[5] Rensselaer Polytechnic Institute, founded in 1824, was the first higher education institution to instruct students in the applied sciences of husbandry, mechanics, and domestic science and the first degree-granting technological university in the English-speaking world. *See* www.Rensselaer.edu/About/Welcome/history.html. The first state agricultural college founded in 1855 became Michigan State University.

[6] The Morrill Act enacted by Congress in 1962 donated land among the states that would be sold for the purpose of establishing colleges of agriculture and mechanical arts and was amended in 1890 to prohibit payments of federal funds to states that prohibited admission of blacks to tax-supported institutions.

[7] Section 1 of the Fourteenth Amendment declares, in part, that "[n]o State shall make or enforce any law which shall … deprive any person of life, liberty, or property without due process of law … "

[8] 42 U.S.C. Section 1983 provides in part: "Every person who, under color of any statute, ordinance, regulation, custom or usage, of any State … subjects, or causes to be subjected, any citizen of the United States or other person within the jurisdic-

tion thereof to the deprivation of any rights, privileges, or immunities secured by the Constitution and laws, shall be liable to the party injured ... "

[9] For a comprehensive list, see RALPH MAWDSLEY, LEGAL PROBLEMS OF RELIGIOUS AND PRIVATE SCHOOLS 96 (2000).

[10] 941 F. Supp. 192 [113 EDUC. L. REP. 1191] (D.D.C. 1996).

[11] 443 F.2d 121 (6th Cir. 1971).

[12] 776 F. Supp. 189 [71 EDUC. L. REP. 83] (E.D. Pa. 1991), *aff'd* 996 F.2d 125 [75 EDUC. L. REP. 1024] (3d Cir. 1992).

[13] *See* PA. CODE § 40.33 where a state-aided university must sign an agreement with the state department of education.

[14] 407 F.2d 73 (2d Cir. 1968).

[15] *See* Isaacs v. Bd. of Trs. of Temple Univ. of Commonwealth Sys. of Higher Educ., 385 F. Supp. 473 (D.C. Pa. 1974) (Temple Univ.).

[16] *See* Doe v. Hackler, 316 F. Supp. 1144 (D. N.H. 1970) (private academy directly accepted state money as tuition payments in return for educating secondary school students, and state board of education had authority to see that academy's facilities were such as would be approved as comprehensive high school).

[17] *See* ILL. REV. STAT. 110 § 30/2.

[18] *See* OHIO REV. CODE § 1702.59 (corporation required to file a verified statement of continued existence).

[19] *See* ILL. REV. STAT. 110 § 30/1.

[20] *See* TEX. CIV. STAT. § 1302-3.02

[21] *See* OHIO REV. CODE § 1702.20 (all members entitled to vote subject to articles of incorporation).

[22] *See* OHIO REV. CODE § 1702.26 (unless changed by articles of incorporation, only nominated persons can be elected and no voting by proxy permitted).

[23] *See* ILL. REV. STAT. 110 § 30/5 (3 years).

[24] *See* OHIO REV. CODE § 1710.05 (articles of incorporation are to provide for meetings).

[25] *See* OHIO REV. CODE § 5709.121(A)(2).

[26] *See* OHIO REV. CODE § 5739.02(B)(3) ("sales tax - sales of food sold to students only in a cafeteria, dormitory, fraternity, or sorority maintained in a private ... college or university"); TEX. TAX CODE § 171.061 (franchise tax); FLA. STAT. ANN. § 199.183 (tax exemptions applies to "nonprofit private ... colleges or universities conducting regular classes and courses of study required for accreditation by, or membership in, the Southern Association of Colleges and Schools, Department of Education, or the Florida Council of Independent Schools"); Va. CODE ANN. § 58.1-401 (exempt from state income tax); MINN. STAT. ANN. § 272.02 (property taxes).

[27] *See* Stern v. Webb Hayes Nat'l Training Sch. For Deaconesses and Missionaries, 381 F. Supp. 1003 (D.S.C. 1974). The *Stern* standard was cited with apparent approval in O'Donnell v. Sardegna, 646 A.2d 398 (Md. 1994).

[28] 371 S.E.2d 858 [49 EDUC. L. REP. 446], (Ga. 1988), *abrogated on other grounds*, Warren v. Bd. of Regents of Univ. Sys. of Ga., 527 S.E.2d 563 (Ga. 2000).

[29] *Id.* at 860-61.

[30] *See* Bache Halsey Stuart v. Univ. of Houston, 638 S.W.2d 920 [6 EDUC. L. REP. 1164] (Tex. Ct. App. 1982) (board of regents required to reimburse a brokerage firm for $500,000 in losses when the firm liquidated securities at the direction of a university employee).

[31] 64 S.E.2d 524 (S.C. 1951) (the transaction in this case involved a purchase of corporation property by a board member).

[32] *Id.* at 531.

[33] 791 A.2d 990 [162 EDUC. L. REP. 853]] (N.H. 2002).

[34] *Id.* at 995.

[35] 737 A.2d 941 138 EDUC. L. REP. 1999] (Conn. Ct. App. 1999).

36  *See* Holt v. Coll. of Osteopathic Physicians and Surgeons, 394 P.2d 932 (Cal. 1964) (minority trustees of a charitable corporation can sue to enjoin the improper use of corporate assets because of their fiduciary duty).

37  *See* A. Scott, TRUSTS (4th ed. 1989) § 348.1.

38  *See* CONN. REV. STAT. § 33-1038 (authorizes a member or director of a corporation to challenge a decision of the board).

39  *See* Steeneck v. Univ. of Bridgeport, 668 A.2d 688 [106 EDUC. L. REP. 203] (Conn. 1995) (a life trustee did not have authority under state law to bring a lawsuit challenging a board agreement with a religious entity whereby the entity would give $55 million in exchange for selection of 60 percent of the board).

40  *See* Forum Fin. Group v. President and Fellows of Harvard Coll., 173 F. Supp. 2d 72 [159 EDUC. L. REP. 576] (D. Me. 2001) (College's motions to dismiss denied as to whether faculty member investment decisions pertaining to financial transactions of plaintiff in Russia were the responsibility of the College).

41  The Trs. of Dartmouth Coll. v. Woodward, 4 Wheat. (U.S.) 518 (1819).

42  FREDERICK RUDOLPH, THE AMERICAN UNIVERSITY 209 (1962) (it was also in this argument that Daniel Webster made the memorable comment that "It is ... a small college, and yet there are those that love it...."). *Id.* at 210.

43  *Id.*

44  42 U.S.C. § 2000e.

45  29 U.S.C. § 621.34.

46  20 U.S.C. § 206.

47  29 U.S.C. § 706; 42 U.S.C. §§ 12101 *et seq.*

48  209 U.S.C. §§ 2601-2654.

49  8 U.S.C. §§ 1324. 1324a, 1324b.

50  20 U.S.C. § 794.

51  42 U.S.C. § 2000d.

52  20 U.S.C. §§ 1681-86.

53  42 U.S.C. § 6101.

54  20 U.S.C. § 1232g.

55  *See* 34 C.F.R. 97.102 *et seq.*

56  *See* the Animal Welfare Act - 7 U.S.C. § 2131 *et seq.*

57  17 U.S.C. § 101 *et seq.*

58  Lanham Act–15 U.S.C. §§ 1051-1127.

59  *See e.g.*, Resource Conversation and Recovery Act (RCRA–42 U.S.C. § 6901 *et seq.*); Comprehensive Environmental Response, Compensation and Liability Act [CERCLA [Superfund Act] (42 U.S.C. § 9601 *et seq.*); Clean Air Act (42 U.S.C. §§ 1857 *et seq.*, 7551 *et seq.*, and 7623), and Toxic Substances Control Act (15 U.S.C. 1251 *et seq.*).

60  *See e.g.*, WASH. REV. CODE § 49.60.030 that prohibits discrimination on the basis of "race, creed, color, national origin, sex, or the presence of any sensory, mental, or physical disability or the use of a trained dog guide or service animal by a disabled person."

61  *See* Kirsch v. Prince George's County, 626 A.2d 372 [83 EDUC. L. REP. 1037] (Md. 1993) ("mini-dorm" zoning ordinance which regulated the rental of residential property to students pursuing higher education deprived students of equal protection under both Federal and Maryland Constitutions).

62  *See e.g.*, VA. CODE ANN. § 2.1-715; MINN. STAT. ANN. § 363.03(2) (prohibit discrimination on the basis of marital status). For an example of an interpretation of a marital status statute as applied to a religious institution, *see* Parker-Bigbach v. St. Labre Sch., 7 P.3d 361 [146 EDUC. L. REP. 1129] (Mont. 2000) (termination of counselor living with a man without being married not marital status discrimination).

63  *See* Gay Rights Coalition v. Georgetown Univ., 536 A.2d 1 (D.C. Cir. 1987) (religious university had to provide gay/lesbian student access to facilities because of District of Columbia ordinance protecting that category); Levin v. Yeshiva Univ., 730 N.Y.S.2d

15 [156 Educ. L. Rep. 1255] (N.Y. Ct. App. 2001) (lesbian medical students denied permission to live with their partners in school-owned housing state disparate impact claim under state and city human rights laws).

[64] For example, Title VII contains three exemptions for religious institutions entitling them to make employment decisions based on religious preferences. For a comprehensive discussion of how these exemptions impact religious colleges and universities, *see* Ralph Mawdsley, Legal Problems of Religious and Private Schools 214-227 (2000). However, state statutes may exempt religious institutions from coverage from discrimination on the basis or religion in certain categories for which religion or sexual orientation involves a bona fide occupational requirement for employment. *See* Minn. Stat. Ann § 363.02(2).

[65] 29 U.S.C. § 141 *et seq*. LMRA defines "employer" to exclude "any state or political subdivision thereof," thereby removing public colleges and universities from its coverage. 29 U.S.C. § 152(2).

[66] *See* N.L.R.B. v. Catholic Bishop of Chi., 440 U.S. 490 (1979) (Supreme Court held that religious schools not covered under NLRA because Congress had not manifested an intent to include them); University of Great Falls v. N.L.R.B., 278 F.3d 1335 [161 Educ. L. Rep. 118] (D.C. Cir. 2002) (Relying on *Catholic Bishop*, Catholic university not subject to NLRA and the National Labor Relations Board could not inquire into the religious character of the university).

[67] *See* South Jersey Teachers Org. v. Diocese of Camden, 789 A.2d 682 [161 Educ. L. Rep. 880] (N.J. Super. Ct. 2000) (individual schools within a diocese can have their own bargaining units under state collective bargaining statute).

[68] *See* Midwestern Coll. of Massotherapy v. State Med. Bd. 675 N.E.2d 31 [115 Educ. L. Rep. 471] (Ohio Ct. App. 1996).

[69] *See* Kensington Univ. v. Council for Private Postsecondary and Vocational Educ., 62 Cal. Rptr. 582 [117 Educ. L. Rep. 230] (Cal. Ct. App. 1997).

[70] 695 So. 2d 709 (Fla. Dist. Ct. App. 1995) (even though not accredited by a regional accrediting agency, the college was recognized by the U.S. Department of Education and the Council on Postsecondary Accreditation (COPA), which the court determined met the requirements of state law).

[71] Under the Higher Education Act of 1965 regulations, 34 C.F.R. § 600.2 (2001), a correspondence course is one that is "provided by an institution under which the institution provides instructional materials, including examinations on the materials, to students who are not physically attending classes at the institution. When students complete a portion of the instructional materials, the students take the examinations that relate to that portion of the materials, and return the examinations to the institution for grading."

[72] One of the leaders in learning centers and technology in delivering coursework is the University of Phoenix. *See* www.uoponline.com/default.asp (last visited May 26, 2002). One of the leaders in the use of videotapes to deliver courses is Liberty University. *See* www.liberty.edu (last visited May 27, 2002).

[73] *See generally*, Elizabeth D. Kaiser, The Legal Implications of Online Universities, 8 Rich. J. L. & Tech. 19 (Spring 2002).

[74] *See* 20 U.S.C. § 1001 *et seq*.

[75] 34 C.F.R. § 600.7(a)(1)(i-ii) and (b) (2000).See 20 U.S.C. § 1091(k)-(l)(1)(A)(2000). Subsection k provides: "Special rule for correspondence courses. A student shall not be eligible to receive grant, loan, or work assistance under this ... title for a correspondence course unless such course is part of a program leading to an associate, bachelor or graduate degree." According to subsection (l), a student will not be considered enrolled in correspondence "unless the total amount of telecommunications and correspondence courses at such institution equals or exceeds 50 percent of the total amount of all courses at the institution."

[76] *See* 20 U.S.C. § 1091(L)(1)(a).

77 34 C.F.R. § 668.8(b)(3)(ii)(A-B).

78 *See e.g.,* Ohio Rev. Code, § 1703.27; Ill. Ann. Stat. 805 § 5/13.10.

79 870 P.2d 222 [89 Educ. L. Rep. 1240] (Or. Ct. App. 1994).

80 Article I, section 8, clause 3 of the United States Constitution provides that Congress shall have the power "[t]o regulate Commerce ... among the several States."

81 Or. Rev. Stat. § 348.835(2)(c)(2).

82 City Univ. v. Office of Educ. Policy & Planning, 870 P.2d at 224.

83 *Id., quoting from* Pike v. Bruce Church, Inc., 397 U.S. 137, 142 (1970).

84 Following the *City University* case, the Oregon legislature repealed Or. Rev. Stat. § 348.835 in 1997.

85 Center for Legal Studies, Inc. v. Lindley (Center), 2001 WL 30069 (9th Cir. 2001).

86 Oregon has a separate statute regulating career schools by the Superintendent of Public Instruction. *See* Or. Rev. Stat. § 345.030. The state created an Office of Degree Authorization whose authority is found at Or. Rev. Stat. § 348.603 to regulate degree and certificate granting programs.

87 *Center,* 2001 W.L. 30069 **1. *See* Or. Admin. R. 583-020-0021.

88 483 A.2d 1172 [21 Educ. L. Rep. 558] (D.C. Cir. 1984).

89 D.C. Code § 29-815, recodified as § 29-615. In addition to requiring proof that the members of the governing board are persons "of good repute," the statute requires that "the faculty is of reasonable number and properly qualified and that the institution is possessed of suitable classroom, laboratory, and library." *Id.* at 29-615(a)(4).

90 Nova Univ. v. Educ. Inst. Licensure Comm'n, 483 A.2d at 1176.

91 *Id.* at 1181 (emphasis in original).

92 *Id.* at 1182.

93 *Id.* at 1183 (emphasis in original).

94 *See* New Jersey Bd. of Higher Educ. v. Shelton, 448 A.2d 988 [5 Educ. L. Rep. 1170] (N.J. 1982) (court upheld state's right to deny a New Jersey college, Shelton College, the right to confer degrees).

95 *Nova I*, 283 A.2d at 1181.

96 287 S.E.2d 872 [2 Educ. L. Rep. 872] (N.C. 1982).

97 506 So. 2d 490 [40 Educ. L. Rep.563] (Fla. Dist. Ct. App. 1987).

98 Since *Philip Crosby*, the Florida legislature amended the statute to provide that "[a]n entity shall not use the term "college" or "university" in its name in Florida without approval by the board, unless the board determines that its name is clearly and accurately descriptive of the services provided by the entity and is not one that may mislead the public." Fla. Stat. Ann. § 246.121(4).

99 84 F. Supp. 504 [100 Educ. L. Rep.182] (S.D. Fla. 1995).

100 *Id.* at 510.

101 *See e.g.,* Ga. Code Ann. § 14-3-840.

102 482 A.2d 120 [20 Educ. L. Rep. 905] (D.C. Cir. 1984).

103 *See* G. Bogert, The Law of Trusts and Trustees, § 543, at 216-219 (2d ed. 1978).

104 *See* Grafton v. Brooklyn Law Sch., 478 F.2d 1137 (2d Cir. 1973); Smith v. Duquesne Univ., 612 F. Supp. 72 [26 Educ. L. Rep. 604] (W.D. Pa. 1985); Murphy v. Villanova Univ., 547 F. Supp. 512 [6 Educ. L. Rep. 715] (E.D. Pa. 1982).

105 Blackburn v. Fisk Univ., 443 F.2d 121 (6th Cir. 1971).

106 Browns v. Mitchell, 409 F.2d 593 (10th Cir. 1969).

107 Berrios v. Inter-Am. Univ., 409 F. Supp. 769 (D.P.R. 1975); Grossner v. Columbia Univ., 287 F. Supp. 535 (S.D.N.Y. 1968).

108 Logan v. Bennington Coll., 72 F.3d 1017 [106 Educ. L. Rep. 51] (2d Cir. 1995) (establishing sexual harassment policy required by state law); Missert of Boston Univ., 73 F. Supp. 2d 68 [140 Educ. L. Rep. 554] (D. Mass. 1999) (creating human subjects research board required for federally funded research).

109 Tavolini v. Mt. Sinai Med. Ctr., 984 F. Supp. 196 [123 Educ. L. Rep. 195] (S.D.N.Y. 1997); Mogimzadeh v. Coll. of St. Rose, 653 N.Y.S.2d 198 [115 Educ. L. Rep. 1012]

(N.Y. App. Div. 1997); Gardiner v. Mercyhurst Coll., 942 F. Supp. 1055 [114 Educ. L. Rep. 162] (W.D. Pa. 1996).

[110] Hack v. President and Fellows of Yale Coll., 16 F. Supp. 2d 183 [129 Educ. L. Rep. 1020] (D. Conn. 1998).

[111] 218 Cal. Rptr. 228 [27 Educ. L. Rep. 525] (Cal. Ct. App. 1985).

[112] 391 U.S. 563 (1968) (in determining whether a public school teacher's free speech rights had been violated when he had been dismissed following a letter to a newspaper concerning school district financial management and an upcoming levy, the Court articulated six factors to consider: (1)whether the communication would interfere with close working relationships; (2) whether the communication would provoke conflict or otherwise undermine the employer's operations; (3) whether the communication concerned a topic of public interest; (4) whether there was an opportunity to rebut or refute any errors in the communication; (5) whether the communication shows the employee's incompetence at his position; and, (6) whether the communication was intentionally false).

[113] 429 U.S. 274, 276 (1977) (as a result of termination of a nontenured teacher for several altercations with employees and students and following the leaking of a communication to a radio station of a school memorandum, the Court found that even if an employee has been disciplined following an exercise of a constitutional right, the employer can prevail if it can show by a preponderance of the evidence "that it would have reached the same conclusion ... even in the absence of the protected conduct.").

[114] *See* Flint v. St. Augustine High Sch., 323 So. 2d 229, 235 (La. Ct. App. 1976) (although a student case, the case states the well-founded principle that treatment of persons in nonpublic institutions must satisfy the minimum requirements of due process).

[115] *See e.g.*, Hall v. Baptist Mem'l Health Care Corp., 215 F.3d 618 [145 Educ. L. Rep. 216] (6th Cir. 2000) (religiously affiliated college entitled to religious exemption under title VII after terminating an employee who had been ordained as a lay minister by a church with a large gay and lesbian membership).

[116] *See* Alicia v. New Brunswick Theological Seminary, 608 A.2d 218 [75 Educ. L. Rep. 834] (N.J. 1992) (in contractual claim by faculty member not provided tenure-track position, court held that it had no jurisdiction under Free Exercise Clause to review employment decisions regarding faculty in religiously controlled seminary where faculty teach only religious subjects). *But see,* Welter v. Seton Hall Univ., 128 N.J. 279, 608 A.2d 206 [75 Educ. L. Rep. 822] (N.J. 1992) where court could address breach of contract claim by two nuns who taught for Seton Hall University but did not teach religious subjects or perform religious functions.

[117] 866 F.2d 438 [51 Educ. L. Rep. 740] (D.C. Cir. 1989).

[118] Academic freedom is a term that eludes clear definition. While the term carries the idea of faculty members' right to teach and do research pursuant to the AAUP's 1940 "Statement of Principles of Academic Freedom and Tenure," it also carries the idea of self-governance. In Piarowski v. Ill. Cmty. Coll. Dist. 515, 759 F.2d 625, 629 [24 Educ. L. Rep. 46] (7th Cir. 1985), the court noted the equivocal nature of academic freedom by observing that "[i]t is used to denote both the freedom of the academy to pursue its ends without interference from the government ... and the freedom of the individual teacher (or in some versions-indeed, in most cases-the student) to pursue his ends without interference from the academy; and these two freedoms are in conflict."

[119] 818 F.2d 58 [39 Educ. L. Rep. 502] (D.C. Cir. 1987) (tenured faculty member dismissed following an on-going, in-class dispute with a student was entitled under faculty handbook to a trial as to whether the university had followed the language in the handbook).

[120] *Id.* at 69.

[121] *See* Maguire v. Marquette Univ., 627 F. Supp. 1499 [30 Educ. L. Rep. 1141] (E.D. Wis. 1986) (female applicant with theological position antithetical to Catholic Church's beliefs did not have to be offered position in theology department, which represents the

core of Catholic beliefs in the university); McEnroy v. St. Meinard Sch. of Theology, 713 N.E.2d 334 [136 EDUC. L. REP. 541] (Ind. Ct. App. 1999) (court had no jurisdiction to resolve alleged breach of contract claim involving statement of faculty opposing a position of the Pope where academic freedom at the seminary included religious doctrine and ecclesiastical law).

[122] *See* Roberts v. Wake Forest Univ., 286 S.E.2d 120 [2 EDUC. L. REP. 296] (N.C. Ct. App. 1982) (indefinite contract for golf coach considered to be employment-at-will under state law).

[123] *See* Tramontozzi v. St. Francis Coll., 649 N.Y.S.2d 43 [114 EDUC. L. REP. 252] (N.Y. App. Div. 1996) (athletic director an employee-at-will and could be dismissed for no cause at all).

[124] *See* Heinritz v. Lawrence Univ., 535 N.E.2d 81 [101 EDUC. L. REP. 1120] (Wis. Ct. App. 1995) (contract withdrawn by university due to insurance problems related to prospective employee's handicapped son could be withdrawn before the applicant began work; the applicant was not able to overcome presumption that a contract for an indefinite period is an employment-at-will contract).

[125] *See generally*, H. OLSEN AND R. DUSTIN, EMPLOYMENT AT WILL: A GUIDE TO AN ERODING DOCTRINE (CUPA 1987).

[126] *See* Tuamala v. Regent Univ., 477 S.E.2d 501 [113 EDUC. L. REP. 1337] (Va. 1996) (all faculty had fixed-term, five-year contracts renewable each of the five years).

[127] 777 So. 2d 1242 [151 EDUC. L. REP. 714] (La. Ct. App. 2001).

[128] Conway v. Pac. Univ., 879 P.2d 201, 203 [94 EDUC. L. REP. 531] (Or. Ct. App. 1994).

[129] 663 N.Y.S.2d 701 [121 EDUC. L. REP. 1126] (N.Y. App. Div. 1997). *See also*, Muhitch v. St. Gregory Church and Sch., 659 N.Y.S.2d 679 [119 EDUC. L. REP. 632] (N.Y. App. Div. 1997) (former teacher with one-year contract could not sue for breach of contract).

[130] *See* United States *ex rel.* Yesudian v. Howard Univ., 946 F. Supp. 31 [114 EDUC. L. REP. 1062] (D.D. Cir. 1996) (conflict among the provisions in a faculty handbook regarding the rights of probationary employees prior to termination prevented the university from being granted summary judgment).

[131] *See* Johnson v. Coll. of Art and Design, Inc. v. Nulph, 453 S.E.2d 80 [97 EDUC. L. REP. 521] (Ga. Ct. App. 1995).

[132] 663 N.Y.S.2d 735 [121 EDUC. L. REP. 1132] (N.Y. App. Div. 1997).

[133] In the public sector, *see* Mueller v. Univ. of Minn., 855 F.2d 555 [48 EDUC. L. REP. 1093] (8th Cir. 1988) (tenured faculty member dismissed after being found to have used university resources to promote his private business).

[134] For cases including the handbook as part of the employment contract, *see* Moffice v. Oglethorpe, 367 S.E.2d 112 [46 EDUC. L. REP. 837] (Ga. Ct. App. 1988) (faculty handbook incorporated by reference into contract); Fogel v. Trs. of Iowa Coll., 446 N.W.2d 451 [56 EDUC. L. REP. 590] (Ia. 1989) (college employment handbook part of contract but too ambiguous to support cause of action for breach of unilateral contract of employment); Dahlman v. Oakland Univ., 432 N.W.2d 304 [50 EDUC. L. REP. 895] (Mich. Ct. App. 1988) (failure of faculty member to exhaust grievance procedure in faculty handbook prohibited breach of contract action). For cases where handbook was not part of employment contract, *see* Wall v. Tulane Univ., 499 S.E.2d 375 [36 EDUC. L. REP. 1041] (La. Ct. App. 1986) (university's change in tuition waiver benefit not violation of contract where staff handbook not part of employment contract); Hannon v. Bepko, 684 F. Supp. 1465 [47 EDUC. L. REP. 150] (S.D. Ind. 1988) (handbook did not apply to hourly employee); Faur v. Jewish Theological Seiminary of Am., 536 N.Y.S.2d 516 [51 EDUC. L. REP. 586] (N.Y. App. Div. 1989) (admission policies not part of employment contract so seminary could decide to admit women).

[135] 824 F. Supp. 18 [84 EDUC. L. REP. 219] (D. Mass. 1993).

[136] *Id.* at 22.

[137] 731 So. 2d 983 [135 EDUC. L. REP. 284] (La. Ct. App. 1999).

[138] *See* Leikvold v. Valley View Cmty. Hosp., 688 P.2d 1170 (Ariz. 1984) (handbook that does not state that it is not part of employment contract creates implied obligation of employer to honor entire handbook if it selectively attempts to enforce only part of handbook against employee).

[139] 640 F. Supp. 42 [34 Educ. L. Rep. 467] (S.D.N.Y. 1986).

[140] 502 So. 2d 735, 739 [37 Educ. L. Rep. 999] (Ala. 1987).

[141] 437 A.2d 1257 [1 Educ. L. Rep. 867] (Pa. Super. Ct. 1981).

[142] Braidfoot v. William Carey Coll., 793 So. 2d 642 [157 Educ. L. Rep. 432] (Miss. Ct. App. 2000) (no breach of good faith where the party received all that was bargained for).

[143] *See* Talley v. Flathead Valley Cmty. Coll., 857 P.2d 701 [85 Educ. L. Rep. 295] (Mont. 1993).

[144] *See* Willitts v. Roman Catholic Archbishop of Boston, 581 N.E.2d 475 [70 Educ. L. Rep. 1207] (Mass. 1991).

[145] *See* Tollefson v. Roman Catholic Bishop of San Diego, 268 Cal. Rptr. 550 [59 Educ. L. Rep. 803] (Cal. Ct. App. 1990).

[146] Logan v. Bennington Coll., 72 F.3d 1017 [106 Educ. L. Rep. 51] (2d Cir. 1995.

[147] *See* Bruno v. Detroit Inst. of Tech., 215 N.W.2d 745 (Mich. Ct. App. 1974).

[148] *See* Silva v. Univ. of N.H., 888 F. Supp. 293 [101 Educ. L. Rep. 704] (D.N.H. 1994) (faculty member in public university entitled to reinstatement following discipline for terms used in class that allegedly constituted sexual harassment).

[149] *See* Harvey v. Palmer Coll. of Chiropractic, 363 N.W.2d 443, 444 [23 Educ. L. Rep. 667] (Iowa Ct. App. 1984) ("requirements imposed by the common law on private universities parallel those imposed by the due process clause on public universities").

[150] 869 F. Supp. 238 [96 Educ. L. Rep. 419] (D. Vt. 1994).

[151] *Id.* at 246.

[152] *See* Aronson v. N. Park Coll., 418 N.E.2d 776 (Ill. App. Ct. 1981) (student dismissal upheld pursuant to handbook language, "undesirable and whose continuation in the school is detrimental to himself or his fellow students."); Carr v. St. John's Univ., 187 N.E.2d 18 (N.Y. App. div. 1962) (expulsion of four students for conduct not "in conformity with ideals of Christian education and conduct [that] the university reserved the right to dismiss a student at any time on whatever grounds the university judged advisable.").

[153] *See* Galiani v. Hofstra Univ., 499 N.Y.S.2d 182 [30 Educ. L. Rep. 1247] (N.Y. App. Div. 1986).

[154] *See* Ahlum v. Adm'rs of Tulane Educ. Fund, 617 So. 2d 96 [82 Educ. L. Rep. 1021] (La. Ct. App. 1993) (failure of university to make a tape recording of a student disciplinary hearing as provided in student handbook, due to a tape recorder failure, was not fatal as long as the student had an opportunity to present his version of the facts and was informed of the charges against him); Life Chiropractic Coll. v. Fuchs, 337 S.E.2d 45 [29 Educ. L. Rep. 416] (Ga. Ct. App. 1985) (college bulletin statement that "due process is followed in all disciplinary cases" had been met in a student discipline situation even though the student had been denied a request to confront witnesses).

[155] 418 N.E.2d 776 (Ill. App. Ct. 1981).

[156] *Id.* at 781.

[157] 747 A.2d 205 [142 Educ. L. Rep. 980] (Md. Ct. App. 2000).

[158] *Id.* at 211.

[159] 56 F. Supp. 2d 129 [137 Educ. L. Rep. 619] (D. Mass. 1999) (students were suspended for one year after being found guilty of taking money from a student account and were not permitted to participate in the 1999 commencement).

[160] Martin v. Pratt Inst., 717 N.Y.S.2d 356 [149 Educ. L. Rep. 872] (N.Y. App. Div. 2000).

[161] *See* Parraway v. Andrews Univ., 50 B.R. 316 [26 Educ. L. Rep. 304] (W.D. Mich. 1984); *In re* Scroggins, 209 B.R. 727 [119 Educ. L. Rep. 170] (D. Ariz. 1997); *In re* Lanford, 10 B.R. 132 (D. Minn. 1981).

[162] 999 S.W.2d 213 [137 EDUC. L. REP. 1132] (Ark. Ct. App. 1999).

[163] *Id.* at 217.

[164] 546 F. Supp. 1342 [6 EDUC. L. REP. 653] (S.D.N.Y. 1982).

[165] 750 A.2d 1020 [144 EDUC. L. REP. 314] (Vt. 2000).

[166] Britt v. Chestnut Hill Coll., 632 A.2d 557 [86 EDUC. L. REP. 905] (Pa. Super. Ct. 1993).

[167] *Id.* at 560.

[168] 431 N.Y.S.2d 60 (N.Y. Sup. Ct. 1980).

[169] *Id.* at 61.

[170] 453 A.2d 263 [8 EDUC. L. REP. 74] (N.J. Super. Ct. 1982).

[171] *Id.* at 278.

[172] *See* Susan M. v. N.Y. Law Sch., 556 N.E.2d 1104 [61 EDUC. L. REP. 716] (N.Y. 1989).

[173] *See* Sharick v. Southeastern Univ. of The Health Sciences, Inc., 780 So. 2d 136 [152 EDUC. L. REP. 448] (Fla. Dist. Ct. App. 2000).

[174] Goodman v. President and Trs. of Bowdoin Coll., 135 F. Supp. 2d 40 [152 EDUC. L. REP. 660] (D. Me. 2000).

# 3 Religious Colleges and Universities

Ralph Mawdsley

## Introduction

The early higher education institutions in the United States were started for religious purposes. The first three universities (Harvard – 1636; William and Mary – 1693; and Yale – 1701) have been characterized as "establishments of the Protestant Reformation."[1] Each was formed to train persons for the ministry or to proselytize among the Native Americans. The departure of these three higher education institutions from their religious roots[2] reflected the secularizing trend among many colleges and universities founded in the seventeenth and eighteenth centuries as the percentage of students studying for the ministry shrunk from 50 percent in the first half of the Eighteenth Century to only 6.5 percent in 1901.[3] By the mid-eighteenth century, colleges such as Yale, the College of New Jersey (Rutgers), and Kings (Columbia) were broadening their curricula and offering a significant number of courses, such as math, geography, and English, not related to religion.[4]

Not all colleges and universities, however, have left their religious roots. Georgetown University, established in 1791 by the Jesuits, is the oldest college founded by a religious group that has retained its religious ties.[5] Hundreds of other religious higher education institutions established since 1791 have retained at least some connection to their religious origins. A cursory review of one of the many descriptive catalogs on colleges and universities reveals that approximately one-third of the four-year higher education institutions in the United States still claim to have some religious connection.

Religious colleges and universities are variously referred to as "religious," "sectarian," and "church-related." While the first two have similar meanings, not all religious institutions are necessarily church-related. Although most sectarian higher education institutions have a connection to a specific church,[6] church denomination,[7] or other religious-based organization,[8] a few have no such connection.[9]

The purpose of this chapter is to discuss legal issues that relate to the governance and management of religious higher education institutions. References will be made, where possible, to statutes, regulations, and court decisions that pertain only to religious colleges and universities. However, some references to nonreligious, private institutions may be necessary where the law would clearly be the same, whether the college or university is religious or not.

## Changing Nature of Religious Colleges and Universities

Most religious universities were started with clear religious beliefs and standards of conduct for faculty and students.[10] For example, faculty and students not only might be required to assent to the institution's religious beliefs as expressed in its doctrinal statement, but might also have to agree to abide by standards of conduct, such as abstaining from objectionable substances and participating in mandatory religious activities, which could include chapels and religious services. However, the pervasive religious character of many of these colleges and universities has eroded over the years and relatively few, if any, can claim that they adhere to the same degree of religious rigor as at their founding.

Whether a college or university is religious today may vary across a wide continuum of activities and connections. At one end of the continuum, a university's claim to being religious may be largely historical with publication in its handbooks of its religious founding by a particular religious group. The university may continue to identify itself with the founding group and receive part of its funding from the group, but with no control by the group over its operations. At the other end of the continuum, the university may be tightly controlled by the founding group, with members of that group controlling the board and having the power to determine curriculum and to hire and fire employees who disagree with the group's (and thus, the university's) religious beliefs. In between these two ends of the continuum exists an almost infinite number of variations.

Courts generally refer to all colleges and universities with religious connections as sectarian, whether or not they are church-related. However, those with extensive religious connections and church control have the additional appellation of "pervasively" sectarian. Whether a higher education institution is pervasively sectarian depends on the facts. The extent to which a higher education institution is pervasively sectarian can affect the relationship of the institution with government. One of the most important issues concerns eligibility of a religious higher education institution to receive government aid, an eligibility that is framed by the Establishment Clause of the First Amendment.

Courts have not prohibited the granting of aid to an institution simply because it is sectarian, but aid to pervasively sectarian colleges and universities is suspect. In *Tilton v. Richardson*,[11] the Supreme Court upheld federal construction grants for Roman Catholic colleges and universities, where the buildings financed with the funds would not be used for sectarian instruction or religious worship. However, nonreligious use was not sufficient to pass muster under the Establishment Clause, and the Court had to determine whether the colleges were pervasively sectarian. The Court reasoned that the colleges were not because they subscribed to the 1940 AAUP Statement of Academic Freedom and Tenure, they admitted non-Catholic students, they hired non-Catholic faculty, and they taught religion courses that were other than the Catholic religion.[12] Similarly, two years later, the Supreme Court upheld the eligibility of a Baptist college to receive funds from state tax-exempt revenue bonds as part of a state program to assist colleges and universities as long as the funds were not used for sectarian instruction or a place of worship.[13] The Court specifically found that the college was not pervasively sectarian even though the board of trustees was elected by the state's Baptist Convention, approval of certain college financial transactions was required by the Convention, and the college's charter could be amended only by the Convention. What the Court found dispositive as to the lack of pervasiveness was the absence of religious qualifications for faulty membership or student admission and the 60 percent Baptist representation among the students being the same as the percentage of Baptists in the area where the college was located.

Recent Supreme Court decisions cast doubt as to whether a college's pervasive sectarianism would be a bar at all to participating in direct government assistance. In *Witters v. Washington Department of Services for the Blind*,[14] the Court upheld a state financial grant to a student attending a Bible college (clearly pervasively sectarian) for the purpose of preparing for the ministry. The Court reasoned that the sectarian nature of the college was not relevant since the grant went directly to the student and not the college. *Witters* reflects the difficulty in using direct versus indirect analysis in determining whether aid benefits a pervasively sectarian college. Three subsequent K-12 decisions have lent support for the notion that pervasively religious institutions can benefit from government aid as long as the aid can also be seen to benefit students. In *Zobrest v. Catalina Foothills School District*,[15] the Court found no Establishment Clause violation where a public school assigned a sign-language interpreter to a religious school (pursuant to the child's IEP), even though religion permeated most of the courses in the school. In *Agostini v. Felton*,[16] the Court upheld public school district assignment of publicly paid Title I teachers to inner-city religious schools. Finally, in *Mitchell v. Helms*,[17] the Court upheld the direct loan of instructional equipment and materials to urban, religious schools. However, as a caution, the Supreme Court in *Locke v. Davey*[18] upheld under the State of Washington Constitution the refusal of the state to provide a grant to a student majoring in theology at a religious higher education institution over the claim of the student that prohibiting this expenditure violated his free exercise of religion right. *Locke v. Davey* underscores the notion that enforcement of state constitutional provisions more restrictive than the federal Establishment Clause may mean that not all students at religious colleges and universities will necessarily have equal access to public funds.

In the wake of *Witters*, *Zobrest*, *Aguilar*, and *Mitchell*, federal and state courts have upheld the eligibility of religious colleges and universities to receive funds from tax-exempt revenue bonds and to receive state grants for expenses as part of a post-secondary high school option program.[19] Although the revenue bond funds cannot be used for chapels or other campus places for religious worship, there is no way that these funds can be viewed as other than going directly to the religious institution. Similarly, funds reimbursing colleges for some of the expense in permitting high school students to take college credits for high school credit go directly to defer operating costs related to the program. Whether this line of precedents suggests a disincentive for pervasively religious colleges and universities to dilute their religious nature is a critical issue.

There are some benefits that come to colleges and universities because they are regarded as pervasively religious. Pervasively religious colleges and universities are generally exempt from state unemployment compensation statutes,[20] and church-controlled universities can be exempt from Social Security[21] and ERISA requirements.[22]

While religious colleges and universities may be subject to collective bargaining requirements in selected states, judicial precedent exempts these institutions from the requirements of the National Labor Relations Act. In *Universidad Central de Bayamon v. National Labor Relations Board* ("NLRB"),[23] the First Circuit refused to enforce an order of the NLRB directing a Catholic university to bargain collectively with a faculty union. Relying on an earlier Supreme Court decision, *National Labor Relations Board v. Catholic Bishop*,[24] that held that Congress had not expressed a clear intention for religious educational institutions to be subject to the National Labor Relations Act, the First Circuit looked to factors that established Catholic control over the University: the University was part of a larger complex that included a seminary and elementary and secondary schools, the latter of which were used by University education students for student teaching; the Dominican Order, founders of the University, provided gifts of land, scholarships, and administrative salaries; the president of the University was required by by-laws to be a Dominican priest; a majority of the five-member executive committee was required to be Dominican priests; and the Board of Directors must include the Regional Vicar of the Dominican Order, the Prior of the Convent of Our Lady of the Rosary, and the University president, all of whom were Dominican priests.[25]

However, even with these benefits attached to being pervasively sectarian and even assuming that pervasively religious colleges and universities today can participate in many government programs, there is no certainty that religious colleges and universities will keep intact the intensity of their religious character. In some cases, erosion of religious requirements occurs because of voluntary choices by the governing bodies of religious colleges or universities or by their controlling organizations.[26] Thus, faculty or student subscription to a set of religious beliefs may no longer be required for employment or admission, or certain religious activities, once mandatory, may become voluntary.

## Changes in Religious Colleges and Universities Resulting from Laws and Court Decisions

However, even if religious institutions do not choose voluntarily to dilute their religious character, laws or court decisions can affect the ability of religious colleges or universities to retain their religious distinctiveness. Thus, when the Supreme Court in *Bob Jones University v. U.S.*[27] held that the Internal Revenue Service's decision to revoke the tax-exempt status of the University for its religiously based, racially segregated dating and marriage policies was constitutional, the University faced a choice of either changing its religious beliefs or maintaining its religious beliefs and operating without tax exempt status. It chose the latter course. Such a clear option is not always possible. In *Gay Rights Coalition v. Georgetown University*,[28] student gay/lesbian groups sued the University, a Jesuit university, under a District of Columbia ordinance prohibiting discrimination in the use of or access to facilities and services based wholly or partially on sexual orientation. When the University refused to permit use of its facilities and services on the grounds that it could not recognize organizations that were contrary to its religious position opposing homosexuality, the D.C. appeals court opined that the University would not have to change its beliefs by permitting the groups to use its facilities and services. In other words, the court reasoned that the University's religious beliefs applied to not having to recognize the groups, not to having them present on campus using facilities and services. While the court used reasoning similar to *Bob Jones University*, that government has an interest in eradicating discriminatory conduct, the result left Georgetown University in the religiously difficult position of having to tacitly acknowledge that which it opposed.

One of the key distinctions between religious and secular private colleges and universities is that courts are frequently called upon to determine whether religious beliefs are sufficient to justify university conduct engaged in pursuit of those beliefs. The question is the extent to which courts can apply civil law to religious institutions. Although the U.S. Supreme Court has held that courts cannot resolve civil disputes that turn on interpretation of aspects of religious doctrine,[29] courts have considerable latitude in applying and interpreting civil law that does not implicate religious doctrine. However, the extent to which religious or doctrinal beliefs serve as a buffer protecting the college or university from judicial inquiry is not a well-defined line. Nonetheless, religious beliefs provide a defense to religious colleges and universities not available to their private secular counterparts.

## Governance of Religious Colleges and Universities: State Regulation

Religious colleges and universities are like all other higher education institutions in that they must have a governing board for the purpose of making rules and regulations.[30] Boards derive their authority to act on behalf of their universities from state charters granted as part of the incorporation process.[31] The state incorporation statute and charter identify the broad authority of the board to act in the interest of a university.[32] Although state legislatures can impose requirements on the formation and operation of religious colleges and universities,[33] the Supreme Court long ago recognized that they cannot change unilaterally the governance structure so as to alter the private nature of the college or university.[34] However, states can reserve the right in the granting of a charter to amend, alter, or repeal the same. Where religious doctrine is inconsistent with the state's requirements for incorporation, a state may declare that the doctrine will prevail over state statute.[35]

One of the most important interests that a higher education institution has is the granting of degrees. If a state's limitation on the conferring of degrees conflicts with a religious college's views, questions are raised under the Free Exercise and Establishment Clauses. In *New Jersey State Board of Education v. Board of Directors of Shelton College* ("Shelton"),[36] a pervasively religious college operated by the Bible Presbyterian Church[37] objected to a state requirement that all higher education institutions in the state had to secure a license from the State Board before conferring any degrees.

In this lawsuit, the College objected on Free Exercise and Establishment Clause grounds to the authority of the state to regulate the right of a religious college to confer baccalaureate degrees, even though the College had earlier lost free speech, equal protection, and state constitution challenges to the state's authority.[38] In upholding the authority of the state to regulate conferring of degrees, the state's supreme court observed that, even though the statute had no exemptions for sectarian colleges, the legislature must have been "aware of the existence of religiously oriented colleges;" and therefore, the statute demonstrated "legislative intent to regulate the conferring of baccalaureate degrees by religious as well as secular institutions."[39] Regarding the free exercise claim, the court rejected the state's claim that its regulation imposes "no direct interference with religious practice ... [simply] because [the College's ] religion does not require attendance at Shelton College."[40] However, even though the regulation imposed "some burden on the exercise of religion," it was, none-theless, constitutional because it represented the least-restrictive means for the state to carry out its interest in "maintaining minimum academic standards and preserving the basic integrity of the baccalaureate degree."[41] The court rejected the College's excessive entanglement argument under the Establishment Clause because the College had declined to participate in the licensing process. *Shelton* stands for the important principles that states have the authority to intrude into the governance responsibilities of college and university boards,[42] and the Religion Clauses will not exempt such regulation unless there is evidence of legislative intent to exempt religious institutions or unless a substantial burden in the institution's religious mission can be proved.

Any private college, religious ones included, however, can alter their own relationship with the state so that they become state entities. In *Braden v. The University of Pittsburgh* ("Braden"),[43] a University, once nonsectarian and private, became a part of the state's public university system. The state legislature, upon request from the University's board for state funds to correct dire financial straits, made state money contingent on the University becoming "an instrumentality of the Commonwealth [of Pennsylvania] to serve as a State-related institution in the Commonwealth system of higher education."[44] The change in *Braden* from private to public would apply to religious colleges and universities, with the result that special conditions that had been imposed on governance, such as representation on the board by certain religious persons or control of the board by outside religious organizations, would cease.

## Governance: Religious Responsibilities and Fiduciary Duty

Generally, the determination of who serves on the board of a religious college and university, how those persons are appointed and reappointed, and what their term of office will be is determined by the institution's constitution and bylaws. Frequently, membership on the board includes representatives from religious organizations, and states may expressly grant to those organizations the right to appoint some or all trustees.[45] It is important to note that the boards of controlling religious organizations (such as churches or associations of churches) could be liable under the principle of ascending liability for defaults of the college or university under circumstances in which the higher education institution shares a common purpose and a common name with the controlling religious organization.[46]

At least some members of governing boards in religious colleges and universities are selected for their ability to monitor and direct the religious life of the institution.[47] The relationship between governance, in terms of policy-making, and management, generally the difference between board functions and officer responsibilities, can be a fine, if not nonexistent, line at religious institutions. Faculty at religious colleges or universities may find that overriding policy concerns directed at maintaining religious integrity can restrict management discretion. In *Tuomala v. Regent University*,[48] three law school faculty members at a religious university sought injunctive relief to enforce their alleged right to tenured contracts based on the University president's statement to an accrediting agency (American Bar Association ["ABA"]) that the three-year contracts for law faculty were renewable except for good cause. In rejecting relief for plaintiffs, the Virginia Supreme Court noted that at this University, "the power to set university policy is vested in the Board ... the president's function is to carry out the Board's broad policy directives within the policy guidelines, and that Regent's presidents are not permitted to take any unauthorized action."[49] The University's Chancellor testified that, had the board known of the president's representations to the ABA, the board "would have shut down the law school."[50] Although college and university officers are always constrained by the limitations of their boards, the desire of boards at religious institutions to preserve the right to non-renew faculty who are no longer compatible with the university's religious doctrine represents yet another layer of board control with which public and nonsectarian private university officers do not have to contend.

Board members of religious colleges and universities, like members of all higher education boards, have a fiduciary duty in their dealings with the institution. They are expected to disclose to the board any conflicts of interest in their business dealings with the university. Failure to do so will void any action taken.[51] Board members are expected to be diligent in making decisions with the institution's money. In *Jarvis Christian College v. National Union Fire Insurance Company*,[52] the College lost $2,000,000 of its endowment when a board member with an undisclosed interest in an investment company persuaded other board members to transfer the money to his company, where he invested and lost it in speculative investing. When the board secured an unrecoverable judgment against the board member for the money lost, it tried unsuccessfully to recover from its liability insurer for the "wrongful acts" of its director. In upholding the insurer's position, the Fifth Circuit reasoned that the policy exempted any claim "arising out of the gaining of personal profit or advantage," and, even though the errant board member had realized no profit, the opportunity to realize a profit was sufficient to exclude the College from coverage.

When the decisions of board members are challenged, they are likely be held to a corporate standard of care rather than to charitable trust principles. In *Corporation of Mercer University v. Smith*,[53] the Georgia Supreme Court upheld the decision of the University board of directors to close the campus of a woman's college that had recently merged with the University, both of which were affiliated with the Georgia Baptist Convention. The court agreed with the University that universities are businesses and, as such, need administrative flexibility to make day-to-day decisions including the ability to acquire and sell assets.

Although a corporate, as opposed to trust, standard of care gives board members greater latitude in managing and disposing of institutional assets, the lesser standard still imposes an expectation of good faith in business dealings. In *Stern v. Lucy Webb Hayes National Training School for Deaconesses and Missionaries*,[54] patients in a hospital sued board members for breach of fiduciary duties of care and loyalty where board members who were also board members of banks and investment firms allegedly enriched themselves and their businesses. The gravamen of the lawsuit was that the twenty-five to thirty-five member board had deferred decision-making regarding investments to a finance committee that was dominated by two trustees, the hospital administrator and the treasurer. Even though the court found no breach of standard of care, it did iterate the responsibilities of board members:[55]

1. Board members can delegate financial decisions to committees as long as the board periodically supervises their work.

2. Board members who fail to supervise or even attend board meetings breach their fiduciary duty.

3. Board member reliance on the advice of corporate officers does not replace review of officer reports.

4. A board member who permits negligent mismanagement of the corporation to go unchecked has committed an independent wrong against the organization.

5. Board members should not only reveal interlocking responsibilities but also refrain from voting or influencing the corporation to do business with a company with which they have an interest.[56]

Involvement on a board where mismanagement by certain board members or officers has occurred can have financial implications for other board members. In a non-education case, *Teague v. Bakker*,[57] two board members who were sued along with James Bakker regarding the fraudulent sale of hotel shares at a religious organization's theme park were found not liable in the $129,618,000 judgment against Bakker for common law fraud, plus the same amount for punitive damages. However, even though the two board members were found not guilty, they incurred considerable legal expenses in their defenses. In adding pain to the injury of being subjected to a much-publicized lawsuit, the trial court awarded the costs of defense to only one of the two successful board members, as a prevailing party, against the 160,000 plaintiffs, a decision that was upheld on appeal to the Fourth Circuit. Obviously, to incur considerable expense in defending oneself successfully without the certainty of recovery of those costs in the end represents a financial risk to a board member. The lesson from *Teague* would seem to be that a person's membership on a religious organization's board can create both visibility and vulnerability, even if the person is not involved in financial mismanagement. Board members cannot afford to be silent and/or acquiescent with regard to the decisions of officers or the opinions of other board members when it comes to financial matters.

## Faculty in Religious Colleges and Universities

Legal issues concerning faculty occur in three areas: constitutional, statutory, and contractual. Constitutional issues relate to whether faculty have constitutional rights and whether government requirements pertaining to faculty violate the constitutional rights of religious colleges and universities. Statutory issues relate to whether federal and state statutes apply to faculty in religious higher education institutions. Contractual issues relate to the interpretation of employment contracts under state contract law principles.

Absent an unusual set of facts, faculty in religious colleges (as in all nonpublic higher education institutions) do not have constitutional rights under the U.S. Constitution. The Fourteenth Amendment, assuring that rights of life, liberty, and property will not be abridged, applies only to state governments and their agencies.[58] Litigants who cannot make a claim directly under the Fourteenth Amendment may attempt to achieve the same result using Section 1983 of the Civil Rights Act of 1964,[59] but the absence of state action will serve as a bar.

Where a faculty member in a religious (or any nonpublic) higher education institution alleges a constitutional violation, he or she has a formidable burden of proof to demonstrate that the institution is implicated with the state under one of four theories: state entanglement,[60] state or public function,[61] symbiotic relationship,[62] and state entwinement.[63] Courts have consistently held that a wide range of relationships between nonpublic institutions and state government agencies are not sufficient to invoke liability under a state action theory: reception of state and/or federal assistance;[64] accreditation or state licensure;[65] granting of a state charter;[66] tax exemption;[67] filing of state forms;[68] performance of a state function, viz. education;[69] establishing policies required by government;[70] state inspection and regulation;[71] and service of government officials on governing boards.[72] In the leading case of *Rendell-Baker v. Kohn*,[73] the Supreme Court refused to find state action to support constitutional claims of faculty discharged allegedly for exercise of free speech because there was no state action, even though the employing school for maladjusted students received 90 percent of its funds from the federal government, received all student referrals from public schools, and complied with a variety of public regulations.

However, to declare that faculty in religious higher education institutions have no constitutional rights does not mean that they forsake all fairness in the manner in which the institutions deal with them. Where a faculty member alleges a violation of a substantive constitutional right, courts are likely to scrutinize the employee's contractual rights through the lens of constitutional fairness. A private college or university cannot immunize itself from scrutiny under the institution's employment contract by claiming that the constitution protects its right to decide tenure and promotion.[74] Normally, however, the degree of judicial scrutiny is not onerous, and university decisions will be upheld as long as "there is color of due process."[75] A constitutional level of review will take place only where a private university claims that it provides the same rights as faculty at public universities[76]

The other side of the constitutional question is whether courts can intervene in employee disputes and apply civil law without violating the religious college or university's First Amendment rights. In *Welter v. Seton Hall*,[77] a Catholic university alleged that awards of damages for breach of contract to two nuns after they had been discharged intruded into the doctrinal control of the Catholic Church over those involved in religious service. However, in upholding the damages awards, the Supreme Court of New Jersey reasoned that, where the nuns were computer-science instructors and not involved in a ministerial function at the university, the court could apply common law contract principles without intruding into the University's religious tenets. Generally, courts have protected religious higher education institutions under the First Amendment from judicial inquiry only as to employees involved with ministerial functions.[78] Application of civil law, be it common law or statutes, to religious institutions will generally be upheld where the civil law can be applied without changing religious beliefs.[79] However, even the most sincerely held religious beliefs can be overridden where government has important interests, such as eradicating discrimination, to pursue.

Aside from constitutional issues relating to the application of civil law to religious colleges and universities, issues also arise as to whether the statutes themselves exempt the institutions from judicial inquiry. Title VII's[80] prohibitions on employment discrimination contain broad exemptions from coverage for religious organizations. Other federal statutes, such as the Age Discrimination in Employment Act (ADEA)[81] or Title I of the Americans with Disabilities Act (ADA),[82] and the Family Medical and Leave Act (FMLA),[83] either contain no exemption[84] or contain only a limited exemption.[85]

Three exemptions within Title VII provide some protection for employment decisions by religious higher education institutions. Although Title VII does not apply to employers with fewer than fifteen employees,[86] most colleges and universities will have more than that number, either on their own payrolls or by including the employees of controlling religious organizations.[87]

The three important religious exemptions are

1.  Title VII exempts hiring, discharge, or classification based on religion, sex, or national origin where "religion, sex, or national origin is a bona fide occupational qualification [BFOQ] reasonably necessary to the operations of that particular business or enterprise."[88] The burden is on the employer to prove the necessity of the BFOQ[89] and the Equal Employment Opportunity Commission (EEOC) narrowly interprets whether a BFOQ exemption is appropriate. In general, the EEOC will give favorable treatment where an employee is involved in religious instruction[90] but not to differences of treatment where gender[91] or nonreligious factors[92] are involved.

2.  Title VII exempts employment of persons of a particular religion if the institution is "in whole or in substantial part, owned, supported, controlled, or managed by a particular religious corporation, association, or society, or if the curriculum of such school, college, university, or other educational institution or institution or learning is directed toward the propagation of a particular religion."[93] Although the burden is on the institution to prove its religious preference, this exemption is more broadly interpreted than BFOQ. In *Wirth v. College of the Ozarks*,[94] a nondenominational "Christian-based college" could terminate a Catholic faculty member because his views were different from those of the College. Employment decisions will be upheld even if the connection between a college or university and a religious organization is only one of limited financial support rather than control over the governing board.[95] In *Hall v. Baptist Memorial Health Care Corporation*,[96] the Baptist Memorial College of Health Sciences' discharge of an employee who had been ordained by a church with a large homosexual congregation was upheld because "the College does not have to hire only Baptists or follow a strict policy of religious discrimination to be eligible for the Title VII exemption."[97] When an employee at a religious higher education institution alleges hiring discrimination on one of the other protected grounds under Title VII, EEOC's inquiry is limited to whether the institution has presented proof of its preference to hire persons of a particular religion.[98] For a higher education entity, such as a seminary, by definition an institution involved in the preparation of persons to carry out the religious mission of a particular group, EEOC's jurisdiction is further circumscribed. Whether or not seminaries are located on the premises of religious colleges and universities, EEOC's request under Title VII for record-keeping demographic information about their employees is limited to support personnel and administrators not involved with academics but does not include anyone who "fit[s] the definition of 'ministers.'"[99] Many colleges or universities have a religious

heritage but no longer seek to further that heritage by hiring persons generally of a particular religion. Nonetheless, courts will uphold, under Title VII, hiring preferences within certain departments in those institutions that teach the religion's doctrine or theology.[100]

3.  Title VII exempts "a religious corporation, association, educational institution, or society with respect to the employment of individuals of a particular religion to perform work connected with the carrying out by such corporation, association, educational institution, or society of its activities."[101] The Supreme Court has upheld the extension of this exemption to all employees within a religious organization, even those working in subsidiary units of the organization not involved in propagating the organization's religious message.[102] Qualifying for this exemption does not require a rigid sectarianism. In *Killinger v. Samford University*,[103] the Eleventh Circuit upheld a teaching reassignment of a faculty member based on differences of religious views between the faculty member and the Dean of the Divinity School. The court found controlling a cumulative set of factors identifying the Baptist religious preference for instruction within the Divinity School compatible with Baptist theology: ninety-five percent of the faculty and eighty-eight percent of the students were Baptist; its trustees were Baptist; seven percent of its budget was received from the Alabama Baptist Convention; it submitted financial reports to, and was audited by, the Convention; it belonged to the Association of Baptist Colleges and Schools; and its faculty handbook and contracts contained affirmations and commitments advancing Christianity.

Other federal statutes, such as Title IX,[104] Equal Pay Act,[105] Title VI[106] and Section 504 of the Rehabilitation Act of 1973,[107] apply to religious colleges and universities only if they receive federal funds. Of these statutes, only Title IX contains an exemption for "an educational institution that is controlled by a religious organization if the application of this subsection would not be consistent with the tenets of such organization."[108] However, the burden is on the institution to apply for the exemption and to identify which parts of the regulations conflict with specific religious tenets.[109] As a practical matter, Title IX may have very limited application to gender-based employment issues in light of an indication that employees alleging gender discrimination must bring their claims under Title VII rather than Title IX, which means that the broader religious exemptions under Title VII are available to the institutions.[110] However, religious defenses under Title VII are not likely to be upheld where the effect of an employment practice is to treat one protected class differently than another.[111]

In addition to federal statutes, religious colleges and universities may be subject to state and local laws that can include protected categories, such as marital status[112] and sexual orientation,[113] that are not covered under federal law, as well as state whistleblower statutes.[114] Employees of religious institutions may also find that they can pursue claims of employment discrimination under state laws comparable to federal statutes.[115]

Except where statutes or regulations impose requirements on religious colleges or universities, these institutions can establish employment relationships under common law contract principles. The contractual rights that faculty at religious colleges and universities have may vary with the faculty member's status. On a continuum, that status can include employee-at-will,[116] term, probationary (non-tenured), and tenured. The status generally affects the rights that the faculty enjoy regarding notice and a hearing. Faculty with one-year term contracts generally have no claim for breach of contract when the term expires,[117] even if they have not received notice provided in the contract.[118] The contractual rights of nontenured, tenure-track faculty will depend on written language in the employment contract and handbooks as well as oral statements made prior to or during the employment relationship.[119]

Generally, faculty contract rights are contained in an employment contract and a faculty handbook. However, whether a handbook is considered part of the employment contract depends on the intent of the institution. Not all handbooks have been held to be part of the employment contract. In *Dunfey v. Roger Williams University*,[120] an involuntarily discharged admissions administrator had no claim under the university's employment manual for severance pay because "the Personnel Policy Manual [could] be amended, modified, or superseded at any time." In rejecting the faculty member's claim, a federal district court reasoned that the Manual did not create any contractual rights since it could be altered at any time, and, therefore, the administrator could not have relied on its statements. As *Dunfey* suggests, determining whether an employment contract exists depends on the usual elements of offer, acceptance, consideration, and mutuality of obligation or benefit, even though many courts would probably disagree with *Dunfey* and find an enforceable contract with consideration based on justifiable reliance[121] because handbooks are often regarded as a part of the employment contract.[122]

Religious colleges and universities can reasonably be expected to incorporate faculty handbooks into the employment contract since the handbooks will contain the most recent expectations for compliance with religious requirements. Courts are likely not to intrude, under the free exercise or establishment clauses, into discipline or discharge of faculty for violations of religious requirements.[123] However, courts will intervene, despite religious defenses, where the institution has failed to make religion a condition for employment[124] and where litigation of faculty members' claims can be pursued without intruding into an interpretation of religious requirements.[125]

## Students in Religious Colleges and Universities

The rights of students at religious colleges and universities parallel those for faculty. Unless courts can find state action, students have no substantive or procedural constitutional rights. Despite efforts by students to allege state action because of a variety of connections between a college and the state, courts have refused to find state action to support a constitutional theory.[126] However, courts expect that students will be dealt with fairness that may mimic due process.[127] At the heart of due process is the expectation that persons will be treated reasonably and will be subject to fair rules. As is the case for faculty, students are subject to rules in handbooks, but these rules can be attacked either facially[128] or as interpreted and applied to students.[129]

As in the case for faculty, federal anti-discrimination statutes, such as Titles IX, VI, and section 504, apply only where religious college and universities receive funds administered by the federal government. Since virtually all institutions participate in the Department of Education's Title IV student aid programs, this requirement is met. Title IX has become especially significant in higher education in prohibiting sexual harassment and prohibiting discrimination in athletic programs. In light of the Supreme Court's decisions in *Franklin v. Gwinnett County Public Schools*[130] permitting direct action damages claims under Title IX for sexual harassment by employees of students and *Davis v. Monroe County Board of Education*[131] permitting direct action damages claims for student-on-student sexual harassment, religious colleges and universities are as vulnerable under harassment claims as any other public or private institution. Similarly, religious higher education institutions are just as responsible as their private, nonsectarian counterparts to meet Title IX's equity requirements for men's and women's athletic programs.[132] Students with disabilities are protected under Title III of ADA's prohibition of discrimination in public accommodations. Title III contains an exemption for "any religious entity"[133] which it defines as "a religious organization, including a place of worship."[134] This exemption is broad enough to cover seminaries[135] and perhaps even pervasively religious colleges and universities. However, all colleges and universities participating in federal student aid programs would be covered under Section 504 of the Rehabilitation Act of 1973. Since Title III of ADA is patterned after Section 504,[136] an institution exempt under ADA will still encounter the same requirements under 504.

In addition to federal statutory remedies under these same statutes as applied to faculty, students are protected under the Family Educational Rights and Privacy Act (FERPA).[137] This statute affords confidentiality for education records and protects them from impermissible disclosure; this applies to all institutions receiving funds distributed by the Department of Education (e.g., Title IV). In the past, courts have permitted enforcement of FERPA by private action under the statute. However, this ended with *Gonzaga University v. Doe* in which the Supreme Court held that no private right of action existed under FERPA, nor could a claim be brought under section 1983.[138] Gross violations of the principles of confidentiality under this act can result, however, in loss of federal funds through federal agency action.

Student contract claims present many of the same issues as for faculty. Students facing disciplinary action may be dealing with broad prohibitions of unacceptable conduct in student handbooks. One of the important concepts in dealing with student disciplinary action is that of notice. Notice includes notification as to what conduct is considered unacceptable and what handbook provision the conduct violates. Courts will give religious institutions great latitude and uphold disciplinary action, including suspensions or expulsions, as long as the alleged misconduct at issue can fit within the broad language of published student disciplinary policies.[139] However, students must be informed regarding which of the handbook provisions the disciplinary action is proceeding under, and failure to provide this kind of notice can result in a new hearing.[140] In an older case, a New York court upheld, in *Carr v. St. John's University*,[141] expulsion of two university students married in a civil ceremony, as well as two students acting as witnesses, under a University regulation stating that "in conformity with ideals of Christian education and conduct the university reserved the right to dismiss a student at any time on whatever grounds the university judged advisable." Although the case may seem somewhat archaic in terms of higher education's current more permissive environment, it does illustrate that courts are not unresponsive to religious requirements for student conduct. To the extent that acceptable student conduct is framed in terms of religious standards, courts are unlikely to intrude into either the standard or application of the standard to student misconduct as long as the student had notice of the institution's standard and the misconduct covered by that standard.[142]

The process to which students are entitled during a disciplinary proceeding will generally depend on the language in the student handbook. Courts will hold higher education institutions to the process in student handbooks[143] but, otherwise, will require only that students have an opportunity to present their version of the facts.[144] Once courts are satisfied that the college or university had followed the procedures in its handbook, they will not attempt to second-guess the institution's decision.[145] However, failure to follow handbook procedures can subject the higher education institution to a trial on that issue.[146]

Beyond the issues regarding student misconduct, students may have contractual claims against the institution flowing from their status as a consumer. Students have been successful under a variety of legal theories, breach of contract, fraud, and misrepresentation, where they have not received the instruction promised in university promotional material.[147] In addition, students may have a claim under a state's deceptive practice statute where the course as delivered was different than one that had been advertised.[148] In general, students are entitled to expect higher education institutions to honor the commitments that they have made to them[149] and not to engage in conduct that breaches either a contractual or fiduciary relationship between the student and the institution.[150]

## Conclusion

Religious colleges and universities are the oldest form of higher education in the United States, even though many of the early institutions have long since become secular. The transition from religious colleges and universities to secular ones mirrors the general secularizing trend in higher education. However, many of the religious institutions started in the nineteenth and twentieth centuries have maintained their religious ties, albeit not with the same intensity as the original founders intended. The erosion of religious distinctiveness has been, in most cases, a gradual process as religious colleges and universities have struggled to integrate such secular influences as accreditation, academic freedom, and due process into the religious matrix of their founding charters. For institutions that have continued to be controlled by a specific religious body or group of religious entities, change has been more gradual but, nevertheless, irresistible and irretrievable.

Other than the internal dynamic associated with religious change, religious colleges and universities have been affected by the practical realities of attracting students and faculty whose intensity of religious commitment may vary considerably. The necessity for change has been driven by factors beyond the control of the institutions. State legislatures and the Congress have passed a wide range of statutes that affect the manner in which colleges and universities manage their affairs with employees, students, and the public at large.

With all of the regulation, the wonder is that religious colleges and universities have been able to maintain a religious distinction at all. The fact that many have is a testament to efforts by college and university administrators, faculty, and board members to make the commitment to their religious roots.

## Endnotes

[1] H. EDWARDS AND V. NORDIN, HIGHER EDUCATION AND THE LAW 7 (1979).

[2] William and Mary is a public university, part of the Commonwealth of Virginia university system, and Harvard and Yale are private, secular institutions.

[3] J. BRUBACHER AND W. RUDY, HIGHER EDUCATION IN TRANSITION (1976), P. 7

[4] *Id.* at 12.

[5] Zygano, Sectarian Universities, Federal Funding, and the Question of Academic Freedom, 85 RELIGIOUS FREEDOM 136 (1990).

[6] There are 237 colleges and universities in the United States that claim affiliation with the Catholic Church, even though most of these were founded by religious orders within the Catholic Church and are independent of episcopal control. F. A. Foy AND R. Avato, 1997 Catholic Almanac 536 (1997).

[7] For example, Baylor University in Waco TX, the largest Baptist university in the world, is affiliated with the Baptist General Convention of Texas, which elects 25 percent of the members of the Board of Trustees. *See* http://www.baylor.edu/

[8] For example, Appalachian Bible College is the operating arm of an independent mission organization, Appalachian Bible Fellowship. *See* http://www.abc.edu/ last visited Feb. 8, 2002).

[9] For example, see Grove City College, Grove City, PA is "committed to Christian principles," even though it does not have a specific affiliation with a religious church or denomination. *See* www.gcc.edu.

[10] For a comprehensive review of all religious colleges and universities in the United States, see Thomas Hunt and James Carper (eds.), Religious Higher Education in the United States (1996).

[11] 403 U.S. 672 (1971).

[12] For another Roman Catholic case, *see* Roemer v. Bd. of Pub. Works of Md., 426 U.S. 736 (1976) (Court upheld state subsidy to four Catholic colleges because none of them received funds from, or reported to the Catholic Church, Catholic representation on the boards of trustees did not influence college decisions, attendance at religious services on the campuses was not required, mandatory religion courses were taught within the 1940 AAUP Principles of Academic Freedom, before class prayer was miniscule and not required, and the faculty was hired without having to be Catholic).

[13] Hunt v. NcNair, 413 U.S. 734 (1973).

[14] 474 U.S. 481 [29 Educ. L. Rep. 496] (1986) (on remand, however, to the state, its supreme court found that, even though the grant did not violate the federal Establishment Clause, it violated the state constitution; *see* Witters v. Dep't of Servs. for the Blind, 771 P.2d 1119 [53 Educ. L. Rep. 278] (Wash. 1989)).

[15] 509 U.S. 1 [83 Educ. L. Rep. 930] (1993).

[16] 521 U.S. 203 [119 Educ. L. Rep. 29](1997).

[17] 530 U.S. 1296 [145 Educ. L. Rep. 44] (2000).

[18] 540 U.S.712 (2004)

[19] *See* Va. Coll. Bldg. Auth. v. Lynn, 538 S.E.2d 682 [149 Educ. L. Rep. 918] (Va. 2000), (a pervasively religious university, Regent University, was eligible to participate in the state's tax-exempt revenue bond program even though secular courses were taught from a religious perspective, effectively reversing an earlier decision, Hebel v. Indus. Dev. Auth. of the City of Lynchburg, Va., 400 S.E.2d 516 [65 Educ. L. Rep. 621] (Va. 1991), declaring another pervasively religious university, Liberty University, ineligible to participate in the same tax-exempt revenue bond program). *See also*, Minnesota Fed'n of Teachers v. Mammenga, 500 N.W.2d 136 [83 Educ. L. Rep. 409] (Minn. Ct. App. 1993) (state could reimburse pervasively religious college for tuition, textbook, and materials costs of high school students attending the college pursuant to the state's Post-Secondary Enrollment Options Act). *See also* Columbia Union Coll. v. Oliver, 254 F.3d 496 [155 Educ. L. Rep. 24] (4th Cir. 2001) (college affiliated and controlled by Seventh Day Adventist Church entitled to state grant money because of secular purpose of academic program; however, although not required in this case, appeals court also agreed with the district court that college did not satisfy requirements of being pervasively sectarian).

[20] *See, e.g.*, Ohio Rev. Code §4140.01(B)(h)(i) (exempt from unemployment compensation are employees "in the employ of a church or convention or association of churches, or in an organization which is operated primarily for religious purposes and which is operated, supervised, controlled, or principally supported by a church or convention of churches."). *See* Czigler v. Bureau of Employment Servs., 501 N.E.2d 56 [36 Educ.

L. Rep. 426] (Ohio Ct. App. 1985) (teacher of Hebrew and Jewish religious subjects at Hillel Academy denied unemployment compensation benefits because the following elements made the school "pervasively sectarian" even though not controlled by a specific Jewish congregation: reception of funds from Jewish community fund; recognition of traditional holidays and Jewish holy days; student body exclusively Jewish; and included among the board of directors were rabbis from each Jewish congregation serving in ex officio capacity.).

[21] 42 U.S.C. §410(a)(8)(B) ("Service performed in the employ of a church or qualified church-controlled organization," provided an exemption has been filed by the organization with IRS, is exempt from coverage under Social Security.).

[22] 29 U.S.C. §§1002 (A)(33); 1321(B)(3); 26 U.S.C. §414(e)(3)(B) (church benefit plans exempted from reporting and disclosure requirements of Employment Retirement Income Security Act [ERISA] for "a church or … a convention or association of churches by or associated with a church or a convention or association of churches." Under §414(e) a church or convention or association of churches is one "which is exempt from tax under section 501," which would distinguish organizations claiming tax exemption only as educational institutions.).

[23] 793 F.2d 383 [33 Educ. L. Rep. 46] (1st Cir. 1985).

[24] 440 U.S. 490 (1979).

[25] *Id.* at 399-400.

[26] For example, regarding the battle between Baylor University and the Texas Baptist Convention for control of the University's board of trustees, see *Trustees Limit Baptist Control Over University*, N.Y. Times, Oct. 21, 1990, at 47; *Baptists Board Oks New Governing Plan for Baylor University*, Houston Post, Sept. 11, 1991, at A1.

[27] 461 U.S. 574 [10 Educ. L. Rep. 918] (1983).

[28] 536 A.2d 1 [44 Educ. L. Rep. 309] (D.C. Cir. 1987).

[29] *See* Presbyterian Church v. Hull Church, 393 U.S. 440, 449 (1969) (Court invalidated state law that permitted juries to determine ownership of church property based on whether a controlling church organization had departed from church doctrine. "[The] First Amendment values are plainly jeopardized when church property litigation is made to turn on the resolution by civil courts of controversies over religious doctrine and practice.").

[30] *See e.g.*, Ga. Code Ann. § 14-3-801; Va. Code Ann. § 23-9.2:3 (2001); Fla. Stat. Ann. § 623.02 (incorporation and changes under supervision of circuit judge in county in which school is located); Mich. Comp. Laws Ann. § 450.178 (religious schools called "ecclesiastical corporations").

[31] *See* Fla. Stat. Ann. § 246 .081 (the authority to act as a nonpublic higher education institution in the state requires a license from the State Board of Nonpublic Career Education; the articles of incorporation do not confer authority to function).

[32] See Ohio Rev. Code Ann. § 1702.12 (among the authority of nonpublic corporations is the right to sue and be sued, to hold and dispose of property, and to indemnify officers).

[33] As part of its nonpublic corporation statute, Ohio permits indemnification of any party to a lawsuit only if the party acted in "good faith" and prohibits indemnification where a party has been liable for negligence or misconduct in the performance of duties to the corporation. Ohio Rev. Code § 1702.12 (E) (1) and (2) (a) and (b).

[34] The Trustees of Dartmouth Coll. v. Woodward, 4 Wheat. (U.S.) 518 (1819) (Court struck down state statutes that increased number of trustees, giving appointment power of the new trustees to state officials).

[35] *See* Ga.Code Ann. § 14-3-180.

[36] 448 A.2d 988 [5 Educ. L. Rep. 1170] (N.J. 1982).

[37] The College clearly seemed to meet the criteria as pervasively sectarian. It operated as part of the Bible Presbyterian Church's mission, infused religion throughout the curriculum, and required students "to conform their behavior to religiously derived codes of conduct." *Id.* at 990.

[38] Shelton Coll. v. State Bd. of Educ., 226 A.2d 612 (N.J. 1967).

[39] *Shelton*, 448 A.2d at 992, 993.

[40] *Id.* at 994.

[41] *Id.* at 994, 996.

[42] See § 110 ILCS 1010/6 (2001) (no educational institution in Illinois can confer a degree until one year after it has provided notice to the Board of Higher Education and has received approval; among the information to be provided are the names and addresses of the president and board members, which must be reported annually as to any changes).

[43] 552 F.2d 948 (3d Cir. 1977).

[44] *Id.* at 959 (the issue as to whether the University was part of the state system of education arose in the context of a civil rights claim against the University under section 1983 of the Civil Rights Act of 1964, which required a finding of state action)

[45] *See* Ohio REV. CODE ANN. § 1713.22 (Anderson 2001); KY. REV. STAT. ANN. § 273.070 (incorporated school can organize branch campuses).

[46] *See* Barr v. United Methodist Church, 153 Cal. Rptr. 322 (Cal. Ct. App. 1979) (denomination held financially responsible following bankruptcy of nonprofit organization that operated fourteen retirement homes).

[47] *See e.g.*, *supra*, note 7 where the Texas Baptist Convention appoints 25 percent of Baylor University's trustees. *See also supra* note 19 and accompanying text where individuals occupying designated church positions were required to serve on a Catholic university's board.

[48] 477 S.E.2d 501 [113 EDUC. L. REP. 1337] (Va. 1996).

[49] *Id.* at 504.

[50] *Id.* The case does not discuss the University's reasons for opposing tenure, but one reason may be to eliminate any limitation on the University's ability to nonrenew faculty whose conduct is inconsistent with underlying moral and religious tenets without having to go through the process of demonstrating good cause.

[51] *See* Gilbert v. McLeod Infirmary, 64 S.E.2d 524 (S.C. 1951) (the business dealing will be void even if there is no fraud and even if the university suffered no harm).

[52] 197 F.3d 742 [140 EDUC. L. REP. 105] (5th Cir. 1999).

[53] 371 S.E.2d 858 [49 EDUC. L. REP. 446] (Ga. 1988).

[54] 381 F. Supp. 1003 (D.S.C. 1974).

[55] *Id.* at 1013-14.

[56] For a broader discussion of the legal duties of board members, see R. MAWDSLEY LEGAL PROBLEMS OF RELIGIOUS AND PRIVATE SCHOOLS 139-49 (2000).

[57] 35 F.3d 978 (4th Cir. 1994), *cert. denied*, 513 U.S. 1153 (1995).

[58] The Fourteenth Amendment, through which the substantive and procedural rights of the Fourteenth Amendment are made applicable to states, provides in part that: "No State shall make or enforce any law which shall abridge the privileges or immunities of citizens of the United States; nor shall any State deprive any person of life, liberty, or property, without due process of law; nor deny to any person within its jurisdiction the equal protection of the laws."

[59] 42 U.S.C. § 1983 provides in part: "Every person who, under color of any statute, ordinance, regulation, custom or usage, of any State ... subjects, or causes to be subjected, any citizen of the United States or other person with the jurisdiction thereof to the deprivation of any rights, privileges, or immunities secured by the Constitution and laws, shall be liable to the party injured ... "

[60] *See* Howard v. Pine Forge Acad., 678 F. Supp. 1120 [45 EDUC. L. REP. 115] (E.D. Pa. 1987) (compliance with state requirement applicable to all public and nonpublic institutions not state action).

[61] *See* Hawkins v. NCAA, 652 F. Supp. 602 [37 EDUC. L. REP. 811] (N.D. Ill. 1987) (NCAA regulatory applicable to a private university not traditionally and exclusively a state function even though public interest may be served).

[62] *See* Stone v. Dartmouth Coll., 682 F. Supp. 106 [46 EDUC. L. REP. 194] (D.N.H. 1988) (college discipline of underage drinking not a proxy for criminal prosecution that state could bring).

[63] *See* Brentwood Acad. v. Tenn. Secondary Sch. Ass'n, 531 U.S. 288 [152 EDUC. L. REP. 18] (2001) (state athletic association rule-making authority as limiting free expression rights of a private school where association controlled by public schools considered state action for purposes of section 1983 damages claim).

[64] *See* Rendall-Baker v. Kohn, 457 U.S. 830 [4 EDUC. L. REP. 999] (1982).

[65] *See* Huff v. Notre Dame High Sch., 456 F. Supp. 1145 (D. Conn. 1978).

[66] *See* Fischer v. Driscoll, 546 F. Supp. 861 [6 EDUC. L. REP. 545] (E.D. Pa. 1982); Blackburn v. Fisk Univ., 443 F.2d 121 (6th Cir. 1971).

[67] *See* Bright v. Isenbarger, 314 F. Supp. 1382 (N.D. Ind. 1970); Brown v. Mitchell, 409 F.2d 769 (10th Cir. 1969).

[68] *See* Albert v. Carovano, 851 F.2d 561 [48 EDUC. L. REP. 35] (2d Cir. 1988).

[69] *See* Berrios v. Inter-Am. Univ., 409 F. Supp. 769 (D.P.R. 1975); Grossner v. Trs. of Columbia Univ., 287 F. Supp. 535 (S.D.N.Y. 1968).

[70] *See* Logan v. Bennington Coll., 72 F.3d 1017 [106 EDUC. L. REP. 51] (2d Cir. 1995); Missert v. Trs. of Boston Univ., 73 F. Supp. 2d 68 [140 EDUC. L. REP. 554] (D. Mass. 1999).

[71] *See* Moghimzadeh v. Coll. of St. Rose, 653 N.Y.S.2d 198 [115 EDUC. L. REP. 1012] (N.Y. App. Div. 1997); Gardiner v. Mercyhurst Coll., 942 F. Supp. 1055 [114 EDUC. L. REP. 162] (W.D. Pa.1996).

[72] *See* Hack v. President and Fellows of Yale Coll., 16 F. Supp. 2d 183 [129 EDUC. L. REP. 1020] (D. Conn. 1998).

[73] 457 U.S. 830 [4 EDUC. L. REP. 999] (1982).

[74] *See* Kyriakopoulos v. George Washington Univ., 866 F.2d 438 [51 EDUC. L. REP. 740] (D.C. Cir. 1989).

[75] Flint v. St. Augustine High Sch., 323 So. 2d 229, 235 (La. Ct. App. 1976).

[76] See Franklin v. Leland Stanford, Jr. Univ., 218 Cal. Rptr. 228 [27 EDUC. L. REP. 525] (Cal. Ct. App. 1985).

[77] 608 A.2d 206 [75 EDUC. L. REP. 822] (N.J. 1992).

[78] *See* Alicea v. New Brunswick Theological Seminary, 608 A.2d 218 [75 EDUC. L. REP. 834] (N.J. 1992); EEOC v. Southwestern Baptist Theological Seminary, 485 F. Supp. 255 (N.D. Tex. 1980), *rev'd in part* 651 F.2d 277 (5th Cir. 1981).

[79] *See* Russell v. Belmont Coll., 554 F. Supp. 667 [9 EDUC. L. REP. 143] (M.D. Tenn. 1982) (Equal Pay Act applied to church-controlled college regarding differential pay for women over free exercise and establishment clause objections because no religious belief of the college would be hampered); Geary v. Visitation of Blessed Virgin Mary Parish Sch., 7 F.3d 324 [86 EDUC. L. REP. 623] (3d Cir. 1993) (ADEA claim of 50-year-old teacher discharged after marrying divorced man applied to religious school because issue of alleged age discrimination could be addressed without challenging religious views on divorce). *But see,* Boyd v. Harding Acad. Of Memphis, Inc., 88 F.3d 410 [110 EDUC. L. REP. 981] (6th Cir. 1998) (discharge of out-of-wedlock teacher upheld pursuant to religious belief against extramarital sex where school had enforced its belief with regard to both men and women).

[80] 42 U.S.C. § 2000 *et seq.*

[81] 29 U.S.C. § 621 *et seq.*

[82] 42 U.S.C. § 12101 *et seq.*

[83] 29 U.S.C. § 2611 *et seq.*

[84] *See* Soriano v. Xavier Univ., 687 F. Supp. 1188 [47 EDUC. L. REP. 989] (S.D. Ohio 1988) (ADEA applicable to religious university over free exercise and entanglement arguments because no evidence in statute that Congress intended to exclude religious universities); Gargano v. Diocese of Rockville Ctr., 80 F.3d 87 [108 EDUC. L. REP. 78] (2d Cir. 1996) (breach of contract award upheld over establishment clause defense

where school had violated its handbook in not considering plaintiff for new position). *But see,* Cochran v. St. Louis Preparatory Seminary, 717 F. Supp. 1413 (E.D. Mo. 1989) (ADEA not applicable to seminary where faculty member, performing ministerial functions, was discharged because there was no legislative intent to include religious institutions).

85 *Cf.* McGrehaghn v. St. Denis Sch., 979 F. Supp. 323 [122 Educ. L. Rep. 455] (E.D. Pa.) (Title I of ADA applicable to employees in religious schools) *with* White v. Denver Seminary, 157 F. Supp. 2d 1171 [156 Educ. L. Rep. 871] (D. Colo. 2001) (seminary exempt as "religious organization" under Title III of ADA).

86 42 U.S.C. § 2000e(b)

87 Title VII uses a "single employer doctrine" which can include employees of organizations other than educational institutions where there is interrelation of operations, common management, centralized control of labor relations, and common ownership or financial control. *See* EEOC v. St. Francis Xavier Parochial Sch., 20 F. Supp. 2d 66 [130 Educ. L. Rep. 611] (D.C. Cir. 1999), *rev'd on other grounds,* 117 F.3d 621 [120 Educ. L. Rep. 915], *on remand,* 77 F. Supp. 2d 71 [140 Educ. L. Rep. 913] (D.D.C. 1999) (ADA case that followed title VII jurisdictional requirements).

88 42 U.S.C. § 2000e-2(e)(1).

89 *See* Hernandez v. St. Thomas Univ., 793 F. Supp. 214 [76 Educ. L. Rep. 403] (D. Minn. 1992) (university had burden of proving a factual basis for privacy considerations of BFOQ for hiring only female custodians for female dorm).

90 *See* Maguire v. Marquette Univ., 627 F. Supp. 1499 [30 Educ. L. Rep. 1141] (E.D. Wis. 1986); Pime v. Loyola Univ. of Chi., 585 F. Supp. 435 [17 Educ. L. Rep. 1128] (N.D. Ill. 1984).

91 *See* Vigars v. Valley Christian Ctr. of Dublin, Cal., 805 F. Supp. 802 [79 Educ. L. Rep. 100] (N.D. Cal. 1992) (discharge of librarian on the basis of out-of-wedlock pregnancy because of "role model"); EEOC v. Fremont Christian Sch., 609 F. Supp. 344 (N.D. Cal. 1984), *aff'd* 781 F.2d 1362 (9th Cir. 1986) (denial of health insurance to employees not "head of household.").

92 *See* Ritter v. Mount St. Mary's Coll., 495 F. Supp. 724 (D. Md. 1980) (tenure denial had nothing to do with religious doctrine of college).

93 42 U.S.C. § 2003-2(e)(1).

94 26 F. Supp. 2d 1185 [131 Educ. L. Rep. 197] (W.D. Mo. 1998).

95 *See* Killinger v. Samford Univ., 113 F.3d 196 [118 Educ. L. Rep. 48] (11th Cir. 1997).

96 145 F. Supp. 216 [145 Educ. L. Rep. 216] (6th Cir. 2000).

97 Hall v. Baptist Mem'l Health Care Corp., 27 F. Supp. 2d 1029, 1037 [131 Educ. L. Rep. 385] (W.D. Tenn. 1998).

98 *See* EEOC v. Miss. Coll., 626 F.2d 477 (5th Cir. 1980) (female applicant not hired because she was not Baptist had no title VII discrimination claim on the basis of gender if College had a preference in hiring Baptists).

99 *See* EEOC v. Southwestern Baptist Seminary, 485 F. Supp. 255 (N.D. Tex. 1980), *rev'd in part* 651 F.2d 277 (5th Cir. 1981) (among those that EEOC could not request record-keeping information about were all faculty, the president and vice president, the chaplain, deans of men and women, the academic deans, and those persons supervising faculty).

100 See Pime v. Loyola Univ., 803 F.2d 351 [35 Educ. L. Rep. 646] (7th Cir. 1986) (refusal to hire Jewish part-time instructor for a full-time position in philosophy department upheld where the university with connections to the Jesuits could maintain a "Jesuit presence" within the department); Maguire v. Marquette Univ., 627 F. Supp. 1499 [30 Educ. L. Rep. 1141] (E.D. Wis. 1986) (female applicant not hired in theology department because of her view on abortion upheld because the definition of what is Catholic theology is protected by the First Amendment).

101 42 U.S.C. § 2000e-1.

[102] *See* Amos v. Corporation of the Presiding Bishop, 483 U.S. 327 (1987) (five employees employed by organizations wholly owned by the Mormon Church could be discharged for not meeting the Church's requirements for a temple recommend).

[103] 113 F.3d 196 [118 EDUC. L. REP. 48] (11th Cir. 1997).

[104] 20 U.S.C. § 1681 *et seq.*

[105] 29 U.S.C. § 206(d)(1).

[106] 42 U.S.C. § 2000d.

[107] 20 U.S.C. § 794.

[108] 20 U.S.C. § 1681(a)(3).

[109] 45 C.F.R. § 86.12(b).

[110] *See* Gardner v. St. Bonaventure Univ., 171 F. Supp. 2d 118 [159 EDUC. L. REP. 25] (W.D.N.Y. 2001) (former employee could proceed with gender discrimination claim under Title IX, but not Title IX).

[111] *See* Cline v. Catholic Diocese of Toledo, 199 F.3d 853 [140 EDUC. L. REP. 880] (6th Cir. 1999) (court refused to uphold summary judgment for *Diocese* because question of fact existed as to whether school enforced its policy against pre-marital sex solely by observing pregnancy of female teachers); EEOC v. Tree of Life Christian Schs., 751 F. Supp. 700 [64 EDUC. L. REP. 765] (S.D. Ohio 1990) (EPA had minimal impact on religious educational institution's beliefs regarding familial roles of men and women to extent head of household allowance paid to married male faculty members with dependents but not to female faculty members; institution free to practice religious beliefs that did no unlawfully discriminate in wage scale on basis of gender).

[112] *See* Parker-Bigbach v. St. Lubre Sch., 7 P.3d 361 [146 EDUC. L. REP. 1129] (Mont. 2000) (school subject to state marital status law but not in violation when it terminated a counselor for living with a man without being married).

[113] *See* Gay Rights Coalition v. Georgetown Univ., 536 A.2d 1 [44 EDUC. L. REP. 309] (D.D.C. 1987) (city ordinance applied to gay student request to meet on university campus despite Catholic religious views opposing homosexuality). *Cf.* Walker v. First Presbyterian Church, 22 FEP 762 (Cal. Super. Ct. 1980) (city ordinance prohibiting discrimination on basis of sexual orientation did not apply to church organist who was member of worship team).

[114] *See* Keefe v. Youngstown Diocese of Catholic Church, 698 N.E.2d 1009 [128 EDUC. L. REP. 850] (Ohio Ct. App. 1997) (employee entitled to go to trial as to whether her discharge had violated the state Whistleblower Act).

[115] *See* Gallo v. Salesian Soc'y, Inc., 676 A.2d 580 [109 EDUC. L. REP. 1286] (N.J. Super. Ct. 1996) (lay teacher could sue religious school under state statute prohibiting age and sex discrimination).

[116] *See* Roberts v. Wake Forest Univ., 286 S.E.2d 120 [2 EDUC. L. REP. 296] (N.C. Ct. App. 1982) (golf coach discharged after seven months had contract for an indeterminate term, which under state law meant an employment-at-will); Tramontozzi v. St. Francis Coll., 649 N.Y.S.2d 43 [114 EDUC. L. REP. 252] (N.Y. App. Div. 1996) (athletic director an employee-at-will and could be discharged at any time).

[117] *See* Muhitch v. St. Gregory the Great Catholic Church and Sch., 659 N.Y.S.2d 679 [119 EDUC. L. REP. 632] (N.Y. App. Div. 1997) (former teacher with one-year contract could not sue for breach of contract).

[118] *See* DiSimone v. Sienna Coll., 663 N.Y.S.2d 701 [121 EDUC. L. REP. 1126] (N.Y. App. Div. 1997) (probationary faculty member with contract that stated that it was for one year and nonrenewable had no breach of contract claim even it he received notice of nonrenewal two days late).

[119] *Cf.* Lewis v. Loyola Univ. of Chi., 500 N.E.2d 47 [35 EDUC. L. REP. 1199] (Ill. App. Ct. 1986) (preemployment letter promising submission of candidate for early tenure created contractual obligation) *with* Conway v. Pac. Univ., 879 P.2d 201 [94 EDUC. L. REP. 531] (D. Mass. 1993) (dean's incorrect statement about status of prior student evaluations in tenure process could not be basis for negligent misrepresentation).

[120] 824 F. Supp. 18 [84 Educ. L. Rep. 219] (D. Mass. 1993).

[121] *See* Fairbank v. Tulane Univ., 731 So. 2d 983 [135 Educ. L. Rep. 284] (La. Ct. App. 1999) (student of deceased parent-faculty member had contractual claim on tuition waiver provision in effect when student's parent died, not at a later date when student enrolled in graduate program after the waiver had been removed)

[122] *See* Moffice v. Oglethorpe Univ., 367 S.E.2d 112 [46 Educ. L. Rep. 837] (Ga. Ct. App. 1988) (handbook incorporated by reference into contract).

[123] *Cf.* Gabriel v. Immanuel Evangelical Lutheran Church, Inc., 640 N.E.2d 681 [94 Educ. L. Rep. 907] (Ill. App. Ct. 1994) (contract offered to teacher could be withdrawn with First Amendment protection where teacher's service considered a "call" and selection of ministers was a responsibility of congregation).

[124] *See Welter* (two discharged nuns each entitled to $45,000 breach of contract awards because employment contract contained no language requiring that they secure permission of religious order to teach and no reference to Canon Law).

[125] *See* Bassinger v. Pilarczek, 707 N.E.2d 1149 [133 Educ. L. Rep. 240] (Ohio Ct. App. 1997) (even though court could not inquire into breach of contract claim as to whether two discharged faculty members had violated their contract by entering into canonically invalid marriage, the court could determine whether the breach of contract was a pretext for age discrimination under ADEA).

[126] Ben-Yonatan v. Concordia Coll., 863 F. Supp. 983 [94 Educ. L. Rep. 1321] (D. Minn. 1994) (suspended student had no constitutional protection despite college's reception of considerable amounts of state and federal funds); Albert v. Caravano, 851 F.2d 561 [48 Educ. L. Rep. 35] (2d Cir. 1988) (students suspended after seizing administration building had no constitutional claims even though state required all private colleges to submit disciplinary rules and penalties).

[127] *See* Harvey v. Palmer Coll. of Chiropractic, 363 N.W.2d 443, 444 [23 Educ. L. Rep. 667] (Iowa Ct. App. 1984) ("requirement imposed by the common law on private universities parallel those imposed by the due process clause on public universities.").

[128] *See* Bob Jones Univ. v. U.S., 461 U.S. 574 [10 Educ. L. Rep. 918] (1983) (rule regarding interracial dating and marriage facially unenforceable as discriminatory, although challenge to rule was by IRS and not students).

[129] *See* Gay Rights Coalition v. Georgetown Univ., 536 A.2d 1 [44 Educ. L. Rep. 309] (D.C. Cir. 1987) (handbook provision limiting student group use of university facilities and services not enforceable as applied to gay student group despite religious objection to homosexuality).

[130] 503 U.S. 60 [72 Educ. L. Rep. 32] (1992).

[131] 526 U.S. 629 [134 Educ. L. Rep. 477] (1999).

[132] The leading case has become Cohen v. Brown Univ., 101 F.3d 155 [114 Educ. L. Rep. 394] (1st Cir. 1996) where the eliminating of two men's and two women's teams violated Title IX where the proportion of women to men in athletics remained considerably lower than the proportion of men to women on campus.

[133] 28 C.F.R. § 36.102(e).

[134] 28 C.F.R. § 36.104.

[135] White v. Denver Seminary, 157 F. Supp. 2d 1171 [156 Educ. L. Rep. 871] (D. Colo. 2001).

[136] *Cf.* the identical categories of persons protected under section 504 [29 U.S.C. § 706(8)(B)] and ADA [42 U.S.C. § 12102].

[137] 20 U.S.C. § 1232(g) *et al.*

[138] 536 U.S. 273 (2002).

[139] *See* Aronson v. N. Park Coll., 418 N.E.2d 776 (Ill. App. Ct. 1981) (student who had been diagnosed as a chronic paranoid and who had refused to report for treatment could be dismissed as a student who is "undesirable and whose continuation in the school is detrimental to himself and his fellow students").

[140] *See* Fellheimer v. Middlebury Coll., 869 F. Supp. 238 [96 Educ. L. Rep. 419] (D. Vt. 1994).

[141] 187 N.E.2d 18 (N.Y. App. Div. 1962).

[142] *See* Dlaiken v. Roodbeen, 522 N.W.2d 719 [94 Educ. L. Rep. 945] (Mich. Ct. App. 1994) (parish priest's decision not to readmit children unreviewable under First Amendment); Gaston v. Diocese of Allentown, 712 A.2d 757 [127 Educ. L. Rep. 354] (Pa. Super. Ct. 1998) (court did not have subject matter jurisdiction in tort suit brought after children expelled for violation of church doctrine).

[143] *See* Harvey v. Palmer Coll. of Chiropractic, 363 N.W.2d 443 [23 Educ. L. Rep. 667] (Iowa Ct. App. 1984) (expelled student presented jury question as to whether college had followed its own regulations).

[144] *See* Galiani v. Hofstra Univ., 499 N.Y.S.2d 182 [30 Educ. L. Rep. 1247] (N.Y. App. Div. 1986).

[145] *See* Lyon Coll. v. Gray, 999 S.W.2d 213 [137 Educ. L. Rep. 1132] (Ark. Ct. App. 1999) (awarding student an "F" in a course and suspending him for balance of school year); Dinu v. President and Fellows of Harvard Univ., 56 F. Supp. 2d 129 [137 Educ. L. Rep. 619] (D. Mass. 1999) (requiring students to withdraw who had completed all graduation requirements but had not graduated); Harwood v. Johns Hopkins Univ., 747 A.2d 205 [142 Educ. L. Rep. 980] (Md. Ct. App. 2000) (denial of graduation where student had murdered another student between completing requirements and graduation).

[146] *See* Schaer v. Brandeis Univ., 716 N.E.2d 1055 [137 Educ. L. Rep. 1091] (Mass. Ct. App. 1999) (student entitled to a trial as to whether university had followed its procedures in suspending him for sexual harassment); Goodman v. President and Trustees of Bowdoin Univ., 135 F. Supp. 2d 40 [152 Educ. L. Rep. 660] (D. Me. 2001) (white student had breach of contract claim concerning alleged unfair treatment following his suspension after a fight with a Asian student).

[147] *See* Idress v. Am. Univ. of the Carribean, 546 F. Supp. 1342 [6 Educ. L. Rep. 653] (S.D.N.Y. 1982); Dezick v. Umpqua Cmty. Coll., 599 P.2d 444 (Or. 1979).

[148] *See* Andre v. Pace Univ., 618 N.Y.S.2d 975 [96 Educ. L. Rep. 192](N.Y. City Ct. 1994).

[149] Britt v. Chestnut Hill Coll., 632 A.2d 557 [86 Educ. L. Rep. 905] (Pa. Super. Ct. 1993).

[150] James v. SCS Bus. and Technical Inst., 595 N.Y.S.2d 885 [82 Educ. L. Rep. 166] (N.Y. Civ. Ct. App. 1992).

# 4 Faculty
## Joseph Beckham

## Faculty Employment Issues

Litigation involving the relationship between higher education institutions and faculty is typically fact-intensive, unique to a particular context, and complicated by a range of legal issues. Despite reluctance to intervene in the academic decision-making process, judges are regularly compelled to resolve disputes between institutions and aggrieved faculty. The range of issues presented in appellate decisions begins with interpreting the nature of the contract between the parties and extends to a host of legal challenges to institutional decisions that may include allegations of arbitrary and capricious action, denial of First Amendment rights to free speech and association, and violation of state and federal anti-discrimination law.

Public and private institutions face similar contract challenges, with the notable exception that faculty in public institutions may assert protected constitutional rights involving due process and equal protection guarantees that relate to the contract of employment. In addition, the public employee's entitlement carries with it the right to assert First Amendment constitutional rights to free speech. Although private institutions are not typically burdened with protecting the employee's First Amendment rights, it is conceivable that the private institution may contractually obligate itself to extend rights to due process or academic freedom.

### Employment Contracts

Faculty contracts are based on an offer by the institution and an acceptance by the prospective employee. A valid contract will include express terms or conditions, specifying the period of employment, the duties and status of the employee, and the amount of compensation. A faculty member's contract may incorporate the provisions of a bargaining agreement or institutional policies, such as provisions that are contained in a personnel handbook or faculty manual.[1] Public higher education institutions may be governed by state statutory mandates or agency regulations that are influential in determining the rights and obligations of employees.

## Express and Implied Contracts

An express contract is a written document specifically containing the terms and conditions of the employment agreement. In the absence of an express contract, a judge may consider the actions of the parties, oral communications, and institutional documents in order to determine whether an employment agreement may be implied. The judge's foremost concern will relate to whether there was a meeting of the minds on the terms of the agreement that signals a mutual intent to enter into a contract.[2] In an illustrative case, a community college teacher was offered an annual contract in which performance criteria were stipulated. When the teacher reviewed the performance criteria in the contract, she added a statement rejecting the criteria and signed the contract. The reviewing court ruled that the stipulation of performance criteria constituted a material element of the contract, and the teacher had indicated by her modification that she was unwilling to accept the institution's contract offer.[3]

The contract may require interpretation in light of other institutional documents on which the faculty member might reasonably have relied. When the employment contract incorporates specific reference to faculty handbooks, institutional policies, or bargaining agreements, judges refer to these documents as part of the employment contract and hold the institution to substantial compliance with the terms express in those documents.[4] This rule has been particularly applicable to colleges and universities that fail to comply with institutional procedures when making termination and tenure decisions.[5]

## Oral Representations

Judges prefer to adopt a literal interpretation of express contract terms and are reluctant to permit the introduction of oral testimony when a comprehensive written employment agreement is introduced in evidence. In a representative case, a former assistant professor was denied the opportunity to present proof of an oral tenure agreement when the court ruled that the parties had entered into a fully integrated written contract that contained no tenure provision.[6] The refusal to admit oral testimony qualifying the written terms of a contract is referred to as the parole evidence rule. The rule was developed to protect the integrity of written contracts and prohibits a party to a written contract from contradicting the terms of the agreement with evidence of alleged oral representations.[7]

However, there are exceptions to the parole evidence rule that permit a judge to consider additional evidence going beyond the express terms and conditions of a written agreement. Ambiguous terms in the contract of employment may require additional evidence concerning the intent of the parties.[8] Judges may rely on the representations of the parties to determine the nature of an employment contract. In one case, the intent of the parties was determined by judicial reference to letters and oral statements by the dean who assured a faculty member recruited for a post as professor and department chair that he would be recommended for tenure. The professor prevailed by showing that the letters and oral representations of the dean were part of the employment agreement that induced the faculty member to come to the institution.[9]

Oral representations by authorized agents of the institution may influence the interpretation of the contract, but this is more likely to occur in the absence of a written contract and under circumstances in which it was reasonable for the employee to rely on such representations.[10] For example, a professor's assertions that her academic dean promised her lifetime employment did not create de facto tenure in the opinion of a federal court of appeals. The court found the professor's reliance on such an assertion to be unreasonable, given that her employment contract incorporated by reference the university's written policies, which stipulated a formal policy and procedure for the award of tenure.[11]

## Agency

If the faculty member is to demonstrate that the institution should be bound by the acts of an agent acting beyond the scope of actual authority, the institution must have clothed the agent with apparent authority, and the agent's promise must have been one that the institution could make and perform lawfully.[12] The faculty member must also demonstrate that the institution accepted and retained the benefit it received in return for the agent's promise and the faculty member's reliance on that promise was reasonable in light of his or her knowledge and experience with the academic enterprise.

A memorandum from an individual in apparent authority may be sufficient to bind an institution to an offer of employment. In one case, a community college instructor received a written notice of reemployment for the upcoming academic year. The president of the college had signed the memo and directed the instructor to accept or reject the reappointment, date, sign, and return the document to the college. The instructor complied but received a second letter sixteen days later that informed him he would not be tendered a formal contract of employment because of insufficient student enrollment. In ruling for the instructor, a state appeals court found that the president could have conditioned the offer of employment on whether enrollment was sufficient to justify hiring, but his failure to do so created an employment agreement that justified the court in providing equitable relief to the employee.[13]

In contrast, a faculty appointee who sought to enforce a four-year term of employment negotiated with the director of university program failed to bind the university to the negotiated agreement. Although claiming that the director had apparent authority to contract for the four-year period, the state appeals court rejected the claim.[14] The appeals court noted that state law granted the authority to extend contracts beyond a year solely to the university chancellor and reasoned that with the appointee's interpretation, "any multi-year contract made by an agent on behalf of a state institution of higher education would be valid unless expressly countermanded."[15] Such an interpretation and application of the law would turn the chancellor's power of prospective appointment into a retrospective veto power that would be inconsistent with the state law.

While the general rule is that an institution cannot be contractually bound by the promises of an agent absent express authority, judges have artfully interpreted this standard. In one case, state law granted the authority to university presidents to make appointments and provide for compensation and other conditions of employment, but state law also provided that the president's designee could give salary increases. Deans regularly performed these functions, making appointments to the faculty and granting discretionary increases to faculty during the budget year. When a dean received express authorization from the university provost in the form of a promise to support whatever measures the dean took to retain a professor, the state appeals court held that the dean was acting within the scope of his employment when he entered into a contract with the professor and was an authorized agent of the university. In the state appeals court's view, the dean possessed both the general authority (under state statute law) and the specific authority (delegated by the provost) to commit the institution to the terms of a salary increase.[16]

## Contract Types

Employment contracts are typically distinguished as "at will," "term," or "continuing contracts." Employment at will is employment for an indefinite term and terminable at the will of either party. A term or probationary contract is one in which the faculty member has no entitlement to employment beyond the period specified in the contract. The award of tenure grants a property right in the form of an entitlement to continuing contract.

At-will status is often associated with administrative positions in colleges and universities. Judges reason that, absent a specific contract agreement establishing a fixed term of employment, an employer is free to dismiss an employee at any time and for any reason without liability.[17] Similarly, the employee may abandon the position without notice to the employer. Under the at-will doctrine, a plaintiff cannot state a claim for breach of the employment contract if the position was for no specified or guaranteed period of time.[18] However, the at-will employee may be entitled to some limited protection in a dismissal. For example, in private sector institutions, an internal grievance procedure may apply to the institution's adverse employment decision. In a public sector institution, either a grievance procedure or the stigmatizing nature of allegations against the employee may be such that an opportunity for a name-clearing hearing may be available under state administrative procedures or federal law.[19]

Probationary faculty are typically appointed under a term contract. In public institutions, these contracts may require timely notice of nonrenewal prior to the ending date of the contract, but no additional due process protection is available unless state law grants additional entitlements.[20] In one case, a federal appeals court ruled that even though the faculty handbook was not expressly incorporated in the contract of employment, a probationary faculty member could reasonably rely on timely notice, given handbook provisions and the custom and practice of the institution. Failure to provide timely notice of nonrenewal meant that the institution was required to show cause for termination since a legitimate expectancy of another annual contract was created.[21]

If a term or annual contract employee were subject to an adverse employment decision during the period of the contract, the employee could claim a breach of contract. In a public institution of higher education, Fourteenth Amendment due process protections, principally notice and hearing, would be applicable to the employee's entitlement. Thus, annual contract faculty in public institutions have a protected property right to employment and a concomitant due process right to notice and hearing if they are subject to dismissal during the period of employment.[22]

### Tenure

Tenure is a form of continuing contract, designed to create a contractually enforceable institutional commitment to appointment for an indefinite term that can be terminated only for good cause in accordance with procedures specified as part of the contract of employment. The institution's agents can specify tenure in the institution's governing documents, faculty handbooks, collective bargaining agreements, or individual contracts of employment. The traditional basis for award of tenure is excellence in teaching, research, and service.

The American Association of University Professors (AAUP) has played a formidable role in defining tenure in the American college and university. Many faculty handbooks have adopted the language of the AAUP's 1940 Statement of Principles[23] as part of institutional policy. Even in the absence of a specific reference, ambiguities in faculty employment contracts will often be resolved by reference to AAUP guidelines as representing custom and practice in the academic profession.

Judges grant considerable discretion to institutions in the context of tenure decisions if the institution has the foresight to establish express and relevant criteria. For example, despite a faculty recommendation to grant tenure, one institution's president and board denied tenure to an assistant professor on the basis of predicting shifts in student enrollment and declining interest in the program with which the assistant professor was associated. A New York appeals court affirmed the award of summary judgment to the institution and rejected the assistant professor's challenge to the denial of tenure on the basis that the faculty handbook made it inescapable that the institution could consider future institutional need in tenure decisions.[24]

Affirming institutional discretion, a Maryland appeals court agreed with the university that collegiality is a factor that may be considered in promotion and tenure review even though it is not expressly included in the institution's promotion and tenure policy.[25] The court reasoned that collegiality plays an essential role in the categories of both teaching and service and found error in the trial court's failure to hold, as a matter of law, that collegiality was an appropriate consideration in the context of an assistant professor's review for tenure and promotion.[26]

Although judicial deference to academic decision-making applies to the decision to grant or deny tenure, these employment issues are not beyond judicial scrutiny. While the management of a higher education institution is uniquely the province of faculty and administrators within the institution, university agents are required to follow internal rules and procedures, and a court may determine whether institutional representatives violated the terms of the institution's handbook or acted arbitrarily and capriciously. In a case in which the faculty handbook provided that classroom performance is the prime criteria for tenure at the institution and required that institutional representatives make classroom visitations as part of a tenure evaluation, the department chair's failure to undertake the requisite classroom visits was regarded by the court as an insufficient evaluation in light of the direction of the handbook, requiring the court to grant a de novo tenure review to the faculty member.[27]

In a similar breach of contract claim related to the denial of tenure, the Supreme Court of Connecticut noted that despite the faculty handbook's directive for the evaluation committee to be as specific as possible about an employee's tenure prospects, the committee was positive about the faculty member's work, vague about her deficiencies, and negligent in clarifying the criteria that would apply to award of tenure. Under these circumstances, it was reasonable for the assistant professor to rely on the assurance that she should continue along the course of scholarship she had established. The court, in ruling that the institution had breached the contract of employment, concluded that if the college had been more specific in its evaluation of the plaintiff's candidacy, she might have been able to more judiciously allocate her time and energies in a fashion that would more closely address the institution's tenure requirements.[28]

## De Facto Tenure

Beginning with the United States Supreme Court decision in *Perry v. Sindermann,*[29] federal courts have recognized that a faculty member may plead and prove that the institution maintained a custom and practice of de facto tenure. In the *Perry* decision, the Court weighed the lengthy service of a community college faculty member, the institution's repeated assurances that satisfactory performance would result in continuous employment and the institution's failure to develop a formal tenure policy in holding that the faculty member had established a claim of de facto tenure.

However, institutions that specifically provide formal policies and procedures for award of tenure may avoid these claims.[30] For example, in a case in which a probationary faculty member asserted that she had obtained tenure through completing a seven-year period of service at the institution, the reviewing court evaluated the claim in relationship to a faculty handbook that expressly provided that it was the institution's prerogative to award tenure. Given the specific terms of the handbook, the court rejected the professor's assertion that university officials had assured her of automatic tenure once she completed seven years of probationary service.[31] In a similar case, an untenured assistant professor who was not renewed for a third probationary year claimed an entitlement protected by due process and a requirement that good cause accompany the non-renewal. The Seventh Circuit rejected the claim, emphasizing that the contract of employment reserved broad discretion relative to reappointment in the institution's representatives and general statements in the faculty handbook that reappointment would be guided by criteria related to teaching, scholarship, and service did not establish an entitlement to continued employment.[32]

## Collective Bargaining

The contract of employment may be significantly influenced by collective bargaining agreements, but the applicable laws governing faculty collective bargaining differ between public and private sector institutions. State law regulates public institutions of higher education, while private institutions are governed by the National Labor Relations Act of 1935 as amended by the Labor-Management Relations Act of 1947.[33]

State laws vary significantly in the extent to which faculty may bargain collectively. In some jurisdictions, bargaining may be nothing more than a right to meet and confer with institutional management, while other states may authorize bargaining over a range of subjects that include mandatory items such as wages, hours, and a potentially inclusive category consisting of "conditions of employment." Permissive subjects may be negotiated when both parties agree to the negotiation.

What constitutes mandatory or permissive subjects for negotiation will be subject to judicial interpretation of applicable state or federal law. Certain items may be beyond the scope of bargaining in a particular state because legislative pronouncement has preempted the topic or the topic is a nondelegable function of the governing board. For example, the Supreme Court of South Dakota has ruled that a state appropriations statute providing for faculty salary increases to be made exclusively by the institutional governing board was constitutional and rejected a faculty union's claim that the board could not exercise that discretion absent a negotiated agreement.[34] In another case, the Ohio legislature was justified in imposing a faculty workload policy that was held by the United States Supreme Court to be an inappropriate subject for collective bargaining.[35]

While private sector institutions may elect to voluntarily recognize faculty representatives of a union and commence bargaining, the usual approach to faculty collective bargaining in both the private and public sector is to insist that faculty representatives seeking recognition petition for a certification election and establish, usually by majority vote, that they represent the interest of faculty for purposes of collective negotiations. As a part of this process, defining the community of interest among employees will result in determining the nature of the bargaining unit. For example, the Supreme Court of Vermont held that adjunct faculty did not share a community of interest with full-time faculty and could be excluded from the faculty bargaining unit at Vermont public institutions.[36]

Faculty in private sector institutions may be restricted from the application of federal collective bargaining law if language in institutional handbooks appears to grant broad managerial and supervisory responsibilities to faculty.[37] This "managerial exclusion" from bargaining would apply when faculty participate broadly in institutional governance, effectively determining "the product to be produced, the terms upon which it will be offered, and the customers who will be served."[38] However, the exclusion has not precluded collective bargaining in all private sector institutions as judges weigh limits on faculty influence over institutional decision-making in assessing managerial status.

Recognition as the official bargaining agent for a particular unit carries a presumption of exclusive status for purposes of bargaining.[39] Exclusive status permits the designated faculty union to charge non-members an agency fee to underwrite the costs of union services,[40] but non-union faculty are not obligated to pay for the costs of union political activity with which the non-union faculty disagree.[41] Although the determination of what constitutes "political activity" that is not germane to collective bargaining is often speculative, it would include subsidies for legislative lobbying outside the scope of contract ratification or implementation of the terms of the agreement.[42]

The application of collective bargaining agreements to contract disputes has resulted in mixed legal precedent. Faculty may be foreclosed from asserting rights under an implied contract when the bargaining agreement contains language expressly providing that the agreement constitutes the complete agreement between the parties.[43] Similarly, a grievance and arbitration provision in the bargaining agreement may limit the options available to a faculty member for redress of a breach of contract claim. Negotiated agreements often provide for a grievance procedure to resolve disputes related to the administration of the agreement. Arbitration is typically a final step in resolving disputes, and the agreement will define the powers and duties of the arbitrator.

### Adverse Employment Decisions

Just as institutional governing boards are vested with the authority to hire, assign, and award tenure, these governing bodies may undertake adverse employment decisions against faculty. In the context of employee discipline, an adverse employment decision may include reprimand, suspension with or without pay, demotion, nonrenewal, lay off or dismissal for cause. Judicial review of an adverse employment decision involves a series of inquiries: Did the institution comply with the contractual obligation to the employee? Were procedures for undertaking an adverse employment decision followed? Was substantial evidence provided in proof of the alleged facts justifying the adverse employment decision? Did the facts establish good cause under the terms of the contract?

While adverse employment decisions involving faculty at public institutions of higher education are subject to review based on constitutional constraints, judicial review of disciplinary decisions involving faculty of private colleges or universities is limited to whether the institution failed to comply with its own internal procedures and whether a decision was made arbitrarily, capriciously, or in bad faith. Whether the institution is public or private, judges recognize that some discretion must be afforded to the institution in determining whether an adverse employment decision is warranted. Stress on overly detailed written criteria and unnecessarily literal interpretation of those criteria cannot be permitted to eliminate consideration of relevant, but subjective, factors in evaluating employees.

As a corollary, judges emphasize that a court may not substitute its judgment for the judgment and discretion properly exercised by college administrators. For example, a state appeals court affirmed a ruling that a president's reprimand of a tenured faculty member was consistent with the terms of the institution's faculty handbook and made in good faith. Despite the fact that the president's decision contravened the recommendation of a review committee that proposed the reprimand be invalidated, the court held that the president's final determination sufficiently set forth job-related reasons for the adverse employment decision based on continued neglect of academic duties and was supported by the record. It found no basis for further judicial intervention with respect to the exercise of administrative discretion.[44]

## Progressive Discipline

Unless employee misconduct is so egregious or extreme that a single instance would justify cause for dismissal, the range of adverse employment decisions permits a system of progressive discipline.[45] Under such a system, an employee's single instance of misconduct might result in a written reprimand. If the behavior continues, an escalation of penalties, to include suspension or demotion, could be implemented. A documented pattern of continuing misconduct would result in dismissal. One state court reasoned that a record of progressive discipline effectively documented a history of repeated correction, counseling, and training of the employee about job-related deficiencies. In view of the evidence that the employee had not adequately conformed her conduct to the requirements of the job, the court found that dismissal was justified. [46]

## Good or Just Cause

The American Association of University Professors (AAUP) proposes "adequate cause" as the standard for dismissal of faculty,[47] but it is the institution's burden to define the concept and relate it to the performance of faculty. Under the AAUP definition, dismissal is possible only if the institution can show demonstrated incompetence or dishonesty in teaching or research, manifest neglect of duty, or conduct that substantially impairs the individual's job-related responsibilities.[48] Among the specific grounds that are often incorporated in institutional disciplinary policies, unprofessional conduct, insubordination, immorality, neglect of duty, and incompetence are typically identified.

If the institution's policy or the employment contract does not specify a particular ground or relies solely on a vague standard for adequate cause, the faculty member may challenge an adverse employment decision on the basis that the standard is so vague that reasonable people might disagree on its meaning.[49] An assertion that the grounds for an adverse employment decision are vague will be subject to a test of reasonableness. For example, a tenured university professor was dismissed for failure to maintain "standards of sound scholarship and competent teaching" because of his inappropriate and abusive treatment of visiting Chinese scholars; his failure to comply with a superior's directive; and his dishonesty in dealing with payroll, federal grant funds, and applications for an academic position. The federal appeals court rejected a challenge based on vagueness, reasoning that a tenured professor should "be expected to behave decently towards students and coworkers, to comply with a superior's directive, and to be truthful and forthcoming in dealing with payroll, federal research funds, or applications for academic positions. Such behavior is required for the purpose of maintaining sound scholarship and competent teaching."[50]

## Unprofessional Conduct

Unprofessional conduct includes a range of inappropriate behaviors. It may be implicated when a faculty member's lack of collegiality, harassment of department personnel, refusal to heed prior warnings regarding his conduct, and excessive filing of grievances are documented.[51] Intellectual dishonesty, including charges of plagiarism, may serve as a basis for unprofessional conduct leading to dismissal.[52]

In one instance, a tenured faculty member in a community college was properly dismissed for "capricious disregard of accepted standards of professional conduct" based on instances of arbitrary treatment of students, rude and discourteous behavior to peers and staff, and insubordination toward supervisors. In response to complaints from students, faculty and administrative personnel, the department chair initially substantiated the complaints, then met with the faculty member and identified problems that, if not corrected, would result in termination. When this approach failed, the chair recommended termination, and extensive due process procedures were set in motion. The faculty member received written notice of the charges against her, and a faculty committee began an inquiry that led to a finding of cause for dismissal. Following a formal hearing, a recommendation for dismissal was advanced to the governing board, which affirmed discharge. The state supreme court ruled that the charges were established by clear and convincing evidence and held that dismissal was justified because the faculty member had received repeated counseling, specific warnings, and reprimands about the behavior that ultimately led to her dismissal.[53]

Unprofessional conduct was addressed in a case involving a tenured professor who had concealed his dual employment as a member of the faculty at two separate institutions. In responding to inquiries from his dean at one of the institutions, the professor misled the administrator by suggesting that the appointment at the other institution was temporary and part-time when in fact it was a tenured appointment. After resigning the post at one institution, the professor was subject to termination proceedings at the other on the basis that he failed to maintain a relationship of trust with professional colleagues. The state appeals court rejected the professor's contention that the institution must prove impairment in his teaching, research, or service, concluding that what constituted "unprofessional conduct" was best left to the determination of the professional community of which the individual was a part.[54]

In a Minnesota case, a state appeals court affirmed dismissal of two university gymnastics coaches on the basis of clear and convincing evidence of unprofessional conduct. Testimony from students and staff confirmed that one of the coaches had, on more than one occasion, directed students to lie concerning her failure to conform to university policies on student transportation to athletic activities. Further testimony confirmed that the other coach had, either intentionally or negligently, allowed students to view sexually explicit videotape footage that had been included on tapes of students participating in gymnastic competition. In the latter case, the court found that even if the distribution of the tape to students had been unintentional, the coach's negligent conduct seriously compromised his effectiveness as a representative of the university and a guide and teacher of young people.[55]

Unprofessional conduct would also apply to dismissal for harassing students.[56] A tenured faculty member's insulting and demeaning letters to a former student who sought to receive a grade change were deemed "unprofessional" by a faculty panel convened to hear evidence of the professor's conduct. The professor challenged the hearing recommendations and filed suit when he was subject to demotion and reduction in salary. On review, a federal appeals court viewed the professor's letters to the student as attempts to compel or coerce an apology from the student and concluded that in balancing the professor's right to comment, the university's interest in ensuring that its students receive a fair grade and are not subject to demeaning, insulting, and inappropriate comments would outweigh the professor's interests.[57]

In another instance of unprofessional conduct, dismissal was justified in a case that involved allegations that a professor had sexually harassed a student while on an international studies program. The professor challenged the cause for dismissal from the private college, alleging that it breached the contract of employment in terminating him. The federal appeals court looked to the college's faculty handbook, noting that there was no mention of cause for dismissal in the document, but recognizing that, under the board-approved sexual harassment policy, a hearing committee could recommend termination if charges of sexual harassment were substantiated. The court held that the provisions of the sexual harassment policy stated grounds for dismissal in the instant case and ruled that the dismissal should stand.[58]

Failure to effectively document instances of misconduct at the time they occur may jeopardize an institution's effort to undertake dismissal for unprofessional conduct. Judges often apply a whole record test that spans the faculty member's employment and considers evidence that supports the adverse employment decision as well as contradictory evidence. In ruling that a decision to dismiss was arbitrary and capricious, one court reviewed a record of six incidents allegedly involving harassing and threatening behavior on the part of a tenured faculty member. These incidents spanned a fifteen-year period and, in most cases, had not been documented at the time they occurred and did not lead to administrative reprimand or other progressive discipline. The length of time between the alleged misconduct and the disciplinary action taken in connection with that misconduct was considered by the reviewing court to be an indication of bad faith on the part of the university in its attempt to dismiss the professor.[59]

## Insubordination

Dismissal for insubordination involves evidence of a repeated, constant, or continuing refusal to obey reasonable orders. Evidence of insubordination may be regarded as insufficient to sustain dismissal absent documentation that the employee was given a reasonable directive regarding his or her conduct and that the alleged misconduct was constant or continuous. Institutional administrators must make directives concerning the conduct that is prohibited as clear and unequivocal as possible in order to avoid a factual dispute in which the employee asserts that he or she effectively complied with a directive or the directive failed to warn of the prohibited conduct.[60]

Progressive discipline in cases involving insubordination is recommended as a means of providing notice of prohibited conduct. Written directives and reprimands provide a documentary record of previous instances of inappropriate behavior and corroborate testimony that the employee has been advised of what conduct is acceptable and what conduct would result in termination if continued.[61]

## Neglect of Duty

Neglect of duty involves the repeated failure to perform duties prescribed by law or to comply with reasonable directives or institutional policies relating to employee responsibilities. Instances of neglect of duty are often appropriate for a plan of progressive discipline. For example, a faculty member's persistent absenteeism would justify an initial warning, followed by a formal reprimand and heightened oversight to insure compliance with directives. If the behavior continued, the documented evidence of excessive absenteeism would constitute "good and sufficient reason" to suspend without pay or demote, and future instances might justify termination.

Repeated warnings, coupled with a persistent failure to comply with reasonable directives, were illustrated in a case in which a tenured professor of nursing challenged discharge for "significant neglect of duty." The record established the professor had been relieved of her teaching assignment and directed to develop two new graduate courses. However, syllabi and other materials for these courses were not developed, and requests for the submission of these materials were ignored. When the professor left the university for a stay in Florida, she was repeatedly contacted by university officials, advised that she was absent without permission, and directed her to report immediately and complete her assignments. On her return, she submitted no written materials related to the task of developing the graduate courses. The state appeals court found that the record provided clear and convincing proof that the professor's discharge was warranted.[62]

In all cases involving good cause for dismissal, it is the institution's burden to establish evidence to justify the adverse employment decision. For example, the dismissal of a tenured faculty member for neglect of duty was accompanied by evidence the professor had disclosed confidential student information to a classroom of students and neglected her teaching duties by ending a course one month prior to the conclusion of the academic term. A state court affirmed the decision of an administrative law judge that the institution met its burden to establish by clear and convincing evidence that there was adequate cause for dismissal.[63]

However, in a case in which an institution's decision to dismiss for "neglect of professional responsibilities" was not affirmed, the reviewing court ruled the institution failed to evaluate the faculty member's actions according to appropriate professional standards. The faculty member refused to teach a class until the institution disciplined a disruptive student, and the governing board rejected a faculty grievance committee's recommendation and moved to terminate his employment. The reviewing court remanded the case with an admonition that the professor should be allowed to present evidence that his conduct was within the bounds of reasonable behavior for the profession. In essence, the court determined that the phrase "neglect of professional responsibilities" includes consideration of whether the faculty member's actions were reasonable in refusing to teach the class given the institution's failure to take steps to resolve the incident with the disruptive student.[64]

## Immorality

Allegations of immorality involve conduct sufficiently egregious and notorious to bring the individual concerned or the higher education institution into public disgrace or disrespect and impair the individual's performance. In many cases, the immoral conduct would be so extreme that a single instance is sufficient for dismissal. Factors to be weighed in assessing a basis for immorality as a cause for dismissal would include: (1) the likelihood of recurrence of the questioned conduct; (2) the extenuating or aggravating circumstances, if any; (3) the effect of notoriety and publicity; (4) any impairment of teacher-student relationships; (5) any disruption of the educational process; (6) motive; and (7) the proximity or remoteness in time of the conduct.[65]

When the employee is a faculty member, documenting impairment will often require demonstrating a nexus between the behavior and the individual's fitness to continue his or her professional responsibilities. The requirement for nexus is intended to balance the faculty member's right to privacy against the interest of the institution in insuring efficiency and realizing its mission as an educational institution. In an illustrative case, a teacher's misdemeanor convictions for possession of marijuana and cocaine and her actions in allowing drug sales to take place in her home provided just cause for dismissal. As in most cases of this type, once the arrest became public, the college suspended the teacher with pay pending the outcome of the criminal trial. In the administrative hearing held by the college, it was determined by extensive testimony that the teacher's effectiveness was substantially impaired. The board's review of testimony from other faculty and its conclusion that the teacher's conduct directly contradicted her teaching role as a psychologist preparing students for careers in drug counseling were significant factors on which the court relied in affirming dismissal.[66]

In a case in which a teacher in a California community college was arrested and charged with possession and intent to sell cocaine, errors by law enforcement resulted in an acquittal. However, on review in an administrative proceeding, dismissal was regarded as the appropriate sanction for the teacher, who, on the standard of substantial evidence, was found to have participated in the sale of cocaine at a private residence being monitored by police. The California appeals court affirmed dismissal based on a record that included extensive testimony from faculty and administrators that the conduct of the teacher compromised his effectiveness as teacher, colleague, and role model for students.[67]

## Competency

Faculty competency is associated with effective classroom teaching, knowledge of subject matter, and skill in the conduct of research. When dismissal for incompetence is implicated, it involves a pattern of behavior, and the institution must provide the necessary documentation to support the cause.[68] An important dimension of documentation is observation and evaluation of performance, an activity that is increasingly mandated by requirements for accountability in both public and private institutions of higher education. In an illustrative case, low student evaluations, testimony concerning student complaints, high withdrawal rates and low student enrollments in the professor's classes, and repeated efforts by superiors to improve the professor's performance were documented to warrant the adverse employment decision.[69]

Incompetence involves job-related performance falling below an acceptable standard and typically includes a remedial opportunity to correct deficiencies if those deficiencies do not pose a significant and immediate risk of harm to students or compromise close working relationships with colleagues. When teacher competence is at issue, progressive discipline is replaced by the identification of performance deficiencies, assistance to correct deficiencies, a reasonable opportunity for remediation, and assessment of whether performance has improved.

As a formative process, evaluation requires that reasonable, job-related performance criteria be set and that the institution, through a process of observation, evaluation, and conferencing, assist the employee to improve. When efforts to correct deficiencies and improve performance fail, the evaluation process becomes a system for documenting deficiencies and justifying an adverse employment decision based upon lack of competence. A recommendation to dismiss may be compelled when the system of assessment documents that significant deficiencies persist in spite of reasonable efforts to improve performance.

Evaluation systems must yield a documentary record that confirms the fairness and reasonableness of the process, compiles with legal mandates, and meets the test of substantial evidence. Unsubstantiated claims of inadequate performance, conflicting appraisals of performance, or lack of uniform standards in the evaluation process may contribute to the view that there is insufficient evidence to support an adverse employment decision. Competent and substantial evidence, which may include classroom observations, student evaluations or complaints, testimony of colleagues, anecdotal memoranda, or a combination of sources will sustain the legitimacy of the process and justify an adverse employment decision.

Proper notice of deficiencies and time in which to correct those deficiencies conforms to essential requirements of due process and helps rebut claims that the evaluation system is arbitrary or capricious. In an illustrative case, a reviewing court noted that the institution provided formal and informal notification to the professor of specific deficiencies in his performance over a four-year period. Periodic evaluations established that the professor did not improve performance, and letters, memoranda, and oral warnings to the professor described how his performance was deficient, using language congruent with that later used in the formal charges involving lack of competence. This documentation was persuasive in convincing the court that the professor had adequate notice of the standard of performance required, sustaining dismissal.[70]

In a similar case, a cumulative record of the employee's problems with three different supervisors confirmed instances of complaints about a librarian's failure to complete assigned tasks and lack of skills, particularly computer literacy skills, necessary to perform his job. The state supreme court found that the collective bargaining agreement governing the institution's relationship with its employees stipulated that "just cause" for dismissal included incompetency. The employee had been given notice of performance deficiencies and an opportunity for remediation, but in a two-month period of remediation, there was no evidence that he had improved performance relevant to job requirements. The state court ruled that the cumulative evidence in the record sustained the dismissal decision.[71]

## Reduction-in-force

While most adverse employment decisions relate to employee performance involving misconduct, incapacity, or incompetence, lay-off decisions involving bonafide financial exigency may compel the institution to justify the necessity for lay-off and the process for selecting employees. Declining enrollments and loss of program funding are two frequent justifications for a reduction-in-force (RIF). In considering these justifications, courts attempt to grant reasonable discretionary authority to the institution while construing RIF policies narrowly in order to balance the protections of tenure. Expressly incorporating policies on RIF in faculty handbooks or negotiated agreements can help insure that fair and reasonable procedures are applied to the selection of employees subject to layoffs when conditions of economic stringency are imposed on the institution.[72]

In a case in which a college met its burden to justify layoffs based on a system-wide reduction, a federal appeals court found the RIF was related to declining enrollment. In response to a faculty member's claim that he was selected for layoff because of a disability, the court affirmed that there was no evidence presented that the college deviated from the announced plan for the RIF or that anything other than objective criteria for the selection of employees to be laid off was applied. Although the instructor asserted that a subsequent job posting for an electronics instructor established the college's intent to discriminate against him, the court rejected this contention, noting that the later posting was undertaken to comply with an immigration regulation and that the position was already filled by an immigrant whose job description did not match the former instructor's.[73]

### Constructive Discharge

Constructive discharge occurs when the employer makes the employee's work environment so intolerable that the employee resigns. Claims of constructive discharge are evaluated under a reasonable person standard by most state and federal courts. It is not sufficient to assert that working conditions are difficult or unpleasant. The former employee must seek to establish that working conditions were so intolerable that a reasonable person would feel compelled to resign.[74] In other words, given the conditions, a reasonable person in the same or similar circumstances as that of the employee would have no other choice than to quit.[75]

One federal appeals court distinguished constructive discharge from constructive resignation. A tenured faculty member, reassigned to research activities after student complaints about his teaching, objected to reassignment and failed to report for work. The federal appeals court affirmed the university's determination to treat this refusal as a resignation, noting that constructive resignation refers to situations in which the employee abandons his or her position without formally resigning, and the employer treats the employee as if he had formally resigned.[76]

## Contract Rescission

The employee's fraudulent conduct in procuring the contract may result in rescission of the employment contract,[77] but an institution should be prepared to provide appropriate due process in the event rescission is rejected by a court of competent jurisdiction.[78] The Supreme Court of Vermont concluded that a faculty member's misrepresentation regarding his past work history and references warranted rescission of the employment contract and supported just cause dismissal.[79] The faculty member had failed to report his criminal conviction and incarceration and had misrepresented his work history in that time period. Because honesty is an implicit duty of every employee, the plaintiff had notice that his misrepresentation was grounds for dismissal.

### Due Process

Standards of fundamental fairness dictate that when the institution adopts a rule or guideline establishing a procedure for its employees, institution must substantially observe that procedure and any inquiry involving allegations of misconduct will proceed in good faith.[80] While private institutions are governed by the standard of good faith in adhering to the material elements of the contract of employment relative to disciplinary procedures,[81] a public institution may be held to constitutional due process standards related to the Fourteenth Amendment.

Minimal constitutional standards required of public institutions when dismissal of tenured faculty is contemplated would involve notice of the cause for dismissal, notice of the names of witnesses and their testimony, meaningful opportunity to be heard, and an impartial panel with appropriate academic expertise.[82] Other protections extended to a faculty member may include allowing objections to any prospective hearing panel member, permitting cross-examination of witnesses and providing opportunities for the presentation of testimony and evidence on the faculty member's behalf.[83] The right to have representation by an attorney in a termination decision will often depend on the law of the particular jurisdiction. One federal appeals court approved an institution's policy allowing counsel to be present and advise but prohibited the attorney from conducting cross-examination of witnesses. The court's justification for this policy was that due process did not require a full-fledged remediation trial.[84]

The question of whether a post-termination hearing can remedy the failure to provide an adequate pretermination hearing for an employee who possesses an expectation of continued employment (e.g. tenure) has been resolved differently in different jurisdictions.[85] The best advice to college administrators is to insure that a sound and minimally adequate pretermination hearing is provided to employees who have protected property interests in continued employment in order to avoid future litigation of that due process issue. Note, however, that the United States Supreme

Court has ruled that a public employee who is charged with a sufficiently serious crime need not receive a hearing before being suspended without pay. In that case, the university acted immediately to suspend a campus police officer who was arrested on drug-related charges, and the Court reasoned that the employee was provided with a timely post-termination hearing and the institution's interest in acting to suspend an employee accused of a felony was significant.[86]

A faculty member's failure to comply with institutional procedures for instituting due process protections may bar the employee from establishing a denial of due process. In reviewing one faculty member's claim, a federal appeals court found that although the professor filed complaints and letters of protest with the administration of the institution, he did not comply with the two-step grievance process established by the university. The court reasoned that in order to state a claim for failure to provide due process, the professor must have taken advantage of the processes that are available. In other words, a procedural due process violation cannot have occurred when the state university provides apparently adequate procedural remedies and the employee has not availed himself of those remedies.[87]

## Property and Liberty Interests

To state a claim for violation of due process, a faculty member must show that he or she was deprived of a right protected by due process of law and then identify an official action that caused that denial. The faculty member may claim a right to due process, including a hearing prior to the implementation of discipline, when the effect of a public institution's administrative action would be to deny a property entitlement under the contract of employment.[88] Alternately, stigmatizing statements disseminated by the institution may so injure the faculty member's reputation as to implicate a liberty interest under due process of law. If such a stigma were to have the effect of foreclosing other employment opportunities, then the faculty member might successfully claim a right to a name-clearing hearing.[89]

Most allegations of a denial of an entitlement arise from adverse employment decisions related to the discipline of employees, but other deprivations of a property right may implicate due process. For example, minimal due process, including notice of the reasons for a proposed deprivation of property rights and some opportunity to respond to those reasons, was required when administrators determined to reduce a faculty member's compensation from a discretionary fund and advised him that he must generate the lost compensation through grant funds.[90] However, claims of a denial of committee appointments or denial of certain research, lecturing, and publishing opportunities would be unlikely to establish a constitutionally protected entitlement. A contention that denying these opportunities would influence "chances for tenure" was considered unsupportable as a basis for creating an entitlement by one federal court.[91]

A faculty member alleging violation of a liberty interest must establish that the institution or its agents disseminated a false statement of a stigmatizing nature that precipitated an adverse employment decision without providing the employee a meaningful opportunity to clear his or her good name. While a stigma might be found if the institution publicly accused a faculty member of dishonesty, immorality, criminality, or racism, allegations that a faculty member was a poor performer and could not get along with colleagues have not been sufficient to raise a liberty interest[92] nor was a provost's statement quoted in the student newspaper that the faculty member's removal was in the best interests of the department.[93] Denial of tenure or non-renewal of appointment would not constitute so significant a stigma as to create a right to due process. While judges reason that these decisions may reflect negatively on the employee, this negative effect is insufficient, absent evidence of charges that would seriously damage reputation or foreclose other employment, to warrant due process protections.[94]

To prevail on a claim of stigma, there must be evidence that the institution publicly disclosed accusations against the employee[95] and there was a deprivation of an employee interest.[96] In a representative case, a Florida court rejected a professor's claim that denial of promotion to full professor had a stigmatizing effect that would require due process protection. The state appellate court found the denial of the professor's promotion left his legal status unaltered in that he remained a tenured associate professor.[97]

### Substantial Compliance

Substantial compliance with institutional due process procedures is the applicable standard in employee discipline.[98] "Substantial," however, does not mean that compliance must be so rigorous that any deviation will result in overturning an adverse employment decision. In a North Dakota case, a faculty member challenged a nonrenewal decision on the grounds that the department failed to adequately follow the evaluation format outlined by the department. The written policy stipulated that nontenured faculty were to be evaluated at the end of the first semester of their first year and again at the end of their first year. The faculty member asserted that her second evaluation, coming in February, occurred several months before the end of the second semester. The reviewing court held that there was substantial compliance with the department's written evaluation procedures and that the purpose of evaluation, to inform the faculty member of her job performance, was accomplished.[99]

Even in cases in which the institution adopts ad hoc policies and procedures to address an initial instance of misconduct, judges have shown deference to institutional practices if fundamental due process protections are applied. In a case in which a tenured university professor was publicly censured and barred from administrative positions as a sanction for "seriously negligent scholarship," a federal appeals court examined the institution's ad hoc procedures involving plagiarism and found that the professor had adequate notice of charges against her, an opportunity to challenge for cause any of the panel members who heard her case, to present evidence, call witnesses, challenge witnesses, and bring a colleague to the hearings to assist her. At the conclusion of the hearings, the committee recommended censure and forwarded its report to the academic dean. The dean asked the professor to respond in writing to the report, and this response was incorporated along with the panel's recommendations and findings in a report to the provost. The court regarded the university's procedures as providing appropriate due process safeguards.[100]

The standard of substantial compliance has also been applied to annual performance evaluation in the context of tenure decisions. In a West Virginia case, tenure denial was challenged on the basis that the institution failed to afford the candidate the requisite annual evaluations and third-year review required by the university handbook. The reviewing court found that third year reviews were wholly discretionary under the terms of the handbook and that any failure to conduct annual evaluations in selected years was overshadowed by annual evaluations that provided the candidate with repeated notices of her deficiencies throughout the period of her university service. The court affirmed a judgment that the university had substantially complied with evaluation and tenure procedures and any procedural irregularities were harmless.[101]

University administrators may sometimes find that there are alternative due process procedures under institutional policy for dealing with issues of employee discipline. In one case, a tenured professor subject to suspension based on allegations of sexual harassment of students, challenged the notice and hearing provided on the basis that it failed to conform to the specific requirements of the sexual harassment policy. The reviewing court ruled that the institution's decision to follow the due process procedures set forth in the bargaining agreement, rather than those established under the sexual harassment policy, did not violate constitutional standards and emphasized that there is no requirement under the Fourteenth Amendment that an employee receive due process procedures of his or her choice.[102]

## Free Speech

The topic of employee free speech is addressed in detail elsewhere in this text, but free speech challenges to the employment decisions of public colleges and universities requires a brief primer on the topic within this chapter. When a faculty member challenges an adverse employment decision on the basis that the decision violates freedom of speech, the determination of whether speech is protected and the application of an appropriate balance between individual rights and a public institution's interests are essential. In a leading constitutional decision, *Pickering v. Board of Education,*[103] a public school teacher, dismissed for a controversial letter to the editor that was critical of the local school board and superintendent, prevailed in establishing that the board's action violated First Amendment free speech. The United States Supreme Court ruled that absent evidence that the teacher's published letter contained intentionally false or misleading statements, or that the statements would interfere with close working relationships or disrupt school operations, the board could not punish the teacher for speaking out on a matter of public concern.

However, federal courts have restricted the application of *Pickering* in public higher education. A judge's first inquiry involving a free speech claim is whether the speech involved a matter of public concern as revealed by the content, form, and context of the speech.[104] If the speech can reasonably be characterized as relating to private interests rather than public concerns, then no constitutional protection for the speech is available. If the speech is related to a matter of public concern, then the judge must strike a balance "between the interests of the [employee], as a citizen, in commenting upon matters of public concern and the interest of the State, as an employer, in promoting the efficiency of the public services it performs through its employees."[105]

The exercise of free speech cannot insulate the faculty member from an adverse employment decision based on conduct unrelated to First Amendment protections. In *Mt. Healthy City School District v. Doyle,*[106] the United States Supreme Court concluded that a teacher's disclosure of a proposed teacher dress code policy via a local radio talk show could not serve as the basis for an adverse employment decision, as the speech was on a matter of public concern and constitutionally protected. However, the case was remanded to allow the board to establish that the adverse employment decision was justified absent consideration of the protected speech. The Court reasoned that the teacher should not be able, by engaging in the exercise of free speech, to prevent the employer from assessing performance unrelated to free speech and reaching a decision not to rehire the employee on the basis of that record.

Even when an adverse employment decision is predicated on a faculty member's exercise of free speech, the public institution's interest may outweigh the faculty member's free speech rights, particularly when the speech itself can reasonably be forecast to create a substantial disruption or material interference within the workplace. When weighing the value of the employee's speech against the impact on government operations, a four-judge plurality of the United States Supreme Court, in *Waters v. Churchill,*[107] indicated the public employer need only show that the speech is likely to be disruptive before the speaker may be punished.[108] This decision would appear to permit an institution to punish an employee for speech on a matter of public concern if institutional representatives had a reasonable belief that the speech would disrupt efficient operations and the potential interference with institutional operations would outweigh the free speech rights of the employee. The plurality opinion suggests that the public institution could fire a faculty member for disruptive speech based on its reasonable belief as to what the faculty member said, regardless of what may actually have been said.

### Public Concern

Using a "whole record" test, a judge must initially determine whether a faculty member's speech is related to a matter of public concern. Matters of public concern recognized by federal courts include a professor's public disclosure of grade fraud allegations,[109] a college professor's scholarly writings expressing controversial views on racial differences,[110] and public protest concerning closing of a branch campus and the university's spending priorities.[111]

To be protected, a faculty member's speech must relate to matters that embrace the First Amendment right to religious, political, or philosophic speech rather than personal interests.[112] While faculty criticisms about large class sizes, lack of adequate course offerings, and the institution's overemphasis on increasing enrollment might be characterized as public concerns,[113] it is questionable whether the First Amendment protects criticism of internal management decisions.[114] For example, evidence that a faculty member criticized a dean or department chair might easily be tied to a personal grievance outside the realm of public concern when the comments are narrowly focused on employee dissatisfaction with administrative policies.[115] Similarly, complaints about a faculty member's reassignment and reduction in length of appointment are more likely to reflect a matter of private interest.[116]

Public criticism of the institution, even when couched in general terms, may be regarded by a court as a veiled attempt to address personal grievances.[117] One federal appeals court acknowledged that allegations that a public official had misused public funds or made misrepresentations to the public would implicate a matter of public concern but found an assistant professor failed to meet her burden to show that her public criticism of the institutional governing board and president rose to the level. The court characterized the faculty member's criticism of the president and governing board as challenges to the policies and governance of the institution that "rarely transcend the internal workings of the university to affect the political or social life of the community."[118]

Although utterances in a closed forum may be less likely to be regarded as matters of public concern, the nature of the forum is seldom controlling in a case involving faculty speech.[119] In an illustrative case, a faculty member's speech criticizing colleagues for maintaining close relationships with the local business community and thus compromising ethical standards for objectivity in the academy was directed only to colleagues. Despite the fact that the criticism was not directed to the general public, the court found the forum was not controlling on the determination of whether the speech was protected. [120]

Judges attempt to discriminate between a disgruntled employee's intent to redress a personal grievance and the faculty member's inquiry into or discussion of an issue pertinent to a broader public or community interest.[121] In one case, a faculty member who protested the conditions in his laboratory on the basis that the handling of toxic chemicals raised questions of safety was regarded as having addressed a matter of public concern even though he brought his criticism to his employer and would himself benefit if laboratory conditions were improved.[122] However, two faculty members who were denied tenure and not renewed alleged that the primary reason they were subject to an adverse employment decision involved letters they sent to university officials requesting an external examination of the review process within their department. Assessing the employees' motivation in seeking the external review, the court noted that the context in which the letters were written was one in which departmental infighting might affect chances for tenure. While the court agreed that having some personal interest in calming tensions within the department would not preclude the letters from reflecting public concern, the court characterized the letters as "much more akin to an effort to resolve an internal squabble than to statements by individuals speaking out as citizens."[123]

## Speech as a Motivating Factor

In addition to establishing that the speech involved a matter of public concern, the faculty member has the initial burden of showing that his or her constitutionally protected speech was a "substantial" or "motivating factor" in the adverse employment decision. In an illustrative case, a federal appeals court held that although an assistant dean's comments critical of affirmative action initiatives might presumptively be related to a matter of public concern protected by the First Amendment, there was insufficient evidence from which a jury could reasonably infer that the speech was a substantial or motivating factor in termination. The court rejected the contention that the close proximity in time between the employee's speech and his discharge was sufficient to give rise to an inference that the speech motivated the employment decision.[124]

## Conduct Unrelated to Free Speech

The public higher education institution may justify an adverse employment decision if it can establish sufficient cause unrelated to the faculty member's exercise of free speech.[125] For example, evidence that a professor had repeatedly refused to comply with reasonable requests to report his work-related activity and to establish and maintain a full-time presence in a university laboratory led one federal appeals court to find that the university would have taken the same action absent consideration of any protected speech, and this defeated the professor's claim.[126] In another case, a federal appeals court reasoned that a professor's discharge was based on a persistent decline in enrollment rather than his public statements to an investigating committee.[127] Although a federal district court found that a faculty member's criticisms of arbitrary conduct, nepotism, and racism within his department were constitutionally protected, the court characterized the professor's insistence that he was retaliated against to be grounded on a "muddled conspiracy theory."[128] Ruling for the university, the court concluded that the institution's basis for denying promotion, although a subjective assessment, related to lack of scholarly productivity, which was a valid, neutral reason to deny promotion.

A non-tenured professor asserted that his nonrenewal was predicated on his views of diversity and multiculturalism presented in classroom discussions, comments in faculty meetings, and articles and cartoons posted outside his office. The federal district court found that the professor's comments on issues of diversity were matters of public concern protected by the First Amendment but held that his interjection of diversity issues in his classroom disrupted the uniformity of instruction in the department, created divisions within the faculty, and encroached upon courses offered in other departments of the university. The institution was held to have met its burden to show that the professor's difficulty in working with colleagues, together with his disruption of the delivery of courses, justified the institution in relieving him of his teaching assignments and not renewing his contract.[129]

One court found abundant evidence to sustain the conclusion that a professor's censure and dismissal was unrelated to any free speech rights the professor may have invoked.[130] The dismissed faculty member alleged violation of his free speech rights under the First Amendment, but the federal district court reviewed an extensive record, finding that the professor had made harassing, coercive, and threatening statements to colleagues and administrators and had falsely accused the university president and a number of other administrators of criminal misconduct. While the professor had exercised free speech rights on a matter of public concern in criticizing certain institutional policies, the court found that the bulk of his "speech" was unprotected.

However, judges remain sensitive to the possibility that an institution may be using an adverse employment decision for the purpose of punishing a faculty member for the exercise of constitutionally protected rights. In one case, a non-tenured faculty member was notified of non-renewal shortly after she testified on behalf of a plaintiff in a discrimination lawsuit brought against the university. Although the university claimed the reason for the nonrenewal was related to opening a faculty line so the institution could hire a professor to help secure accreditation for a doctoral program, divergent and conflicting statements about the reasons for selecting the professor for non-renewal created a strong suspicion on the part of the reviewing court that the reason was pretextual and that the institution was motivated by a desire to retaliate against the professor for an exercise of free speech.[131]

## Balancing Interests

Courts carefully scrutinize a faculty member's speech in an attempt to balance the employee's interest in commenting on matters of public concern against the institution's interest in efficiency.[132] Concerns about the potential disruption of the institution's efficient operation may relate to whether the speech (1) impairs discipline or control by superiors, (2) disrupts coworker relations, (3) erodes close working relationships premised on personal trust and confidentiality, (4) interferes with the speaker's performance of his or her duties, or (5) obstructs the routine operation of the office.[133]

Absent evidence that a faculty member's criticisms introduced discord in his or her relations with colleagues or adversely affected classroom performance, institutions may be prohibited from undertaking adverse employment decisions against outspoken faculty. For example, a university employee's criticism of the institution's affirmative action efforts was regarded by one federal appeals court as a matter of public concern protected by the First Amendment and speech that outweighed the employer's interest in efficient operation. The appeals court rejected the notion that the employee's speech had a disruptive impact on the university's operations, and found no discernible impact on close working relationships.[134]

Courts recognize fostering and maintaining mutual respect among faculty as a powerful and substantial interest of an academic employer.[135] Conduct that may interfere or disrupt close working relationships essential to organizational effectiveness may justify weighing the institution's interest over the free speech rights of the employee.[136] While this principle is particularly true when the employee speaking out holds a key policy-making position,[137] it can also apply to the conduct of faculty who create dissension within their academic units.

False accusations, bitter attacks on colleagues or superiors, and threats or encouragement of unlawful or disorderly conduct would certainly implicate a level of discord that would justify an adverse employment decision. In an illustrative case, tenured professors who were transferred to another department based on an open letter critical of the department's leadership, funding, and facilities were unsuccessful in challenging the transfer. The federal appeals court found no demonstrated property interest on which to base a claim of a denial of due process, and, while the criticism of the department leveled by the professors implicated public concerns, the court held that the disruption in efficient operations caused by the speech justified the transfer. The court regarded the professors' criticism as significantly hampering departmental morale, harmony, and communication among colleagues.[138] In a similar case, evidence of low morale, staff hostility, and lack of communication between directors justified the institution's decision to implement administrative transfers and overcame the employee's public allegations of a misappropriation of grant funds.[139]

While a charge of academic misconduct in a public institution is more likely to be a matter of public concern rather than private interest, one federal court of appeals has held that an assistant professor's unsubstantiated claims of academic misconduct would not outweigh the institution's decision to refuse to renew his contract. In this case, the assistant professor charged a colleague with academic misconduct, and the university investigated the charges, found they were unsubstantiated, vindicated the colleague, and chose not to renew the assistant professor. The court characterized the unsubstantiated charge of academic misconduct not only as a waste of time for other members of the faculty, but as a reflection on the judgment of the accuser. The court reasoned that the assistant professor's unsubstantiated claim of academic misconduct was so central to the university's mission to judge the fitness of faculty that the institution was entitled to weigh his speech in its decision not to renew his contract.[140]

An institution may properly consider a faculty member's incendiary public speech in a public forum in relation to the potential for workplace disruption. In considering a university's decision to limit the term of a department chair because of a controversial speech he had given off campus, a federal appeals court found the adverse employment decision was justified because the institution had made a substantial showing that the chair's speech would disrupt university operations. In the speech, the department chair had criticized public school curriculum as racially biased and made several derogatory comments, particularly about Jews. While the speech clearly involved matters of public concern, the court balanced the interest of the chair in commenting on a matter of public concern against the institution's interest in promoting the efficiency of its services. Proposing that when a speech is clearly on a matter of public concern, the institution may make a substantial showing of "likely interference" and not actual disruption, the appeals court reasoned that the institution need only show that the speech "threatened" to interfere with government operations in order to justify an adverse employment decision.[141]

## Academic Freedom

Academic freedom denotes both the freedom of the academy to pursue its objectives without undue external interference and the freedom of the individual faculty member to pursue professional objectives without interference from the academy.[142] As Justice Frankfurter described the institution's prerogatives in *Sweezy v. New Hampshire*,[143] "It is the business of the university to provide …'four essential freedoms'… to determine for itself on academic grounds who may teach, what may be taught, how it shall be taught, and who may be admitted to study."[144] The faculty interest may be inferred from the language of the majority in *Keyishian v. Board of Regents*,[145] "The vigilant protection of constitutional freedoms is nowhere more vital than in the community of American schools."[146]

Since academic freedom involves the right of the institution and its representatives to function with reasonable independence from government interference, one might presume that the doctrine would enable a public institution to assert its prerogatives as a government employer and reasonably restrict the free speech of employees. This principle supported one federal court's conclusion that the institution's academic freedom to set assignments for teaching and the performance of other duties deserves some protection from judicial intervention when the alleged harm to the faculty plaintiffs was not sufficiently detailed to show a pecuniary loss. The institution acted in response to an internecine battle within an academic unit that appeared to have disrupted scholarship and teaching. The court reasoned that faculty warfare would warrant institutional intervention in order to restore decorum, and transfers or reassignments to ease tensions appeared justified.[147]

On the other hand, the doctrine as applied to faculty rights would appear to free individual faculty from interference by administrators or others within the academy. In dealing with this paradox, courts have elected to regard academic freedom as a special concern of the First Amendment and not an independent, fundamental right.[148] Given the lack of a precise judicial definition of the construct and the uncertainty of its application under the First Amendment, judges often acknowledge that principles of academic freedom inform judicial determinations involving free speech under the First Amendment by recognizing that the context for exercising free speech in institutions of higher education is influenced by institutional norms associated with academic freedom.

In a provocative decision interpreting academic freedom prerogatives, one federal appeals court examined whether a Virginia statute restricting faculty access to material on the Internet through state-owned computers violated academic freedom or the right of access to ideas that might reasonably relate to First Amendment free speech. The court's majority reasoned that the speech at issue in this case, access to materials on state-owned or leased computers used for the purpose of carrying out employment duties, was viewed as speech in the employee's role as employee, rather than private citizen. As to the professors' academic freedom challenge, the majority concluded that whatever academic freedom exists is possessed by the institution rather than the individual. Since, in the majority's view, most of the judicial decisions on academic freedom have addressed the autonomy of the institution in undertaking its mission without undue interference from government, there was little precedent to support the faculty members' insistence that their right to access information on computers owned or leased by the institution was constitutionally protected.[149]

The right to assign grades can create a conflict between the institution and the faculty member's exercise of academic freedom and has resulted in mixed judicial treatment. A dean's directive compelling a professor to change a student's grade was regarded by a federal appeals court as violating the professor's free speech and academic freedom privileges. The court reasoned that the assignment of a grade is symbolic speech intended to communicate a message to the student. By compelling the professor to change the grade rather than acting to change it by administrative fiat, the dean had violated the professor's right to free speech in the unique context of the academic environment.[150] However, in a later case, a federal appeals court found no violation of speech rights in an institution's decision to reassign a faculty member who failed to follow a directive to change a student's grade from failing to "incomplete." The appeals court ruled that a university professor in the public setting does not have a First Amendment right to expression through the medium of the institution's grading procedures.[151]

## Classroom Speech

In determining whether a faculty member's classroom speech is constitutionally protected, it is essential that institutional leaders give consideration to the institution's educational mission and the unique role academic freedom plays within the academy. Recognizing that a faculty member's academic freedom may extend to the authority to utilize a particular pedagogical approach, evaluate student performance, and experiment with innovative practices in the classroom, judges insist that institutional officials exercise reasonable restraint in limiting the range of faculty speech in the classroom setting.

Judges appear protective of the faculty member's right to address controversial subjects with demonstrated relevance to subject matter and can be persuaded that a classroom practice is acceptable when shown to have relevance to curricular content or a legitimate pedagogical objective. In an illustrative case, a tenured faculty member who was reprimanded for discussing unionization activities at the college in his political science class claimed that the reprimand had a chilling effect on First Amendment free speech. The federal district court recognized the faculty member's academic freedom as a special dimension of the First Amendment and emphasized that the teacher's speech involved a matter of curricular relevance. Reasoning that while the institution may regulate the curriculum, it does not have the right to dictate the teacher's pedagogical method, the court rejected a motion to dismiss the professor's claim.[152]

In another case in which a legitimate pedagogical purpose outweighed the institution's interest in punishing speech, a federal appeals court vindicated a faculty member's decision to initiate a classroom discussion of socially controversial words. The appellate court ruled that the professor's in-class use of the objectionable speech was germane to the subject matter of his lecture on the power and effect of language, and noted the offensive language was suggested by the students in the context of the class, not gratuitously used by the professor in an abusive manner. In balancing the competing interests involved, the court took into account the robust tradition of academic freedom in American higher education, noting that judges have recognized that educational institutions occupy a unique place in First Amendment jurisprudence.[153]

A professor's right to academic freedom is not a "license for uncontrolled expression at variance with established curricular content and internally destructive of the proper functioning of the institution."[154] For example, a university's decision not to renew a non-tenured teacher because her teaching style conflicted with the institution's pedagogical approach did not implicate free speech or academic freedom. The federal appeals court reasoned that the nontenured teacher's teaching philosophy, rather than any particular classroom speech, was the basis for the institution's decision not to renew her contract and concluded that academic freedom does not entitle a faculty member to adopt a teaching style in conflict with that of the institution.[155] Another federal appeals court emphasized that the First Amendment does not place restrictions on the authority of a public university to determine the content of the education it will provide, and the institution is free to regulate what subject matter will be approved and taught.[156] Similarly, while a faculty member may have philosophical objections to grading standards or testing requirements implemented by the institution, those objections do not justify refusal to conform to institutional directives to modify grading practices or administer standardized examinations.[157]

Institutions that seek to regulate a faculty member's classroom speech should do so with sensitivity to institutional norms and should impose a system of progressive discipline when appropriate.[158] For example, a state appeals court, in reviewing the history of a professor's repeated use of sexual innuendos in the classroom, found evidence of formal student complaints, repeated warnings and reprimands, and peer observations confirming sexually oriented comments to students. In the court's view, the institution proceeded in good faith, properly found that the professor's behavior was inappropriate, provided adequate warning of prohibited conduct, and was justified in acting to dismiss. The documentation clearly established that the classroom conduct violated institutional policy and the system of progressive discipline provided the faculty member with sufficient notice of the prohibited conduct.[159]

A public university's reprimand prohibiting a professor from inter-jecting his religious views into course material presented during instructional time was justified based on the institution's interest in maintaining a separation of church and state under the Establishment Clause of the First Amendment. The federal appeals court concluded that the limitations were narrowly tailored and would not restrict the faculty member from responding to student questions about his religious opinions in other settings[160] but affirmed the institution's "authority to reasonably control the content of its curriculum, particularly that content imparted during class time."[161]

A business school could prohibit a faculty member from introducing his views of the need to increase racial and gender diversity in the business community into classroom discussions. Even though the reviewing court concluded the classroom speech was on a matter of public concern, the court imposed a balancing test in holding that the institution's interest in determining the content of the curriculum and organizing the content of courses outweighed the faculty member's right. The court reasoned that restricting the professor's speech was necessary to avoid divisions among the faculty of the department with regard to responsibility for teaching the components of the curriculum and in order to insure the school effectively delivered the required content to its students.[162]

Finding that a faculty member's use of profanity served only to re-flect his negative attitude toward students, another federal court held that a faculty member failed to establish that the use of profanity had "any purpose other than cussing out his students as an expression of frustration with their progress."[163] Characterizing students in a college classroom as a "captive audience," the court regarded the professor's use of profanity as a "deliberate attack" with no educational justification.[164] The appeals court reasoned that the First Amendment did not protect the classroom use of profanity since it did not touch on a matter of public concern and was not shown to be relevant to the subject matter of the course.

While faculty may raise due process challenges to disciplinary sanc-tions based on charges of sexual harassment,[165] it is unlikely that faculty could challenge an investigation into allegations of sexual harassment in the classroom by claiming that the investigation itself violates free speech or academic freedom.[166] When classroom comments may reasonably be forecast to create a sexually charged, hostile environment[167] and cannot be shown to be germane to the curriculum or relevant to matters of public concern, faculty are unlikely to be insulated by an academic freedom privilege,[168] and institutions may overcome a faculty member's assertion of a free speech or academic freedom prerogative.[169] However, if the professor's classroom comments advance valid pedagogical objectives relating to the subject matter of his course and can be shown to relate to matters of public concern, then classroom comments may be constitution-ally protected speech, and the faculty member's academic freedom may outweigh the institution's interest in punishing his speech.[170] (Editor's Note: Chapter 6 also discusses speech issues.)

## Discrimination in Employment

Discrimination on the basis of race, religion, national origin, sex, age, or disability is prohibited under federal law and the provisions of many state laws, most of which are applicable to both public and private institutions of higher education. Principal among the federal statutes that cover employment discrimination are Title VII of the Civil Rights Act of 1964,[171] Title IX of the Education Amendments of 1972,[172] Section 504 of the Rehabilitation Act of 1973,[173] the Americans With Disabilities Act,[174] and the Age Discrimination in Employment Act.[175] Since the litigation of employment discrimination claims is highly fact intensive, summary disposition of the charges will be more likely where employment practices include documentary records that support a strong anti-discrimination posture. The principles associated with nondiscrimination in employment are elaborated in the chapter discussing the application of Title VII, but some examination of the employer's burden in employment discriminated is treated below.

### *Legitimate, Non-discriminatory Reasons*

The employer's burden in cases involving allegations of discrimination based on disparate treatment is to articulate a legitimate non-discriminatory reason for the adverse employment decision.[176] The requirement to "articulate" rather than prove, requires the employer to produce some evidence in support of the stated reason for the adverse employment decision. In order to meet the burden of production, higher education institutions must institute and uniformly apply evaluation and documentation systems that establish reasonable, job-related rationales for adverse employment decisions. For example, conference memoranda and formal complaints that a professor was repeatedly absent and tardy, failed to make arrangements for his absences to be covered, and failed to complete and turn in student grades on time overcame a claim of disparate treatment.[177] One institution met its burden to articulate a legitimate non-discriminatory reason for discharging a clinical nurse supervisor by presenting evidence that it had lost two nursing home training sites and was threatened with the loss of two more because of the nurse's ineffective supervision of nursing students.[178] A disability discrimination claim was overcome with evidence of corroborating evaluations indicating valid performance deficiencies in teaching.[179] An institution's decision to terminate was properly based on testimony and memoranda confirming unsatisfactory job performance, disregarding university directives, and misusing university resources.[180]

Assessments of teaching performance may be sufficient to rebut a prima facie case of employment discrimination if they are effectively documented.[181] For example, the use of student evaluations and classroom observation to substantiate inadequate teaching skills has been relied on to rebut a professor's discrimination claims.[182] In another case, a college's concerns about an ethnic minority professor's lack of organization in lecture and difficulty in communicating with students were factors that were reflected in the record of the college's committee on promotion and tenure. When the professor challenged the committee's recommendation not to offer him a tenure track position, the federal appeals court acknowledged that the committee's minutes provided the documentation for the articulation of a legitimate, non-discriminatory reason for the adverse employment decision.[183]

A faculty member's lack of research and scholarship has been cited as a nondiscriminatory reason for an adverse employment decision.[184] For example, an institution's showing that the reason for denial of tenure and nonrenewal was the professor's failure to obtain research funding has rebutted claims of discrimination.[185] In a case involving allegations of sex discrimination, a federal appeals court noted the faculty member's failure to publish in top-tier journals, a publication record of largely coauthored articles, and criticism of her publication record by outside reviewers, in holding the university's proffered reasons for denying promotion and tenure were not pretextual.[186] Another federal appeals court recognized that failure to earn the Ph.D. degree and lack of scholarly productivity were all relevant considerations contributing to legitimate, non-discriminatory reasons for a faculty member's non-renewal.[187]

The articulated reason for an adverse employment decision should include a clear and reasonably specific factual basis for the employment decision.[188] Standards of quality should not be so subjective that they cannot be effectively communicated and consistently assessed in the faculty evaluation process. For example, if the proffered reason for an adverse employment decision is ineffective teaching performance, then the institution must establish that it maintains a policy in which teaching competence is a performance criterion and that it uniformly relies on a reasonable measure of teaching performance, such as student evaluations.[189]

## Conclusions

While the level of judicial scrutiny applicable to a college or university's employment decisions will vary, judges are unlikely to interfere when the adverse employment decision is based upon criteria reasonably related to job requirements, free of impermissible discrimination or the denial of a constitutional right to free speech or association, reached by proper procedures, and supported by substantial evidence. Judicial intervention would necessitate review of a host of factors used by the academy to make employment decisions, a role courts have neither the competency nor the resources to undertake.

Nevertheless, if responsible administrators do not have reasoned, ascertainable standards for making adverse employment decisions or if they fail to apply those standards in a particular employment decision, the consequences may implicate legally protected rights and result in legal challenge. Judicial review of the employment decision-making process can be anticipated when employment decisions appear arbitrary or capricious, lack supporting evidence, or deny the faculty member's legally protected rights.

Sound employment practices provide a record of events, incidents, appraisals, discussions, interviews, admonitions, and directives that can be relied upon to support the evidentiary sufficiency and credibility of an employment decision. When efforts to correct or improve a faculty member's performance have failed and an adverse employment decision is compelled, that decision must be predicated upon standards reasonably related to job requirements and upon substantial adherence to the procedural requirements established by law, contract, collective agreement, and institutional policy.

It is recommended that faculty and professional staff be included in the process of establishing professional competencies and encouraged to participate in every phase of the employment decision-making process. From policy formulation to implementation, employee participation in employment decision-making enhances employee relations, provides for more informed decision-making, and contributes to a perception of fundamental fairness and reasonableness that can deter lawsuits and reduce judicial intervention.

Development and implementation of legally sound employment practices and procedures will not eliminate legal disputes but should yield a documentary record that substantiates the fairness and reasonableness of the process, establishes the proper predicate for an adverse employment decision, and elaborates the procedural integrity of the process. Evaluative criteria must be developed that are sufficiently specific and reasonably job-related to enable faculty to guide their conduct and provide a standard by which the faculty member's conduct can be evaluated. Systematic and uniform application of those criteria must characterize the process that will ultimately be relied upon to support employment decisions. Finally, employment practices must be procedurally correct, whether that procedure is express in institutional policies or implicit in the provision of due process of law.

# Endnotes

[1] *See* Zuelsdorf v. Univ. of Alaska, 794 P.2d 932 (Alaska 1990) for a case in which the university's personnel regulations were a part of the contract of employment, and failure to give timely notice of nonrenewal breached the probationary employee's contractual rights.

[2] Dixon v. Bhuiyan, 2000 OK 56, 10 P.3d 888, 891 (Okla. 2000).

[3] Caldwell v. Linker, 901 F. Supp. 1010 (M.D.N.C. 1993).

[4] Brady v. Bd. of Trs. of Neb. State Colls., 196 Neb. 226, 242 N.W.2d 616 (Neb. 1976).

[5] *See* Bennett v. Wells Coll., 641 N.Y.S.2d 929 (App. Div. 1996) (tenure denial) and Savannah Coll. of Art and Design v. Nulph, 265 Ga. 662, 460 S.E.2d 792 (Ga. 1995) (termination). *But see* Jacobs v. Mundelein Coll., 256 Ill. App. 3d 476, 628 N.E.2d 201 (Ill. Ct. App. 1993) and De Simone v. Skidmore Coll., 159 A.D.2d 926, 553 N.Y.S.2d 240 (N.Y. App. Div. 1990) in which statements in faculty handbooks concerning criteria for evaluating annual contract employees or establishing procedures for evaluation were not regarded by courts as creating a contractual right protecting the faculty member from an adverse employment decision.

[6] Ozerol v. Howard Univ., 545 A.2d 638 (D.C. App. 1988).

[7] *See* Kashif v. Cent. State Univ., 133 Ohio App. 3d 678, 729 N.E.2d 787 (Ohio Ct. App. 1999) in which the court rejected parole evidence that might alter the unambiguous written contract of the parties.

[8] *See* Tuomala v. Regent Univ., 252 Va. 368; 477 S.E.2d 501 (Va. 1996) in which testimony of members of the institutional governing board was necessary in order to determine the policy-making body's intention with regard to the terms of the agreement.

[9] Lewis v. Loyola Univ. of Chi., 149 Ill. App. 3d 88, 500 N.E.2d 47 (Ill. Ct. App. 1986).

[10] Yates v. Bd. of Regents of Lamar Univ., 654 F. Supp. 979 (E.D. Tex. 1987).

[11] Geddes v. Northwest Mo. State Univ., 49 F.3d 426 (8th Cir. 1995). *See* Gottlied v. Tulane Univ. of La., 529 So. 2d 128 (La. Ct. App. 1988) in which the "apparent authority" of a university administrator to grant tenure did not create a right to tenure in light of the specific and limiting terms of the employment contract agreed to by the professor and the procedures for award of tenure stipulated in the faculty handbook.

[12] This analysis does not address the possibility that an agent's representations may create a basis for that agent's individual liability. See Bicknese v. Sutula, 660 N.W.2d 289 (Wis. 2003) (chair, in making an employment offer to the applicant, was bound to act in accordance with the express terms and conditions of the institution's policies and procedures, and if representations were not consistent with university policies, individual liability could ensue) and Hirsch v. Columbia Univ., 293 F. Supp. 2d 372 (S.D.N.Y. 2003) (dean's statements to candidate, if false and knowingly made, may constitute fraudulent inducement if made in an effort to induce the applicant to accept the position).

[13] Ashcraft v. Dist. Bd. of Trs., 615 So.2d 271 (Fla. Dist. Ct. App. 1993).

[14] Yasnoff v. Hallick, 155 Or. App. 474, 963 P.2d 747 (Or. Ct. App. 1998).

[15] *Id.* at 749.

[16] Parker v. State of Fla. Bd. of Regents, 724 So. 2d 163 (Fla. Dist. Ct. App. 1998). The agreement developed in the dean's memo was a conditional contract to raise the professor's salary "as soon as the budget situation permits." A jury could reasonably find that there were sufficient funds to raise the professor's salary within the first year of the agreement.

[17] *See, e.g.,* McCallum v. Coop. Extension Serv., 142 N.C. App. 485, 42 S.E.2d 227 (N.C. Ct. App. 2001) in which no protected property interest protected by due process was available to an at-will employee; Dunfey v. Roger Williams Univ., 824 F. Supp. 18 (D. Mass. 1993) in which termination of a university administrator was not governed by a covenant of "good faith and fair dealing"; and Rutherford v. Presbyterian Univ.

Hosp., 417 Pa. Super. 316, 612 A.2d 500 (Pa. Super. Ct. 1992) in which the employee's reliance on the general terms of an employee handbook did not create a property entitlement to due process.

18  Kish v. Iowa Cent. Cmty. Coll., 142 F. Supp. 2d 1084 (N.D. Iowa 2001); Murtagh v. Emory Univ., 152 F. Supp. 2d 1356 (N.D. Ga. 2001); and Galloway v. Roger Williams Univ., 777 A.2d 148 (R.I. 2001).

19  Starishevsky v. Hofstra Univ., 161 Misc. 2d 137, 612 N.Y.S.2d 794 (N.Y. App. Div. 1994) (sexual harassment and unethical conduct) and Spiegel v. Univ. of S. Fla., 555 So.2d 428 (Fla. Dist. Ct. App. 1989) (right to hearing for department chair subject to removal under state administrative procedure act).

20  Board of Regents v. Roth, 408 U.S. 564; 92 S. Ct. 2701; 33 L. Ed. 2d 548 (1972).

21  Greene v. Howard Univ., 412 F.2d 1128 (D.C. Cir. 1969).

22  Calhoun v. Gaines, 982 F.3d 1470 (10th Cir. 1992).

23  American Association of University Professors, *Academic Freedom and Tenure, 1940 Statement of Principles and Interpretive Comments*, AAUP REDBOOK (1977).

24  Roklina v. Skidmore Coll., 268 A.D.2d 765, 702 N.Y.S.2d 161 (N.Y. App. Div. 2000).

25  University of Balt. v. Iz, 123 Md. App. 135, 716 A.2d 1107 (Md. Ct. App. 1998).

26  *Id.* at 166-167, 716 A.2d at 1123-1124. *See* Mayberry v. Dees, 663 F.2d 502 (4th Cir. 1981); Stein v. Kent State Univ., 994 F. Supp. 898 (N.D. Ohio 1998), *aff'd w/o opinion*, 181 F.3d 103 (6th Cir. 1999); and Bresnick v. Manhattanville Coll., 864 F. Supp. 327 (S.D.N.Y. 1994) for a similar affirmations that collegiality is implicit in tenure criteria.

27  Sackman v. Alfred Univ., 186 Misc. 2d 227; 717 N.Y.S.2d 461 (N.Y. Sup. Ct. 2000).

28  Craine v. Trinity Coll., 259 Conn. 625, 791 A.2d 518 (Conn. 2002).

29  408 U.S. 593 (1972).

30  *See* Gray v. Bd. of Regents of the Univ. Sys. of Ga., 150 F.3d 1347 (11th Cir. 1998) in which the federal appeals court rejected tenure by default based on express institutional policies on the award of tenure.

31  Paul v. Howard Univ., 754 A.2d 297 (D.C. 2000). *But see* Harris v. Ariz. Bd. of Regents, 528 F. Supp. 987 (D. Ariz. 1981) in which a federal court afforded de facto tenure to a terminated faculty member despite the existence of a formal tenure policy based on an offer letter that stated the employee would receive tenure automatically in his third year of employment.

32  Omosegbon v. Wells, 335 F.3d 668 (7th Cir. 2003).

33  29 *U.S.C.* Sec 141 *et seq.*

34  South Dakota Educ. Ass'n v. S.D. of Regents, 1998 SD 84, 582 N.W.2d 386 (S.D. 1998).

35  Central State Univ. v. Am. Ass'n of Univ. Professors, 526 U.S. 124, 119 S. Ct. 1162, 143 L. Ed. 2d 227 (1999).

36  Vermont State Colls. Faculty Fed'n v. Vert. State Colls., 152 Vt. 343; 566 A.2d 955 (Vt. 1989).

37  NLRB v. Yeshiva Univ., 444 U.S. 672, 100 S. Ct. 856, 63 L. Ed. 2d 115 (1980).

38  *Id.* at 686.

39  *See* Knight v. Minn. Cmty. Coll. Faculty Ass'n., 466 U.S. 284, 104 S. Ct. 1799, 80 L. Ed. 2d 302 (1984) in which the Court rejected a challenge to a faculty union's exclusive right to negotiate subjects of mandatory bargaining.

40  Abood v. Detroit Bd. of Educ., 431 U.S. 209, 97 S. Ct. 1782, 52 L. Ed. 2d 261 (1977).

41  Chicago Teachers' Union v. Hudson, 475 U.S. 292, 106 S. Ct. 1066, 89 L. Ed. 2d 232 (1988).

42  Lehnert v. Ferris Faculty Ass'n, 500 U.S. 507, 111 S. Ct. 1950, 114 L. Ed. 2d 572 (1991).

43  White v. Winona State Univ., 474 N.W.2d 410 (Minn. Ct. App. 1991) and McGough v. Univ. of S.F., 214 Cal. App. 3d 1577, 263 Cal. Rptr. 404 (Cal. 1989).

44  Dalmolen v. Elmira Coll., 279 A.D.2d 929, 720 N.Y.S.2d 573 (App. Div. 2001).

[45] Trimble v. W. Va. Bd. of Dirs., 209 W. Va. 420, 549 S.E.2d 294 (W. Va. 2001).

[46] Reece v. Bd. of Trs. of Marshall Univ., 202 W. Va. 89, 502 S.E.2d 186 (W. Va. 1998).

[47] American Association of University Professors, *Recommended Institutional Regulations on Academic Freedom and Tenure,* ACADEME, Jan.–Feb. 1983, at 15a-20a.

[48] *Id.* Regulation 5(a), at 26.

[49] *See, for example,* Ohio Dominican Coll. v. Krone, 54 Ohio App. 3d 29, 560 N.E.2d 1340 (Ohio Ct. App. 1990); Korf v. Ball State Univ., 726 F.2d 1222 (7th Cir. 1984); and Garrett v. Matthews, 625 F.2d 658 (5th Cir. 1980).

[50] San Filippo v. Bongiovanni, 961 F.2d 1125, 1137 (3d Cir. 1992),

[51] *See* de Llano v. Berglund, 282 F.3d 1031 (8th Cir. 2002).

[52] *See* Agarwal v. Regents of the Univ. of Minn., 788 F.2d 504 (8th Cir. 1986) and Yu v. Peterson, 13 F.3d 1413 (10th Cir. 1993).

[53] Phillips v. State Bd. of Regents, 863 S.W.2d 45 (Tenn. 1993).

[54] Zahavy v. Univ. of Minn., 544 N.W.2d 32 (Minn. Ct. App. 1996). *See* Garner v. Mich. State Univ., 185 Mich. App. 750, 462 N.W.2d 832 (Mich. Ct. App. 1990) in which the state appeals court ruled that a tenured professor alleged to have lied during a preemployment interview was entitled to due process and a right to an adversarial hearing before discharge even though the university sought to rescind the contract.

[55] Deli v. Univ. of Minn., 511 N.W.2d 46, 52 (Minn. Ct. App. 1994).

[56] *See* Korf v. Ball State Univ., 726 F.1222 (7th Cir. 1984).

[57] Keen v. Penson, 970 F.3d 252 (7th Cir. 1992).

[58] Logan v. Bennington Coll., 72 F.3d 1017 (2d Cir. 1995). *See also* McDaniels v. Flick, 59 F.3d 446 (3d Cir. 1995) in which minimal due process procedures in pretermination based on allegations of sexual harassment were adequate to justify summary judgment for the public college. *But see*, Chan v. Miami Univ., 73 Ohio St. 3d 52, 1995 Ohio 226, 652 N.E.2d 644 (Ohio 1995) in which the state supreme court held that a faculty member subject to dismissal under the procedures set forth for the resolution of sexual harassment complaints was denied due process.

[59] Dismissal Proceedings Against Huang, 110 N.C. App. 683, 693, 431 S.E.2d 541, 548 (N.C. Ct. App. 1995).

[60] *See* Howard Univ. v. Baten, 632 A.2d 389 (D.C. Ct. App. 1993) in which evidence of insubordination created a jury question concerning whether the university employee received adequate warning about prohibited non-job related work.

[61] *See* Nelson v. Pima Cmty. Coll., 83 F.3d 1075 (9th Cir. 1996) and Hanton v. Gilbert, 36 F.3d 4 (4th Cir. 1994) in which consistent documentation of misconduct and clear administrative directives justified adverse employment decisions.

[62] Josberger v. Univ. of Tenn., 706 S.W.2d 300 (Tenn. Ct. App. 1985).

[63] Peterson v. N.D. Univ., 678 N.W.2d 163 (N.D. 2004).

[64] McConnell v. Howard Univ., 818 F.2d 58 (D.C. Cir. 1987).

[65] Morrison v. State Bd. of Educ., 1 Cal. 3d 214; 461 P.2d 375; 82 Cal. Rptr. 175 (Cal. 1969).

[66] Board of Dirs. of Des Moines Area Cmty. Coll. v. Simons, 493 N.W.2d 879 (Iowa Ct. App. 1992).

[67] West Valley-Mission Coll. v. Concepcion, 16 Cal. App. 4th 1766, 21 Cal. Rptr. 2d 5 (Cal. App. 1993).

[68] *See* Bevli v. Brisco, 211 Cal. App. 3d 986, 260 Cal. Rptr. 57 (Cal. Ct. App. 1989) in which a community college chemistry teacher was dismissed for evident unfitness based on evaluation of her teaching competency.

[69] Cotter v. Trs. of Pensacola Jr. Coll., 548 So. 2d 731 (Fla. Dist. Ct. App. 1989).

[70] Riggin v. Bd. of Trs. of Ball State Univ., 489 N.E.2d 616 (Ind. Ct. App. 1986).

[71] McCauley v. Sch. of Mines, 488 N.W.2d 53 (S.D. 1992). *See* Trejo v. Shoben, 319 F.3d 878 (7th Cir. 2003) for a case in which a professor's coarse commentary and ribald comments to graduate students while attending an academic conference were not protected by the First Amendment.

[72] *See* Katz v. Georgetown Univ., 246 F.3d 685 (D.C. Cir. 2001).

[73] Cable v. Ivy Tech State Coll., 200 F.3d 467 (7th Cir. 1999).

[74] *See* Hart v. Univ. Sys. of N.H., 938 F. Supp. 104 (D.N.H. 1996) in which a federal district court ruled there was sufficient evidence to support a finding of constructive discharge when a former department chair presented circumstantial evidence of discriminatory treatment.

[75] Lighton v. Univ. of Utah, 209 F.3d 1213 (10th Cir. 2000).

[76] Patterson v. Porch, 853 F.2d 1399 (7th Cir. 1988).

[77] Morgan v. Am. Univ., 534 A.2d 323 (D.C. 1987).

[78] Garner v. Mich. State Univ., 185 Mich. App. 750, 462 N.W.2d 832 (Mich. Ct. App. 1990) in which the institution was required to provide due process to professor consistent with university policies.

[79] Sarvis v. Vt. State Colls., 172 Vt. 76, 772 A.2d 494 (Vt. 2001).

[80] *See* Levenstein v. Salafsky, 164 F.3d 345 (7th Cir. 1998) in which the court agreed that the procedures used to investigate and hear charges were a sham intended to force the faculty member's resignation and Harrington v. Harris, 118 F.3d 359 (5th Cir. 1997) in which the court reasoned that administrative manipulation of the evaluation system to arbitrarily favor black faculty violated plaintiff's substantive due process rights to a "rationale application" of the institution's merit pay policy.

[81] *See* Fox v. Parker, 98 S.W.3d 713 (Tex. App. 2003) holding that the private university carefully followed the procedural steps in the faculty handbook in dismissing a tenured faculty member for inappropriate sexual conduct with students.

[82] McDaniels v. Flick, 59 F.3d 446 (3d Cir. 1995) and Levitt v. Univ. of Tex., 759 F.2d 1224 (5th Cir. 1985).

[83] Johnson v. Ala. Agric. and Mech. Univ., 481 So. 2d 336 (Ala. 1985).

[84] Frumkin v. Bd. of Trs., Kent State Univ., 626 F.2d 19 (6th Cir. 1980).

[85] *See* Ross v. Med. Univ. of S.C., 328 S.C. 51, 492 S.E.2d 62 (S.C. 1997) in which a state court found that deficiencies in a pre-termination hearing relative to the right to respond to charges was remedied in the extensive due process permitted in the post-termination hearing. *But see* Stallworth v. City of Evergreen, 680 So.2d 229 (Ala. 1996), *cert. denied*, 519 U.S. 1007, 117 S. Ct. 509, 136 L. Ed. 2d 399 (1996) holding that a post-termination hearing cannot remedy due process violations that occur in a pre-termination hearing.

[86] Gilbert v. Homar, 520 U.S. 924, 117 S. Ct. 1807, 138 L. Ed. 2d 120 (1997).

[87] Alvin v. Suzuki, 227 F.3d 107 (3d Cir. 2001).

[88] Cleveland Bd .of Educ. v. Loudermill, 470 U.S. 532, 105 S. Ct. 1487, 84 L. Ed. 2d 494 (1985). *But see*, Gilbert v. Homar, 520 U.S. 924, 117 S. Ct. 1807, 138 L. Ed. 2d 120 (1997) in which a post termination hearing was sufficient to protect the rights of a university employee charged with drug possession.

[89] Wells v. Doland, 711 F.2d 670 (5th Cir. 1983).

[90] Williams v. Tex. Tech Univ. Health Sciences Ctr., 6 F.3d 290 (5th Cir. 1993).

[91] Miller v. Bunce, 60 F. Supp. 2d 620 (S.D. Tex. 1999).

[92] *See* Meyer v. Univ. of Wash., 105 Wn.2d 847, 719 P.2d 98 (Wash. 1986) and Harris v. Ariz. Bd. of Regents, 528 F. Supp. 987 (D. Ariz. 1981).

[93] Garvie v. Jackson, 845 F.2d 647 (6th Cir. 1983).

[94] Bunger v. Univ. of Okla. Bd. of Regents, 95 F.3d 987 (10th Cir. 1996).

[95] Simonson v. Iowa State Univ., 603 N.W.2d 557 (Iowa 1999) in which the court found no evidence that would establish the institution had publicly disclosed the reason (alleged sexual harassment of students—ongoing investigation) for an employee's paid administrative leave.

[96] Edwards v. Cal. Univ. of Pa., 156 F.3d 488 (3d Cir. 1998).

[97] Herold v. Univ. of S. Fla., 806 So. 2d 638 (Fla. Dist. Ct. App. 2002)

[98] *See* Tonkovich v. Kan. Bd. of Regents, 159 F.3d 504 (10th Cir. 1998) in which the court emphasized that while the institution's representatives might have failed to

adhere to certain evidentiary rules or institutional polices, they did nothing to change the fact that the professor received notice, an opportunity to be heard by an impartial tribunal, and a full-blown evidentiary hearing with post-termination protections such as the right to counsel, to cross examine witnesses, and to present witnesses in his behalf and Deli v. Univ. of Minn., 511 N.W.2d 46 (Minn. Ct. App. 1994) in which a state appeals court held that failure to conform to specified procedures in termination is reversible only where a party's substantial rights have been prejudiced.

[99] Smith v. State, 389 N.W.2d 808 (N.D. 1986).

[100] Newman v. Burgin, 930 F.2d 955 (1st Cir. 1991) *See also* Agarwal v. Regents of the Univ. of Minn., 788 F.2d 504 (8th Cir. 1986), which identifies four elements of due process in a plagiarism hearing: (1) notice of reasons for termination of tenure, (2) notice of names of accusers, (3) opportunity to present evidence in defense, and (4) impartial tribunal.

[101] Karle v. Bd. of Trs., 575 S.E.2d 267 (W. Va. 2002).

[102] Shub v. Hankin, 869 F. Supp. 213 (S.D.N.Y.1994).

[103] 391 U.S. 563, 88 S. Ct. 1731, 20 L. Ed. 2d 811 (1968).

[104] Connick v. Myers, 461 U.S. 138, 146, 103 S. Ct. 1684, 75 L. Ed. 2d 708 (1983),

[105] 391 U.S. at 568.

[106] 429 U.S. 274, 97 S. Ct. 568, 50 L. Ed. 2d 471 (1977).

[107] 511 U.S. 661, 114 S. Ct. 1878, 128 L. Ed. 2d 686 (1994). In this case, a nurse employed at a state-run hospital was terminated for criticizing department policies to a potential department employee.

[108] *Id.* at 1890.

[109] Powell v. Gallentine, 992 F.2d 1088 (10th Cir. 1993).

[110] Levin v. Harleston, 966 F.2d 85 (2d Cir. 1992).

[111] Kurtz v. Vickrey, 855 F.2d 723 (11th Cir. 1988). *See also* Jacobs v. Meister, 108 N.M. 488, 775 P.2d 254 (N.M. Ct. App. 1989) in which a decision not to renew a nontenured professor was improperly based on his public criticism of the university administration.

[112] Dishnow v. Sch. Dist. of Rib Lake, 77 F.3d 194, 197 (7th Cir. 1996).

[113] *See* Johnson v. Lincoln Univ., 776 F.2d 443 (3d Cir. 1985) and Daulton v. Affeldt, 678 F.2d 487 (4th Cir. 1982).

[114] *See* Kurtz, 855 F.2d at 730, *but see* Schweitzer v. Univ. of Tex. Health Ctr., 688 F. Supp. 278 (E.D. Tex. 1988) in which an employee's efforts to inform her superiors of waste in the payroll accounting system was regarded as constitutionally protected speech.

[115] Pressman v. Univ. of N.C. at Charlotte, 78 N.C. App. 296, 337 S.E.2d 644 (N.C. Ct. App. 1985). *See* Harris v. Merwin, 901 F. Supp. 509 (N.D.N.Y. 1995) in which an assistant professor's speech critical of the appointment of a new chairperson was not a matter of public concern so as to protect him from nonrenewal.

[116] Leachman v. Rector and Visitors of the Univ. of Va., 691 F. Supp. 961 (W.D. Va. 1988).

[117] *See* de Llano v. Berglund, 282 F.3d 1031 (8th Cir. 2002) in which the professor's public criticism related primarily to matters of department conflicts and were regarded as a public airing of his private interests.

[118] Clinger v. N.M. Highlands Univ., 215 F.3d 1162 (10th Cir. 2000), quoting Bunger v. Univ. of Okla. Bd. of Regents, 95 F.3df 987, 992 (10th Cir. 1996).

[119] *But see* Schneider v. Indian River Cmty. Coll., 684 F. Supp. 283 (S.D. Fla. 1987). In this case, the federal district court held that employees of the college's public radio station were not denied free speech rights when they were dismissed for failure to conform to a directive prohibiting reporting on certain topics on the air. The court emphasized that the licensee of the state-owned public television station has the right to make editorial decisions and, as a closed forum, those decisions may be enforced against employees who are informed of the prohibitions and defy them.

[120] Mumford v. Godfried, 52 F.3d 756 (8th Cir. 1995). *See also* Corum v. Univ. of N.C., 330 N.C. 761, 413 S.E.2d 276 (N.C. 1992) in which a dean's comments to the administrative staff (opposing a directive relocating artifacts in a university collection) was based on a matter of public concern and constitutionally protected speech.

[121] *See* Ayoub v. Tex. A & M Univ., 927 F.2d 834 (5th Cir. 1991), *cert. denied* 502 U.S. 817, 112 S. Ct. 72, 116 L. Ed. 2d 46 (1991) and Stevenson v. Lower Marion County Sch. Dist., 327 S.E.2d 656 (S.C. 1985).

[122] Bloch v. Temple Univ., 939 F. Supp. 387 (E.D. Pa. 1996).

[123] Colburn v. Trs. of Ind. Univ., 973 F.2d 581, 587 (7th Cir. 1992). *See* Peterson v. State of N.D. *ex rel.* N.D. Univ., 240 F. Supp. 2d 1055 (D.N.D. 2003) for a case in which a faculty member's disapproval of the university's removal of her department chair was regarded as a matter of personal interest amounting to a grievance that was job-related and not a matter of public concern.

[124] Roberts v. Broski, 186 F.3d 990 (7th Cir. 1999).

[125] *See* Gerhart v. Hayes, 217 F.3d 320 (5th Cir. 2000) in which the institution justified dismissal on the basis regular supervisory evaluations that established the employee failed to meet legitimate, job-related objectives.

[126] Nicholas v. Penn. State Univ., 227 F.3d 133 (3d Cir. 2000).

[127] Hamer v. Brown, 831 F.2d 1398 (8th Cir. 1987).

[128] Curtis v. Univ. of Houston, 940 F. Supp. 1070, 1078 (S.D. Tex. 1996).

[129] Scallet v. Rosenblum, 911 F. Supp. 999 (W.D. Va. 1996).

[130] Fong v. Purdue Univ., 692 F. Supp. 930, 959 (N.D. Ind. 1988).

[131] Roos v. Smith, 837 F. Supp. 803 (S.D. Miss. 1993).

[132] *See* Kurtz v. Vickery, 855 F.2d 723, 732 (11th Cir. 1988).

[133] Rankin v. McPherson, 483 U.S. 378, 388, 107 S. Ct. 2891, 97 L. Ed. 2d 315 (1987).

[134] Johnson v. Univ. of Cincinnati, 215 F.3d 561 (6th Cir. 2000).

[135] *See* Carleton Coll. v. Nat'l Labor Relations Bd., 230 F.3d 1075 (8th Cir. 2000) in which the decision not to renew an adjunct faculty member was not an unfair labor practice and was justified on the basis that the adjunct's behavior in a meeting with the dean provided substantial evidence of disrespect for the department and the college and unwillingness to act in a professional manner.

[136] Hall v. Ford, 856 F.2d 255 (D.C. Cir. 1988).

[137] *Id.* at 261.

[138] Maples v. Martin, 858 F.2d 1546 (11th Cir. 1988).

[139] Propst v. Bitzer, 39 F.3d 148 (7th Cir. 1994).

[140] Feldman v. Ho, 171 F.3d 494, 498 (7th Cir. 1999).

[141] Jeffries v. Harleston, 52 F.3d 9 (2d Cir. 1995).

[142] *See* Piarowski v. Ill. Cmty. Coll. Dist. 515, 759 F.2d 625 (7th Cir. 1985), *cert. denied*, 474 U.S. 1007 (1985).

[143] 354 U.S. 234 (1957), 77 S. Ct. 1203, 1 L. Ed. 2d 1311.

[144] *Id.* at 263.

[145] 385 U.S. 589, 87 S. Ct. 675, 17 L. Ed. 2d 629 (1967).

[146] *Id.* at 603.

[147] Webb v. Bd. of Trs. of Ball State Univ., 167 F.3d 1146 (7th Cir. 1999)

[148] Keen v. Penson, 970 F.2d 252, 257 (7th Cir. 1992) and Piarowski v. Ill. Cmty. Coll., 759 F.2d 625, 629 (7th Cir. 1985).

[149] Urofsky v. Gilmore, 216 F.3d 401 (4th Cir. 2000).

[150] Parate v. Isibor, 868 F.2d 821 (6th Cir. 1989).

[151] Brown v. Armenti, 247 F.3d 69 (3d Cir. 2001).

[152] Mahoney v. Hankin, 593 F. Supp. 1171 (S.D.N.Y. 1984). *See* DiBona v. Matthews, 269 Cal. Rptr. 2d 882 (Cal. Ct. App. 1990) in which the college's cancellation of a drama class and prohibition on production of a controversial play led to a holding that the institution failed to present a sufficient justification for denying the faculty member's First Amendment free speech right to select classroom materials.

153 Hardy v. Jefferson Cmty. Coll., 260 F.3d 671 (6th Cir. 2001). *But see,* Vega v. Miller, 273 F.3d 460 (2d Cir. 2001) in which institutional administrators were entitled to qualified immunity for their actions in terminating an instructor who undertook a classroom exercise that involved vulgar and profane language.

154 Clark v. Holmes, 474 F.2d 928, 931 (7th Cir. 1972), *cert. denied*, 411 U.S. 928 (1973).

155 Hetrick v. Martin, 480 F.2d 706 (6th Cir. 1973), *cert. denied*, 414 U.S. 1075 (1973).

156 Edwards v. Cal. Univ. of Pa., 156 F.3d 488 (3d Cir. 1998) in which the appeals courts ruled that a professor did not have a constitutional right to choose curriculum related to his religious views in contravention of the university's curriculum policies.

157 Lovelace v. Southeastern Mass. Univ., 793 F.2d 419 (1st Cir. 1986) (grading policy) and Wirsing v. Bd. of Regents of the Univ. of Colo., 739 F. Supp. 551 (D. Colo. 1990), *affirmed w/o opin.*, 945 F.2d 412 (10th Cir. 1991) (testing requirements).

158 *See* Trimble v. W. Va. Bd. of Dirs., 209 W. Va. 420, 549 S.E.2d 294 (W. Va. 2001) in which the court noted a tenured professor's history of satisfactory performance would not justify dismissal for a single instance of relatively minor insubordinate conduct.

159 Holm v. Ithaca Coll., 682 N.Y.S.2d 295 (App. Div. 1998).

160 Bishop v. Aronov, 926 F.2d 1066 (11th Cir. 1991).

161 *Id.* at 1074.

162 Scallet v. Rosenblum, 911 F. Supp. 999 (W.D. Va. 1996).

163 Martin v. Parrish, 805 F.2d 583 (5th Cir. 1986).

164 *Id.* at 585. In a concurring opinion, one justice emphasized that the professor's remarks, considering the totality of the circumstances, were unrelated to any educational purpose.

165 *See* Cohen v. San Bernardino Valley Coll., 92 F.3d 968 (9th Cir. 1996) in which an appellate court reversed the judgment of a district court and held that the terms of the sexual harassment policy were unconstitutionally vague, thus violating the professor's free speech rights.

166 *See* Goldbarth v. Kan. State Bd. of Regents, 9 P.3d 1251 (Kan. 2000) in which an investigation of classroom sexual harassment was not regarded as creating a chilling effect on the exercise of free speech.

167 McClellan v. Bd. of Regents, 921 S.W.2d 684 (Tenn. 1996) and Wexley v. Mich. State Univ., 821 F. Supp. 479 (W.D. Mich. 1993).

168 *See* Rubin v. Ikenberry, 933 F. Supp. 1425 (C.D. Ill. 1996) in which the professor's frequent classroom reference to sexual topics and inappropriate inquiries to students justified in discipline.

169 *See* Bonnell v. Lorenzo, 241 F.3d 800 (6th Cir. 2001) in which the appeals court emphasized that neither the First Amendment nor academic freedom is a shield that grants faculty the absolute right to use a superior position to harass or intimidate students.

170 *See* Silva v. Univ. of N.H., 888 F. Supp. 293 (D.N.H. 1994) in which the professor's use of sexual analogy to convey competencies in effective writing was protected.

171 42 *U.S.C.* Section 2000e *et seq.*

172 20 *U.S.C.* Section 1681 *et seq.*

173 29 *U.S.C.* Section 794.

174 42 *U.S.C.* Section 12101 *et seq.*

175 29 *U.S.C.* Section 621 *et seq.*

176 Texas Dep't of Cmty. Affairs v. Burdine, 450 U.S. 248, 101 S.Ct. 1089, 67 L. Ed. 2d 207 (1981).

177 Sinha v. State Univ. of N.Y. at Farmingdale, 764 F. Supp. 765 (E.D.N.Y. 1991) (failure to promote).

178 Hayes v. Invesco, 907 F.2d 853 (8th Cir. 1990) (discharge).

179 Mayer v. Univ. of Minn., 940 F. Supp. 1474 (D. Minn. 1994) (alleged disability discrimination).

180 Randall v. Howard Univ., 941 F. Supp. 206 (D.C. 1996).

[181] *See* Soares v. Univ. of New Haven, 154 F. Supp. 2d 365 (D. Conn. 2001) in which the professor's substandard performance evaluations justified the adverse employment decision and Schneider v. Northwestern Univ., 925 F. Supp. 1347 (N.D. Ill. 1996) in which the denial of tenure was upheld on the basis that the institution's proffered reason was related to subjective factors that were reasonably related to scholarship and teaching.

[182] Akeyo v. O'Hanlon, 75 F.3d 370 (8th Cir. 1996); Lutz v. Purdue Univ., 133 F. Supp. 2d 1101 (N.D. Ind. 2001); and Favetz v. Bd. of Control, Grand Valley State Univ., 903 F. Supp. 1181 (W.D. Mich. 1995).

[183] Bina v. Providence Coll., 39 F.3d 21 (1st Cir. 1994). *See* Byerly v. Ithaca Coll., 290 F. Supp. 2d 301 (N.D.N.Y.2003) in which student assessments of the faculty member's teaching justified denial of tenure.

[184] Anderson v. Univ. of N. Iowa, 779 F.2d 441 (8th Cir. 1985) and Lynn v. Regents of the Univ. of Cal., 656 F.2d 1337 (9th Cir. 1981).

[185] Bernofsky v. Tulane Univ. Med. Sch., 962 F. Supp. 895 (E.D. La. 1997).

[186] Lawrence v. Curators of the Univ. of Mo., 204 F.2d 807 (8th Cir. 2000).

[187] Jiminez v. Mary Wash. Coll., 57 F.3d 369 (4th Cir. 1995).

[188] Morris v. Wallace Cmty. Coll.-Selma, 125 F. Supp. 2d 1315 (S.D. Ala. 2001).

[189] Girma v. Skidmore Coll., 180 F. Supp. 2d 326 (N.D.N.Y. 2001).

# 5 Non-Academic Personnel
## Luke Cornelius and Gus Douvanis

## Introduction

Although professors and instructors are the college and university employees that are most visible in higher education, they represent only a portion of the campus employees necessary for an institution to function. Even the smallest of colleges requires a range of non-academic employees, from secretaries and groundskeepers to presidents and senior administrators. A large university can, in many regards, resemble a small city government in terms of the complexity of its operations and the range of its employees. Many schools operate their own hospitals, business enterprises, police departments, and even nuclear power plants. While the legal rights and administrative requirements of such employees may closely mirror those of the instructional staff, there are some significant differences that merit consideration.

This chapter will attempt to generally detail the legal status and treatment of these non-academic employees. Although the best legal analogy for such employment may be to compare the situation to that of a municipal government, a private company, or a religious denomination, depending on the type of institution, there are additional considerations that place unique challenges on the administration of such personnel. A unique consideration in college and university employment are the large number of personnel whose status as non-academic employees are complicated by their status as students, especially graduate students, or as faculty members. Another consideration, which cannot be fully addressed in an overview such as this, is the diversity of higher education organizations and their individual terms and conditions of employment. At some institutions, particularly small private colleges, nearly all non-academic employees may essentially have the status of "at-will" employees. On the other hand, in certain public universities, depending on state law, the majority of these employees will be covered by the state civil service system requiring competitive examinations and objective hiring procedures and affording employees rights of job tenure and due process that rival, or even exceed, the protections afforded to the academic faculty.

## Organization

As indicated above, the nature of a particular employment relationship can vary depending on the type and location of an institution of higher learning. However, there are certain standard methods of classifying non-academic staff that, with variations in terminology and application, are generally utilized by many educational organizations. "Classified Personnel" refers to that large body of workers hired to carry out specific support functions of the college or university. In a public institution, these employees may also be part of a state or local Civil Service System. Classified personnel are typically hired to perform specific duties on campus and are selected on the basis of possessing and demonstrating job-specific knowledge, skills, and abilities. Examples of classified personnel, typically the largest group of employees on campus, can include clerks and secretaries, groundskeepers and maintenance persons, police or security officers, lab technicians, bus drivers and vehicle operators, warehousemen, nurses and medical assistants, and computer technicians. In most cases, such employees must demonstrate specific competencies in performing various duties through either work experience or entrance examinations. For some highly skilled or sensitive positions, the possession of external certifications, such as in law enforcement or nursing, may also be necessary.

Another large group of employees are those known as "Administrative and Professional Personnel" or "A&P" employees. In a civil service system, these employees are often classified as Exempt Employees. These members of the college or university staff are those that, as a requirement of their employment, usually must possess high levels of formal education and experience. They are also employed based upon more subjective considerations such as their potential to make a positive impact on the institution's operations and their ability to successfully work with other senior A&P staff. Examples of A&P personnel would include presidents, provosts, vice-presidents, deans, and directors, as well as medical doctors, engineers, and curators. One characteristic of these employees is their lack of job security. While A&P employees may enjoy high pay and prestige in their positions, they are usually referred to as "at-will" employees. Should their supervisor or the institution's governing board decide that such an employee is no longer effective in their role, or should they simply decide a change of personnel is desirable, they may simply dismiss an A&P employee in accordance with any contractual guarantees the employee may have had.

Although classified and A&P staff may make up the majority of a school's non-academic employees, there are still several other categories that must be considered. Colleges and universities commonly make use of contract employees. Often such employees are hired to complete specific recurring or non-recurring tasks. They may also be hired to work with related campus organizations and enterprises such as student government or school-related businesses. In addition, colleges and universities make use of considerable numbers of temporary employees. Grant-funded employees make up a closely related class of workers. These employees are hired to help an institution, or some sub-agency or even individual professor of that institution, fulfill the obligations of a grant provided by some outside agency or organization. Frequently, these grants involve research activities that require the facilities and expertise of a university and its faculty. Such employment is very similar to contract employment in the sense that the expectation of employment cannot be considered to exceed the expiration or exhaustion of the grant funding.

Those workers who are also enrolled as students in an institution constitute a particularly nebulous class of employees. Colleges and universities traditionally hire large numbers of their own students as workers in a variety of temporary and part-time roles. Some of these are fairly unrestricted workers, hired under a grant or contract to fulfill some general duty. Others are employed as a condition of receiving financial aid such as students hired under college work-study programs. Graduate assistants are a particularly unique type of student employee. Graduate assistants are typically hired in a variety of sub-categories such as Teaching Assistants and Research Assistants, which delineate the type of work they perform for the college or university. As with work-study students, graduate assistants usually receive tuition assistance in addition to their salary or hourly pay. However, many graduate assistants are employed for reasons other than a need for financial aid. Graduate assistants often are employed as part of their educational programs. Thus, while they receive payment as employees for performing a useful, or even vital, service to the institution, they are also receiving valuable training and instruction. For many professors and professional researchers, the graduate student's assistantship is a vital apprenticeship considered necessary to pursue career goals. This dual role of the assistantship is highlighted by the policies of many graduate degree programs that require students to serve as teaching or research assistants as a graduation requirement.

## Hiring and Promotion

Both public and private institutions of higher education must conform to a series of federal laws related to employment. Of particular significance to the hiring and promotion process is Title VII of the Civil Rights Act of 1964.[1] Title VII operationalizes the protections not only of the Civil Rights Act regarding discrimination based on race, color, gender, and national origin, but also those of subsequent legal enactments such as the Age Discrimination in Employment Act,[2] the Equal Pay Act,[3] Section 504 of the Rehabilitation Act of 1973,[4] and the Americans with Disabilities Act.[5] Title VII applies to all employers of more than 15 employees, including all state and local public institutions.[6] The intended reach of Title VII, the number of employees required by even a small college to operate, and the prevalence of federal funding in colleges and universities insures that these federal anti-discrimination laws cover virtually all institutions of higher education.

State and local statutes and regulations, as well as the provisions of collective bargaining agreements, provide additional protections and requirements that govern the status of non-academic personnel. For example, while not explicitly protected in federal statutes, many states bar both public and private employers from discrimination based upon sexual orientation.[7] Specific state protections can cover a variety of potential employment issues. For example, Wisconsin bars discrimination based on marital status, arrest and conviction records, or the use or non-use of "lawful products" when not at the work site or performing work-related tasks.[8] New York[9] and New Jersey[10] go so far as to ban any employment decisions based upon the individual's genetic history and information.

It should be noted that these restrictions apply to all aspects of the employment relationship, from initial recruiting to termination. Particular care must be exercised at two specific junctures: recruitment and the application/interview process. Under Executive Order 11246,[11] issued in 1965, all employers in federally assisted or contracted programs, such as higher education, must not only avoid invidious discrimination, but they must also state in all recruiting materials that they do not discriminate with regard to race, color, religion, sex, or national origin.[12] Care must be taken to engage in recruitment practices that will address a diverse population and not utilize recruitment media that excessively targets only specific applicant pools. For example, a college using radio advertisements to seek employees should insure that its advertisements are not disproportionately played on music stations which appeal to persons of specific ages, races, genders, religions, or national origins. Employers should also be sensitive to the availability of specific media, such as trade publications or the Internet, among various populations, especially with regard to race and national origin.

These restrictions apply even more significantly in the application and interview process. Except when related to a Bona Fide Occupational Qualification or to achieve affirmative action goals, employment applications and interviewers should avoid questions related to an employee's status as a member of a protected class. If a requirement of a position might cause conflict with an applicant's potentially protected status, then the employment process should focus on the requirement as opposed to the individual's personal attributes or beliefs. For example, if a position requires working on weekends, which may cause conflicts with religious beliefs, an application or interviewer should ask if the applicant is available to work weekends or is available for such work, as opposed to asking the applicant directly about their beliefs. Also, it is important to remember that it is permissible to deny employment based on membership in a protected class when no reasonable employment accommodations can be made. For example, if an applicant for a position as a football coach indicates that he or she cannot work on Saturdays due to his or her religious beliefs, he or she can be excluded, as it is axiomatic that working on Saturday is an essential duty of a college football coach. By contrast, if the applicant was seeking employment as a librarian, the question must be asked of how essential such scheduling is for every applicant? Unless the librarian position is so specialized as to preclude scheduling another employee in the applicant's place, it would not seem essential that every librarian be available for Saturday work. Unless it relates to an essential requirement of a position, for which accommodations might be sought, questions should not be asked on applications or in interviews that would compel an applicant to declare their membership in a protected class.

## Federal Protections

To operationalize the above discussion, it is appropriate to review the various federal protections active in college employment. While these statutes are critical to insure compliance with federal civil rights standards, it must also be remembered that state and local statutes, collective bargaining agreements, and institutional policies, such as anti-discrimination declarations, may also protect potential employees. What follows are brief summaries of the appropriate federal statutes that are universally applicable, under Title VII, to both public and private employers.

### Title VII

Title VII is one of the most powerful and sweeping federal laws affecting employment. Applying to any organization with more than fifteen employees, it provides a sweeping mandate against discrimination on the basis of race, color, gender, national origin, or religion. This statute is controlling on all personnel actions from the initial advertisement of vacancies through disciplinary and termination decisions. One significant aspect of Title VII is that it can be invoked using two different legal doctrines: *disparate treatment* and *disparate impact.*[13] Disparate treatment is normally applied when an applicant or employee can show they were members of a protected class under Title VII and they were treated differently than non-class members in employment decisions. Disparate treatment implies clear discrimination against an individual or specific group of protected persons. By contrast, disparate impact requires that a plaintiff show that an employer's personnel policies have an undue impact on persons of one or more protected classes. Rather than alleging a specific incident of discrimination, disparate impact requires the plaintiffs to demonstrate a pattern of discriminatory hiring overall, regardless of intent.

A good example of the reach of Title VII in the employment of non-academic employees can be found in the ongoing litigation and consent decrees in *Shuford v. Alabama State Board of Education.*[14] Here allegations were made that in administrative and support staff positions in a statewide system of higher education, colleges and universities had consistently, through local action, failed to hire and promote African-Americans in general and African-American females in particular. When these protected individuals werc hired, they were often given lower job titles and pay than previous incumbents in their positions. Although the courts accepted that in many of the specific cases listed, the reasons for these decisions were legitimate and non-discriminatory, overall, the courts found a general pattern of discrimination sufficient to support a decree requiring affirmative action in the recruiting of minorities, especially minority women, system-wide. In addition, widespread re-classification of current employees was also deemed a necessity. *Shuford* illustrates Title VII's application to two protected categories, race and gender.

### The Age Discrimination in Employment Act (ADEA) of 1967[15]

This congressional enactment effectively expanded the protected classes defined in Title VII to include employees and job seekers over the age of forty. As with other Title VII actions, age discrimination can be proven through either disparate treatment or disparate impact. Not only does the ADEA prohibit discrimination in hiring decisions, but it also protects the jobs of older workers from arbitrary termination to eliminate the salary or benefits burden of employing senior staff. For example, in *Burger v. New York Institute of Technology,*[16] a reduction in force led to the lay-off of the oldest and most senior employee in an accounting department. Although the college claimed that its decision was based on the fact that several of the employee's responsibilities were being eliminated, a federal appeals court affirmed a lower federal court's determination that the older employee met her initial burden to show that the lay-off occurred under circumstances giving rise to an inference of age discrimination. The appeals court noted that many of her duties were not eliminated but were simply transferred to younger employees and the institution had failed to establish that the job duties of these employees were so different from hers as to justify retaining a younger and less senior employee instead of her.

Employers need to be especially conscious of the protections of the ADEA when making reduction in force decisions or dealing with older employees who have above-average absences for illness and disability. The act can also apply to older job seekers who apply for positions, such as student affairs and residence hall services, which are traditionally filled by younger employees. As a general policy, it is preferable to avoid the appearance of discrimination by asking potential employees if they meet a minimum age to work, usually eighteen, rather than to ask them to disclose their age or provide a specific date of birth.[17]

## The Equal Pact Act of 1963[18]

The Equal Pay Act (EPA) sought to eliminate traditional pay disparities that existed between men and women by requiring that employees receive equal pay when performing jobs of substantially equal skill, effort, and responsibility.[19] The EPA does not, however, require that the jobs compared be identical. The legal comparison, therefore, focuses more on the relative difficulty and performance of two positions, as opposed to specific job duties and functions. To be enforceable, the EPA requires that jobs be "equal," which in practice means virtually identical; any difference allows different, less-favorable treatment, which is not considered to be discriminatory. Since few jobs are virtually identical, the judicial tendency to conflate equality with sameness has bedeviled plaintiffs who seek a remedy under this law. Although this act has been difficult to implement, it has proven successful in several challenges. For example, a Tennessee university was required to raise the salary of its female administrative managers in several departments when a male administrative manager was hired at a higher salary in one department of the same college.[20]

## Section 504 and the Americans with Disabilities Act

These two laws, Section 504 of the Rehabilitation Act of 1973[21] and the Americans with Disabilities Act (ADA),[22] provide similar protections to college employees depending on the nature of their employment. In its 1987 precedent, *School Board of Nassau County, Florida v. Arline*,[23] the Supreme Court held that Section 504 protected educational employees in federally funded institutions. Section 504 essentially requires non-discrimination in employment decisions, including hiring, promotion, evaluation, and discipline, based upon an individual's disabilities.[24] In particular, Section 504 and the ensuing ADA, require an employer to make "reasonable accommodations" for disabled employees. As defined, the definition of reasonable is based on whether a particular accommodation would create an unreasonable burden on the institution or risk to others. In order to be protected under Section 504, an individual must be regarded as having a disability that impairs a "major life function." If an employee is qualified, reasonable accommodations may include changes in scheduling, the assignment of duties among similar employees, and the physical modification of the workplace and job-related equipment.

In 2001, the Supreme Court limited the application of the ADA in cases involving public institutions of higher education that may be considered "arms of the state" and protected by the U.S. Constitution's Eleven Amendment. In *Board of Trustees of University of Alabama v. Garrett,*[25] the Court concluded that Congress, in passing the ADA, had not properly abrogated the rights of states and their agencies to immunity from federal laws under the Eleventh Amendment. Consequently, although Section 504 remains applicable to public higher education institutions and private institutions receiving over $10,000 in federal aid,[26] the ADA does not extend to those public institutions clothed with "arm of the state" status under the immunity provided by the Eleventh Amendment. However, as the ADA makes similar requirements in terms of both eligibility and accommodations, the requirements for private institutions under the ADA are essentially the same as those for employers covered by Section 504.

While both laws protect employees with a range of disabilities, both physical and mental, there is one area of protected disability that merits particular mention. In the *Arline* ruling the Supreme Court held that an individual infected with a serious disease, even if asymptomatic, was considered disabled within the meaning of Section 504. The case of *Bragdon v. Abbott*[27] expanded this definition by also applying the ADA to individuals infected by the HIV/AIDS virus. In employment cases involving infected employees, employers must demonstrate an unreasonable risk of disease transmission to justify excluding persons from employment or restricting their employment duties.[28] It must be noted that the Supreme Court standard requires the establishment of a significant risk of transmission, not merely some possibility, a standard that would typically require the expert testimony of competent medical personnel in order to substantiate the risk.

## Bona Fide Occupational Qualifications

As previously stated, under ordinary circumstances, college employers should avoid asking questions on applications and during pre-employment interviews that would implicate a protected status. The exception is when such a question concerns a Bona Fide Occupational Qualification. In general, Bona Fide Occupational Qualifications, or BFOQ's, must relate to a legitimate job requirement. BFOQ's can include the possession of specific certification or licenses, possession of specific job-related skills, or the ability to perform particular tasks, such as lifting a particular weight or working irregular hours. Some BFOQ's may also require inquiry into protected characteristics and may allow discrimination based on those characteristics, but courts narrowly treat an employer's claim of a BFOQ to restrict the application of this exception to employment discrimination. BFOQ's may sometimes apply to sex, religion, national origin, and age, but not to race.

The classic example of this is the provision within Title VII that provides that the law "shall not apply … to a religious corporation, association, educational institution, or society with respect to the employment of individuals of a particular religion to perform work connected with the carrying on by such corporation, association, educational institution, or society of its activities."[29] This provision allows religious institutions to advertise and fill positions with persons who are members of a specific faith and to inquire about the religious beliefs of potential employees. It can also permit the termination of employees who subsequently perform their duties or behave in a manner inconsistent with the doctrines of the employer.[30] Care should be exercised with this exception as it applies specifically to those employees whose duties are directly connected with the college's religious purpose, such as administrators, chaplains, and counselors. At the same time, however, institutions have broad discretion in making these doctrinal decisions. In *Serbian Eastern Orthodox v. Milivojevich*[31] the Supreme Court held that the First Amendment's requirement of separation of church and state forbids the courts from inquiring into the legitimacy and sincerity of doctrines asserted by religious organizations in making employment decisions.

The concept of BFOQ's offers employers a great deal of guidance in making hiring and promotion decisions. For this reason, many organizations followed a detailed system of classification for their non-academic positions that includes a job analysis intended to detail the knowledge, experience, and competencies required for each job. By defining the essential functions and BFOQ's for a given job and then designing application materials and processes around them, it is possible to not only avoid improper inquiries, but irrelevant ones as well. BFOQ's also offer legal protection for employment decisions by basing those decisions on well-developed objective criteria. Finally, under certain conditions, BFOQ's may necessitate inquiries and adverse decisions based upon otherwise protected status.

## Evaluation, Discipline, and Termination

Given the myriad of employment conditions experienced by employees in institutions of higher education, it is difficult to generalize the procedures to be used in employee evaluation, discipline, and termination. The obligations of state employment laws, collective bargaining agreements, and contract provisions all serve to dictate the procedures and protections available to college employees. Furthermore, there is again a clear distinction between public and private institutions.

Public employment precedents such as *Perry v. Sindermann*[32] and *Branti v. Finkel*[33] clearly establish a right to due process before terminating an employee who has some legitimate expectation of continuing employment. In general, long-term public employees and those with contracted periods of employment cannot be terminated or disciplined in an arbitrary fashion. Typically they enjoy a right to receive notice of their alleged shortcomings and violations and a right to some impartial process of review in which they can contest specific allegations. Public employees are also protected from arbitrary discipline based upon the exercise of rights protected under federal and state laws and constitutions. Such employees may also enjoy special statutory protection in the form of "Whistleblower" laws. In many states, statutes specifically protect employees who bring to light allegations of malfeasance by their employers.[34] However, these protections are general in nature. For public employees hired in a clearly "at-will" position, typically high-profile persons such as university presidents, these protections may not apply. For example, in *Idoux v. Lamar University System,*[35] a federal district court upheld the termination of a university president for speaking out on unethical practices.

Private university employees do not enjoy the constitutional protections afforded to public employees. Absent protective state laws, union agreements, or contract provisions, all such employees must be considered "at-will." As previously mentioned, this holds especially true in sectarian institutions where courts are hesitant to intervene in matters of internal governance and faith, even when contract protections are present.[36] Otherwise, private colleges and universities are bound to follow their own internal procedures for discipline and evaluation. Furthermore, although a private college may enjoy relative legal freedom in making these employment decisions, care must still be exercised to insure that these actions do not violate the federal employment laws cited previously including Title VII, ADA, ADEA, and the Equal Pay Act. And because private institutions operate primarily under contract law rather than constitutional law, an institution's obligations under contract law require good faith in performance, thus binding the private institution to principles of fairness that may mirror some of the elements of constitutional due process in the public institution.

## Unions and Collective Bargaining

The rights of non-academic personnel to collective bargaining generally follow those of faculty.[37] As such, the law regarding employee organization and collective bargaining essentially creates three identifiable classes of colleges and universities. Public colleges and universities, as arms of the state, are explicitly excluded from coverage under federal labor laws and the National Labor Relations Act.[38] As a result, public colleges and universities are governed exclusively by state laws regarding rights to organize employees, collectively bargain, and strike. Predictably, while such rights have been extended in states with strong traditions of private labor unions, such as those in the Upper Midwest and the Northeast, the rights of all public employees, including those in higher education, to unionize are considerably weaker in other parts of the country, especially the South.[39] As a result, some states such as Minnesota and Michigan permit the establishment of exclusive bargaining units and even closed shop provisions for public employee representation. By contrast, many states, especially again those in the South, have statutes which guarantee public employees the "right to work," thus preventing the mandatory membership of state employees in unions or associations. These states also maintain their statutory exemption from mandatory collective bargaining and make strikes and work stoppages by public employees illegal, further weakening both the effectiveness and appeal of unions in these states.

Private colleges and universities must be sub-divided into two sub-categories: Secular and Sectarian. In 1970, the National Labor Relations Board (NLRB) extended the reach of the National Labor Relations Act (NLRA) to private colleges and universities when it intervened to insure the recognition of employee bargaining units at Cornell University and Syracuse University in 1970. As such, private colleges and universities, regardless of any non-profit status, must accept the provisions of the NLRA and the jurisdiction of the NLRB. This act, which represents a series of federal laws dating back to the original Wagner Act of 1935, provides federal oversight to insure private employees the right to organize, collectively bargain, pursue grievances against their employer, and conduct legal strikes and work stoppages under certain conditions.[40]

Specifically, the NLRA guarantees the rights of private secular university employees to organize into collective bargaining units. Although subject to specific circumstances, the NLRB has generally upheld the right of these employees to organize in the workplace and to use university property for these purposes, as long as they are not impeding the business of the employer.[41] The law also requires employers to bargain in good faith with the identified representative units, permits election to organize and govern these units, and prohibits any interference with union organization or retaliation or discrimination against employees based upon union membership or activities.[42] The NLRB also exercises control over any grievances or disputes concerning union organization and activities and can protect the employment of workers who strike under certain circumstances.

However, the Supreme Court has limited the application of the NLRA to private colleges and universities that are operated by religious organizations. In the landmark ruling of *NLRB v. Catholic Bishop of Chicago*,[43] the Court ruled that the application of the NLRA to religious institutions would implicate a serious potential for conflicts between Church and State. The Court decided in that case, which involved lay employees in schools operated by the church, that lacking a clear intent by Congress to extend the NLRA to religious institutions, the NLRB was barred from exercising its authority over religious colleges and schools. Consequently, collective bargaining is not legally protected in sectarian institutions and remains a purely internal issue to be resolved by these institutions without the interference of federal or state authorities.

It is especially important, given the diversity of the college employment spectrum, that colleges and universities understand the concept of the representative bargaining unit. Although the NLRA only requires the employer to negotiate with the unit that represents the majority of its employees, it must respect certain precedents and procedures in this regard. The determination of the representative collective bargaining unit is a matter for the employees alone to determine, not the employer. Additionally, disputes regarding which organization represents certain employees must be referred to the NLRB regional offices for resolution and cannot be resolved by the employer. Furthermore, although the law recognizes exclusive bargaining units, the Supreme Court has ruled that employers may have to recognize multiple representative units representing distinct groups or classifications of employees, especially in medical centers.[44] Therefore, it is possible that a university would have to separately recognize and collectively bargain with different unions or associations representing different types of employees such as nurses, maintenance workers, and police or security officers.

Colleges and universities must also be careful to respect the rights of non-union employees covered by their collective bargaining agreements. In *Abood v. Detroit Board of Education*,[45] the United States Supreme Court required employers to refund to non-union employees any dues collected under the collective bargaining agreement to support union political activities that they do not support. Although closed shop agreements may require such non-members to pay dues to support the collective bargaining process, they cannot require non-members to support other union activities that implicate their First Amendment rights. Recent case law supports the proposition that colleges and universities that help collect union fees under an agreement by means such as automatic payroll deductions must provide clear and well-publicized procedures for employees to exempt themselves from these additional dues for unsupported political or other union speech activities.[46] This requirement is best met either by an up-front exemption from these deductions or a prompt refund of any deductions at employee request.

## Students as Employees

Traditionally, colleges and universities have employed large numbers of their own students to perform a myriad of tasks. Most of these student employees are hired as part-time temporary workers receiving an hourly wage to serve as intramural sports officials, food service workers, ushers, bus drivers, and cashiers. Students are hired through normal procedures and paid an hourly wage, often derived from the revenues generated by activity fees or university enterprises. These employees are also appropriately classified simply as hourly employees and treated the same way, in terms of hiring, benefits, and other employee rights.

However, colleges and universities also employ two general classes of students under a hybrid system that combines employment and financial aid: graduate assistants and work-study students. Work-study students are recipients of funds provided by the federal College Work Study Program funded under the Economic Opportunity Act of 1964.[47] Generally, these are undergraduates who perform various clerical or service tasks in return for a stipend and assistance in paying tuition and other expenses. Graduate assistants are a more diverse group. They can perform a variety of highly technical and skilled duties, ranging from conducting scientific research to teaching large sections of undergraduate courses. They also are paid from numerous sources including institutional funds or outside research grants. Their pay and benefits can also vary widely. Some receive a modest stipend and remission of a portion of their tuition payments. Others can receive payment comparable to that of some full-time employees, allowances for room and board, full-tuition, and even health and retirement benefits. All of these workers present several legal complexities to colleges and universities.

Traditionally, the courts have treated such workers as recipients of financial aid and students, not employees. In the case of federal work-study students, the statute authorizing the program specifies that such workers are not employees in the traditional sense but recipients of financial aid. However, the case law regarding federally funded work study students has not always been consistent in this regard.

In many cases, the courts have cited the Economic Opportunity Act in establishing that funds paid to student workers under the College Work Study Program constitute federal aid and not wages, regardless of the duties performed, and therefore work study students should be excluded from all other benefits and legal protections extended to other classes of employees. In *Murphy v. Villanova University,*[48] a district court twice held that students employed under the College Work Study Program were not eligible for any benefits or wages from any source outside the financial aid program. As such, work-study employees whose funding was terminated could not vindicate preferential employment claims for regular university employment and could not sue for wrongful termination. In an Arizona unemployment compensation dispute, a state court extended this limitation to bar the receipt of unemployment compensation by terminated work study students.[49] Even parallel case law, in areas such as welfare eligibility, has accepted that monies earned under the work-study program cannot be construed as wages due to employment.[50] Likewise, in *N.L.R.B. v. Certified Testing Laboratories,*[51] a federal appeals court upheld a determination that work-study students employed in off-campus training programs could not participate in certification votes to determine collective bargaining units, even when they performed the identical work of other eligible employees. Work-study students have also been denied eligibility for workman's compensation benefits.[52]

However, support for this proposition has not been universal. In *Richman v. Ross,*[53] a New York appellate court found that a student's receipt of federal work-study funds did constitute employment so as to limit eligibility for unemployment compensation from a previous employer. Another New York ruling found work study students were, in fact, eligible under state law as employees for purposes of receiving workman's compensation.[54] And, in one of the most fully developed cases involving work-study students, the Eighth Circuit held that a student injured while working in a federal facility under the similar Vocational Education Act was to be considered a federal employee and eligible for compensation under the Federal Employees Compensation Act.[55]

The Eight Circuit decision also raises a cautionary point about the treatment of work-study recipients as students instead of employees. In the unique circumstances of that case, based upon work location, the student was treated as an employee. However, in *Grant v. Tulane,*[56] a former work-study student filed a tort claim against the university and a private oil company regarding her work as a lab assistant in a jointly sponsored project. The company moved to dismiss her claims arguing that compensation for her illnesses, allegedly the result of poisoning in the lab, was limited to the state workman's compensation system. In rejecting this contention, and therefore allowing the student to proceed on her claims for damages, the court noted that the traditional interpretation of the College Work Study Program as a form of financial aid meant that the plaintiff was not an employee under the law and, therefore, her claims could not be limited by workman's compensation. Colleges and universities should be aware that while the usual legal interpretation of the Economic Opportunity Act limits their responsibility under a host of employee's rights laws, this same interpretation may open them to more general torts for workplace injuries, especially in private universities and public institutions not protected by strong state sovereign immunity laws.

The legal situation regarding graduate assistants of all types used to be very similar to that of college work-study students. A classic case example would be the situation that occurred at Yale University in the mid-1990s.[57] After years of agitation and attempts to organize and gain university recognition, teaching assistants at Yale held a dramatic "grade strike." Late in the fall semester, they voted to withhold all term grades until the university recognized the Graduate Employees and Students Association (GESO) as a collective bargaining unit. The university refused to bargain, instead firing all of the striking teaching assistants and proceeding to expel several. Eventually, the strike fell apart, and most of the graduate students were re-hired. Although the strike failed, the GESO filed a complaint with the NLRB claiming unfair practices. The NLRB eventually settled the claim by finding that the strike, regardless of the legal status of the GESO, constituted an illegal strike under the NLRA.

However, a larger issue confronted the NLRB regarding the Yale strike. Although its tactics may have violated the NLRA, the Yale GESO was attempting to gain the same recognition as a legitimate employee bargaining unit that faculty and staff at private universities enjoyed since the 1970s. By virtue of its ruling on the strike tactics the NLRB was able to sidestep this issue briefly. Prior to the incident at Yale, the NLRB had employed what was referred to as a "primary purpose test" in classifying graduate assistants.[58] Under this test the question the NLRB posed was what was the primary purpose of graduate student employment? In every instance, it was found that the main goal of such employment, as asserted by the universities, was to facilitate graduate education by providing students with financial aid and giving them experiences in teaching, research, or service that would serve to better prepare them for their professional and academic careers.

However, this test has recently been abandoned by the NLRB. In *Boston Medical Center,*[59] the NLRB replaced the "primary purpose test" with a "compensated services test." In this test, the simple question is whether or not a person provides services or work for someone else in return for compensation.[60] Based upon this definition, the NLRB found that medical residents and interns, while undoubtedly fulfilling educational requirements, were being compensated for providing medical services to the university hospital. Applying this definition, it was not difficult for the NLRB to then extend its ruling to university graduate assistants. In *New York University,*[61] the NLRB rejected the university's attempt to draw distinctions between medical residents and academic graduate assistants. Although the latter did not yet possess terminal degrees, the NLRB found that under its simple definition, graduate students performed work under the supervision of other university employees and, in return, received wages and other compensation. As such, the NLRB found that graduate assistants, fellows, proctors, and other paid categories of graduate student workers were employees and were, therefore, eligible to organize and collectively bargain under the NLRA.

The impact of the *New York University* decision remains to be seen. As with other employees, the NLRB's authority is limited to private, non-sectarian institutions. Furthermore, other decisions that appear to extend this precedent are very likely to be appealed to the federal courts, which have yet to speak directly on this issue. Nonetheless, the effects are already apparent. According to the Coalition of Graduate Employee Unions, a network of U.S. and Canadian graduate student organizations, some two-dozen U.S. universities recognize collective bargaining units for graduate students.[62] What is interesting is that many of these are located at public universities outside the purview of the NLRB. Although the NLRB ruling in *New York University* does not apply to these institutions, the logic of this ruling has been adopted by state labor-relation boards and state courts in many locations. For example, in Illinois, the state courts have required the Illinois Educational Labor Relations Board to hold elections to certify a collective bargaining unit for graduate student employees at the University of Illinois at Urbana-Champaign.[63] Two of the nation's largest multi-unit university systems, the State University of New York and the City University of New York, have also recognized collective bargaining units for graduate students.

The long-term implications of this movement remain uncertain. Some argue that extending collective bargaining protections to graduate students recognizes the vital labor they provide in return for little compensation. Alternate arguments contend that this trend, if not blocked by the federal courts, will lead to financial crisis, damage to academic freedom, and an end to the traditional mentoring relationship between faculty and graduate student.[64] Recognition of graduate assistants as employees may extend to them other employee rights and protections. For example, courts have not traditionally treated this form of employment as a property interest that bestowed due process rights to graduate assistants.[65] While the temporary nature of such employment is generally recognized, it is possible that either the courts or collective bargaining agreements may extend additional due process protections to graduate assistants for the duration of a degree program.

## Conclusion

The legal treatment of non-faculty and non-academic employees is at least as variable as the diversity of institutional types and organizational missions in American higher education. Factors such as public or private governance, religious or secular control, and the applicability of federal and state collective bargaining laws all affect the status of these employees and serve to make legal generalizations all but impossible, save in the area of federal anti-discrimination law. Religiously operated institutions would appear to have the fewest legal restrictions regarding their employee relations. Exemption from mandatory collective bargaining under federal and state law, combined with specific doctrine-based exemptions under the Civil Rights Act, leaves these institutions relatively free to operate within the sphere of contract law. By contrast, secular private institutions fall under the jurisdiction of nearly all federal and state employment and civil rights acts as well as compulsory collective bargaining under the NLRA. And, while public institutions may be beyond the reach of the NLRA, they are fully bound by the federal statutes and constitutional protections that apply to all public employees and possibly extensive state legal protections as well.

Colleges and universities must also be extremely cautious regarding the employment of students on campus. While many may fall into the category of temporary and part-time employment, others present special challenges. Jurisdictions across the country continue to grapple with the question of the nature of the employment of college work-study students. While most have not viewed them as employees, this legal perspective has not been universal. Furthermore, even if the language of the Economic Opportunity Act is ultimately upheld, the interpretation that work-study students are not employees may actually increase the tort liability risks for colleges and universities when these students are injured while on the job.

Finally, special attention must be paid to ongoing litigation and legislation regarding the employment status of graduate students. Although traditionally viewed legally in the same way as college work-study recipients, recent decisions of the NLRB and various state courts and agencies, accompanied by the rising militancy of graduate students on some campuses, may culminate in increased legal recognition for these students and greater challenges for the institutions that employ them. In addition to growing legal protections, these changes may also force institutions to re-examine the traditional academic relationships between graduate students, faculty, and other staff in their advanced degree programs.

# Endnotes

1. 42 U.S.C. §§ 2000e *et seq.*
2. 29 U.S.C. § 621 *et seq.*
3. Pub. L. 88-38, June 10, 1963, 77 Stat. 56
4. 29 U.S.C. § 793.
5. 42 U.S.C. § 12101 *et seq.*
6. Under the Equal Employment Opportunity Act of 1972 (Pub. L. 92-261, Mar. 24, 1972, 86 Stat. 103). *See* JAMES A. BUFORD, PERSONNEL MANAGEMENT AND HUMAN RESOURCES IN LOCAL GOVERNMENT, at 25-26.
7. Most notably Connecticut, Maryland, Nevada, Massachusetts, New Jersey, Minnesota, Wisconsin, California, Oregon, Rhode Island, Vermont, Hawaii, New Hampshire, and the District of Columbia.
8. W.S.A. § 111.31.
9. MCKINNEY'S EXECUTIVE LAW § 296.
10. N.J.S.A. 10:5-12.
11. 41 C.F.R. § 60.
12. *See* Buford, *supra*, at 39-40; William J. Rosenthal and Stephen D. Shawe, *Employment Law Deskbook*, § 2.03[1].
13. L. Dean Webb and M. Scott Norton, *Human Resources Administration*, at 255-256.
14. 968 F. Supp. 1486 [119 EDUC. L. REP. 985] (M.D. Ala. 1997), *et al.*
15. 29 U.S.C. §§ 621 *et seq.*
16. 94 F.3d 830 (2d Cir. 1996).
17. *See also*, Wichmann v. Bd. of Trs. of S. Ill. Univ., 180 F.3d 791 (7th Cir. 1999); Hurd v. Pittsburg State Univ., 109 F.3d 1540 (10th Cir. 1997); Kalvinskas v. Cal. Inst. Of Tech., 96 F.3d 1305 (9th Cir. 1996); Cella v. Fordham Univ., 644 N.Y.S.2d 53 (N.Y. App. Div. 1996).
18. 29 U.S.C. § 206(d).
19. Buford, *supra*, at 37.
20. Hatton v. Hunt, 780 F. Supp. 1157 (W.D. Tenn. 1991).

[21] 29 U.S.C. § 793.

[22] 42 U.S.C. §§ 12101 *et seq.*

[23] 480 U.S. 273, 107 S. Ct. 1123, 94 L. Ed. 2d 307, 55 USLW 4245, 43 Fair Empl. Prac. Cas. (BNA) 81, 42 Empl. Prac. Dec. P 36,791 [37 EDUC. L. REP. 448] (1987).

[24] Rosenthal, *supra*, at §18.02(7).

[25] 531 U.S. 356, 121 S. Ct. 955, 148 L. Ed. 2d 866, 69 USLW 4105 [151 EDUC. L. REP. 35, 11 A.D. Cases 737] (2001).

[26] 29 U.S.C. 793 (Section 503).

[27] 524 U.S. 624, 118 S. Ct. 2196, 141 L. Ed. 2d 540, 66 USLW 4601, 8 A.D. Cases 239 (1998).

[28] Rosenthal, § 18.02[7].

[29] 42 U.S.C. § 2000e-1(a).

[30] *See, e.g.*, *Pime* v. Loyola Univ. of Chi., 803 F.2d 351, 55 USLW 2275, 42 Fair Empl. Prac. Cas. (BNA) 1, 41 Empl. Prac. Dec. P 36,567 [35 EDUC. L. REP. 646] (7th Cir. 1987).

[31] 426 U.S. 696, 96 S. Ct. 2372, 49 L. Ed. 2d 151 (1976).

[32] 408 U.S. 593, 92 S. Ct. 2694, 33 L .Ed. 2d 570, 1 IER Cases 33 (1980).

[33] 445 U.S. 507, 100 S. Ct. 1287, 63 L. Ed. 2d 574, 1 IER Cases 91 (1980).

[34] *See, e.g.*, Swain v. Elfland, 550 S.E.2d 530 (N.C. App. 2001), operationalizing N.C. GEN. STAT. § 126-85 (1999).

[35] 828 F. Supp. 1252 [85 EDUC. L. REP. 793] (E.D. Tex. 1993).

[36] *See, e.g.*, Killinger v. Samford Univ., 113 F.3d 196 (11th Cir. 1997).

[37] *See, e.g.*, 183 NLRB 329 (1970); Abood v. Detroit Bd. of Ed., 97 S. Ct. 1782 (1977); Minnesota State Bd. for Cmty. Colleges v. Knight, 104 S. Ct. 1058 (1984), *et al.*

[38] 197 NLRB 291 (1989); National Labor Relations of 1935, a.k.a. the Wagner Act, Section 2(2).

[39] Buford, *Supra*, at 380-1.

[40] The National Labor Relations Act, the NLRA, is a combination of the Wagner Act of 1935, the Taft-Hartley Act of 1947, and the Landrum-Griffin Act of 1959.

[41] NLRA Section 7.

[42] Rosenthal, *supra*, at §17.06.

[43] 99 S. Ct. 1313 (1979).

[44] American Hosp. Assoc. v. NLRB, 499 U.S. 606, 111 S. Ct. 1539, 113 L. Ed. 2d 675 (1991).

[45] 431 U.S. 209, 97 S. Ct. 1782, 52 L. Ed. 2d 261 (1977*); See also*, Lehnert v. Ferris Faculty Ass'n, 500 U.S. 507, 111 S. Ct. 1950 114 L. Ed. 2d 572 (1991).

[46] *See* Swanson v. Univ. of Haw. Prof'l Assembly, 269 F. Supp. 2d 1252 (D. Haw. 2003).

[47] 42 U.S.C. §§ 2251-2256.

[48] 520 F. Supp. 560 (D. Pa. 1981); 547 F. Supp. 512 (D. Pa. 1982).

[49] Pima Cmty. Coll. v. Ariz. Dep't of Econ. *Sec.*, 714 P.2d 472 (Ariz. App. 1986).

[50] Brown v. Bates, 363 F. Supp. 897 (D. Ohio 1973).

[51] 387 F.2d 275 (3d Cir. 1967).

[52] Grant v. Tulane Univ., 2001 WL 245785 (E.D. La. 2001).

[53] 412 N.Y.S.2d 222 (N.Y.A.D. 1979).

[54] Lopez v. CUNY, 750 N.Y.S.2d 194 (N.Y. A.D. 3 Dept. 2002).

[55] Waters v. U.S., 328 F. Supp 812 (D. Ark. 1971), *aff'd.* 458 F.2d 20 (8th Cir. 1972).

[56] 2001 U.S. Dist. LEXIS 3041 (E.D. La. 2001).

[57] Joshua Rowland, *'Forecasts of Doom': The Dubious Threat of Graduate Teaching Assistant Collective Bargaining to Academic Freedom*, 42 B.C. L. REV. 941 (July 2001).

[58] Grant M. Hayden, *'The University Works Because We Do': Collective Bargaining Rights for Graduate Assistants*, 69 FORDHAM L. REV. 1233 (March 2001); Gregory Gartland, *Of Ducks and Drakes: A Call for a Return to the National Labor Relations Board's 'Primary Purpose Test' in Determining the Status of Graduate Students Under the National Labor Relations Act*, 4 U. PA. J. LAB. & EMP. L. 623 (Spring 2002).

[59] 330 NLRB 152 (1999).

[60] Gartland, *supra*, at 635.

[61] 332 NLRB 111 (2000).

[62] Source: The Coalition of Graduate Employee Unions, http://cgeu.org (2004).

[63] Graduate Employees Organization, IFT/AFT, AFL-CIO v. Ill. Educ. Labor Relations Bd., 315 Ill. App. 3d 278, 733 N.E.2d 759, 248 Ill. Dec. 84, 164 L.R.R.M. (BNA) 2807 [147 EDUC. L. REP. 651] (Ill. App. 1 Dist. 2000).

[64] Gartland, *supra note 60*; Hayden, *supra*; Rowland, *supra*.

[65] *See* Hupp v. Sasser, 490 S.E.2d 880 (W. Va. 1997).

# 6 Faculty Speech
## Patrick Pauken

## Introduction

> The essentiality of freedom in the community of American
> universities is almost self-evident. No one should underes-
> timate the vital role in a democracy that is played by those
> who guide and train our youth. To impose any strait jacket
> upon the intellectual leaders in our colleges and universities
> would imperil the future of our Nation. No field of education
> is so thoroughly comprehended by man that new discoveries
> cannot yet be made.... Scholarship cannot flourish in an
> atmosphere of suspicion and distrust. Teachers and students
> must always remain free to inquire, to study and to evalu-
> ate, to gain new maturity and understanding; otherwise our
> civilization will stagnate and die.[1]

Grand statements like this one set quite an inviting scene for dialogue
among college and university leaders, faculty, students, and community
members. The issues at the discussion tables in academic settings have
varied widely in their specifics over the years. In the 1950s and 1960s,
there were investigations of faculty members who may have been members of alleged "subversive organizations" and disciplinary actions taken
against students and faculty who engaged in allegedly disruptive political
protests and rallies.[2] In the 1990s and 2000s, there are cases of faculty
members accessing questionable information on World Wide Web sites,[3]
controversial classroom conversations and other activities, and the production of highly controversial plays.[4] Despite the variation in specific
factual contexts, the general sentiment remains the same: "The classroom
is peculiarly the marketplace of ideas."[5] As the Court of Appeals for the
Third Circuit stated in a 1980 case,

> The academic process entails, at its core, open communica-
> tion leading to reasoned decisions. Our society assumes,
> in almost all cases with good reason, that different views

within the academic community will be tested in an atmosphere of free debate. It is the dialectic process which
underlies learning and progress.[6]

Similar to the discussion of speech issues affecting students, presented
in the previous chapter, a discussion of the expression rights of faculty
and staff involves the balance between the rights and responsibilities of
employees and the institutions themselves, for both parties have messages
to contribute to the larger academic dialogue. This balance is best met
through an analysis of the capacities the speakers have taken to express
their views. On one end of the balance, we must ask whether the faculty
or staff member is speaking as a citizen, an employee, or as an educator.
On the other end, we must ask whether the college or university's interest
is inspired by its role as sovereign, employer, educator, or patron.[7]

## Faculty/Staff as Citizen

A discussion of the expression rights of public college and university
employees as citizens finds much of its foundation in the loyalty oath
cases of the 1950s and 1960s. A loyalty oath is a statement signed by a
government employee, wherein the individual "declares his allegiance to
his government and its institutions and disclaims any support of foreign
ideologies or associations."[8] Loyalty oaths can be "affirmative," whereby
they demand that the employee support the constitution, laws, policies, and
other regulations of the employer itself and/or of the larger government
system as a whole. They may also be "negative," whereby they restrict or
prohibit certain acts of government employees, even within the employees'
personal lives. It is particularly in the employee's role as a *private citizen*
where such oaths raise significant legal questions. As such, the lessons
learned from the loyalty oath cases have easy application to other aspects
of the private lives of public college and university employees.

The United States Supreme Court, in an early loyalty oath case, decided, simply, that mere membership in certain groups or organizations
was not enough to deny government employment or to impose any other
penalty.[9] In order for a government employer to restrict outside group
membership or government employment opportunities, the group membership must be accompanied by knowledge of any unlawful intentions or
purposes that the group may have. At issue in *Wieman v. Updegraff* was
an Oklahoma state statute that required each state officer and employee
to sign a loyalty oath stating that he or she is not a member and has not
been a member for the preceding five years of any organization listed
by the Attorney General as a "communist front" or "subversive". The
Supreme Court invalidated the law and held that the Due Process Clause
does not permit a state to classify "innocent association" with "knowing
association." In a similar case eight years later, the Court struck down an
Arkansas statute that required every teacher employed in a state-supported

school or college to file an annual affidavit listing every organization to which the teacher belonged within the preceding five years.[10] While the state does have the right to investigate the competence and fitness of its teachers in state-supported institutions, this right does not carry with it the right (or the necessity) to compel disclosure of every associational tie that the teachers have.

Two other related United States Supreme Court cases addressed loyalty oaths signed by public school and university teachers. The state statutes at issue in *Sweezy v. New Hampshire*[11] and *Keyishian v. Board of Regents*[12] did not differ significantly from those challenged in earlier loyalty oath cases, but the Courts in *Sweezy* and *Keyishian* analyzed the issue with a little more attention paid to the educator roles played by the challengers. In *Sweezy*, a university employee (Sweezy) was subjected to two interrogations under a state statute that forbade "subversive persons" from working for the state. Before the first interrogation, Sweezy read a lengthy statement expressing his disagreement with the questioning. Among his messages was a statement indicating that the mere fact that he had nothing illegal to hide did not diminish his disagreement with having to answer questions about his alleged "subversive" activity. Despite the statements, Sweezy answered many of the questions asked but refused to answer several others including questions on the content of a lecture he delivered at the state university on an article he co-authored in which he labeled himself a "classical Marxist" and a socialist and on the knowledge of the Progressive Party and its members. He refused to answer the same questions in a court of law and was judged to be in contempt. The State Supreme Court affirmed the judgment against Sweezy and argued that the state government needed to be informed on such matters for its own self-preservation, in spite of the constitutional rights of the accused. According to the lower courts, the content of Sweezy's university courses was relevant to his character as a teacher. The United States Supreme Court disagreed and held for Sweezy. "We believe that there unquestionably was an invasion of [Sweezy's] liberties in the areas of academic freedom and political expression—areas in which government should be extremely reticent to tread."[13] The Court noted that teachers and students must be free to read, write, study, and speak without undue suspicion and distrust from authority.

> Our form of government is built on the premise that every citizen shall have the right to engage in political expression and association ... All political ideas cannot and should not be channeled into the programs of our two major parties. History has amply proved the virtue of political activity by minority, dissident groups, who innumerable times have been the vanguard of democratic thought and whose programs were ultimately accepted. Mere orthodoxy or dissent from the prevailing mores is not to be condemned.

The absence of such voices would be a symptom of grave illness in our society.[14]

In *Keyishian*, several members of the faculty and staff at the State University of New York (SUNY) at Buffalo challenged a law and a university policy that prevented the appointment or retention of government employees who were members of "subversive organizations," including the Communist party or any organization that advocated the violent overthrow of state or federal government.[15] Similar to its holding in *Wieman*, the Supreme Court held that the government may not deny employment to knowing members of such groups without showing that those employees intend to further any unlawful aims of those groups. The Court remained respectful of the commitment of higher education to the notion of academic freedom and condemned laws and policies that perpetuate the notion of guilt by association. According to the Court, policies such as SUNY's deter not only unlawful activity, but also lawful activity: "The *threat* of sanctions may deter almost as potently as the actual application of sanctions."[16]

A discussion of union membership as free speech is not easily placed on a point in the spectrum between "teacher as citizen" and "teacher as educator." But for the sake of discussion and for their stronger relationship with loyalty oath cases than with cases involving alleged wrongful terminations and nonrenewals, two Supreme Court cases addressing the constitutional implications of union membership and restrictions on that membership deserve attention here. First, in *Minnesota State Board for Community Colleges v. Knight*, the Court upheld a state statute restricting certain meetings of faculty to only those meetings that involve the faculty's exclusive bargaining representative.[17] Again engaging a constitutional balance, the Court held that the statute did not infringe on the free speech and associational rights of faculty. In effect, the plaintiffs still had the right to speak on education-related issues.[18] But the Court did not recognize a First Amendment right of individual faculty to participate in academic policymaking. Instead, the Court favored the state's interest in ensuring that its employers have only one voice with which to communicate on contract negotiations.

Second, in *Lehnert v. Ferris Faculty Association*,[19] the Court upheld a Michigan statute that permitted a faculty union to charge fair share fees to all faculty members, regardless of whether the faculty members had joined the union. According to the Court, these fees are permissible if they are germane to collective bargaining activity, justified by the government's interest in positive labor relations and the avoidance of free riders, and not overly burdensome to the dissenters' freedom of speech. Some additional charges, even if not directly related to collective bargaining activities, may be permissible as well. These include charges related to the faculty association's relationships with the state and national parent associations (e.g., for magazine production and annual convention expenses). Costs for political lobbying activities and other activities that relate more to philosophical ideologies, on the other hand, may not be charged as part of the employees' pro-rata shares.

Even with the inclusion of the above cases involving loyalty oaths and union activity, there are not many cases or judicial trends in free speech that can truly be categorized as wholly unrelated to the professional roles that college and university employees play. The court in *Denius v. Dunlap*[20] raised the issue of how much information an employer may request on a release form used for criminal background checks. A retired Air Force technical sergeant who was employed to teach several courses at a federally funded, eighteen-month program for sixteen-to-eighteen-year-old high school dropouts, signed his employment contract but refused to sign a release form that would allow his employer to access records that would effectively waive any attorney-client privilege the employee had in any of the requested information. While the court held for the defendant on qualified immunity grounds, it did note that the right to consult with an attorney is protected by the First Amendment, and the ability to maintain confidentiality in attorney-client communications is an important component of this right. In another case touching on what public college and university employees do with their free time, the Court of Appeals for the Fifth Circuit in *Hoover v. Morales* struck down a policy that prohibited university professors from taking employment as consultants or expert witnesses, even when doing so could create a conflict with the interests of the state as a whole.[21]

## Faculty/Staff as Employee

For purposes of free speech analysis, the difference between a faculty/staff member's role as citizen and his or her role as employee is a small one. The judicial determination of what role the speaker is playing, however, is assuredly an important one, almost entirely dependent on one threshold question: is the speech at issue related to a matter of public concern? If the answer is "yes," the courts tend to favor the speaker as a citizen and restrict employer suppression of the expressive activity. If the answer is "no," the courts will generally find in favor of the employer and allow the employer wide latitude in the governance of its internal affairs. While the "marketplace of ideas" sentiment of *Keyishian* remains alive and well, the faculty/staff member's status as "employee" adds a well-litigated wrinkle to the balance, starting with the landmark decision in *Pickering v. Board of Education*.[22]

In *Pickering*, a public school teacher was dismissed after writing a letter to the editor of a local newspaper criticizing his board of education for the board's appropriation of funds and its handling of two failed tax levy campaigns. The board countered with accusations that the statements in the letter were false and had a negative impact on the efficient operation of the schools. In reality, the community and many of Pickering's co-workers greeted the letter with a good measure of apathy and disbelief. The letter itself was not directly critical of any particular board members or school administrators. Pickering appealed the termination, but the Illinois state courts rejected his First Amendment claims and affirmed the district's decision. On appeal to the United States Supreme Court, the Court reversed. In one of its initial statements, the Court rejected the argument that public employees give up their constitutional rights as citizens upon acceptance of government employment. "The problem in any case is to arrive at a balance between the interests of the teacher, as a citizen, in commenting upon matters of public concern and the interest of the State, as an employer, in promoting the efficiency of the public services it performs through its employees."[23] To arrive at this balance, the Court weighed several factors:

(1) whether the subject of the speech was a matter of public concern;

(2) the closeness of the working relationships between the speaker and those he or she criticized;

(3) whether there was a detrimental impact on the administration of the schools;

(4) whether the performance of the employee suffered as a result of the expression and its response; and

(5) whether the employee was speaking in his or her professional capacity or as a private citizen.[24]

On application of these factors to the facts in *Pickering*, the Court found that the letter to the editor dealt with a matter of public concern: the use of taxpayer money in the operation of public schools. Because the relationship between Pickering, a teacher, and the board members he criticized was not close on a daily basis, the Court found in favor of the plaintiff teacher on the second factor, as well. Compounded with that finding, the Court held that there was no detrimental impact on either the performance of the district or the performance of Pickering. There was no levy on the ballot at the time of the letter, nor was there any evidence of disruption at Pickering's school. Also significant to the speech issue in *Pickering* was the Court's discussion of the board's claim that Pickering's statements were false. To the extent that the statements were false, the statements must have led to some detriment on the part of the employer's operation. In *Pickering*, there was no detriment. Furthermore, an accusation that the board was mismanaging funds, even from an employee of the district, reflected a difference of opinion on a matter of general public interest. "[A]bsent proof of false statements knowingly or recklessly made by him, a teacher's exercise of his right to speak on matters of public importance may not furnish the basis for his dismissal from public employment."[25]

While the *Pickering* Court includes, among the other balancing factors, the question of whether the speech was on a matter of public concern, the Supreme Court in *Connick v. Myers*[26] placed special attention on that factor and made it a threshold question before applying a balancing test. In *Connick*, a district attorney (Connick) dismissed an assistant district attorney (Myers) for her refusal to accept an inter-office transfer and for then distributing a questionnaire to coworkers requesting opinions on transfers, office morale, the need for a grievance committee, the level of confidence in supervisors, and the pressure to work on political campaigns. After the lower courts held for Myers, the Supreme Court reversed in favor of the employer. On the threshold question of whether Myers' speech related to a matter of public concern, the Court held that the discharge of a state employee for speaking on matters of *internal* concern is not prevented by the First Amendment:

> When employee expression cannot be fairly considered as relating to any other matter of political, social, or other public concern, government officials should enjoy wide latitude in managing their offices, without intrusive oversight by the judiciary in the name of the First Amendment.[27]

To answer the question of whether the speech relates to a matter of public concern, the court looks at the content, context, and form of the speech. The Court in *Connick* found that, with the exception of the questionnaire items dealing with political campaigns, Myers' speech constituted a matter of internal concern. Applying the *Pickering* balancing test, the Court ultimately held that the public aspects of Myers' speech were outweighed by Connick's interest and necessity in the efficient and successful operation of the D.A.'s office and the maintenance of close-working relationships with superiors.

Private communications on matters of public concern are protected under the First Amendment.[28] In other words, matters of public concern need not be publicized to the community or media to be considered "public concerns." The inquiry depends more on the role of the speaker than it does on who is the primary audience. In *Milman v. Prokopoff*,[29] an adjunct curator (Milman) of a university art museum filed a grievance against the director of the museum when the director deleted a substantial portion of a brochure the curator had written for an upcoming exhibit and then cancelled a second exhibit altogether. Both exhibits were funded by federal grants that the curator had obtained. The grievance was a protest over the authority the administration has over the intellectual content and integrity of the product of a grant. The court held for Milman. Under the grants, Milman was expected to carry a large part of the responsibility for producing the shows. The speech was both personal and public. It also dealt with the proper discharge of the art museum director's duties pursuant to both university policy and a federally funded grant.

In addition to content, time, place, and manner of the speech, courts may also focus on the motive of the speaker. Is the speech calculated to redress personal grievances, or does it have a broader public purpose? Does the employee wish to move the public to speak out on the matter as well? To make these points, each case in the *Pickering-Connick* line does not need full discussion here. But in introducing these factors, courts continue to investigate whether the employee's speech concerns public or private matters. Examples of public concerns in college and university speech include a grievance over the abrupt cancellation of a military history exhibit;[30] criticism of curriculum, inadequate facilities, low faculty-to-student ratio, poor performance of graduates on a licensing exams, the ability of the department to prepare students for professional careers, and the status of accreditation;[31] criticism by a tenured professor of the current president and board of trustees based on financial management and accreditation concerns;[32] statements made by a college program administrator to an investigating committee regarding the money management and program funding decisions of the university's central administration;[33] participation in a faculty vote of "no confidence" for their dean;[34] an assistant dean's public criticism over the university's budgetary decisions and minority student recruitment efforts;[35] a law school professor's speech advocating the legalization of marijuana, criticizing national drug policy, and debating civil disobedience on its face;[36] classroom statements about diversity;[37] and a professor's discussion of pornography in class.[38]

Examples of non-public concerns in faculty and staff expression include speech on obtaining priority funds from the College to supplement the budget of an academic department;[39] personal grievances about the new Dean or chair of an academic department;[40] complaints about the method by which faculty members are elected to the Graduate Council;[41] speech on the policy for internal evaluation of tenure and promotion applications;[42] a professor's in-house criticism of a particular English text;[43] a psychology professor's casual, sexually-charged conversations with graduate students and colleagues from other universities at an international research conference;[44] and a professor's memo to departmental graduate students disparaging one of his colleagues over comments the colleague made about the termination of two university employees.[45] Of particular note in this list of non-public concerns is a small line of cases involving faculty disputes with central administration over grading policies. Largely, courts have held that such disputes are matters of internal concern that are best decided by "competition among systems of evaluation at different universities, not federal judges." [46]

Four relatively recent cases that apply the *Pickering* and *Connick* balance illustrate these points. The first case, *Bauer v. Sampson*,[47] highlights particularly the *Pickering* factors addressed after the threshold *Connick* "public concern" question is answered. In *Bauer*, the chancellor of the South Orange County Community College District (Sampson) sought to discipline a tenured professor of ethics and philosophy (Bauer) for writings and illustrations prepared and circulated by Bauer. The writings and illustrations were inspired by a time of great turmoil in the District, including financial trouble and a powerful board of trustees deeply involved in the day-to-day operations of the college. Bauer's writings and illustrations, while only a part of this turmoil, depicted the dictatorship, injury, and death of the newly appointed president and many members of the Board of Trustees. They were all published within one month of each other under fictitious bylines in a campus newspaper called *Dissent*. Sampson responded with a letter to Bauer stating that Bauer had violated the college's policy on workplace violence and racial harassment. Bauer refused to adhere to the terms of the discipline and filed suit instead. The Ninth Circuit held that threats are not protected by the First Amendment but that a "substantial amount of 'overtones' are not threats."[48] It was unconstitutional for Sampson to attempt to forbid the expression. "[T]hough at times adolescent, insulting, crude, and uncivil, Bauer's publication focuses directly on issues of public interest and importance."[49] His statements were not true threats and the institution's rights as an employer were not unduly burdened by Bauer's speech. On the *Pickering* balance, the court noted that Bauer's statements did contribute to disharmony among colleagues. However, the court also noted that the College's turbulent times were hardly due solely to Bauer's conduct. "[I]ndeed, anyone who has spent time on college campuses knows that the vigorous exchange of ideas and resulting tension between an administration and its faculty is as much a part of college life as homecoming and final exams."[50] There was no negative impact on Bauer's job performance. Finally, the statements were disseminated through a campus publication distributed exclusively to the college community.

The second case, *Boyett v. Troy State University*,[51] also involves a university employee angry with the decisions made by his administration. But the *Boyett* court makes the important point that the mere fact that the speech occurs at a public university does not make the speech related to a matter of public concern. Boyett, an associate professor and dean of CIS/Mathematics, worked on successive, one-year contracts for six years. In his fifth-year, he announced that he would resign as dean and return to the faculty. The new dean was a colleague that Boyett had evaluated poorly. In December of his sixth year, Boyett received notice that his contract would not be renewed. Boyett alleged that the nonrenewal was based, in part, on speech on a matter of public concern: (1) expression related to the fight for additional department funding, (2) comments made on an employee evaluation, (3) personal grievances, (4) methods by which faculty members are chosen for internal governing bodies, and (5) comments made about the review procedures of tenure and promotion applications. The court held that each of these matters was of internal concern. The mere allegation that the speech concerned the operation of a public university is not enough. "[T]aken to its logical conclusion, the plaintiff's argument means that any time a person's speech will have an effect on the public, regardless of how small or unlikely that effect may be, that speech relates to a matter of public concern."[52]

The third case, *Trejo v. Shoben*, makes a similar point to the one in *Boyett*, in that the mere fact that the speech occurs among university personnel does not transform the speech into speech related to a matter of public concern.[53] But it adds a contextual factor that is necessary to highlight. In *Trejo*, the University of Illinois Urbana-Champaign terminated the contract of an untenured assistant professor of psychology after receiving several complaints about the professor's conduct on the job. Specifically, a large number of complaints stemmed from his conduct at a research conference in Toronto, Canada, where he, colleagues from Stanford University and Wichita State University, and several graduate students from the University of Illinois engaged in casual conversations over dinner and drinks, and again over card games. The discussions were decidedly sexual in nature, with Trejo advocating extramarital affairs, making several sexual comments, and soliciting female companionship including from his university's graduate students. In his documents for trial, Trejo argued that the conversations were intellectual in nature, based in human sexuality, and started with comments about a television documentary on the sexuality of primates. The district court dismissed Trejo's suit and the Court of Appeals for the Seventh Circuit affirmed. In its decision, the court of appeals held that Trejo's speech related to matters of private concern only—Trejo's "flirtatious chit-chat"—giving the University of Illinois leeway to terminate Trejo's contract. What makes this case important is not the ground-breaking rule of law, but rather the slippery slope that comes from idle conversation among colleagues and students while on the job, albeit often in social situations. What may have started as an academic conversation related to the subject matter of the participants' teaching and research agendas (though the court of appeals in *Trejo* doubted this) turned quickly into a conversation jeopardizing a faculty member's job.

The final example in this illustration of the *Pickering-Connick* line of cases is *Burnham v. Ianni*.[54] In *Burnham*, students in the history club at the University of Minnesota-Duluth decided to use the history department's display case to display photographs of history professors in costumes and props related to teaching and research interests. Two of the eleven professors who participated posed with weapons.[55] The popular photographs and the accompanying written material also placed in the display case were thought to communicate matters of public interest to the many students, staff, faculty, and campus visitors who passed by the display case every day. But there was a complaint relayed from the university's affirmative action officer who claimed that the two photos of professors with weapons re-aggravated a threat sent to an unrelated professor several weeks earlier. She also claimed that the display constituted sexual harassment and demanded that the two photos with weapons be removed. The history department refused to remove the photos, but after a couple of meetings with Chancellor Ianni, the chancellor ordered campus police to remove the pictures. The two professors filed suit. The Eighth Circuit Court of Appeals held that the expressive conduct here—the posting of photos—is constitutionally protected speech.[56] The dispute over the abrupt cancellation of the military history exhibit was more than just an internal employee grievance. It involved a content-based cancellation of a history department's public display. Chancellor Ianni also attempted to apply the *Pickering* balancing test, and contended that his removal of the photos was to preserve an efficient and harmonious workplace. But the court held that Ianni failed to provide evidence that the speech activity had an adverse effect on the operation of the public employer. It was unreasonable to assert that two photos containing historical weapons in a display case with nine other photos exacerbated an atmosphere of fear on the campus. Furthermore, there was no adverse action taken against the professors, against which their speech might be balanced.

Related to both *Pickering* and *Connick* is another landmark decision by the Supreme Court in the area of public employees and free expression. In *Mount Healthy City School Board of Education v. Doyle*,[57] an untenured public school teacher (Doyle) sued his employer alleging that his nonrenewal was in retaliation for his constitutional exercise of free speech. Among the incidents the school district listed as reasons for his nonrenewal were Doyle's arguments with fellow teachers and staff members, derogatory and obscene comments and gestures to students, and a phone call to a local radio station to discuss the contents of a school district dress code for teachers. In holding for the school district, the Supreme Court adopted the following burden-shifting test:

(1) The employee must show that

   (a) his or her conduct was protected under the Constitution; and

   (b) the protected conduct was the substantial motivating factor in the employer's decision.

(2) If the employee satisfies this burden, then the employer must show that the employee would have been disciplined (e.g., nonrenewed, terminated, etc.) anyway.[58]

The school district in *Doyle* admitted that the phone call to the radio station was one of the reasons for the decision to nonrenew. However, according to the Court, the mere fact that protected speech was used in the employment decision is not enough to warrant reinstatement and/or back pay. The district successfully demonstrated that it would have recommended norenewal in light of the other incidents. Basically, the Court held that an employee cannot use a free speech claim to overcome a record of unsatisfactory performance justifying an employer's adverse employment decision:

> While a borderline or marginal employee should not have employment decisions weigh against him because of constitutionally protected conduct, that same employee ought not to be able to prevent the employer from reviewing his performance record by adding constitutionally protected conduct to it.[59]

The *Doyle* burden-shifting test has seen much application in higher education settings. The Fifth Circuit Court of Appeals, for example, made the important statement that the plaintiffs must actually suffer some job detriment in order to prevail under a *Doyle* analysis. In *Harrington v. Harris*,[60] three veteran professors at Thurgood Marshall School of Law participated in a vote of no confidence against the school's dean and wrote a letter to the university president asking that the dean be removed. When the professors received comparatively low salary merit increases, they filed free speech, due process, and race discrimination claims. The trial court held for the plaintiffs on each of the three issues, but the Court of Appeals reversed on the free speech issue. The court applied *Doyle* and assumed, first, that the First Amendment protected the professors' statements. However, the court held that the plaintiffs had not suffered any adverse employment decision that could support retaliation claims. All three were still employed as full-time, fully tenured professors. No one was terminated, demoted, or threatened with either termination or demotion. None of the plaintiffs suffered a reduction in pay.

Similar to *Doyle*, many cases also involve adverse employment decisions that may be inspired, in part, by protected employee speech. However, in some of these cases, the employer is able to show that the protected speech was not the substantial motivating factor in its decision. In *Gerhart v. Hayes*, for example, the University of Houston fired its director of the Research Institute for Computing and Information Systems (RICIS).[61] She had been hired to diversify and increase the sources of RICIS funding. During her tenure, she complained to senior administrators and her colleagues that finance and administration funds had been inadequately allocated. After she worked for two years on the job, she was informed by letter that she was being fired for her failure to broaden the funding base for the institute. She admitted that the funding had declined but argued that the termination was due to her expression of opinion about funding allocation. In its first opinion, the Fifth Circuit held that the employee's speech did not relate to a matter of public concern, as she was speaking in her role as an employee on the university's allocation of discretionary funding. However, upon rehearing, the court vacated that portion of the opinion and engaged in a partial *Doyle* analysis, whereby it held that the speech, whether or not it related to a matter of public concern, was not the substantial or motivating factor in the decision to terminate. The court held that the real reason for her termination was that she failed to do the job she was asked to do when she was hired. This case may be an indication that it is permissible for a court to jump over the first step of *Doyle* (often a tough question) and get to an easier question—whether the expression was a substantial factor in the employment decision. The problem with this analysis is that it not only jumps over the first step of *Doyle* (whether the speech is constitutionally protected), it stands to trump the very well-regarded holding of *Connick* which states that the courts will not intervene in the internal day-to-day decision-making of government employers on speech issues unless that speech is related to a matter of public concern. Absent consideration of the threshold question, courts may be judging employer decisions based on purely internal concerns.

In a case similar to *Gerhart*, a former assistant dean of a college of dentistry sued his college's chancellor and claimed that his contract reduction and demotion were in retaliation for his public criticism over the university's budgetary decisions and minority student recruitment efforts.[62] One of the duties as Assistant Dean included the recruitment of minority candidates under the university's Urban Health Program. The program had met its enrollment goals early, but the numbers declined rapidly after that. At a series of meetings of the college's community advisory council, Assistant Dean Roberts attributed the decline, in part, to the college's failure to provide the program with sufficient funds. On the retaliation claim against the chancellor, the court of appeals applied *Doyle*. Assuming that Roberts' speech was constitutionally protected, the Court of Appeals agreed that Roberts' expression was not the substantial or motivating factor behind the university's decision to terminate. While *Roberts* is a fairly typical *Doyle* application, the court made a telling state-ment with respect to the chronology and timing of speech and employ-ment decisions. When answering the "substantial or motivating factor" prong of *Doyle*, the chronological relationship between an employee's speech and the adverse employment decision made against the employee does not, by itself, give rise to an inference that the speech motivated the employment decision.

In 1996, the Tenth Circuit Court of Appeals combined the rulings in *Pickering, Connick*, and *Doyle*, into a single four-step test:

(1) The court must determine whether the employee's speech can be characterized as constituting speech on a matter of public con-cern;

(2) If yes, then the court must engage a balancing test between the employee's rights as a citizen in commenting on matters of public concern and the state's rights in promoting the effective efficient provision of public service (the *Pickering* balance);

(3)  If the *Pickering* balancing test favors the employee, then the employee must show that the constitutionally protected speech was a substantial or motivating factor in the employer's adverse employment decision made against him; and

(4)  If the employee makes that showing successfully, then the employer must show, by preponderance of the evidence, that the decision would have been made even in the absence of the protected conduct.[63]

This test, while useful as a way to establish a frame from which to analyze free speech concerns of public higher education employees, has not been explicitly adopted in another higher education case. Moreover, the four prongs fail to include a reference to another significant Supreme Court decision involving the speech of public employees. In *Waters v. Churchill*,[64] a nurse was terminated after her employer, a public hospital, investigated some negative comments that the nurse made to a colleague about her boss and her department. A plurality of the Supreme Court indicated that, regarding the regulation of speech, the government may treat its own employees differently than it does private citizens:

> The government's interest in achieving its goals as effectively and efficiently as possible is elevated from a relatively subordinate interest when it acts as sovereign to a significant one when it acts as employer. The government cannot restrict the speech of the public at large just in the name of efficiency. But where the government is employing someone for the very purpose of effectively achieving its goals, such restrictions may well be appropriate.[65]

Effectively, *Waters* supports the view that even when an adverse employment decision is predicated on a government employee's exercise of free speech, the public institution's interest may outweigh the employee's free speech rights, particularly when the speech itself can reasonably be forecast to create a substantial disruption or material interference with workplace efficiency. Even when the employee's speech is on a matter of public concern, the plurality opinion in *Waters* grants the government as employer some good faith leeway in determining that the employee's speech is likely to be disruptive to the operations of the employer. In other words, as long as the employer has a reasonable belief that the speech would disrupt efficient operations, the employer may punish the employee, regardless of what the employee actually said. Note, though, that the punishment must be based on the potential disruption and not in retaliation for the speech.

The case law applying *Waters* explicitly in higher education contexts is sparse. Two cases provide guidance. First, in *Jeffries v. Harleston*,[66] the longtime chair of the Black Studies department at the City University of New York delivered an off-campus speech concerning racial bias in New

York State's public school curriculum. In the speech, he made several derogatory comments directed at Jews. Despite favorable reviews of Jeffries' job performance from the Dean and provost, university president Harleston investigated and recommended that Jeffries' current three-year term as chair be limited to one year. The board of trustees agreed, and Jeffries sued Harleston and each member of the board individually. The district court found in favor of Jeffries, and the Court of Appeals for the Second Circuit, in its first opinion in the case, applied the *Doyle* test and affirmed. Upon the defendants' petition, the Supreme Court granted certiorari, vacated the first Court of Appeals decision, and remanded the case for reconsideration in light of the Court's decision in *Waters*.[67] Upon reconsideration, the Second Circuit held that the defendants did not violate the speech rights of Jeffries when they voted to demote him. In its opinion, the court of appeals made a distinction between the defendants who voted to demote Jeffries in retaliation for Jeffries' speech (seemingly prohibited under *Waters*) and those who voted to demote on the basis of the potential disruption the speech would cause (permitted under *Waters*). The jury found that the majority of the defendants limited Jeffries' term on the basis that the speech would harm the university. The court of appeals found the expectation of harm to be reasonable and held against Jeffries. On a side note, the court of appeals said that the academic freedom rights of Jeffries were not violated, as the detriment he suffered came in the form of a lost administrative position and not a faculty position.

Second, in *Hennessy v. City of Melrose*, 194 F.3d 237 (1st Cir. 1999), the court upheld a college's decision to remove a student from the teacher certification program after the public school where he was student teaching terminated his assignment. During student teaching, the student had expressed his strong views against abortion and homosexuality, made inappropriate presentations to the students and called the principal the devil and the principal's staff her disciples. Applying *Waters*, the court held that the school's interest in preserving a collegial and harmonious atmosphere for its staff and a healthy respect for the school's curriculum outweighed Hennessy's interests in expressing his views.

## Faculty/Staff as Educator: Faculty Academic Freedom

Generally, academic freedom is the "right to teach as one sees fit, but not necessarily the right to teach evil."[68] According to Richard Hofstadter and Walter P. Metzger,[69] the traditional German notion of academic freedom was composed of two concepts. *Lehrfreiheit* is the freedom to teach for teachers. *Lernfreiheit* belongs to students as their right to determine the course of their own studies. In 1940, the American Association of University Professors (AAUP) adopted a statement of principles declaring academic freedom as a right that belonged to professors. In part, the AAUP proclaims the following:

> Institutions of higher education are conducted for the common good and not to further the interest of either the individual teacher or the institution as a whole. The common good depends upon the free search for truth and its free exposition.
>
> Academic freedom is essential to these purposes and applies to both teaching and research. Freedom in research is fundamental to the advancement of truth. Academic freedom in its teaching aspect is fundamental for the protection of the rights of the teacher in teaching and of the student to freedom in learning. It carries with it duties correlative with rights.[70]

In practice, naturally, academic freedom is not without its limits. Moreover, the amount of case law on the asserted academic freedom rights of college and university personnel is high, and the developing judicial standards applied to academic freedom claims are not without their controversy. From the faculty member's perspective, early cases involved conduct and content in the classroom.[71] Recent applications expand on those traditional scenarios and discuss the rights of faculty members to develop their own grading policies[72] and to conduct controversial research in cyberspace on university-provided computer systems.[73]

## Classroom Speech of Faculty

As the list of academic freedom cases grows, so does the significant disparity among courts as to what legal standard ought to apply to such controversies. On one hand, courts may apply the "matter of public concern" standard of the *Pickering/Connick* duo, or the burden-shifting test of *Doyle*. Under each of these standards, it may be argued that the classroom speech of college and university faculty competes well against the claims of the employing public institutions. In other words, on speech related to matters of public concern, faculty members' rights are more likely to be protected. On the other hand, public colleges and universities may assert *Hazelwood* and its restrictive non-public forum analysis. Under such a standard, public institutions need only relate their speech restrictions to legitimate pedagogical concerns.

There are no recent Supreme Court decisions specifically addressing academic freedom rights of faculty members in the classroom. But among federal appeals court opinions, the Eleventh Circuit set the dialogue in motion in 1991 with its decision in *Bishop v. Aronov*.[74] Bishop, a professor of health, physical education, and recreation at the University of Alabama, taught exercise physiology to undergraduates and graduates. In his classes,

Bishop occasionally made comments on his Christian religious bias and its relationship to human physiology. According to his own testimony, Bishop told his students that his relationship with Jesus Christ was much more important than the production of papers and articles for tenure and promotion. He did not require his students to believe as he did, but he did tell his students that everything he did and said in the classroom should be understood to travel through a Christian lens. Bishop also organized special discussion sessions with any students and staff members who were interested in exploring the Christian relationship with exercise physiology. After receiving several complaints from students, Bishop's department chair wrote him a letter asking that he refrain from interjecting his religious beliefs in classes and from scheduling the optional class sessions. Bishop filed suit alleging that the letter was in violation of his First Amendment rights. The district court held for Bishop, but the Court of Appeals reversed.

The *Bishop* court explicitly adopted *Hazelwood* as its analytical frame. First, it considered the context and noted that, during instructional time, a university classroom is not an open forum.

> This context ... leads us to consider the coercive effect upon students that a professor's speech inherently possesses and that the University may wish to avoid. The University's interest is most obvious when student complaints suggest apparent coercion—even when not intended by the professor.[75]

Second, the court considered the university's curricular mission and the university's authority to control the content of its curriculum, particularly during class time. As long as it does so reasonably, a college or university has the authority to direct the curriculum-based conduct of teachers both in and out of the classroom.

Finally, the court considered Bishop's claims of academic freedom. Because the memo was written in direct response to particular circumstances (in-class comments and separate class sessions), the court interpreted the department chair's instructions narrowly. According to the court, there are some topics that produce more apprehension than comfort. The court cited to *Tinker* and *Hazelwood* and made the quick distinction that when the teacher is the speaker, the resulting speech is more closely connected to the school itself than it is for the otherwise independent speaker. The letter did not say that Bishop could not hold these views, speak on these views, or even publish and present on these views. He simply was not permitted to discuss his religious views under the guise of university courses. The court narrowed the memo even more to say that Bishop was not prevented from scheduling special on-campus discussions or conversations on the evidence of God in human physiology; he was simply prevented from doing so in relation to the courses he teaches in classrooms or in like settings on campus.

> Though we are mindful of the invaluable role academic
> freedom plays in our public schools, particularly at the
> post-secondary level, we do not find support to conclude
> that academic freedom is an independent First Amendment
> right. And in any event, we cannot supplant our discretion
> for that of the University.... In this regard, we trust that the
> University will serve its own interests as well as those of its
> professors in pursuit of academic freedom. University of-
> ficials are undoubtedly aware that quality faculty members
> will be hard to attract and retain if they are to be shackled
> in much of what they do.[76]

One year following *Bishop*, the Second Circuit heard a claim from another contentious professor. This time, the court held in favor of the professor, disfavoring the university's actions designed to shield students from the professor's controversial views. In *Levin v. Harleston*,[77] Levin, a tenured professor at the City University of New York had published three controversial writings containing a number of denigrating comments concerning the intelligence and social characteristics of African Americans. After the third publication, the Dean of the College of Humanities created alternate or "shadow" sections of Levin's courses for any of Levin's students who wished to transfer. Levin was not informed of these new sections. Students also staged demonstrations outside of Levin's classrooms. A faculty committee found Levin's writings to be inappropriate, unprofessional, and harmful to the College's educational process. As a result of the College's determination, Levin feared discipline and turned down several speaking engagements. The Court of Appeals held that the creation of alternate sections of Levin's courses for students who did not like his ideas violated the professor's free speech and due process liberty rights. Instead of applying *Hazelwood*, as the *Bishop* court had, the court applied *Doyle* and held that Levin's protected speech was the motivating factor in the university's decision to discipline Levin.[78] The court held that the notion of tenure is lost without the opportunity to freely explore and write and speak on topics of scholarly interest, even if those topics are controversial.

Several recent cases continue to recognize *Pickering/Connick* as the applicable standard for faculty classroom speech. Making the point that much higher education classroom speech, while often heated and controversial, does not lose its public nature, a Virginia federal district court judge argued that "[t]o suggest that the First Amendment, as a matter of law, is never implicated when a professor speaks in class, is fantastic."[79]

An interesting pair of cases from the Sixth Circuit in 2001 illustrates how tricky (and unpredictable) the *Pickering/Connick* balance can be. First, in *Bonnell v. Lorenzo*, a student filed a complaint with Macomb Community College, stating that professor Bonnell had consistently engaged in extreme profanity and other vulgar conduct and language in class.[80]

As the college had received similar complaints in the past, administrators informed Bonnell of the complaint and ordered him to stop engaging in such conduct, as it was a potential violation of college policy and could render the college liable under Title IX for sexual harassment. Bonnell claimed that the language was germane to content and the discussion in the English classes he taught. Eight months later, the college received another letter with similar complaints. In it, the student asked for an apology and argued that Bonnell should be terminated. Bonnell offered an apology—an eight-page satirical essay entitled "An Apology: Yes, Virginia, There is a Sanity Clause". Bonnell's asserted sanity clause was the First Amendment. He circulated a copy of the complaint (with names blacked out) and his essay to all of his students, 200 faculty members, and to television and print media. Bonnell was then suspended with pay, pending further investigation. He filed suit. The district court granted Bonnell's injunction. The court of appeals applied the *Pickering/Connick* balancing test and reversed. On the question of whether the speech touched on matters of public concern, the court addressed the content, form, and context of the speech. In doing so, however, the court noted that Bonnell was speaking as both a citizen and as an employee—a case of "mixed speech" related to both public and private concerns. On one hand, Bonnell's essay on allegations of sexual harassment and arguments on the importance of academic freedom in higher education, circulated to students, faculty, and the media, is a matter of public concern. On the other hand, the classroom speech that gave rise to the sexual harassment complaint and the disciplinary measures did not relate to a matter of public concern. According to the court, however, if any part of the speech at issue involves matters of public concern, then a court will apply the *Pickering* balancing test to weigh the mixed speech and its impact on the employer's interests. With respect to the speech in *Bonnell*, the court held that the defendants' interests in maintaining confidentiality of sexual harassment claims, avoiding institutional liability for allowing such harassment to continue, and providing safe and hostility-free classrooms for its students outweighed Bonnell's interests in academic freedom.

In the second Sixth Circuit case, in a divergent decision, another panel of the Sixth Circuit held that "[b]ecause the essence of a teacher's role is to prepare students for their place in society as responsible citizens, classroom instruction will often fall within the Supreme Court's broad conception of 'public concern.'"[81] In *Hardy v. Jefferson Community College*, an adjunct instructor was nonrenewed after he led a classroom discussion on the impact of oppressive and disparaging words, including "girl," "lady," "faggot," "nigger," and "bitch". Hardy was a teacher in the college's communications program, teaching a class on Introduction to Interpersonal Communication. In the discussion, students examined how language is used to marginalize minorities and other oppressed groups in society. One student complained that the discussion was racist, sexist, and offensive.

Like Bonnell, Hardy argued that the use of such words was germane to the discussion on language and social constructivism and to the course on communications. Applying *Pickering/Connick* and distinguishing the decision in *Bonnell*, the court agreed with Hardy.[82]

The Second Circuit has addressed a case similar to *Hardy*. In *Vega v. Miller*, however, a critical factual difference led to an opposite result.[83] Vega, a non-tenured teacher at New York Maritime College, was dismissed for leading his class in a word association exercise. The goal of the word association exercise was to help students avoid being repetitive in essay writing. The students selected "sex" as the topic. The administrators asserted that Vega acted unprofessionally when he failed to end the exercise, which led to students standing on chairs and shouting vulgarities and sexually explicit terms. Vega was writing some of the terms in words or initials on the blackboard. The college claimed that the exercise violated the college's sexual harassment policy. Upholding the termination, the court found that the vulgarities used in Vega's class were not political expression. Unlike the instructor in *Hardy*, Vega's use of such language was not designed as an exploration of the words' origins or uses in society. The particular subject matter used for the classroom exercise was not necessary to complete the lesson Vega wished to teach. According to the court, "[e]ven though no students complained, what students will silently endure is not the measure of what a college must tolerate or what the administrators may reasonably think that a college need not tolerate."[84]

## Grading Policies

A small but telling set of cases may represent additional evidence that whatever academic freedom rights ever existed for individual faculty members may be dwindling. In the late 1980s, in an early decision favoring faculty, the Sixth Circuit held that forcing a university faculty member to sign a memorandum changing a student's grade constituted compelled speech and was unlawful.[85] In *Parate v. Isibor*, the court held that the "assignment of a letter grade is a symbolic communication intended to send a specific message to the student ... [and] is entitled to some measure of First Amendment protection."[86] According to the court, a professor's assignment of grades is central to the professor's teaching methods. Therefore, they should retain wide discretion over the evaluation of their students.

In 2001, in cases similar to *Parate*, the Third and Seventh Circuits held in favor of the higher education institutions, with both courts holding that grading falls within the institution's freedom to determine how courses will be taught. In *Brown v. Armenti*,[87] a tenured professor was suspended from teaching after he refused to follow an order to change the grade of a student. He was later fired for writing a letter to the board of trustees criticizing the president.[88] On the allegation that the suspension was in retaliation for refusing to change the grade, the court of appeals held for the university. "'In the classroom' refers to those settings where the professor is acting as the university's proxy, fulfilling one of the functions involved in the university's 'four essential freedoms': choosing 'who may teach, what may be taught, how it shall be taught, and who may be admitted to study.'"[89] The court noted that had the professor been speaking generally on the issue of grade inflation, the speech might have been protected as a matter of public interest. However, the court found that the professor was essentially expressing his dissatisfaction with the internal office decision of his supervisor. In *Wozniak v. Conry*,[90] a long-time professor at the University of Illinois at Urbana-Champaign submitted his semester grades, but refused to submit grading materials, despite many requests to do so. The dean of the college of engineering barred him from teaching any more classes, canceled his research funds, and reassigned him to manage the departmental web site. The court held that the plaintiff had refused to follow reasonable university rules and, with many opportunities to comply without effect, such insubordination was unprotected by the Constitution.

## Institutional Academic Freedom

> Our Nation is deeply committed to safeguarding academic freedom, which is of transcendent value to all of us.... That freedom is therefore a special concern of the First Amendment, which does not tolerate laws that cast a pall of orthodoxy over the classroom. The Nation's future depends upon leaders trained through wide exposure to that robust exchange of ideas which discovers truth out of a multitude of tongues, (rather) than through any kind of authoritative selection.[91]

The above statement, from the 1967 Supreme Court decision in *Keyishian v. Board of Regents*, is surely a source of great pride for higher education faculty. It is also, however, a source of great controversy, as the notion of academic freedom has been recently mired in a battle of ownership. In other words, is academic freedom an individual right or and an institutional one? Despite the volume of earlier claims and discussions to the contrary, an emergent trend seems to favor academic freedom as an institutional right.

In 2000, the Fourth Circuit made one of the most important statements on the issue of academic freedom for faculty and advanced the notion that academic freedom is an institutional right and not an individual one.[92] What makes *Urofsky v. Gilmore* noteworthy is that it does not involve a challenge to an isolated decision made by a university administrator against an individual employee. The plaintiffs, instead, challenged a university policy and a state statute that made it illegal for state employees to access sexually explicit material on computers that are owned or leased by the state. Furthermore, the case represented a challenge to speech in cyberspace, a valuable teaching and research arena for higher education audiences. In the case, the District Court held for the professors, and the Court of Appeals reversed. According to the federal appeals court, the state law did not restrict government employees from accessing sexually explicit sites on computers that are not owned or leased by the government;[93] nor did it attempt to restrict speech engaged by the speakers in their roles as citizens. The law only restricted speech in the role of employee. To make the point, the court stated:

> This focus on the capacity of the speaker recognizes the basic truth that speech by public employees undertaken in the course of their job duties will frequently involve matters of vital concern to the public, without giving those employees a First Amendment right to dictate to the state how they will do their jobs.[94]

The plaintiffs argued that their academic freedom rights outweighed the interests of the state as employer, that university professors have the right to determine the subjects of their research, writing, and teaching, without oversight by the institution. The appeals court concluded that "any right of academic freedom above and beyond the First Amendment rights to which every citizen is entitled, the right inheres in the University, not in individual professors."[95] Focusing again on the critical role of the speaker, the court distinguished *Sweezy v. New Hampshire* by noting that the challenger in *Sweezy* was speaking as a private citizen and not as a government employee.[96]

Cases such as *Urofsky v. Gilmore, Brown v. Armenti,* and *Bishop v. Aronov* indicate broadening judicial support for public college and university policies and decisions controlling the teaching and classroom activities of faculty members. In each of these cases and several more like them, courts have held that it is the academic institution that has control over what curriculum is taught, how it is taught, and who may teach it. Beyond application to traditional classroom activity, the notion of academic freedom as an institutional right has been applied to a range of institutional decision-making including student admissions, tenure review, student activity fees, ethics codes, the production of plays, the display of artwork, required reading lists for freshman orientation, and acceptable use policies for university-sponsored computers and Internet technology.

One Supreme Court decision, in *University of Pennsylvania v. EEOC,*[97] set the judicial standard for the relationship between academic freedom and tenure review. In *Pennsylvania,* a female faculty member of Asian descent at the University of Pennsylvania was denied tenure and filed a complaint with the EEOC under Title VII, alleging race, national origin, and sex discrimination. As part of its investigation of the claims, the EEOC requested the faculty member's tenure review file and the tenure review files of five male professors whom the plaintiff argued had received more favorable treatment. The university requested that the EEOC modify its request so that the university could keep the peer-reviewed tenure files confidential. The EEOC responded with a subpoena and an application for an enforcement order from the District Court. The District Court issued the enforcement order and the Court of Appeals for the Third Circuit and the Supreme Court affirmed. The Court held that a university does not have a special privilege against disclosure of materials relevant and necessary for the investigation of race, sex, and national origin charges. The university claimed, in part, that disclosure would violate its rights to academic freedom. According to the university's argument, there would be a chilling effect on truthful candid tenure evaluations as more and more peer evaluations become public and, as a result, the quality of university instruction would suffer. The Court disagreed and held that the subpoena is not directly related to any content-based restriction on the academic work of the university. It does not provide any criteria that the university must use in selecting teachers. It merely requires that the university use criteria that do not violate Title VII.

The Court's opinion in *Pennsylvania* certainly has its impact on the tenure and promotion review process. However, in a technical sense, the Court did not do great harm to the institutional right to review and supervise a college teacher's classroom activities when deciding whether to grant or deny tenure, as such a right does not belong to the courts themselves. As the cases in the earlier sections on faculty speech rights illustrate, institutional rights to review and supervise extend to the evaluation of the relationship between the teacher's pedagogical content, style, and method and the college or university's institutional standards and philosophies. For example, in *Webb v. Board of Trustees of Ball State University*,[98] Webb, a tenured professor, filed a complaint accusing a colleague of sexually harassing a student. The assistant provost, whom Webb had been dating, requested only a reprimand for the accused colleague. Webb then accused the assistant provost and other administrators of ethical lapses for not taking stronger action. During the following months, Webb launched a massive campaign against university administrators and faculty members, leading a few to quit. Webb's teaching schedule was then altered, and he complained about that, saying that the changes were in retaliation for his free speech. The court upheld the university's decision to terminate Webb. "Universities are entitled to insist that members of the faculty (and their administrative aides) devote their energies to promoting goals such as research and teaching. When the bulk of a professor's time goes over to fraternal warfare, students and the scholarly community alike suffer, and the university may intervene to restore decorum and ease tensions."[99]

The college or university itself is a speaker, a contributor to higher education dialogue along with students and faculty. While many judicial pronouncements make this point, an excerpt from the Supreme Court's opinion in *Rosenberger v. The University of Virginia* states it succinctly:

> When the state is the speaker, it may make content-based choices. When the University determines the content of the education it provides, it is the University speaking, and we have permitted the government to regulate the content of what is or is not expressed when it is the speaker or when it enlists private entities to convey its own message.[100]

The authority of a state university to make content-based choices regarding school-sponsored curricular and extracurricular activities and events has been addressed recently in a few controversial cases involving alleged hostility toward Christianity. In each of these cases, the university's authority prevailed. In *Linnemeir v. Board of Trustees of Purdue University*,[101] residents of the state of Indiana filed a motion to prevent a state university from producing Terrence McNally's play *Corpus Christi*. The play depicts Jesus Christ as a homosexual who has sexual relations with his disciples. The plaintiffs argued that the university would violate the First Amendment by publicly endorsing anti-Christian beliefs. The court denied the plaintiffs' motion and held that the First Amendment does not prevent a state university from providing a venue for the expression of views contrary to traditional Christianity. To hold otherwise would "imply that teachers in state universities could not teach important works like Voltaire, Hobbes, Hume, Darwin, Mill, Marx, Nietzsche, Freud, Yeats, Heidegger, Sartre, Camus, John Dewey, and countless other staples of Western culture."[102] A specific policy promoting a certain religion or a certain philosophy contrary to all religions would violate the First Amendment. But that was not the case here. "The government's interest in providing a stimulating, well-rounded education would be crippled by attempting to accommodate every parent's hostility to books inconsistent with their religious beliefs."[103] According to the majority, there is no doubt that "Corpus Christi" will be offensive to many patrons, but "the quality or lack thereof of Corpus Christi and other post-modernist provocations is a matter for the state university, not for federal judges, to determine."[104]

Making similar statements in a case involving a sculpture placed on public university grounds as part of an annual outdoor sculpture exhibition, the United States District Court for the District of Kansas, in *O'Connor v. Washburn University*, held that a controversial sculpture did not violate the Establishment Clause, despite its allegedly anti-Catholic message.[105] The sculpture was one of five chosen by the university's campus beautification committee to be placed in various public spaces on campus for the 2003-04 school year. According to the student and faculty plaintiffs, the sculpture, entitled *Holier Than Thou*, conveyed a message of hostility toward the Catholic community, particularly through a written statement from the artist mounted below the sculpture.[106] In response to an early round of local and national complaints, the university's president made an important statement regarding the speech rights of the institution as a whole and the opportunities such events present to the individual members of a university community:

> One of the purposes of art is to engage us intellectually and emotionally. This work apparently has fulfilled that function as there is a wide variety of commentary on the piece, ranging from support to opposition.... As a university, we should take this opportunity to create a positive educational experience. Seminars can be organized surrounding this work of art and its symbolism. Speakers could address the aesthetic elements, religious perspectives and issues facing contemporary religions. Different points of view must and can be represented....[107]

After another round of complaints, the university's board of regents voted 5-2 to keep the sculpture. Addressing the Establishment Clause claim, the district court supported the president and the board of regents and held that the university had a secular purpose for the decisions it made regarding the art work and that a reasonable observer viewing the sculpture would not believe the university placed it on campus as an attack on Catholicism. The context was not anti-religion; it was an annual artistic competition and campus beautification.

In a twist on the religion-based claims to the institutional decisions made by public universities in the cases described above, a presentation of the widely publicized case involving the 2002 freshmen orientation at the University of North Carolina and the required readings from the Qur'an is necessary. In *Yacovelli v. Moeser*, two taxpayers and three incoming freshmen filed suit against the university, asking for injunctive relief and claiming violations of the Establishment and Free Exercise clauses, not for an alleged direct attack on Christianity, but for endorsement of Islam. Procedurally, the taxpayers' claims were dismissed for lack of standing and the injunctive relief was denied for mootness.[108] Substantively, applying the popular *Lemon* test,[109] endorsement test, and coercion test, the court also dismissed the Establishment Clause claims.[110] The stated secular purpose was to engage students in critical thinking and writing exercises on a current topic. According to the court, the use of the book at the orientation did not endorse religion, as the book was written and read in an effort to understand history, culture, and art, none of which is impermissible under the Establishment Clause. Finally, the orientation program did not require the participation in any religious exercise. "It was a scholarly discourse, not a proselytizing mission."[111] In a later decision in the same case, the court dismissed the student plaintiff's free exercise claims, as the university's orientation program did not impair the plaintiffs' ability to practice or profess their beliefs.[112]

The discussion of institutional academic freedom and the end of the second chapter on freedom of speech issues seems a good place to engage a brief discussion on, thus far, the largest library available to students, staff, faculty, and visitors to college and university campuses: the Internet. As courts continue to emphasize the *institution* as the primary authority over the time, place, manner, and sometimes the content of student and faculty speech, *cyberspace* continues to expand and affect the way teaching, learning, research, and service are conducted in higher education. Combining these institutional and technological forces yields a predictable path. The university retains the control over the technological forums it provides to students, staff, faculty, and visitors. In other words, the institution controls, through policy and practice, the acceptable use of its computer networks—the newest, most expandable forum for discussion. Acceptable use policies are sets of rules, regulations, rights, and responsibilities that govern student, staff, faculty, and visitor use of the Internet and the World Wide Web at colleges and universities.[113] Most institutions of higher education have adopted such policies and have incorporated them into student and faculty codes of conduct, as well as general library regulations. An example from Eastern Michigan University is included in this text.[114] Typical acceptable use policies apply to personal computers, workstations, mini- and mainframe computers, and voice, data, and video communication networks. Generally, they will apply to any technology provided by or attached to the college or university network. In other words, if a user is connected to the institution's service provider, then he or she is subject to the acceptable use policy (AUP).

AUPs are governed by standard ethical and legal principles such as ownership, copyright, privacy, and network security. For example, most AUPs do not allow users, without proper authorization, to access, alter, damage, or destroy the work of other users or the property of the institution. In addition, the AUPs will forbid the use of college or university information technology systems when such use is for personal financial gain and unrelated to legitimate academic pursuits. Exceptions may exist on a case-by-case contractual basis. Among typical acceptable uses are the following:

(1) use for exchange of data or information for personal development, to maintain currency, or debate issues in a professional or academic field;

(2) use for disciplinary, professional, association, or advisory activities related to the user's research and instructional activities;

(3) use in applying for or administering grants or contracts for research or instruction; and

(4) use for general administrative activities and communication in support of research and instruction.

Typical unacceptable uses include the following:

(1) establishment of network connections that create routing patterns inconsistent with the effective and shared use of the institution's network;

(2) malicious use of any kind including, but not limited to, harassment of other users, attempts to cause system outages, or attempts to discover passwords;

(3) uses that violate applicable laws, regulations, or institutional policies;[115]

(4) unsolicited advertising;

(5) use of institutional resources for profit-making activities; and

(6) use of institutional resources for recreational games when such use restricts access of those resources by other users.

Case law involving acceptable use policies in educational institutions is sparse, to be sure. However, policymakers are not without some guidance with respect to the freedom of speech in cyberspace. The United States Congress has attempted several times in the past decade to effect regulations restricting the access, transmission, and display of certain content over the Internet.[116] Each of the attempts has been challenged as vague, overbroad, and violative of the First Amendment. With one recent exception, the statutes have been struck down.[117]

Within discussions of free speech, the primary challenge to AUPs from students, staff, and faculty stem largely from claims of academic freedom. First, there is the general right to academic inquiry and the access to information. Indeed, cyberspace represents a rather limitless library for a college or university community. While not a cyberspace case, a plurality in *Board of Education, Island Trees Union Free School District v. Pico* articulated this sentiment. The Court observed the students' freedom "to inquire, to study and to evaluate, and to gain new maturity and understanding."[118] While *Pico* involved a challenge to the removal of library books from a school's library, the reasoning of the Court applies nicely in cyberspace. The Court even quoted James Madison:

> A popular Government, without popular information, or the means of acquiring it, is but a Prologue to a Farce or a Tragedy; or perhaps both. Knowledge will forever govern ignorance: and a people who mean to be their own Governors, must arm themselves with the power which knowledge gives.[119]

Against the general right to speak freely and the claimed right to access information, the college or university has several legitimate responses, each of which has been fully discussed in this chapter and throughout this text.[120] Even in the most open of forums, universities are permitted to impose reasonable time, place, and manner restrictions on the speech of visitors to the forum. Provisions of AUPs, arguably, fall within this realm of reasonableness. Certainly, the obligation of students, staff, faculty, and campus visitors to respect applicable copyright, privacy, and criminal laws is not excessive. Add the argument that the institution owns its information technology network and, therefore, has the right to control it even more tightly than it could an open forum, and the speech claims of network users lose considerably more weight. The primary judicial example is *Urofsky v. Gilmore.*[121] In *Urofsky*, the Fourth Circuit Court of Appeals upheld a Virginia state statute that made it a crime to access sexually explicit material on computers owned or leased by the state. University of Virginia faculty members challenged the statute as infringing on their academic teaching and research and violative of the First Amendment. The court held that academic freedom rights belong to the university and not to the individual faculty members and students. Similarly, the Court of Appeals for the Tenth Circuit, in *Loving v. Boren*, held that the university computer and Internet services do not constitute a public forum, as long as the university does not open the facilities to the general public.[122] According to the court, "[t]he state, no less than a private owner of property, has the right to preserve property under its control for the use to which it is lawfully dedicated."[123] With some speculation, college and university AUPs similar to the one reproduced in the Appendix will likely be upheld against similar First Amendment challenges.

# Endnotes

1. Sweezy v. N.H., 354 U.S. 234, 250 (1957).
2. *See, e.g.*, Dixon v. Ala. State Bd. of Educ., 294 F.2d 150 (5th Cir. 1961).
3. Urofsky v. Gilmore, 216 F.3d 401 (4th Cir. 2000).
4. Linnemeir v. Bd. of Trs. of Purdue Univ., 260 F.3d 757 (7th Cir. 2001).
5. Keyishian v. Bd. of Regents, 385 U.S. 589, 603 (1967).
6. Trotman v. Bd. of Trs., 635 F.2d 216, 218-219 (3d Cir. 1980).
7. For the sake of argument, the "university as sovereign" role presumes that the inquiry involves *public* colleges and universities. The "university as patron" analogy is discussed in full below.
8. BLACK'S LAW DICTIONARY 947 (6th ed. 1990); *see also* SPERRY, D.J.; DANIEL, P.T.K.; HUEFNER, D.S.; & GEE, E.G., EDUCATION LAW AND THE PUBLIC SCHOOLS: A COMPENDIUM (2d ed. 1998).
9. Wieman v. Updegraff, 344 U.S. 183 (1952).
10. Shelton v. Tucker, 364 U.S. 479 (1960).
11. 354 U.S. 234 (1957).
12. 385 U.S. 589 (1967).
13. 354 U.S. at 250.
14. *Id.* at 250-251.

[15] The University of Buffalo had been a private university. Upon merging with the SUNY system, the university automatically became subject to state laws and SUNY regulations.

[16] 385 U.S. at 604 (internal quotation marks omitted) (emphasis added).

[17] 465 U.S. 271 (1984). The meetings at issue were "meet and confer sessions"—opportunities for public employees to offer policy advice to their employers.

[18] The Court distinguished cases like *Shelton* and *Wieman*. *Knight* dealt with speech by employees on academic policymaking, not the general right to speak with others for purely communicative purposes.

[19] 500 U.S. 507 (1991).

[20] 209 F.3d 944 (7th Cir. 2000).

[21] 164 F.3d 221 (5th Cir. 1998). Some of the plaintiffs in this case had been retained as expert witnesses in the state's lawsuit against tobacco companies. The testimony of the plaintiffs in cases such as this relates to matters of public concern. "The notion that the State may silence the testimony of state employees simply because that testimony is contrary to the interests of the State in litigation or otherwise, is antithetical to the protection extended by the First Amendment." *Id.* at 226.

[22] 391 U.S. 563 (1968).

[23] *Id.* at 568.

[24] *Id.* at 568-574. *See also* SPERRY & DANIEL, ET AL., EDUCATION LAW AND PUBLIC SCHOOLS: A COMPENDIUM 503 (2d ed. 1998).

[25] 391 U.S. at 576.

[26] 461 U.S. 138 (1983).

[27] *Id.* at 146.

[28] "Private communications are often the most effective way to bring about policy changes and the least disruptive to the delivery of government services." Gardetto v. Mason, 100 F.3d 803, 815 (10th Cir. 1996).

[29] 100 F. Supp. 2d 954 (S.D. Iowa 2000).

[30] Burnham v. Ianni, 119 F.3d 668 (8th Cir. 1997) (en banc).

[31] Maples v. Martin, 858 F.2d 1546 (11th Cir. 1988).

[32] Bauer v. Sampson, 261 F.3d 775 (9th Cir. 2001).

[33] Hamer v. Brown, 831 F.2d 1398 (8th Cir. 1987).

[34] Honore v. Douglas, 833 F.2d 565 (5th Cir. 1987).

[35] Roberts v. Broski, 186 F.3d 990 (7th Cir. 1999).

[36] Blum v. Schlegel, 18 F.3d 1005, 1012 (2d Cir. 1994).

[37] Scallet v. Rosenblum, 911 F. Supp. 999 (W.D. Va. 1996).

[38] Cohen v. San Bernardino Valley Coll., 92 F.3d 968 (9th Cir. 1996).

[39] Boyett v. Troy State Univ., 971 F. Supp. 1403 (M.D. Ala. 1997). Speech was not about the misuse of university funds, which may have qualified as a matter of public concern.

[40] *Id.*

[41] *Id. See also* Bunger v. Univ. of Okla., 95 F.3d 987 (10th Cir. 1996) (a dispute over whether tenured and untenured professors can serve on such councils is a matter of internal concern).

[42] Boyett v. Troy State Univ., 971 F. Supp. 1403 (M.D. Ala. 1997).

[43] Williams v. Ala. State Univ., 102 F.3d 1179 (11th Cir. 1997).

[44] Trejo v. Shoben, 319 F.3d 878 (7th Cir. 2003).

[45] Simons v. W. Va Univ., No. 95-1712, 1996 U.S. App. LEXIS 10425 (4th Cir. May 7, 1996).

[46] Wozniak v. Conry, 236 F.3d 888, 891 (7th Cir. 2001). *See also* Brown v. Armenti, 247 F.3d 69 (3d Cir. 2001) and Lovelace v. Southeastern Mass. Univ., 793 F.2d 419 (1st Cir. 1986). A discussion on the academic freedom implications of such disputes appears later in the chapter.

[47] 261 F.3d 775 (9th Cir. 2001).

[48] *Id.* at 782.

[49] *Id.* at 783.

[50] *Id.* at 785.

[51] 971 F. Supp. 1403 (M.D. Ala. 1997).

[52] *Id.* at 1416.

[53] 319 F.3d 878 (7th Cir. 2003).

[54] 119 F.3d 668 (8th Cir. 1997).

[55] One professor posed with a .45 caliber military pistol and a coonskin cap, and one wore a laurel wreath and posed with an ancient Roman sword.

[56] Nonverbal conduct qualifies as speech "if it is intended to convey a particularized message and the likelihood is great that the message will be understood by those who view it, regardless of whether it is actually understood in a particular instance in such a way." 119 F.3d at 674 (citing to Spence v. Washington, 418 U.S. 405, 411(1974)).

[57] 429 U.S. 274 (1977).

[58] *Id.* at 287.

[59] *Id.* at 286.

[60] 118 F.3d 359 (5th Cir. 1997).

[61] 201 F.3d 646, *reh'g en banc denied and opinion amended*, 217 F.3d 320 (5th Cir. 2000).

[62] Roberts v. Broski, 186 F.3d 990 (7th Cir. 1999).

[63] Gardetto v. Mason, 100 F.3d 803, 811 (10th Cir. 1996) (a college administrator's public criticism of the college's central administration and its policies and her public campaign for three, non-incumbent candidates for the Board of Trustees is protected speech and was not disruptive of college affairs).

[64] 511 U.S. 661 (1994).

[65] *Id.* at 675.

[66] 21 F.3d 1238 (2d Cir. 1994).

[67] 115 S. Ct. 502 (1994).

[68] BLACK'S LAW DICTIONARY 11 (6th ed. 1990).

[69] J. W. Ward, "The Development of Academic Freedom in the United States," PUB. OPIN- ION Q., Vol. 20, pp. 353-386 (1956).

[70] The full statement from the AAUP appears in the Appendices. *See also* http://www. aaup.org/statements/Redbook/1940stat.htm.

[71] *See, e.g.*, Clark v. Holmes, 474 F.2d 928 (7th Cir. 1972) and Riggin v. Bd. of Trs. of Ball State Univ., 489 N.E.2d 616 (Ind. Ct. App. 1986).

[72] *See, e.g.*, Brown v. Armenti, 247 F.3d 69 (3d Cir. 2001) and Wozniak v. Conry, 236 F.3d 888 (7th Cir. 2001).

[73] *See, e.g.*, Urofsky v. Gilmore, 216 F.3d 401 (4th Cir. 2000).

[74] 926 F.2d 1066 (11th Cir. 1991).

[75] *Id.* at 1074.

[76] *Id.* at 1075.

[77] 966 F.2d 85 (2d Cir. 1992).

[78] Levin was warned that his future conduct would remain under scrutiny but did not have an opportunity to defend himself.

[79] Scallet v. Rosenblum, 911 F. Supp. 999, 1013-1014 (W.D. Va. 1996). On the *Picker- ing* balance, the court held that the teacher's use of certain materials and methods in a graduate business course did, in fact, cause a substantial disruption and were not protected.

[80] 241 F.3d 800 (6th Cir. 2001).

[81] Hardy v. Jefferson Cmty. Coll. and Ky. Cmty. and Tech. Coll. Sys., 260 F.3d 671, 679 (6th Cir. 2001).

[82] The court also distinguished Dambrot v. Central Mich. Univ., 55 F.3d 1177, 1189 (6th Cir. 1995) (upholding the termination of a football coach who used the word "nigger"

in a locker room talk with his team). For a discussion of hate speech codes, see the chapter on student speech issues.

[83] 273 F.3d 460 (2d Cir. 2001).

[84] *Id.* at 468.

[85] Parate v. Isibor, 868 F.2d 821 (6th Cir. 1989).

[86] *Id.* at 827.

[87] 247 F.3d 69 (3d Cir. 2001).

[88] Professor Brown had been teaching at California University of Pennsylvania for almost three decades and had been tenured since 1972. He gave a failing grade to a student in a practicum class after the student attended only three of fifteen required meetings. Armenti, the president of the university, ordered that the grade be changed to an "incomplete".

[89] 247 F.3d at 75 (quoting Regents of Univ. of Cal. v. Bakke, 438 U.S. 265, 312 (1978)).

[90] 236 F.3d 888 (7th Cir. 2001).

[91] Keyishian v. Board of Regents, 385 U.S. 589, 603 (1967).

[92] Urofsky v. Gilmore, 216 F.3d 401 (4th Cir. 2000).

[93] However, the Act does allow the state to give employees permission, subject to some review procedures, to access such sites on government-owned or leased equipment.

[94] *Urofsky*, at 409.

[95] *Id.* at 410.

[96] Two years before *Urofsky*, the Court of Appeals for the Tenth Circuit, in Loving v. Boren, 133 F.3d 771 (10th Cir. 1998), upheld a similar law. University officials had blocked access to a number of Internet news groups that contained allegedly obscene material.

[97] 493 U.S. 182 (1990).

[98] 167 F.3d 1146 (7th Cir. 1999).

[99] *Id.* at 1150. *See also* Hetrick v. Martin, 480 F.2d 705 (6th Cir. 1973) (The court held that the First Amendment does not prevent the termination of an untenured teacher whose pedagogical style and philosophy did not conform to those of the school's administration. Academic freedom does not give teachers the right to have their teaching styles "insulated from review" by the superiors.)

[100] 515 U.S. 819, 833 (1995).

[101] 260 F.3d 757 (7th Cir. 2001).

[102] *Id.* at 759.

[103] *Id.*

[104] *Id.* at 760. For a discussion on a related issue, *see* Piarowski v. Prairie State Coll., 759 F.2d 625 (7th Cir. 1985) (upholding a college's decision to move offensive faculty-created artwork away from a heavily-traveled public space to a less-traveled one).

[105] 305 F. Supp. 2d 1217 (D. Kan. 2004).

[106] The message stated, "I was brought up Catholic. I remember being 7 and going into the dark confessional booth for the first time. I knelt down, and my face was only inches from the thin screen that separated me and the one who had the power to condemn me for my evil ways. I was scared to death, for on the other side of that screen was the persona you see before you." *Id.* at 1220.

[107] *Id.* at 1220-1221.

[108] Yacovelli v. Moeser, No. 1:02CV596, 2004 U.S. Dist. LEXIS 9152 (M.D.N.C. May 20, 2004).

[109] *See* Lemon v. Kurtzman, 403 U.S. 602 (1971).

[110] Yacovelli v. Moeser, 2004 U.S. Dist. LEXIS 9152 (M.D.N.C. 2004).

[111] *Id.* at *45.

[112] Yacovelli v. Moeser, 324 F. Supp. 2d 760 (M.D.N.C. 2004).

[113] For a full discussion of acceptable use policies in K-12 settings, see Daniel, P.T.K. and Pauken, P.D., *Educators' Authority and Students' First Amendment Rights on the Way*

[footnote cont.] *to Using the Information Highway: Cyberspace and Schools*, 54 Wash. Univ. J. of Urb. & Contemp. L. 109 (1998).

[114] *See* http://www.emich.edu/public/It/acceptable.html.

[115] Institutions of higher education that also serve as Internet service providers for their students, staff, faculty, and visitors must promulgate and enforce policies to educate college and university personnel about copyright law. See the related discussion of the Digital Millennium Copyright Act of 1998 and the Technology, Education, and Copyright Harmonization Act of 2002 in the chapter on intellectual property.

[116] The Communications Decency Act of 1996 (CDA), 47 U.S.C. § 223, Pub. L. No. 104-104 § 502-552, 110 Stat. 56 (1996); Child Pornography Prevention Act of 1996 (CPPA), 18 U.S.C. § 2256(8), Pub. L. No. 104-208, 110 Stat. 3009-3129 (1996); The Children's Online Protection Act (COPA), 47 U.S.C. § 231, Pub. L. No. 105-277, 112 Stat. 2681-736 (1998); and The Children's Internet Protection Act (CIPA), 20 U.S.C. § 6301 (2002), Pub. L. 106-554, 114 Stat. 2763, 2763A-335 (2000).

[117] *See* Reno v. ACLU, 521 U.S. 844 (1997) (invalidated the CDA); Ashcroft v. Free Speech Coalition, 122 S. Ct. 1389 (2002) (invalidated the CPPA); Ashcroft v. ACLU, 122 S. Ct. 1700 (2000) (invalidated the COPA); and United States v. American Library Association, 123 S. Ct. 2297 (2003) (upheld the CIPA in a 4-Justice plurality, allowing the federal government to withhold funding until libraries install blocking software on their computers).

[118] 457 U.S. 853, 868 (1982).

[119] *Id.* at 867 (from G. Hunt, 9 *Writings of James Madison* 103 (1910)).

[120] For example, see the sections on student and faculty speech issues for a discussion of university organizations, student publications, and academic freedom.

[121] 216 F.3d 401 (4th Cir. 2000).

[122] 133 F.3d 771 (10th Cir. 1998).

[123] *Id.* at 955.

# 7 Tort Liability
## Nathan Roberts, Richard Fossey, and Todd DeMitchell

## Introduction

At one time, American higher education institutions were substantially insulated from legal claims, and the courts treated them with great deference. Today, however, this judicial deference to higher education has eroded. As Bickel and Lake observed, "Courts today enforce business-like responsibilities and rights while preserving some uniqueness in college affairs. Judges are increasingly willing to apply traditional negligence and duty rules to university life and activities and increasingly less willing to view the university as subject to traditional insularity rules."[1] Judicial deference is still afforded to colleges and universities regarding their academic decision-making. However, little deference or differentiation is given to institutions of higher education for the risks associated with many of their activities.

## Influence of Tort Law on Higher Education

A major risk to higher education is exposure to tort suits, particularly suits arising from personal injuries associated with negligence. Broadly defined, a tort is a civil wrong, other than breach of contract, for which the court will provide a remedy in the form of an action for damages.[2] Torts reflect basic policies of equitability and justice in human relations. Individuals can be held legally accountable for their actions or failure to act. "The common thread woven into all torts is the idea of unreasonable interference with the interests of others."[3]

Torts are broadly categorized into three types:

1. Negligence torts-conduct that falls below an acceptable standard of care and results in injury.

2. Intentional torts-actions that are committed with intent, a volitional act,[4] and include such actions as defamation and fraudulent misrepresentation. Some intentional torts, such as assault, battery, trespass, and false imprisonment, may also constitute criminal acts.

3. Strict liability-injuries that result from the creation of unusual hazard such as storage of explosives.

In some jurisdictions, public colleges can avoid tort liability by asserting sovereign or governmental immunity.[5] The applicability of this defense varies from state to state and does not provide the protection it once did. Private colleges cannot claim governmental immunity; however, sometimes they can assert a limited charitable immunity defense that also varies from state to state.

This chapter will focus on three common torts: negligence, defamation, and fraudulent misrepresentation. In addition, it will discuss legal issues surrounding negligence release forms and discuss the duties associated with campus crime.

# Negligence

The law of torts is concerned with the allocation of losses arising out of human activities. The word tort is derived from the Latin word *tortus,* which means twisted. In common use, it is a synonym for wrong. The purpose of the law of torts is to adjust these losses, and to afford compensation for injuries sustained by one person as the result of the conduct of another.

Another influence on a court's decision may be the relative ability of the respective parties to bear a loss. This influence is commonly referred to as the "deep pocket" theory. Often juries and judges show a tendency to favor the poor against the wealthy. However, a more distinct aspect of this theory relates to a party's capacity to avoid the loss, absorb it, or pass it along and distribute it in smaller portions among a larger group. For example, a university with 30,000 students can increase tuition by ten dollars and pass along a $300,000 judgment. Institutional defendants, by price increases and insurance, are better able to distribute to the public the losses that are inevitable in a complex civilization. Rather than place the loss on the shoulders of an individual plaintiff who would be ruined by the loss, the courts have often found ways to shift the burden of the loss to institutional defendants.

## Elements of Negligence

The basic tort concept of negligence consists of the following elements: (1) duty, (2) breach of duty, (3) causation, and (4) damages.[6] Common law holds that everyone is responsible not only for the results of his or her willful acts, but also for injuries to another caused by lack of ordinary care. "Negligent conduct is conduct which involves an unreasonable risk of causing harm."[7]

As a general rule, a person has no affirmative duty to aid or protect another, although there are situations in which a duty of reasonable, prudent care may be owed to another. The existence of a legal duty depends on numerous factors including the status of and relationship between the injured party and the institution. An institution owes a duty to someone if the institution can foresee an unreasonable risk of harm arising from its activities.[8] This inquiry is both factual and legal. The factual review can be called foreseeability in fact, *i.e.*, it is the possibility of harm from a particular type of conduct of such magnitude that a reasonable person would take it into consideration in determining how he or she should act. The legal review balances the likelihood and severity of the harm from the conduct against the alternatives available to the actor, such as the cost of acting in a different manner. Generally, duty is considered a question of law for the court to decide. This is particularly true where the issue turns upon policy factors.

There are three levels of duty: no duty, ordinary duty, and special duty.[9] No duty is often portrayed by the example that there is no duty to come to the aid of a stranger. If there is no duty, there is no liability. An ordinary duty requires one to exercise some care for others' safety. To identify the appropriate level of care, courts postulate a standard of care that, if matched or exceeded, satisfies the duty owed. In most situations, the standard of care that is owed is the level of care that an ordinary and prudent person would exercise in like or similar circumstances. This standard is often called the "reasonable person" standard. The reasonable person possesses ordinary sense, uses ordinary care, and possesses ordinary skills.

Special circumstances sometimes create special duties. For example, while there is no ordinary duty to aid a stranger, if a person's conduct or instrumentality caused the need for aid, then a duty may arise.[10] Sometimes a special duty is owed because a person is a professional, like a doctor, lawyer, or accountant,[11] and owes a special professional level of care. It is important to remember that the term "duty" refers to the first element in a prima facie case of negligence. Accordingly, it is the foremost consideration in a negligence case because without duty there is little more to discuss. However, duty should not be confused with liability. Duty is simply the first element of negligence and the other aspects of a negligence case must also be established.

In *Fox v. Board of Supervisors of Louisiana State University,*[12] a rugby player sued his Minnesota college and Louisiana State University (LSU) after his neck was broken in a rugby tournament, which was sponsored by LSU's rugby team. The Louisiana Supreme Court ruled that the state university was in no special relationship to the plaintiff, and thus the university had no affirmative duty to act in protection of his safety. Further, the court found the university did not have a duty to monitor the actions of the rugby team regarding the tournament at which the player suffered injury.

However, a seventeen-year-old, special student attending a pre-season summer soccer program at the University of Southern Maine successfully asserted on appeal that the university owed her a duty. A male she met at a fraternity party sexually assaulted the student athlete in her university dormitory room. The male accompanied her back to the dormitory. She used her key and let both of them into the dorm. He later came back to her room and assaulted her. The Supreme Judicial Court of Maine held, "[t]he University owed plaintiff as a business invitee, 'a duty to exercise reasonable care in taking such measures as were reasonably necessary for her safety in light of all the existing circumstances.'"[13] Similarly, in *Davidson v. University of North at Carolina Chapel Hill*, a state court found that the university owed a duty to a junior varsity cheerleader who was injured in a regular practice session.[14] The court reasoned that the university owed the junior varsity cheerleader the same level of supervision and safety precautions as provided to members of the cheerleading team because both teams provided valued services to the institution.

If a legal duty is established, the next issue to be determined is whether the institution breached its duty. Breach asks whether the defendant, who owed a duty, acted reasonably. The breach inquiry focuses upon what the institution did compared with what it could have done to avoid harm to the plaintiff. For example, the plaintiff in *Bowden v. City University of New York*[15] slipped and fell on a walkway following a snowstorm at the campus of Kingsborough Community College. A duty is owed "for a hazardous condition created on its premises by precipitation only if the landowner had actual or constructive notice of the conditions and had a reasonably sufficient time from cessation of the precipitation to remedy the condition caused by it."[16] To determine whether the duty owed was breached, the record needed to clarify the amount of time that passed between the end of the snowstorm and the time of the accident. In addition, the record must establish the college's snow and ice removal procedures.

Before negligence is found, an institution's breach of duty must be shown to have been the proximate cause of the injury.[17] In most jurisdictions, "cause" is subdivided into two separate elements: (1) cause-in-fact and (2) legal or proximate cause. The question to be answered regarding the first element is: was the defendant's negligent act (breach of duty) a cause-in-fact of the plaintiff's injuries? This factual inquiry is generally resolved by applying either the "but for" or the "substantial factor" test.[18] The issue is generally decided by the jury, which must determine whether the defendant's action or inaction was a substantial factor in the plaintiff's injury.

The second element (proximate or legal cause) is a shorthand way of asking: as a matter of policy, does society want to allow this plaintiff to recover from this defendant for these particular injuries arising in this particular manner? The court may elect to relieve the defendant of liability because to make the defendant pay for specific damages related to an injury occurring in a certain manner would offend some valid societal policy such as fairness, the proper allocation of resources, or the promotion of some societal value.

Foreseability answl to ? of prox case

Foreseeability is central to the question of proximate cause.[19] If a particular harm is foreseeable, the actor who owes a duty to the one situated in foreseeable harm must take reasonable steps, such as issuing a warning, to reduce the likelihood of that harm. For example, in *Mullins v. Pine Manor College,* the Supreme Judicial Court of Massachusetts recognized that the "concentration of young people, especially young women, on a college campus creates a favorable opportunity for criminal behavior, … and thus the threat of criminal behavior is self-evident."[20]

*damages*

Finally, damages are essential to the negligence tort. The damage issue may be subdivided into two parts: (1) can the victim recover these particular damages inflicted in this particular way, and (2) if so, what is the measure (amount) of such damages? The first question is whether the plaintiff injured this defendant in the manner claimed by the defendant. Sometimes this is a question of law for the judge. The second question— the measure of damage—essentially is a fact issue within the somewhat limited discretion of the fact-finder.[21]

*possible defenses*

If a plaintiff substantiates a prima facie case of negligence, an institution may still be relieved of liability by asserting particular defenses such as contributory negligence, comparative negligence, and assumption of the risk. Contributory negligence historically barred a plaintiff's recovery in a tort action. The doctrine of contributory negligence provides that a plaintiff who is negligent is denied any recovery, even if his or her negligence is slight when compared to that of the defendant. Under the doctrine of contributory negligence, the plaintiff must act as a reasonably prudent person for his or her own safety and the safety of others.

*comparative neg = reduces amount of recovery in proportion to plaintiff's fault*

Within the past four decades, many states have abandoned the concept of contributory negligence in favor of a comparative negligence standard. In comparative negligence jurisdictions, the plaintiff's contributory negligence is not a complete bar to recovery but reduces the award of damages in proportion to the plaintiff's fault. Thus, a plaintiff who is 40 percent at fault may recover 60 percent from a defendant, such as a university, if the institution and its agents are found to be 60 percent at fault. In considering the comparative fault of a party, the court assesses the nature of the conduct of the parties.[22] Accordingly, under the doctrine of comparative fault, the fault of all persons who contributed to the injury must be determined, and the partial fault of the plaintiff may limit the amount of damages awarded but will not bar a recovery.

*assumption of risk*

Liability will not be imposed when it is determined that a plaintiff has assumed the risk of the injury that occurred. For example, in *Rubtchinsky v. State University of New York,*[23] a student was injured in a game between first and second year students that was conducted as part of an orientation program. The court found that the student, who had been offered several orientation activities, chose to play the game and ruled that by voluntarily assuming the risks of the game, he assumed the risks of his injury as a participant.

The American system of jurisprudence places the economic loss incident to any misfortune on one of three individuals absent insurance: (1) the person suffering the misfortune (anything from a broken bone to damaged property); (2) the person or institution who negligently or deliberately causes the misfortune to occur; and (3) under certain statutory schemes, the party deemed by the legislature to be appropriate (*e.g.* Workman's Compensation).

There is no way to transfer the pain, annoyance, or distress that accompanies any misfortune; however, insurance serves to distribute the risk of economic loss to as many parties as possible among those who are subject to the same kind of risk. By paying a pre-set amount (premium) into a general fund out of which payment will be made for an economic loss of the defined type, each member contributes to a small degree toward compensation for losses suffered by any member of the group. The member has no way of knowing in advance whether he or she will receive in compensation more than was contributed or whether she or he will merely be paying for the losses of others in the group; but the primary goal is to exchange the gamble of doing it alone for the opportunity to pay a fixed amount into an insurance fund, knowing that the amount is the maximum that the insured party will lose on account of the particular type of risk insured against.[24]

This broad sharing of economic risk is the principle of risk distribution and can be applied to losses that occur from property damage (such as a fire-demolished building) or injuries to students or other individuals on campus.[25] In the context of higher education institutions insuring against losses to equipment or buildings or losses due to institutional negligence, the premium paid into the fund is considered a cost of providing services and is computed into the institution's normal operating expenses.

## Institutional Duty of Care

*In loco parentis*[26] is a Latin term that conveys the idea that colleges and universities have a parental relationship with students and act in actual parents' absence to protect the students' welfare. Over time, *in loco parentis* suggested the notion that most student problems are quietly handled within the college or university without involving outside authorities, such as the police or the courts.

In the United States, courts recognized the concept of *in loco parentis* through the middle part of the last century. For example, in *Gott v. Berea College,* the court wrote, "College authorities stand *in loco parentis* concerning the physical and mental training of their students."[27] During this period, the courts did not scrutinize the activities of colleges and universities very closely. However, while *in loco parentis* was the most prominent feature of the student-institutional relationship in this period, the legal rules of *in loco parentis* were just a feature of an overall system protecting colleges and universities. Courts protected universities by drawing upon a variety of legal paradigms from other recognized areas of insularity. Universities were viewed as part family, part charity, part government, part public, and part private.

However, as time progressed, these notions of insularity were subject to legal attack. Colleges and universities, like other social institutions, have increasingly been compelled to come to the legal system and explain their conduct. This new perspective views the relationship between student and university as one of shared responsibility and a balancing of university authority and student freedom.[28] Duty is the method of monitoring the balance.

Cases involving the hazing of students highlight the modern college or university's potential for liability based on an emerging duty of care. Historically, courts were reluctant to impose a duty on higher education institutions for injuries to students that arose from hazing activities by other students. However, in *Furek v. University of Delaware,*[29] the Supreme Court of Delaware determined that the magnitude of the foreseeable risk and the institution's policies towards hazing imposed a duty of reasonable care for the safety of students. *Furek* involved a student who was injured in a hazing incident involving alcohol use. The university had a policy against hazing, which mirrored state laws prohibiting these practices, but the university's hazing policy was not properly implemented. Campus police were not properly instructed concerning the university's policy. There were formal policy statements and announcements regarding fraternity-related disorder and discipline, but the court found little evidence of affirmative steps by the institution to implement these formal policies. The court reasoned that the university's policies against hazing and the university's knowledge of previous hazing incidents in fraternities created a special duty. *Furek* established that a university, when undertaking a duty, must do so properly when people (mainly students) have come to rely on what the university undertook to do.

In *Knoll v. Board of Regents,*[30] the Supreme Court of Nebraska used reasoning that paralleled the *Furek* decision. In this case, a student who was injured in a hazing activity filed suit against the university, alleging that it acted negligently in failing to enforce prohibitions against hazing, alcohol consumption, and physically abusive behavior. The state supreme court reversed a grant of summary judgment to the university, finding that the hazing activities were foreseeable by the university, which had knowledge of previous instances of hazing by other fraternities and of specific instances of possession of alcohol, alcohol abuse, and assaults involving the fraternity that had subjected the student to hazing. The court took the view that it is the risk reasonably to be perceived that is the determinant of whether a duty is owed.

Adopting a different rationale justifying institutional liability for hazing, the Vermont Supreme Court, in *Brueckner v. Norwich University,*[31] examined the experience of a student attending a military college who was subjected to incidents of hazing that included verbal and physical harassment by upperclassmen known as "the cadre." The student reported the hazing incidents to university officials but eventually withdrew from the institution, thinking that his situation would not improve. His scholarship was terminated, and he brought suit against the institution. A lower court found the institution liable for assault and battery, negligent infliction of emotional distress, intentional infliction of emotional distress, and negligent supervision.

The Vermont Supreme Court affirmed the lower court's decision holding the institution liable for the tortuous conduct of the cadre and affirmed an award of compensatory damages. The court ruled that the university would be liable for the actions of the cadre if these cadets were acting within the scope of employment as agents of the institution. Although the institution had adopted policies against hazing, it had charged the cadre members with indoctrinating and orienting new students. The court reasoned that a jury could find that the members of the cadre were performing a general duty to indoctrinate and orient on behalf of the institution and the cadre's hazing activities were within the scope of employment. The institution was liable for the tortuous acts of the cadre both because the institution had authorized the indoctrination and orientation and because the institution was negligent in meeting a duty of reasonable care to control and supervise the cadre.

While courts have acknowledged the possibility that a special duty relationship will create a basis for negligent liability, it is generally the rule that colleges and universities are not insurers of students' safety or the safety of guests on their campuses. A prime example of this analysis is found in *Bradshaw v. Rawlings.*[32] Bradshaw was rendered a quadriplegic when a car in which he was a passenger struck a parked vehicle on the return trip from a class picnic. The sophomore class advisor, who was a faculty member, participated in planning the picnic and signed a check, drawn on class funds, that was later used to purchase beer. Additionally, flyers announcing the picnic and featuring drawings of beer mugs were prominently displayed on campus. However, neither the advisor nor any other faculty or staff member attended the picnic. The jury found in favor of Bradshaw and awarded damages against Rawlings (the driver of the car), the college, the beer distributor, and the local municipality.

In charging the jury, the trial court did not hold the college to any greater duty of care than that of a reasonable person. However, because under the common law, no duty exists to control the conduct of third persons (such as Rawlings) to prevent them from causing harm to others (such as Bradshaw), a special relationship would have to be recognized between the college and either Bradshaw or Rawlings in order for the college to be found liable.

The Court of Appeals for the Third Circuit held that in submitting the liability question to the jury under the simple negligence standard, "the district court assumed that such a duty existed ..."[33] Further, the appellate court, in an effort to determine whether a duty existed on the part of the university, proceeded to examine "the competing individual, public, and social interests implicated" in the case.[34] Beginning with the oft-quoted statement that the modern American college is not an insurer of the safety of its students, the appellate court reviewed at some length the changes in the student-college relationship from the days of *in loco parentis* through the change in the voting age to eighteen and student rights cases in the 1970s.

The court found that, as a result of this change of relationship and reallocation of responsibilities, society now considered college students to be adults rather than children. The court concluded that students had no special relationship with their university per se; if a specific duty of care existed, it would have to be proven by some other special interest or relationship. Therefore, the college could not be held liable for Bradshaw's injuries.

However, a special relationship has been found to exist in some cases. For example, in *Tarasoff v. Regents of the University of California,*[35] a university psychotherapist failed to warn his patient's victim of the patient's dangerous tendencies after the patient had stated he would kill the victim. When he did in fact kill the victim, the court held that the patient-therapist relationship created a duty of reasonable care to warn others of the foreseeable risks of the patient's homicidal threat.

While the duty to warn of a danger was predicated on a special relationship in *Tarasoff,* courts have been reluctant to extend the concept of special duty in cases involving students and higher education institutions. The Supreme Court of Utah rejected a special duty of supervision in *Beach v. University of Utah.*[36] Beach, a twenty-year-old student, was severely injured during a geology field trip when she fell off a cliff at night while others slept. The faculty members in charge of the expedition knew she had been drinking before the accident and, in fact, had drunk alcohol. The Utah Supreme Court held that neither the university nor the faculty members breached any special duty by failing to supervise the student's conduct, failing to enforce laws and school rules against underage drinking, or refraining from drinking themselves. The Court declared that colleges must not be saddled with unrealistic, unenforceable duties of supervision that undermine the educational goals of a college education.

Student-institutional relationships involving some degree of institutional supervision or control may create a special duty relationship. Judges have recognized that higher education institutions owe a legal duty to students to provide proper instruction and adequate supervision in classroom contexts that involve high risks, foreseeable harm, and the instructor's special expertise.[37] Because of the degree of supervision and control exercised over school-sponsored intercollegiate athletic programs, several courts have imposed a special duty relationship in this particular context of student-institutional relationships. For example, in *Kleinknecht v. Gettysburg College*,[38] a federal appeals court upheld liability specifically predicated on a special duty relationship. After a student who had been recruited to play lacrosse suffered a fatal heart attack during practice, the parents of the student brought a negligence action against the college, arguing that a special relationship existed between the student and the college by virtue of the student's status as a member of the intercollegiate athletic team. A federal appeals court agreed, reasoning that because the student was recruited to play lacrosse and, at the time of his heart attack he was participating in a scheduled athletic practice for a college-sponsored intercollegiate team, a special relationship existed that was sufficient to impose a duty of reasonable care.

Having determined that a special relationship existed, the court then reviewed the record to evaluate whether the incident was foreseeable and assess whether a duty of care was owed. The court determined that it was foreseeable that a member of the College's interscholastic lacrosse team could suffer a serious injury during an athletic event and concluded the college owed a duty to the student to take precautions against the risks of injury. In making its determination, the federal court clearly intended to set limits on the class of students to which this decision would apply, stating:

> There is a distinction between a student injured while participating as an inter-collegiate athlete in a sport for which he was recruited and a student injured at a college while pursuing his private interests, scholastic or otherwise. This distinction serves to limit the class of students to whom a college owes the duty of care that arises here. Had (the student) been participating in a fraternity football game, for example, the College might not have owed him the same duty or perhaps any duty at all.[39]

Universities may be susceptible to liability pursuant to a special relationship that can exist if the university is the owner of land (a landlord). Several cases that followed *Mullins* support the contention that the landlord-tenant relationship creates a special duty to protect students residing in residence halls. In the case of *Cutler v. Board of Regents of State of Florida*,[40] a state appeals court allowed a female university student who was assaulted and raped in her residence hall room to amend her complaint, asserting that "recent Florida decisions have held that a landlord, who recognizes and assumes the duty to protect his tenants from foreseeable criminal conduct, may be liable if he fails to take reasonable precautions to prevent injury to his tenants from this conduct."[41] In *Miller v. State*,[42] the Court of Appeals of New York affirmed negligence on the part of the university for failing to protect a female student from rape in a residence hall. The appeals court noted:

> As a landowner, the State must act as a reasonable (person) in maintaining property in a reasonably safe condition in view of all the circumstances ... Under this standard, a landlord has a duty to maintain minimal security measures, related to a specific building itself, in the face of foreseeable criminal intrusion upon tenants ... Thus, defendant here had a duty to take the rather minimal security measure of keeping the dormitory doors locked when it had notice of the likelihood of criminal intrusions.[43]

Negligence predicated on the landlord-tenant relationship was affirmed in *Nero v. Kansas State University*[44] in which a female student who was sexually assaulted in her residence hall persuaded the Supreme Court of Kansas that Kansas State University owed a duty of reasonable care to students in residence halls once it exercised its discretion to make such housing available to students. While declining to hold that the university-student relationship itself imposes a duty on institutions to protect students, the court did rule that a university has a duty to regulate and supervise foreseeable dangers occurring on its property. Finding that the trial court erred in granting summary judgment to the institution, the state supreme court reversed and remanded the case, emphasizing that the trial court must resolve the question of whether, at the time of the attack, the institution's agents should have foreseen the attack on the student.

## Release of Liability

Some colleges and universities prepare liability release forms that they require students to sign before permitting them to participate in varsity sports, extramural sport competition, field trips, study abroad programs, or other institution-sponsored activities that involve some risk of physical injury.[45] Do such release forms compose part of a good risk management strategy or are such documents unenforceable and, thus, just worthless pieces of paper?

The courts are split on the validity of negligence release forms when used by colleges or universities to reduce their exposure to students' injury claims. At least two courts have upheld the validity of such releases,[46] and at least one court concluded that a university's negligence release was invalid as a violation of public policy.[47]

*Lemoine v. Cornell University*[48] is a representative case in which a New York state court honored a release form. In *Lemoine*, a student sued Cornell University for negligence arising from injuries she suffered when she fell from a climbing wall during the first session of a seven-week, rock-climbing course offered by the university's outdoor education program.

The student had signed a contract agreeing to follow climbing wall safety policies and to hold the university harmless for any injuries she suffered from using the climbing wall, including injuries caused by the university's negligence. The university moved to dismiss the case, citing the negligence-release contract the student signed, and the student responded by arguing that the contract was void as a violation of public policy. She also cited a state law that prevented amusement parks and recreational facilities from enforcing negligence release clauses.[49] The state appellate court ruled in favor of the university, finding that the state law on which the student relied did not apply to higher education institutions offering instruction in recreational activities. In the court's view, the release form was a contract the student signed which unambiguously acknowledged the inherent risks of rock climbing and the use of climbing walls, and the language holding the university harmless for injuries incurred during rock climbing instruction was legally enforceable.

On the other hand, the West Virginia Supreme Court of Appeals refused to enforce an "anticipatory release" signed by a student as a condition of participating in the West Virginia University Rugby Club.[50] In that release, the student agreed to waive "any and all claims, both present and future, arising from my participation in rugby club activities, including but not limited to negligence, property damage, personal injury, and wrongful death."[51] After the student was injured while playing rugby, he sued the University of West Virginia, but his suit was dismissed by the trial court on the grounds that the release he had signed absolutely barred him from recovery. On appeal, however, the West Virginia Supreme Court of Appeals reversed. In the appellate court's view, the university was performing a public service by sponsoring the rugby club and could not exculpate itself from tort liability.

The university had argued that rugby was merely a recreational activity and did not constitute an essential service. But the West Virginia court disagreed. "This court has long held athletics are integral and important elements of the educational mission at West Virginia University."[52] By providing recreational activities to students, the court said, the university was performing a public service for which it owed the students a duty of care.[53] Furthermore, the court reasoned the university held a decisive bargaining advantage when it required the plaintiff to sign the anticipatory release as a condition of playing rugby. The university had utilized an attorney in drafting the release, while the student apparently had not had the benefit of legal counsel. Concluding that the university violated public policy in seeking to enforce its negligence release against the student in such circumstances, the appellate declared the release void as a matter of West Virginia public policy.

Given the disagreement among the courts, colleges and universities that wish to require students to sign negligence releases as a condition of participating in a particular activity should consult legal counsel to determine whether such releases are enforceable in their jurisdiction. If exculpatory releases are used, they should be simple and easily understandable. Furthermore, although some courts will uphold negligence releases against a claim of simple negligence, they will generally not enforce such releases against a claim of reckless behavior, intentional misconduct, or gross negligence.[54] Finally, while negligence release forms may form a part of a valid risk management plan, they are no substitute for adequate insurance. Under no circumstances should an institution drop or reduce its liability insurance coverage under a mistaken belief that negligence release clauses will shield them from tort liability.

## Campus Crime Reporting

Under the provisions of the Clery Act,[55] initially passed in 1990, all colleges and universities receiving federal funds must file annual reports with the U.S. Department of Education about criminal activity on their campuses, their off-campus property, and certain public property areas. The Clery Act requires that institutions also establish procedures for responding to campus sexual assaults. In addition, several published court opinions issued over the last twenty years make clear that institutions can be civilly liable for criminal acts committed against their students if campus security is handled negligently.

In short, college and university officials now have definite responsibilities in connection with campus crime. These responsibilities fall into three broad categories: 1) reporting crime incidents in accordance with federal law, 2) minimizing the risk of civil liability for crimes that occur on campuses, and 3) instituting comprehensive crime prevention policies and procedures for their respective institutions.

Although media attention in recent years may give the impression that college campuses are crime-prone environments, the nation's colleges and universities are relatively safe places to be. For example, according to a report issued by the U.S. Department of Education, the homicide rate on the nation's college campuses was only 0.07 per 100,000 enrolled students in 1999, compared to 14.1 per 100,000 persons ages seventeen to twenty-nine and 5.7 per 100,000 persons overall. In other words, "students on the campuses of postsecondary institutions [are] significantly safer than the nation as a whole."[56]

Nevertheless, although relatively rare, campus crime has particular characteristics. These characteristics, if known, can help campus administrators better plan their crime-prevention strategies. First of all, most campus crime is committed by students against other students, not by outside intruders.[57] By and large, student-on-student crime involves relatively minor offenses—theft and alcohol-related offenses, for example. Freshman women are more likely to be rape victims than college women as a whole, probably due to the fact that first-year female students are less likely to have developed good self-protection strategies.[58] Alcohol is frequently a factor in campus crimes, with both victims and perpetrators to be more likely than not to be under the influence of alcohol at the time the crime is committed.[59]

Currently, institutions are required to provide statistics on the following crimes that are reported to campus security officials or the police within the three most recent calendar years: homicide, forcible and non-forcible sex offenses, robbery, aggravated assault, burglary, motor vehicle theft, and arson. Liquor law violations, illegal weapons possession, and drug violations must also be reported as well as certain hate crimes.[60]

In addition, the Clery Act requires colleges and universities to provide sexual assault victims with information about their option to notify law enforcement agencies of the crime against them and to notify victims that campus personnel will assist them in contacting these agencies. Under the Act, institutions are required to provide sexual assault victims with a change in their academic or living situation if so requested, and other options are reasonably available. Victims are also entitled to receive notification of campus disciplinary procedures for sex offenses. Both accused and accuser are entitled to the same opportunities to have others present during disciplinary procedures, and institutions are required to notify both the accuser and the accused of the outcome of any institutional disciplinary proceeding alleging a sex offense.

Finally, and perhaps most importantly, higher education institutions are required to give students and employees timely warnings about criminal activity that may constitute an ongoing threat to the campus community. For example, a college would be required to notify staff and students if a serial rapist were operating in the area or a particular campus locale had become the scene of repeated muggings. A detailed discussion of the Clery Act's obligations are beyond the scope of this chapter, but all campus administrators who work in the area of student services should have a thorough understanding of their individual responsibilities under the Act. Institutions that violate the Clery Act's provisions may be fined or suspended from participation in federal student financial aid programs.[61]

## Crime Prevention Checklist

Institutions should develop a comprehensive crime prevention plan, involving not only campus law enforcement authorities, but student services and housing personnel, grounds keeping and maintenance departments, college counselors, and medical staff. At a minimum, the following issues should be addressed:

- A campus security plan should reflect the institution's efforts to prevent campus crime. The plan should address lighting, shrubbery, police patrols, escort services, call boxes in isolated areas, and residence hall security.[62]

- A routine procedure should be put in place to notify the campus community about serious criminal activity that constitutes an ongoing threat to students and employees. The Cleary Act requires this.
- Campus disciplinary procedures should be reviewed to make sure they are adequate to address complaints of serious sexual misconduct. All persons participating in campus adjudications should be trained and thoroughly cognizant of their roles.
- The institution should develop a clear policy about which kinds of student sexual offense accusations will be handled internally and which will be turned over to outside law enforcement agencies.
- Institutions should develop routine procedures for collecting and reporting crime data in compliance with the Clery Act.

## Defamation

Defamation is a type of tort distinguishable from negligence because it is associated with an intentional act. Defamation may take one of two forms, oral (slander) or written publication (libel). A defamatory statement, either verbal or written, is one that injures a person's reputation and diminishes the respect, esteem, and goodwill in which the person is held with a community.[63] The statement must be published to some third party and must be capable of defamatory meaning and be understood as referring to the plaintiff in a defamatory sense.[64] A communication is defamatory if it tends to harm the reputation of another as to lower him in the estimation of the community or to deter third persons from associating or dealing with him.[65]

A prima facie case for defamation includes the following elements: (1) the material must be published to a third party;[66] (2) the matter must be capable of a defamatory meaning;[67] (3) the third party person must have understood the publication as referring to the plaintiff; and (4) the matter must have been understood in a defamatory sense.[68]

However, there are factors that affect these four elements. "Ordinarily, the defendant is not liable for any publication made to others by the plaintiff himself, even though it was to be expected that he might publish it."[69] Every repetition of a defamatory statement is a publication in itself," even if the publishing party tries to make it clear that he or she does not believe the defamation.[70] Usually there is no recovery for statements of pure opinion, which does not assert by implication the existence of false, defamatory facts to justify the opinion. Mere abusive language and ridicule, obviously not intended to be taken literally, has not been regarded as defamatory. Similarly, insults and invective directed to the plaintiff but not communicated to a third party are not considered defamatory.

Defamation is organized into two concepts: *per se* and *per quod.* Defamation *per se* does not require the plaintiff to prove actual injury or loss, and this rule applies to both slander and libel. As one state appeals court noted, "When a publication is libelous *per se*, a prima facie case presumption of malice and a conclusive presumption of legal injury arise entitling the victim to recover at least nominal damages without proof of special damages."[71]

Under common law principles four categories are considered defamatory *per se*: (1) words that impute the commission of criminal offense; (2) words that impute a loathsome or communicable disease; (3) words that impute an inability to perform one's lawful trade, profession, or business, and (4) words that impute lack of chastity to a woman.[72] An affirmative defense of qualified privilege can be asserted in response to a *per se* finding. Truth and good motive can also be raised as defense.[73]

The second concept, defamation *per quod*, requires that the plaintiff show actual damage in order to recover. The plaintiff is required to prove that the publication of the statement was the cause of loss or harm. Basically, *per quod* means that the words on their face are not harmful. Plaintiff must establish the harm, whereas in *per se* defamation harm is presumed.

Defenses to defamation include truth, opinion privilege, absolute privilege, and qualified privilege.[74] The defendant carries the burden of properly asserting these defenses, which are applied in those situations in which there are public policy reasons for permitting freedom of expression.[75] In general, one who publishes a defamatory statement of fact is not subject to liability for defamation if the statement is substantially true. While substantial truth is normally a question for the jury, where no reasonable jury could find that substantial truth had not been established, the question is one of law. When a faculty member composed a memorandum to an associate about a colleague's lack of fitness to serve in the capacity of department chair, the memorandum pointed out that the colleague had been an inpatient in a psychiatric unit due to a sleep disorder and used infertility drugs. In response to a defamation claim, the university contended that since the plaintiff admitted certain facts stated in the memorandum to be truthful, she could not support her defamation claim. The Appeals Court of Illinois found that the plaintiff corroborated the veracity of a number of the claims and ruled that inasmuch as the contents of the disparaging memorandum were "substantially true," her defamation claims must fail.[76]

While in one sense all opinions imply facts, the question of whether a statement of opinion is actionable as defamation is one of degree. The more generalized the opinion, the more likely the opinion is not actionable as a matter of law. The emphasis in the test for determining the opinion privilege is on whether the statement contains an objectively verifiable assertion: if the statement is not capable of verification, it is protected as purely a statement of opinion. For example, if the faculty member in the previous case expressed the view that the colleague lacked fitness to serve in that role, the statement, standing alone, might be regarded as a statement of opinion. Similarly, a court could find that a general accusation of "unprofessional conduct" might be protected opinion, but if the opinion was accompanied by additional allegations of sexual misconduct with colleagues that permitted an inference the opinion was based on facts, then the opinion privilege would not apply. In a case reflecting this principle, a reviewing court reasoned that the additional allegations would permit a claim for libel per se.[77]

An absolute privilege is limited to six situations: (1) judicial proceedings, (2) legislative proceedings, (3) executive communications, (4) consent of the plaintiff,[78] (5) husband and wife communications, and (6) political broadcasts.[79] Absolute privilege applies to those situations where "the importance of the unrestricted exchange of information is so great that even defamatory statements made with actual malice are privileged."[80] However, absolute privilege has its limits. For example, a student might be insulated from liability for utterances made against a professor in a campus disciplinary hearing, but the privilege would not apply to statements the student then repeated outside the hearing.[81]

Qualified privilege is the more commonly asserted privilege. Qualified privilege for higher education professionals must meet the following standards in their job-related communications: (1) they must be performing acts within their duties; (2) they must only release the allegedly defamatory information to individuals or officials who have the right to receive such information; and (3) they must act in good faith and without malice.[82] For example, a university president wrote in a report to the board of trustees that "administrative personnel in place in March 1995 are inadequate for the job."[83] Although the administrator was not named, there was no dispute that the statements were made about the plaintiff. The Ohio court found that the communication between the president and the board of trustees was made in the "interest of the defendant, limited to the scope of plaintiff's duties with defendant, and that it was published on a proper occasion and in a proper manner."[84] Therefore, the communication was protected by qualified privilege. However, the qualified privilege could be defeated if the plaintiff proves actual malice. The court defined actual malice as a publication made "with knowledge that it was false or with reckless disregard of whether it was false or not."[85]

Since chairs, deans, and presidents often comment on the work of employees as a part of the responsibilities of the position, an entitlement to a qualified privilege regarding their communications is often asserted. For example, when a staff member in a university department was terminated for insubordination, the chair wrote and disseminated a memo to members of the department explaining the dismissal. The memorandum included an explanation of the sequence of events leading to the dismissal, including accusations that the employee had brought false charges against the chair and had been insubordinate. When the former employee alleged defamation, the department chair was insulated from liability by a qualified privilege. The state court reasoned that the chair's memo was made in good faith and upheld an important interest. The chairman had an interest in the department's operation and sought to protect against the undermining of employee morale. He distributed the memo in question to members of the department in order to put an end to misleading rumors and inaccurate accounts of the employee's dismissal. Viewed in this light, the appeals court held the memo was limited in its scope and communicated on in proper form and to appropriate parties.[86]

Faculty may also assert a qualified privilege. In one case, a faculty member's critical comments in letters of reference were protected by a qualified privilege as long as the author did not act with malicious purpose, bad faith or recklessness in making a negative recommendation.[87] Alternately, a faculty memorandum circulated in a department that urged removal of the chair following a vote of "no confidence" by the faculty, was protected by a qualified privilege. The court ruled that, broadly applied, the common-interest, qualified privilege would insulate professors in a college or university setting in which a common interest in preserving academic reputation and faculty integrity would motivate these employees to communicate with each other.[88]

In many ways, higher education, and perhaps all education, is a communicative enterprise. Information is conveyed and judgments are continually made orally and in writing. The statements often have consequences. Harm can result in the form of poor evaluations and lost tenure bids. While defamation law provides a remedy or a vindication for words that are false or injurious to reputation, the law provides affirmative defenses that attempt to balance the interests of the individual with the organization's need to insure effective communication.

## Fraudulent Misrepresentation

Colleges and universities are in the business of providing information for the guidance of others. Students and their parents often rely on statements from institutional personnel as well as information contained in brochures and websites when making decisions and planning courses of action. Claims of fraud arise when institutional representatives misrepresent a material fact in an effort to deceive and the student may be said to have reasonably relied on the misrepresentation leading to an economic loss.[89]

While judges have been reluctant to recognize claims of fraudulent misrepresentation involving non-profit higher education institutions, proprietary institutions have been vulnerable to these suits, in part because the profit motive for encouraging students to enroll may lead to intentional misrepresentations of programs and services. In one case involving a for-profit business and technical institute, the court rescinded a contract between the student and institute based on evidence the institution's agents failed to provide the promised training and induced the student to enroll using deceptive practices.[90] In another instance, a student with limited English language skills prevailed on a claim that he was deceived about his aptitude for a computer course by agents of a private, proprietary school that then failed to provide the requisite instruction at his ability level.[91]

Claims of fraud may implicate institutional liability when all the elements of the claim are well pleaded. In *Craig v. Forest Institute of Psychology*,[92] a state appeals court identified the elements of a fraud claim to include a false representation of a material fact upon which the party reasonably relied to his or her detriment and injury. Student-plaintiffs presented evidence that the institute represented the students would be able to obtain masters and doctoral degrees in psychology and be licensed in the state. The students contended that the representatives of the institute knew it could not continue to operate the branch campus serving the students when enrollment of the previous institute's students fell, but the institute continued to recruit students while failing to disclose its precarious financial position. These allegations and the evidence on which they were based created a question of whether the representatives of the institute had defrauded the students and justified returning this question to the trial court for further proceedings.

In general, a claim of fraudulent misrepresentation must be predicated upon specific representations that were known to be false by those making the representations. When a student, relying on the advice of an employee of the college or university, establishes that the employee made a misrepresentation of a material existing fact upon which the student reasonably relied and which proximately caused injury, a claim of fraudulent misrepresent may be established. For example, when a dean and Vice-President for Academic Affairs gave assurances to a student that he could enroll in a specific degree program, despite knowing that the institution did not plan to offer such a program, the student's detrimental reliance on those promises created a basis for personal liability for the dean and vice-president.[93]

Courts have generally rejected fraud claims because the proof of justifiable reliance on a false assertion of fact leading to actual injury is difficult to establish.[94] For example, in *Lidecker v. Kendall College*,[95] students in the nursing program at the institution filed suit alleging fraud when the program failed to receive accreditation. They argued that the fact that the program was not accredited was not mentioned in the catalog. An Illinois appeals court found that the institution had not committed fraud when it omitted a statement about accreditation in the catalog, as the omission was not intended to induce the students to enroll or to deceive them. The lack of accreditation did not cause injury, as other graduates of the program had obtained employment, and the students failed to show that the omission was a material one. Also, statements made by the president and program director assuring them that accreditation would be obtained were found by the court to be statements of opinion and not actionable in fraud.

However, courts will recognize claims for fraud or misrepresentation that allege than an educational institution failed to provide specifically promised educational services, such as the failure to provide promised courses in a particular subject.[96] Courts generally will not inquire into whether an institution properly performed a promised educational service, but they will rule on claims that the institution failed to perform the service at all. The key inquiry is whether the issue involves the nuances of educational processes and theories or an objective assessment of whether the institution made a good-faith effort to perform on its promise.[97]

In *Alsides v. Brown Institute, Ltd.*,[98] a student sued his educational institution, alleging that it had agreed but (1) failed to provide instruction on the installation and upgrade of Unix operating system software, (2) failed to provide hands-on training, (3) did not have enough computers to teach the courses, and (4) did not deliver the number of hours of instruction described in the materials given to students. The state appeals court adopted the view that a student may bring an action against an educational institution for fraud or misrepresentation if the institution failed to perform on specific promises it made to the student and the claim would not involve an inquiry into the nuances of education processes or theories.[99]

While a non-profit college or university's exposure to claims of fraudulent misrepresentation has been restricted, employees of these institutions may be vulnerable for individual liability in some unique circumstances. In *Minger v. Green*,[100] a federal appeals court reversed an immunity defense advanced by a housing administrator based on a finding that the complaint stated a claim for intentional misrepresentation that could create individual liability for the death of a student. The federal appeals court reasoned the parent's pleading was sufficient to allege an act on the part of the housing director that involved intentionally misleading the parent concerning the cause and seriousness of a residence hall fire. In order to establish a claim, the parent was obligated to allege a material misrepresentation that was known to be false and made with the intent that the statement would be acted upon. The housing official had responded to the parent's requests to know the cause of a fire in the residence hall where her son, a student with dyslexia and perceptual/spatial disorientation, resided. The court noted that the parent alleged that the housing administrator never responded to the parent's requests to know the cause of the fire, discouraged her from further investigation, knew or should have known that the parent would rely on his statements, and as a result, that the parent and student would fail to take steps to protect the student from the risk of another fire. Finally, the complaint alleged that, as a result of reliance on director's statements, those statements became a substantial factor in the student's death. Since these allegations were sufficient to state a claim for intentional misrepresentation on the part of the housing administrator, the case was returned to the lower court for further proceedings.

Misrepresentation and fraud claims are no longer novel issues. Universities and colleges must carefully review information about programs and degrees to insure accuracy. Recruiters and other institutional representatives should be adequately trained to accurately report programs and services. Finally, all faculty and staff should provide adequate and accurate verbal and written responses to inquiries, regularly update all brochures, and include date disclaimers on written materials. Websites that are likely to be utilized and relied upon by parents and students in their decision-making should also have effective date disclaimers. When the institution is no longer using a web site, it should be disconnected or deleted.

## Concluding Remarks

Colleges are institutions that have responsibilities to large numbers of individuals including recently emancipated adults and significant numbers of employees. These institutions have a plethora of outside business arrangements. All these relationships highlight the need for colleges to be proactive in risk management. Our society's proclivity to litigate real damages and trivial inconveniences highlights the need for vigilance. The number of lawsuits filed against colleges and universities is not abating. "As a result, the time and expense spent on litigation and defense of claims by higher education institutions, administrators, faculty members, trustees, regents, in-house counsel have also continued to increase."[101]

Increased awareness of the contours of duties owed, both ethical and legal, on the part of all who may be subject to suits is an important step. Adopting a risk management stance, which "includes a variety of efforts by legal counsel and others to identify risks and develop appropriate policies and strategies in advance of any legal dispute,"[102] is an excellent beginning point. A commitment to a safe campus that extends policy pronouncements to include habits of action and habits of mind provides a foundation for managing the risk associated with the activities and life of institutions of higher education.

## Endnotes

[1] ROBERT D. BICKEL & PETER E. LAKE, THE RIGHTS AND RESPONSIBILITIES OF THE MODERN UNIVERSITY—WHO ASSUMES THE RISKS OF COLLEGE LIFE 105 (1999).

[2] "A civil action for tort is initiated and maintained, by the injured for the purpose of obtaining compensation for the injury suffered, whereas in a criminal proceeding the action is brought by the state to protect the interests of the public from actions of a wrongdoer." KERN ALEXANDER & M. DAVID ALEXANDER, AMERICAN PUBLIC SCHOOL LAW 549 (5th Ed. 2001).

[3] WILLIAM PROSSER & W. PAGE KEETON, PROSSER AND KEETON ON TORTS 6 (5th ed. 1984).

[4] "If the actor knows that the consequences are certain, or substantially certain, to result from an act and still goes ahead, he or she is treated by the law as if he or she had, in fact, desired to produce the result." KERN ALEXANDER & M. DAVID ALEXANDER, AMERICAN PUBLIC SCHOOL LAW 549 (5th Ed. 2001).

[5] *For example see*, Mississippi (Miss. Code Ann § 11-46-1 et seq. (Supp. 1999), Ohio (R.C. 2744.03(A)(5), and South Carolina (S.C. Code Ann. § 15-78-60(25) (Supp. 1999).

[6] *See* Frank L. Maraist & Thomas Galligan, Louisiana Tort Law (1996).

[7] Todd A. DeMitchell, *The Educator and Tort Liability: An Inservice Outline of a Duty Owed*, 154 Educ. L. Rep. 417, 421 (2001).

[8] For a discussion of the limits of a university's liability, *see* Korellas v. Ohio State Univ., 779 N.E.2d 1112 (Ohio Ct. Cl. 2003) in which a student athlete who assaulted a delivery person was found not to be an employee, and thus the university was not responsible for his actions.

[9] Bickel & Lake, *supra* note 1.

[10] Restatement (Second) Of Torts §§ 314, 322 (1965).

[11] *See* Board of Trs. v. Coopers & Lybrand, 775 N.E.2d 55 (Ill. App. 1 Dist. 2002), in which a community college district brought an action against auditors alleging professional negligence.

[12] 576 So. 2d 978 (La. 1991).

[13] Stanton v. Univ. of Me. Sys., 773 A.2d 1045, 1049 (Me. 2001).

[14] Davidson v. Univ. of N.C. at Chapel Hill, 544 S.E.2d 920 (N.C. 2001).

[15] 743 N.Y.S.2d 119 (A.D. 2 Dept. 2002).

[16] *Id.* at 120.

[17] *Res ipsa loquitur* ("the thing speaks for itself"), although rare, allows a plaintiff to demonstrate breach without a specific factual finding of breach. In certain cases negligence can be inferred from the facts. For example, in *Byrne v. Boadle*, 159 Eng. Rep. 299 (1863), breach was established when a barrel rolled out of a warehouse's second story window and hit a passerby. The court concluded that barrels do not roll out of windows on their own. Therefore some unspecified negligent act caused the barrel to roll out the window. In an education case, *res ipsa loquitur* was applied when a metal encased frame of glass fell on a student while she was seated in a mobile-unit classroom (Douglas v. Bd. of Educ., 468 N.E.2d 473 (1984)).

[18] *See*, Thomas Galligan, *A Primer on the Patterns of Negligence*, 53 La. L. Rev. 1509 (1993).

[19] *See, e.g.*, Palsgraf v. Long Island R.R., 248 N.Y. 339,162 N.E.99 (1928). Judge Cardozo articulated the doctrine of zone of danger as an essential element of foreseeability.

[20] 449 N.E.2d 331, 335 (1983).

[21] Youn v. Maritime Overseas Corp., 623 So. 2d 1257 (La. 1993).

[22] Maraist & Galligan, *supra* note 6.

[23] 260 N.Y.S.2d 256 (N.Y. Ct. Cl., 1965).

[24] John F. Dobbyn, Insurance Law In a Nutshell (1996).

[25] For an informative discussion of risk management in higher education *see* Brett A. Sokolow, *Risk Management in the Community College*, in Robert C. Cloud (ed.) Legal Issues in the Community College (2004), 85-94.

[26] Sir William Blackstone, in 1769, articulated the doctrine of *in loco parentis*. Blackstone asserted that part of the authority of the parent is delegated to the schoolmaster. According to the *in loco parentis* doctrine, "a parent may … delegate part of his parental authority, … to the tutor or schoolmaster of his child; who is then *in loco parentis*, and has such a portion of the power of the parent committed to his charge, … that of restraint and correction as may be necessary …" 1 William Blackstone Commentaries on the Laws of England, 441 (1769).

[27] 161 S.W. 204, 206 (Ky. 1913).

[28] Bickel & Lake, *supra* note 1.

[29] 594 A.2d 506 (Del. 1991).

[30] 601 N.E.2d 757 (Neb. 1999).

[31] 730 A.2d 1086 (Vt. 1999). *But see* Alton v. Tex. A & M Univ., 168 F.3d 196 (5th Cir. 1999), in which a federal appeals court rejected a claim that hazing by members of university's military training organization violated a student's due process rights.

[32] 612 F. 2d 135 (3d Cir. 1979, *cert. denied*, 446 U.S. 909 (1980).

[33] *Id.* at 138.

[34] *Id.* at 138.

[35] 17 Cal.3d 425, 551 P.2d 334 (1976).

[36] 726 P.2d 413 (Utah 1986).

[37] *See generally,* Fu v. State, 643 N.W.2d 659 (Neb. 2002) (explosion in chemistry laboratory); Garrett v. Northwest Miss. Junior Coll., 674 S.2d 1 (Miss. 1996) (injury in using milling machine) and Delbridge v. Maricopa County Cmty. Coll., 893 P.2d 55 (Ariz. App. 1994) (fall from utility pole in training class).

[38] 989 F.2d 1360 (3d Cir. 1993).

[39] *Id.* at 1368.

[40] 459 So. 2d 413 (Fla. App.1984).

[41] *Id.* 414-415.

[42] 478 N.Y.S.2d 829 (App. Div. 1984).

[43] *Id.* at 883.

[44] 861 P.2d 768 (Kan. 1993).

[45] Mary Ann Connell & Frederick G. Savage, *Releases: Is There Still a Place for Their Use by Colleges and Universities?* J.C. & U.L. 579, 579 (2003). *See also generally,* Richard Fossey, *School Districts' Negligence Release Forms: Are They Worth the Paper They're Printed On?* 177 Educ. L. Rep. 755 (2003) (discussing the use of negligence release forms by public school districts).

[46] Lemoine v. Cornell Univ., 2 A.D.3d 1017, 769 N.Y.S.2d 313(2003) (student injured in rock climbing course offered by university); Terry v. Ind. State Univ., 666 N.E.2d 87 (Ind. Ct. App. 1996) (student injured in motorcycle training course offered by university). *See also generally,* Sharon v. City of Newton, 769 N.E.2d 738 (Mass. 2002) (involving injury of high school cheerleader).

[47] Kyriazis v. Univ. of W. Va., 450 S.2d 649 (W. Va. 1994) (release signed by university student as condition of participating in rugby invalid as violation of public policy). *See also generally,* Wagenblast v. Odessa Sch. Dist. No. 105-157-166, 758 P.2d 968 (Wash. 1988) (holding school district release forms that students were required to sign as condition of participating in interscholastic sports to be violation of public policy).

[48] 769 N.Y.S.2d 313 (App. Div. 2003).

[49] *Id.* at 315.

[50] Kyriazis v. Univ. of W. Va., 450 S.E.2d 649, 651 (W. Va. 1994).

[51] *Id.* at 652, n. 1.

[52] *Id.* at 655.

[53] *Id.*

[54] Connell & Savage, *supra* note 38, at 603-04.

[55] 20 U.S.C. §1092(f) (2003).

[56] U.S. Dep't Of Educ., Office Of Postsecondary Educ., The Incidence Of Crime On The Campuses Of U.S. Postsecondary Institutions 5 (January 2001).

[57] Security on Campus, Inc., Campus Safety Audit http://www.securityoncampus.org/students/audit.pdf (April 28, 2003) (stating that 80 percent of all felonies are student-on-student).

[58] Colleen Finley & Eric Corty, *Rape on Campus: The Prevalence of Sexual Assault While Enrolled in College,* 34 J. C. Student Dev. 113, 116 (1993).

[59] Michael Clay Smith & Richard Fossey, Crime On Campus: Legal Issues And Campus Administration 147 (1995).

[60] The U.S. Department of Education has promulgated regulations that explain the Clery Act's crime reporting obligations in detail. 34 C.F.R. 668.46(b) and (c) (2003).

[61] This discussion about the Jeanne Clery Disclosure of Campus Security Policy and Campus Crime Statistics Act is taken from the web site of Security on Campus, Incorporated, http://www.securityoncampus.org. (April 25, 2003). Other discussions of the Act include: Donald D. Gehring, *Campus Crime, College Policy, d Federal Laws*, in ADM'R'S GUIDE FOR RESPONDING TO CAMPUS CRIME: FROM PREVENTION TO LIABILITY, 17-28 (Richard Fossey & Michael Clay Smith eds., 1996); CAROL BOHMER & ANDREA PARROT, SEXUAL ASSAULT ON CAMPUS (1993).

[62] For a comprehensive checklists of campus security precautions *see* SMITH & FOSSEY, *supra* note 109, at 233-35; Richard Fossey & Michael Clay Smith, *Responding to Campus Rape: a Practical Guide for Campus Administrators* 29, 40-41, in ADM'R'S GUIDE FOR RESPONDING TO CAMPUS CRIME: FROM PREVENTION TO LIABILITY (Richard Fossey & Michael Clay Smith eds. 1996); Fossey & Smith, *supra* note 117, at 398-401. *See also generally*, Security on Campus, Inc., Campus Safety Audit http://www.securityoncampus.org/students/audit.pdf (Accessed April 28, 2003) (campus security checklist for parents).

[63] PROSSER & KEETON, *supra* note 3, at 773.

[64] For example, the Appellate Court of Illinois in a defamation case involving a varsity high school football coach used the following definition: "A statement is considered defamatory if it tends to cause such harm to the reputation of another that it lowers that person in the eyes of the community or deters third persons from associating with him." Myers v. Levy, 808 N.E.2d 1139, 1147 (Ill. App. 2 Dist. 2004). The Court of Appeals in Ohio described defamation as "false publication causing injury to a person's reputation, or exposing the person to public hatred, contempt, ridicule, shame or disgrace or affecting him adversely in his trade or business." Mitikas v. The Univ. of Dayton, 788 N.E.2d 1108, 1115 (Ohio Ct. App. 2003).

[65] However, see, James v. DeGrandis, 138 F. Supp. 2d 402 (W.D.N.Y. 2001) in which a university soccer coach brought a defamation action against a team member and his father but the court found that if the plaintiff already has a low reputation the statements are not actionable. In other words, it is only your good name that can be defamed. If you do not have a good name, there may well be nothing to defame.

[66] The publication must be intentional and made with "the intent to discredit another." Prosser, supra note 3, at 802. Furthermore, Prosser writes, "Courts have never imposed strict liability on the defendant for accidental and non-negligent publication of defamatory matter. There is in fact no liability for which the defendant did not intend and could not reasonably anticipate ...." at 803. However, Prosser seems to leave open the door for the negligent publication of a defamatory statement.

[67] "Courts determine if a statement is capable of a defamatory meaning; juries determine if the statement can be understood by reasonable people to be defamatory." DAVID J. SPERRY, PHILIP T. K. DANIEL, DIXIE SNOW HUEFNER, & E. GORDON GEE, EDUCATION LAW AND THE PUBLIC SCHOOLS: A COMPENDIUM 215 (2d ed. 1998).

[68] PROSSER & KEETON, *supra* note 3, at § 113.

[69] *Id.* at 802. However, Prosser and Keeton note that a letter sent to an individual who is knowingly blind might reasonably have to seek assistance in reading the letter, thus publishing the defamatory statement to a third party, *Id.*.

[70] *Id.* at 799. "The courts have said many times that the last utterance may do no less harm than the first, and that the wrong of another cannot serve as an excuse to the defendant." *Id.*

[71] Hanton v. Gilbert, 486, S.E.2d 432, 436-437 (N.C. Ct. App. 1997).

[72] PROSSER & KEETON, *supra* note 3, at § 112. Prosser notes that even though this per se rule has not been applied to a man the Second Restatement of Torts, § 574 and Comment c have made actionable actionable oral imputations of serious sexual misconduct, at 793.

[73] Wynne v. Loyola Univ. of Chi., 741 N.E.2d 669 (Ill. App. Ct. 2000).

[74] Some states have enacted statutory provisions requiring that the publication, even if true, must have been made for good motives or for justifiable ends (California Penal Code, libel § 251 and slander, § 260).

[75] PROSSER & KEETON, *supra* note 3, at 816.

[76] Wynne, 741 N.E.2d at 676.

[77] Chiavarelli v. Williams, 681 N.Y.S.2d 276 (App. Div. 1998).

[78] *See* Baker v. Lafayette Coll., 504 A.2d 247 (Pa. Super. Ct. 1986).

[79] *Id.* at § 114.

[80] Wagner v. Miskin, 660 N.W.2d at 596.

[81] Wagner v. Miskin, 660 N.W.2d 593, 596 (N.D. 2003).

[82] SPERRY, DANIEL, HUEFNER, & GEE, *supra* note 70, at 223.

[83] Washington v. Cen. State Univ., 699 N.E.2d 1016, 1019 (Ohio Ct. Cl. 1998).

[84] *Id.* at 1020.

[85] *Id.*

[86] Hanton, 486, S.E.2d at 437.

[87] Ostaz v. Med. Coll. of Ohio, 683 N.E.2d 352 (Ohio App. 1996).

[88] Anas v. Brown, 702 N.Y.S.2d 732 (App. Div. 2000)

[89] Blane v. Ala. Cmty. College, 585 So. 2d 866 (Ala. 1991).

[90] James v. SCS Bus. and Tech. Inst., 595 N.Y.S.2d 885 (N.Y. Civ. Ct. 1992).

[91] Albert Merrill Sch. v. Godoy, 357 N.Y.S.2d 378 (N.Y. Civ. Ct. 1974).

[92] 713 So. 2d 967 (Ala. App. 1997)

[93] Byrd v. Lamar, 846 So. 2d 334 (Ala. 2002)

[94] *See* Brody v. Finch Univ., 698 N.E.2d 257 (Ill. App. 1998) in which a state appeals court found that complaining students failed to prove that the allegations of fraud were proved by clear and convincing evidence, and upheld the trial court's decision that the students did not establish this claim.

[95] 550 N.E.2d 1121 (Ill. App. 1990).

[96] Cavaliere v. Duff's Bus. Inst., 605 A2d 397 (Pa. Super. Ct. 1992) (recognizing no policy consideration against claims for misrepresentation where trade school represents that certain curriculum will be offered and it is not or that the school is accredited to give certain degree when it is not).

[97] Ross v. Creighton Univ., 957 F.2d 410 (7th Cir. 1992).

[98] 592 N.W.2d 468 (Minn. Ct. App. 1999).

[99] Alsides v. Brown Inst., Ltd., 592 N.W.2d at 474.

[100] Minger v. Green, 239 F.3d 793, 800 (6th Cir. 2001).

[101] William P. Hoye, *What a Difference a Millennium Makes: Tort Litigation in Higher Education, Circa Y2K,* 147 EDUC. L. REP. 767 (2000).

[102] Paul Ward & Nancy Tribbensee, *Preventive Law on Campus*, CHANGE 35(3) 16-21 (2003) at 18.

# 8 Contracts With Students
## Kerry Brian Melear

## Introduction

The contractual relationship between student and university has undergone an evolutionary process through which it has become firmly established as a characterization of the relationship between institutions of higher learning and their students. In the nineteenth and early twentieth century, the doctrine of *in loco parentis* framed the relationship between the institution and the student in American higher education.[1] Colleges and universities exercised strict control not only over the academic lives of their students, but also the moral, spiritual, and social aspects of a student's daily life.[2] Twentieth century shifts in social policy and the changing nature and composition of the student population in American higher education, however, led to a retooled legal concept of the relationship between institutions of higher learning and their students. Arthur Levine and Jeanettte Cureton have written that contemporary postsecondary students, many of whom are "older, part-time, and working students, especially those with children, often say they want a different type of relationship with their colleges from the one undergraduates have historically had," one resembling a consumer-provider orientation.[3] In their comprehensive study of the institution-student relationship, Robert Bickel and Peter Lake delineated the myriad shifts through which the connection between college and student has evolved, arguing that the "new image is one of *shared* responsibility and a balancing of university authority and student freedom."[4]

The constitutional theory of the relationship between student and institution, which applies within the context of publicly supported higher education, was a catalyst for the proliferation of contemporary contract cases filed against postsecondary institutions.[5] *Dixon v. Alabama State Board of Education*[6] is the case often considered the "death knell" of *in loco parentis* and the genesis of the constitutional theory.[7]

Constitutional theory advances the philosophy that students at public colleges and universities possess rights under the United States Constitution, particularly under the Fourteenth Amendment's due process guarantees concerning notice and hearing. Relative to these due process protections, a federal appeals court in *Dixon* held that students at state-supported institutions had the right to notice and a hearing prior to any disciplinary action that might result in dismissal. Publicly funded higher education, it was reasoned, was no longer a privilege extended to the student but an entitlement protected by due process of law. Constitutional theory analysis is thus restricted to cases involving public higher education institutions because independent institutions are not government agents and thus not bound to provide constitutional protections. As a result, private college and university students rely more heavily on a contractual analysis, which has been increasingly applied since the advent of *Dixon* in 1961.

The idea of higher education as an entitlement ushered in by *Dixon* conditioned the subsequent conception of students as possessing contractual rights. The *Dixon* case became the foundation for a contract orientation in that it applied due process protections guaranteeing procedural fairness when the state would deprive an individual of his or her liberty or property, suggesting that students in public institutions possess an entitlement to receive certain services from higher education institutions. The characterization of students as consumers with a property interest in their education was introduced, giving rise to a contractual interpretation embraced by students in both public and private sectors of higher education.

Contract theory has provided students a means to seek redress of their disagreements with colleges and universities, and courts have embraced the contractual relationship in an effort to frame the reciprocity of rights and obligations between student and institution.[8] Hazel G. Beh has argued that "the work horses of contract law, the implied obligations of good faith and fair dealing, hold the potential to define and to police the student-university relationship while avoiding the pitfalls of judicially second-guessing and intruding into the management of the institution or its academic freedoms."[9]

Courts have held that contracts between student and institution can be created expressly in written or oral form or created impliedly from the conduct of the parties.[10] Although the relationship between institution and student has been frequently characterized as contractual in nature, courts have cautioned against the rigid application of classic contract principles in the higher education setting. One federal district court expressed this caution:

> The judicial inquiry should be directed toward the *bona fides* of the decision-making and the fairness of its implementation: whether the institution acted in good faith and dealt fairly with its student body should be the polestar of the judicial inquiry. This approach will give courts broader authority for examining university decision-making in the administrative area than would a modified standard of judicial deference and will produce a more legally cohesive

body of law than will application of classic contract doctrine with its many judicially created exceptions, varying as they must from jurisdiction to jurisdiction.[11]

Similarly, some scholars have argued that the breadth of contract theory precludes uniform application to higher education because of the multi-faceted nature of college and university operations. Courts appear to adhere closely to contract theory in some areas and apply it more liberally in others. Beh noted that in academic and disciplinary decisions, courts tend to defer to the institution, while simultaneously regarding the relationship between student and institution as contractual. She contended that "[t]he fit between contract and higher education has never been comfortable ... Scholars have long complained that the lack of a unifying legal doctrine has led to confusing and unpredictable legal decisions."[12] Others have suggested that materials such as catalogs and bulletins are not drafted to be contracts and are, therefore, vague and amended with ease at the will of the institution.[13] Theodore C. Stamatakos asserted that students and institutions do not enter into an arm's-length agreement, as not all potential students have the wherewithal to attend the college or university of their choice, and students are unable to negotiate the terms indicated in the institution's bulletin or catalog.[14]

Controversies over contracts for housing, food service, and other auxiliary enterprises of a college or university are most likely to involve classic contract principles in defining the relationship between the student and the institution, as typically does litigation involving disputes over tuition, fees, scholarships, loans, and related pecuniary matters.[15] In these cases, judges tend to examine the express terms and specific language of the contract contained within the "four corners" of the contract document and issue opinions accordingly.

While the treatment of cases regarding financial matters or auxiliary enterprises typically involves a rendering of classic contract principles, the contractual relationship developed between student and institution in the academic and disciplinary context is given a greater breadth of interpretation by the courts.[16]

## The Student-Institution Contract: Case Law

### Academic Issues

#### *Judicial Deference to Academic Decisions*

Due to the traditional deference of the courts to the judgment and expertise of members of the academy, decisions concerning academic matters are typically made with a relative degree of insulation from judicial scrutiny, except in cases of the overt abuse of authority or arbitrary and capricious institutional action.[17] In cases regarding academic matters filed by students at public colleges and universities, the judiciary has typically upheld the institution's authority to conduct its academic programs, regularly citing *Regents of the University of Michigan v. Ewing*[18] and *Board of Curators of the University of Missouri v. Horowitz*.[19]

In *Ewing*, the Supreme Court upheld an institutional decision to dismiss a student, reasoning that the focus of the student's argument was that the university had misjudged his ability to remain in a special medical education program. The Court, in holding for the institution, upheld judicial deference to academic decisions and stated:

> When judges are asked to review the substance of a genuinely academic decision, such as this one, they should show great respect for the faculty's professional judgment. Plainly, they may not override it unless it is such a substantial departure from accepted academic norms as to demonstrate that the person or committee responsible did not actually exercise professional judgment.[20]

In *Horowitz*, the Supreme Court established that, in the adjudication of academic disputes, the degree of due process afforded to students is less rigorous than the protections required of disciplinary matters. In the context of procedural due process, informal notice and review are sufficient to satisfy constitutional requirements for academic policy or procedure at public institutions. This standard mandates only notice of deficiencies and an opportunity to remedy those deficiencies, rather than the traditional requirement of notice of charges against the student and fair and impartial hearing required in the disciplinary context. The Court stated that "a hearing may be useless or harmful in finding out of truth as to scholarship"[21] and that "informal review and evaluation sessions between student and faculty meet constitutional requirements"[22] for the satisfaction of due process. These cases provide a foundation for judicial reluctance to intervene in academic matters.

Judges are disposed to intervene on behalf of the student, however, when institutional decisions are made arbitrarily or capriciously. For example, in *Sylvester v. Texas Southern University*,[23] the United States District Court ruled in favor of a law student who was not afforded the opportunity to address a grade dispute that precluded her from maintaining her class rank and jeopardized her status as valedictorian. The court ruled that the student was deprived of her right to procedural and substantive due process, noting that the university had afforded a meaningful review in other student appeals and must provide the same benefit to her.[24]

Thus, against the background of *Ewing* and *Horowitz*, courts are particularly hesitant to intervene in academic decisions. They are poised to review student contract claims in the academic context, but will only intervene on behalf of the student if arbitrary or capricious institutional action resulted in violation of an implied or express contractual commitment.[25] This deference to academic expertise is consistently expressed in judicial opinions in which students advance contractual claims.

## Admissions

The concept of the offer and acceptance of tuition and fees as the genesis of a binding contract to admit is delineated in *Steinberg v. Chicago Medical School*,[26] the benchmark case in the application of contract theory to the admissions process. In *Steinberg*, the Illinois Supreme Court affirmed a rejected applicant's ability to bring a breach of contract suit against an institution for failing to follow stated admissions procedures. In this case, a student applied for admission to medical school and paid the application fee. The application was rejected, and the student filed suit, claiming breach of contract and alleging that the university had used non-academic criteria in the application process: namely, the ability of the student or his family to make substantial financial contributions to the medical school. The trial court ruled in favor of the university; the student appealed, and the appellate court reversed the decision of the trial court, holding that a rejected applicant could file suit under contract theory if the institution failed to follow its stated admissions criteria.[27] The university appealed, and the Supreme Court of Illinois affirmed the appellate court ruling, stating that there was a contractual relationship between the student and institution, predicated on the medical school's obligation to evaluate applicants according to the criteria published in the bulletin:

> The description in the brochure containing the terms under which an application will be appraised constituted an invitation for an offer. The tender of the application, as well as the payment of the fee pursuant to the terms of the brochure, was an offer to apply. Acceptance of the application and fee constituted acceptance of an offer to apply under the criteria defendant had established.[28]

The Illinois high court ruled that the institution's failure to meet this obligation was a breach of contract because the school was contractually obligated to evaluate applicants by the established and publicly documented standards of admission set forth in institutional publications.

In *Steinberg*, the court was willing to order the return of the student's application fee in remedy of the breach of contract; however, cases in which students seek to compel the university to admit them often meet with little success. For example, an appellate court in North Carolina ruled in favor of the institution regarding the existence of a contract to permit a student to change enrollment status in a graduate program. In *Elliot v. Duke University*,[29] a student brought an action against Duke University to compel the institution to admit her to regular student status in the master's degree program in religious education. She had initially enrolled as a special student and, after a year, informed the director of admissions of her desire to become a regular student in the program. At a subsequent meeting, he informed her that a decision had been made to admit her to the regular program and delineated a sequence of appropriate courses for her consideration. She enrolled, believing she was in a period of transition from special student to regular student status but was later informed that she had never applied to become a regular student as specified in the university catalog. She then submitted an application, which was rejected. She filed suit, arguing that she had fulfilled her part of the agreement by paying tuition and completing the required courses, and was "entitled to specific performance of the alleged contract to admit her to the degree program."[30] The Court of Appeals of North Carolina, however, concluded that an agreement regarding her admission had never existed because a valid contract exists only when there is mutual assent to the same agreement between the parties.[31] The court concluded that there was never any mutual assent between the student and any university official empowered with the ability to admit her into the regular program. The student's unilateral belief that the parties had reached an agreement was insufficient to prove the existence of a contract.

## Grades

Although courts recognize the contractual nature of the relationship between institutions of higher learning and students, they also apply the doctrine of judicial deference to academia in cases regarding specific grading policies and procedures. For example, in *Davis v. Regis College*,[32] a nursing student was removed from and failed the clinical portion of a course due to substandard performance as evaluated by faculty members. This resulted in the student's failure of the entire course, which caused his cumulative grade point average to fall below the college requirements, precluding him from advancing to his senior year until passing the course and restoring his GPA. He filed suit arguing that the grading policy was a form of arbitrary punishment, but the college maintained that the grade was an academic judgment developed by faculty members within the discretionary authority granted to educational institutions, not a punitive measure.[33] Finding no evidence of arbitrary or capricious action, the lower court ruled in favor of the university, and the student appealed.

The Colorado Court of Appeals first noted that although the relationship between the student and college "is grounded in contract, indicating some kind of reciprocal relationship,"[34] the judiciary will not interfere with an institution's academic evaluation of its students without evidence that a decision was made arbitrarily, capriciously, or in bad faith: "Most courts have long refrained from interfering with the authority vested in school officials concerning matters of academic evaluation including the awarding of grades and the establishment of academic standards."[35] The court examined the clinical records and found that the student's performance had been below average in several instances; it also found that he had, at times, been unprepared and unprofessional. Because the student did not present evidence that the decision was made in violation of the academic contract and because the clinical records concerning his performance were clear, the court ruled in favor of the college.[36]

### Degrees

Academic decisions involving the conferral or withholding of degrees fall well within the umbrella of protection offered by the doctrine of judicial deference to the judgments of the institution. The judiciary is reluctant to review cases involving academic decisions regarding degrees, and students are generally unsuccessful in bringing suits to mandate the granting of (or to enjoin the withholding of) a degree. The courts, in cases involving degrees, tend to scrutinize the contractual relationship closely and to limit its decisions to the four corners of the academic contract. Only in overt cases of abuse of discretion on the part of the institution will the judiciary intervene on behalf of the student.

A case illustrative of the hesitancy of the court to intrude upon academic decisions, *Olsson v. Board of Higher Education of the City of New York*,[37] demonstrates that the judiciary will intervene in decisions regarding the granting of degrees only when the institution has acted arbitrarily or capriciously. In this case, a graduate student failed a comprehensive examination required for his degree program and was precluded from graduation on that basis. He argued that he had relied upon a misleading statement made by a professor relative to the grading procedures for the examination, specifically that a passing score required answering at least three of five questions correctly, when the actual criteria was four of five correct responses. The student stated that he had allocated his time in taking the examination in reliance on this statement and argued that he had achieved a passing score under that criterion. Although the university declined to change his score, it offered to allow him to retake the examination. He filed suit to prevent the university from applying the more stringent standard, and both the trial court and appellate court ruled in favor of the student, ordering the university to shoulder the burden of the professor's erroneous statement and to award the student his degree.[38]

The Court of Appeals of New York, however, reversed this decision, articulating traditional concerns about judicial intervention in academic contexts and cautioning that the judicial mandate of a degree should be employed in only "the most egregious of circumstances."[39] With regard to the relationship between the student and institution, the court ruled that "the essence of the implied contract is that an academic institution must act in good faith in its dealing with its students"[40] and that in the case at hand, the college acted in good faith and fulfilled this obligation when it offered the student an opportunity to retake the examination.[41]

## Changes in Degree Requirements

Courts again adhere to the doctrine of judicial deference in cases turning on changes in degree requirements and are hesitant to intervene unless changes in program requirements are made in an arbitrary or capricious fashion or without proper notice. In *Mendez v. Reynolds*,[42] a number of community college students were precluded from graduation due to a change in program requirements. Prior to 1996, the college required students in its bilingual education program to pass a writing assessment test in order to enroll in a final English course required for graduation. A waiver system was implemented that allowed students who failed the writing test an optional course of study that would qualify them to enroll in the final English course and then to graduate. During that year, however, the college governing board rescinded the waiver program and returned to the mandatory passage of the writing assessment as a prerequisite for graduation. As a consequence, students who participated in the waiver system were not eligible for graduation, and the students filed suit. The lower court granted a preliminary injunction allowing students who had not passed the writing assessment test to graduate.

A New York appellate court, however, reversed the lower court's decision. Citing *Olsson v. Board of Higher Education of the City of New York*,[43] the court ruled that "it would contravene public policy to force an institution of higher learning to award degrees where the students had not demonstrated the requisite degree of academic achievement."[44] The court found no arbitrary or capricious action on the part of the college governing board and reasoned that those students who had participated in the waiver system, but completed the final English course, would be in an even better position to pass the written assessment test. The court did mandate, however, that the college provide tuition-free remedial assistance to students who were affected by the change in requirement.[45]

## Academic Dismissals

The judiciary is hesitant to overturn an institution's dismissal of a student for academic reasons.[46] To be successful, the student must demonstrate the existence of a contractual relationship with the institution and evidence of arbitrary or capricious action on the part of the college or university in dismissing the student. In the absence of such evidence, courts are unlikely to intervene in an academic dismissal. In *Pham v. Case Western Reserve University*,[47] a dental student was dismissed for poor academic performance several months prior to his graduation. The student had previously been enrolled in the dental program for three years at another institution, at which he was required to repeat his first year of study. He was later dismissed from that institution, and Case Western Reserve University (CWRU) accepted him conditioned upon his repeat of the second year of study there. The student's subsequent academic and clinical performance were considered marginal during his tenure at CWRU, and he was notified of his deficient performance but allowed to continue his studies on academic review, a classification referring to students who failed to achieve a certain level of performance. His performance the following year was also judged deficient, and he was again notified and later dismissed from the program. The student filed suit alleging, among other charges, that the university had breached its contractual obligation to him by arbitrarily dismissing him from the program. Finding no contract violation, the trial court ruled in favor of the university, and the student appealed.[48]

The Court of Appeals of Ohio, citing *Board of Curators of the University of Missouri v. Horowitz*[49] and *Regents of the University of Michigan v. Ewing*,[50] proffered traditional judicial reservations with regard to the review of academic decisions. Citing *Behrend v. State*,[51] however, the court recognized the nature of the relationship between student and institution as contractual and ruled that "[w]hen a student enrolls in a college or university, pays his or her tuition and fees and attends the school, the resulting relationship may reasonably be construed as being contractual in nature."[52] The court noted that the institution's catalog contained a reservation of rights clause that specifically provided the university power to dismiss a student for any reason it deemed pertinent and found this sufficient to justify the student's expulsion.[53]

The specific terms of the academic contract can be amended by mutual assent of the parties, i.e. the student and the university. In *Bleicher v. University of Cincinnati College of Medicine*,[54] a medical student was dismissed for failing the pharmacology course. The university provided him the option to substitute his National Board of Medical Examiners (NBME) pharmacology score for the final examination in the pharmacology course, and he accepted this offer. A remedial class was offered during the next summer term, but the student declined to enroll. His NBME score ultimately proved insufficient, and the student then asked to take the final examination of the remedial pharmacology class offered the following term, in which students had already taken their mid-term examination. He was granted permission but was required to take both the mid-term and final examinations in the same time period allotted the other students for the final examination. He failed these examinations and was dismissed from the university. The student filed suit against the institution, alleging that the university breached a contract through failure to follow its own educational guidelines by substituting his NBME score for the final examination in the pharmacology course. Because the student agreed to the use of his NBME score, however, the trial determined that the university did not breach its contract and ruled in favor of the university.[55] The student appealed the decision.

The Court of Appeals of Ohio held that the relationship between the student and the institution is contractual in nature, the terms of which are to be found in statements published by the university but that the terms of that contract can indeed be altered if the involved parties agree: "Where the contract permits, the parties may alter its terms by mutual agreement, and any additional terms will supersede the original terms to the extent the two are contradictory."[56] The *Bleicher* opinion was cited in *Elliot v. University of Cincinnati*,[57] in which a doctoral student in music was dismissed for failure to pass comprehensive examinations and filed suit alleging that the university violated its own rules as set forth in the handbook. Finding no arbitrary action on the part of the institution, the trial court ruled in favor of the university, and the student appealed. The Ohio appeals court stated that the standard of review of academic matters is deference to the authority of the university and determination of whether it acted "arbitrarily and capriciously."[58]

In some instances, judges have ruled that institutional catalogs and bulletins do not constitute binding, contractual agreements when applied to academic dismissal. In *Love v. Duke University*,[59] a Hispanic doctoral student at Duke University failed to perform satisfactorily and was subsequently dismissed. He filed suit alleging that he had been removed from the program due to his ethnicity and that the university breached a contractual agreement with him that was clearly specified in the university bulletin.

The United States District Court echoed the familiar sentiment of judicial deference to academia, noting, "Since academic dismissals are wholly discretionary, great deference must be given to these decisions."[60] The court further found that no contract existed between the student and the university, particularly because "the academic bulletin is not a binding contract."[61] Interestingly, however, the court ruled in favor of the university on the basis that the student did not perform to the level of the guidelines delineated in the bulletin. Thus, although the court found no contract in existence, it looked to the specific language printed in the university publication as a supporting rationale for its decision.

## Program Termination

Courts are intolerant of arbitrary program closures, and have established that a student may demonstrate a breach of contract if the institution fails to provide timely and sufficient information concerning the pending elimination of a program or institutional closure. For example, in *Galton v. College of Pharmaceutical Sciences of Columbia University*,[62] a group of pharmacy students filed suit in the Supreme Court of New York, New York County, against the College of Pharmaceutical Sciences and the university, alleging breach of contract for the pending closure of the program. Due to dire financial conditions, the pharmacy program threatened closure unless substantial outside assistance could be obtained. Columbia

University, noting that the College of Pharmaceutical Sciences was a separate entity governed by its own board of trustees, stated that it, too, was experiencing financial difficulties and that it had neither the authority nor duty to provide assistance.

The students argued that the implied contractual relationship that existed between the parties precluded the College from "arbitrarily closing its doors and refusing to permit further attendance."[63] Both the college and university argued that the students had no standing to sue because only the board of regents had the power to suspend, revoke, or alter the charter of the college and moved for dismissal of the complaint.

The trial court, however, determined that the students had established a prima facie case of financial distress sufficient to deny the university's motion to dismiss the claims, set the matter for immediate trial, and cast a protective shadow over the students in ruling:

> Students presently attending the College should not be peremptorily cast out of the College, and their education interrupted for an indefinite time, perhaps forever, if such action is arbitrary. Students are entitled to consideration from educational institutions who invite them to pursue their education in the halls of learning of such institutions. Upon admission of a student to a college there is some obligation upon the part of the college to permit the student to continue his studies to graduation if willing and eligible to continue. Of course, if circumstances beyond the control of the College, such as lack of finances, prevent the College from continuing, the issue is concluded. But there must be an opportunity to inquire into the basis of the determination. The court must provide it. This does not appear to be the function of the Board of Regents.[64]

Institutions may avoid liability, however, if they provide timely and adequate notice of any impending program closure or elimination and demonstrate that the closure was precipitated by an impossibility of continued performance, an issue often subsumed in budgetary considerations. In *Beukas v. Farleigh Dickinson University*,[65] students filed suit alleging breach of contract when the university decided to permanently close the dental college as well as the graduate studies program leading to the Doctor of Dental Medicine Degree. The decision to terminate the program was based upon a financial exigency and was communicated promptly to students and faculty. Furthermore, students were given a number of options concerning degree completion, including transfer to other institutions that were, in some cases, state-subsidized. The Graduate Studies Bulletin contained a reservation of rights clause permitting the university to make changes to programs and curriculum as it deemed necessary, including a statement that "The foregoing changes may include, without limitation, the elimination of colleges, schools, institutes, programs, departments, or courses ..."[66]

The students filed suit for breach of contract, arguing that a contract to educate was created by the university bulletin and other publications and that it was breached by the elimination of the dental program. The university argued that the doctrine of judicial deference should apply and that even if a contractual relationship were to be found, the reservation of rights clause included in the bulletin would prohibit the students from establishing a contract breach.

The Superior Court of New Jersey cautioned against applying classic contract principles to this case. The court acknowledged that there were prior cases concerning program termination that involved a contractual analysis but said that the theoretical underpinnings of these decisions have been criticized as lacking in a coherent and unified application of the law.[67] In reaching its conclusion, the court rejected the application of classic contract theory but stated that even if it were applied, the university reserved the right to eliminate programs in the bulletin. Lacking a showing of bad faith, arbitrary action, or insufficient notice given to students, the court saw no reason to force the application of contract principles only to reject them.[68]

## Disciplinary Policies

As the evolution of the relationship between university and student has shifted away from the philosophy of *in loco parentis* and toward a contractual perspective, student-plaintiffs have exploited new avenues to challenge institutional disciplinary policies. As the following cases indicate, judges tend to apply strict standards of construction and substantial compliance to express statements made in university publications concerning disciplinary procedures and are consistent in requiring that colleges and universities follow their stated disciplinary procedures.[69] In particular, when due process protections are extended to students, judges will hear disciplinary cases to determine whether the institution's agents acted in an arbitrary or capricious manner and will examine controversies to ensure that no violations of a student's due process rights took place that could result in a breach of contract between student and institution.

The application of contract principles in disciplinary cases is particularly germane to private institutions. While due process protections secured under the Fourteenth Amendment are relevant to public institutions of higher education, these constitutional due process protections do not extend to students at private institutions. Thus, private institutions are bound by the disciplinary standards of their institution only to the extent that a contractual obligation has been created.[70]

## Judicial Deference to Disciplinary Decisions

The courts remain hesitant to intervene in academic decision-making but must balance judicial deference to institutional expertise with intrusion into the disciplinary decision-making process through examination of institutional policies and determination of the extent of college or university compliance with these stated policies. In some cases, the balance is a fine one, and courts at the various levels of appeal find themselves in disagreement on the permissible extent of intrusion into academia. For example, in *Schaer v. Brandeis University*,[71] the Supreme Judicial Court of Massachusetts reversed an appellate court's decision that had ruled against a university for failure to follow the stated procedures outlined in its student code. The university board on student conduct found an undergraduate at this private institution guilty of violating several provisions of the student handbook after engaging in a sexual encounter with a female student.[72] The student argued that the encounter was consensual and that he was not interviewed prior to his hearing, a requirement clearly stated in university policy as part of the judicial process. Also, the student alleged that the hearing was not properly recorded and was not conducted in strict compliance with the institution's student code.[73] The student was suspended for three months and ordered to serve probation for his remaining tenure at the university. His university appeal of this decision was denied, and he filed suit for injunctive relief. The lower court dismissed his complaint on the grounds that he did not state a claim for which relief could be granted.[74] A state appeals court determined that the lower court had erred in dismissing the student's claim and ruled that the university failed to follow the disciplinary procedures outlined in its student code.[75]

The Supreme Judicial Court of Massachusetts, however, disagreed with the lower appellate court and affirmed the ruling of the trial court, concluding that the student had failed to state a claim on which relief could be granted.[76] The state high court's majority emphasized that the judiciary is "chary about interfering with academic and disciplinary decisions made by private colleges and universities."[77] In addressing the claims for breach of contract, the majority ruled that the student had failed to demonstrate sufficient evidence of specific breach in the disciplinary process, stating that "[a] university is not required to adhere to the standards of due process guaranteed to criminal defendants or to abide by rules of evidence adopted by courts."[78] The court concluded that institutions of higher learning must have broad discretion in the construction of appropriate disciplinary sanctions and that while a university should adhere to its stated policies, the student failed to present sufficient evidence of a material breach.[79]

Dissenting justices, however, embraced contract theory and emphasized that institutions must follow their own express procedures:

> While the university's obligation to keep the members of
> its community safe from sexual assault and other crimes is

of great importance, at the same time the university cannot
tell its students that certain procedures will be followed then
fail to follow them. In a hearing on a serious disciplinary
matter there is simply too much at stake for an individual
student to countenance the university's failure to abide by
the rules it has itself articulated.[80]

In another dispute turning on disciplinary matters, a Maryland appeals court addressed the importance of judicial deference to academia
in dictum but granted a narrow window of review regarding institutional
compliance with established procedures. In *Harwood v. Johns Hopkins
University*,[81] a student, who had murdered a fellow student and been
convicted, filed suit against a private university after being expelled and
denied his degree. During the fall term of 1995, the student had completed
all degree requirements necessary for graduation; however, because the
university holds the graduation ceremony only once annually, after the
spring semester, he was compelled to wait until May 1996 to receive
his degree. It was during this interim period that he murdered the other
student and was expelled. He filed suit arguing that he was not subject to
the university's disciplinary action after he had completed all degree requirements and that the university had acted in an arbitrary and capricious
fashion by declining to confer his degree. Finding no arbitrary action on
the part of the institution, the trial court ruled in favor of the university,
and the student appealed.[82]

The Court of Special Appeals of Maryland first sounded traditional
concerns of judicial deference regarding the role of the courts in the examination of academic matters, and cited the difference between public and
private institutions relative to the due process protections afforded students
in each context: "Although the actions of public universities are subject to
due process scrutiny, private universities are not bound to provide students
with the full range of due process protection."[83] The court then limited
itself to the contractual standards of review employed when scrutinizing
judicial actions of private institutions: whether Johns Hopkins University
(JHU) had the authority to withhold the student's diploma after he had
completed the required coursework and whether JHU acted in an arbitrary
or capricious fashion in expelling the student. The precise language of the
university handbook was relied upon to resolve both issues.[84]

The *Schaer* and *Harwood* decisions underscore the balance of judicial
deference to university decision-making exhibited by the courts. These
cases demonstrate the reluctance of the courts to intervene in academia,
allowing only a narrow window of review in disciplinary cases to determine whether the institution acted arbitrarily or capriciously or whether
express policies and procedures were followed.

### Express Disciplinary Standards

Despite judicial reluctance to intervene in academia, however, the precise language of university publications can be construed in favor of the student when the institution does not follow published procedures. Courts look to the explicit language of institutional publications in addressing whether an institution's actions were arbitrary or violated a contract between student and institution.

For example, in *Fellheimer v. Middlebury College*,[85] a student was suspended from a private institution after disciplinary proceedings for the alleged sexual assault of a fellow student. Prior to the hearing, the student was informed he was being charged with "Rape/Disrespect for Persons."[86] The student alleged that he contacted the dean, expressed confusion over the charges, and was told to concentrate on the rape charge. After the hearing, the student received a letter indicating that the university had found him not guilty of rape but guilty of "Disrespect for Persons." The student filed suit for breach of contract, alleging that the university failed to provide him adequate notice of all charges. A federal district court ruled in favor of the student, noting that the handbook specifically stated that the charges against a student must state the nature of the charges with sufficient particularity to permit the accused student to prepare a defense against the charges.[87] In the court's view, the charge "Disrespect of Persons" was never mentioned in such a way as to give the student sufficient time to prepare his defense, and the court found the college in breach of its contract with the student with respect to providing adequate notice of charges.[88]

Courts have construed various institutional publications related to campus disciplinary policies as creating a contract between an institution and its students. In *Warren v. Drake University*,[89] the Eighth Circuit Court of Appeals upheld a jury verdict finding that provisions of the student handbook, the honor code, and the university catalog created a contract between the student and institution. A law student was suspended after being arrested for attempting to purloin goods using a stolen credit card. He later petitioned for readmission, but the institution refused. He filed suit; the trial court ruled in favor of the university; and on appeal, the court concluded that the provisions of the student handbook and honor code formed a contract between student and institution and that the university had not breached this contract when it suspended him and denied his readmission.

As demonstrated by the decisions in these cases, the statements made or actions taken by an institution or its representatives can establish the basis for the creation of a contractual relationship between student and university. In the disciplinary context, courts will look to the precise language of institutional publications and communications made by those who possess the authority to bind the institution and balance these statements against institutional actions to determine whether a college or university complied with its own policies or violated a contract through an arbitrary or capricious departure from clearly delineated institutional policy.

## Educational Malpractice and Consumer Issues

The system of American jurisprudence has been awash with claims related to the violation of consumer rights. Charges of educational malpractice, breach of contract, and fraud have been tied to issues of consumer protection, but the application of consumer protection law is controlled by the jurisdictional requirements of particular state statutes and the interpretation of those statutes by judges within that jurisdiction. In cases involving higher education institutions, the burden of proof remains with the student to establish sufficient evidence that a university violated a consumer code. Broad claims of consumer protection violations are typically construed as veiled arguments for educational malpractice, a theoretical tort that has been consistently rejected by appellate courts. However, some courts have recognized the student as a consumer of services and have allowed for amended complaints that implicate contractual rights. Many consumer protection laws permit recovery of attorney's fees for the prevailing party and allow a plaintiff to seek certification as a representative of a larger class of aggrieved plaintiffs.

The elaboration of breach of contract claims has given rise to alternative claims of educational malpractice and violation of a consumer relationship between student and institution. Courts do not recognize educational malpractice as a viable claim against an institution of higher learning for policy reasons stemming from reluctance to expand the tort liability of educational, non-profit corporations and the tradition of judicial deference to academia.[90] Accordingly, students have looked to contract theory to bring actions that mirror the claim of educational malpractice against colleges and universities, although courts consistently pierce this veil and reject such cases. If, however, a student emphasizes specific instances in which a college or university has breached the contract to educate, courts have recognized these specific allegations.

### *Educational Malpractice Claims Veiled As Contract Claims*

The court in *Gally v. Columbia University*[91] ruled that "Not every dispute between a student and a university is amenable to a breach of contract claim."[92] In a case filed by a dental student who was dismissed after failing a required course, the student argued that the university breached its contract with her on a number of levels. The United States District Court ruled that her claim was actually an argument for educational malpractice veiled in contract theory, ruling "Where the essence of the complaint is that the school breached its agreement by failing to provide an effective education, the complaint must be dismissed as an impermissible attempt to avoid the rule that there is no claim in New York for 'educational malpractice.'"[93] The court found that the contract argument advanced in this case, when stripped to its essence, failed to state a claim for breach of contract and that "[t]he application of contract principles to the student-university relationship does not provide judicial recourse for every disgruntled student."[94]

As demonstrated in *Paladino v. Adelphi*,[95] a student can circumvent the judicial rejection of a theory of educational malpractice by citing specific promises that were breached by the institution rather than a broad assertion that the quality of education fell below a standard of reasonable, prudent care. In this case, which involved a student in a private elementary school but which has been applied to higher education by the judiciary,[96] a parent filed suit on behalf of his son, alleging an inferior quality of education at the private school. The trial court, holding that the established policy of refusing to entertain educational malpractice suits did not bar actions in contract, ruled in favor of the student, and the school appealed.[97] The Appellate Division of the Supreme Court of New York reversed the decision, echoing the prevailing sentiment that the judiciary should not address issues of educational malpractice for public policy reasons.

> Professional educators—not judges—are charged with the responsibility for determining the method of learning that should be pursued for their students. When the intended results are not obtained, it is the educational community—and not the judiciary—that must resolve the problem. For, in reality, the soundness of educational methodology is always subject to question and a court ought not in hindsight, substitute its notions as to what would have been a better course of instruction to follow for a particular pupil. These are determinations that are to be made by educators and, though they are capable of error, their integrity ought not be subject to judicial inquiry.[98]

However, the appellate court addressed the idea that a contract exists between student and institution and recognized that, although broad claims of educational malpractice do not fall within the scope of review because they would engender judicial assessment of educational methodology, remedies could be available under contract theory if the claims were specific to the service breached:

> If in a case such as this, a private school were simply to accept a student's tuition and thereafter provide no educational services, an action for breach of contract might lie. Similarly, if the contract with the school were to provide for certain specified services,

such as for example, a designated number of hours of instruction, and the school failed to meet its obligation, then a contract action with appropriate consequential damages might be available.[99]

Such a circumstance is evident in *Ross v. Creighton University*,[100] in which a former scholarship basketball player filed suit against the university for breach of contract and educational malpractice. The student, who came from an academically disadvantaged background, argued that the university had contracted to provide him adequate tutoring and other academic assistance. The trial court dismissed the charges of educational malpractice as well as the contract charges, noting that the relationship between student and institution is a contractual one but that no specific promises had been breached.

The Seventh Circuit Court of Appeals affirmed the trial court's reluctance to address the theory of educational malpractice for several reasons:

> First, there is a lack of a satisfactory standard of care by which to evaluate an educator. Second, inherent uncertainties exist in this type of case about the cause and nature of damages. A third reason for denying this cause of action is the potential it presents for a flood of litigation against schools. A final reason courts have cited for denying this cause of action is that it threatens to embroil the courts into overseeing the day-to-day operations of schools. This oversight might be particularly troubling in the university setting where it necessarily implicates considerations of academic freedom and autonomy.[101]

With regard to the former student's contract claims, however, the appellate court disagreed with the trial court's dismissal of the charges. The court acknowledged the contractual nature of the student-institution relationship, although cautioning against allowing educational malpractice claims to be recast as contract arguments. Citing *Paladino*, the court noted that to "simply allege that the education was not good enough"[102] is insufficient and emphasized that the student must identify specific contractual promises that were breached. In reversing and remanding the lower court's decision relative to the student's contract claims, the appellate court held that the student's claims alleged more than simply an inadequate education; rather, the student asserted that the university knew of his deficiencies, offered him specific services to assist him academically, and breached its promise by failing to provide those services. This interpretation would permit the court to "adjudicate Mr. Ross' specific and narrow claim that he was barred from *any* participation in and benefit from the University's academic program without second-guessing the professional judgment of the University faculty on academic matters."[103]

### Consumer Protection

The application of consumer protection law is generally controlled by the jurisdictional requirements of the particular state in which the suit is filed. Courts are skeptical of broad claims of consumer protection violations and typically view them as veiled assertions of educational malpractice claims. For example, in *Finstad v. Washburn University of Topeka*,[104] the Supreme Court of Kansas recognized students as consumers but ultimately ruled against them in a suit seeking damages under the Kansas Consumer Protection Act and for educational malpractice. The university's bulletin erroneously stated that the court reporting program was accredited, when in fact the program was in the process of seeking accreditation. The university deleted this statement from all undistributed catalogs and made announcements to students. Some students filed suit claiming they had been aggrieved by paying tuition to receive instruction in an unaccredited program.

The court stated that a consumer must be aggrieved by a violation in order to successfully argue fraud under the Consumer Protection Act and that these students were not aggrieved by the catalog misstatement because they did not rely on it as a basis for enrollment, nor did they exhibit injury due to reliance on the statement. Citing *Ross v. Creighton University*,[105] the court further cautioned against judicial review of educational malpractice claims.[106]

## Conclusion

The contract theory applicable to higher education has undergone an evolutionary process through which it has become firmly ensconced as a viable legal descriptor of the relationship between institutions of higher learning and students. In its nascent period, it existed as a simple compact through which a student pledged to uphold the rules, regulations, and codes of the college. In its current manifestation, contract theory has provided students an outlet to seek redress against their colleges and universities that was previously unavailable. Now often characterized as consumers, students have certain and precise expectations concerning institutional performance and actively seek judicial relief through contract theory for perceived abrogation of these expectations. For institutions of higher education and their agents, contractual relationships with students create binding legal responsibilities that cannot be ignored.

Courts have cautioned against the uniform application of classical contract principles across all areas of the academic relationship, however.[107] Some characterize the relationship between institutions and students as too complex for the application of classical contract theory, suggesting that the law of contracts lacks coherent and unified application in this sphere.[108] Other courts adopt a position of deference to academic decision-making and defer to the expertise of the institution unless the student exhibits evidence of a breach of contract or can show that the actions of the college or university were arbitrary, capricious, motivated by ill-will, or wholly inconsistent with academic norms.[109] These courts suggest reliance on a quasi-contractual relationship that emphasizes reciprocity of good faith and reasonableness between student and institution that would more accurately reflect the nature of the university-student relationship than would the rigid application of purely contractual principles.

Private universities are not bound to provide students with constitutional due process protections, but they must adhere to the rules and regulations delineated by the institution. Contract theory is thus embraced by students at private colleges and universities as a means to seek redress against their institutions in lieu of due process protections. The judiciary is particularly exact in adjudication of cases against private colleges and universities in ascertaining whether these institutions follow the disciplinary procedures, as well as other rules and regulations, they promulgate within the context of published materials.[110]

Claims of educational malpractice are not recognized by the courts for policy reasons; however, contract theory offers an alternative to a claim of educational malpractice.[111] Courts will intervene if the student provides evidence of a breach of a specific promise made or the non-performance of a specific service purported to be available to the student.[112]

Students are often characterized as consumers of educational services, but there has been a limited application of consumer protection law to higher education in United States courts, largely because these laws focus on evidence of fraud and intentional misrepresentation. Application of consumer protection laws varies from state to state, given the requirements of a particular state's code, and the burden of proof to establish a breach of consumer protection law remains with the student. Most consumer protection cases brought by students involve a claim of fraudulent misrepresentation, as an alternative theory to a breach of contract claim. Consumer protection legislation typically requires proof of fraudulent activity on the part of the institution, and student litigants assert this claim in addition to an allegation of contract breach.[113]

While the future direction of the institution-student relationship may manifest itself in a number of ways, analysis of contemporary case law suggests that contract theory has attained prominence as a viable legal descriptor of the relationship between institutions of higher learning and their students. The elaboration of a contractual relationship between student and institution has engendered the conception of the student as a consumer of goods and services and framed reciprocity of obligation between the two parties. Students have embraced contract theory as a means of redress against arbitrary or capricious action on the part of the institution, and, although the judiciary has adhered to tradition deference to the institution in cases regarding academic matters, it has recognized that much of the legal relationship between student and institution is aptly characterized as contractual.

# Endnotes

1  FREDERICK RUDOLPH, THE AMERICAN COLLEGE AND UNIVERSITY: A HISTORY (Athens, GA: University Press of Georgia, 1962). *See also* Perry A. Zirkel and Henry F. Reichner, *Is the 'In Loco Parentis' Doctrine Dead?* 15 J. L. & EDUC. 3, 281 (1986), in which the authors quote *Gott v. Berea Coll.*, 156 Ky. 376, 379-380, 161 S.W. 204, 206 (1913), a Kentucky case from 1913 in which a state court upheld a college's rule forbidding students to frequent certain restaurants and brasseries: "[C]ollege authorities stand *in loco parentis* concerning the physical and moral welfare and mental training of the pupils … [T]here is no question that the power of school authorities over pupils is not confined to the schoolroom or grounds, but to extend to all acts of pupils which are detrimental to the good order and best interest of the school."

2  CHRISTOPHER J. LUCAS, AMERICAN HIGHER EDUCATION: A HISTORY (New York: St. Martin's Griffin, 1994).

3  ARTHUR LEVINE & JEANETTE S. CURETON, WHEN HOPE AND FEAR COLLIDE: A PORTRAIT OF TODAY'S COLLEGE STUDENT (San Francisco: Jossey-Bass Publishers, 1998) at 50.

4  ROBERT D. BICKEL AND PETER F. LAKE, THE RIGHTS AND RESPONSIBILITIES OF THE MODERN UNIVERSITY: WHO ASSUMES THE RISKS OF COLLEGE LIFE? (Durham, NC: Carolina Academic Press, 1999), 105.

5  Other theoretical interpretations of the legal relationship have been advanced, including status, privilege, and fiduciary theories. For a discourse on fiduciary theory, *see* Kent Weeks & Rich Haglund, *Fiduciary Duties of College and University Faculty and Administrators*, 29 J.C. & U.L. 1, 153 (2002). *See also* Bickel and Lake at *supra* note 6 for a comprehensive discussion of alternate theoretical interpretations.

6  294 F. 2d 150 (5th Cir.), *cert. denied*, 368 U.S. 930 (1961).

7  Gerard A. Fowler, *The Legal Relationship Between the American College Student and the College: An Historical Perspective and the Renewal of a Proposal*," 13 J.L. & EDUC. 3, 408 (1984). *See also* Elizabeth L. Grossi & Terry D. Edwards, *Student Misconduct: Historical Trends In Legislative and Judicial Decision-Making in American Universities*, 23 J.C. & U.L. 4, 829 (1997).

8  C. Robert Lawson & Jack L. Daniels, *Procedural Due Process in Higher Education: A Protection of Students' Rights*, 12 THE S. Q. 3, 217 (1974); Zirkel & Reichner at *supra* note 3; B. Jackson, *The Lingering Legacy of 'In Loco Parentis:' An Historical Survey and Proposal for Reform*, 44 VAND. L. REV. 1135 (1991). *See also* R. RATLIFF, CONSTITUTIONAL RIGHTS OF COLLEGE STUDENTS: A STUDY IN CASE LAW (Metuchen, NJ: Scarecrow Press, 1972), at 38-39, in which the author stated, "The courts have often looked to contract law—or at least a semblance of it—to rationalize decisions growing out of campus conflicts. Contract, with its broad implication of property-like rights, falls within the ready comprehension of any court. The concept has been seized, given broad construction, and enforced by the courts to which it was addressed."

9  Hazel G. Beh, *Student Versus University: The University's Implied Obligations of Good Faith and Fair Dealing*, 59 MD. L. REV., 183, 184-85 (2000).

10  ROBERT M. HENDRICKSON, THE COLLEGES, THEIR CONSTITUENCIES AND THE COURTS (Topeka, KS: National Organization On Legal Problems Of Education, 1991).

11  Beukas v. Farliegh Dickinson Univ., 605 A.2d 776, 784 (N.J. Super. 1991).

12  Hazel G. Beh, *Downsizing Higher Education and Derailing Student Educational Objectives: When Should Claims for Program Closures Succeed?,* 33 GA. L. REV. 155, 178 (1998).

13  Eileen K. Jennings, *Breach of Contract Suits by Students Against Post-Secondary-Education Institutions: Can They Succeed?*, 7 J.C. &U.L. 191 (1980-81).

[14] Theodore C. Stamatakos, *The Doctrine of In Loco Parentis: Tort Liability and the Student-College Relationship*, 65 IND. L. J. 471 (1990).

[15] *See, e.g.,* Thornton v. Harvard Univ., 2 F. Supp. 2d 89 (D. Mass. 1998) (court examined the precise language of a student aid program in determining a student's ineligibility.); Hysaw v. Washburn Univ. of Topeka, 690 F. Supp. 940, 946 (D. Kan. 1987) (Football players on athletic scholarships who were dismissed for boycotting football practice filed suit alleging that the university breached their scholarship contracts. The court ruled in favor of the institution, noting that the language of the written scholarship contracts did not promise that the athletes would be allowed to play football: "In fact, the only promises in those written contracts were that the players would receive money. [The students] provide no evidence, other than 'understandings' and 'expectations' that they were promised a position on the 1986 team."); Reynolds v. Sterling Coll., Inc., 750 A.2d 1020 (Vt. 2000) (Supreme Court of Vermont concluded that tuition policy was contractually binding between student and institution).

[16] *See* Ferdinand Dutile, *Disciplinary Versus Academic Sanctions in Higher Education: A Doomed Dichotomy?*, 29 J.C. & U.L. 3, 619, 652 (2003). The author argues that, in many instances, the distinction between academic and disciplinary cases is blurred and that the courts have provided little guidance in establishing a clear delineation. He promotes, as a remedy, a consolidated standard of review of academic and disciplinary decisions, based on a "careful and deliberate assessment" of the offense in question and a hearing, the extent of which would vary according to the extent of potential loss to the student. This standard would strike a balance "between the substantial interests that both the student and the university bring to academic and disciplinary cases." *See* James v. Wall, 83 S.W.2d 615 (Tex. App. 1989) (contractual analysis was used to determine the outcome of a case involving both disciplinary and academic elements stemming from the same student offense).

[17] *See* K.B. Melear, *Judicial Intervention in Postsecondary Academic Decisions: The Standards of Arbitrary and Capricious Conduct*, 177 EDUC. L. REP. [1] (July 31, 2003).

[18] 474 U.S. 214 (1985), 106 S. Ct. 507 (1985), 88 L. Ed. 2d 523 (1985).

[19] 435 U.S. 78 (1978), 98 S. Ct. 948 (1978), 55 L. Ed. 2d 124 (1978).

[20] *Ewing*, 106 S. Ct. 507, 513 (1985).

[21] *Horowitz*, 98 S. Ct. 948, 955 (1978).

[22] *Id.* at 953.

[23] 957 F. Supp. 944 (S.D. Tex. 1997).

[24] *Id.* at 947. *See also* Susan M. v. N.Y. Law Sch., 544 N.Y.S.2d 829 (N.Y. App. Div. 1989), *rev'd*, 556 N.E.2d 1004 (N.Y. 1990). This case also exemplifies the judiciary's reluctance to intervene in grading matters. The New York Court of Appeals ultimately overturned the lower court's decision, but the case merits examination as it represents judicial intervention later rebuffed for its intrusion into academia. *See also* Johnson v. Schmitz, 119 F. Supp. 2d 90 (D. Conn. 2000) (claims of specific breaches of academic policies overcame judicial deference).

[25] *See* Kraft v. W. Alanson White Psychiatric Found., 498 A.2d 1145 (D.C. App. 1985); Clifton-Davis v. State, 930 P.2d 833 (Okla. App. 1996); Banks v. Dominican Coll., 42 Cal. Rptr. 2d 110 (Cal. App. 1 Dist. 1995); Lewis v. St. Louis Univ., 744 F.2d 1368 (1984); Giles v. Howard Univ., 428 F. Supp. 603 (D.D.C. 1977); Baldridge v. State of N.Y., 293 A.D.2d 941 (2002). In these cases, the courts were reluctant to overturn an academic decision without clear evidence of unreasonable or arbitrary or capricious action on the part of the university.

[26] 371 N.E.2d 634 (1977).

[27] *See* Steinberg v. Chi. Med. Sch., 354 N.E.2d 586, 591 (1976).

[28] Steinberg v. Chi. Med. Sch., 371 N.E.2d 634, 639 (Ill. 1977).

[29] 311 S.E.2d 632 (N.C. App. 1984).

[30] *Id.* at 636.

[31] *Id.* at 636. *See also* Long v. Univ. of N.C. at Wilmington, 461 S.E.2d 773 (N.C. App. 1995); Keles v. Yale Univ., 889 F. Supp. 729 (S.D.N.Y. 1995).

[32] 830 P.2d 1098 (Colo. App. 1991).

[33] *Id* at 1099.

[34] *Id.* at 1100.

[35] *Id* at 1100.

[36] *Id. See also* Harris v. Blake, 798 F.2d 419 (10th Cir. 1986).

[37] 402 N.E.2d 1150 (N.Y. Ct. App. 1980).

[38] *Id.* at 1152.

[39] *Id.* at 1154.

[40] *Id.* at 1153.

[41] *Id.* at 1153. *See also* DeMarco v. Univ. of Health Sciences, 352 N.E.2d 356 (Ill. App. 1976); Williams v. Franklin & Marshall Coll., 2000 U.S. Dist. LEXIS 691; and Harwood v. Johns Hopkins Univ., *infra* note 83 (court upheld the denial of a student's degree, concluding that the student provided insufficient evidence to demonstrate that the university failed to follow its stated procedures).

[42] 681 N.Y.S.2d 494 (1998).

[43] *Supra* note 39.

[44] Mendez v. Reynolds, 681 N.Y.S.2d 494, 497 (1998)

[45] *See also* Crabtree v. Cal. Univ. of Pa., 606 A.2d 1239 (Pa. Commw. Ct. 1992); University of Tex. Health Sci. Ctr. at Houston v. Babb, 646 S.W.2d 502 (Tex. Ct. App. 1982). In these cases, it is demonstrated that the decision may favor the student where he or she reasonably and justifiably relied on statements made in the catalog concerning course requirements and curricular issues.

[46] *See Ewing* and *Horowitz* at *supra* notes 20-24 and accompanying text.

[47] 1997 Ohio App. LEXIS 1307.

[48] *Id.* at *3-4.

[49] *Horowitz*, 435 U.S. 78 (1978), 98 S. Ct. 948 (1978), 55 L. Ed. 2d 124 (1978).

[50] *Ewing*, 474 U.S. 214 (1985), 106 S. Ct. 507 (1985), 88 L. Ed. 2d 523 (1985).

[51] 55 Ohio App. 2d 135 (Ohio Ct. App. 1977).

[52] Pham v. Case W. Reserve Univ., 1997 Ohio App. LEXIS 1307, at *8.

[53] *Id.* at *10. *See also* Betts v. Rector & Visitors of Univ. of Va., 967 F. Supp. 882 (D. Va. 1997); 1999 U.S. App. LEXIS 23105 (a reservation of rights clause in an institutional publication successfully negated a student's contract claim); Eiland v. Wolf, 764 S.W.2d 827, 838 (1989) ("A basic requisite of a contract is an intent to be bound, and the catalog's express language negates, as a matter of law, an inference of such intent on the part of the university."); *See also* Law v. William Marsh Rice Univ., 123 S.W.3d 786 (Tex. App. 2004) (appellate court concluded that disclaimer in private university's catalog precluded creation of an enforceable contract between student and institution).

[54] 604 N.E.2d 783 (Ohio App. 10 Dist. 1992).

[55] *Id.* at 788.

[56] *Id.* at 787.

[57] 703 N.E.2d 996 (Ohio Ct. App. 1999).

[58] *Id.* at 998.

[59] 776 F. Supp. 1070 (M.D.N.C. 1991).

[60] *Id.* at 1075. *See also* Mittra v. Univ. of Medicine, 719 A.2d 693, 697 (N.J. Super. A.D. 1998), in which the court reasoned that "… the role of the courts in resolving disputes involving the dismissal of a student for academic reasons was limited to a determination whether the university complied with its own regulations and whether the institution's decision was supported by the evidence."

[61]  *Id.* at 1075. *See also* Raethz v. Aurora Univ. 805 N.E. 696 (Ill. App. 2d Dist. 2004) (appellate court noted that the relationship cannot be categorized in purely contractual terms, but that courts can intervene in an arbitrary or capricious academic dismissal).

[62]  332 N.Y.S.2d 909 (N.Y. App. Div 1972).

[63]  *Id.* at 911.

[64]  *Id.* at 912. *See also* American Computer Inst. v. State, 995 P.2d 647 (Alaska 2000).

[65]  605 A.2d 776 (N.J. Super. L. 1991). *See supra* note 13 and accompanying text.

[66]  *Id.* at 778.

[67]  *Id.* at 781. The court cited *In re* Antioch Univ., 418 A2d 105 (1980); Behrend v. State, 379 N.E.2d 617 (1977), *supra* note 53; Peretti v. Mont., 464 F. Supp. 784 (D. Mont. 1979), *rev'd on other grounds*, 661 F.2d 756 (9th Cir. 1981). The court opined that "[a]lthough the result in each of the foregoing cases has not been questioned, the theoretical bases underlying these decisions have been criticized as lacking in a unified and legally consistent application of the law." *See* Virginia D. Nordin, *The Contract to Educate: Toward a More Workable Theory of the Student-University Relationship*, 8 J.C. & U.L. 2, 141, 179 (1981-82); See *also* Jennings at *supra* note 15.

[68]  *Id.* at 784. *See* HARRY T. EDWARDS & VIRGINIA C. NORDIN, HIGHER EDUCATION AND THE LAW (Cambridge, MA: Institute for Educational Management, Harvard University, 1979) at 421, in which the authors state that "The courts in … quasi-contract cases use contract law as an analogy to define and describe university-student relations. This approach allows a court to pick and choose those aspects of contract law which it feels can be applied with validity to the student-university relation, without adhering rigidly to ramifications of contract law and theory …"

[69]  *See* Schaer v. Brandeis Univ., *infra* note 73; Harwood v. Johns Hopkins Univ., *infra* note 83; and Fellheimer v. Middlebury Coll., *infra* note 87.

[70]  *See* Boehm v. Univ. of Pa. Sch. of Veterinary Med., 573 A.2d 575 (1990) (the opinion emphasized that a majority of courts characterize the relationship between students and private institutions as contractual and that these students are entitled only to the procedural safeguards outlined in institutional publications).

[71]  735 N.E.2d 373 (Mass. 2000).

[72]  Schaer v. Brandeis Univ., 716 N.E.2d 1055, 1058 (Mass. App. 1999).

[73]  *Id.* at 1058-1059.

[74]  *Id.* at 1058.

[75]  *Id.*

[76]  *Schaer, supra* note 73 at 381.

[77]  *Id.* at 381.

[78]  *Id.* at 381.

[79]  *Id.* at 381.

[80]  *Id.* at 385. A second dissenting justice responded to the concerns of the majority opinion regarding judicial interference in disciplinary decisions made by private colleges and universities but also embraced the application of contract theory: "I share the court's concern, but its disinclination to interfere with university governance should not alter basic contract law and the traditional standard for evaluating the sufficient of a complaint. I agree with the dissenting opinion that the university, like any other, must abide by its contracts." *See* Melvin v. Union Coll., 600 N.Y.S.2d 141 (A.D. 2 Dept. 1993) (New York appellate court ruled that a student who had been suspended from a private college for academic dishonesty was entitled to an injunction precluding her suspension because the college did not conform to its disciplinary guidelines as delineated in the student handbook). *See also* Ebert v. Yeshiva Univ., 780 N.Y.S.2d 283 (N.Y. Supp. 2004) (court noted that deference should be granted in disciplinary matters, but courts can review for failure to follow stated guidelines).

81 747 A.2d 205 (Md. Ct. Spec. App. 2000).

82 *Id.* at 208.

83 *Id.* at 209.

84 *Id.* at 211. *See also* Benyonatan v. Concordia Coll. Corp., 863 F. Supp. 983 (D. Minn. 1994) (the private college satisfied all contractual obligations to a suspended student when it followed the judicial terms outlined in its publications).

85 869 F. Supp. 238 (D. Vt. 1994).

86 *Id.* at 244.

87 *Id.* at 245.

88 *Id.* at 247.

89 886 F.2d 200 (8th Cir. 1989).

90 *See* Andre v. Pace Univ., 665 N.Y.S.2d 777 (1996). *See also* Miller v. Loyola Univ. of New Orleans, 829 So. 2d 1057 (La. App. 2002) (appellate court noted that there is no legal recognition of claims of educational malpractice).

91 22 F. Supp. 2d 199 (S.D.N.Y. 1998).

92 *Id.* at 206.

93 *Id.* at 207.

94 *Id.* at 208. *See also* Lawrence v. Lorain County Cmty. Coll., 713 N.E.2d 478 (Ohio App. 9 Dist. 1998) (appellate court found a student's contract claim against the institution to be a veiled claim for educational malpractice).

95 454 N.Y.S.2d 868 (N.Y. 1982).

96 *See also* Andre v. Pace Univ., 665 N.Y.S.2d 777 (1996); 618 N.Y.S.2d 975 (1994); Bittle v. Okla. City Univ., 6P.3d 509 (Okla. Civ. App. Div. 3 2000); Cavaliere v. Duff's Bus. Inst., 605 A.2d 397 (Pa. Super. Ct. 1992); Clarke v. Trs. of Columbia Univ., 1996 U.S. Dist. LEXIS 15620; Ross v. Creighton Univ., 957 F.2d 410 (Ill. App. Ct. 1992); and Sirohi v. Lee, 634 N.Y.S.2d 119 (App. Div. 1995).

97 *Paladino,* 454 N.Y.S.2d 868, 870 (N.Y. 1982)

98 *Id.* at 873.

99 *Id* at 873.

100 957 F.2d 410 (7th Cir. 1992).

101 *Id.* at 414.

102 *Id.* at 416-417.

103 *Id.* at 417. *See* Andre v. Pace Univ., 665 N.Y.S.2d 777 (1996); 618 N.Y.S. 2d 975 (1994); Cavaliere v. Duff's Bus. Inst., 605 A.2d 397 (Pa. Super. Ct. 1992); Clark v. Trs. of Columbia Univ., 1996 U.S. Dist. LEXIS 15620; Bird v. Lewis & Clark Coll., 104 F. Supp. 2d 1271 (D. Or. 2000); Alsides v. Brown Inst., 592 N.W.2d 468 (Minn. Ct. App. 1999) (students were successful in suits against their institutions by evidencing specific instances in which the university failed to deliver specific, promised services); *See also* Bittle v. Okla. City Univ., 6 P.3d 509 (Okla. Civ. App. Div. 3 2000) (if a student demonstrates both a contractual agreement with a private institution that delineates a specific procedure for grievance resolution as well as the institution's failure to follow its own procedure, a cause for breach of contract may arise).

104 845 P.2d 685 (Kan. 1993).

105 *Supra* note 123.

106 *See also* Villarreal v. Art Inst. of Houston, 20 S.W.3d 792 (Tex. App.—Corpus Christi 2000); Chiaka v. Rawles, 525 S.E.2d 162 (Ga. Ct. App. 1999) (a student's fraud and contract claims were dismissed because she failed to show specific instances of reliance on any misstatements or any resulting injury); Lidecker v. Kendall Coll., 550 N.E.2d 1121 (Ill. App. 1 Dist. 1990) (students' fraud claim failed because they could know provide evidence that the institution intended to deceive).

107 *See supra* notes 13-16.

[108] *See* Beukas v. Farleigh Dickinson Univ. at *supra* notes 13 and 67 and accompanying text; Love v. Duke Univ. at *supra* note 61; and Gally v. Columbia Univ. at *supra* note 93 and accompanying text.

[109] *See* Hazel G. Beh, *Downsizing Higher Education and Derailing Student Educational Objectives: When Should Student Claims for Program Closures Succeed?,* 33 GA. L. REV. 155, 178, in which the author noted that courts will defer to the authority of the institution in making academic and disciplinary decisions, while simultaneously regarding the relationship between student and institution as contractual. She stated that "[t]he fit between contract and higher education has never been comfortable. Scholars have long complained that the lack of a unifying legal doctrine has led to confusing and unpredictable legal decisions." *See also* Dutile, *supra* note 18.

[110] *See supra* note 72 and accompanying text.

[111] *See supra* note 92 and accompanying text.

[112] *See supra* notes 94-106 and accompanying text.

[113] *See supra* notes 106-108 and accompanying text.

[114] *See supra* notes 106-108 and accompanying text.

# 9 Student Speech
## Patrick Pauken

## Introduction

As with all discussion of constitutional rights, the resolution of legal conflict in free speech and expression cases in institutions of higher education boils down to a balance of rights. On one hand, there is the *institutional right* to restrict or suppress an individual's exercise of freedoms, where this exercise may hamper the efficient, effective, well guided, and well-defined operation of a state-supported college or university. Along with this right comes the institutional right to form its own voice as an institution: to share with its community its own code, its own message, and its own mission and vision. On the other hand, there is the *individual right* to exercise freedoms so important to the foundation and definition of this country, among them the freedom of speech, freedom of association or assembly, and freedom of religious worship. Within the context of the freedom of speech and association, the next two chapters explore the balance of rights among all college and university players, both individual and institutional, as those players search for, develop, define, modify, and proclaim their respective voices and messages. In particular, the present chapter on student speech issues covers all aspects of expressive activity among students, from personal speech not associated with university-sponsored activities or curricula to speech associated with student organizations and student publications, and, finally, speech contained in the classroom curricular activities of students.

## Student Protest

> Struggles to coerce uniformity of sentiment in support of some end thought essential to their time and country have been waged by many good as well as by evil men.... As governmental pressure toward unity becomes greater, so strife becomes more bitter as to whose unity it shall be.... Those who begin coercive elimination of dissent soon find them-

> selves exterminating dissenters. Compulsory unification of
> opinion achieves only the unanimity of the graveyard.... If
> there is any fixed star in our constitutional constellation, it
> is that no official, high or petty, can proscribe what shall be
> orthodox in politics, nationalism, religion, or other matters
> of opinion or force citizens to confess by word or act their
> faith therein.[1]

Much student protest activity is silent, passive, and respectful. In fact, a review of the student protest case law from all levels of education reveals that very few cases involve genuinely violent or disruptive behavior on the part of the protestors themselves.[2] Often, it is the responses to the protestors and the content of their protests that cause the disruption.[3] In the end, the familiar "disruption" standard applies on college campuses, where a college or a university may restrict the expressive activity of students if that activity is substantially interfering or materially disruptive to the rights of others or the operation of the college or university.[4]

This disruption standard can be defined and applied in numerous ways. An early example, from *Cox v. Louisiana*,[5] illustrates two challenges to a policy: one "on its face" and one "as applied". In *Cox*, a leader of a civil rights demonstration and twenty-three university students were arrested following courthouse picketing and a sit-in at racially segregated lunch counters in Baton Rouge, Louisiana. In a protest involving at least 1,500 people, the arrestees were charged under state law with peace disturbance, obstructing public passages, and courthouse picketing. The Supreme Court overturned the conviction on a couple grounds. First, the Court found that the protest activity, as applied, did not actually breach the peace. Despite the large number of people involved, the protesters followed all orders and engaged in typical nonviolent protest activities such as picketing, chanting, singing, and praying. Second, the Court struck down the statute on its face as being unconstitutionally vague and overbroad and in violation of free speech and free association. Louisiana defined "breach of the peace" as "to agitate, to arouse from a state of repose, to molest, to interrupt, to hinder, to disquiet." But, according to the Court, one of the very functions of free speech is to invite dispute. Speech "may indeed best serve its high purpose when it induces a condition of unrest, creates dissatisfaction with conditions as they are, or even stirs people to anger. Speech is often provocative and challenging."[6] While the convictions in *Cox* were overturned, it is important to note that the Court gave higher education administrators valuable policymaking guidance. Prohibitions against obstructing public passages are acceptable, as speech and assembly rights are not unlimited:

> The rights of free speech and assembly, while fundamental
> in our democratic society, still do not mean that everyone
> with opinions or beliefs to express may address a group

at any public place and at any time. The constitutional guarantee of liberty implies the existence of an organized society maintaining public order, without which liberty itself would be lost in the excesses of anarchy."[7]

*Tinker v. Des Moines Community School District*[8] is regarded as *the* landmark case for student free speech. In *Tinker*, public school parents and students decided to wear black armbands to publicize their objections to United States involvement in Vietnam. School administrators adopted a policy forbidding the armbands and suspended students who wore them. Students filed suit, alleging that the policy violated their free speech rights. The Supreme Court held for the students. In this case, the students' speech was silent and passive and yielded no evidence of disruption or interference. The restriction was based on the administrator's fear and apprehension of the unpleasantness that might come from an unpopular viewpoint. But the Court held that such undifferentiated fear is not enough. "It can hardly be argued that either students or teachers shed their constitutional rights to freedom of speech or expression at the schoolhouse gate."[9] Any word spoken in a classroom that disagrees with the views of another has the power to disturb. But, according to the Court, this is a risk that society must take. "Schools may not be enclaves of totalitarianism.... Students may not be regarded as closed-circuit recipients of only that which the State chooses to communicate."[10]

The popular "schoolhouse gate" statement from *Tinker* provides strong support for similar sentiment at the higher education level. In fact, unlike students' rights in K-12 settings, students' rights to free expression on college campuses may parallel the rights of adults in public forums. For example, in *Healy v. James*, the Supreme Court reviewed the legality of a university's decision to deny a student petition to form a chapter of Students for a Democratic Society (SDS).[11] In holding for the students, the Court held that the disagreement of university administrators over the views expressed by students and mere fear of what might come from the divergent views are not enough to suppress student speech. The burden to justify suppression of speech is on the institution, but such suppression may not be based on a philosophical disagreement with the group's message. According to the Court, it may not even be based on the group's expression of views condoning violence and disruption.

> As repugnant as these views may have been, especially to one with President James' responsibility, the mere expression of them would not justify the denial of First Amendment rights.... The College, acting here as the instrumentality of the State, may not restrict speech or association simply because it finds the view expressed by any group to be abhorrent.[12]

Similar to their rulings in K-12 cases, however, courts have held that universities may suppress student speech if it is unlawful or disruptive—if it advocates views directed to inciting or producing imminent lawless action and likely to incite or produce such action. In a case like *Healy*, for example, recognition may be denied to a student group that violates reasonable campus rules. Reasonable time, place, and manner restrictions—even in a marketplace of ideas—must be respected, so long as they are content-neutral, narrowly-tailored to serve a significant governmental interest, and leave open ample alternative channels of communication. "A college has the inherent power to promulgate rules and regulations; that it has the inherent power properly to discipline; that it has the power appropriately to protect itself and its property; that it may expect that its students adhere to generally accepted standards of conduct."[13] A public higher education institution must be careful, however, in the enforcement of these speech policies.

In *Orin v. Barclay*,[14] plaintiff Benjamin Orin and two of his associates wished to use Olympic Community College (OCC) campus property to protest abortion. The Interim Dean of Students granted them the right to protest, but only if they did not create a disturbance, interfere with students' access to building, or base their protest in overtly religious terms. After the protestors left for the campus quad, the Dean dispatched two security guards to monitor the event. During the four-hour protest, the Dean's office received several complaints. The crowd around the protestors ranged from five to over 100. Eventually, a security guard asked Orin to leave because he was violating the conditions imposed by the Interim Dean. Orin refused, and the college called city police who arrested Orin when he again refused to leave. The demonstrators alleged that the college restricted the protest due to the religious content of the speech. The college alleged that the restriction was based on verbal assaults on spectators and impending physical conflict. Orin sued the Dean and the security officer who demanded him to end the protest and alleged First Amendment violation of free speech and freedom of religion. The district court held that the defendants were entitled to qualified immunity. On appeal, the court of appeals addressed each of the three restrictions the Dean imposed on Orin's protest. The first two—not to create a disturbance and not to block access to campus buildings—are legal as content-neutral restrictions narrowly tailored to meet the college's legitimate governmental and pedagogical interests. The third condition—to refrain from religious worship or instruction—was a different story. The college did create a forum for the protestors' expression. Having done so, the college could not limit the expression based on viewpoint to only secular content. Because the Dean's third condition was content-based, the college must narrowly tailor the restriction to meet a compelling governmental interest. Dean Barclay argued that the First Amendment's requirement for separation of church and state required the religion-based condition. The Court of Appeals rejected this argument.[15]

In addition to the alleged viewpoint discrimination in policy enforcement as seen in *Orin*, a college or university must also be careful not to impose unreasonable prior restraints on student speech. "A prior restraint exists when the enjoyment of protected expression is contingent upon the approval of government officials."[16] Prior restraints are not unconstitutional per se, but they bear a "heavy presumption" against constitutional validity.[17] To withstand constitutional scrutiny, a prior restraint must contain certain procedural safeguards. In particular, the administrator issuing or denying a petition or license to engage in expressive activities must make the decision in a reasonable amount of time. "Promptness is essential because undue delay compels the speaker's silence while the applicant awaits a decision.... Unreasonable and indefinite delay is tantamount to the complete suppression of speech."[18]

One challenge to a prior restraint arose in *Burbridge v. Sampson* where South Orange County Community College adopted a policy regulating the time, place, and manner of speech and other advocacy activities on campus.[19] Under the policy, non-district individuals and organizations could use district property for commercial purposes only with prior approval of the President, provided that the activities did not interfere with the normal functioning of the district. Non-commercial speech conducted for personal or private gain was restricted. The policy also required that speech that may generate an audience of greater than twenty people and/or speech that needs amplification required advance reservation and is restricted to three designated areas on campus.[20] Plaintiffs argued that the policy was vague, overbroad, and unconstitutional as a prior restraint. The court agreed and held that the defendants failed to articulate any governmental interest furthered by the designation of specific free-speech areas.[21] The court also held that the policy was overbroad in that there were many commercial and noncommercial aspects of speech that are inextricably intertwined.

Two-and-a-half years after the court's decision in *Burbridge*, the parties returned in a dispute over South Orange County Community College's new speech policy.[22] In response to the adverse ruling in *Burbridge*, the community college adopted new time, place, and manner restrictions on the expressive activities of both students and members of the public who wish to use campus facilities. The plaintiffs, one of whom was Burbridge, filed suit alleging that the new policy acted as a prior restraint, violated free speech rights, and was unconstitutionally overbroad for all speakers. The court first held that the students had standing only to sue on behalf of the students and not members of the general public, and while the court noted that some provisions were constitutional and others were not, it eventually struck down all of the provisions affecting students, holding that the unconstitutional provisions were not severable. The primary substantive concern noted by the court was that the policy gave largely unfettered discretion to the community college campus presidents to determine which expressive activities would be permitted. Accordingly, with such a high level of discretion resting with only one government official and no procedures to guide their administrative decisions, the policy violated speech rights of students.

Importantly, the defendant community college in *Khademi* argued that the college policy was written to comply with a California state statute requiring institutions of higher education to protect the free speech rights of students.[23] But interestingly, the court found a compelling governmental interest in only the part of the college's policy designed to prevent the "commission of unlawful acts on community college premises" and "the substantial disruption of the orderly operation of the community college."[24] In other words, blanket imposition of all the terms of a state statute requiring community colleges to draft speech policies was not narrowly tailored to the few governmental interests the court found compelling. With respect to specific content-based provisions, the court struck down the provision restricting the posting of advertising materials. This provision was lawful only as related to the posting of ads for goods and services already criminally unlawful in California or the United States. Content-neutral provisions, such as those restricting speech activities when lawn maintenance is an issue and/or when there are preexisting reservations for use of the same space, are permissible. Lastly, the court ruled on the alleged overbreadth of the policy. It upheld the defamation provisions and the extension of the policy to off-campus school-sponsored speech that materially disrupts the work of the college or the rights of others but struck down the provision prohibiting leaflets on windshields, in parking lots, and inside buildings.[25]

## Recognized Student Groups

> Effective advocacy of both public and private points of view, particularly controversial ones, is undeniably enhanced by group association.... Of course, it is immaterial whether the beliefs sought to be advanced by association pertain to political, economic, religious or cultural matters, any state action which may have the effect of curtailing the freedom to associate is subject to the closest scrutiny.[26]

Similar to restrictions on non-sponsored student expression, public college and university policies governing the recognition and activities of student groups and the benefits they receive are subjected to high constitutional scrutiny. *Healy v. James*,[27] discussed above, illustrates this point. Students formed a local chapter of the Students for a Democratic Society and filed for status as an official student organization. The college president denied the application because the group's philosophies were antithetical to the college's mission. On a First Amendment challenge, the Supreme Court held that the denial of a student group may be based on the failure to comply with reasonable campus regulations, but it may not be based on an assumed relationship with the national chapter, a disagreement with the group's philosophy, or a mere unsubstantiated fear of disruption.[28]

While universities may promulgate policies to guide the expressive activities of student groups, those policies must be viewpoint and content neutral, based on a compelling governmental interest, and narrowly tailored to meet that interest. In *Pro-Life Cougars v. University of Houston*, for example, the United States District Court for the Southern District of Texas applied this strict scrutiny standard to a "Disruption of University Operations and Events" policy.[29] Under the policy, events deemed "potentially disruptive" were subject to specific time, location, and content restrictions. The Pro-Life Cougars student organization had applied to use a certain university plaza, typically and historically used for student expressive events, for its pro-life "Justice for All" exhibit. Among other collisions between the student group and the policy, the particular plaza requested was not on the approved list for potentially disruptive activities. The dean of students deemed the exhibit potentially disruptive and denied the application. The exhibit included eight, two-sided signs, each of them three feet by four feet, which held photographs and educational messages.[30] In a holding similar to that in *Khademi v. South Orange County Community College District*,[31] the court struck down the policy as an unlawful prior restraint that gives one governmental official overly broad discretion without objective guidelines. In a related point, the court held that the contentious term of the policy, "potentially disruptive," was not narrowly tailored to reach a compelling governmental interest.

Often, an institution will assert the avoidance of a First Amendment Establishment Clause violation as a compelling governmental interest. In *Widmar v. Vincent*,[32] a state university excluded, from student organization recognition, any group desiring to use facilities for religious worship and religious discussion or teaching. A student religious group that had been meeting on campus for four years filed suit. The trial court held for the university, the circuit court of appeals reversed and held for the students, and the Supreme Court upheld in favor of the students. The Court held that while the avoidance of an Establishment Clause violation may be compelling, a policy of equal access for all student groups would not necessarily have been incompatible with the law. The Court applied the then-popular, three-part test adopted in *Lemon v. Kurtzman*.[33] According to the Court, a policy recognizing religious student organizations would have a secular purpose, would not have the primary effect of advancing religion, and would avoid excessive entanglement with religion. The forum for student organizations is open to all forms of discourse and, as such, does not advance religion, even if there are incidental religious benefits to some of the forum's participants. An open forum in a public university does not confer any imprimatur of state approval with respect to the views of the speakers. Comparing *Widmar* to cases like *Healy*, the Court held, finally, that a policy allowing a student religious group to use university facilities does not commit the university to the religious goals of that group any more than allowing minority political groups to use facilities would attribute certain political views to the institution as a whole.[34]

## Student Activity Fees

On one end of the activity fee debate, perhaps Thomas Jefferson said it best: "To compel a man to furnish contributions of money for the propagation of opinions which he disbelieves, is sinful and tyrannical."[35] But, of course, in tight financial times, an argument on the other side is that, in order to offer comprehensive successful programs and activities, students may have to contribute to the cause through a mandatory fee. Two significant Supreme Court cases in the past decade tend to favor the institution's argument. But the legal claims that continue this debate do not come from doubting a college or university's need for the fees; they come from institutional decisions over which groups would be permitted to access the pooled fees and what the groups are doing with the money once it is accessed. In other words, how much say should a student have in where or how his or her money is being spent?

In 1995, in *Rosenberger v. Rector and Visitors of the University of Virginia*,[36] the University of Virginia imposed a mandatory student activity fee, whereby the fees were pooled for distribution to independent student organizations for printing costs for their publications.[37] Students filed a suit when the university denied funding to their organization. The organization, Wide Awake Publications, wrote a newsletter entitled *Wide Awake: A Christian Perspective at the University of Virginia*. The students argued that the university's refusal to authorize payment violated their rights to free speech. The university argued that to authorize the payment would endorse religion in contravention of the Establishment Clause. The university cited to its student activities fund policy, which denied funds to any group that "primarily promotes or manifests a particular belief in or about a deity or an ultimate reality." The lower courts held for the university, agreeing with the university's legitimate interest in avoiding an Establishment Clause violation.

The Supreme Court reversed and held for the students. The University of Virginia's policy governing the distribution of student activity funds was not viewpoint neutral. In the realm of private speech or expression, the government may not favor one speaker over another. The policy did not specifically exclude religion as a subject matter, but the university treated unfavorably those student organizations with religious viewpoints.[38] The Court also noted significant problems with the wording of the policy's exceptions: "promotes" and "manifests." "It is difficult to name renowned thinkers whose writings would be accepted, save perhaps for articles disclaiming all connection to their ultimate philosophy."[39]

On the Establishment Clause concerns, the *Rosenberger* Court found no evidence that the university intended to favor or disfavor religion. The purpose was to keep the marketplace of ideas open and diverse. The institution's disclaimer that all eligible student organizations are independent of the university secures neutrality. Under the policy, the money goes to the organization's outside printer and not to the organization's own accounts. Any benefit to religion is purely incidental in a viewpoint-neutral funding program. The Court also held that the university's concern about violating the Establishment Clause was unfounded. In fact, the denial of funding could be a violation, as it risks pervasive bias or hostility to religion. According to the Court, to censor public university students' religious speech would be more harmful to the dictates of the Establishment Clause than to provide printing services to student publications on a neutral basis.

The second significant Supreme Court case on the activity fee issue, *Board of Regents of the University of Wisconsin v. Southworth*, raised a related claim.[40] Similar to the argument made by Thomas Jefferson, the plaintiffs in *Southworth* argued that a mandatory fee charged to students at the University of Wisconsin was unconstitutional on its face, as it funded expressive activities with which they disagreed. The university claimed that the fee is consistent with the institution's missions of promoting and supporting extracurricular activities, stimulating advocacy and debate on diverse points of view, enabling participation in political activity, and promoting opportunity to develop social skills.[41] The lower courts struck down the policy, holding that a public university may not compel particular speech with a mandatory activity fee.

The Supreme Court reversed and upheld the policy. According to the Court, provided that the policy is viewpoint neutral (and the parties in *Southworth* conceded that it was), the policy does not violate the First Amendment. In fact, it enhances the free exchange of ideas in that it provides student activity funds to various student groups in a viewpoint-neutral fashion.

> The University may determine that its mission is well served
> if students have the means to engage in dynamic discussions
> of philosophical, religious, scientific, social, and political
> subjects in their extracurricular campus life outside the
> lecture hall. If the University reaches this conclusion, it
> is entitled to impose a mandatory fee to sustain an open
> dialogue to these ends.[42]

The Court was sympathetic to the arguments of the complaining students, however. These students are entitled to certain safeguards with respect to expressive activities that they are required to support. The Court determined that the appropriate safeguards are provided through the doctrine of viewpoint neutrality in allocation of the funds. In a follow-up decision to *Southworth* one year later, the District Court for the Western District of

Wisconsin invalidated the University of Wisconsin's allocation procedures under the student fee policy. According to the court, the review procedure for the allocation of funds gave a student government committee too much discretion and was not viewpoint neutral.[43]

## Student Publications

In the spirit of decisions like *Tinker*, *Healy*, and even *Rosenberger*, courts are likely to support student-produced newspapers, as long as the publications do not give rise to material or substantial disruption of institutional operations or the rights of others. In addition, any policies promulgated by the public college or university for production and distribution of student newspapers must be content-neutral and viewpoint-neutral; restriction on speech in student publications may not be based on mere disagreement with the content or fear of apprehension and conflict. The decision in *Papish v. Board of Curators of the University of Missouri* illustrates these points.[44] The University of Missouri expelled a graduate student for distributing a publication allegedly containing "indecent speech". The newspaper, the *Free Press Underground*, had been sold on campus for four years pursuant to an agreement with the University Business Office. The particular issue in question contained two troubling items. One was a political cartoon, with the caption "With Liberty and Justice for All", depicting policemen raping the Goddess of Justice. The second item was an article entitled "M—f—Acquitted", which discussed the trial and acquittal of a New York City youth charged with assault. The Student Conduct Committee found that the student had violated the student code of conduct. The student code prohibited indecent speech and required students "to observe generally accepted standards of conduct". The Chancellor and the Board of Curators affirmed the expulsion. The district court and court of appeals upheld the university's decision. The Supreme Court applied *Healy* and reversed. "[T]he mere dissemination of ideas—no matter how offensive to good taste—on a state university campus may not be shut off in the name alone of 'conventions of decency.'"[45] Dissenting Justices in *Papish* argued differently. Justice Burger argued that the decision to discipline the student for "obscene and infantile" speech was not unreasonable even in light of the recognized right of students to criticize their university, faculty, and government as a whole.[46]

An argument can be made that student publications, produced under agreements with an institution's administration and under the aegis of student codes of conduct, are actually institution-sponsored and, therefore, subject to stricter speech rules than those adopted by the Court in *Tinker*, *Healy*, and *Rosenberger*. With that argument comes the possibility that the landmark K-12 student newspaper case, *Hazelwood Independent School District v. Kuhlmeier*, is applicable to public college and university publications as well.[47] In *Hazelwood*, high school students filed suit after their

principal cut two pages from the school-sponsored and classroom-pro-
duced newspaper. The principal's decision to cut the pages was due to the
controversial content of a couple student-written articles.[48] The Supreme
Court held in favor of the school. First, the Court held that the school
newspaper was a nonpublic forum, not opened, by policy or by practice,
to indiscriminate use by the general public. Second, the Court held that
a school may exercise greater control over speech that the public might
perceive to bear the imprimatur of the school. Finally, the Court held that
school administrators may exercise editorial control over the content and
style of student speech in school-sponsored, expressive activities so long
as their actions are based on legitimate pedagogical concerns.

The applicability of *Hazelwood* to higher education was challenged
in *Kincaid v. Gibson*.[49] Kincaid and Coffer were staff members on the
committee for *The Thorobred*, the student yearbook at Kentucky State
University (KSU). With a depleted staff, Coffer significantly redirected
the style and content of the publication. Gibson, the university's Vice
President for Student Affairs, objected to several aspects of the yearbook,
including the cover, the theme ("destination unknown"), and the lack of
captions on many of the pictures.[50] She ordered that the yearbook copies
be confiscated and not distributed. The district court held that the yearbook
was not a public forum, in that the intended audience was limited to KSU
students and the yearbook was not intended as a journal of expression and
communication in the sense of a public forum. Consequently, the district
court held that the actions of the university were reasonable. A divided
panel of the Sixth Circuit affirmed the decision.

The en banc Court of Appeals reversed and held that the university
yearbook was a limited public forum (or a "designated public forum").
*Hazelwood* did not apply; the actions of the university must be judged
under strict scrutiny and not under the "legitimate pedagogical concerns"
standard of a closed forum. To determine whether the yearbook constituted
a limited public forum, the court looked at the policy and practice of the
university officials. The publications policy opens with the following self-
imposed restraint: "The Board of Regents respects the integrity of student
publications and the press, and the rights to exist in an atmosphere of free
and responsible discussion and of intellectual exploration." Testimony
from both sides indicated that students had control over content. This was
not a college course taken for a grade. The court further distinguished
*Hazelwood*, stating that this is not a K-12 setting with young people.

In an interesting case discussing the investigative rights of a university
publication, a North Carolina appeals court held that a student newspaper
does not have a First Amendment right to access student disciplinary
proceedings. In *DTH Publishing Corporation v. University of North
Carolina*,[51] two students were charged with removing about 1,500 copies
of the university's student magazine from the racks used for distribution
of the magazine. The publisher of the newspaper filed suit and requested

access to the disciplinary proceedings involving the two students. Both the trial court and the court of appeals held for the university.

## Student Government

Colleges and universities regularly promulgate rules and regulations regarding student government activities including elections. Primary among them are the restrictions placed on election campaigns. In the area of campaign funding, one recent case may tell the representative story. In *Welker v. Cicerone*,[52] the University of California-Irvine Student Elections Code had restricted campaign spending to $100 for students running for spots on the university's Legislative Council. Violations of the code resulted in disqualification. Welker, a senior, was running unopposed for a seat on Legislative Council, and spent $233.40. The Elections Commission disqualified Welker and the University Judicial Board affirmed. Welker filed suit for reinstatement to the Legislative Council and expungement of the disciplinary record. The court applied *Buckley v. Valeo*,[53] and held for the student. The *Buckley* Court had found that limits on campaign spending directly affect free speech in quantity and in diversity.[54] Accordingly, defendants responding to challenges like Welker's must show that their funding limits are narrowly tailored to meet a compelling governmental interest. In *Welker*, the defendants offered four such interests. The court held that the first one, to increase socio-economic equality, was not compelling. The court rejected each of the remaining three asserted interests because the elections code was not narrowly tailored to meet them. First, the university's interest in encouragement of academic pursuits was fine, but was not related to student elections.[55] Second, the university imposed the limits to decrease the influence of private corporate sponsors. The court agreed with the interest, but held that the code already provided for it, in that there were limits on the amount a candidate could get from any one source. Finally, the university argued that a limit on campaign funding would increase students' creativity (i.e., do more with less). The court found that there was no direct correlation between creativity and spending limits and even if there were, such a limit would stifle creativity, not increase it.

Related to campaign funding limits are restrictions on campaign activity and the distribution of literature. These limits are governed by the standards adopted and applied in cases like *Tinker* and *Healy*: content-neutral and viewpoint-neutral time, place, and manner restrictions are permissible. Policies inspired by the maintenance and fair distribution of scarce institutional resources are permissible as well.[56]

## Fraternities and Sororities

Does the First Amendment protect fraternities and sororities in the same way that it might protect student publications and other student groups? In order for the answer to be "yes," a fraternity or sorority must convince a court that its activities are designed to be expressive and associational for First Amendment purposes. This may be a tall order for the group to meet. The Third Circuit Court of Appeals, in a recent opinion, held that a fraternity chapter was "social," not "expressive," and was not protected under the First Amendment. In *Pi Lambda Phi v. University of Pittsburgh*, the university revoked the chapter of a fraternity after a 1996 police raid yielded drugs and drug paraphernalia including heroin, cocaine, opium, and date rape drugs.[57] A couple of internal appeals failed and the Chapter filed suit. Ultimately, the Court of Appeals affirmed the trial court's decision to uphold the university's decision.

The Court of Appeals noted that there are two types of free association and held that the fraternity chapter does not qualify under either one. First, intimate association, generally equated with family-based relationships, receives protection as a fundamental element of personal liberty. To determine whether a group qualifies here, a court will examine the group's size, purpose, policies, selectivity, congeniality, and other related characteristics. The court found that when it's at full force, the fraternity chapter is not small (eighty members). Similarly, it is not very selective, taking its members from the entire student body.

Second, expressive association recognizes the right to associate for the purpose of engaging in speech, assembly, petition for the redress of grievances, and the exercise of religion. The right of expressive association is a generous one. It is not reserved merely for advocacy groups. But there must be some expressive activity. Even with this broad definition, the fraternity chapter in *Pi Lambda Phi* failed to show evidence of expressive association. Despite the existence of a national parent chapter that would likely qualify under this standard, there was no evidence that the fraternity ever took a stand on any issue of public, political, social, or cultural importance. A few minor acts of charity work and community service were not enough. In an important move, the court also noted that even if the fraternity had qualified as an expressive association, the court would have denied its claims. The university's restrictions significantly outweighed the fraternity's interests. "Associational activities need not be tolerated where they infringe reasonable campus rules, interrupt classes, or substantially interfere with the opportunity of other students to obtain an education."[58]

## Hate Speech

A function of the First Amendment is to invite dispute. "Speech is often provocative and challenging. It may strike at prejudices and preconceptions and have profound unsettling effects as it presses for acceptance of an idea. That is why freedom of speech, though not absolute, is nevertheless protected against censorship or punishment."[59] As grand as this statement is, this chapter has illustrated consistently that rights to freedom of expression are not without their limits. Hate speech codes and hate crime laws cover harmful unlawful conduct committed on account of the victims' race, gender, ethnicity, religion, disability status, military status, and/or sexual orientation. Universities' versions of these codes were particularly susceptible to successful First Amendment challenge in the early 1990s. In other words, attempts by educational institutions to restrict harmful, harassing conduct of members of the university community have not been successful when placed against the freedom of expression.[60] On the other end of the policymaking spectrum, however, schools, colleges, and universities are required under Title IX of the Education Amendments of 1972 to promulgate policies prohibiting sexual harassment.[61] In the late 1990s, the Supreme Court opened the door to institutional liability under Title IX for deliberate indifference to known sexual harassment.[62]

In discussions of hate speech laws, the applicable landmark Supreme Court case is *R.A.V. v. City of St. Paul*.[63] In *R.A.V.*, the Supreme Court struck down the city of St. Paul's hate speech ordinance, under which it was a crime to display symbols that "aroused anger, alarm or resentment in others on the basis of race, color, creed, religion, or gender." The Court held that the ordinance was not neutral, in that it allowed speech that advanced the ideas of racial and ethnic equality but prohibited speech by those who express views on disfavored subjects. One year later, the Supreme Court visited a related case and upheld a statute that imposed a harsher prison sentence on criminals who engage in crimes where the victim is targeted because of race.[64] According to that Court, the increase in sentence went beyond mere disagreement with defendants' beliefs and biases. The prospect of enhanced penalty under the criminal law does not chill free speech. The First Amendment does not prohibit the use of speech as evidence in establishing the required elements of the crime. The state's desire to redress individual and societal harm caused by bias-motivated crimes provided an adequate defense for penalty enhancement.

Courts have addressed campus hate speech codes only a few times. In 1989, in *Doe v. University of Michigan*, a psychology graduate student filed suit challenging the legality of the university's hate speech code.[65] The policy prohibited physical or verbal behavior that stigmatized or victimized an individual "on the basis of race, ethnicity, religion, sex, sexual orientation, creed, national origin, ancestry, age, marital status, handicap, Vietnam-era veteran status."[66] The plaintiff argued that under the policy, the classroom discussion of certain controversial theories positing the biological differences between men and women and among races may be perceived as "sexist" or "racist" under the policy. The court held for the plaintiff, striking down the policy as vague and overbroad. According to the court, it was impossible to determine the scope of the policy as it related to classroom speech, academic discussions, and research. Two years later, in *UWM Post, Inc. v. Board of Regents of the University of Wisconsin*, the district court for the Eastern District of Wisconsin struck down a similar anti-discrimination policy at the University of Wisconsin.[67] Adding to the string of court rulings disfavoring university decisions to restrict alleged "hate speech," the Fourth Circuit Court of Appeals, in *Iota Xi Chapter of Sigma Chi Fraternity v. George Mason University*, upheld a summary judgment in favor of a fraternity that staged an "ugly woman contest" as part of its "Derby Days Events."[68] Applying *Texas v. Johnson*,[69] the court held that such activity, while immature and sophomoric, constituted protected expression. The court also applied *R.A.V.* and held that the university could not punish the speakers in this case merely because university officials disapproved of the ideas contained in the students' conduct.

Despite the good intentions of policymakers who draft and implement hate speech codes and despite the legal lessons they have learned from earlier cases, one recent attempt to solidify a school anti-harassment policy failed as well.[70] In *Saxe v. State College Area School District*, a school district attempted to blend the protected groups highlighted in earlier codes, like the ones in the Michigan and Wisconsin cases, with the recent Title IX liability standards of *Gebser v. Lago Vista Independent School District*[71] and *Davis v. Monroe County Board of Education*.[72] The policy result was a provision that prohibited verbal or physical conduct that has the effect of creating an intimidating, hostile, or offensive environment. The legal result was the same; the code was struck down. The court argued that "harassment," as defined by federal anti-discrimination statutes like Title IX, is not necessarily unprotected expression under the First Amendment.[73] Moreover, the policy at issue extended the definition of harassment too far to include teasing, name-calling, joke telling, and mimicking. As a result, the policy was declared overbroad and unconstitutional.

## Student Speech in Academic Contexts

Given the litigious nature of free expression claims and the history of student speech issues on college and university campuses, the case law explicitly involving the classroom work and academic freedom of students is surprisingly sparse. Instead, much of the legal direction in the law of student speech comes from challenges to campus-wide policies on protest activity, student publications, and recognized student organizations, each discussed earlier in this chapter. Nonetheless, a few points should be made regarding the classroom work of students and the application of the popular K-12 decision in *Hazelwood Independent School District v. Kuhlmeier*.[74] As discussed above, the Court of Appeals for the Sixth Circuit, in *Kincaid v. Gibson*,[75] held that *Hazelwood* did not apply to speech associated with a university yearbook. The court in *Kincaid* held that the yearbook was a limited public forum, that the students had control over the content, that this activity was not a course taken for a grade, and that the students were adults. So what about a situation in which there is a course for a grade and the students are not the only people in control of content? With the low number of such cases at the college and university setting, courts have tended to look to the case law from K-12 and, whether or not the factual situations are representative of those found in higher education, have drawn narrow bounds on the speech rights of students in higher education arenas.

In *Brown v. Li*,[76] for example, Christopher Brown decided to include a "Disacknowledgments" section at the end of his master's thesis. It began as follows: "I would like to offer special *Fuck You's* [sic] to the following degenerates for being an ever-present hindrance during my graduate career...." The disacknowledgments named the dean and staff of the university's graduate school, the staff at the university library, and a former California governor. His thesis committee did not accept the thesis, withheld granting the degree, and placed Brown on academic probation for failing to complete the degree in a timely manner. After several months of probation, the university relented and granted the degree when Brown agreed to submit the thesis without the offending section. Brown, however, did not submit the thesis to the university library and, as a result, it was never placed in the library's archives. Brown filed suit arguing that the withholding of his degree violated his free speech rights. He requested an injunction to compel the university to place his thesis in the library. The district court granted summary judgment for the defendants and, in a divided opinion, the Ninth Circuit affirmed on the First Amendment claims.[77] The court of appeals' lead opinion re-framed the central legal issue—whether the defendants violated Brown's free speech rights when they refused to accept his disacknowledgments section—and applied *Hazelwood* in the context of university classroom/curricular assignments. The court distinguished curricular activities from extracurricular activities and deferred to the authority of an educational institution to establish its curricular standards:

> ... [A]n educator can, consistent with the First Amendment, require that a student comply with the terms of an academic assignment.... [T]he First Amendment does not require an educator to change the assignment to suit the student's opinion or to approve the work of a student that, in his or her judgment, fails to meet a legitimate academic standard.[78]

The court in *Brown* made special note of a college student's age and maturity. But, instead of favoring the speech of the student on these accounts, the court drew the student and his speech closer to college control:

> The Supreme Court's jurisprudence does not hold that an institution's interest in mandating its curriculum and in limiting a student's speech to that which is germane to a particular academic assignment diminishes as students age. Indeed, arguably the need for academic discipline and editorial rigor increases as a student's learning progresses.[79]

Applying the *Hazelwood* standard, the court found that a master's thesis is part of the university's curriculum and that the procedural and substantive rules applicable at the University of California-Santa Barbara, where Brown was a student, were reasonably related to legitimate pedagogical concerns associated with the completion of a master's thesis. Additionally, the court held that the defendants acted within their discretion when they refused to accept Brown's addendum.[80]

Factually, the result in *Brown* may be satisfactory to college and university personnel, in that some level of professional discipline and academic standard must be met—standards established under the discretionary authority of college and university academic leaders. But on the level of student free speech in the higher education context, the right and opportunity of a student to direct learning or to contribute to learning outcomes or the overall knowledge base in a classroom setting may be hampered by the extensive application of *Hazelwood* in the college classroom. The lead opinion in *Brown* deferred to the curricular missions and the syllabi of faculty members and their necessary inclusion of material that enhances the critical thinking abilities of students. "For example, a college history teacher may demand a paper defending Prohibition, and a law school professor may assign students to write 'opinions' showing how Justice Ginsburg and Justice Scalia would analyze a particular Fourth Amendment question."[81] Continuing in this vein, the opinion indicated that college students, in particular, as their "learning progresses," need a stronger guiding hand when it comes to oral and written expression. The partial dissent in *Brown*, on the other hand, disagreed vigorously with the application of *Hazelwood* to college and university student speech. The dissenting judge, instead, cited cases like *Healy v. James*,[82] *Rosenberger v. Rector and Visitors of the University of Virginia*,[83] and *Kincaid v. Gibson*[84] to illustrate the point that college and university students are typically more mature and independent than their K-12 counterparts and that the courts have regularly afforded them more speech rights. The dissent argued that, perhaps, a limited public forum analysis would better suit the college and university classroom, where reasonable time, place, and manner restrictions are permissible; viewpoint discrimination is not; and where content-based restrictions are subject to strict scrutiny. And, at the very least, he argued for intermediate judicial scrutiny over the reasonableness standard of *Hazelwood*.

So, the impact of the sharply divided decision in *Brown* has yet to be measured. Until more cases involving the academic speech rights of students are litigated, it will be difficult to tell whether the result was motivated by the legitimate balance of rights between institutional curricular authority and student free speech or by the obvious misstep in professionalism on the part of the student. One post-*Brown* decision, however, seems to indicate the comfort level courts may have in applying *Hazelwood* to higher education classrooms. Interestingly, *Axson-Flynn v. Johnson* involved a student who, instead of using profane language to make her points, wished to refrain from doing so.[85] In *Axson-Flynn*, a former student in the University of Utah's Actor Training Program (ATP) filed suit against the program faculty alleging that the faculty violated her rights to free speech and free exercise of religion when they required her to perform monologues and other scenes that contained what the student (Axson-Flynn) argued were offensive words. Axson-Flynn, a Mormon, told the faculty as early as her audition for the program that there were things she felt uncomfortable doing as an actor. She would not take her clothes off, take the name of God or Christ in vain, or "say the four-letter expletive beginning with the letter F." ATP admitted her to the program, but Axson-Flynn's first semester would be her last. During the semester, Axson-Flynn reiterated her discomforts and even omitted offensive language from one of her classroom monologues without anyone noticing. While she received very good grades on assignments, instructors told her that she would have to "get over" her misgivings if she wished to grow as an actor. At her semester review, defendant faculty members reportedly recommended that Axson-Flynn "talk to some other Mormon girls who are good Mormons, who don't have a problem with this."[86] The faculty members said that Axson-Flynn would have to modify her values or consider leaving the program. Axson-Flynn was never explicitly asked to leave the program; but she did, indeed, leave the ATP and the university one month into her second semester. The district court granted summary judgment to the defendants on both the speech and religion claims, but the Tenth Circuit reversed on both accounts.

On Axson-Flynn's free speech claim, the Tenth Circuit explicitly held that *Hazelwood* applied, in that the University of Utah's classrooms were nonpublic forums and the associated speech by students and faculty was university-sponsored.[87] "Few activities bear a school's imprimatur and involve pedagogical interests more significantly than speech that occurs within a classroom setting as part of a school's curriculum."[88] The court expressed great deference to instructors' curricular decisions. And while admitting that the ATP compelled Axson-Flynn to speak, an action that would be scrutinized heavily in a more public forum, the court held that some compulsion to speak is expected in academic work at all levels of education and often reasonably to legitimate pedagogical concerns. In this case, the ATP faculty argued that the compulsion to speak is intimately related to professional work in theater and was necessary in this instance. The court did not disagree, but held that there was a factual dispute over whether the compulsion to speak was reasonably related to a legitimate pedagogical concern or was a pretext for religious discrimination. As a result, the court reversed the grant of summary judgment and remanded the case. The court also remanded Axson-Flynn's free exercise claim, in that there was a factual dispute as to whether the faculty had treated the student unfairly with respect to religious exemptions made on assignments.[89]

# Endnotes

[1] West Va. State Bd. of Educ. v. Barnette, 319 U.S. 624, 640, 642 (1943).

[2] West Va. State Bd. of Educ. v. Barnette, 319 U.S. 624 (1943) (Jehovah's witnesses protested mandatory salute of the American flag) and Tinker v. Des Moines Cmty. Sch. Dist., 393 U.S. 503 (1969) (students protested U.S. involvement in Vietnam by wearing black armbands to school), are fine examples from K-12 education.

[3] *See, e.g.,* Gilligan v. Morgan, 413 U.S. 1 (1973) (Supreme Court held that a claim filed following the civil unrest and killings at Kent State University in May 1970 was not justiciable, in that it asked for an injunction to monitor the governor's training and deployment of the National Guard). *See also* Orin v. Barclay, 272 F.3d 1207 (9th Cir. 2001).

[4] This judicial standard is also well known from a landmark case from K-12 education. *See* Tinker v. Des Moines Cmty. Sch. Dist., 393 U.S. 503 (1969).

[5] 379 U.S. 536 (1965).

[6] *Id.* at 551-552 (*quoting* Terminiello v. City of Chi., 337 U.S. 1, 4-5 (1949)).

[7] *Id.* at 554. On a related issue, traditional due process rights of notice and an opportunity to be heard apply to university-based discipline of students. *See* Dixon v. Ala. State Bd. of Educ., 294 F.2d 150 (5th Cir.), *cert. denied*, 368 U.S. 930 (1961).

[8] 393 U.S. 503 (1969).

[9] *Id.* at 506.

[10] *Id.* at 511.

[11] 408 U.S. 169 (1972).

[12] *Id.* at 187-188. For a popular judicial opinion on a related issue, *see* Texas v. Johnson, 419 U.S. 397 (1989) (the Court struck down a statute criminalizing the burning of the American flag as a form of protest). According to the *Texas* Court, "the government may not prohibit the expression of an idea simply because society finds the idea itself offensive or disagreeable." 419 U.S. at 414.

[13] Esteban v. Cent. Mo. State Coll., 415 F.2d 1077, 1089 (8th Cir. 1969), *cert. denied*, 398 U.S. 965 (1970).

[14] 272 F.3d 1207 (9th Cir. 2001).

[15] *See* subsection "Facilities Usage and Public Forum Doctrine," *supra.*

[16] Near v. Minn., 283 U.S. 697, 713 (1931).

[17] FW/PBS, Inc. v. City of Dallas, 493 U.S. 215, 225 (1990) and Pro-Life Cougars v. Univ. of Houston, 259 F. Supp. 2d 575, 583 (S.D. Tex. 2003).

[18] Baby Tam & Co., Inc. v. City of Las Vegas, 154 F.3d 1097, 1101 (9th Cir. 1998).

[19] 74 F. Supp. 2d 940 (C.D. Cal. 1999).

[20] The three designated speech areas did not include the spaces on campus traditionally and historically used for speech activities.

[21] The college offered two compelling government interests: (1) promotion of a safe and secure educational atmosphere over a commercial one and (2) prevention of fraud and harassment of students and staff. But the college failed to show that its policy furthered those interests.

[22] Khademi v. S. Orange County Cmty. Coll. Dist., 194 F. Supp. 2d 1011 (C.D. Cal. 2002).

[23] *See* Cal. Educ. Code § 76120. The statute, while protective of speech rights, also contains a provision prohibiting student speech that is typically unprotected (e.g., speech that is obscene, libelous, slanderous, inciting of clear and present danger, in violation of lawful campus regulations, and substantially disruptive to college operation).

[24] 194 F. Supp. 2d at 1027 (words taken directly from the California Education Code)

[25] Upholding a broadly worded provision banning the posting of leaflets could, for example, ban the posting and distribution of class notes.

[26] NAACP v. Ala. *ex rel.* Patterson, 357 U.S. 449, 460-461 (1958).

[27] 408 U.S. 169 (1972).

[28] In a similar case, *Gay Student Services v. Tex. A & M Univ.*, 737 F.2d 1317 (5th Cir. 1984), the university asserted a similar defense, that a gay student organization was inconsistent with university mission. The court of appeals reversed a decision in favor of the university and held that the university's failure to recognize the group was a violation of the First Amendment. The court noted that, even though homosexuality was illegal in Texas at the time, the student group was not formed for such activity. It was not illegal to be homosexual. Moreover, there was no evidence of illegal activity on the part of the group.

[29] 259 F. Supp. 2d 575 (S.D. Tex. 2003).

[30] Notably, a few months preceding the pro-life group's application, the university had granted permission to the Free Speech Coalition, a different student organization, to display the same exhibit on the requested plaza for three consecutive days.

[31] 194 F. Supp. 2d 1011 (C.D. Cal. 2002).

[32] 454 U.S. 263 (1981).

[33] 403 U.S. 602 (1971).

[34] *See also* Lark v. Lacy, 43 F. Supp. 2d 449 (S.D.N.Y. 1999), *vacated in part on other grounds*, 87 F. Supp. 2d 251 (S.D.N.Y. 2000), in which the court held, in part, that the revocation of a non-student group's right to use a public university's facilities violated the group's First Amendment rights. The group, affiliated with the International Church of Christ (COC), had used the facilities for some time along with several other non-student users. But some COC members had fallen out of favor with university administration, and the court emphasized the evidence that the university used its disdain for the individuals to take action against the COC. As a result, the COC's motion for preliminary injunction to reinstate its license to use the facilities was granted.

[35] *See* Keller v. State Bar of Cal., 496 U.S. 1, 10 (1990) (*quoting* I. Brant, James Madison: The Nationalist 354 (1948)).

[36] 515 U.S. 819 (1995).

[37] Under a disclaimer required by the policy, the organizations are independent of the university as a whole.

[38] *See also* Lamb's Chapel v. Ctr. Moriches Union Free Sch. Dist., 509 U.S. 384 (1993) and Good News Club v. Milford Cent. Sch. Dist., 121 S. Ct. 2093 (2001).

[39] 515 U.S. at 837.

[40] 529 U.S. 217 (2000).

[41] The activity fees are pooled and available for disbursement to student organizations, subject to university approval. Money is distributed by application for reimbursement.

[42] 529 U.S. at 233.

[43] Fry v. Bd. of Regents of the Univ. of Wis., No. 96-C-0292-S, 2001 U.S. Dist. LEXIS 3346 (W.D. Wis. Mar. 15, 2001).

[44] 410 U.S. 667 (1973).

[45] *Id.* at 670. For more discussion on content-nonneutral restrictions in university publications, *see* Stanley v. Magrath, 719 F.2d 279 (8th Cir. 1983); Schiff v. Williams, 519 F.2d 257 (5th Cir. 1975); and Joyner v. Whiting, 477 F.2d 456 (4th Cir. 1973).

[46] 410 U.S. at 672. Justice Rehnquist, in a second dissent, argued that the language used in the paper was lewd and obscene and was not protected by the First Amendment.

[47] 484 U.S. 260 (1988).

[48] One article involved the impact of divorce on children where the article contained some disparaging comments about the father of a student and one on teenage pregnancy where the identities of pregnant students could be discovered.

[49] 191 F.3d 719, *rev'd en banc*, 236 F.3d 342 (6th Cir. 2001).

[50] Coffer created a purple cover, while the school's colors were green and gold.

[51] 496 S.E.2d 8 (N.C. Ct. App. 1998).

[52] 174 F. Supp. 2d 1055 (C.D. Cal. 2001).

[53] 424 U.S. 1 (1976).

[54] *But see* McConnell v. Fed. Elections Comm'n, 124 S. Ct. 619 (2003), where the Supreme Court upheld major provisions of the McCain-Feingold Bipartisan Campaign Reform Act of 2002 against a First Amendment challenge.

[55] Furthermore, there was already a minimum GPA requirement to run for office.

[56] *See* Alabama Student Party v. Student Gov't Ass'n of the Univ. of Ala., 867 F.2d 1344 (11th Cir. 1989).

[57] 229 F.3d 435 (3d Cir. 2000). Four fraternity members were arrested, and one was convicted and expelled for drug possession and trafficking.

[58] 229 F.2d at 445 (*quoting* Healy v. James, 408 U.S. at 189).

[59] Terminiello v. City of Chi., 337 U.S. 1, 4 (1949).

[60] *See, e.g.*, UWM Post, Inc. v. Bd. of Regents of the Univ. of Wis., 774 F. Supp. 1163 (E.D. Wis. 1991); Doe v. Univ. of Mich., 721 F. Supp. 852 (E.D. Mich. 1989).

[61] 20 U.S.C. § 1681(a) (2002). For an example from Antioch College, see http://www. antioch-college.edu/cat2002/com_stand.html.

[62] *See* Gebser v. Lago Vista Indep. Sch. Dist., 524 U.S. 274 (1998) (teacher-to-student harassment) and Davis v Monroe County Bd. of Educ., 526 U.S. 629 (1999) (student-to-student harassment).

[63] 112 S. Ct. 2538 (1992).

[64] Wisconsin v. Mitchell, 508 U.S. 476 (1993).

[65] 721 F. Supp. 852 (E.D. Mich. 1989).

[66] *Id.* at 856.

[67] 774 F. Supp. 1163 (E.D. Wis. 1991).

[68] 993 F.2d 386 (4th Cir. 1993).

[69] 491 U.S. 397 (1989) (a statute that criminalized the burning of the American flag was declared unconstitutional).

[70] Saxe v. State Coll. Area Sch. Dist., 240 F.2d 200 (3d Cir. 2001).

[71] 524 U.S. 274 (1998).

[72] 526 U.S. 629 (1999).

[73] *Id.* at 204.

[74] 484 U.S. 260 (1988).

[75] 236 F.3d 342 (6th Cir. 2001).

[76] 308 F.3d 939 (9th Cir. 2002), *cert. denied*, 538 U.S. 908 (2003).

[77] The case yielded three opinions: one denying the First Amendment claim on a formal *Hazelwood* analysis, one concurring opinion denying the claim on Brown's attempt to deceive his thesis committee, and a partial dissent disagreeing whole-heartedly with the application of *Hazelwood* in the college and university setting.

[78] 308 F.3d at 949.

[79] *Id.* at 951.

[80] The lead opinion applied *Hazelwood* to make this point. The concurring judge argued that Brown's speech rights did not include the right to deceive his committee by adding a new section to the thesis.

[81] *Id.* at 953.

[82] 408 U.S. 169 (1972).

[83] 515 U.S. 819 (1995).

[84] 236 F.2d 342 (6th Cir. 2001).

[85] 356 F.3d 1277 (10th Cir. 2004).

[86] *Id.* at 1282.

[87] *See also* the discussion of *Bishop v. Aronov*, 926 F.2d 1066 (11th Cir. 1991), and related discussion of faculty academic freedom in the next chapter.

[88] 356 F.3d at 1289 (internal quotations and citations omitted).

[89] Axson-Flynn had presented evidence that a Jewish student received an exemption from a group assignment to be performed in class on Yom Kippur.

# 10 Student Equal Protection and Due Process

## Charles Russo and William Thro

## Introduction

It almost goes without saying that without students, an institution of higher learning cannot exist. In the day-to-day lives of colleges and universities, issues involving students are a constant, making this one of the more expansive areas in a review of higher education. Rather than attempt to survey the entire universe of topics under the penumbra of students in higher education, this chapter embraces a more modest goal by focusing on selected issues related to the Fourteenth Amendment's provision of equal protection of the laws and due process of law as applied to public institutions of higher education.

In light of recent Supreme Court activity, this chapter first explores equal protection with particular attention to affirmative action in admissions and then turns to selected due process issues.

## Levels of Judicial Review Under Equal Protection

The Equal Protection Clause of the Fourteenth Amendment to the United States Constitution reads as follows: "No State shall ... deny to any person within its jurisdiction the equal protection of the laws."[1] When state action, whether statute, regulation, policy, or practice, is challenged as a violation of the Equal Protection Clause, courts have historically invoked one of three standards for judicial review. The most forgiving standard, that of rational basis review, asks only that a rational relationship between the state action and a legitimate state interest be established. The intermediate level of review, sometimes called "intermediate scrutiny," requires that the state action be upheld if the regulation is substantially related to an important governmental interest.[2] The highest level of review, invoking strict judicial scrutiny, demands that the state action be permitted only if it is a narrowly tailored means to achieve a compelling governmental interest.[3]

Intermediate scrutiny has been used in several cases involving gender classifications. In a higher education context, the Supreme Court recognized gender as a suspect classification that requires more than mere rational basis review under the Equal Protection Clause in *Mississippi University for Women v. Hogan*.[4] In *Hogan*, the Court held that a public university's all-female nursing school's denial of admission to men was unconstitutional, finding that the purported important governmental objective—remedying past discrimination—was not genuine because women had not been discriminated against in the context of the nursing school, and instead, the school's policy perpetuated the "stereotyped view of nursing as an exclusively woman's job."[5] Most recently, in *United States v. Virginia*,[6] the Court reaffirmed *Hogan*. In response to a suit alleging sex discrimination against the Virginia Military Institute (VMI), the sole single-sex school among Virginia's public institutions, VMI proposed a parallel program for women located at a private liberal arts school for women. Striking down this alternative to the creation of opportunities for women to attend VMI, the Supreme Court held:

> Parties who seek to defend gender-based government action must demonstrate an "exceedingly persuasive justification" for that action…. The justification must be genuine, not hypothesized or invented post hoc in response to litigation. And it must not rely on overbroad generalizations about the different talents, capacities, or preferences of males and females.[7]

While gender classifications are scrutinized to determine whether they are substantially related to the achievement of important government objectives, racial, expungement, and national origin classifications are scrutinized under the strict scrutiny test to determine if they are narrowly tailored to further compelling government objectives.[8] Strict scrutiny is the most rigorous form of judicial review applied under equal protection analysis. Strict scrutiny review applies to government actions that discriminate on the basis of suspect classifications. The Supreme Court's pronouncements on affirmative action in college and university admissions reflect a contemporary application of the strict scrutiny standard.

## Equal Protection and Affirmative Action in Admissions

*Regents of University of California v. Bakke*,[9] the most prominent Supreme Court case involving racial preferences in education prior to its 2003 rulings in *Grutter v. Bollinger*[10] and *Gratz v. Bollinger*,[11] is a logical starting point at which to begin an examination of strict scrutiny in admissions. In *Bakke*, a fractured Supreme Court considered a challenge to a medical school program filed by a white applicant who was denied admission under a racial preference program that set aside sixteen seats out of one hundred openings for specified minority groups, defined as African, Mexican, Asian, and Native-American. The white male was initially excluded, then later ordered admitted by the Supreme Court of California, even though his qualifications were substantially equivalent to those who were admitted in his place. In a plurality opinion, in which the Justices failed to reach the requisite five-member majority necessary to make its opinion binding precedent in similar cases, the Court held that while the program was illegal and the white student should have been admitted, the consideration of race per se was not constitutionally forbidden in admissions decisions.

A plurality in *Bakke* found that the white applicant was unlawfully excluded in violation of Title VI of the Civil Rights Act of 1964, which prohibits recipients of federal funding from discriminating based on race, color, or national origin. This plurality did not review, and maintained that it should not have considered, the white applicant's right to Equal Protection under the Fourteenth Amendment since it was able to resolve the dispute on the basis of statutory interpretation. Justice Powell, relying on the Equal Protection Clause of the Fourteenth Amendment, joined this plurality in concluding that the plaintiff should have been admitted to the medical school but reasoned that the university had unconstitutionally discriminated against the applicant.

However, Justice Powell contended the Constitution did not prohibit taking race or ethnic origin into consideration as one of a number of factors in an admissions program because a university's quest for a diverse student body can be considered of paramount importance in the fulfillment of its mission. He declared that a state university's interest in a diverse student body may legitimately be served by weighing race and ethnic origin as competitive factors in an institution's admissions program.

Following *Bakke*, the Court addressed racial preference programs in a variety of settings. In non-education cases, the Court reached mixed results where the federal government sought to assist various minority groups,[12] was largely unfavorable in the context of legislative reapportionment,[13] and refused to permit affirmative action to be a factor in a case involving public school teachers.[14]

Lower federal courts have generally reached mixed results over the use of racial preferences in higher education. Prior to *Gratz/ Grutter*, the Fourth, Fifth, and Eleventh Circuits have struck down racial preference plans while the Sixth and Ninth Circuits rejected such challenges. For example, the Fourth Circuit, in *Podberesky v. Kirwan*,[15] struck down a scholarship program at the University of Maryland that was open only to African-American students as violating the Equal Protection Clause. The court reasoned that the goals of the race-conscious scholarship program could not be used to lower effective minimum acceptance criteria in creating an applicant pool since such an approach was insufficiently narrowly tailored to meet its goal in the absence of evidence that university officials tried, without success, to employ a race-neutral solution. Similarly, the Fifth Circuit invalidated an admissions plan at the University of Texas School of Law that granted substantial preferences to racial minorities in *Hopwood v. Texas*.[16] The court held that a preference system based on race did not survive strict scrutiny under the Equal Protection Clause and rejected Justice Powell's opinion in *Bakke* that a higher education institution's interest in a diverse student body could meet a test of compelling state interest. Moreover, in *Johnson v. Board of Regents of the University of Georgia*,[17] the Eleventh Circuit upheld a lower court's decision that a state university's admissions policy was unconstitutional. The court affirmed that the plan, which awarded an arbitrary but fixed numerical diversity bonus to non-white applicants at a decisive stage in the admissions process, failed the strict scrutiny test and thus violated the Equal Protection Clause.

On the other hand, the Ninth Circuit rejected a challenge from unsuccessful white applicants who charged that a state law school engaged in racially discriminatory admissions practices in *Smith v. University of Washington Law School*.[18] The court affirmed that the plaintiffs' class action suit was properly decertified—essentially ending their claim—when a state initiative was passed which prohibited the state from offering preferential treatment to any individual or group based on race, sex, color, ethnicity, or national origin. In dicta, the court voiced its opinion that a properly designed and operated race-conscious admissions program would not violate either equal protection or Title VI. The Supreme Court refused to hear appeals in all four of the preceding cases.

The companion cases that reached the Supreme Court, *Grutter v. Bollinger*[19] and *Gratz v. Bollinger*,[20] both originated at the University of Michigan. *Grutter* was filed by an unsuccessful forty-three-year-old, white female applicant with a 3.8 (on a scale of 4.0) undergraduate Grade Point Average (GPA), a Law School Admission Test score that put her in the 86th percentile nationally, and who challenged the law school's use of race as a factor in admissions decisions. During the course of the litigation, school officials conceded that the plaintiff probably would have been admitted had she been a member of one of the under-represented minority groups, defined as African-Americans, Hispanics, and Native Americans.

A federal trial court in Michigan entered an injunction in *Grutter* that temporarily prevented the university from applying its policy on the basis that it violated both the Equal Protection Clause and Title VI insofar as it was insufficiently tailored to further its stated goal of achieving diversity. On appeal, an en banc panel of the Sixth Circuit, in a five-to-four judgment, vacated the injunction and reinstated the policy since it was convinced that it was narrowly tailored to achieving the stated goal of a diverse student body.

*Gratz* was filed by two unsuccessful, white applicants, one female and the other male, who had applied to undergraduate programs at the University of Michigan's College of Literature, Science, and the Arts. The students claimed that the use of race as a factor applied a more stringent standard to non-minorities. In fact, during the year that the female plaintiff applied for admission, the university accepted all forty-six applicants from the preferred minority group, all of whom had the same adjusted grade point average and test scores as the non-preferred candidates, while only 121 of 378 of the non-preferred candidates were selected.[21] In addition, the policy gave members of the same minority groups as in *Grutter* a bonus of twenty points on a 150-point admissions scale, an amount roughly equivalent to one full grade on a four-point GPA scale.[22]

In *Grutter v. Bollinger*[23] the Court upheld the Law School's use of a system of racial preference that permitted applicants with lower Law School Admissions Test (LSAT) scores and Grade Point Averages (GPA) to be admitted over non-minority candidates based on the view that diversity is a compelling governmental interest. Conversely, in *Gratz v. Bollinger*,[24] the Court struck down the University's undergraduate admissions process using a point system that allocated twenty points based on race or ethnicity on the basis that it was insufficiently narrowly tailored to achieve its goal.

Writing for the five-member majority in *Grutter*, Justice O'Connor, relying heavily on Justice Powell's opinion in *Bakke*, concluded that obtaining the educational benefits of diversity was a compelling governmental interest. However, the Court emphasized that any use of race to achieve the educational benefits of diversity must be narrowly tailored. If an institution wished to consider race, then it must (1) provide for individualized consideration; (2) be undertaken only after a serious good-faith consideration of the viability of non-racial alternatives; (3) not unduly burden non-minorities; and (4) be periodically reviewed and of limited duration.[25]

The stringent nature of the narrow tailoring requirement is illustrated by *Gratz*,[26] in which Chief Justice Rehnquist, writing for the majority, struck down the undergraduate admissions policy at the University of Michigan on the basis that it was not sufficiently narrowly tailored to achieve the state's compelling interest in achieving the educational benefits of a diverse student body. In particular, he found that the Michigan system did not provide for the individualized consideration that Justice O'Connor described in *Grutter* or that Justice Powell called for in *Bakke*. Under the facts of *Gratz*, the Chief Justice reasoned that adding twenty points to an undergraduate applicant's score based solely on race made race decisive for even the most minimally qualified minority candidate.

The United States Supreme Court's decisions in these companion cases reaffirmed the constitutionality of weighing race in higher education admissions policies intended to foster a diverse student body in higher education institutions. However, it is clear that only a narrowly tailored policy designed to consider race in admissions will withstand the Court's application of strict scrutiny to racial classifications.

## Due Process in the Disciplinary Context

In addition to ensuring equal protection of the laws, the Fourteenth Amendment to the Constitution protects life, liberty, and property interests from arbitrary government action and extends the protection of due process of law.[27] A student's interest in pursuing an education is included within the Fourteenth Amendment's protection of liberty and property.[28] Particularly in a disciplinary due process context, the interests of a properly admitted student in completing his or her education, as well as avoiding unfair or mistaken exclusion from the educational institution and the accompanying stigma that may be associated with suspension or expulsion, are among the interests that due process is intended to protect.

The historic evolution of a student's disciplinary due process rights has its genesis in a series of cases that begin with *Dixon v. Alabama State Board of Education.*[29] In *Dixon*, several students were expelled from Alabama State College in 1961 for participating in a civil rights protest off campus. The college undertook the expulsions without any prior notification or hearing, and the students argued that because their activity was constitutionally protected, they should have been extended the due process protections of notice of the charges against them and a hearing at which they could respond to the charges.[30]

A federal district court, following the concept of *in loco parentis*, approved the institution's action, but the federal appeals court rejected the insulation afforded to public institutions of higher education against judicial review by ruling that students at a publicly supported state college were entitled to fundamental due process when an expulsion or long-term suspension was implicated. By characterizing the student's interest in higher education as an entitlement, not a privilege, the *Dixon* ruling established that a public higher education institution could not condition the student's admission and matriculation on a waiver of the fundamental constitutional right to due process, thus squelching the traditional institutional prerogatives surrounding *in loco parentis*.

In the disciplinary due process context, the Fourteenth Amendment requires that public higher education institutions provide students with notice and an opportunity to be heard.[31] The Supreme Court in *Goss v. Lopez*[32] considered the procedural due process issue in the context of disciplinary action taken by a public educational institution. In that case, students challenged the statutory authority of administrators to suspend for up to ten days without prior notice or a hearing. The Court held that a ten-day suspension was not a *de minimus* deprivation of the students' property or liberty interests in an education and could not be imposed in "complete disregard of the Due Process Clause."[33] The Court reasoned that at a minimum, students must be given "*some* kind of notice and afforded *some* kind of hearing."[34]

The degree of due process extended to the student depends upon the nature of the interest affected and the circumstances of the specific case. As one federal appeals court has noted, while "notice and opportunity to be heard have traditionally and consistently been held to be the essential requisites of procedural due process ... beyond the right to notice and hearing, the span of procedural protections required to ensure fairness becomes uncertain."[35] In other words, beyond the essential requisites, notice and hearing, the requirements of disciplinary due process remain flexible and responsive to the procedural protections that a particular situation demands. One test applied to determine the extent of required due process, delineated by the Supreme Court in *Mathews v. Eldridge*[36] requires the application of a balance between three factors:

> First, the private interest that will be affected by the official action; second, the risk of an erroneous deprivation of such interest through the procedures used and the probable value, if any, of additional or substitute procedural safeguards; and finally, the Government's interest, including the function involved and the fiscal and administrative burdens that the additional or substitute procedural requirement would entail.[37]

Notice and hearing, to be fair in the disciplinary due process sense, require that the student adversely affected be adequately informed of the charges, afforded the opportunity to respond to charges, to explain conduct, and to defend against the allegations of misconduct. Beyond these elements, courts have granted institutions considerable flexibility in the application of due process standards, requiring no more than substantial compliance with standards of notice and hearing and allowing institutions to "cure" defects in the processes when procedural errors occur. For example, in *Tigrett v. Rector and Visitors of the University of Virginia*,[38] student-plaintiffs pointed to the process afforded by the public university in claiming a violation of rights under the Fourteenth Amendment. Three of the students involved in a fight were scheduled for a hearing, which was postponed pending resolution of criminal charges involving disorderly conduct and assault and battery. Notwithstanding a postponement, the student judiciary committee held a hearing and ordered expulsion, but these expulsions were not carried out, and a second hearing was scheduled. This second hearing was cancelled when the committee chair recused herself, and the institution's Vice-President for Student Affairs appointed a hearing panel of student, faculty, and administration representatives to hear the case because the second hearing committee found it would be unable to hear the case in a timely manner. This panel convened, the students appeared, witnesses gave testimony, evidence was presented, and factual findings were made that led to a one-semester suspension for two students and a two-semester suspension for one student. However, the university president, on review of the record, rejected the panel's recommendations and imposed a one-year suspension on one student and a two-year suspension on another. An appeal of the president's decision to a judicial review board led to an affirmation of the president's penalties.

Although the federal appeals court recognized a student's right to attend a college or university was an entitlement protected by due process once the students were properly admitted, the court ruled the students were not deprived of their right to continued enrollment until after a full evidentiary hearing and appeals had been resolved against them. Because the initial expulsion was never enforced, there was no deprivation of a property right in the initial hearing. Although the students argued that the president was the "ultimate fact finder" in this case and they had a right to appear before him to explain their conduct, the court held the hearing committee was the ultimate fact finder and the president was the final decision maker. No legal precedent supported the contention that the student's should have a right to appear at the appeals stage. Since the students received a meaningful hearing at the earlier stage of the proceedings, their claim of a due process violation was rejected.

The flexible due process standards applicable to student disciplinary hearings contrast them from the rigorous standards applicable to criminal prosecutions. One illustration of this difference is the role of legal counsel in student disciplinary hearings.[39] Generally, if a student retains legal counsel when faced with disciplinary action, the role of counsel in such proceedings is limited to serving the student in an advisory capacity, not as an advocate who is free to question witnesses, challenge evidence or testimony, or present either an affirmative defense or rebuttal.[40] In *Gabrilowitz v. Newman,*[41] the First Circuit was called upon to decide whether due process required that a student have the assistance of counsel in a disciplinary hearing. The student sought to have counsel present at his hearing on allegations of assault and attempted rape in order to advise him of the ramifications of any statements he might make that could be prejudicial to him in a pending criminal trial. Balancing the factors set forth in *Mathews*, the First Circuit held that in this context, in which the student faced disciplinary action and concomitant criminal charges, due process required that counsel be present for the limited role of advising the student in order to protect his rights at the criminal trial.[42] Although acknowledging that the ruling was intended to apply to a limited context, the federal appeals court emphasized that the risk of an erroneous deprivation of a protected interest, the constitutional right to freedom from self-incrimination, justified the presence of legal counsel in an advisory capacity.[43]

In other cases, courts have applied the *Mathews* balancing test to affirm that more extensive participation by legal counsel in student disciplinary hearings is not required by due process of law.[44] While acknowledging that students have the right to be advised by counsel in circumstances in which a contemporaneous criminal proceeding could subject them to a risk of self-incrimination, courts rejected suggestions that counsel should be allowed to address the hearing board, present and object to documents, and cross-examine witnesses.[45] In one case, the federal district court emphasized that if legal counsel were permitted liberal involvement in student disciplinary hearings, the burden on the institution would outweigh a student's interest in due process. The court noted the fiscal burden on the university would be insubstantial because the student would bear the expense, but the active role of an attorney at the hearing would be intrusive in that the college might find it necessary to have counsel present to represent the college's interests and to insure that the college's witnesses were not harassed by the student's counsel during cross-examination.[46]

## Due Process in the Academic Context

In *Board of Curators of the University of Missouri v. Horowitz*,[47] the Supreme Court considered the degree of due process owed by a public university to a medical student dismissed on academic grounds. The Court held that the dismissal of the medical student was predicated on academic,[48] rather than disciplinary, grounds because it "rested on the academic judgment of school officials that she did not have the necessary clinical ability to perform adequately as a medical doctor[.]"[49] While a disciplinary dismissal might involve the violation of institutional rules of conduct, an academic dismissal was characterized as "more subjective and evaluative" than the "typical factual questions presented in the average disciplinary decision."[50] In light of the characterization of an academic dismissal as one requiring "expert evaluation ... and historic judgment of educators" and bearing "little resemblance to ... judicial and administrative fact-finding proceedings,"[51] the Court held that procedural due process does not require any form of hearing before a decision-making body, either before or after the termination decision is made.

The *Horowitz* Court concluded that great deference must be given to a public institution's academic decisions.[52] The student's claims of deprivation of liberty due to the dismissal's effect on future employment in the medical field and violation of procedural due process were regarded as groundless. In the context of procedural due process, notice and informal review is all that is necessary to satisfy constitutional requirements for academic policy or procedure rather than the more rigorous requirements of notice of charges against the student and fair and impartial hearing. In an academic dismissal, it is sufficient that the student was informed of the nature of the faculty's dissatisfaction and that the ultimate decision to dismiss was "careful and deliberate."[53] By telling the student of the problem, offering her reasonable opportunities to remediate the behaviors, and carefully deliberating over whether to dismiss her, the university met due process requirements in an academic context.

Decisions after *Horowitz* have followed the Supreme Court's reasoning regarding the procedural difference between academic and disciplinary violations. In *Harris v. Blake*,[54] the Tenth Circuit upheld a Colorado university's decision to require one of its students to withdraw due to his academic deficiencies. Because *Harris* was involved an academic violation rather than a disciplinary problem, less-stringent procedural protections applied, and a hearing was not required to satisfy due process. Following *Horowitz,* the Tenth Circuit reasoned that notice, followed by a careful and deliberate determination, satisfied due process requirements.[55]

While hearings in academic due process cases are not required, providing the student with an opportunity to appear and explain behavior has been acknowledged as an act of good faith reflecting the institution's effort to ensure fundamental fairness.[56] In one case, a student subject to dismissal following repeated negative evaluations based upon "non-cognitive" factors that included criteria such as maturity in professional relationships and timeliness was permitted to appear before a review committee, make an oral argument, and answer questions. The federal appeals court emphasized that the institution exceeded the traditional requirements of academic due process because, in addition to being advised of deficiencies and the consequences of failure to correct the deficiencies, the student had an opportunity to meet with the committee, availed himself of that opportunity and was invited to develop his own plan of remediation.[57]

The Supreme Court reiterated its judicial deference to academic decision-making in *University of Michigan v. Ewing,*[58] which involved a dismissal due to poor academic performance and a low score on medical board exams. The plaintiff, a student enrolled in a six-year special studies program of combined undergraduate and medical education, developed academic deficiencies and failed the National Board of Medical Examiners' Examination (NBME). Following the failure, the promotion and review board of the institution voted to dismiss the student. The student alleged that the university had violated his constitutional rights by dismissing him without providing him an opportunity to retake the examination. The United States Supreme Court determined that the focus of the student's claim was that the university had misjudged his fitness to remain a student. In its analysis, the Court's majority emphasized that truly academic decision-making is uniquely the province of a faculty's professional judgment. Cautioning that judges should show great respect for this judgment, the majority held that the student's dismissal should not be overridden "unless it is such a substantial departure from accepted academic norms as to demonstrate that the person or committee responsible did not actually exercise professional judgment."[59] The Court held that, even if the student had a property interest in continued enrollment, the student's due process rights were not violated since the record did not indicate arbitrary action by the university.[60]

## Substantive Due Process

In *Ewing*, the plaintiff-medical student challenged his dismissal from medical school as arbitrary and capricious in violation of his substantive due process rights. In his concurrence in that case, Justice Lewis Powell noted that "[w]hile property interests are protected by procedural due process even though the interest is derived from state law rather than the Constitution, substantive due process rights are created only by the Constitution."[61] Substantive due process protects specific fundamental rights to individual freedom and liberty from deprivations based upon arbitrary and capricious government action. In *Washington v. Glucksberg*,[62] the Supreme Court identified two controlling features of substantive due process:

> First, we have regularly observed that the Due Process Clause specially protects those fundamental rights and liberties which are, objectively, deeply rooted in this Nation's history and tradition, and implicit in the concept of ordered liberty, such that neither liberty nor justice would exist if they were sacrificed. Second, we have required in substantive-due-process cases a careful description of the asserted fundamental liberty interest. Our Nation's history, legal traditions, and practices thus provide the crucial guideposts for responsible decision-making that direct and restrain our exposition of the Due Process Clause.[63]

The Sixth Circuit has noted that substantive due process and equal protection, though defined differently, are similar concepts:

> "[b]oth stem from our American ideals of fundamental fairness and both enmesh the judiciary in substantive review of governmental action. The spheres of protection offered by the two concepts are not, to be sure, coterminous. However, they will overlap in certain situations so that a violation of one will constitute a violation of the other. [64]

To establish a violation of substantive due process, a student must, at a minimum, either demonstrate that a fundamental right guaranteed by the Constitution has been denied or that the conduct of the state institution's representatives can be characterized as so arbitrary and capricious as to "shock the conscience." The United States Supreme Court has noted that there is no right to an education in the Constitution,[65] and this reasoning would appear to foreclose a claim that a violation of substantive due process could be established by proving the denial of an entitlement to an education. On the other hand, establishing that the actions of college and university administrators were so arbitrary and capricious as to shock the conscience would place an extraordinary burden of proof on a student plaintiff.

In an illustrative case, students claimed that institutional representatives induced them to enroll in a Master of Social Work program by knowingly and falsely representing to them that the program was approved for accreditation. They further alleged that the institutional defendants failed to take the steps necessary to ensure that the program would gain accreditation. Through hiring unqualified faculty and maintaining an inadequate curriculum, the institutional defendants were alleged to have knowingly prevented the program from gaining accreditation. In response to these allegations, the Seventh Circuit expressed sympathy for the students' situation but rejected the substantive due process claim as the alleged conduct was not sufficiently egregious to "shock the conscience" as that phrase is employed in substantive due process analysis.[66]

Student-plaintiffs may allege that the severity of a punishment creates the basis for a substantive due process claim, an assertion that requires the court to weigh the "severity of the punitive effect … against the severity of the conduct which occasioned the suspension."[67] However, judicial review of an institution's suspension or expulsion decision would only be available if there were no rational relationship between the punishment and the offense.[68] In a case in which a public university determined that student-plaintiffs had engaged in sexual abuse of a fellow student and suspended them from the university, the student-plaintiffs contended that substantive due process was violated because the severity of the suspensions included loss of student scholarship funds, opportunities as student athletes, and other consequential damages. The federal district court determined that, far from "shocking the conscience," the university's decision to suspend the student-plaintiffs was well within the substantive due process protections of the Fourteenth Amendment.[69]

## Due Process in Degree Revocation

The revocation of a degree by a public college or university implicates a full range of due process protections. Courts apply a higher level of scrutiny in degree revocation cases and show less deference to academic decision-making because the revocation of a degree is the most severe penalty that an institution can take against a current or former student. Because the penalty of degree revocation is more severe than that involved in suspension or expulsion, it may implicate both procedural and substantive due process claims. Degree revocation may involve a purely academic determination that the student did not meet established requirements for the degree, or the revocation may be a penalty for misconduct. Stricter procedural requirements providing for a hearing in academic degree revocations may be required because of the more serious nature of the penalty and the student's substantial property interest in the degree.

In a case illustrating degree revocation for academic reasons, the Ohio Supreme Court in *Waliga v. Kent State University*[70] held that a university was empowered to revoke a degree provided there was a justifiable cause and the revocation was accompanied by "constitutionally adequate procedure."[71] The institution discovered that two graduates had not satisfied substantive degree requirements, and after providing notice and an opportunity to appear at a hearing, revoked the degrees. The issue before the court was whether the public university had the power to revoke a degree awarded some fifteen years earlier. The court stated,

> We consider it self-evident that a college or university acting through its board of trustees does have the inherent authority to revoke an improperly awarded degree where (1) good cause such as fraud, deceit, or error is shown, and (2) the degree-holder is afforded a fair hearing at which he can present evidence and protect his interest. Academic degrees are a university's certification to the world at large of the recipient's educational achievement and fulfillment of the institution's standards. To hold that a university may never withdraw a degree, effectively requires the university to continue making a false certification to the public at large of the accomplishment of persons who in fact lack the very qualifications that are certified.[72]

The application of due process in degree revocations involving misconduct was addressed in *Crook v. Baker*,[73] in which the Sixth Circuit determined that the University of Michigan had satisfied the due process requirements in revoking an academic degree from a graduate who was alleged to have procured the degree by fraud as a result of the discovery that the student had fabricated data for his master's thesis. In this case, the university appointed an ad hoc hearing panel of professors who scheduled a hearing and notified the former student of the allegations and the potential disciplinary penalties. The former student appeared with his legal counsel[74] and was allowed to review and respond to the evidence of fraud. The panel found that the former student was guilty of fraud but made no specific recommendation for revocation of degree. That decision was approved, and administrative authorities recommended that the student's degree be revoked. The Sixth Circuit first determined that the university was authorized to rescind a degree, then went on to assess the degree of procedural due process required in degree revocation cases. Emphasizing that the hearing process was informal, but the range of protections afforded to the former student extensive, the appeals court stated:

> With respect to Crook's opportunity to be heard, it is without dispute that, in addition to the abundant notice we have just

described, he had counsel from the beginning who dealt with the University, he had the opportunity to and did file a response to the charges that was supplemented after the hearing, he had the opportunity to present witnesses and to have an expert with him at the hearing, he and his counsel both made opening statements at the hearing and his counsel was free to advise him, and he made statements and asked questions of the other witnesses. Moreover, Crook filed exceptions to the Committee's findings and his attorney argued his case before the Regents.[75]

The federal appeals court also reversed a lower court's determination that the former student's right to substantive due process was denied. The appeals court reviewed an extensive transcript of the eight-hour proceedings, together with materials submitted to the ad hoc faculty panel by the parties prior to its hearing and concluded that the panel report finding the thesis data to be fabricated was neither arbitrary nor capricious. The court went on to emphasize that the decision to revoke the degree was supported by a rational basis test, and the finding of fraud by the hearing panel was accompanied by clear and convincing evidence.[76]

Degree revocation for nonacademic reasons was also addressed in *Goodreau v. Rector and Visitors of the University of Virginia.*[77] In this case, a short time after awarding the degree, the university discovered that a former student had used his position as president of a student club to embezzle more than $1,500 in university funds. The student admitted the embezzlement and pled guilty to a criminal misdemeanor. The university honor committee sent the student a certified letter explaining that he was accused of an honor violation, and failure to respond in a timely fashion would be presumed to be an admission of guilt. When the former student did not respond, a recommendation went forward from the committee to rescind the degree. No action was taken on this recommendation, but five years later, the student attempted to enroll in a master's degree program at the university and was denied admission due to a notation that his enrollment had been "discontinued." When the former student sought to have the transcript notation removed, the university not only refused to change his enrollment status, but it reinstituted the degree revocation process. The president of the university notified the former student of the proceedings and offered him an opportunity to present any documents but did not offer an opportunity to appear. After receiving notice of degree revocation, the student appealed.

A federal district court rejected the university's motion for summary judgment on the student's due process claims[78] and found that the student presented at least four areas in which a question of fact for a jury needed resolution. First, it was questionable whether the former student received adequate notice of the possible consequence of degree revocation when initially notified that he had been accused on an honor violation. Second, there was sufficient evidence that the university had deviated from existing practice in resolving disciplinary matters to raise a question of whether the deviations resulted in a denial of due process. Third, the delay between consideration of degree revocation and actual revocation of the degree implicated a due process violation. Finally, there was sufficient evidence to suggest that the former student's evidence was not properly considered by the institution in the degree revocation hearings held by the general faculty.

## Conclusions

The Fourteenth Amendment's provisions guaranteeing equal protection of the laws and due process of law are applicable to students in public higher education institutions, but these protections are not absolute and must be balanced with the state's legitimate interest in maintaining the efficiency and effectiveness of its colleges and universities. Balancing competing interests requires case-by-case analysis and cautious application of general legal principles by courts. While legal precedent can inform practice and guide judicial decisions, issues related to equal protection and due process are unlikely to diminish, as students are more sensitive to the need to advance their constitutional rights in these domains. Institutional representatives should be responsive to new and emerging issues in this area and vigilant in conforming institutional policies and procedures to contemporary legal precedents.

## Endnotes

[1]  U.S. Const. amend. XIV, § 1.

[2]  *Compare* United States v. Va., 518 U.S. 515, 534 (1996) (invalidated the state of Virginia's policy of excluding women from the Virginia Military Institute under intermediate scrutiny standard, finding that the state did not present an "exceedingly persuasive justification" for its use of a sex-based classification), with Nguyen v. Immigration and Naturalization Serv., 533 U.S. 53, 60 (2001) (majority applied the traditional intermediate scrutiny test, which requires that a sex-based classification be "substantially related" to an "important governmental objective" to pass constitutional muster).

[3]  *See* City of Richmond v. J.A. Croson Co., 488 U.S. 469, 493 (1989) ("The purpose of strict scrutiny is to 'smoke out' illegitimate uses of race by assuring that the legislative body is pursuing a goal important enough to warrant use of a highly suspect tool."); Wygant v. Jackson Bd. of Educ., 476 U.S. 267, 274 (1986) (school district's plan to lay off white teachers with more seniority before minority teachers with less seniority invalidated because general societal discrimination insufficiently compelling objective under strict scrutiny test absent showing of prior discrimination by the actual governmental unit involved); and Brown v. Bd. of Educ., 347 U.S. 483 (1954) (eliminating public school segregation based on racial classification).

[4]  458 U.S. 718 (1982).

[5]  *Id.* at 729.

[6]  518 U.S. 515 (1996).

[7] *Id.* at 531, citations omitted.

[8] *See* City of Richmond v. J.A. Croson Co., 488 U.S. 469 (1989) (strict scrutiny standard applied to review Richmond's minority "set-aside" program, under which a percentage of government construction contracts were reserved for minority-owned contractors); Loving v. Va., 388 U.S. 1, 11 (1967) (strict scrutiny-like review applied to state miscegenation statute that criminalized marriage of white person to non-white person); and Korematsu v. U.S., 323 U.S. 214, 216 (1944) (legal restrictions curtailing civil rights of single racial group are immediately suspect and "courts must subject them to "the most rigid scrutiny").

[9] 438 U.S. 265 (1978).

[10] 123 S. Ct. 2325 (2003).

[11] 123 S. Ct. 2411 (2003).

[12] *See* Fullilove v. Klutznik, 448 U.S. 448 (1980) (plurality upholding a federal public works projects that gave preferences to businesses owned by members of racial minorities) and Metro Broad. v. Fed. Communications Comm'n, 497 U.S. 547 (1990), rehearing denied, 497 U.S. 1050 (1990) (upholding a preference policy with regard to minority ownership of new radio or television stations on the basis that it had a substantial relationship to an important Congressional interest). *But see* Richmond v. J.A. Crosson, Co., 488 U.S. 469 (1989) (striking down a federal law that would have increased the number of minority-owned businesses that were awarded construction contracts); Adarand Constructors Inc. v. Pena, 515 U.S. 200 (1995) (vitiating a program that would have granted preferences to minority contractors in building projects could not be upheld unless it could pass strict scrutiny).

[13] United Jewish Orgs. v. Carey, 430 U.S. 144 (1977) (plurality upholding a plan authorized by a New York statute to create districts in which minority voters were in the majority). *But see* Shaw v. Reno I, 509 U.S. 630 (1993) (holding that where the legislature in North Carolina took race into consideration in creating congressional districts wherein minorities constituted a majority of voters, it was subject to strict scrutiny). *See also,* Miller v. Johnson, 515 U.S. 900 (1995) (striking down a legislative plan from Georgia, which would have created a congressional district based on race absent proof that the scheme on the basis that it was not narrowly tailored to achieve a compelling governmental interest); *Shaw v. Reno II,* 517 U.S. 899 (1996).(holding that since race was the predominant reason for creating the districts, the plan was invalid because it was not sufficiently narrowly tailored to correct past instances of governmental discrimination against minorities; and Bush v. Vera, 517 U.S. 952 (1996) (plurality striking down the creation of three Congressional districts in Texas where race was a key factor).

[14] Wygant v. Jackson Bd. of Educ., 476 U.S. 267 (1989) (holding that a layoff of non-minority teachers based solely on race violated equal protection). *See also,* Taxman v. Bd. of Educ. of the Township of Piscataway, 91 F.3d 1547, 1547 (3d Cir. 1996), *cert. granted,* 521 U.S. 1117, 117 S. Ct. 2506 (1997), *cert. dismissed,* 522 U.S. 1010 (1997).

[15] 38 F.3d 147 (4th Cir. 1994), *rehearing denied,* 46 F.3d 5 (4th Cir. 1994); *cert. denied,* 514 U.S. 1128 (1995).

[16] 78 F.3d 932 (5th Cir. 1996), *rehearing and suggestion for rehearing denied,* 84 F.3d 720 (5th Cir. 1996), *cert. denied sub nom.* Thurgood Marshall Legal Soc'y v. Hopwood, 518 U.S. 1033 (1996); *appeal on remand,* 95 F.3d 53 (5th Cir. 1996), *on remand,* 78 F. Supp. 2d 932 (W.D. Tex. 1998).

[17] 263 F.3d 1234 (11th Cir. 2001).

[18] 233 F.3d 1188 (9th Cir. 2000), *cert. denied,* 532 U.S. 1051 (2001).

[19] 137 F. Supp. 2d 821 (E.D. Mich. 2001), *stay denied,* 137 F. Supp. 2d 874 (E.D. Mich. 2001), *hearing en banc ordered,* 277 F.3d 803 (6th Cir. 2001), *reversed,* 288 F.3d 732 (6th Cir. 2002), *opinion after hearing en banc,* 309 F.3d 329 (6th Cir. 2002), cert. granted, 123 S. Ct. 617 (2002).

[20] 135 F. Supp. 2d 790 (E.D. Mich. 2001).

[21] U.S. Amicus Brief, Gratz v. Bollinger, 2003 WL 151258 (2003). 2003, p. *21.

[22] *Id.* at *10. The same scale awarded only twelve points for a perfect score of 1,600 on the Scholastic Aptitude Test.

[23] 123 S. Ct. 2325 (2003).

[24] 123 S. Ct. 2411 (2003).

[25] Grutter, 123 S. Ct. at 2329-30.

[26] 123 S. Ct. 2411.

[27] Stewart v. Bailey, 7 F.3d 384, 392 (4th Cir. 1993).

[28] *See* Goss v. Lopez, 419 U.S. 565, 574-75, 42 L. Ed. 2d 725, 95 S. Ct. 729 (1975).

[29] 294 F.2d 150 (5th Cir. 1961), *cert. denied*, 368 U.S. 930 (1961).

[30] The university expelled the students without ever giving a specific reason for the expulsion other than "this problem of Alabama State College" following demonstrations. *Id.* at 158-159.

[31] In the private university setting, contractual and associational rights rather than constitutional safeguards may protect students from expulsion or suspension. *See, e.g.,* Tedeschi v. Wagner Coll., 404 N.E.2d 1302, 1306 (N.Y. 1980) (holding that because the private college's guidelines required a hearing, the student was entitled to a hearing before the board and the president before she could be suspended) and Schaer v. Brandeis Univ., 716 N.E.2d 1055 (Mass. App. Ct. 1999), *rev'd in part*, 432 Mass. 747 (Mass. 2000) (holding that a private college must comply with the procedures they establish in the student conduct code to ensure fundamental fairness to students).

[32] 419 U.S. 565, 42 L. Ed. 2d 725, 95 S. Ct. 729 (1975).

[33] *Id.* at 576.

[34] *Id.* at 579 (emphasis in original).

[35] Gorman v. Univ. of R.I., 837 F.2d 7, 13-14 (1st Cir. 1988). In this case, the appeals court was responding to the student's insistence on the right to legal counsel in the disciplinary hearing. The court rejected a right to representation by counsel at disciplinary hearings, unless the student is also facing criminal charges stemming from the incident in question.

[36] 424 U.S. 319, 47 L. Ed. 2d 18, 96 S. Ct. 893 (1976).

[37] *Id.* at 335.

[38] 290 F.3d 620 (4th Cir. 2002)

[39] In some cases, courts have rejected any role of legal counsel in student disciplinary cases. *See* Gorman v. Univ. of R.I., 646 F. Supp. 799, 806 (D.R.I. 1986), *aff'd in part and rev'd in part,* 837 F.2d 7, 16 (1st Cir. 1988) (both courts noting that weight of authority is against the right of the student to have counsel present at disciplinary proceeding); Jaksa v. Regents of the Univ. of Mich., 597 F. Supp. 1245 (E.D. Mich. 1984), *aff'd*, 787 F.2d 590 (6th Cir. 1986) (holding that student did not have right to counsel because the university did not proceed against student through counsel); and Garshman v. Pa. State Univ., 395 F. Supp. 912, 921 (M.D. Pa. 1975) (noting that medical student is literate and intelligent individual who understands his rights and can express himself and therefore concluding that student does not have due process right to be represented by counsel).

[40] Esteban v. Cent. Mo. State Coll., 277 F. Supp. 649 (W.D. Mo. 1967), *appeal after remand,* 290 F. Supp. 622 (W.D. Mo. 1968) (dismissing student's lawsuit), *aff'd,* 415 F.2d 1077 (8th Cir. 1969) (Blackmun, J.), *cert. denied,* 398 U.S. 965 (1970). The district court required that the college permit students to have counsel present with them at the hearing to advise them, but the attorney would not be allowed to question witnesses brought against the students.

[41] 582 F.2d 100 (1st Cir. 1978).

[42] *Id.* at 106-07.

[43] *Id.* at 105. The court emphasized that the burden on the university would be slight because the student's attorney would only be present at the hearing to advise the student and would not participate in the presentation of evidence.

[44]   Osteen v. Henley, 13 F.3d 221 (7th Cir. 1993) and Hart v. Ferris State Coll. 557 F.
       Supp. 1379 (W.D. Mich. 1983).

[45]   *Id.* at 225, Hart, 557 F. Supp. at 1385-88.

[46]   Hart, 557 F. Supp. at 1388.

[47]   435 U.S. 78, 55 L. Ed. 2d 124, 98 S. Ct. 948 (1978).

[48]   *Id.* at 80. The student was informed of the faculty's dissatisfaction with her progress
       and the possibility that she would not graduate because of it. In addition to providing
       the student with a remedial opportunity to correct deficiencies, the university took
       additional steps to ensure that its decision was sound by having seven independent
       doctors evaluate the student.

[49]   *Id.* at 89-90.

[50]   *Id.* at 90.

[51]   *Id.* at 89-90.

[52]   *Id.* at 91 "'Judicial interposition in the operation of the public school system of the Na-
       tion raises problems requiring care and restraint.'" (*quoting* Epperson v. Arkansas, 393
       U.S. 97, 104 (1968)).

[53]   *Id.* at 85.

[54]   798 F.2d 419 (10th Cir. 1986).

[55]   *Id.* at 423.

[56]   *See* Ku v. State of Tenn., 322 F.3d 431 (6th Cir. 2003) in which a medical school
       student placed on leave of absence due to unsatisfactory performance did not have an
       opportunity to appear before the faculty committee making the initial recommenda-
       tion but was allowed to appeal the decision to a faculty review panel, and the panel
       heard his response to the recommendation. The federal appeals court held the medical
       school's decision to place a student on leave and to require remediation of identified
       deficiencies before readmission to the program did not violate the student's academic
       due process rights. The court reasoned that when the student is fully informed of
       faculty dissatisfaction with progress and the decision to dismiss is careful and deliber-
       ate, the Fourteenth Amendment due process requirement is met. *See also* Shaboon v.
       Duncan, 252 F.3d 722 (5th Cir. 2001) in which a medical student subject to dismissal
       was provided with opportunities to explain her side of events, which included having
       an attorney present.

[57]   Richmond v. Fowlkes, 228 F.3d 854 (8th Cir. 2000). Although the student contended
       the faculty member who had given him the last of three negative evaluations had
       participated in the committee's deliberations and biased the committee, all that was
       confirmed about her participation was that she was an ex officio member of the com-
       mittee, did not vote or participate in the deliberative process, and acted solely as a
       source of historical information. Absent evidence going beyond the student's allega-
       tion, the court was unwilling to find that the presence of the faculty member biased the
       committee's deliberations.

[58]   474 U.S. 214 (1985).

[59]   *Id.* at 226.

[60]   *See id.* at 227-28 (holding that the university had adequate grounds for dismissing the
       student).

[61]   *Id.* at 229 (citation omitted) (Powell, J., concurring).

[62]   521 U.S. 702, 138 L. Ed. 2d 772, 117 S. Ct. 2258, 117 S. Ct. 2302 (1997),

[63]   *Id.* at 720-721.

[64]   Gutzwiller v. Fenik, 860 F.2d 1317, 1330 (6th Cir. 1988).

[65]   *See* San Antonio Indep. Sch. Dist. v. Rodriguez, 411 U.S. 1, 34, 36 L. Ed. 2d 16, 93
       S. Ct. 1278 (1973) in which the Court expressly declined the invitation to hold that
       education is a fundamental right under the Due Process Clause.

[66]   Galdikas v. Fagan, 342 F.3d 684, 692 (7th Cir. 2003). *See also* Butler v. Rector and
       Bd. of Visitors of the Coll. of William and Mary, 2005 U.S. App. LEXIS 2001 (4th Cir.
       2005) in which the appeals court rejected an expelled student's claim that her exonera-

tion by a student honor council foreclosed a faculty committee from establishing remediation plan and ongoing evaluation that ultimately resulted in expulsion. The appeals court affirmed the lower court's dismissal of the student's action, holding the student failed to persuade that the faculty's conduct "shocks the conscience" or otherwise rises to the level of a substantive due process violation.

[67] Board of Educ. of Rogers v. McCluskey, 458 U.S. 966, 969, 73 L. Ed. 2d 1273, 102 S. Ct. 3469 (1982).

[68] Brewer v. Austin Indep. Sch. Dist., 779 F.2d 260, 264 (5th Cir. 1985).

[69] Gomes v. Univ. of Me. Sys., 304 F. Supp. 2d 117 (D. Me. 2004).

[70] 488 N.E.2d 850 (Ohio 1986).

[71] *Id.* at 853.

[72] *Id.* at 852.

[73] 813 F.2d 88 (6th Cir. 1987).

[74] The role of counsel in this case was that of an advisor to the student who did not take an active role in the former student's defense. *Id.* at 97.

[75] *Id.* at 98-99.

[76] *Id.* at 101.

[77] 116 F. Supp. 2d 694 (W.D. Va.2000).

[78] *Id.* at 707.

# 11 Sexual Harassment
## Martha McCarthy and Suzanne Eckes

## Introduction

According to a 1997 study conducted by the National Coalition of Women and Girls in Education, approximately 30 percent of undergraduate students and 40 percent of graduate students have experienced some form of sexual harassment, with student-to-student harassment being the most common. The National Coalition also graded the nation's efforts in attaining gender equity over the prior quarter century and gave its lowest grade, D+, to achieving equity in terms of the elimination of sexual harassment.[1] If one questions the prevalence of sexual harassment in higher education, a look at the growing number of cases addressing such claims should remove any doubts. There have been more than 350 reported sexual harassment suits against colleges and universities, most rendered since 1985, and the legal challenges show no signs of dissipating.[2]

## Legal Context

This section provides a framework for the subsequent discussion of sexual harassment claims initiated by employees and students in higher education. Specifically, the Supreme Court's interpretations of the central grounds to challenge sexual harassment in colleges and universities are reviewed.

### Title VII of the Civil Rights Act of 1964

During the past few decades, there has been a steady increase in employment discrimination litigation pertaining to sexual harassment. Moreover, the legal standards have steadily become more favorable toward aggrieved victims. Most of the sexual harassment cases involving employees have been brought under Title VII of the Civil Rights Act of 1964, which bars public and private employers from discriminating against employees based on various characteristics, including gender.[3]

Initially, courts recognized that individuals could get relief under Title VII for *quid pro quo* sexual harassment—repeated and unwelcome sexual advances or derogatory statements, gestures, or actions based on sex—if pay raises, promotions, or other benefits were conditioned on submission to the sexual advances.[4]

In 1986, the Supreme Court in *Meritor Savings Bank v. Vinson* recognized that a second type of sexual harassment is actionable under Title VII.[5] The Court held that severe and persistent harassment (e.g., sexual advances, abusive language, demeaning behavior based on sex) resulting in a *hostile work environment* also could be the basis for a successful Title VII claim. Citing the 1980 guidelines issued by the Equal Employment Opportunity Commission,[6] the Court ruled that employers could be liable for hostile environment harassment without evidence that the victims have suffered economic or other tangible losses.[7] The Court further noted that simply because the victim submits to sex-related conduct does not necessarily mean it was welcomed.[8]

Subsequently, the Court held in *Harris v. Forklift Systems* that the hostile environment does not have to cause a diagnosed psychological injury to be actionable under Title VII.[9] In this case, the Court identified factors to use in judging whether an environment is sufficiently hostile to abridge Title VII. These factors include the persistence or severity of the harassing conduct, whether it is physically threatening or humiliating, and the conduct's interference with an employee's work performance.[10] Until 1998, to obtain relief under Title VII the aggrieved employee at least had to substantiate the employer's negligence by showing that the employer knew or should have been aware of the harassment (constructive notice) and failed to take corrective action.[11]

Then, in a trilogy of sexual harassment cases in 1998, the Supreme Court made it easier for victims to secure damages from their employers. In two of these cases, *Burlington Industries v. Ellerth* and *Faragher v. City of Boca Raton*, the Supreme Court held that the employer's intentional acts or negligence are not always required for liability to be assessed; under certain circumstances, the employer can be liable for sexual harassment initiated by supervisors *without any showing of negligence or fault*.[12] Recognizing that the employer includes its agents (i.e., supervisors) for Title VII purposes, the Court concluded that the employer can be liable for a supervisor's harassment if the supervisor purports to act on behalf of the employer, relies on apparent authority, or is aided in accomplishing the harassment by the employment relationship.[13]

If the victim experiences tangible loss (e.g., demotion, dismissal), the employer is strictly liable for the supervisor's behavior and cannot assert the defense that reasonable precautions were taken. However, the Court held that if the employee experiences no tangible loss or change in job status, employers can avoid liability by demonstrating that they exercised reasonable care to prevent the harassment and took prompt corrective action and that the employee unreasonably failed to use the internal grievance procedures. Thus, employers who have acted appropriately are not completely vulnerable to liability for harassment initiated by their supervisors.[14] And employer liability for harassment among coworkers continues to be evaluated based on the "knew or should have known" constructive notice standard.[15]

In the third Supreme Court decision rendered in 1998, *Oncale v. Sundowner Offshore Services*, the Court held that Title VII's prohibition of discrimination based on sex does not preclude a same-sex harassment claim.[16] The court further noted that while the harassment must be severe and persistent to be actionable under Title VII, it does not have to be motivated by sexual desire. As a result of *Oncale,* same-sex harassment suits can be initiated under Title VII if they meet the standards of proof applicable to sexual harassment claims generally. Taken together, these three 1998 rulings have made it easier for employees to establish that they are victims of actionable sexual harassment and have made it more difficult for employers to build a defense.

While the terms *quid pro quo* harassment and *hostile environment* harassment are still used in Title VII cases, the differences between the two types of harassment has become less distinct. The Supreme Court in 1998 cast some doubt on continuing to use these categories, recognizing the "limited utility" of distinguishing "threats that are carried out" from "bothersome attentions" that are so persistent and severe that they create a hostile work environment.[17] The Office for Civil Rights (OCR) in the Department of Education also acknowledges in its *Sexual Harassment Guidance* that "in many cases the line between *quid pro quo* and hostile environment discrimination will be blurred."[18]

## Title IX of the Education Amendments of 1972

Since Title VII remedies are confined to employment discrimination, some student harassment victims may use this provision if they are employed by their college or university (e.g., research associates, teaching assistants). But in the absence of an employment relationship, students must find other grounds to use in challenging sexual harassment. The most commonly used provision is Title IX of the Education Amendments of 1972. Title IX specifies that "no person in the United States shall, on the basis of sex, be excluded from participation in, be denied the benefits of, or be subjected to discrimination under any education program or activity receiving federal financial assistance."[19] Student victims of sexual harassment may assert Title IX claims against education institutions by (1) suing the institution for money damages, (2) suing the institution for injunctive or declaratory relief, and (3) seeking administrative compliance by filing a complaint against the institution through an internal grievance process or with the U.S. Department of Education.[20]

Title IX has generated a number of Supreme Court rulings interpreting congressional intent in enacting the law, and some of these rulings have, in turn, evoked congressional responses.[21] Also, questions have been raised regarding how Eleventh Amendment restrictions apply in Title IX disputes, and Congress attempted to clarify this issue by abrogating state immunity from Title IX suits in a 1986 law.[22]

In 1992, the Supreme Court delivered a significant decision, *Franklin v. Gwinnett Public Schools*, holding for the first time that students can use Title IX to seek monetary damages from school districts for sexual harassment by school personnel.[23] In this case, a female student alleged that school authorities took no action even though they were aware that a teacher/coach was harassing her, which included coercive intercourse on school grounds. The student further asserted that school personnel discouraged her from pressing charges against the teacher/coach. The unanimous Supreme Court held that Congress did not intend to restrict the remedies available to individuals for Title IX violations, and therefore, students could use Title IX to seek monetary damages for gender discrimination in the form of sexual harassment by school employees.[24] But the Court was not precise as to the conditions that abridge Title IX, spawning a range of lower-court decisions.[25]

In 1998, the Supreme Court finally clarified the Title IX standard in *Gebser v. Lago Vista Independent School District*, holding that school officials with authority to take corrective action must have actual knowledge of the harassment and be deliberately indifferent toward the victim to establish a Title IX violation.[26] The Court ruled that Title IX essentially entails a contract in that school districts promise not to discriminate based on gender in educational programs receiving federal funds. Since Title IX attaches conditions to the receipt of federal aid, the Court concluded that educational institutions must be aware of any requirements accompanying such funds. The Court further held that the school district's failure to adopt a sexual harassment policy and effective grievance procedure did not necessarily constitute a Title IX violation, even though the U.S. Department of Education guidelines for Title IX require such policies and procedures.[27]

In *Gebser*, a female student sued the school district for failing to stop her long-term sexual relationship with a teacher. The student did not report the relationship to school officials, but after a policeman caught the teacher and student having sexual relations, the teacher was subsequently terminated. The Supreme Court concluded that the student's claim did not satisfy the threshold of "actual knowledge" and "deliberate indifference" on the part of school authorities. The Supreme Court majority rejected basing Title IX liability on a constructive notice standard (i.e., the employer should have known of the inappropriate behavior) or on a theory of vicarious liability (i.e., the school district is liable for intentional acts of its teachers, regardless of the employer's fault) that are used to assess Title VII claims of sexual harassment in employment.

The Court emphasized the distinction between conditional spending laws like Title IX and Title VII, which is a regulatory law and includes a direct prohibition on gender discrimination in employment. However, a number of commentators have questioned whether such structural differences justify the significantly different liability standards the Supreme Court has articulated for the two laws. For example, William Kaplan has asserted: "In particular, nothing about these acknowledged differences between Title IX and Title VII undermines the basic point ... that in terms of public policy and statutory purposes (and, it might be added, common sense) it is unlikely that Congress would have contemplated or intentionally provided for such a divergence between the protections for students and the protections for employees."[28]

The standard to establish Title IX liability that was announced in *Gebser* is difficult, but not impossible, to satisfy. Also, the OCR maintains that it will continue to be diligent in investigating possible Title IX violations where students allegedly have been harassed by educational personnel and in terminating federal aid to institutions that are not in compliance with the law. In 1997, the OCR issued detailed Title IX guidelines regarding the responsibilities of educational institutions receiving federal financial assistance to recognize and effectively respond to sexual harassment.[29] These guidelines were more stringent than the Supreme Court's subsequent interpretation of Title IX, so the OCR revised the document in 2001 to reflect the Court's position. In other respects, the revised document is identical to the 1997 guidelines.[30]

The most recent Supreme Court decision addressing sexual harassment against students, *Davis v. Monroe County Board of Education*, pertains to student-to-student harassment.[31] The Court in this 1999 ruling held that education institutions can be liable for damages under Title IX in connection with peer sexual harassment but adopted the high threshold that it announced in *Gebser*. In short, educational institutions have an affirmative duty to protect students from sexual harassment inflicted by their peers if school personnel with the power to do something about the harassment have actual knowledge of the behavior and exhibit deliberate indifference toward the rights of the victim. To establish a Title IX violation for peer harassment, the education institution must exercise substantial control over both the harasser and the environment in which the known harassment takes place, and the inaction of school personnel must at least make the victim more vulnerable to the harassment. The Supreme Court held that this duty is triggered only if the harassment is severe and persistent and if it interferes with the victim's ability to benefit from educational opportunities. This is a heavy burden of proof for student victims of peer harassment to secure damages under Title IX, but this burden can be met, just as it can in cases involving employee-to-student harassment. It is also important to note that same-sex harassment is actionable under Title IX, like Title VII, as long as the harassment is based on gender and not sexual orientation.[32]

Both *Gebser* and *Davis* were five-to-four decisions, and only Justice O'Connor, who wrote both majority opinions, was in the majority in both cases.[33] The other four in the majority in *Gebser*, who supported the "actual knowledge" and "deliberate indifference" standards to award damages, were not convinced that similar criteria should be used to evaluate peer-harassment claims. The *Davis* dissenters contended that Title IX was not designed to make educational institutions liable for third-party, peer harassment, which may make them vulnerable to frivolous peer-harassment suits.[34] But this has not happened, given plaintiffs' heavy burden of proof. Nonetheless, these decisions left unresolved issues as to precisely how indifferent the response of school authorities must be to abridge Title IX. Also, some ambiguity remains regarding what educational personnel are authorized to take corrective action, especially in connection with peer harassment.

*Gebser* and *Davis* involved elementary and secondary school students, but the Title IX principles developed in the majority opinions apply to higher education as well. However, colleges and universities will have less risk of liability for peer harassment under Title IX because they generally exert less control over students and the environment than is the case in elementary and secondary schools.[35] Another issue complicating the applicability of *Davis* in higher education pertains to free speech protections. In *Davis*, the dissenting justices noted the potential conflict between protecting college students' First Amendment, free speech rights and shielding them from peer harassment, and they emphasized that the university's "power to discipline its students for speech that may constitute sexual harassment is also circumscribed by the First Amendment." [36] Even though several hate-speech policies have been struck down in institutions of higher education because the provisions have been vague or overly broad,[37] unlawful sexual harassment is not shielded by free speech protections.[38]

## Other Grounds to Challenge Sexual Harassment

Although sexual harassment victims in higher education usually seek remedies under Title VII for employees and Title IX for students, there are other legal avenues for relief. For example, state tort cases can be initiated for intentional acts or if negligent supervision results in such harassment.[39] To establish negligence, the plaintiff must show that the defendant breached a duty to protect the plaintiff, which resulted in harm. This burden was satisfied in a negligence suit against a Louisiana community college that was required to pay damages to a student because she was raped by the culinary arts supervisor, who was a convicted felon.[40]

Plaintiffs also can initiate suits claiming that sexual harassment implicates their Fourteenth Amendment rights if state actors are involved. They may assert that such behavior impairs their equal protection rights to be free from purposeful governmental discrimination or their substantive due process rights to bodily security. Usually such constitutional claims are initiated under section 1 of the Civil Rights Act of 1871, codified as 42 U.S.C. section 1983 and commonly referred to as "section 1983." This law does not create substantive rights but instead provides a remedy when a state official, acting under color of state law, deprives an individual of federally protected rights.[41]

The standards that are applied in Title IX sexual harassment cases are comparable to the standards used under section 1983.[42] A defendant can be liable under section 1983 if the plaintiff can prove that the state actor had notice of a pattern of unconstitutional acts and reflected deliberate indifference to or tacit authorization of the offensive acts without taking sufficient remedial action.[43] Section 1983 suits are appealing in some situations because they can be directed toward individuals as well as the educational institution, whereas Title IX damages suits can be brought against only the institutional grant recipients. In a section 1983 suit, individual defendants can assert the defense of qualified (good faith) immunity unless the actions violate clearly established federal rights.[44] The qualified immunity defense is available only to individuals, however, and cannot be used by the educational institutions[45]

Whether claimants can bring suit under both Title IX and section 1983 remains controversial. Courts have not spoken with a single voice as to whether Congress intended to extinguish the right to sue under section 1983 by enacting Title IX. The Supreme Court in 1980 recognized that section 1983, though typically used to enforce federal constitutional rights, reaches infringements of federal statutory rights as well.[46] This ruling opened up the possibility that even where there is a federal statutory remedy available, individuals who have been subjected to harm under color of state law could also bring suit under section 1983. One year later, the Court limited this decision, recognizing that "it is hard to believe that Congress intended to preserve the section 1983 right of action when it created so many specific statutory remedies."[47] The Court concluded that federal laws with comprehensive remedies may demonstrate congressional intent to preclude section 1983 suits. Circuit courts are split regarding whether Title IX supplants section 1983 suits against school officials responsible for a policy or practice that violates Title IX.[48] And the Supreme Court has not resolved this issue.

## Recent Litigation Involving Higher Education

During the 1980s, sexual harassment in university settings typically involved male faculty members harassing female students.[49] While this form of harassment continues to be prevalent, charges of sexual harassment now involve a wide range of abuses of power.[50] This section addresses litigation involving both employees and students as victims. Due to the increase in litigation surrounding these issues, only selected cases are highlighted to illustrate the most frequently cited issues.

## Employees as Victims

Employees in higher education have brought both *quid pro quo* and hostile environment harassment claims under Title VII. The vast majority of these cases are brought by female plaintiffs, though a few claims have been initiated by men. Despite the evidence of sexist university power structures and evolving legal standards more favorable to harassment victims, most university employees have been unsuccessful in their sexual harassment claims.[51]

To illustrate, in *Holly D. v. California Institute of Technology*, an administrative secretary at the California Institute of Technology (CIT) alleged that a faculty member engaged in unwelcome sexual advances toward her.[52] The employee brought suit under Title VII against both the university and the faculty member. The Ninth Circuit affirmed the district court's grant of summary judgment to the defendants. The appeals court noted that the employee produced no evidence demonstrating a connection between her job duties and the faculty member's requests that she engage in sexual acts with him.[53] The court did recognize, however, that the employee's allegations against the university properly would have supported a hostile environment claim under Title VII, but the university established that it had taken reasonable care to prevent the sexually harassing behavior, which is an affirmative defense. Specifically, the court noted that CIT implemented a written harassment policy with detailed procedures. The court also reasoned that since Title VII addresses actions of employers in responding to the harassment, the victim in this case could not use Title VII to get damages from the faculty member who was the actual harasser.

In *Okruhlik v. University of Arkansas*, a female faculty member also was unsuccessful in challenging the alleged hostile work environment.[54] She and three other faculty members complained to the dean about tension with some of the program's male faculty and administrators. The dean then initiated an investigation, but the alleged harassment continued; in one instance, the female faculty member overheard dirty jokes and negative comments about her. Eventually, she took a leave because of the alleged emotional and psychological impact of the harassment. After being denied tenure, which she claimed was a form of retaliation, she filed a lawsuit against the university, the dean, and others for retaliation and a hostile work environment. Although the jury returned a verdict in favor of the female faculty member on both claims, the district court entered a judgment for the university and dean, and the Eighth Circuit affirmed this decision.[55] Similarly, in *Gupta v. Florida Board of Regents*, a university faculty member was unsuccessful in an action alleging sexual harassment and retaliation under Title VII.[56] Reversing the district court's decision, the Eleventh Circuit held that harassment of the faculty member was not so frequent, severe, or pervasive to constitute actionable sexual harassment under Title VII. The harassed faculty member failed to present evidence that a reasonable person would consider the conduct toward her to be severe.[57] Other courts have taken a similar approach, finding challenged behavior not to be severe or pervasive enough to constitute sexual harassment under Title VII.[58]

Despite the poor record of females prevailing in such suits, they have been successful in some cases. In one case, a tenured faculty member at the University of Iowa alleged a hostile work environment, denial of promotion, and retaliation for making a sexual harassment claim.[59] She contended that there were false rumors created by male faculty about her receiving beneficial treatment from the university's department head because of her sexual relationship with him. The federal district court agreed with the female faculty member, finding that she was the victim of unwanted sexual harassment based on her gender. The district court reasoned that a hostile environment was created by cartoons posted outside a classroom concerning the alleged sexual liaison and several other instances regarding remarks concerning the sexual affair.[60] The university attempted to avoid liability by relying on the First Amendment, but the court was not persuaded. The court noted that

> [f]ree speech and academic freedom considerations might preclude Title VII liability if the sexual relationship rumors were true, but … [they] were not true. Rights of free speech and academic freedom do not immunize faculty members from liability for slander or their universities from Title VII liability for a hostile work environment generated by sexual-based slander.[61]

As noted, there have also been a few cases where male employees allegedly have been victims of harassment inflicted by women or other men. In *Bowman v. Shawnee State University* (SSU), a former male instructor filed a suit against the university and its former Dean of Education, alleging sexual harassment, discrimination, and retaliation.[62] Among causes of action, the plaintiff brought suit under Title VII, claiming that the female dean had touched him inappropriately, made several sexual remarks, and frequently telephoned him. The district court dismissed the case in favor of the university. On appeal, the Sixth Circuit affirmed, holding that the former male instructor had suffered no adverse employment action while at the university. The appellate court also reasoned that, even though the alleged incidents did constitute sexual harassment, taken together they were not severe or pervasive enough to create a hostile work environment.[63]

There have also been a few same-sex harassment cases filed. In *Mota v. University of Texas at Houston Health Science Center*, a male faculty member sued the university, alleging same-sex harassment and retaliation under Title VII.[64] He alleged that he was harassed by his male supervisor and that the university retaliated against him for making complaints with both the university and the Equal Employment Opportunity Commission. He described the harassment by the supervisor as "unwanted and offensive sexual conduct." The Fifth Circuit affirmed the district court's decision, holding that the faculty member had been harassed and experienced retaliation.[65]

## Students as Victims

University students can be victims of harassment initiated by university employees or by their peers. Several cases have addressed faculty-to-student harassment, and most have involved allegations of Title IX violations. Since appropriate university officials must have actual notice of the harassment for a Title IX claim to succeed, questions have arisen regarding who in the university setting has authority to take corrective action. One federal district court found that the director of financial aid and the director of the graduate history program were not officials with the proper authority to take corrective action against the alleged harassment of a graduate student, even though the student argued that both were aware of her relationship with a faculty member.[66] The court found that the financial aid officer was aware only that the student and faculty member were casually seeing each other. Also, there was insufficient evidence regarding whether the director of the graduate history program knew of the relationship.[67]

Similarly, in *Delgado v. Stegall*, a former student at Western Illinois University (WIU) alleged sexual harassment by a faculty member, for whom she worked as an office assistant.[68] At first, she expressed her concerns to a fellow teacher and a counselor, neither of whom reported the faculty member's misconduct to WIU officials. It was not until after transferring to another university that the female student filed a complaint with WIU; the institution responded by forcing the faculty member to undergo sexual harassment training and placing a letter of reprimand in his file. The student sought relief in district court, alleging violations of Title IX by WIU. She also sued the faculty member under section 1983 to vindicate the alleged impairment of her Title IX rights.[69] The district court granted summary judgment for both defendants, ruling that the student had failed to establish a violation of Title IX by WIU and that Title IX was the exclusive remedy for a teacher's misconduct, thereby freeing the faculty member of any potential liability under section 1983. The Seventh Circuit affirmed the district court's decision in part, holding that the student failed to prove under the *Gebser* standard that WIU had either actual knowledge of the actions of the faculty member or was deliberately indifferent toward the victim.[70] However, the appeals court disagreed with the district court's conclusion that Congress, by enacting Title IX, intended to foreclose the right to sue under section 1983. The Seventh Circuit reasoned that it was doubtful that Congress intended this result since it created Title IX without any mechanism to sue individuals for relief. Therefore, the proposition that Title IX eliminated a right to sue persons in their individual capacities under section 1983 would not serve any of the goals contemplated by Congress in passing Title IX.[71]

Likewise, in *Pociute v. West Chester University*, a student claimed that she was harassed by a faculty member while she was enrolled at West Chester University (WCU).[72] The student brought suit against WCU, the faculty member, and the WCU president. During discovery, the district court dismissed all claims against the president but allowed the student to proceed with a Title IX claim and a state law claim against WCU. The jury returned a verdict in favor of WCU, concluding that the student had failed to find "an appropriate person with authority to institute corrective measures at [WCU]." [73] On appeal to the Third Circuit, the court affirmed the district court's decision. The appeals court reasoned that the student victim had not established both prior notice and a lack of appropriate response on the university's part.[74]

Some cases have focused on the "deliberate indifference" aspect of the Title IX standard. Specifically, once it is established that university authorities had actual notice, courts will consider if the university acted with deliberate indifference to the allegations of sexual harassment. In a case where a college investigated a student's claim that she was harassed by a faculty member, the federal district court held that the student failed to demonstrate that the college acted with deliberate indifference.[75] Similarly, in *Wills v. Brown University*, the First Circuit found the university's "reasonably firm" reprimand of a faculty member charged with sexually harassing a student to be sufficient for Brown to avoid liability under the "deliberate indifference" standard.[76] The court upheld the inadmissibility of evidence regarding the university's responses to other harassment allegations against the same faculty member.

As with cases where employees are victims, some harassment cases involving student victims also have addressed First Amendment issues. For example, in a Virginia case, a student alleged that a faculty member had sexually harassed her on several occasions and that some of the harassing statements were made during class.[77] The court dismissed the idea that judicial interference in a professor-to-student interaction could stifle academic speech.[78] The court noted that "[a]cademic freedom, while intended to encourage creativity, should never be used to shield illegal, discriminatory conduct."[79] Other courts have recognized that universities exercise broad authority over faculty members' classroom expression, which represents the institution.[80]

In addition to students bringing claims against faculty members, there have also been a series of cases involving coaches. In *Klemencic v. Ohio*

*State University*, a former track and cross-country athlete for Ohio State filed a sexual harassment lawsuit against her coach and the university.[81] In this case, the coach attempted to establish a romantic relationship with her while she was still training with the team. Later that year, the student alleged that the coach prevented her from training with the team because she refused to date him, which amounted to *quid pro quo* sexual harassment. She brought these grievances to the attention of the Athletic Director, who reprimanded and admonished the coach and also provided the student with psychological services. Unhappy with this result, the student filed a sexual harassment claim in district court against Ohio State, the coach, and the Athletic Director in their official capacities. She alleged that she was a victim of *quid pro quo* harassment and a hostile work environment under Title IX. She also charged that both the coach and the Athletic Director were liable within their individual capacities under section 1983. The district court entered final judgment in favor of the coach and granted summary judgment to the university. The Sixth Circuit Court of Appeals affirmed.[82]

In higher education, the line is not as clear between employee-to-student and peer harassment as it is at the K-12 level. For example, graduate students often are also university employees. In an illustrative case, *Morse v. Regents of the University of Colorado*, two female students at the University of Colorado at Colorado Springs (UCCS) claimed that they were subjected to harassment committed by both a higher-ranking cadet and an ROTC officer while they were participating in the ROTC program.[83] The female students alleged that such harassment created a sexually hostile environment, and they reported the harassment to UCCS representatives. Unsatisfied with the response, the female students filed a claim in district court under Title IX, section 1983, and a few other grounds. UCCS argued that it did not exercise control over the ROTC department. The district court agreed and dismissed the Title IX and other claims against the university.

On appeal, the Tenth Circuit found that the district court erred in failing to consider documents provided by the female students in response to UCCS' contention that it had no control over the alleged harassers. The court reasoned that the ROTC program was offered and sanctioned by UCCS, and thus the university was liable for the hostile environment created by the fellow student and the ROTC instructor because UCCS knew of the harassment and did not adequately respond.[84]

The Supreme Court's *Davis* decision left questions regarding how its opinion would apply to peer harassment in the higher education context.[85] Since universities do not exert the degree of control over students that is evident at the K-12 level, it is not surprising that peer-harassment claims are not as prevalent among higher education students. However, there have been some cases involving allegations that colleges and universities are responsible for peer harassment on campus.

In *Adusumilli v. Illinois Institute of Technology* (IIT), a female student alleged that six male students and four male faculty members had sexually harassed her. The student had reported two of the student incidents to school officials. In her lawsuit, she claimed that the school knew and refused to respond to this harassment. She also claimed that the school responded to her allegations with retaliation, such as unfair grades. Applying *Davis*, the Seventh Circuit concluded that despite the student's assertion that there were twelve incidents of sexual harassment, only two of those were reported to IIT. Of the two incidents reported, only one was given to a school official with authority to take corrective action. As a result, actual knowledge was not established. Additionally, the court did not find the harassment to be severe, pervasive, and objectively offensive.[86]

Likewise, a Kansas federal district court did not find challenged harassment to be severe enough to evoke liability under the *Davis* standard. In this case, a student alleged that another student touched her once in the mid-thigh area and three times on her shoulder or back area.[87] The female student alleged that the college was deliberately indifferent to her complaints. A university official told her that she could not file a complaint just because a classmate was "creeping" her out. Unhappy with this reaction, she wrote a note to the vice-president of the college, who organized a meeting with her to discuss the harassment. During this meeting, the vice president said he would speak with the alleged harasser. Although the college officials met with the male student and took measures to prevent further harassment, the female student was not satisfied and sought his suspension from school.[88] The court did not find that the college acted with deliberate indifference because it met with the alleged harasser, notified the students' instructors, and took measures to prevent encounters between the two students. The court further found that the four instances of unwelcome touching did not rise to the level of severe and pervasive harassment.[89]

It is not impossible, however, for university students to be successful in peer-harassment lawsuits under Title IX. For example, Yale University was denied summary judgment where a student argued that the university created a hostile environment in the aftermath of her complaints that she was raped by a male student.[90] The victim filed a complaint with the Sexual Harassment Committee, requesting that the Committee remove the male student from the course in which they both were enrolled. In accordance with its written Grievance Procedures, the Committee researched the incident and recommended that the male student be required to take a leave of absence until the female student graduated. Throughout the grievance process, the female student contended that she made repeated requests for academic accommodations and that Yale never responded to these requests, thus creating a hostile environment in violation of Title IX. The court reasoned that although Yale was not liable for the rape of which it had no notice, a reasonable jury could conclude that further encounters of any sort between the rape victim and her attacker could create an environment sufficiently hostile to deprive the victim access to educational opportunities provided by the university. The female student, therefore, raised an issue of material fact, and the court denied Yale's motion for summary judgment under Title IX.[91]

From the growth in sexual harassment litigation in higher education since the early 1990s, one might think that the incidents of such harassment involving students have increased dramatically. But the expansion of law suits is more likely attributed to the Supreme Court's recognition in 1992 that individuals can use Title IX to sue educational institutions for sexual harassment.[92] Perhaps the continued threat of legal action will cause institutions of higher education to become more assertive in trying to prevent sexual harassment on campus.

## Guidance for University Personnel

It is important for faculty, administrators, and students in institutions of higher education to know the legal requirements under Title VII and Title IX and to comply with them. Moreover, institutional policies prohibiting sexual harassment should clearly articulate what behaviors are prohibited and should include explicit employee and student grievance procedures. There must always be more than one avenue to file sexual harassment complaints to ensure that victims do not have to submit their claims to the alleged harasser. The policies should also be clear regarding who will investigate complaints, how investigations will be conducted, and what disciplinary action will be taken when harassment is substantiated.[93]

Adopting appropriate institutional policies and procedures is essential but not sufficient to curtail sexual harassment. Such policies must be widely disseminated so that potential victims know their rights and potential perpetrators know what penalties they may face for engaging in sexual harassment. Edward Stoner and Catherine Ryan have observed that "all supervisors, including department chairs and professors, must be educated thoroughly on all aspects of the policy, emphasizing their special obligation not to engage in discrimination or harassment and to deal with, rather than to ignore, potential discrimination and harassment."[94]

The legal standards outlined by the Supreme Court under Title VII and Title IX should be viewed as the minimum institutional response.[95] There are many things colleges and universities should do to combat sexual harassment that may not be legally required. For example, college and university administrators should be aggressive in offering students, faculty, and staff educational programs regarding sexual harassment, such as assemblies and workshops.[96] These programs not only should address the legal requirements and complaint procedures, but also should focus on the negative consequences of sexual harassment for the individuals and institutions involved. Such educational efforts may discourage incidents of sexual harassment and reduce potential university liability.[97] Moreover, counseling programs should be in place for victims when harassment does occur.

Despite recent efforts to strengthen institutional policies and enhance educational programs and other preventive efforts, sexual harassment remains a significant problem on college and university campuses.[98] This is an important issue, and all members of the higher education community should feel a commitment as well as a responsibility to work toward the elimination of sexual harassment.

# Endnotes

[1] NATIONAL COALITION FOR WOMEN AND GIRLS IN EDUCATION, TITLE IX AT 25: REPORT CARD ON GENDER EQUITY. A REPORT OF THE NATIONAL COALITION FOR WOMEN AND GIRLS IN EDUCATION, 31 (1997).

[2] *See* BILLIE W. DZIECH & MICHAEL W. HAWKINS, SEXUAL HARASSMENT IN HIGHER EDUCATION 163-172 (1998); Julie Davies, *Assessing Institutional Responsibility for Sexual Harassment in Education*, 77 TUL. L. REV. 387 (2002); Linda Eyre, *The Discursive Faming of Sexual Harassment in a University Community*, 12 GENDER & EDUC. 3 (2000); Gregory M. Petouvis, *Student-on-Student Sexual Harassment in Higher Education: The Effect on Davis v. Monroe County Board of Education*, 8 VA J. SOC. POL'Y. & L. 397 (2001).

[3] 42 U.S.C. § 2000e (2005). Title VII specifically prohibits employers with fifteen or more employees from discriminating on the basis of race, color, religion, gender, or national origin in hiring, promotion, and compensation practices including fringe benefits and other terms and conditions of employment. Title VII is enforced by the Equal Employment Opportunity Commission, and individuals can bring suits for remedies including compensatory and punitive damages.

[4] *See, e.g.,* Miller v. Bank of Am., 600 F.2d 211 (9th Cir. 1979); Barnes v. Costle, 561 F.2d 983 (D.C. Cir. 1977); Tomkins v. Pub. Serv. Elec. and Gas Co., 568 F.2d 1044 (3d Cir. 1977).

[5] 477 U.S. 57 (1986).

[6] 29 C.F.R. § 1604.11(a) (2005).

[7] *See Meritor,* 477 U.S. at 69-71.

[8] *Id.* at 68.

[9] 510 U.S. 17 (1993).

[10] *Id.* at 22-23.

[11] *See, e.g., Meritor,* 477 U.S. at 70-73.

[12] Burlington Indus., Inc. v. Ellerth, 524 U.S. 742 (1998); Faragher v. City of Boca Raton, 524 U.S. 775 (1998).

[13] *See* RESTATEMENT (SECOND) OF AGENCY § 219(2)(B)-(D)(1958).

[14] *See Burlington,* 524 U.S. at 765; *Faragher,* 524 U.S. at 805-08.

[15] *See* 29 C.F.R. § 1604.11(c), (d) (2005).

[16] 523 U.S. 75 (1998).

[17] *Burlington,* 524 U.S. at 751.

[18] SEXUAL HARASSMENT GUIDANCE: Harassment of Students by School Employees, Other Students or Third Parties, 62 Fed. Reg. 12034, 12039 (1997, *rev'd* 2001).

[19] 20 U.S.C. § 1681 *et seq.* (2005).

[20] William A. Kaplan, *A Typology and Critique of Title IX Sexual Harassment Law After Gebser and Davis,"* 26 J. C. & U. L. 615, 636 (2000).

[21] *See* Grove City Coll. v. Bell, 465 U.S. 555 (1984) (finding Title IX program specific in that it applied only to educational programs directly receiving federal aid); North Haven Bd. of Educ. v. Bell, 456 U.S. 512 (1982) (clarifying that Title IX protects employees as well as students, since both are "beneficiaries" of educational programs); Cannon v. Univ. of Chi., 441 U.S. 677 (1979) (recognizing a private right to bring suit under Title IX). In response to the *Grove City* decision, Congress responded to the Court's misinterpretation of Title IX by clarifying that this law and three other similarly worded federal laws cover entire institutions if any of their programs receive federal aid Civil Rights Restoration Act of 1987, 20 U.S.C. § 1687 (2005). Currently, the Supreme Court is addressing whether employees in educational institutions can pursue retaliation claims under Title IX for their treatment after filing a Title IX complaint on behalf of students. Jackson v. Birmingham Bd. of Educ., 309 F.3d 1333 (11th Cir. 2002), *cert. granted,* 124 S. Ct. 2834 (2004).

[22] In Litman v. George Mason Univ., 186 F.3d 544, 548-57 (4th Cir. 1999), the federal appellate court discussed at-length why it was an appropriate exercise of congressional power to enact the Civil Rights Remedies Equalization Act, 42 U.S.C. § 2000d-7(a)(1) (2005), amending Title IX as well as several other laws to make explicit that states are not immune under the Eleventh Amendment from suits alleging Title IX viola-tions. The court reasoned that states and their political subdivisions know that as a consequence of accepting federal funds they must comply with Title IX's antidiscrimi-nation provisions and must consent to federal suits to resolve disputes. *Id.* at 551-52. In addition to congressional authority to abrogate states' immunity under its powers granted by Section 5 of the Fourteenth Amendment, states can waive their immunity by consenting to be sued in federal court. For a discussion of whether Congress can attach a waiver of immunity to states' receipt of federal aid under its Article I spending powers, *see* Martha McCarthy, *Students as Targets and Perpetrators of Sexual Harass-ment: Title IX and Beyond,* 12 HASTINGS WOMEN'S L. J. 177, 181-82, n. 23 (2001).

[23] 503 U.S. 60 (1992).

[24] *Id.* at 70.

[25] For a discussion of these cases, see McCarthy, *supra* note 22, at 184-87.

[26] 524 U.S. 274 (1998).

[27] *Id.* at 291-92. *See also* 34 C.F.R. § 106.8(b) (2005).

[28] Kaplan, *supra* note 20, at 624.

[29] SEXUAL HARASSMENT GUIDANCE, 62 Fed. Reg. at 12034. The legal standards seem to favor Title IX victims compared to Title VII victims in one area, at least when minors are involved. "Welcomeness" is a significant factor in determining whether Title VII claims will be successful, but this is not true if an adult and minor are involved. The judiciary has supported the *Guidance* in stipulating that there is always an element of coercion in a sexual relationship between an adult and child, so such relation-ships between school employees and elementary students can never be defended as consensual, and there is a strong presumption that such relationships with secondary school students are not consensual. In connection with postsecondary students, the *Guidance* states that a number of factors will be considered in determining whether an employee's sexual advances could be considered welcome, such as the nature of the conduct and the relationship of the employee to the student, including the control or authority the employee has over the student. *Id.* at 12040-41.

[30] REVISED SEXUAL HARASSMENT GUIDANCE: Harassment of Students by School Employ-ees, Other Students or Third Parties, 66 Fed. Reg. 5512 (2001).

[31] 526 U.S. 629 (1999).

[32] *See* Nabozny v. Podlesny, 92 F.3d 446 (7th Cir. 1996) (distinguishing between gender discrimination and sexual orientation discrimination); *see also* Oncale v. Sundowner Offshore Serv., 524 U.S. 75 (1998); *supra* text accompanying note 16.

[33] *Id.* at 654 (Kennedy, J., dissenting). Chief Justice Rehnquist and Justices Thomas and Scalia joined the dissent.

[34] *Id.* at 672-77.

[35] *See infra* text accompanying note 85.

[36] 526 U.S. at 668-69.

[37] *See, e.g.*, Dambrot v. Cent. Mich. Univ., 55 F.3d 1177 (6th Cir. 1995) (striking down university harassment policy as overbroad and vague, but holding that the coach's use of the term "nigger" during locker-room talk was not protected by the First Amendment); UWM Post, Inc. v. Bd. of Regents of Univ. of Wis. Sys., 774 F. Supp. 1163 (E.D. Wis. 1991) (striking down university speech code that prohibited the creation of an intimidating, hostile, or demeaning educational environment).

[38] *See* Petouvis, *supra* note 2.

[39] In *Gebser*, 524 U.S. 274, 292 (1998), the Supreme Court observed that the stringent standard it adopted for relief under Title IX "does not affect any right of recovery than an individual may have ... as a matter of state law."

[40] Harrington v. La. State Bd. of Elem. & Second. Educ., 714 So. 2d 845 (La. Ct. App. 1998) (finding institutional negligence for failing to conduct a proper background check prior to hiring the felon).

[41] 42 U.S.C.S. § 1983 (2005).

[42] *See* Hendrichsen v. Ball State Univ., 2003 U.S. Dist. LEXIS 3710 (S.D. Ind. March 12, 2003).

[43] *See* Kinman v. Omaha Pub. Sch. Dist., 94 F.3d 643 (8th Cir. 1996).

[44] *See* Harlow v. Fitzgerald, 457 U.S. 800, 815-19 (1982); Bruneau v. S. Kortright Cent. Sch. Dist., 163 F.3d 749, 755-56 (2d Cir. 1998); Crawford v. Davis, 109 F.3d 1281, 1284 (8th Cir. 1997). *See also* Oona, R.-S. v. McCaffrey, 143 F.3d 473, 477-78 (9th Cir. 1998) (recognizing that failure to take reasonable steps to curtail sexual harassment of students represents bad faith because the law in this regard has been clearly established at least since 1992); Kimberly Bingaman, *Fourth Annual Review of Gender and Sexuality Law*, 4 GEO. J. GENDER & L. 329 (2002).

[45] Owen v. City of Independence, Mo., 445 U.S. 622 (1980). Courts have reasoned that public universities are immune from section 1983 claims because they are arms of state government and therefore are subject to Eleventh Amendment prohibitions on federal suits against states. *See* Rounds v. Ore. State Bd. of Higher Educ., 166 F.3d 1032 (9th Cir. 1998) (reasoning that because the defendant was a state university, it was entitled to immunity on a section 1983 claim); Johnson v. Univ. of Cincinnati, 215 F.3d 561 (6th Cir. 2000) (affirming summary judgment to the university on Eleventh Amendment immunity grounds for section 1983 claims).

[46] Maine v. Thiboutot, 448 U.S. 1 (1980).

[47] Middlesex County Sewerage Auth. v. Nat'l Sea Clammers Ass'n, 453 U.S. 1, 20 (1981).

[48] *See* Delgado v. Stegall, 367 F.3d 668 (7th Cir. 2004). *Compare* Pfeiffer v. Marion Ctr. Area Sch. Dist., 917 F.2d 779, 789 (3d Cir. 1990); *and* Bruneau v. S. Kortright Cent. Sch. Dist., 163 F.3d 749 (2d Cir. 1998); *with* Crawford v. Davis, 109 F.3d 1281 (8th Cir. 1997); Seamons v. Snow, 84 F.3d 1226, 1233-34 (10th Cir. 1996); *and* Lillard v. Shelby County Bd. of Educ., 76 F.3d 716, 722-24 (6th Cir. 1996).

[49] *See generally* Eyre, *supra* note 2.

[50] *See id.*

[51] *See* Mark Bartholomew, *Judicial Deference and Sexual Discrimination in the University*, 8 BUFF. WOMEN's L.J. 55, 57 (1999).

[52] Holly D. v. Cal. Inst. of Tech., 339 F.3d 1158 (9th Cir. 2003).

[53] *Id.* at 1181.

[54] Okruhlik v. Univ. of Ark., 395 F.3d 872 (8th Cir. 2005).

[55] *See id.* at 876.

[56] 212 F.3d 571 (11th Cir. 2000).

[57] *Id.* at 586.

[58] *See e.g.*, Johnson v. Galen Health Inst., 267 F. Supp. 2d 679 (W.D. Ky. 2003) (finding that the instructor's conduct was not pervasive in the sense that there was severe harassment on a regular basis); Hendrichsen v. Ball State Univ., 2003 U.S. Dist. LEXIS 3710 (S.D. Ind., March 12, 2003) *aff'd*, 2004 U.S. App. LEXIS 18127 (7th Cir. Aug. 19, 2004) (holding that the student did not prove that the harassment was severe and pervasive). *But see* Mota v. Univ. of Tex. at Houston Health Sci. Ctr., 261 F.3d 512, (5th Cir. 2001) (holding that the harassment was sufficiently severe and pervasive enough in a same-sex Title VII harassment suit).

[59] Jew v. Univ. of Iowa, 749 F. Supp. 946 (S.D. Iowa, 1990).

[60] *Id.* at 958-63.

[61] *Id.* at 961.

[62] 220 F.3d 456, 458 (6th Cir. 2000).

[63] *Id.* at 463-66.

[64] 261 F.3d 512, 515 (5th Cir. 2001).

[65] *Id.* at 530.

[66] Liu v. Striuli, 36 F. Supp. 2d 452, 466 (D.R.I. 1999).

[67] *Id.*

[68] 367 F.3d 668, 670 (7th Cir. 2004).

[69] *Id.* at 670.

[70] *Id.* at 672.

[71] *See id.* at 675.

[72] 2004 U.S. App. LEXIS 26638, (3d Cir. December 21, 2004).

[73] *Id.* at *4.

[74] *Id.* at *9-10.

[75] Frederick v. Simpson Coll., 149 F. Supp. 2d 826, 839-41 (S.D. Iowa 2001).

[76] 184 F.3d 20 (1st Cir. 1999); *but see* Chantos v. Rhea, 29 F. Supp. 2d 931, 934-38 (N.D. Ill. 1998).

[77] Kadiki v. Va. Commonwealth Univ., 892 F. Supp. 746 (E.D. Va. 1995).

[78] Bartholomew, *supra* note 51, at 64.

[79] *Kadiki*, 892 F. Supp. at 755.

[80] Bishop v. Aronov, 926 F.2d 1066 (11th Cir. 1991) (holding that university classrooms are not an open forum and faculty members can be prohibited from expressing their religious viewpoints in the classroom). Several courts have relied on a K-12 decision, Hazelwood Sch. Dist. v. Kuhlmeier, 484 U.S. 260 (1988), to conclude that faculty members' classroom expression represents the institution and can be regulated for pedagogical reasons. *See, e.g.,* Vanderhurst v. Colo. Mt. Coll. Dist., 208 F.3d 908 (10th Cir. 2000) (recognizing that professors at public institutions of higher education do not have a First Amendment right to decide what will be taught in the classroom but finding that the defendant college waived appellate review because it had failed to assert before the district court that the faculty member's termination was based on legitimate pedagogical concerns).

[81] 263 F.3d 504, 507 (6th Cir. 2001).

[82] *Id.*

[83] 154 F.3d 1124, 1126 (10th Cir. 1998).

[84] *Id.* at 1128.

[85] *See* Karen E. Edmonson, *Davis v. Monroe County Board of Education Goes to College: Holding Post-Secondary Institutions Liable Under Title IX for Peer Sexual Harassment*, 75 NOTRE DAME L. REV. 1203 (2000).

[86] 191 F.3d 455 (7th Cir. 1999) (unpublished decision) ("*Adusumilli II*"). *See also* Adusumilli v. Ill. Inst. of Tech., 1998 WL 601822 (N.D. Ill. Sept. 09, 1998) ("*Adusumilli I*").

[87] Cubie v. Bryan Career Coll., 244 F. Supp. 2d 1191 (D. Kan. 2003).

[88] *Id.* at 1202-04.

[89] *Id.*

[90] Kelly v. Yale Univ., 2003 U.S. Dist. LEXIS 4543 (D. Conn. Mar. 26, 2003).

[91]  *Id.* at *17.

[92]  *See* Franklin v. Gwinnett Pub. Schs., 503 U.S. 60 (1992); *supra* text accompanying note 23.

[93]  Each educational institution has a legal obligation to designate at least one employee to coordinate Title IX compliance. *See* 34 C.F.R. § 106.8(a) (2005).

[94]  Edward N. Stoner & Catherine S. Ryan, *Burlington, Faragher, Oncale, and Beyond: Recent Developments in Title VII Jurisprudence,* 26 J. C. & U. L. 645, 662 (2000).

[95]  *See* Kaplan, *supra* note 20, at 641-42.

[96]  *Id.* at 643. *See also* Susan Hippensteele & Thomas C. Pearson, *Responding Effectively to Sexual Harassment: Victim Advocacy, Early Intervention, and Problem Solving,* CHANGE (Jan.-Feb. 1999), at 48.

[97]  Eyre, *supra* note 2, at 3.

[98]  *See* Nikki C. Townsley & Patricia Geist, *The Discursive Enactment of Hegemony: Sexual Harassment and Academic Organizing,* 64 W. J. OF COMM. 2 (2000).

# 12 Employment Discrimination Under Title VII

Joseph Beckham and
Carole de Casal

## Introduction

Discrimination on the basis of race, religion, national origin, sex, age, or disability is prohibited under federal law and the provisions of many state laws, most of which are applicable to both public and private institutions of higher education. Principal among the federal statutes that cover employment discrimination are Title VII of the Civil Rights Act of 1964,[1] Title IX of the Education Amendments of 1972,[2] Section 504 of the Rehabilitation Act of 1973,[3] the Americans With Disabilities Act,[4] the Equal Pay Act,[5] and the Age Discrimination in Employment Act.[6] While sexual harassment and claims under Section 504 and the ADA are addressed elsewhere in this text, employment discrimination continues to be guided by the burden of proof developed in litigation under Title VII of the Civil Rights Act. This chapter addresses the burden of proof applicable to cases of employment discrimination, as developed in litigation involving Title VII and applicable to other federal laws prohibiting discrimination in employment.

Section Five of the Fourteenth Amendment[7] grants Congress the authority to enforce the equal protection clause and enact federal anti-discrimination law. The theme of federal employment discrimination law is that similarly situated employees or prospective employees should receive equal treatment by employers. These laws are intended to insure equality in the employment relationship for groups or individuals who are different in some respect. Because these laws have broad application to institutions of higher education (exceptions for private religious institutions are discussed in earlier chapters) and considering that many of these laws are mirrored in corresponding state statutes, this chapter will focus on the principal federal statute forbidding employment discrimination in colleges and universities, Title VII.

## Title VII Overview

Title VII of the Civil Rights Act of 1964 (Title VII) is the most comprehensive of the federal anti-discrimination statutes and prohibits discrimination in employment on the basis of race, sex, religion, and national origin.[8] As the United States Supreme Court has pointed out, "(I)n enacting Title VII of the Civil Rights Act of 1964, Congress intended to prohibit all practices in whatever form which create inequality in employment opportunity due to discrimination on the basis of race, religion, sex, or national origin."[9] The law prohibits discrimination in individual employment decisions as well as employer policies or patterns of conduct that discriminate broadly against members of protected groups.

Within the protected classifications of Title VII, it is unlawful to discriminate against any employee or applicant for employment with regard to hiring, termination, promotion, compensation, job training, or any other term, condition, or privilege of employment. The law extends to employment decisions based on stereotypes and assumptions about abilities, traits, or the performance of individuals. Discrimination on the basis of an immutable characteristic associated with race, such as skin color; hair texture; or certain facial features violates Title VII, even though not all members of the race share the same characteristic.

Title VII prohibits both intentional discrimination and neutral job policies that disproportionately exclude minorities and that are not job related. Equal employment opportunity cannot be denied because of marriage to or association with an individual of a different race; membership in or association with ethnic-based organizations or groups; or attendance or participation in school or places or worship generally associated with certain minority groups. The statute's standard of nondiscrimination is found in Section 703(a) and makes it unlawful for an employer

1. to fail or refuse to hire or to discharge any individual, or other wise to discriminate against any individual with respect to his compensation terms, conditions, or privileges or employment, because of such individual's race, color, religion, sex, or national origin; or

2. to limit, segregate, or classify his employees or applicants for employment in any way which would deprive or tend to deprive an individual of employment opportunities or otherwise adversely affect his status as an employee, because of such individual's race, color, religion, sex, or national origin.[10]

The Act also prohibits discrimination on the basis of a condition that predominately affects a protected group, unless the practice is job-related and consistent with business necessity, termed a Bona Fide Occupational Qualification or BFOQ. BFOQ's may apply to situations involving religion or sex.[11] The protected characteristics of race and national origin are excluded as a BFOQ for college and university positions.[12]

Title VII gives employees two possible causes of action. Under a theory of disparate impact, plaintiffs allege that an employer's facially neutral policies have a discriminatory effect on a protected group, and the employer cannot justify the policies by business necessity. Under a theory of disparate treatment, plaintiffs allege that an employer intentionally discriminated against a member or members of a protected group and a shifting burden of proof applies to the determination of liability.

## Disparate Impact

A plaintiff proves disparate impact by establishing that a particular employment practice has an adverse effect on employees of the plaintiff's race or sex, regardless of the employer's intent. In *Griggs v. Duke Power Company*,[13] for example, the employer required workers seeking promotion to achieve a particular score on aptitude tests.[14] The plaintiffs established that the test had an adverse effect on African-American workers because they passed at a significantly lower rate than did other workers. The test was not shown to bear a reasonable relationship to the requirements of the job, as a passing score on the test was not predictive of success on the job. In *Griggs*, the test led to the employer's selection of a significantly greater proportion of white employees than of African-Americans for promotional opportunities within the company. The test was said to have a disproportionate adverse effect on African-Americans, and by using the test as the basis for selection, the employer effectively discriminated against the plaintiffs because of their race.

What distinguishes disparate impact claims based on the reasoning established in *Griggs* is that the plaintiffs were successful without proving that the employer intended to discriminate on the basis of race. The test was neither job-related, nor did it select employees for promotion opportunities at random. If the test had selected at random, the success rates of African-Americans and other employees would have been representative of the proportions of these employees taking the test. The test would have had no adverse effect and would have been legal. Since the test was shown to have a disparate impact on a minority, the employer's use of the test to decide whom to promote, meant the employer effectively made decisions based on race, whether it was the employer's intention to do so or not.[15]

The *Griggs* Court unanimously concluded that a facially neutral employment practice that has a disproportionately adverse effect on a minority cannot be used unless it is justified by a standard known as "business necessity.[16] Section 703(k)(1)(A) of Title VII, as amended by the Civil Rights Act of 1991, provides:

> An unlawful employment practice based on disparate impact is established under this subchapter only if (i) a complaining party demonstrates that a respondent uses

a particular employment practice that causes a disparate impact on the basis of race, color, religion, sex, or national origin and the respondent fails to demonstrate that the challenged practice is job related for the position and consistent with business necessity.[17]

Disparate impact analysis has not been extensively litigated in higher education, and courts have provided little guidance on the nature of plaintiff's proof and the requirements of an employer's business necessity defense.[18] Several factors may account for the lack of reliance on disparate impact theories. The Civil Rights Act of 1991 mandated that no compensatory or punitive damages are available under this theory, and this limitation on damages may discourage plaintiffs who seek more than equitable relief.[19] In addition, disparate impact claims involve compliance with the rigorous requirements of class-action lawsuits under federal law, and this may tend to restrict the number of individual plaintiff's who seek relief under this theory. Perhaps most significantly for higher education institutions, however, is the fact that selection devices such as aptitude tests and diploma requirements are seldom used as a basis for employment decisions. For example, faculty selection decisions are more often characterized by subjective, though job-related, criteria related to research, service, and teaching. Even for non-academic personnel, employment decisions are typically based on selection devices that have been validated as job-related and screened to reduce the possibility of invidious bias in test items.

## Disparate Treatment

With respect to disparate treatment, the principal United States Supreme Court decisions interpreting Title VII have involved how to prove discriminatory intent. Under the standard most invoked in litigation, *McDonnell Douglas Corp. v. Green,*[20] a test of circumstantial evidence has evolved. However, in *Price Waterhouse v. Hopkins,*[21] a standard of "direct evidence" has received judicial recognition. With guidance from these two cases, lower federal courts applied a standard in which a plaintiff may establish a claim of Title VII discrimination either by introducing direct evidence of discrimination or by proving circumstantial evidence that would support an inference of discrimination. A plaintiff need only prove direct evidence or circumstantial evidence because the two claims were mutually exclusive. Under the direct evidence approach, once the plaintiff introduced evidence that the employer terminated him or her because of his or her race or other protected status, the burden of persuasion shifts to the employer to prove that it would have terminated the plaintiff even had it not been motivated by discrimination.[22]

Direct evidence is "evidence, which if believed, proves [the] existence of [the] fact in issue without inference or presumption."[23] When a plaintiff offers direct evidence and the trier of fact accepts that evidence, the plaintiff has proven discrimination.[24] However, a proof based on direct evidence of discrimination is often difficult to establish in a higher education context because vague and subjective judgments related to employee qualifications and performance are prevalent, particularly when faculty issues are involved.[25]

The influence of the *McDonnell Douglas* standard in application to federal anti-discrimination law has been pervasive. The first step of the standard required a plaintiff to meet a modest proof in support of a prima facie case and seemed to favor the plaintiff. After the employee established a prima facie case, the employer must articulate a legitimate, non-discriminatory reason for the adverse employment decision. Once the employer does so, the plaintiff must demonstrate that the proffered reason was pretextual, a subterfuge masking intent to discriminate. Applications of the test in higher education settings abound.

## Racial and National Origin Discrimination

Historically, racial discrimination has been a primary issue in Title VII cases. Under the shifting burden of proof, also known as the "tripartite test" first articulated in *McDonnell Douglas,* a plaintiff challenging an employer's hiring practices must first carry an initial burden of proof.

> The complainant in a Title VII trial must carry the initial burden under the statute of establishing a prima facie case of racial discrimination. This may be done by showing (i) that he belongs to a racial minority; (ii) that he applied and was qualified for a job for which the employer was seeking applicants; (iii) that, despite his qualifications, he was rejected; and (iv) that, after his rejection, the position remained open and the employer continued to seek applicants from persons of complainant's qualification.[26]

The plaintiff's initial burden of proof in disparate treatment cases involving race or national origin is illustrated in a number of cases in which higher education institutions were defendants. In one case, an African-American environmental research analyst was given a negative performance rating by a white supervisor. The analyst was subject to disciplinary measures that included restrictions on funding for professional conferences and was required to maintain daily written logs of his activity. His white male supervisor called him "space pilgrim," "lazy," and accused him of "shifting positions all the time." Alleging that these comments were racial slurs, the analyst filed an internal grievance alleging discrimination by the supervisor. On the recommendation of the university's grievance committee, the analyst was reassigned to another supervisor, but negative evaluations of his performance continued. When he was terminated in what the institution described as a lay-off occasioned by a reduction-in-force, he filed a claim alleging disparate treatment. A federal appeals court affirmed a summary judgment motion for the university, concluding that the analyst failed to establish a prima facie claim of disparate treatment.[27] The appeals court found that the analyst relied on his own perceptions and the findings of the institution's grievance committee in building his case but reasoned that his perceptions are not evidence and the grievance report failed to provide the required inference of bias behind the institution's actions stipulating only that personality conflicts appeared to motivate the supervisor's actions.

In another case, the Eighth Circuit applied the *McDonnell Douglas* test in granting summary judgment to a higher education institution. An African-American chair and professor claimed direct evidence of racial discrimination as well as disparate treatment when his institution failed to promote him to a position as dean and hired a white applicant from outside the institution. The professor had not applied for the position at the time it was filled and claimed that the institution had not provided a definitive application process yet had a history of appointing from within. The federal appeals court found that the circumstances provided no direct evidence of discrimination, but the court proceeded to evaluate the professor's claim under the shifting burden of proof. Despite the fact that the institution had hired several senior administrators from within, the court adopted the view that many positions at universities are necessarily filled in different ways, depending on the nature of a position, its responsibilities, and other factors. The court concluded that a reasonable fact-finder could not infer intentional race discrimination from the decision to consider outside applicants when seeking a qualified individual for a position as dean and, given the professor's failure to make timely application for the position, summary judgment was granted in favor of the university.[28]

If the plaintiff is successful in establishing a prima facie case, the burden then shifts to the employer to articulate a legitimate, non-discriminatory reason for the employment action.[29] Although a higher education institution must articulate a legitimate, non-discriminatory reason for its employment decision, given the subjective and scholarly nature of judgments that typically apply to employment decisions in academe and the reluctance of courts to intervene in employment decisions that involve faculty qualifications, an institution generally meets this requirement. For example, in a case in which a former business professor, who was an African male of Ethiopian origin, contended his nonrenewal was a pretext for Title VII disparate treatment, the institution prevailed by articulating a legitimate, non-discriminatory reason for non-renewal, namely student evaluations of the professor's instructional performance that were regarded as below college standards.[30]

To compound the plaintiff's difficulties, once the institution articulates its reason for the adverse employment decision, the burden shifts back to the plaintiff to persuade the court that he or she has been the victim of intentional discrimination and the institution's proffered reason is a veil to disguise the intent to discriminate. For lower federal courts, it has frequently not been enough for the plaintiff to prove that the employer's legitimate, nondiscriminatory reason is pretextual; the plaintiff must also show that it is a pretext concealing a discriminatory motivation. This standard has led some federal courts to require a proof of discriminatory intent, while other courts have adopted the position that if the employer's reason in unworthy of belief, it can be assumed to disguise a discriminatory motivation.

By way of illustration, a candidate for a position as director of a language program at a New York university challenged the decision of a selection committee that rejected his candidacy in favor of an external candidate. The candidate, who was on the institution's faculty and had served in the role of interim director, met the burden to establish a prima facie case under Title VII and challenged the institution's proffered reason for the hiring decision, which related to teaching effectiveness. The rejected candidate contended that the institution's claim that it simply appointed the best candidate was pretextual in light of evidence that the process of recruitment and selection deviated from normal institutional procedures, the search committee was made up of individuals who could not speak Spanish and yet was charged to assess the candidates on the basis of their teaching competence in a model Spanish lesson, and this atypical search committee was created because of the administration's belief that the interim director would likely win the position if normal procedures were followed. Although a federal district court granted summary judgment to the institution, a federal appeals court reversed, noting that the plaintiff's evidence permitted an inference of discrimination on the basis of national origin and remanded for further findings. The court noted that the articulated reason for the employment decision was that an evaluation had been made that one candidate was better than another, yet the challenged decision was made only after the institution had deviated from its normal selection procedures, had appointed advisors who lacked proficiency in the skills they were asked to evaluate, and had informed another potential candidate that the interim director's candidacy would not be considered seriously. From this evidence, the appeals court concluded that there were genuine issues of fact as to whether the institution's explanation was a pretext to mask unlawful discrimination.[31]

The fact-intensive inquiry involved in the tripartite test is illustrated in a case in which a black assistant professor from the West Indies, who was hired on a tenure track, was issued a one-year contract and ultimately released by the institution. The trial court held the assistant professor met his initial burden of proof and went on to consider whether the institution articulated a legitimate, non-discriminatory reason and assess whether that reason was pretextual. The institution defended its decision by presenting evidence of substandard performance evaluations, negative student evaluations, and failure to produce scholarly work and obtain the doctoral degree, which was expressly determined to be a requirement for maintaining the assistant professor's tenure track position. The assistant professor presented evidence to rebut the institution's articulated reasons for the adverse employment decision, including evidence that the college had retained a white professor who did not have his doctorate and that student evaluations of teaching were tainted by a conspiracy among white students. While the trial court ruled in favor of the black professor, the federal appeals court reversed this ruling on the basis that the court's factual findings were clearly erroneous. The Fourth Circuit Court of Appeals held that the comparison with the white professor was inappropriate because he had been hired at an earlier time when the requirement for an advanced degree was not required. It also concluded that the trial court erred in inferring that the student evaluations were tainted, finding, for example, that student expressions indicating the assistant professor was difficult to understand might reasonably be interpreted as expressing a concern about effective communication rather than discriminatory animus based on race or national origin.[32]

## Religious Discrimination

Title VII prohibitions on disparate treatment also extend to religious discrimination,[33] although religious institutions that are owned, supported, controlled, or managed by a religious organization or that have a curriculum that is generally directed toward the propagation of a particular religion are permitted to exercise religious preferences. Issues of religious discrimination have prompted several cases at religious institutions. A Catholic faculty member was fired from a Presbyterian college for conducting surveys of other faculty members. After the survey incident, he allegedly did not receive raises or received less than the average faculty member for seven years. He sued, and the court dismissed his suit. The court held that if the college discharged him because of his religious views, it could lawfully do so under Title VII.[34] In a similar situation, a private university that established a divinity school hired a professor to teach in both the divinity school and in the departments of religion and English. Differing theological views came between the professor and the dean of the divinity school, causing the professor to be released from his position in the divinity school. The professor filed suit under Title VII.[35] As the university received a portion of its annual budget from the Alabama Baptist Convention, the court held that the university qualified as an educational institution that was protected by the exemptions of Title VII.[36]

The issue of preferential hiring by religious or religiously affiliated institutions has been the subject of several lawsuits. For example, when preferential treatment was used for hiring by a religious university, the university was challenged by a Jewish faculty member. In this instance, a Jewish part-time lecturer in the university's philosophy department objected when the university began requiring that seven of the department's thirty-one, tenure-track faculty positions be held by Jesuit priests, arguing that their presence enhanced the character of the university. The court found that membership in a preferred religious denomination can be a bona fide occupational qualification falling within the meaning of Title VII.[37] In a related case at another Catholic university, a rejected applicant for a theology position claimed the university's actions constituted sex discrimination. Twenty-seven, full-time faculty positions in the theology department were held by Jesuits. The court ruled that its action fell within Title VII's Section 702 exemption allowing religious schools/groups to hire employees of a particular religion, here Catholic. The trial court dismissed the case, and the appellate court affirmed, based on the plaintiff's failure to establish a prima facie case of sex discrimination.[38]

In cases in which Title VII's exemptions for religious institutions are not applicable, employees may assert alternative theories of religious discrimination: disparate treatment and failure to accommodate. In general, higher education institutions are required to reasonably accommodate employee's religion unless the employer can demonstrate an undue hardship.[39] The Equal Employment Opportunity Commission has issued guidelines on the duty employers have under Title VII to provide reasonable accommodation for religious practices of their employees and applicants.[40] A non-higher-education case offers guidance relative to the employer's burden in cases involving religious accommodation. A public school teacher requested to use the personal days provided in the union contract agreement allowing for paid leave for religious holiday observance. Additional days for religious observance would be afforded, but the employer would grant the additional days as unpaid leave. The schoolteacher sued the board of education, arguing religious accommodation should include additional days of paid leave. The United States Supreme Court held that an employer does not need to accede to the preferred accommodations of the employee and may offer its own accommodations as long as they met a standard of reasonableness.[41]

To prove a claim of religious discrimination under the disparate treatment theory, the evidentiary burdens of an employee alleging religious discrimination mirror those of an employee alleging race or national origin discrimination. In *Rubinstein v. Administrators of the Tulane Educational Fund*,[42] a plaintiff, who was Russian and Jewish, had been denied salary increases and promotion to full professor. The associate professor established his prima facie case and presented evidence that a senior faculty member within the department referred to him as a "Russian Yankee" and made an anti-Semitic remark concerning Jewish frugality. The institution justified the employment decisions on the basis that the professor's teaching evaluations were low and his service record was inadequate. The appeals court affirmed summary judgment on the disparate treatment claim for the institution, finding that the evidence of student evaluations demonstrated that the associate professor was a poor teacher and was not entitled to the promotions he sought. The court reasoned that since salary increases were predicated upon merit and the available funds were limited, it was not improper for the institution to rely on these evaluations, together with memoranda and faculty reviews substantiating the professor's ineffective mentoring of students and his low participation rate on faculty committees, as a basis for denying him salary increases. The appeals court's judgment ultimately turned on the professor's failure to substantiate that the institution's articulated reasons for denying him promotion and salary increases were a pretext for discrimination. The appeals court agreed with the district court that the evidence of poor teaching performance was so overwhelming that the suggestion some of the evaluations had been tampered with could not overcome the manifest weight of the evidence. As to the lack of service on committees, the appeals court recognized that discriminatory animus on the part of the department chair might have influenced the associate professor's opportunities for committee assignments, but this was not regarded as sufficient evidence of discriminatory intent. The court also concluded that the discriminatory comments by a faculty member who served on the promotion and pay-raise committees would not defeat summary judgment on the claims of discrimination. In this case, the comments of the faculty member, alluding to the associate professor as a "Russian Yankee" and stating that "Jews are thrifty," were stray remarks not shown to be proximate in time or otherwise related to the employment decisions at issue.

However, there are instances in which the institution's articulated reasons may permit an inference that the employment decision was motivated by a discriminatory intent. In a representative case, *Abramson v. William Paterson College of New Jersey*,[43] the college hired the plaintiff, an Orthodox Jew, as a tenure-track associate professor. At the beginning of her first year at the college, the professor informed her department chair that she would not be able to teach on Jewish holidays, and accommodations in her teaching schedule were permitted. However, a new department chair took exception to the arrangement and this issue became a matter of contention between the administration and the professor as she progressed towards a tenure decision. Relations with the department chair and dean continued to strain over the issue of the professor's religious absences, leading to a recommendation to discontinue the professor's employment. After filing a grievance under the institution's guidelines and initiating a complaint with the EEOC, the professor litigated under Title VII.

The Third Circuit Court of Appeals reversed a lower federal court decision granting summary judgment to the institution. In addition to establishing a claim based on a hostile work environment, the professor succeeded in convincing the appeals court that she met the requirements for a prima facie case under disparate treatment and the institution's articulated reason for the adverse employment decision had shifted in the course of her dismissal. The appellate court stated that if a plaintiff demonstrates that the reasons given for termination do not remain consistent, beginning at the time they are proffered and continuing throughout the administrative proceedings, this may be viewed as evidence tending to demonstrate pretext. Based on the record as a whole, the appellate court ruled that the professor successfully established that the college's justification for tenure denial was sufficiently implausible and inconsistent enough that a fact-finder could reasonably disbelieve the articulate reasons.

## Sex Discrimination

The shifting burden of proof in employment discrimination cases has application to claims of disparate treatment based on gender discrimination. A substantial number of these cases have involved allegations of gender discrimination in tenure denial. In many of these cases, institutions prevail on the basis that the proffered reasons for denying promotion and tenure were not pretextual. The college or university's rationale for tenure denial typically involves a judgment of faculty and administrative leadership that courts are reluctant to overturn in the absence of compelling evidence of pretext.[44] It is also unlikely that irregularities in the tenure review process will invalidate an adverse decision. While some irregularities, such as falsifying hiring criteria or documentary records, might lead to an inference of discrimination, subjective evaluative criteria, changes in the criteria over time, or lack of uniformity in procedures have been regarded as insufficient to establish pretext.[45] However, while institutions enjoy substantial discretion and judicial deference in making tenure and promotion decisions, institutional policies should be refined to reduce the possibility of unequal treatment and to insure a documentary record that will provide evidence of consistency in the evaluation process. Standards of quality should not be so subjective that they cannot be effectively communicated and consistently assessed at any stage of the faculty evaluation process.

Evidence of lack of uniformity in the treatment of similarly situated male and female candidates can be a significant factor in judging the likelihood of discriminatory intent under Title VII. Evidence substantiating discrimination based on gender in tenure and promotion decisions has included a showing that similarly situated male candidates received counseling to assist them in the tenure process and were advised of a requirement for a terminal degree when the female candidate was not so advised.[46] In another instance, a court upheld the claim of an assistant professor and awarded tenure to her based on a finding that the university president's sexist remarks about the English Department had established gender bias.[47] In this latter case, the university had denied tenure despite unanimously favorable endorsement from department colleagues and support at administrative levels.

In general, an institution's tenure and promotion process is extensive and multi-layered. It will require distinction in research or teaching, depending on institutional mission, and no evidence of significant deficiencies in any of the three relevant categories of research, teaching, and service. While plaintiffs in these cases may raise a number of issues, the burden to establish sufficient evidence that the institution's proffered reason is a pretext for discrimination is difficult to carry. For example, in *Bickerstaff v. Vassar College*,[48] a female, African-American associate professor challenged the institution's decision to deny her promotion to full professor. Because the associate professor held positions in both the African studies and education departments, institutional policy required two separate advisory committees to make recommendations on promotion, with one committee voting for the candidate's promotion and the other rejecting it. Based on internal and external appraisals of the candidate's research and evidence from student evaluations, the institution denied promotion. The candidate presented statistical evidence indicating differences in salary paid to faculty based on sex and race and further statistical evidence tending to show that racial bias influenced student evaluations of her performance. Affirming summary judgment for the institution, the federal appeals court reasoned that the candidate failed to demonstrate "that the proffered reason was not the true reason for the employment decision and that race was."[49] In the appeals court's view, the associate professor's burden was to persuade the trier of fact that she was the victim of intentional discrimination in that an illegal discriminatory reason played a motivating role in the decision not to promote. On this question, the court found that no genuine issue of material fact existed that would support the associate professor's claim of intentional discrimination.

The appeals court emphasized that while statistical reports may establish an inference of discrimination, the statistical evidence in this case was so incomplete as to be inadmissible as irrelevant since it failed to account for all the relevant variables that might account for the perceived disparities in salary and evaluation outcomes. While reliance on these student evaluations of instruction may involve subject judgments and hair-splitting when it comes to determining the point at which evaluations indicate "marked distinction," the appeals court noted, first, that the institution possesses the expertise and the discretion to make such judgments and the evidence in this case clearly reflected the candidate's declining effectiveness in the classroom. Finally, the court reviewed evidence from a visiting faculty report that concluded there was opposition to the African studies program at the college and that the program was subject to hostility by some departments. However, when the full report was reviewed, the court noted that the visiting faculty had commented favorably on the program's support from the college administration and from other departments on the campus. Moreover, the court emphasized that any perceived resistance to the African studies program cannot establish discriminatory intent in the candidate's promotion process.

In cases involving disparities in compensation, statistical evidence may play a role in establishing a plaintiff's prima facie case and meeting the burden to show the institution's reason is a pretext to mask discrimination.[50] When a female professor in a medical science field challenged the institution's decision to pay a similarly situated male professor at a significantly higher level of compensation, she presented two statistical studies that indicated gender significantly affected faculty salaries at the university. After adjusting for confounding factors such as rank, degree, tenure, duration at the institution, and age, women tended to earn lower salaries than men. The institution countered that the studies failed to distinguish faculty salaries among medical specialties.

When a jury subsequently returned a verdict for the plaintiff on the issues of sex discrimination under Title VII and unequal pay under the Equal Pay Act (EPA), a federal appeals court reasoned that statistics evidencing an employer's pattern and practice of discriminatory conduct, though not determinative of an employer's reason for the action, are still helpful to confirm a general pattern of discrimination. Since the university failed to present evidence at trial rebutting the conclusions of the reports, the reports were sufficient to establish a prima facie case of sex discrimination.

Having met the initial burden of proof, the plaintiff then rebutted the university's affirmative defenses to explain the wage differential. The university first contended that the newly hired male professor was more productive in his ability to secure grants than the plaintiff, but the female professor established pretext by showing that the amount of grant funding she generated exceeded that of the new professor. As a second articulated reason for the disparity in compensation, the institution asserted the new male professor was offered a higher salary than that of the plaintiff as an incentive to retain the male professor's wife based on market forces. However, the appeals court rejected this defense by noting that market forces were not a tenable argument in this case since they simply served to perpetuate the salary discrimination that Congress sought to alleviate in both Title VII and the EPA.[51]

While both Title VII and the EPA apply the same burden-shifting standard articulated in *McDonnell Douglas*, if the plaintiff is successful in demonstrating a prima facie case under the EPA, the employer may then respond with an affirmative defense to establish that the pay differential is due to (1) a seniority system; (2) a merit system; (3) a system measuring earnings by quantity or quality of production; or (4) any factor other than gender. For example, in *Markel v. Board of Regents of Univ. of Wisconsin*,[52] a plaintiff successfully demonstrated a pay disparity between herself and a similarly situated male consultant, thus establishing a prima facie case. The burden then shifted to the institution to provide evidence to justify the disparity in compensation, and the university explained that the male colleague's pay was based on the longer number of years he had worked for the institution and the fact that he had held a higher position.

This was a legitimate rationale, not based on gender, for the disparity in compensation, a finding that harmonized both the requirements of the EPA and Title VII.

Statistical models tending to show disparities in compensation between a plaintiff and a class of institutional employees are not typically sufficient to establish a claim of disparate treatment, unless the plaintiff can also produce an actual male comparator for purposes of the Title VII or EPA claim.[53] However, once the plaintiff has identified an actual male comparator, statistical models may be employed to show disparities provided that the analysis incorporates relevant variables that could account for salary disparities on the basis of factors unrelated to gender bias.[54]

## Retaliation

Punishing an employee for exercising the right to challenge an employment decision under Title VII is prohibited.[55] However, lower federal courts have divided on the degree of harm the employee must suffer before retaliation claims are actionable. As to retaliation claims, the United States Court of Appeals for the Ninth Circuit, in *Ray v. Henderson*,[56] explained that the federal circuits have developed different standards for assessing the severity of an adverse employment decision. As the Ninth Circuit characterized the issue, the circuits have aligned themselves with either a broad, restrictive, or intermediate position as to what constitutes an adverse employment decision actionable under Title VII.[57] In addition, employees must establish the causal connection between any adverse employment decision and the exercise of rights under Title VII.[58] In some instances, the close temporal proximity between an employer's knowledge of a protected activity (filing a Title VII claim) and an adverse employment action will be sufficient to establish causality.

The U.S. Equal Employment Opportunity Commission (EEOC), in its Compliance Manual, has interpreted the retaliation provision of Title VII to focus on whether the employer's conduct, even if it falls short of a termination or tangible act, would deter the reasonable person from engaging in protected activity.[59] Although the EEOC's interpretation of Title VII does not have the force of law, it is considered persuasive evidence of congressional intent. The Manual explains that "[t]here is no requirement that the adverse action materially affect the terms, conditions, or privileges of employment."[60]

The question of how much harm the employee must have experienced as a result of an employer's retaliatory action was addressed in *Stavropoulos v. Firestone*,[61] in which the Eleventh Circuit, in considering a First Amendment claim, emphasized that the retaliatory action "must involve an important condition of employment."[62] In that case, the plaintiff alleged she suffered emotional distress when University of Georgia officials sent her negative memos, including a mental illness memo and encouraged faculty members with negative comments about the plaintiff to come forward. Relying on Title VII case precedent, the federal appeals court concluded that the alleged harm was too insubstantial because other agents of the university eventually overrode the decision.

On the other hand, what constitutes an adverse employment action that rises to the level of retaliation under Title VII may include actions that fall short of termination. In *Mota v. University of Texas Houston Health Science*,[63] the university argued, first, that a professor who alleged same-sex harassment did not demonstrate the existence of an adverse employment action. The United States Court of Appeals for the Fifth Circuit disagreed, however, stating that in finding that the university had retaliated against the professor, the jury implicitly found that an adverse employment action had been taken. A rational jury, according to the court, could have concluded both that no tangible employment action resulted from the sexual harassment and that the university subsequently retaliated against the professor for filing a complaint concerning the harassment. In this case, the professor did not lose any job benefits when he refused to comply with requests for sexual favors from his department chair, but he was subject to unfavorable assignments, denied a paid leave, stripped of a stipend he regularly received, removed as the principal investigator on certain grants, and subjected to ridicule when he filed an internal compliant about the harassment.

The university argued that many of the actions asserted by the professor did not rise to the level of "adverse employment actions." The professor proffered eleven separate examples of events that he contended were causally linked to the filing of his complaints with the university, and though the court of appeals found that some of them did not qualify as "ultimate employment decisions," it concluded that at least four of the actions allegedly taken by the university met this definition, giving particular attention to the denial of paid leave and the loss of a stipend he regularly received.[64]

In *Russell v. Board of Trustees of University of Illinois*,[65] the plaintiff alleged that the university hospital in which she worked suspended her for five days in retaliation for her complaints about her supervisor and his treatment of female staff members. She brought the complaints against her supervisor after he initiated a disciplinary proceeding against her for inaccurately completing timecards. The plaintiff, in a disciplinary meeting, was subsequently found to have violated hospital policy and was suspended without pay for five days. She appealed the suspension, arguing that the decision to discipline her was tantamount to sexual harassment in retaliation for her complaints about her supervisor and his treatment of the female staff members.

The federal appeals court reasoned that in order to establish a prima facie case of retaliation under Title VII, the plaintiff must present sufficient evidence that she (1) engaged in statutorily protected activity; (2)

she suffered an adverse employment action; and (3) there exists a causal link between the protected expression and the adverse employment action. Although the appeals court found that a five-day suspension was a sufficiently adverse employment decision to invoke Title VII's retaliation standards, the court found no evidence of a causal link between the punishment and the protected activity. The court affirmed a finding that there was no evidence that the members of the institution's disciplinary committee had any reason to believe that the supervisor triggered the disciplinary proceedings for reasons turning on retaliation, nor was there any record that they were aware of the plaintiff's complaint. Thus, the appellate court ruled in favor of the university, concluding that it could not be liable under a theory of retaliation because the plaintiff failed to meet the third prong of a prima facie proof, presentation of evidence of a causal link between the employee's actions and the adverse employment action.

In *Rubinstein v. Administrators of the Tulane Educational Fund*,[66] the Fifth Circuit Court of Appeals affirmed a district court's determination that the evidence of retaliation for filing a discrimination claim was sufficient to overcome a summary judgment claim for the denial of a pay raise. The testimony of the associate professor that his dean had advised him that filing a discrimination claim was not a step a "good colleague" would take was corroborated in part by the testimony of the dean who, although he attempted to distance himself from the meaning of the comment, admitted that he had urged the associate not to bring suit. In the view of the appeals court, this evidence was sufficient to allow a jury to conclude that the institution illegally retaliated against the associate professor.

Similarly, in *Abramson v. William Paterson College of New Jersey*, [67] a federal appeals court found that a professor's complaints of religious discrimination and harassment to the college, formal or informal, oral and written, were sufficient to satisfy the first prong of the prima facie case for retaliation. Further, the professor's termination constituted an obvious adverse employment action, and in light of the timing of her termination and the demonstration of ongoing administrative antagonism that established a causal nexus between the adverse employment action and the protected activity, the court of appeals concluded there was ample evidence from which a reasonable jury could draw inferences establishing a prima facie case for retaliation.

However, in *Mato v. Baldauf*, [68] the Fifth Circuit rejected a claim based on an employee's assertion that her termination in the course of a reorganization was based on her protected activity. The protected activity that the plaintiff alleged involved encouraging and assisting other women to file sexual harassment complaints. The court noted that approximately a year and a half passed between the last sexual harassment complaint and the plaintiff's termination, a time period that did not support an inference of retaliation. Moreover, she failed to present any evidence that the director who initiated the reorganization even knew that she had aided female co-workers in filing sexual harassment claims, all five incidents of which took place before the director began working for institution. The plaintiff contended that the institution's decision to require a Ph.D. for the curator's position and the consequential termination of her employment in the reorganization was the act of retaliation. However, the appellate court found that the plaintiff failed to present sufficient evidence that would allow a jury to conclude that the re-organization decision was a pretext to retaliate against her. The court stated that the first step was to determine whether the director acted independently in deciding that the new curator would be required to hold the Ph.D. degree or whether he was prevailed upon by others in the organization, who were motivated by a retaliatory animus, to create this requirement as a pretext for terminating the plaintiff's employment. The court ruled that plaintiff produced no evidence that would allow a jury to conclude that a retaliatory animus was the impetus for this action.

## Reverse Discrimination/Affirmative Action

The passage of Title VII as part of the Civil Rights Act of 1964 would suggest that it was primarily intended to protect minorities and women from discrimination in the workplace. However, the provisions of the law have also been characterized as applying to all races, religious groups, and members of both genders. In 1976, the United States Supreme Court addressed a case of reverse discrimination in which it concluded that Title VII "was intended to cover white men and women and all Americans."[69] The Court applied Title VII to a case in which two white workers had been fired by their employer for stealing, but a third employee caught stealing, who was black, was not fired. When the two white workers brought suit, the Court stated that Title VII's "terms are not limited to discrimination against members of any particular race."[70]

However, the Court was later to address an affirmative-action plan based on a collective bargaining agreement between the United Steelworkers of America and Kaiser Aluminum & Chemical Corporation that seemed to undercut the "colorblind" reading of Title VII. In *United Steelworkers of America v. Weber,*[71] the Court examined a bargaining agreement that called for company training programs in an effort to promote more black workers and earmarked a percentage of available slots in the training programs for these employees. The plaintiff in this case was a white worker who was denied a place in the training program despite the fact that he was a more senior employee than all of the black employees selected. In deciding *Weber*, a majority of the Supreme Court rejected the view that the private company's affirmative-action program negotiated with a union violated Title VII's prohibitions against racial discrimination in employment. The majority reasoned that Congress did not intend to condemn all private, voluntary, race-conscious affirmative-action plans, and the affirmative-action plan under consideration, which was designed to eliminate traditional patterns of conspicuous racial segregation, was permissible under Title VII. The Court's decision was influenced in part by the fact that the affirmative-action plan did not require the discharge of white workers, and their replacement with new black hirees did not create an absolute bar to the advancement of white employees and was a temporary measure not intended to maintain racial balance but simply to eliminate a manifest racial imbalance.[72]

As these differing opinions would suggest, the application of Title VII has not been easily adapted to claims of reverse discrimination. Claims in which a white male seeks redress under Title VII have resulted in agreement that the reverse discrimination plaintiff may establish a claim under the "direct evidence" standard, but lower courts have not uniformly adopted a similar approach in instances in which the reverse discrimination plaintiff has asserted disparate treatment based on circumstantial evidence. Direct evidence of discrimination could be shown by the employer's admissions of a discriminatory intent, but the likelihood of such an admission against interest seems remote in the more sophisticated academic setting in which subjective hiring and promotion decisions would veil direct evidence of discrimination.

When whites or men are the "minorities" in the institution in which they work, the shifting burden of proof in disparate treatment tends to work in the same way as it would in a traditional *McDonnell Douglas* context. In these cases, a majority plaintiff may show "intentionally disparate treatment when background circumstances support the suspicion that the defendant is that unusual employer who discriminates against the majority."[73] In an illustrative case, a white female professor of home economics at an historically black college established a prima facie case of racial discrimination under Title VII. The faculty member, who was in a racial minority at an institution where blacks outnumbered whites approximately two-to-one both on the faculty and in the student body, claimed constructive discharge in that her decision not to continue at the institution was predicated on the hostility of her superiors. Although the institution insisted that nonrenewal would have been justified based upon charges of incompetence and lack of rapport with students, the faculty member presented compelling evidence that her superior had rejected claims of academic deficiencies and department faculty had engaged in a systematic campaign to remove her from the department, including instigating student unrest and coercing students to sign a petition opposing the white professor's continued employment. When these findings were combined with evidence of the hiring of an African American faculty member to replace the white professor, the federal appeals court affirmed a lower court decision that because of her race, the white professor's failings were treated more harshly than similar failings in a black teacher would have been and that her contract would have been renewed but for the fact that she was white.[74]

When background circumstances confirm that a white employee is suing a predominately white higher education institution under Title VII, different proof would appear to be required. Clearly, the plaintiff is unlikely to establish that the institution typically discriminates against the majority. Initially, the reverse discrimination plaintiff must establish a prima facie case, including a showing that the plaintiff is a member of a protected class under Title VII. Even if this hurdle is overcome, the *McDonnell Douglas* shifting burden of proof has emphasized that an institution of higher education need only meet a burden of production, in-so-far as the employer must articulate a legitimate, nondiscriminatory reason for its employment decision. The plaintiff-employee, however, must meet a burden of persuasion in which the ultimate burden is to persuade the court that the challenged decision was the result of discriminatory motivation.

In some cases, the minority or female plaintiff's proof that the articulated reason put into evidence by the institution was not the true reason is sufficient for the fact-finder to draw the inference that the true reason involved a discriminatory purpose. This inference is plausible because the institution's failure to put into evidence a credible nondiscriminatory reason may suggest that the real reason is discrimination, given the history of societal prejudice against minorities and women. However, when a white male plaintiff challenges an employment decision against a predominantly white higher education institution, it is more difficult to draw the inference that the employer acted because of discrimination against white males, even where a legitimate reason for the adverse employment decision has been negated. For example, a male assistant professor sued when he was denied tenure for failure to publish sufficiently, alleging that women were held to a lesser standard. The jury agreed and found a violation of Title VII, and the predominately white university appealed. On the issue of direct discrimination, the appellate court held that statements by the interim dean, that females and males were judged on different standards, was not probative evidence that the tenure decision was motivated by gender. In addition, the court concluded that the plaintiff did not establish either that he was qualified for tenure or that he was denied tenure in circumstances permitting an inference of discrimination. Because the evidence, in the view of the appeals court, did not support the jury's findings, the case was reversed and remanded.[75]

Many reverse discrimination cases arise in the context of institutionally adopted affirmative-action plans designed to increase the representation of minorities and women in the workforce or to correct alleged inequities in pay and promotion. When these plans are challenged under Title VII, the majority plaintiff can meet the prima facie burden to show unequal treatment, since the institution's plan consciously uses race or gender to advance the employment opportunities of minorities and women. However, if the institution's plan is valid, the institution can advance a legitimate reason for the use of race or sex in employment decisions. This rationale requires a reverse discrimination plaintiff to show that the institution's plan discriminates against the plaintiff and the plan itself is invalid. In many of these cases, the plaintiff will challenge the plan on both equal protection and Title VII grounds. The United States Supreme Court has applied a standard of strict scrutiny to recent cases in which a public employer has adopted an affirmative-action plan favoring minorities.[76]

Reverse discrimination cases in higher education suggest that federal courts may be predisposed to recognize instances of reverse discrimination in affirmative-action plans. In 1980 and 1989, as part of a settlement for gender-based discrimination claims, the University of Minnesota entered into consent decrees. The 1989 decree required female faculty members to take part in the distribution of $3 million. A male professor argued that the provisions of the consent decree discriminated against him because of his sex and sought damages by filing a Title VII and equal-protection claim. The case was complicated because the plan in question was implemented pursuant to a consent decree and was not a voluntary affirmative action plan. However, it was established that the plan mandated by the consent decree was not imposed after a judicial finding of intentional discrimination on the part of the university. After considering three statistical models measuring the differences in salaries between females and males, the district court granted summary judgment to the university on the male professor's claims. However, the appellate court reversed the summary judgment. The male professor met his burden to demonstrate that there was a genuine issue of material fact on the question of whether the variety of statistical models established a manifest or conspicuous imbalance in faculty salaries based on gender. Although this ruling left unanswered the question of whether the salary plan unreasonably discriminated against the male faculty member, the ruling established that the white professor was entitled to pursue his Title VII discrimination claim.[77]

In *Hill v. Ross*,[78] a college dean raised objections to the appointment of a male candidate for a faculty position, insisting that the department fill the position with a female. The dean had imposed hiring goals on the department that included increasing the number of women and minority faculty. He stipulated in email communications that he was unwilling to send male candidates forward, and he ultimately refused to send the name of the male candidate selected by the faculty forward. The university defended its decision to leave the position vacant rather than hire the professor on the basis that the dean's decision was made pursuant to a valid affirmative-action plan.

The Seventh Circuit Court of Appeals reversed a district court's grant of summary judgment, noting three factors in the record that suggested a possible violation of Title VII. First, the appeals court was persuaded that a jury might reasonably conclude that the dean of the college used sex as the sole criterion for his decision not to recommend hiring the male applicant. Reasoning that the dean's imposition of hiring goals involving minorities and women might have exceeded the permissible application of an affirmative-action plan, the court noted that the university did not contend its affirmative-action plan was essential to eradicate the consequences of past discrimination either in the academic department or elsewhere in the institution. Second, the existing affirmative-action plan at the institution did not require that the dean insist upon the hiring of a female candidate. Finally, the court emphasized that the plaintiff carried the burden to show that reliance on the affirmative-action plan may be pretextual. By presenting evidence that the express terms of the affirmative-action plan do not support the dean's decision to block the appointment, coupled with the university's admission that it has not engaged in past discrimination, the plaintiff effectively shifted the burden to the institution to come forth with a justification for the use of sex in the hiring decision. Since neither the university's plan nor its brief addressed that justification, it was compelled to offer an "exceedingly persuasive justification" and plaintiff may then bear the burden of overcoming it.

## Re-examining Plaintiff's Burden

In *Desert Palace, Inc. v. Costa,*[79] a unanimous United States Supreme Court concluded that the 1991 amendments to Title VII allow a plaintiff to advance a mixed- motive discrimination claim against an employer. The essence of a mixed-motive claim is that the plaintiff alleges the employer's adverse employment action is predicated on both legitimate and illegitimate motives. The decision contradicts the generally accepted presumption associated with *Price Waterhouse v. Hopkins*[80] that precludes a finding of mixed-motive discrimination if the employer could prove it would have made the same employment decision with regard to the employee in the absence of discrimination. The essence of the *Costa* decision is that a plaintiff could prevail on a Title VII claim by showing through a preponderance of direct or circumstantial evidence that a discriminatory purpose was a motivating factor in the challenged employment decision.

In *Costa*, the Supreme Court held that the changes in Title VII make no mention of a heightened direct-evidence requirement for a plaintiff.[81] The Court read the statute to require that plaintiff "demonstrate that an employer used a forbidden consideration with respect to any employment practice."[82] The Court noted, "in order to obtain an instruction under § 2000e-2(m), a plaintiff need only present sufficient evidence for a reasonable jury to conclude, by a preponderance of the evidence, that race, color, religion, sex, or national origin was a motivating factor for any employment practice."[83] The requirement for "sufficient evidence" does not contemplate the necessity for "direct evidence" and would permit a plaintiff in a Title VII action to prove discrimination on the basis of circumstantial evidence. By allowing plaintiffs to proceed with a Title VII mixed-motive discrimination claim solely on the basis of circumstantial evidence, the Court's decision in *Costa* may make it easier for plaintiffs in some cases to succeed against employers.

While this decision appears to compromise *Price Waterhouse*, Costa does not modify the shifting burden of proof in *McDonnell Douglas.* The decision does not change the plaintiff's ultimate burden of persuading the fact-finder that he or she was a victim of intentional discrimination. However, the plaintiff may now succeed in this proof either directly by persuading the fact-finder that a discriminatory reason more likely motivated the employer or indirectly by showing that the employer's preferred explanation is unworthy of credence.[84] Whether *Costa* will be interpreted by lower courts to reduce the plaintiff's ultimate burden of persuasion in Title VII cases has yet to be determined, but lower federal courts will be tasked to make that determination on a case-by-case basis.

In one such decision, *Rachid v. Jack In The Box, Inc.*,[85] the Fifth Circuit Court of Appeals applied a new analysis that leaves the initial stages of *McDonnell Douglas* intact. In this modified or merged proof structure, the plaintiff must establish a prima facie case, and the defendant must articulate a legitimate, non-discriminatory reason for the adverse employment action. The Fifth Circuit then proposed that a plaintiff must produce sufficient evidence to create a genuine issue of material fact either that the defendant's articulated reason was a pretext for discrimination (the pretext alternative) or that the defendant's reason is true but another motivating factor for the decision was discrimination based on a protected characteristic (the mixed-motives alternative).[86]

## Conclusion

Title VII remains the principal vehicle for pursuing claims of employment discrimination involving race, religion, national origin, and gender. Particularly in cases involving disparate treatment, the shifting burden of proof applicable to Title VII claims has been adopted as the appropriate standard when pursuing claims under the provisions of other federal and state anti-discrimination laws. However, federal and state courts will continue to refine the shifting burden in response to case-by-case analyses and legislative modifications of Title VII. Two emergent issues will occupy federal courts in the immediate future. First, judges will be compelled to determine the extent to which claims of reverse discrimination will be actionable when brought against predominantly white institutions. It should be anticipated that challenges to affirmative-action hiring and promotion plans will be among the challenges brought by white males under the auspices of both Title VII and the Fourteenth Amendment's equal protection clause. In a larger sense, courts must ultimately assess whether differing standards in reverse discrimination suits are constitutional under the Fourteenth Amendment. Second, the shifting burden of proof as established in *McDonnell-Douglas* seems destined for revision in light of new United States Supreme Court decisions interpreting legislative changes to federal anti-discrimination law.

## Endnotes

1  42 U.S.C. § 2000e *et seq.*
2  20 U.S.C. § 1681 *et seq.*
3  29 U.S.C. § 794.
4  42 U.S.C. § 12101 *et seq.*
5  29 U.S.C. 206(d) (2004).
6  29 U.S.C. § 621 *et seq.* The Age Discrimination in Employment Act of 1967 (ADEA) prohibits age-based discrimination in employment for persons forty years of age or older. The law prohibits age discrimination in hiring, discharge, pay, promotions, and other terms and conditions of employment. As part of the Fair Labor Standards Act, its application is to institutions with twenty or more employees and which affect interstate commerce. The standards for coverage parallel those of Title VII
7  U.S. CONST. amend. XIV, § 5
8  Civil Rights Act of 1964, 701-716, 78 Stat. 241, 253-66 (1964) (current version at 42 U.S.C. 2000e-5 (2000)).
9  Franks v. Bowman Transp. Co., 424 U.S. 747, 763 (1976).
10  42 U.S.C. § 2000e-2(a) (2003).
11  42 U.S.C. § 2000e-2(e)(1).
12  KAPLIN, W. & LEE, B., THE LAW OF HIGHER EDUCATION, 200 (3d ed. 1995).
13  401 U.S. 424 (1971).
14  *Id.* at 427.
15  This reasoning begs the question of whether claims of disparate impact are constitutional under the Section Five enforcement provision of the Fourteenth Amendment. Violations of equal protection require deliberate intention to engage in invidious discrimination. Does a federal law aimed at prohibiting subconscious discrimination qualify as legislation enforcing equal protection?
16  401 U.S. at 432.
17  42 U.S.C.A. § 2000e-2(k)(1)(A).
18  For a discussion of the potential application of disparate impact in employment settings, see E.W. Shoben, *Disparate Impact Theory in Employment Discrimination: What's Griggs Still Good For? What Not?* 42 BRANDEIS L.J. 597 (Spring 2004).
19  *See* M. ROTHSTEIN ET AL., EMPLOYMENT LAW Vol. 1 § 2.31 (3d ed. 2004).
20  411 U.S. 792 (1973).
21  490 U.S. 228 (1989). What suffices as "direct evidence" and whether "direct vs. circumstantial" evidence remains an important issue may have been undercut by the Court's recent decision in Desert Palace, Inc. v. Costa, 539 U.S. 90 (2003).
22  *See* Kline v. Tenn. Valley Auth., 128 F.3d 337, 348 (6th Cir. 1997).
23  Merritt v. Dillard Paper Co., 120 F.3d 1181, 1189 (11th Cir. 1987).
24  McCarthney v. Griffin-Spalding County Bd. of Educ., 791 F.2d 1549, 1553 (11th Cir. 1986).
25  *See* Ben-Kotel v. Howard Univ., 319 F.3d 532 (D.C. Cir. 2003) in which a claim of direct evidence of discrimination under Title VII was dismissed on appeal because the plaintiff, a national origin minority, failed to argue this claim in the district court.
26  411 U.S. at 802.
27  Pilgrim v. Trs. of Tufts Coll., 118 F.3d 864 (1st Cir. 1997).
28  Lockridge v. Bd. Of Trs. of the Univ. of Ark., 294 F.3d 1010 (8th Cir. 2002).
29  Texas Dep't of Cmty. Affairs v. Burdine, 450 U.S. 248, 254 (1981).
30  Girma v. Skidmore Coll., 180 F. Supp. 2d 326 (N.D.N.Y. 2001).

[31] Stern v. Trs. of Columbia Univ. in the City of New York, 131 F.3d 305 (2d Cir. 1997).

[32] Jimenez v. Mary Washington Coll., 57 F. 3d 369 (4th Cir.1995).

[33] 42 U.S.C. § 2000e-2(e).

[34] Wirth v. Coll. of the Ozarks, 26 F. Supp. 2d 1185 (W. D. Mo. 1998).

[35] Killinger v. Samford Univ., 113 F.3d 196 (11th Cir 1997).

[36] 42 USCS § 2000e, et seq.

[37] Pime v. Loyola Univ. of Chi., 803 F. 2d 351 (7th Cir. 1986).

[38] Maguire v. Marquette Univ., 814 F. 2d 1213 (7th Cir 1987).

[39] 42 U.S.C. § 2000e(j).

[40] 29 C.F.R. Part 1605.

[41] Ansonia Bd. of Educ. v. Philbrook, 479 U.S. 60 (1986).

[42] 218 F.3d 392 (5th Cir. 2000).

[43] 260 F.3d 265 (3d Cir 2001).

[44] *See, e.g.,* Lawrence v. Curators of the Univ. of Mo., 204 F.2d 807 (8th Cir. 2000) in which subjective faculty assessments about the "quality of research" were largely unscrutinized by the reviewing court, despite a vigorous dissent by the chief judge of the appeals court.

[45] Aquilino v. Univ. of Kan., 83 F. Supp. 1248 (D. Kan. 2000).

[46] Kunda v. Muhlenberg Coll., 621 F.2d 531 (2d Cir. 1980).

[47] Brown v. Trs. of Boston Univ., 891 F.2d 337 (1st Cir. 1989).

[48] 196 F.3d 435 (2d Cir. 1999)

[49] *Id.* at 446.

[50] Cases involving claims of sex discrimination that involve disparities in compensation often involve both Title VII and the Equal Pay Act. As one federal appeals court has noted, the Equal Pay Act and Title VII must be "construed in harmony, particularly where claims made under the two statutes arise out of the same discriminatory pay policies." Lavin-McEleney v. Marist Coll., 239 F.3d 476, 481 (2d Cir. 2001)

[51] Siler-Khodr v. Univ. of Tex. Health Sci., 261 F.3d 542 (5th Cir. 2001).

[52] *See* Markel v. Bd. of Regents of Univ. of Wis., 276 F.3d 906 (7th Cir. 2002).

[53] See Houck v. Va. Polytechnic Inst. and State Univ., 10 F.3d 204 (4th Cir. 1993).

[54] Lavin-McEleney v. Marist Coll., 239 F.3d 476 (2d Cir. 2001).

[55] 42 U.S.C. 2000e-3(a). The retaliation provision makes it "an unlawful employment practice for an employer to discriminate" against someone who has opposed an employer's unlawful behavior or participated in a Title VII proceeding.

[56] 217 F.3d 1234 (9th Cir. 2000).

[57] *Id.* at 1240-41.

[58] Clark County Sch. Dist. v. Breeden, 121 S. Ct. 1508 (2001)

[59] U.S. Equal Employment Opportunity Comm'n, No. 915.003 Compliance Manual 8-II(D)(3) (1998), *available at* http://www.eeoc.gov/docs/retal.pdf

[60] *Id.* 8, at IV.

[61] 361 F.3d 610 (11th Cir. 2004).

[62] Id. at 619.

[63] 261 F.3d 512 (5th Cir. 2001).

[64] *Id.* at 522-523.

[65] 243 F.3d 336 (7th Cir. 2001)

[66] 218 F.3d 392 (5th Cir. 2000).

[67] 260 F.3d 265 (3d Cir 2001).

[68] 267 F.3d 444 (5th Cir. 2001).

[69] McDonald v. Sante Fe Trail Transp. Co., 427 U.S. 273, 280 (1976).

[70] *Id.* at 276.

[71] 443 U.S. 193 (1979).

[72] *Id.* at 205-206.

[73] Parker v. Baltimore & Ohio R.R. Co., 652 F.2d 1012, 1017 (D.C. Cir. 1981).

[74] Lincoln v. Bd. of Regents, 697 F.2d 928 (11th Cir. 1983)

75  Krystek v. Univ. of S. Mo., 164 F. 3d 251 (5th Cir 1999).

76  *See* Adarand Constructors v. Pena, 515 U.S. 200 (1995) in which the Court held that all racial classifications developed as part of an affirmative action plan by any government—state, local, or federal—are to be strictly scrutinized and Richmond v. J.A. Croson, 488 U.S. 469 (1989) in which the Court applied strict scrutiny under the Fourteenth Amendment's Equal Protection Clause to a city's affirmative action program requiring a thirty percent set-aside for minority subcontractors.

77  Maitland v. Univ. of Minn., 155 F.3d 1013, 1019 (8th Cir. 1998).

78  183 F.3d 586 (7th Cir. 1999).

79  123 S. Ct. 2148, 2155(2003).

80  490 U.S. 228 (1989).

81  *Id.* at 2153.

82  *Id.* (*quoting* 42 U.S.C. § 2000e-2(m) (2002)).

83  *Id.* at 2154-55.

84  Texas Dep't of Cmty. Affairs v. Burdine, 450 U.S. 248, 256 (1981).

85  376 F.3d 305 (5th Cir. 2004).

86  *Id.* at 312.

# 13 Disability Law
## Stephen Thomas

## Introduction

Imagine a scenario in which a surgical technician with HIV is released by a teaching hospital because he refused reassignment. His position required him at times to insert his hands into incisions to make room for the surgeon to work or to provide visibility. Had he been permitted to remain in his role, there was the risk he would eventually be cut or incur a needle prick and thus expose a client.[1] Envision a student who has an unstable personality and anger management issues. She at times explodes and at other times demands not to be called upon as she contends that her responses will make her appear foolish.[2] Consider a professor who sexually harassed students, sexually assaulted a colleague, and provided alcohol to minors. As his defense, he claimed that he has a disinhibitory psychological disorder and that his conduct was due to his disability and therefore not his fault.[3] These and a myriad of other perhaps less-intriguing cases represent challenges to college administrators in their efforts to address the needs of individuals with disabilities yet provide safe and effective learning and working environments.

Although a number of laws have indirect and incidental value when examining the rights of students and employees with disabilities in higher education, two are applied in the vast majority of cases: the Rehabilitation Act (Section 504) and the Americans with Disabilities Act (ADA—Titles I, II, III). Section 504 provides in pertinent part that no "otherwise qualified individual with a disability ... shall ... be excluded from the participation in, be denied the benefits of, or be subjected to discrimination under any program or activity receiving [f]ederal financial assistance...."[4] All public and nearly all private colleges receive either direct or indirect federal financial assistance and therefore must comply.

Title I of the ADA applies to all terms and conditions of employment engaged in by covered employers. Title II prohibits discrimination against the disabled in the provision of services, programs, and activities provided or made available by public entities, including public colleges. In contrast,

Title III applies to private entities, including most private colleges, in their provision of public accommodations.[5]

In addition, it is a violation of federal law to retaliate against any person who made a charge or testified, assisted, or participated in an investigation, proceeding, or hearing regarding a disability claim.[6] As would be imagined, retaliation claims are difficult to prove. By the time a claim reaches the courtroom, college officials seldom confess to wrongdoing and readily identify permissible bases for their adverse actions, both real and imagined.[7] However, the student or employee need not win a disability discrimination suit to prevail in retaliation litigation.

## Students and Applicants

Case law involving college students with disabilities covers a wide range of controversies beginning with admission and ending only when the relationship between college and student has ended (i.e., graduation, withdrawal, or removal).

### Qualifying as Disabled

To qualify as disabled under either Section 504 or the ADA, a student must (1) have a physical or mental impairment that substantially limits a major life activity, (2) have a record of impairment, or (3) be regarded as having an impairment. Unlike K-12 schools that are required to comply with the Individuals with Disabilities Education Improvement Act (IDEIA), at the higher education level, it is the student's responsibility to document his or her disability[8] and to provide officials with timely notice of needed accommodations and modifications.[9]

However, colleges may not establish unnecessarily cumbersome requirements that would limit or delay the enrollment of students with disabilities.[10] A diagnosis from a student-selected physician or psychologist does not end the matter though, as college officials then must determine whether the submitting party (1) is properly credentialed to provide the diagnosis, (2) has provided the necessary documentation, and (3) has made a reasoned assessment as to whether the client's impairment was substantially limiting of a major life activity so as to qualify as a disability.

Accordingly, not every physical impairment or diagnosis by a physician will qualify as a disability under federal statute.[11] The key determination is whether an impairment is substantially limiting[12]—note that the impairment does not have to cause an utter inability to perform the major life activity. Because there is no quantitative approach to determining what qualifies as "substantial," courts have predictably disagreed. Although it is clear that performance must be compared to the average person in the general population, it is unknown just how far below-average a student must be to qualify. Interestingly, some courts have used language that appeared to qualify plaintiffs who simply scored below average or had a mix of scores (some above and others below the norm) arguing that on one of many measures of "learning," the plaintiff was substantially limited.[13] This kind of reasoning appears presumptively invalid, as Congress did not intend half of the population to qualify as disabled. Also, courts are required to consider the positive (e.g., improved endurance due to heart medication) and negative (sleepiness resulting from medication) mitigating factors in resolving whether a given plaintiff is substantially limited.[14]

In a comparatively small number of cases, plaintiffs who do not qualify as currently substantially limited have attempted to qualify for protection under the second and third definitions of disabled when they have been subjected to adverse treatment. Some claimants, for example, have argued that the basis for the treatment was their "record of impairment" (e.g., history of hospitalization due to addiction). Supporting a history or record of impairment is generally easy for plaintiffs to do (e.g., producing hospital and insurance records); showing that the college based its adverse decision on that history, however, is often problematic. The same is true for claims where plaintiffs allege they have been "regarded as having an impairment." Importantly, providing a student with accommodations does not in itself result in the institution regarding the student as disabled,[15] nor will a faculty or staff member suggesting to a student that he or she needs to "seek help."

## Admission/Readmission

As a general rule, applicants with disability must meet the same standards for admission as other students and do so within prescribed deadlines. Nonetheless, college officials should make the application process accessible and convenient, to the extent practical (e.g., on the Internet; through Student Disability Services). Once applicant files are complete, decisions are made regarding admission. Some students with disabilities will be accepted and, in selective programs, some will be denied. Denials typically are based on facially neutral criteria[16] (both objective and subjective) that are administered uniformly (e.g., grade point average (GPA) requirements, blind review of writing sample). Such requirements may have a disparate impact on the disabled (e.g., use of test scores when considering the admission of persons with learning disabilities) but will be permitted if shown to be valid predictors of success in the program.

In comparison, when students seek readmission following a hiatus from campus due to academic or behavioral dismissal or due to their own voluntary withdrawal from the program, college officials not only have the original admissions file with predictive criteria to assist them in determining whether a particular student is now likely to succeed, but also have records of prior (perhaps recent) performance within the program. Such records may militate against rendering a positive admissions decision. Also, once viewed in the aggregate, the student may be considered qualified but be denied readmission, nonetheless, given that he or she is less well qualified than others within the current applicant pool.

Students who are not permitted to matriculate must be denied based on published criteria and not stereotypic assumptions about what they can and cannot do.[17] Those students who are admitted must be able to meet essential program requirements, although they may at times require reasonable accommodations and modifications in so doing.[18]

## Reasonable Accommodations and Modifications

Unless agreed to as a reasonable accommodation or modification, all students must meet the same course and graduation requirements. However, college officials must determine on an individual basis ways that will permit the qualified student to access college programs, activities, and services. The accommodations may be as simple as permission to have extra time on assignments or the use of a segregated quiet room for testing. But, on occasion expectations have been more substantial, some even exhibiting an extraordinary perception of entitlement. For most students, however, requests and resulting accommodations are reasonable and are provided without controversy, cost to the student, or delay. Even then, there is the occasional controversy over when (e.g., transportation availability[19]) or how much of (e.g., time permitted to take a test[20]) the service is to be provided.

Requested accommodations regarding assessments, assignments, and class and degree requirements on occasion are contested. In such instances, professors argue that the requested accommodations will compromise the integrity, if not validity, of the assignment (e.g., class test) or establish an unfair playing field advantaging the disabled. Some professors find it controversial even when asked to provide extra time, and become progressively agitated when requests are made to use open books or notes, supplement multiple choice answers, have take-home tests (rather than in-class), or avoid testing (or even assessment) altogether. Courts, however, will not direct professors or programs to alter their test, course, or degree requirements in ways that would in large part eviscerate academic integrity, assuming such assessments or activities are shown to be essential to the given program or activity.

It should be noted that although colleges are required to make their programs accessible, they are not required to pay for personal attendants, health care providers, general aids, personal devices (e.g., wheelchairs), individually prescribed devices (e.g., prescription eyeglasses or hearing aids), readers for personal use or study, and private tutors, even if the student cannot attend college without such services.[21]

## Waiver of Degree and Program Requirements

Of all requested accommodations or modifications, arguably the most controversial is to waive a requirement outright or to substitute something that clearly does not reflect the same or even similar competency. Some requests are made soon after admission as incoming students learn of mandatory courses they may have difficulty completing (e.g., math, foreign language).[22] Other times, students ask for specific assignment or grade waivers once they have failed the course one or more times.

In an illustrative Sixth Circuit Court of Appeals case, an education major had to earn a grade of "C" or better in math to graduate. After four attempts, she was diagnosed with a math learning disability. She received accommodations but still failed to earn a "C" in two additional efforts. She filed suit, claiming that the University should accept her "D" grade or waive the course outright, given the nature of her disability. Officials had provided a private testing room, a proctor to read exams, extended time, the use of a personal tutor, the use of manipulatives and other physical equipment during exams, the opportunity to repeat a course, and permission to begin student teaching despite her failure to complete the entire curriculum (i.e., the contested math course). The district court had reasoned that educational institutions are not required to lower standards to accommodate the disabled and ruled in favor of the defendant. Plaintiff appealed, arguing that the math course was not a state requirement and therefore should not be required by the University. The circuit court disagreed and affirmed the lower court's ruling, observing that deference should be given to educators when evaluating curricula.[23]

To avoid related litigation, program faculty need to examine their admission and program requirements and make a reasoned and thoughtful determination as to whether each criterion is essential. Substitutions should be allowed for current requirements that are only tangentially related to the program's mission but result in disparate impact on the disabled. However, requirements that are viewed as essential for all applicants and students should be maintained.

## Unreasonable Accommodations and Expectations

As indicated above, at times requested accommodations were found unreasonable, some even unrelated to the disability.[24] On other occasions, previously agreed-to accommodations were altered when officials, over time, developed a better understanding of the student's needs and program requirements.[25] One court even observed that a plaintiff who wanted to use her personal notes while taking a test (in addition to numerous other accommodations that had been provided) had a misunderstanding of disability laws and that they did not create absolute rights to any and all accommodations demanded by the individual with a disability.[26]

In a Ninth Circuit case, a wheelchair-confined student alleged that her college failed to reasonably accommodate her disabilities. On campus, the college had installed ramps at her dormitory, changed inside doors, remodeled the bathrooms, and re-configured the biology lab. When plaintiff enrolled in a field-based program designed to "explore" Australia, officials provided her with private taxis, air line flights (when others used buses and trains), and the use of an accessible van. Two students were hired to serve as her "helpers." Staff purchased a sleeping cot manufactured to her specifications, a small narrow wheelchair for her improved maneuverability, and a special shower head for her use. They also provided more accessible housing when available and scheduled activities and selected sites for the group that ordinarily were not selected but were more accessible to the plaintiff. The court noted that compliance with Title III is determined by viewing a program in its entirety and that the occasional failure to accommodate will not necessarily result in a violation. In the present case, the court found that it was not legal error for the jury to hold that plaintiff had been provided with reasonable accommodation.[27]

## No Reasonable Accommodation Exists.

There will be times when there will be no reasonable accommodation, given the nature of the disability and the type of task to be performed.[28] For example, two applicants to medical programs were denied—one could not independently assess clients as was required by the American Medical Association (i.e., she was blind)[29] and the other had C-5 quadriplegia and would have been unable to complete clinical requirements.[30] Similarly, two deaf applicants were denied admission to their programs of choice—one to a nursing program given that she could not comprehensively receive oral instructions as would be necessary throughout training, particularly in emergency and operating rooms,[31] and the second to a truck-driving school where he had requested the assignment of a sign-language interpreter to ride in the cab to interpret instructions.[32] Accordingly, neither unreasonable accommodations (e.g., those that would place others unnecessarily at risk), nor those that may be theoretically possible but financially or administratively impractical so as to result in hardship, need be provided.

## Duty to Investigate

Prior to making a decision that there is no reasonable accommodation that will enable a prospective student to participate in the college's program or limiting accommodation choices to those routinely provided, many courts have held that officials have an implied duty to investigate possible options.[33] If there were no such duty, colleges would be required to provide only those accommodations that are specifically identified by students that were found reasonable and supported by documentation. Although this approach would certainly help limit expenditures, it likely would restrict meaningful access to programs and activities by qualified students. Many college students know a great deal about their respective disabilities, but a comparative few are knowledgeable about college operations, adaptive technologies, methods of making materials available, and alternative teaching methodologies. As a result, in an effort to demonstrate good faith compliance, it is recommended that officials explore realistic options. Courts do not assume that college staff will have cutting-edge knowledge or know all that is capable of being known. Instead, a more realistic expectation is that staff have "knowledge of that which is generally known to informed professionals."[34]

## Access

Public colleges are required to make services, programs, and activities readily accessible to and usable by the disabled,[35] while private colleges must make changes to existing structures that are readily achievable (i.e., easily accomplished; able to be performed without much difficulty or expense).[36] Renovations and new construction on both public and private campuses must comply with standards identified within the ADA. Nevertheless, disability law does not require that every building or every part of every building be accessible at this time. Rather, the critical issue is whether the service, program, or activity housed within the structure can be accessed. The institution need not incur undue hardship in the process or deface historic structures.

## Dismissal or Removal

Generally, dismissal or removal of a student with a disability from a program or campus should follow the same procedures as are used for other students, whether the dismissal is academic or behavioral.

### Academic Dismissal

Students with disabilities, like all other students, may be dismissed when they fail to meet academic requirements. To prevail in this type of situation, the plaintiff would have to show that (1) the standards had not been applied uniformly (e.g., that other students with lower performance were retained); (2) different, more difficult standards were used when assessing plaintiff's performance; (3) grades were based at least in part on disability; or (4) there had been a miscalculation of the grade (i.e., simple error). Although there are examples of professor misconduct, discrimination, and error, the vast majority of claims challenging grades or academic dismissal have proven unsuccessful.

In a Sixth Circuit case, a student with a diagnosed learning disability had to complete Latin 111, 112, and 113 prior to graduation. Plaintiff alleged that his Latin 112 professor refused to acknowledge his disability, changed the syllabus to cover more material, and gave a longer final exam than previously administered. He received a D- and subsequently failed Latin 113. He sued, demanding an "A" for each of the three classes, $100,000 from each defendant, plus reimbursement for all expenses incurred due to not graduating. The court concluded that the monetary claims against the University were barred by the Eleventh Amendment and that the individual defendants were not subject to action under the ADA. The Section 504 claim also was dismissed, as it does not permit suits against individual defendants, and no claim had been properly made supporting an institutional violation. Moreover, plaintiff was not found to have been discriminated against due to disability, given that the expanded course requirements affected all students.[37]

## Behavioral Dismissal

Neither the ADA nor Section 504 stipulates that additional or different criteria must be used in determining an appropriate penalty for students with disabilities who violate codes of conduct.[38] When students exhibit inappropriate behavior that endangers others (or themselves) or disrupts the educational environment, they may be penalized by restrictions on activities or by removal from the campus, even if the behavior is shown to be a manifestation of the disability. Accordingly, it is irrelevant that a student who uses pervasively vulgar and sexually explicit language in the classroom does so due to having Tourettes or that a student who is bipolar attacks his professor allegedly due to having removed himself from medication. These students would remain responsible for their conduct and may receive an appropriate penalty. Nonetheless, officials *may* elect to consider the "disability relatedness" of the behavior at the penalty or "sentencing" stage of the hearing. At this time, and given the nature and extent of the disability, the administrator may consider whether the student represents a continuing risk to the campus community and whether the behavior is likely to be repeated.

## Postgraduation Testing Accommodations

Prior to engaging in professional practice, several types of employment require the passage of a national or state examination (e.g., attorneys, physicians). Given the range in the quality of college programs, such tests help assure that those who enter the various professions possess at least basic knowledge. Many of these tests are timed and invariably measure reading speed and comprehension in addition to content knowledge. When reading skills are not the skills being measured, given the purpose of the test and projected future practice of those in the profession, test administrators can be required to provide additional time, readers, scribes, and other accommodations depending on the nature of the disability.

As with college admissions, test applicants must document their own respective disabilities prior to receiving accommodations. Once the documentation has been received, test personnel need to determine whether (1) the applicant qualifies as disabled and (2) the requested accommodation is reasonable, given the nature of the disability. Many plaintiffs will fail to meet the first portion of this review, as they will not be considered substantially limited in a major life activity.[39] Indeed, the average person in the population is not capable of successfully completing medical or law school, even with accommodation. Accordingly, it is difficult to argue, if not even disingenuous, that one who has earned an advanced college degree or passed a national standardized exam, with a lower-than-preferred score,[40] is "substantially limited" in learning when compared to "average." Nonetheless, those who do prevail tend to do so by showing that, although they succeeded previously, they did so with the assistance of accommodations and by showing that they were substantially limited in a life activity that affects test performance.

In a Sixth Circuit case, a medical school student was required to take the Step 1 exam to proceed to the third year of medical school. He presented documentation of a learning disability and requested extended test-taking time. University officials refused, reasoning that his impairment was not substantially limiting of a major life activity. He failed the test twice. The district court had denied injunctive relief and concluded that plaintiff was not disabled. He had performed well or at least average on other tests in his academic life and received a 4.3/5.0 GPA in high school, without accommodations. On appeal, the Sixth Circuit affirmed the lower court's ruling.[41]

Even where a test is taken with accommodations, the controversy may not end as testing agencies often place an asterisk on, or otherwise "flag," a test score to indicate that it was derived under nonstandard conditions. In a claim before the Third Circuit, a medical student with multiple sclerosis had received extra time to take an exam, with the score flagged indicating that accommodations were provided, purportedly to insure that those who received the scores would have complete information. Plaintiff contended that this process violated Title III but failed to show that accommodated and nonaccommodated scores were comparable. In contrast, defendant's psychometricians had concluded that with extra time such scores may not be comparable. (Accommodations such as large print were not flagged as test results were considered substantially the same.) The court concluded that plaintiff failed to demonstrate a reasonable likelihood of success and vacated the preliminary injunction ordered by the district court.[42]

## Employees & Employers[43]

Employers that receive federal financial assistance are regulated by Section 504,[44] while those with fifteen or more employees who work twenty or more calendar weeks in the current or preceding year must comply with Title I.[45] The first of these criteria (i.e., recipient status) is fairly easily determined—either the employer receives direct (e.g., research or training grant) or indirect (e.g., student loans) federal financial assistance from the Department of Education (DOE) or not. Qualifying aid does not include procurement contracts, however, as the DOE does not consider such contracts to be "assistance."[46]

The ADA standard is somewhat more problematic, as courts have historically disagreed regarding who counts as an employee (e.g., those on leave, persons working only part-time, those hired as substitutes but not called). The United States Supreme Court addressed this issue in *Walters v. Metropolitan Educational Enterprises*[47] in which it adopted the "payroll method." All that is necessary under this approach is to identify when the employee began employment during the year and when he or she left (if at all). The person is counted as an employee for each working day after being hired and before leaving. Although this case did not involve the ADA, the payroll method has been accepted by lower courts when interpreting this and other federal employment laws.[48]

Title I does not regulate the United States government, corporations owned by the United States, Indian Tribes, or private membership clubs that are exempt from taxation under 26 U.S.C. Section 501(c) but, unlike Title III, does regulate religious institutions. Such institutions may not discriminate based on disability in making employment decisions, although they may discriminate due to religion.[49]

Of particular note is *Board of Trustees of the University of Alabama v. Garrett,*[50] in which the Supreme Court held that Eleventh Amendment Immunity may be claimed as a defense in Title I suits filed in federal court against public employers for monetary awards. In this case, the Court rejected a claim by a former employee of the University of Alabama Medical School, holding that the state university was protected from liability for monetary damages in suits brought under the ADA. However, although the range of relief under the Title I of the ADA is restricted by this decision, plaintiffs may still sue in federal court, but only for relief that is nonmonetary (e.g., an injunction), or a plaintiff may file in state court under state disability law provisions.

## Qualifying as "Disabled" and "Qualified"

As with student issues, to qualify as "disabled" an applicant or employee in an employment context must have a physical or mental impairment that substantially limits one or more major life activities,[51] have a record of impairment[52] (e.g., periodically hospitalized due to tuberculosis[53]), or be regarded as having an impairment.[54] An applicant or employee may support a claim that he or she was "regarded as having a disability" by showing that (1) a covered employer mistakenly believed (perhaps through rumor or unfounded stereotypes) that the applicant's or employee's impairment substantially limited a major life activity (e.g., controlled high blood pressure); (2) he or she has an impairment that is substantially limiting only because of the attitudes of others toward it (e.g., individual has a prominent facial scar or disfigurement); or (3) the applicant or employee has no impairment but is treated as though he or she does (e.g., terminating an employee who is rumored to have AIDS, but the allegation is unfounded and the person has no impairment of any kind).[55] Moreover, the ADA prohibits discrimination against persons who have a family, business, social, or other relationship with a person with a disability.[56] For example, terminating the employment of a parent of a child with a disability for fear of an increase in insurance rates, the loss of insurance, or the loss of production due to the extensive use of leave would violate federal law.

Furthermore, many alleged impairments or characteristics are specifically excluded from coverage unless exceptional circumstances exist: physical characteristics such as eye or hair color, left-handedness, height, weight, muscle tone, pregnancy, predisposition to illness or disease, or age; personality traits such as poor judgment or quick temper; and environmental, cultural, or economic disadvantages such as poverty, lack of education, or prison record.[57] The term disability does not include transvestism, transsexualism, homosexuality, bisexuality, pedophilia, exhibitionism, voyeurism, gender identity disorders not resulting from physical impairments, other sexual behavior disorders, compulsive gambling, kleptomania, pyromania, or psychoactive substance-abuse disorders resulting from current illegal use of drugs.[58] Additionally, employers need not show tolerance for work-related problems that are a consequence of current drug or alcohol use, and are not restricted in terminating the employment of an individual who is in possession of illegal drugs, even if they are engaged in or have completed related rehabilitation programs.[59]

Performance is substantially limited (i.e., the limitation is considerable or is limiting to a large degree[60]) when a person is unable to perform or is significantly restricted in performing a major life activity that can be accomplished by the average person in the general population.[61] The nature, severity, duration (or expected duration), and long-term impact of the impairment are considered when determining whether a limitation is substantially limiting.[62] Such a decision-making process requires a case-by-case analysis, often corroborated by expert testimony, as what may be substantially limiting for one person (e.g., tendonitis, asthma, depression, allergy) may not be for another.

Not only will some impairments not limit major life activities (e.g., a hearing impaired employee who has "average" hearing due to the use of a hearing aid), those that do often restrict the ability to perform only one job rather than a class or broad range of jobs and therefore do not qualify as a disability in regard to "working" when compared to the average person with comparable training, skills, and abilities.[63] The courts will examine the geographic area to which the plaintiff has reasonable access, the nature of the job from which the individual was disqualified, and comparable employment options within the region.[64] Moreover, courts will consider any mitigating or corrective measures the individual may have taken in addressing the disability and in determining whether it has been substantially limiting (e.g., use of state-of-the-art prosthetics; wearing eye glasses).

Qualifying as "disabled" represents only a portion of the burden, as the plaintiff also must show that he or she is "qualified" in spite of the disability. The applicant or employee must satisfy all requisite skill, experience, education, and other job-related requirements and be able to satisfactorily perform all essential job functions, although reasonable accommodations may be necessary.[65]

## The Hiring Process

The hiring process will vary depending on the type of organization and position to be filled, provisions within an applicable collective bargaining agreement, and additional practices identified in other publications. In recruiting and hiring for virtually any position, it is prudent to follow the procedures below in an effort to comply with federal disability law and avoid litigation. This process requires the employer to engage in specific activities at each of five stages of hiring: (1) preemployment, (2) preoffer interview and initial screening, (3) conditional job offer, (4) postoffer interview and examinations, and (5) confirmed job offer.

### Preemployment

The preemployment stage may be the most important of the five in that it provides a foundation for the hiring process and generates data and information used later. This stage includes the identification of essential functions, the preparation of job descriptions, advertising, and recruiting.

Employers should identify the requirements for the position as well as essential and nonessential functions. "Essential functions" are those that are fundamental to the position (i.e., the purpose for which the position was created; those functions the person was hired to perform).[66] The person holding the position must be able to perform all essential functions, either unaided or with reasonable accommodation. In determining whether a function is essential, consideration is given to the employer's perspective (ideally identified in a written job description prepared prior to advertising) as to which functions must be performed by the individual hired, whether other employees are available to perform the particular job function, and whether any of the identified responsibilities is so highly specialized that the person was hired due to his or her ability to perform that particular task. Moreover, the courts will consider the time spent performing the function, consequences of not requiring the function to be performed, terms of the collective bargaining agreement, and the work experience of past incumbents in the same or similar jobs.[67]

Once essential functions have been identified, they should be used in the preparation of job descriptions and advertisements as well as for the basis of structuring interview questions. Job descriptions should be specific regarding qualifications and expectations. The employer must be able to show the business necessity of each selected criterion, particularly if shown to disproportionately screen out applicants with disabilities.[68] For example, if punctuality and regular attendance can be shown to be essential (e.g., an elementary school teacher), it is irrelevant that an applicant has a sleeping, anxiety, or emotional disorder that causes him or her to be routinely late or absent from work. Although the employee's absence may, in fact, be a result of the disorder, such a person is simply not qualified for the position.[69]

The selection of advertising options (e.g., choice of publications to post an opening) and recruiting/hiring procedures are, in large part, dependent on the position being filled and the available budget. At the college or university level, the search process for a custodian, clerk, or secretary will be significantly different than that for a professor, provost, or president. Decisions can be made by single administrators or large search committees. Where committees are used, they typically range in size from three to seven, with efforts made to ensure diversity and representation of stakeholders. One of the first tasks of the committee is to prepare a job description (assuming one does not already exist) that ultimately will be approved by affirmative action and the institution's administration. The committee should be specific as to job expectations, essential functions, and minimum and preferred requirements for initial employment (e.g., required to have a master's degree; prefer to have a Ph.D. degree). Once this is accomplished, the committee needs to agree on the procedures to be followed (e.g., questions to ask candidates; type of interview; number of finalists; criteria to be used in screening out applicants) and then begin the recruitment process.

In addition to paper credentials, employers may require prospective employees to submit to nonmedical examinations or tests (e.g., computer skills test). Physical agility and ability tests that are consistent with business necessity are not considered medical examinations and may be given at any point in the application or employment process if required of all applicants. Only those applicants who meet the employer's legitimate physical criteria for the job will be qualified to receive confirmed offers of employment and to begin work.

## Preoffer Interview and Initial Screening

Once all files have been received, many applicants may be rejected for failure to possess minimum qualifications (e.g., four years of department chair or dean-level experience). No candidate should be considered for employment who does not meet minimum requirements. Eliminating the "unqualified" will reduce the pool, although further reductions will typically be needed prior to interviewing. At this time, search committees often either subjectively rank order remaining candidates or limit the field through the use of quantitative evaluation forms that correspond to the selection criteria. Other times, committee members simply discuss the qualifications of candidates to see if a consensus exists regarding the identification of those who are to become finalists for the position. Obviously, there is not one best way to choose among persons who may appear substantially similar on paper. But, as long as the procedures are fair and do not discriminate in impermissible ways, they will be upheld if challenged in court.

Once finalists have been identified, it is common to conduct personal interviews either by telephone, face-to-face, or both. Until this time, and unless the applicant is personally or professionally known, it is unlikely that committee members will be aware of an applicant's disability status. Even then, phone interviews still will not reveal vision, mobility, dexterity, or other impairments that may have become visually apparent had the interview been conducted face-to-face. Even if a person's disability is self identified or apparent, employers may not generally make inquiries (to the applicant or to persons who know the applicant) about the existence, nature, or extent of the disability; the ability to perform major life activities; workers' compensation history; or current use of legal drugs. However, if an applicant requests an accommodation for the interview process, and the need is not obvious, the employer may require limited documentation to support the existence of a disability.

Notwithstanding the above, the employer may ask questions regarding the applicant's ability to perform job functions and inquire as to how the applicant would perform certain tasks.[70] Also, nonmedical questions regarding qualifications and skills (e.g., work history, licensure) are permitted at this time.

During the screening-out process, an employer may not use selection criteria that disqualify individuals with disabilities unless shown to be job-related and consistent with business necessity. Any tests that are used must accurately reflect the skills, aptitude, or other factors the tests purport to measure, rather than the employee's impaired sensory, manual, or speaking skills, unless those are the skills being measured (e.g., testing the manual skills of an applicant to work as a sign-language interpreter for Student Disability Services would be permitted).[71]

## Conditional Job Offer

Once all data have been aggregated, the committee is responsible for making a selection. When this task has been accomplished, a conditional job offer may be tendered, assuming at least one applicant is sufficiently well qualified. In the selection of the "best" qualified candidate, it is important to note that federal law requires nondiscrimination; it does not require employers to hire unqualified applicants, those who are less qualified, or even those who are equally qualified. Persons not capable of performing each of the "essential functions" and those who do not possess minimum qualifications may be screened out at any time during the process, even if they represent a population that is underrepresented or the target of affirmative action.

In many colleges and universities, faculty and staff serve on a plethora of committees, including hiring committees but seldom are responsible for making final decisions. Often such committees are advisory only with the actual decision being made by someone higher in the hierarchy. Regardless, authorized persons within the organization should make a selection and communicate that decision to the committee and to the successful applicant. At this time, a conditional job offer may be extended, pending the outcome of postoffer interviews and examinations. The conditional job offer may be waived, and a final job offer may be proffered, if the employer so chooses. If not, the applicant proceeds to the next stage.

### Postoffer Interview and Examinations

If necessary, a postoffer interview may be held, and the applicant at that time may be required to submit to medical and other examinations prior to a final job offer and the signing of a contract but only if all employees are required to submit to such additional requirements.[72] Specific disability-related questions (i.e., questions that are likely to elicit information about a disability) may now be asked.[73] However, if a conditional offer is rescinded because interview and/or medical test results indicate that an applicant fails to meet mandatory job requirements, one of two things must be proven: (1) the criteria do not screen out or tend to screen out persons with disabilities or (2) the exclusionary criteria are, in fact, job related and consistent with business necessity. If exclusionary criteria are used, the employer has the additional responsibility of showing that there is no reasonable accommodation that will enable the applicant to perform essential functions.[74] Employers may also at this time inquire as to the applicant's workers' compensation history, previous sick leave use, and general physical and mental health.

### Confirmed Job Offer

Once the applicant who received a conditional job offer has completed required interviews and medical examinations, a final job offer should be extended unless it was discovered through the additional screening procedures that the applicant is not qualified. The offer may not be withdrawn simply because it is discovered that the applicant has a physical or mental impairment that substantially limits a major life activity or will need reasonable accommodations to perform essential job functions.

### Reasonable Accommodation

Where qualified employees have properly documented their respective disabilities, it may be necessary for employers to provide reasonable accommodations.[75] In an employment context, "reasonable accommodation" refers to modifications or adjustments to a job that are necessary to enable an employee to perform essential functions of the position or to enjoy benefits and privileges of employment equal to those enjoyed by persons without disabilities.[76] Dependent on the aggregate of circumstances, reasonable accommodation may at times include practices such as making facilities accessible and usable; restructuring jobs and work schedules; reassigning existing employees with disabilities to vacant positions;[77] acquiring or modifying equipment; making adjustments or modifications to examinations, training materials, and policies; or providing readers or interpreters.[78] The redistribution of marginal (nonessential) functions among several jobs so that the qualified individual with a disability can fill a position also may qualify as a reasonable accommodation.[79] However, an employer is not required to reallocate essential functions or to provide an accommodation that is not causally related to the employee's affected major life activity.[80]

To determine whether an accommodation is both appropriate and reasonable, it is necessary for the employer and employee who has a disability to engage in an informal interactive process to discuss how the employee will perform essential functions.[81] Idiosyncratic preferences of the employee should be considered, although the employer ultimately may select among effective alternatives (e.g., an employer may select a less-expensive, effective accommodation or one that is more easily provided than the one preferred by the employee). However, the individual with a disability is not required to accept the accommodation, aid, service, opportunity, or benefit offered by the employer. Nevertheless, failure to do so may have repercussions if, as a result of that rejection, the employee cannot perform the essential functions of the position.[82] In such an instance, the individual will not be considered qualified and may be removed.

Details about an employee's disability should be shared only on a need-to-know basis. For example, supervisors and managers may be informed about restrictions on work duties and the need for accommodations but generally do not need information about the disability *per se*. In contrast, persons responsible for first aid and safety, under certain conditions, may need to know about the specifics of the disability, required medications, and necessary emergency care.[83]

## Undue Hardship

Given the nature and extent of some disabilities, there are situations when no type of accommodation will enable an applicant to fulfill the requirements of the job (e.g., a blind person wanting to be a bus driver). Other times, the accommodations are "possible" but are financially or organizationally impractical and, if required, would result in hardship on the employer.[84] Whether undue hardship results from a specific accommodation is determined by the courts after a review of the size of the program and its budget; the number of employees; the type of facilities and operation; the type and cost of accommodation; the impact of the accommodation on facility operations, including the affect on other employees to perform their duties; and the impact on the employer's ability to conduct business.[85] Because there is no fixed formula for related calculations, courts have ranged markedly in identifying what is "undue."

## Terms and Conditions of Employment

Federal laws prohibit all forms of employment discrimination against the disabled unless such discrimination is supported by a bona fide occupational qualification (e.g., must have vision to be a surgeon) or, although facially neutral, meets business necessity (e.g., use of a typing skills test to be employed as a typist).

## Compensation and Benefits

Employers may not compensate a person with a disability less than persons without disabilities, unless such differentiation is due to factors such as quantity or quality of work performed, seniority, education, job responsibilities, and the like (e.g., an assembly line worker with manual dexterity limitations may be paid according to output, assuming others are paid in like manner, and as a result receive less than nondisabled peers). Similarly, "leave" opportunities need to be available on a nondiscriminatory basis. However, by the nature of some disabilities, selected employees will require time off from work for physician appointments, therapy, rehabilitation, or rest. As a result, an employee may exhaust all permitted leave. Federal law does not necessarily require an employer to provide employees with disabilities paid or unpaid leave beyond that provided to others, although it may qualify as an accommodation. In some instances, hardship would result if the employer were required to accommodate excessive absences and the employee would be found unqualified for the position.[86]

## Transfer and Reassignment

Transfer or reassignment may be required as a form of reasonable accommodation for existing personnel but not for applicants. An applicant must be qualified for and be able, possibly through the use of accommodations, to perform the essential functions of the position. For existing employees, there will be occasions when transfer or reassignment to an open position may be necessary if they are to continue in employment. A person may have been qualified for his or her current position, notwithstanding limitations imposed by a disability but have experienced a decline in mobility, manual dexterity, vision, or the like to the degree that the essential functions can no longer be performed even with accommodation. In essence, the person is no longer qualified for the current position. That does not necessarily indicate, however, that the employment relationship has ended.

If an appropriate position is vacant, the employee with a disability typically should be reassigned.[87] But, there are limitations to such reassignments as federal law does not require employers to remove an existing employee to create an opening, establish a new position, reassign essential functions,[88] promote the employee to an open superordinate position, or violate collective bargaining agreements regarding "bumping" rights.[89]

### Adverse Employment Decisions

Persons with disabilities both succeed and fail in the workplace, as do persons without disabilities. At times they have been downsized, nonrenewed, suspended, transferred, demoted, not tenured, not promoted, or terminated. In some cases, such adverse decisions were due to violation of policy and directives, poor performance, nonperformance, inappropriate actions while on the job, inadequate skills, or criminal wrongdoing.[90] Other times, the employee's disability was the basis for either an adverse decision or the creation of an environment that was so hostile that the employee was forced to resign (i.e., the employee was constructively discharged).

Where a claim is filed, the challenged action (e.g., demotion, termination) by the employer will be justified if there is a legitimate nondiscriminatory reason (e.g., theft, insubordination, neglect of duty, insubordination, immorality).[91] To prevail, the plaintiff must show that the proffered reason given for the decision was untrue and that the true reason was a form of illegal discrimination (e.g., disability).[92] These represent difficult burdens, with most plaintiffs unable to rise to the occasion, even where actual discrimination is present.

## Recommendations for College and University Practitioners

The following recommendations are provided for college and university administrators when working with students and employees.

## Students

- Establish clear guidelines on how students are to document disability status, including types of supportive data, time lines, and procedures;
- Review documents promptly, and communicate with students regarding eligibility status;
- If qualified as disabled, meet with the student to determine preferences, and then determine effective appropriate accommodations and modifications that are to be provided (i.e., do not provide accommodations that do not address the limitations posed by the disability, even if requested by the student);
- Know that which is generally known to informed professionals regarding disabilities, adaptive technologies, and alternative teaching methodologies;
- Meet with the student periodically to determine if any needs have changed; and
- Review all policies, and seek amendment of those that may result in discrimination against the disabled that are not concomitantly required to address essential aspects of the program or activity.

## Employees

- Identify essential job functions, prepare a job description, advertise, and recruit;
- Narrow the field of applicants; interview the top choices; ask questions based on essential functions; and inquire about the ability to perform the job, rather than the nature of a possible disability;
- Present the best qualified applicant with a job offer;
- Conduct a second interview and medical examination, but only if required of all candidates;
- Make a final job offer unless the interview or exam provides information that would indicate that the applicant is not qualified for the position;
- If the selected individual alleges a disability, review the documentation carefully and timely, requesting additional information if necessary;
- If the employee qualifies as disabled (i.e., the impairment is substantially limiting of a major life activity), meet with the employee to determine preferred accommodations;
- Select effective reasonable accommodations and modifications that will enable the employee to meet essential functions that do not result in undue hardship;
- Periodically review the accommodations with the employee;
- Eliminate disability harassment within the organization, using affirmative education programs and grievance procedures similar to

those used for sexual and racial harassment; and

- Ensure that adverse employment decisions are based on performance or conduct and not on an employee's disability.

## Endnotes

1   Estate of Mauro v. Borgess Med. Ctr., 137 F.3d 398 (6th Cir. 1998).
2   Trznadel v. Thomas M. Cooley Law Sch., No. 5:02-cv-76, 2003 U.S. Dist. LEXIS 9660 (W.D. Mich. May 16, 2003).
3   Motzkin v. Trs. of Boston Univ., 938 F. Supp. 983 (D. Mass. 1996).
4   29 U.S.C. § 794(a) (2005).
5   Title III exempts private religious programs from compliance—28 C.F.R. § 36.102(e) (2005). *See also* White v. Denver Seminary, 157 F. Supp. 2d 1171 (D. Colo. 2001) (holding that a Seminary was pervasively sectarian and thus exempt from Title III).
6   28 C.F.R. § 35.134 (2005); 29 C.F.R. § 1630.12 (2005).
7   *Compare* Bayon v. S.U.N.Y., Buffalo, No. 98-CV-0578E(Sr), 2004 U.S. Dist. LEXIS 5036 (W.D.N.Y. Feb. 6, 2004) (denying summary judgment on the retaliation claims, as plaintiff established a genuine issue of fact as to possible retaliatory conduct); Larson v. Snow Coll., 189 F. Supp. 2d 1286 (D. Utah 2000) (denying a motion to dismiss a retaliation claim) *with* Johnson v. Okla., Nos. 99-6322, 99-6427, 2000 U.S. App. LEXIS 19033 (10th Cir. Aug. 7, 2000) (finding that the plaintiff who was denied an emergency clinical rotation, assigned an "F" for a course, and charged with cheating received low grades due to excessive absences and poor academic performance and not as retaliation for having filed a suit).
8   Carten v. Kent State Univ., 78 Fed. Appx. 499 (6th Cir. 2003); Emerson v. Thiel Coll., 296 F.3d 184 (3d Cir. 2002); Trznadel v. Thomas M. Cooley Law Sch., No. 5:02-cv-76, 2003 U.S. Dist. LEXIS 9660 (W.D. Mich. May 16, 2003).
9   Redden v. Minneapolis Cmty. and Technical Coll., No. A03-1202, 2004 Minn. App. LEXIS 381 (Minn. Ct. App. April 20, 2004); Hash v. Univ. of Ky., 138 S.W.3d 123 (Ky. Ct. App. 2004).
10  Abdo v. Univ. of Vt., 263 F. Supp. 2d 772 (D. Vt. 2003).
11  *See,e.g.,* Branham v. Snow, 392 F.3d 896 (7th Cir. 2004) (finding that although not every plaintiff with diabetes will be disabled, in the present case a trier of fact could determine that the plaintiff's diabetes and treatment regimen are substantially limiting of the major life activity of eating, given the negative side effects of the mitigating measures); Spychalsky v. Sullivan, No. CV 01-0958 (DRH) (ETB), 2003 U.S. Dist. LEXIS 15704 (E.D.N.Y. Aug. 29, 2003), *aff'd,* 96 Fed. Appx. 790 (2d Cir. 2004) (finding that although plaintiff was severely limited in spelling, his overall functioning was "high average" to "superior" and did not qualify as a disability); Swanson v. Univ. of Cincinnati, 268 F. 3d 307 (6th Cir. 2001) (finding that a depressed student failed to qualify as disabled as he was not substantially limited in regard to sleeping or communicating); Allison v. Howard Univ., 209 F. Supp. 2d 55 (D.D.C. 2002) (noting that even if a dismissed student could have supported his "temporary disability"—i.e., temporary emotional distress—which the court doubted, the University had not denied his readmission due to his disability).
12  Davis v. Univ. of N.C., 263 F.3d 95 (4th Cir. 2001) (determining that a teacher education student with multiple personality disorder failed to support the position that she was substantially limited in a major life activity or that she was regarded as being disabled).
13  New York State Bd. of Law Examiners v. Bartlett, 226 F.3d 69 (2d Cir. 2000).
14  Swanson v. Univ. of Cincinnati, 268 F. 3d 307 (6th Cir. 2001) (concluding that medication had improved plaintiff's depression, sleep, and communication skills over time

and that although he was impaired, he was not disabled in comparison to the average person); Wong v. Regents of the Univ. of Cal., 379 F.3d 1097 (9th Cir. 2004) (determining that a dismissed, learning-disabled student was not substantially limited in a major life activity; his ability to complete two years of a medical program mitigated against a ruling on his behalf).

[15] *See, e.g.*, Marlon v. W. New England Coll., No. 01-12199-DPW, 2003 U.S. Dist. LEXIS 22095 (D. Mass. Dec. 9, 2003) (granting summary judgment where a dismissed student with a range of impairments failed to provide documentation showing they were substantially limiting; moreover, providing an accommodation was not evidence that the defendant regarded plaintiff as having a disability); Betts II v. Rector and Visitors of the Univ. of Va., 198 F. Supp. 2d 787 (W.D. Va. 2002) (noting that defendants did not dismiss plaintiff when they learned that he had an impairment or when they mistakenly thought that it qualified as a disability and provided accommodations).

[16] Seldom do college officials facially discriminate against the disabled in making admissions decisions (e.g., denying the admission of a student with quadriplegia because the campus is not wheelchair accessible).

[17] Corey v. W. Conn. State Univ., No. 3:03CV0763, 2004 U.S. Dist. LEXIS 3982 (D. Conn. March 10, 2004).

[18] 28 C.F.R. § 36.309(c)(2) (2005). Possible modifications include changes in length of time permitted for the completion of a course, substitution of specific requirements, or adaptation of the manner in which a course is conducted or materials distributed.

[19] United States v. Bd. of Trs. for the Univ. of Ala., 908 F.2d 740 (11th Cir. 1990).

[20] Robinson v. Univ. of Akron Sch. of Law, 307 F.3d 409 (6th Cir. 2002); Hunt v. Meharry Med. Coll., No. 98 Civ. 7193 (MBM), 2000 U.S. Dist. LEXIS 7804 (S.D.N.Y. June 8, 2000).

[21] 28 C.F.R. § 35.135 (Title II) (2005); 28 C.F.R. § 36.306 (Title III) (2005).

[22] *Compare* Guckenberger v. Boston Univ., 8 F. Supp. 2d 82 (D. Mass 1998) (concluding that a waiver or substitution was not required) *with* Guckenberger v. Boston Univ., 974 F. Supp. 106 (D. Mass. 1997) (requiring a waiver or substitution).

[23] Pangburn v. N. Ky. Univ., No. 99-5474, 2000 U.S. App. LEXIS 6413 (6th Cir. 2000), *cert. denied*, 531 U.S. 875 (2000). *See also* Dicks v. Thomas More Coll., 73 Fed. Appx. 149 (6th Cir. 2003) (determining that the College was not required to waive an algebra course for a student; college officials had provided plaintiff with numerous reasonable accommodations).

[24] Stern v. Univ. of Osteopathic Med. and Health Scis., 220 F.3d 906 (8th Cir. 2000), *rehearing denied*, No. 99-3312SIDM, 2000 U.S. App. LEXIS 23699 (8th Cir. Sept. 21, 2000) (finding that the requested accommodation of a student to supplement his multiple choice answers on exams with either an essay or with responses to oral questions were unrelated to his disability, dyslexia).

[25] Hamilton v. City Coll. of City Univ. of N.Y., 173 F. Supp. 2d 181 (S.D.N.Y. 2001) (granting summary judgment to the defendant where the plaintiff claimed that to change his agreement from "calculator when needed" to "calculator when appropriate" was a violation of due process and disability law).

[26] Hoffman v. Contra Costa Coll., 21 Fed. Appx. 748 (9th Cir. 2001). *But see* Kenny v. Loyola Univ. of Chi., No. 02 C 1006, 2003 U.S. Dist. LEXIS 2597 (N.D. Ill. Feb. 20, 2003) (denying summary judgment where plaintiff was requesting a laptop computer with voice recognition software; visual fire alarm; TTD text phone; area for rescue assistance; power assisted door; wheelchair accessible bathroom with tilted mirror, widened toilet stall with grab bars, a soap holder, a 63-inch hose, ADA compliant shower head, lever-style faucets, and a tub with a seat and grab bars; cafeteria alterations; and expedited cafeteria checkout).

[27] Bird v. Lewis & Clark Coll., 303 F. 3d 1015 (9th Cir. 2002), *cert. denied*, 538 U.S. 923 (2003). *See also*, Maczaczyj v. New York, 956 F. Supp. 403 (W.D.N.Y. 1997) (concluding that a College was not required to provide a student who has panic at-

tacks, anxiety, and social phobia with an entire master's degree program in a distance learning format so that he would not be required to physically attend college).

[28] Falcone v. Univ. of Minn., No. 01-1181, 2003 U.S. Dist. LEXIS 15787 (D. Minn., Sept. 3, 2003) (concluding that a dismissed student who suffered from Crouzon's Syndrome was dismissed due to unsatisfactory clinical ratings, and that plaintiff's inability to synthesize information in a way that would make him a qualified medical student was not capable of being accommodated).

[29] Ohio Civil Rights Comm'n v. Case W. Reserve Univ., 666 N.E.2d 1376 (Ohio 1996).

[30] Thomas Jefferson Univ., 1 Nat'l Disability L. Rep. 229 (OCR 1990).

[31] Southeast Cmty. Coll. v. Davis, 442 U.S. 397 (1979).

[32] Breece v. Alliance Tractor-Trailer Training II, 824 F. Supp. 576 (E.D. Va. 1993).

[33] Wynne v. Tufts Univ. Sch. of Med., 976 F.2d 791, 796 (1st Cir. 1992), *cert. denied*, 507 U.S. 1030 (1993); Nathanson v. Med. Coll. of Pa., 926 F.2d 1368, 1383 (3d Cir. 1991). *But see* Ohio Civil Rights Comm'n v. Case W. Reserve Univ., 666 N.E.2d 1376, 1387 (Ohio 1996) (finding no duty to investigate).

[34] STEPHEN B. THOMAS, STUDENTS, COLLEGES, AND DISABILITY LAW 147 (Dayton, Ohio: Education Law Ass'n, 2002).

[35] 28 C.F.R. § 35.150 (2005).

[36] 28 C.F.R. § 36.304(a) (2005).

[37] Bevington v. Ohio Univ., 93 Fed. Appx. 748 (6th Cir. 2004), *cert. denied*, 125 S. Ct. 316 (2004).

[38] Fedorov v. Bd. of Regents of Univ. of Ga., 194 F. Supp. 2d 1378 (S.D. Ga. 2002) (concluding that a dismissed student, who was caught in possession of illegal drugs, was not protected under federal law—plaintiff entered rehabilitation only upon notice that police would be questioning him).

[39] Powell v. Nat'l Bd. of Med. Exam'rs, No. 02-9385, 2004 U.S. App. LEXIS 19474 (2d Cir. 2004) (noting that a dismissed medical school student with dyslexia, ADD, anxiety, and depression, who had failed the Step I exam three times as well as multiple courses although accommodated, also failed to substantiate that her diagnosed disability was substantially limiting; and concluding that requiring the University to allow the plaintiff to proceed to the next stage of training without passing the test would alter the nature of its program).

[40] Biank v. Nat'l Bd. of Med. Exam'rs, 130 F. Supp. 2d 986 (N.D. Ill. 2000) (concluding that the plaintiff, a student who sought an additional day to take a medical exam, was not substantially limited by dyslexia, as he had scored 192 on Step 1 of the test without accommodation—only 179 was needed to pass).

[41] Gonzales v. Nat'l Bd. of Med. Exam'rs, 225 F.3d 620 (6th Cir. 2000), *cert. denied*, 532 U.S. 1038 (2001).

[42] Doe v. Nat'l Bd. of Med. Exam'rs, 199 F.3d 146 (3d Cir. 1999). Also, issuing a preliminary injunction can in itself be controversial as it in essence permits the plaintiff to prevail (i.e., acquire the opportunity to take the test with accommodation) at the preliminary injunction stage. *Compare* Rothberg v. Law Sch. Admissions Council, 102 Fed. Appx. 122 (10th Cir. 2004) (reversing lower court order that 50 percent additional time be provided a student who had scored 148 out of 180 on the LSAT as she wanted to retake the exam with accommodations to improve the likelihood she could get into the school of choice) *with* Rush v. Nat'l Bd. of Med. Exam'rs, 268 F. Supp. 2d 673 (N.D. Tex. 2003) (issuing preliminary injunction requiring the Board to allow additional time while taking Step 1 given that plaintiff's reading and visual processing skills were below average due to a learning disability).

[43] Portions of this section are similar to and based on chapter 10 in STEPHEN B. THOMAS, STUDENTS, COLLEGES, & DISABILITY LAW (Dayton, Ohio: Education Law Ass'n, 2002).

[44] When a complainant alleges employment discrimination under § 504 or Title I, the standards under Title I are used and will be referred to in this paper—*see* 29 U.S.C. § 794(d) (2005).

[45]  42 U.S.C. § 12111(5)(A) (2005).

[46]  34 C.F.R. §104.3(h) (2005). However, if a procurement contract is for $10,000 or more, the contractor would be responsible for compliance with § 503 of the Act, which requires nondiscrimination by federal contractors.

[47]  519 U.S. 202 (1997).

[48]  Owens v. S. Dev. Council, 59 F. Supp. 2d 1210 (M.D. Ala. 1999).

[49]  29 C.F.R. § 1630.16 (2005).

[50]  531 U.S. 356 (2001).

[51]  29 C.F.R. § 1630.2(i) (2005). Major life activities are functions such as caring for oneself, performing manual tasks, walking, seeing, hearing, speaking, breathing, learning, and working. *See also* Amadio v. Ford Motor Co., 238 F.3d 919 (7th Cir. 2001) (noting that it is not enough for a plaintiff to show that the employer knew of his or her impairment; he or she must also show that the employer believed that the impairment substantially limited a major life activity).

[52]  29 C.F.R. § 1630.2(k) (2005). A record of impairment occurs when the individual has a history of, or has been misclassified as having, a mental or physical impairment that substantially limits one or more major life activities.

[53]  School Bd. of Nassau County, Fla. v. Arline, 480 U.S. 273 (1987).

[54]  29 C.F.R. § 1630.2(l) (2005). *See also* Johnson v. Paradise Valley Unified Sch. Dist., 251 F.3d 1222 (9th Cir. 2001) (concluding that plaintiff need not produce direct evidence that the District regarded her as disabled; plaintiff was a former custodian who was forced to resign given her mobility problems associated with a severe leg injury), *cert. denied*, 534 U.S. 1055 (2001).

[55]  29 C.F.R. § 1630.2(l) (2005).

[56]  29 C.F.R. § 1630.8 (2005).

[57]  29 C.F.R. § 1630 App. (2005).

[58]  29 C.F.R. § 1630.3(d) (2005).

[59]  O'Brien v. City of Hackensack, No. 02-2614, 2003 U.S. App. LEXIS 12434 (3d Cir. April 10, 2003), *cert. denied*, 540 U.S. 1182 (2004).

[60]  Toyota Motor v. Williams, 534 U.S. 184 (2002).

[61]  29 C.F.R. § 1630.2(j)(1)(i) (2005).

[62]  29 C.F.R. § 1630.2(j)(2) (2005).

[63]  29 C.F.R. § 1630.2(j)(3)(i) (2005).

[64]  29 C.F.R. §1630.2(j)(3)(ii) (2005).

[65]  42 U.S.C. §12111(8) (2005); 29 C.F.R. §1630.2(m) (2005).

[66]  29 C.F.R. § 1630.2(n)(1) (2005). *See also* Jacobsen v. Tillmann, 17 F. Supp. 2d 1018 (D. Minn. 1998) (concluding that a teacher who could not pass a math test as part of a licensing examination—14 attempts and accommodations—was not discriminated against due to disability; the ability to demonstrate basic math skills was held to be an essential requirement to be an elementary school teacher).

[67]  29 C.F.R. § 1630.2(n)(2)&(3) (2005).

[68]  29 C.F.R. § 1630.10 (2005).

[69]  Tyndall v. Nat'l Educ. Ctrs., 31 F.3d 209 (4th Cir. 1994) (holding that a former college instructor was not qualified for the position and that her employer did not unlawfully discriminate against her based on her association with her disabled son; an employee who cannot meet attendance requirements is not qualified).

[70]  29 C.F.R. § 1630.14(a) (2005).

[71]  42 U.S.C. § 12112(b)(6)&(7) (2005); 29 C.F.R. § 1630.11 (2005).

[72]  29 C.F.R. §1630.14(b) (2005).

[73]  29 C.F.R. §1630.14(c) (2005).

[74]  29 C.F.R. §1630.14(b) App. (2005).

[75]  Vollmert v. Wis. Dep't of Transp., 197 F.3d 293 (7th Cir. 1999) (finding that employer failed to accommodate a disabled staff member when it transferred her to a position

with fewer opportunities for promotion; such a transfer was inappropriate as reasonable accommodations had not been provided for the previous position).

[76] 29 C.F.R. § 1630.2(o)(1)(ii)&(iii) (2005).

[77] Smith v. Midland Brake, 180 F.3d 1154 (10th Cir. 1999) (en banc) (concluding that the ADA requires an employer to reassign a disabled employee to a vacant position, if the employee is unable to perform the essential functions of his or her current position but is able to perform those of the new position).

[78] 42 U.S.C. § 12111(9) (2005); 29 C.F.R. § 1630.2(o)(2) (2005).

[79] Kiphart v. Saturn Corp., 251 F.3d 573 (6th Cir. 2001) (noting that a reasonable jury could infer that full-task rotation on an assembly line was not an essential function and that job reassignment qualified as a reasonable accommodation).

[80] *See, e.g.*, Felix v. New York City Transit Auth., 324 F.3d 102 (2d Cir. 2003) (finding that accommodations need not be provided that do not address the limitation of the major life activity and flow directly from the disability).

[81] 29 C.F.R. § 1630.2(o)(3) (2005).

[82] 29 C.F.R. § 1630.9(d) (2005).

[83] 42 U.S.C. § 12112(d)(3)(B) (2005); 29 C.F.R. § 1630.14(b)(1) (2005).

[84] 29 C.F.R. § 1630.15(d) (2005); 29 C.F.R. § 1630.9(a) (2005). *See, e.g.*, Merrell v. ICEE-USA Corp., No. 99-4173, 2000 U.S. App. LEXIS 33327 (10th Cir. Dec. 19, 2000) (noting that the only accommodation that would allow a man who supplied and serviced carbonated beverage machines to meet essential functions would be to hire a second individual to accompany him and to perform heavy lifting, resulting in an undue burden).

[85] 42 U.S.C. § 12111(10) (2005); 29 C.F.R. § 1630.2(p) (2005).

[86] EEOC v. Yellow Freight Sys., 253 F.3d 943 (7th Cir. 2001) (holding that an employer was not required to provide an employee with unlimited sick leave); Maziarka v. Mills Fleet Farm, 245 F.3d 675 (8th Cir. 2001) (concluding that an employer was not required to reassign existing workers to compensate for plaintiff's unexpected absences and that dependable attendance was required for his job).

[87] Office of the Architect of the Capitol v. Office of Compliance, 361 F.3d 633 (Fed. Cir. 2004) (finding that transfer to an open position qualified as a reasonable accommodation).

[88] Phelps v. Optima Health & Catholic Med. Ctr., 251 F.3d 21 (1st Cir. 2001) (concluding that the ADA did not require reassignment of essential functions or creation of a new position to enable a nurse who could no longer lift clients to remain employed).

[89] Ozlowski v. Henderson, 237 F.3d 837 (7th Cir. 2001) (observing that an employer is not required to bump a current employee to allow a person with a disability to fill the position or to fill a vacant position it did not intend to fill for reasons independent of the employee's disability).

[90] *See, e.g.*, Newberry v. E. Tex. State Univ., 161 F.3d 276 (5th Cir. 1998) (concluding that a professor was dismissed due to unprofessional conduct, failure to attend meetings, harassment of colleagues, and poor work ethic rather than disability); Curtis v. Univ. of Houston, 940 F. Supp. 1070 (S.D. Tex. 1996) (concluding that a former alcoholic professor was not discriminated against due to his disability but rather was denied promotion to full professor because of his poor academic performance), *aff'd without published opinion*, 127 F.3d 35 (5th Cir. 1997).

[91] 29 C.F.R. § 1630.15(a) (2005).

[92] Reeves v. Sanderson Plumbing Prods., 530 U.S. 133 (2000).

# 14 Intellectual Property
## Philip T.K. Daniel and Patrick Pauken

## Introduction

"Intellectual property" is a product of the human intellect—literary or artistic works, inventions, business methods, or industrial processes—distinct from personal property and real property. Intellectual property law is covered in the law of copyrights, patents, and trademarks. From the words of this definition alone, it can be argued quite easily that nearly every activity engaged by students, staff, and faculty at colleges and universities is in furtherance of the production or protection of "intellectual property."

While the practice of intellectual property (IP) in higher education finds most of its energy in intellectual property policies drafted and enforced by colleges and universities, the inspiration for the law of copyrights and patents comes from the federal Constitution:

> The Congress shall have Power ... To promote the Progress of Science and useful Arts, by securing for limited Times to Authors and Inventors the exclusive Right to their respective Writings and Discoveries.[1]

Central to most constitutional analyses is a balance of rights. With respect to intellectual property in higher education, the balances are twofold. First, the law of intellectual property attempts to strike a balance between an individual's rights to ownership and profit and the public's right to make use of discovered knowledge and inventions. Second, and directly related to IP policies at colleges and universities, there must also be a balance between the ownership rights of the individual author or inventor—generally a faculty member or student—and the ownership rights of the college or university. The legal issues affecting intellectual property in higher education involve both creation and use of intellectual works. Examples include copyright protection for the products of teaching and scholarship, copyright infringement for improper use of protected works, patent ownership and profit for researchers and universities, and trademark licensing and protection of names, logos, symbols, and pictures associated with colleges and universities. There are particular applications and recent legal developments of intellectual property law in cyberspace.

## Copyright

Copyrights are intangible rights granted by federal statute to an author or originator of an artistic or literary work.[2] They are called "copyrights" because many rights are protected within one copyrightable work. These rights, discussed in more detail below, include the right to perform, display, and reproduce the work publicly.

Under 17 U.S.C. § 102(a), copyright protection exists in "original works of authorship fixed in any tangible medium of expression." In copyright law, originality is not difficult to establish; any modicum of originality will suffice.[3] For example, question items on exams are original works of authorship for copyright law purposes.[4] To be fixed, a work must be sufficiently embodied in a copy or a phonorecord—by or under the author's authority—to allow its perception, reproduction, or communication.[5] Important to the concept of "fixed," the statute defines "medium of expression" broadly to include expression made with the aid of a machine or device. Any work prepared by students, staff, or faculty on computers or word processors is not protected until it is saved as a file (on computer or disk) or printed in hard copy. In educational settings, speeches and lectures given by instructors are not generally protected under copyright law, as they are not typically fixed in a tangible medium. The speaker's notes, though (either in hard copy or saved on computer), are copyrightable as items in their own rights. Of course, the speeches and lectures themselves become copyrightable and protected by law if they are original and recorded verbatim under the speaker's authority. These recordings may be more plentiful and regular today with the growing prevalence of teaching by distance education, either on the Internet or via broadcast to off-campus sites.

The Copyright Act lists eight categories of protected works:

(1)  literary works;

(2)  musical works, including any accompanying words;

(3)  dramatic works, including any accompanying music;

(4)  pantomimes and choreographic works;

(5)  pictorial, graphic, and sculptural works;

(6)  motion pictures and other audiovisual works;

(7)  sound recordings; and

(8)  architectural works.[6]

In addition, the subject matter of copyright also includes compilations (collective works) and derivative works, but protection for a work employing preexisting copyrighted material does not extend to any part of the work in which such material has been used unlawfully.[7] The copyright in a compilation or derivative work extends only to the material contributed by the author of such work, as distinguished from the preexisting material employed in the work. Examples of collective works include periodical issues, anthologies, and encyclopedias, in which each contribution is a separate and independent work compiled into a collective whole. A derivative work is a work based on one or more preexisting works, such as a translation, musical arrangement, dramatization, fictionalization, motion picture version, sound recording, art reproduction, abridgment, condensation, or any other form in which a work may be recast, transformed, or adapted.

Copyright does not extend to any idea, procedure, process, system, method of operation, concept, principle, or discovery.[8] But while ideas are not copyrightable, the expression of them is protected, so long as the requirements described above are met. The idea-expression dichotomy  is critical to the work of universities and university personnel. A few examples may suffice. First, computer programs are protected under copyright law, but only the expressive elements of them.[9] Second, data from psychological experiments are copyrightable expressions of facts or processes.[10] Similarly, nonfiction works, often produced by faculty researchers, are protected by copyright as well, as such works require creativity and originality even if the factual elements of the work are not themselves copyrightable.

Of particular importance in the idea-expression debate within copyright law are the roles that free speech and academic freedom play. When does free speech (e.g., on or about the works of other authors) cross the line and infringe copyright? Melville Nimmer, one of the foremost writers on copyright law, spoke to this debate and offered the following as a balance:

> In some degree, [the idea-expression line] encroaches upon freedom of speech in that it abridges the right to reproduce the 'expression' of others, but this is justified by the greater public good in the copyright encouragement of creative works. In some degree it encroaches upon the author's right to control his work in that it renders his 'ideas' per se unprotectable, but this is justified by the greater public need for free access to ideas as part of the democratic dialogue.[11]

First Amendment defenses to copyright infringement claims rarely succeed, and when they do, the rationale favoring the defendants in infringement lawsuits generally tips in favor of "fair use" (discussed below) instead of free speech.

## Exclusive Rights

As any faculty or student researcher/teacher knows, a central feature to academic and professional success is public recognition and acceptance of his or her original work. Copyright law helps to acknowledge authorship by protecting against unauthorized copies, performances, or derivative works. Under the Act, a copyright owner has the exclusive rights to do and to authorize any of the following:

(1)   to reproduce the work in copies or phonorecords;

(2)   to prepare derivative works;

(3)   to distribute copies or phonorecords to the public by sale or other transfer of ownership, or by rental, lease, or lending;

(4)   to perform the work publicly (literary, musical, dramatic, and choreographic works, pantomimes, and motion pictures and other audiovisual works);

(5)   to display the work publicly (literary, musical, dramatic, and choreographic works, pantomimes, and pictorial, graphic, or sculptural works, including the individual images of a motion picture or other audiovisual work); or

(6)   to perform the work publicly by means of a digital audio transmission (sound recordings).[12]

Initially, all of these rights are held in their entirety by the author(s) of the work.[13] But one or more of the exclusive rights may be transferred or licensed to others. In higher education, transfer of copyrights is a common occurrence as institutions draft and enforce IP policies and as journals and book publishers often require an author to assign reproduction and distribution rights in return for publication.

## Limitations on Exclusive Rights

The Copyright Act includes several express limitations on exclusive rights, giving students, staff, and faculty the opportunity to make use of copyrighted works, usually for teaching and research purposes.[14] Three of these statutory limitations are particularly applicable to higher education settings and are discussed here: fair use, reproduction by libraries and archives, and certain performances and displays including those in classrooms and in distance education programs.

## Fair Use

Fair use of a copyrighted work, including reproduction in copies or phonorecords, "for purposes such as criticism, comment, news reporting, teaching (including multiple copies for classroom use), scholarship, or research, is not an infringement of copyright."[15] The spirit of fair use serves to balance the rights between owners and users of copyrighted works—a balance between the creation and discovery of information and the dissemination and use of it—and thereby serves the greater purposes of the copyright laws.

If the use of a copyrighted work is fair, then the user does not need to obtain advance consent of the copyright holder. However, the fair use doctrine is an affirmative defense for alleged copyright infringers. In such cases, the defendants have the burden of proof to show that their use was fair.[16] In determining whether the use made of a work in any particular case is a fair use, the following four factors are applied:

(1) the purpose and character of the use, including whether such use is of a commercial nature or is for nonprofit educational purposes;

(2) the nature of the copyrighted work;

(3) the amount and substantiality of the portion used in relation to the copyrighted work as a whole; and

(4) the effect of the use upon the potential market for or value of the copyrighted work.[17]

Three landmark Supreme Court cases help to outline the fair use doctrine and offer guidance on the proper balance between the rights of copyright holders and users of their works, particularly with respect to the public interest served by the dissemination of information. In *Sony Corporation of America v. Universal Studios*,[18] the Supreme Court held that the sale of VCRs to the general public did not violate the copyrights held on the television programs that are broadcast on public airwaves. The material at issue in the case was broadcast for free to the public at large. The purpose of the use (recording a television program for later viewing) served the public interest in "increasing access to television programming, an interest that is consistent with the First Amendment policy of providing the fullest possible access to information."[19]

A more complete application of the four fair use factors came in the Court's decision in *Harper & Row, Publishers, Inc. v. Nation Enterprises*.[20] In 1977, former President Gerald Ford contracted with Harper & Row to publish his memoirs. Two years later, as the memoirs were nearing completion, Harper & Row (as copyright holders) negotiated a pre-publication agreement with *Time* magazine to publish a 7500-word excerpt of the memoirs in advance of book publication. *Nation Magazine* obtained an unauthorized copy of the memoirs and published an excerpt before *Time*'s scheduled release date. As a result, *Time* canceled its article and refused to pay the remaining fees it owed to Harper & Row. Harper & Row filed suit against the publishers of *Nation Magazine*, alleging a violation of copyright. The Supreme Court held that the use was not fair, ruling that the right of first publication is one of the exclusive rights under Section 106 of the Copyright Act. Under each of the fair use factors, the Court favored Harper & Row. On the first and second factors, despite *Nation*'s claim of "news reporting" as the nature of the use, the Court found that the defendant had, in fact, intended to supplant the plaintiff's right of first publication. Fair use presupposes "good faith and fair dealing."[21] On the third factor, the Court held that while the amount of the taking was not so high quantitatively, the qualitative amount was substantial. Finally, Harper & Row's loss of $12,500 from *Time*'s contract cancellation was enough for the Court to find damage to the market.

More recently, in *Campbell v. Acuff-Rose Music, Inc.*,[22] Acuff-Rose, the holder of the copyright in Roy Orbison's rock ballad, "Oh, Pretty Woman," filed suit against the rap group, 2 Live Crew, after the rap group parodied the classic rock song. In a unanimous opinion, the Supreme Court reversed in favor of the defendant, emphasizing that commercial use of a copyrighted work is only one of the factors in the fair use analysis. The Court noted that the more transformative the new work is, the less significant the other fair use factors become. Here, the heart of any parodist lies in the ability of the listener to recognize enough of the original to know it is a parody; to be declared a fair use, the parody must also be viewed as a new composition that is, in effect, a comment on the original. The Court held, finally, that the markets for the two songs were different enough not to damage Orbison's (Acuff-Rose's) market in the original. *diff markets*

When examining the purpose and character of the use, courts will look at whether the use by the alleged infringer is commercial or noncommercial and whether the use is public or private.[23] Generally, a primarily commercial use will evidence an unfair use,[24] and a primarily noncommercial use will be a fair use, though the determinations are not automatic. For example, direct economic benefit or profit motive is not required for a finding of commercial use. In *American Geophysical Union v. Texaco, Inc.*,[25] the defendant disseminated scientific and technical information to its many researchers by copying the contents of the plaintiff's journals instead of purchasing them. The defendant's stated goal was to disseminate information to researchers rapidly, but the court found that the decision to copy the journals was primarily for business purposes and, hence, an unfair use. Similarly, Napster's provision of the opportunity for computer users to download copyrighted music for free was not a transformative use but a primarily commercial one.[26] More directly related to the work of colleges and universities, the Court of Appeals for the Third Circuit, in *American Medical Colleges v. Mikaelian*, held that the use of exact copies of questions from MCAT medical college tests in the business of preparing students to take the test was an unfair use.[27]

Despite the holding in *Mikaelian*, educational purposes generally lean toward a finding of fair use.[28] The express language of section 107 makes the distinction, though, between nonprofit and for-profit educational uses. In order to make the distinction, the plaintiff (copyright holder) must present evidence of present or future harm to the market for the copyrighted work. Consequently, the fact that students are the ultimate users of the copyrighted works does not automatically dictate a finding of fair use.[29] In higher education, perhaps the biggest controversy arises in cases of course packet copies of multiple works for students to purchase. Largely, the courts are in agreement that commercial copying services must obtain the copyright holders' permission before including copies of protected works in compiled course packets.[30] Although the commercial nature of producing and selling such course packets generally outweighs the educational purposes involved and protects the intellectual property of the copyright holders, there is some sympathy for the creativity of the faculty member in compiling the course packet and the flexibility for the students' access to ideas.[31]

On the second fair use factor, the nature of the copyrighted work, courts will generally weigh two considerations: (1) whether the copyrighted work is published or unpublished; and (2) whether the work is fiction or fantasy, or whether it is nonfiction, factual, or scientific. If the copyrighted work used by the alleged infringer is fantasy or fiction (generally considered high on creativity and originality), then the court will weigh the second factor against a finding of fair use. Some of the determinations seem rather easy. Although certainly worthy of copyright protection, some works are produced and disseminated for informational purposes and designed with fair use in mind.[32] The use of copyrighted informational works leans toward a finding of fair use, but the determination is not so easy when courts must consider the always controversial line between ideas (not protected) and the expression of them (protected). In nonfiction writing, scientific writing, and even in history[33] and biography,[34] multiple authors may interpret the same sets of facts and will often engage similar treatment of them. This does not dictate that a later work is an infringement of all those that came before. There are exceptions, however. Nonfiction, fact-based, and/or scientific works have creativity, originality, and marketability, rendering many uses of them unfair. In *Iowa State University Research Foundation, Inc. v. American Broadcasting Company*, the Second Circuit held that the unauthorized copying and broadcast of a student-produced film on a wrestler was an infringement on the marketability of the film.[35] If the copyrighted work is unpublished, courts will weigh this factor against a finding of fair use.[36] As discussed above, the author has the right to control first publication of his or her work.[37] For example, if a teacher provides her students with an unpublished writing produced by that teacher, future publication rights still belong to the teacher.[38]

The determination for the third fair use factor, the amount and substantiality of the work used, is generally guided by the following principle: The more material taken from the copyrighted work, the more likely a court will be to determine that the use is unfair. However, the measure of "more material taken" is made both quantitatively and qualitatively.[39] For example, the same number of words taken from a novel as from a short poem could certainly give way to different fair use determinations. On the quantitative end of the principle, fair use has been found where the alleged infringer took only twenty-nine words of a 2,100-word magazine article[40] and 4.3 % (7,000 words) of the words in a book.[41] But unfair use has been found in a case where eleven pages of thirty-five were copied[42] and 10 percent of unpublished letters were either closely paraphrased or directly copied.[43] If the quantitative use is high, the fourth fair use factor, effect on the market, may play a role and dictate a finding an unfair use. In *Quinto v. Legal Times of Washington, Inc.*, a federal district court held that the publishing in a legal newspaper of 92 percent of a student's law review article constituted an unfair use in that it preempted the only market for the article.[44]

On the qualitative end of the principle, the key determinant is whether the "heart" of the original work has been taken. Quoting only the factually explanatory material from the copyrighted source may not amount to an unfair use,[45] but when the part taken is the essence of the original work,[46] or the portion with the most popular appeal,[47] the use will likely be unfair. Parodies raise interesting discussions on the third fair use factor. On one hand, too much taking could be considered an unfair use. But in order for the parody to work, the parodist must use enough of the original material for the audience to recognize the source.[48] Following *Acuff-Rose*, the Court of Appeals for the Eleventh Circuit held recently that Alice Randall's "The Wind Done Gone," a parody of Margaret Mitchell's "Gone With the Wind," was not an infringement of copyright.[49] Randall wrote "The Wind Done Gone" as a critique (through parody) of Mitchell's original story's treatment of African Americans. The Court relied on traditional fair use principles and allowed the publication of the parody. The purpose and character of the use, while ultimately in the form of a commercial product, were ones of critique. The court noted that the second factor, the nature of the copyrighted work, is given little weight in parody cases because parodies almost always target well-known expressive works. On factor three, the court ruled the amount and substantiality of the portion used as inconclusive in that a parody must use enough of the original work in order to be effective, but the parody itself must also build on the original work. Finally, the court held that "The Wind Done Gone" is unlikely to displace sales of Mitchell's original work.

In *Harper & Row*, discussed above, the Supreme Court held that the final fair use factor, the effect of the allegedly infringing use on the market for the original work, was the most important element.[50] The Court presented a burden-shifting test for this element. First, the copyright holder must show, with reasonable probability, the causal connection between the infringement and loss of revenue.[51] Then, the alleged infringer must show that the damage would have occurred even without this use. Finally, the plaintiff-copyright holder must show that with continued use by the defendant, the future market will be damaged. Important to the inquiry is the effect not only on the current market for the original work, but also the markets for derivative works.[52] Moreover, if the markets for the two "competing" works are different, then the use by the later work is more likely to be a fair use.[53] With respect to the teaching, scholarship, and research uses of copyrighted works, litigation reveals that fair use will generally be recognized as long as the use does not adversely affect the copyright holder's market.

The use of brief quotes and passages from earlier works in a biography of the author of those works is considered a fair use since the use does not affect the market for the biography subject's pre-existing writings.[54] On the other hand, when suitable copies of works are available from the copyright holders for purchase or license, wholesale copying will not be considered fair, as in cases involving the copying and archiving of scientific research articles,[55] the recording of audio visual works from educational television broadcasts when suitable copies are available for sale,[56] the copying of plaintiff's secure SAT test questions,[57] and copying course packet materials for student study purposes without paying permission fees.[58]

An interesting development in the modern technological age is the effect on multiple markets for copyrighted works. In the newsworthy case of *A & M Records, Inc. v. Napster, Inc.*,[59] the plaintiffs (engaged in the business of recording and distributing copyrighted musical compositions and sound recordings) alleged that Napster was liable for contributory and vicarious copyright infringement when it provided for transmission and retention of sound recordings through the use of digital technology. The court held that these uses were unfair under copyright law. The purpose here was commercial (to avoid the hassle of purchasing music), not trans-formative (downloading is not transformative, it's just a new medium), and wholesale in the amount taken. Finally, there were two markets harmed by Napster: the established traditional sales market and the relatively new online market, both belonging to the authors/creators of the work.

## Library Reproduction

The next limitation on a copyright holder's exclusive rights is a library or archives' right to reproduction of certain works.[60] Under section 108 of the Act, a library or archives may reproduce no more than one copy or phonorecord of a work or to distribute such copy or phonorecord, as long as the reproduction or distribution contains a notice of copyright and is not made for commercial advantage.[61] In order to take advantage of this limitation, the collections of the library or archives must be open to the public or available not only to researchers affiliated with the library or archives, but also to other persons doing research. Higher education libraries will almost certainly qualify here.

Section 108 also allows for additional copies to be made. In the case of unpublished works, three copies or phonorecords may be made for purposes of preservation and security or for deposit for research use in another library or archives. In the case of published works, three copies or phonorecords may be made for the purpose of replacement of a copy or phonorecord that is damaged, deteriorating, lost, or stolen or if the existing format in which the work is stored has become obsolete, as long as the library has determined that an unused replacement cannot be obtained at a fair price. Regardless of whether the work is published or unpublished, any reproduction made in digital format may not otherwise be distributed in that format and may not be made available to the public in that format outside the premises of the library or archives.

Popular in libraries everywhere are the copyright notices on photocopiers. The placement of these notices is a requirement of section 108 and will shield the library or archives from liability for copyright infringement for the unsupervised use of copiers located on its premises. Another important provision in section 108 notes that the rights of reproduction and distribution extend only to the isolated and unrelated reproduction or distribution of a single copy or phonorecord of the same material on separate occasions. If, on multiple occasions, the library or archives is aware or has substantial reason to believe that it is engaging in the related or concerted reproduction or distribution of multiple copies or phonorecords of the same material, then the reproduction and copying rights do not apply. One case is illustrative and offers some reprieve to the libraries and archives. In *Williams & Wilkins Company v. United States*, the Supreme Court held that extensive photocopying by government libraries of medical journal articles at the request of individuals and other libraries was not an infringement of copyright where the copyright holders failed to show harm.[62] Additionally, the Court noted that such copying accommodates the interests of science, medicine, and medical research.

A final, relatively new provision of section 108 grants an additional right to libraries and archives. During the last twenty years of any term of copyright of a published work, a library or archives, including a non-profit educational institution that functions as a library or archive, may reproduce, distribute, display, or perform in facsimile or digital form a copy or phonorecord of such work, or portions thereof, for purposes of preservation, scholarship, or research. This right, however, does not apply if the work is still subject to normal commercial exploitation or a copy or phonorecord of the work can be obtained at a reasonable price or if the copyright owner provides notice that the work is commercially available.

## Classroom Use

An extremely important limitation on the exclusive rights of copyright holders is the allowance of certain performances and displays of copyrighted works in classroom activities.[63] Today, with distance education and online education, the definition of "classroom" is broadened in scope, and recent developments in copyright legislation define that scope.

Section 110(1) speaks to the traditional classroom. This section permits the performance or display of a copyrighted work by instructors or students "in the course of face-to-face teaching activities" of a non-profit educational institution, in a classroom or similar place devoted to instruction. In the case of a motion picture or other audiovisual work, the performance, or the display of individual images, the copy used must be lawfully made, and the person responsible for the performance must not know or have reason to know that the copy is not lawful. Aside from this limitation, there is no other intellectual property constraint on the types of works covered by this provision. As long as other legal requirements are met, teachers and students are free to read aloud from texts, act in a play, sing or play a musical instrument, show a movie, or display text or pictures by way of audio-visual equipment. The definitions of "teachers" and "students" may not be broad enough to include people outside of the professors of record and those students actually enrolled in the course, with the exception of guest lecturers and instructors. As a result, the definition of "teaching activities" is likely not broad enough to include larger educational assemblies and presentations outside of the traditional classroom.

The recent Technology, Education, and Copyright Harmonization Act of 2002, the TEACH Act, broadens significantly the definition of the classroom. The TEACH Act, codified in section 110(2), permits the following educational activities in distance education and/or online settings:

(1)  performance of a nondramatic literary or musical work;

(2)  performance of reasonable and limited portions of dramatic literary works; and

(3)  display of any work in an amount comparable to that which is typically displayed in the course of a live classroom session, by or in the course of a transmission.

The TEACH Act permits in distance education or online environments the same activities as would be permitted in traditional classroom environments. Students may now receive classroom materials at home, from another educational institution, or in school or college computer labs. There are, however, several institutional requirements. First, the performance or display must be made at the direction of or under the actual supervision of an instructor. Second, it must be an integral part of a class session offered as a regular part of the "systematic mediated instructional activities" of an accredited nonprofit educational institution.[64] Third, the performance or display must be directly related and of material assistance to the teaching content of the transmission. Fourth, and particularly important, the transmission must be made solely for, and, to the extent technologically feasible, students officially enrolled in the course and officers or employees of the educational institution as part of their official duties. Fifth, the college or university must institute policies regarding copyright; provide informational materials to faculty, students, and relevant staff members that accurately describe and promote compliance with copyright law; and provide notice to students that materials used may be subject to copyright law. Finally, the college or university must apply technological measures that reasonably prevent the retention and accessibility of the copyrighted work for longer than the class session; reasonably prevent the unauthorized further dissemination of the copyrighted to others; and must not engage in conduct that could reasonably be expected to interfere with technological measures used by copyright owners to prevent such retention or unauthorized further dissemination.[65] Importantly, the exemptions permitted under section 110(2) do not apply to copyrighted works produced or marketed primarily for distance education. These materials (e.g., distance education courses for sale) have their own market and must be legally acquired. Similarly, course reserves are not applicable to these exemptions; their use must be approved elsewhere in copyright law.

## Copyright Ownership, Duration, and Registration

College and university personnel, including students, faculty, staff, and administrators, create countless copyrightable works every day: books, articles, computer programs, lesson plans, exams, class handouts, outlines, lecture notes, term papers, musical compositions, art works, and institutional policies and reports. This section of the chapter discusses the ownership, duration, and registration of these and other copyrightable works.

### Ownership

Under section 201 of the Copyright Act, unless otherwise agreed by parties to a contract, copyright protection vests initially in the author or authors of the work.[66] The authors of a *joint work* are co-owners of copyright in the entire work. Copyright in each separate contribution to a *collective work*, such as a book with individually authored chapters, is distinct from copyright in the collective work as a whole and vests initially in the author or authors of each contribution.

In educational and many other professional settings, the ownership discussion does not stop there, however. The work for hire doctrine is widely applicable in colleges and universities. Section 101 of the Copyright Act defines a "work made for hire" as:

(1) a work prepared by an employee within the scope of his or her employment or

(2) a work specifically ordered or commissioned for use as a contribution to a collective work, as a part of a motion picture or other audiovisual work, as a translation, as a supplementary work, as a compilation, as an instructional text, as a test, as answer material for a test, or as an atlas, if the parties expressly agree in a written instrument signed by them that the work shall be considered a work made for hire.

In the case of a work made for hire, the employer is considered the author and owner of all the rights in the work, unless the parties have expressly agreed otherwise in a written instrument signed by them. The work-for-hire doctrine is often codified in the university's faculty handbook or university charter.

A central issue in work-for-hire cases is whether the employer-employee relationship exists in the first place. If it does, then strict application of the Copyright Act dictates that the employer is the owner of the work made for hire. If the relationship does not exist, then ownership vests in the author of the work. To answer the relationship question, several factors need to be weighed. In *Community for Creative Non-Violence v. Reid*, the Supreme Court addressed over a dozen factors [*Reid* factors] to determine whether the creator of a work is an employee (with ownership vesting in the employer) or an independent contractor (with ownership vesting in the creator):

(1) the hiring party's right to control the manner and means by which the product is accomplished;

(2) the skill required;

(3) the source of instrumentalities and tools;

(4) the location of the work;

(5) the duration of the relationship between the parties;

(6) whether the hiring party has the right to assign additional projects to the hired party;

(7) the extent of the hiring party's discretion over when and how long to work;

(8) the method of payment;

(9) the hiring party's role in hiring and paying assistants;

(10) whether the work is part of the regular business of the hiring party;

(11)   whether the hiring party is in the business

(12)   the provision of tax benefits; and

(13)   the tax treatment of the hired party.[67]

Unless the parties agree otherwise, the *Reid* factors seem to dictate that faculty, staff, and administrators are subject to the work-for-hire doctrine.[68] There is some support for a "teacher exception" to the work-for-hire doctrine, however, meaning that faculty members would retain ownership in their creations, even if they were completed with university resources. In *Hays v. Sony Corporation of America*,[69] two public high school teachers wrote a manual to explain how to use the school's word processors. The teachers distributed the manuals to students and faculty. Later, when the school purchased new word processors from Sony, the school asked Sony to write a similar manual. Sony proceeded to incorporate much of the teachers' previous work in the new manual verbatim. The teachers sued. A federal district court held that the original manual was a work for hire and was owned by the school. The Court of Appeals for the Seventh Circuit dismissed the case on procedural grounds but wrote a lengthy opinion on the ownership of teacher-created materials and advocated a teacher exception to the work-for-hire doctrine. The Seventh Circuit noted three justifications for the teacher exception: (1) tradition in the education field; (2) the lack of congressional action in the Copyright Act to defeat the teacher exception already endorsed by previous courts; and (3) the disruption that would be caused in academic settings with the elimination of the teacher exception.

Under this exception, it can be argued that college and university administrative officials do not directly supervise their faculty in the preparation of academic books and articles and teaching materials. Other courts have endorsed the teacher exception. In *Williams v. Weisser*, a professor (Williams) sued a businessman (Weisser) who employed a student to take notes in Williams' classes.[70] Weisser then reproduced and sold the notes to other students. Weisser defended the lawsuit by arguing that Williams did not own the course materials and, as such, lacked standing. The court supported Williams and held that he held the copyrights in his course materials. Similarly, the court in *Sherrill v. Grieves* held that a teacher of military science courses who had reduced his lectures to writing in the form of a book owned the copyrights in the book.[71]

The teacher exception to the work-for-hire doctrine is technically in direct opposition to statutory language, as well as many university IP policies. Yet it retains strong arguments. First, the spirit of copyright law, stemming from the constitutional provision, grants authorship rights to those who engage in the production and promotion of science and the useful arts—the "sweat of the brow." Second, it is the teacher's initiative and creativity that bring these works to life. Without authorship protection, productive energy and incentive might be lost. Third, the creators are the ones who make the decisions and direct their own work. In effect, it is the faculty members who set their research agendas, write syllabi, and teach courses. Fourth, faculty members are mobile. They often work at more than one college or university over their careers, and they take their work product with them—a prospect made much more feasible if the faculty members themselves own the work product. Fifth, endorsement of the teacher exception is a form of "soft compensation" for the work of faculty members and a good retention tool for universities.[72]

An evenhanded analysis of copyright ownership also supports a work product argument in favor of the university. Along with the express language of copyright legislation, on the side of the university's claim for ownership, one can contend that if the institution owns the work product of its faculty, then the free flow of and access to information throughout the university community is maintained. Under such a set-up, colleges and universities would not have to worry about technical contracts and payment of royalties every time they wanted to use materials created at their own places of business. Institutional ownership also allows colleges and universities to retain the academic benefits of those creations and the prestige that comes with them. Maintaining institutional ownership prevents conflicts of interest among faculty members who may use their positions as stepping-stones for private consulting. Finally, colleges and universities argue that faculty creations are developed on university time with university resources and, as a result, belong to the university.

### Duration

The length of a copyright term depends largely on when the work was created and/or published. Copyright Act amendments over the years have changed the terms of copyright protection. The most recent legislation, the Sonny Bono Copyright Term Extension Act of 1998 (CTEA), extended copyright protection by twenty years for both new works and pre-existing works not yet in the public domain.[73] Works in the public domain are those works that are not protected by copyright law and may be used freely by everyone. The reasons a work may not be protected include: (1) The term of copyright has expired; (2) The author failed to satisfy statutory formalities to perfect the copyright; or (3) The work is a work of the United States Government. The following table outlines copyright durations (*See* Table 14-1):[74]

**Table 14-1**

| Date of Work | Protected From | Term |
|---|---|---|
| Created 1-1-1978 or after | When work is fixed in tangible medium of expression | Life of author + 70 years (or if work is corporate authorship, the shorter of 95 years from publication, or 120 years from creation) |
| Published before 1923 | In public domain | None |
| Published from 1923-1963 | When published with notice | 28 years + could be renewed for 47 years, now extended by 20 years for a total of 67 years; if not so renewed, now in public domain |
| Published from 1964-1977 | When published with notice | 28 years from first term; now an automatic extension of 67 years for second term |
| Created before 1-1-1978 but not published | 1-1-1978, the effective date of the Copyright Act of 1976 which eliminated common law copyright | Life of author + 70 years or 12-31-2002, whichever is greater |
| Created before 1-1-1978 but published between then and 12-31-2002 | 1-1-1978, the effective date of the Copyright Act of 1976 which eliminated common law copyright | Life of author + 70 years or 12-31-2047, whichever is greater |

## Registration

Formal registration is not necessary to gain copyright protection for newly created works.[75] Nor is it necessary to attach the traditional copyright symbol, the letter "c" inside a circle, to the work. As mentioned above, once an original work is fixed in a tangible medium of expression, the work is protected by copyright law. Copyright registration and placement of a copyright notice on the work are encouraged, however, to provide proper notice to users as to the copyright status and date. If a copyright notice appears on the work, then a defendant in an infringement action will have some difficulty claiming innocent infringement.[76] Registration is required if the copyright holder wishes to recover statutory damages and attorneys fees in an infringement lawsuit.[77]

### Copyright Infringement and Remedies

Copyright infringement occurs whenever someone other than a copyright holder exercises one of the exclusive rights of a copyright owner without permission or without a recognized statutory exception to exclusive rights such as fair use.[78] Infringement need not be intentional for the copyright owner to recover. Aside from the intentional/innocent infringement dichotomy, there are three types of infringement: direct, contributory, and vicarious. Direct infringement is infringement by a person or service that actually engages in the infringement of the protected copyright. Direct infringement requires not only imposition, but also volition and involvement.[79] Contributory infringement occurs where one, "with the knowledge of the infringing activity, induces, causes, or materially contributes to the infringing conduct of another" even though "he [or she] has not committed or participated in the infringing acts." This activity often involves copying devices and involves either: (1) personal conduct that encourages or assists the infringement or (2) provision of machinery or goods that facilitate the infringement. To be liable, the alleged infringer must have actual or constructive knowledge of, and must have participated in, the infringing conduct.[80] Finally, vicarious infringement may be imposed on a person or entity that has the right and ability to supervise the infringing activity and has a direct financial interest in the exploitation of the copyright even though he does not have the intent to infringe or the knowledge of the infringement.[81]

The Copyright Act provides several remedies for those whose copyrights have been infringed. First, a successful plaintiff can acquire a temporary or final injunction to stop the infringing action.[82] Second, a court may order the impounding and disposition of infringing articles.[83] Infringing articles include copies or phonorecords of copyrighted works, as well as plates, molds, matrices, masters, tapes, film negatives, or other articles by means of which such copies or phonorecords may be reproduced. Impounding is an available remedy during the pendency of any infringement action, and destruction or other reasonable disposition is an available remedy as part of a final judgment or decree.

Moreover, a copyright owner is entitled to recover any actual damages suffered as a result of the infringing action, plus any additional profits attributable to the infringement that are not taken into account in computing the actual damages.[84] Instead of actual damages and profits, though, the copyright owner may elect, at any time before final judgment is rendered, to recover an award of statutory damages for all infringements involved in the action.[85] Statutory damages are required in cases involving an infringer who is an employee or agent of a nonprofit educational institution, library, or archives acting within the scope of his or her employment who reasonably believed that the infringing use was a fair use. Finally, the court may allow the recovery of full costs by or against any party other than the United States or an officer thereof. Generally, the court may also award reasonable attorney's fees to the prevailing party.[86]

The Copyright Act also provides for criminal action to be taken against anyone who infringes a copyright willfully, either for purposes of commercial or financial gain or by the reproduction or distribution of copies or phonorecords of copyrighted works that have a total retail value of more than $1,000.[87] Punishments have varying ranges of imprisonment and fines, depending on the number of copies made, the financial value of the copyrighted work, and whether the infringer is a repeat-offender. When any person is convicted of any criminal violation, the infringer must also forfeit, destroy, or otherwise dispose of the infringing articles and all equipment used in the manufacture of the articles.

### Copyright Law in the Digital Age: The Digital Millennium Copyright Act

Even with the passage of laws like the Digital Millennium Copyright Act, copyright law does not fit neatly in the digital age. The challenge is to see how traditional, long-standing law can apply to new media. With the Internet, publication and distribution are made even easier, with less time and expense required. Higher Education research can be conducted more efficiently with online libraries and databases. Recall that the requirements for copyright protection are minimal: originality and fixation in any tangible means of expression.[88] Publications in cyberspace vary widely, from quick ideas and email messages to professionally produced corporate newsletters and scholarly articles in online journals.

Internet publishers may be able to restrict their audiences, at least initially. They may make their publications available only to a select group of people: subscribers to an online journal, students enrolled in a course, or direct one-to-one communication such as email. But with or without these early restrictions, the subsequent distribution (and perhaps alteration) of these publications cannot always be controlled or monitored by the copyright holder. In other words, publication, distribution, and infringement are easy, while detection and enforcement are difficult. Nevertheless, the exclusive rights granted to authors under section 106 of the Copyright Act and each of the limitations on exclusive rights—including fair use—apply in cyberspace.[89]

Perhaps the stickiest application of copyright law in cyberspace, as it relates to authorship and ownership of web-created and web-maintained materials, is the work-for-hire doctrine. The teacher exception to the work-for-hire doctrine, accepted by some courts and several commentators, is not recognized in legislation. Without the teacher exception, it is difficult enough to balance the *Reid* factors in favor of faculty members and their creations in the hard copy world. But when these copyrightable documents are created and maintained on university-provided systems (including works created for web-based teaching), the connection to the employer as owner becomes stronger, and the distance from the employee to creator becomes greater. It is strongly encouraged that colleges and universities revisit their intellectual property policies to strike the proper balance between the authorship, ownership, and incentive for the creators and the distribution, use, and promotion of science and useful arts for the consumers. Examples of policy provisions include the following:

(1)  joint ownership of teacher-created works for both the faculty member and the university;

(2)  a "shop right" for the host university, where the faculty member owns the work, but the university has a nonexclusive, nontransferable, royalty-free right to use the work for nonprofit educational purposes;

(3)  a "publicity clause" that requires the faculty member to give the hiring institution credit whenever he or she publishes an article, book, or other educational work;

(4)  a contractual or policy-based recognition of the teacher exception to the work-for-hire doctrine; and

(5)  a contractual or policy provision that grants creators the ownership and the hiring university a percentage of the income;

The Digital Millennium Copyright Act (DMCA) updated United States copyright law to meet the demands of the digital age, combat copyright infringement on the Internet, and conform United States law to the requirements of the World Intellectual Property Organization (WIPO). The DMCA contains within it two central pieces of legislation. The WIPO Copyright and Performances and Phonograms Treaties Implementation Act prohibits the circumvention of technologies that have been installed to prevent online infringement.[90] With some exceptions, the Act also prohibits the manufacture and distribution of circumvention devices. The Online Copyright Infringement Liability Limitation Act primarily creates a safe harbor for online service providers against infringement liability of the provider's subscribers.[91] This act includes a special provision for libraries, archives, and nonprofit educational institutions.[92]

Each of the WIPO treaties obligates the United States to prevent circumvention of technological measures used to protect copyrighted works. As such, the DMCA prohibits the circumvention of any effective "technological protection measure" (e.g., a password or form of encryption) used by a copyright holder to restrict access to its material. Section 1201 divides technological measures into two categories: those for the *restriction of access* to copyrighted works and those for the *restriction of copying* of those works. This categorization was done to assure that fair use continues. In some cases, copying a copyrighted work will be considered fair use. Therefore, circumvention of a technological measure that prevents copying may not be an infringement. Gaining unauthorized access to a work, however, will not be supported by a fair use defense.

The DMCA targets computer programs that are commercially limited and primarily designed and marketed for circumvention. There are exceptions, however. The following circumvention activities are not prohibited by the DMCA and are, therefore, fair uses of copyrighted works:

(1) circumvention by nonprofit library, archive, and educational institutions solely for the purpose of determining, in good faith, whether or not they wish to obtain *authorized* access to the work;

(2) law enforcement, intelligence, or other governmental activities;

(3) encryption research;

(4) testing technological devices that are designed to prevent access by minors to certain material on the Internet;

(5) the collection or dissemination of personally identifying information about the online activities of a natural person; and

(6) testing the security of a computer, computer system, or computer network with the permission of its owner or operator.[93]

A person injured by a violation of section 1201 may bring a civil action for equitable and monetary damages.[94] Special protection is given to nonprofit libraries, archives, and educational institutions, which may be entitled to complete remission of damages in circumstances where the violator proves that he or she was unaware and had no reason to believe the alleged acts were infringing.

The statutory limitations on liability relating to online copyright infringement apply only to Internet service providers (ISP).[95] Most colleges and universities offer Internet access to their students, staff, faculty, and sometimes visitors to libraries. Therefore, colleges or universities qualify for these limitations. In most circumstances, the ISP will not be liable for the infringing acts of its subscribers—acts that include transitory network communication of infringing conduct, intermediate or temporary storage of infringing text or images, and long-term storage of infringing text or images stored at the direction of the user and not the service provider. As long as the Internet service provider plays no substantive roles in the content, direction, or communication of the infringing material, liability will be limited. The provider must establish that it did not have actual knowledge or awareness that the infringing activity was occurring.[96] The college or university must continue to provide access to sites that are pay-per-access or password protected. But it also must act to remove or disable copyright infringing conduct upon notification of claimed infringements. The limitations on liability apply to a service provider only if the ISP has adopted and reasonably implemented, with proper notice to subscribers and account holders, a policy that provides for the termination of subscriptions and accounts of repeat infringers.

The special provision limiting the liability of nonprofit educational institutions contains a few significant points necessary for elaboration.[97] The provision makes a distinction between faculty and graduate students and the institution itself. In order to limit the liability of the institution for the infringing activities of its faculty and graduate student employees,[98] the Act holds that when such faculty and graduate students are performing a teaching or research function, they are considered to be persons other than the institution. In such circumstances, knowledge or awareness of the infringing activities is not to be attributed to the institution if each of the following factors is met:

(1)  such faculty member's or graduate student's infringing activities do not involve the provision of online access to instructional materials that are or were required or recommended, within the preceding three-year period, for a course taught at the institution by such faculty member or graduate student;

(2)  the institution has not, within the preceding three-year period, received more than two notifications described of claimed infringement by such faculty member or graduate student, and such notifications of claimed infringement were not actionable as knowing material misrepresentations of copyright infringement; and

(3)  the institution provides to all users of its system or network informational materials that accurately describe, and promote compliance with, the laws of the United States relating to copyright.

Litigation under the DMCA, to date, has not involved colleges or universities directly. Some coverage of the recent developments is instructive, however. The case law involves First Amendment challenges to the DMCA, particularly the anti-circumvention provisions; infringement lawsuits challenging the service provider's knowledge of the users' infringing conduct; fair use defenses; and the safe harbor limitations on liability for service providers. The free speech defenses from the alleged circumventers have, by and large, failed. While the courts have generally agreed that the circumvention software developed, used, and distributed by the defendants constituted speech, they have held that the DMCA is a valid content-neutral restriction on that speech. For example, in *Universal City Studios, Inc. v. Corley*, the movie industry sued a number of individuals and organizations that distributed a computer program (DeCSS) designed to circumvent the content scramble system (CSS), an encryption system that prevents copying DVDs.[99] The Court of Appeals for the Second Circuit upheld the district court's grant of a permanent injunction prohibiting defendants from posting the DeCSS program on their web site and from posting hyperlinks to other web sites containing DeCSS. The court held that the DMCA was designed to target the program's functional attributes, not its expressive ones. The DMCA does not prohibit making lawful copies of DVDs; it simply prohibits the decryption method of copying.[100] According to the court in *DVD Copy Control Association v. Bunner*, a case with facts similar to those in *Corley*, such an injunction against the distribution of DeCSS "burdens no more speech than is necessary to serve the government's important interest in maintaining commercial ethics."[101]

Online copyright infringement is most certainly a concern for colleges and universities as Internet service providers, whether or not they are aware of the infringing conduct. The Internet access provisions of a college; the popularity and prevalence of Internet music downloads among the college student population; and the noteworthy and newsworthy decisions in *Recording Industry Association of America (RIAA) v. Verizon Internet Servs.*,[102] *A & M Records, Inc. v. Napster, Inc.*,[103] and *In re Aimster Copyright Litigation*[104] have put higher education administrators and students on notice. With a significant recent exception, the DMCA allows a copyright owner to subpoena an Internet service provider (perhaps a college or university) in order to get the name of a user who has allegedly infringed the copyright owner's rights. In the *Verizon* case, the defendant ISP refused to give the name of an alleged infringer who downloaded 600 copyrighted songs in one day.[105] Verizon argued that the DMCA only applied when the infringing materials are stored on the provider's space and not when the service provider's space is used as a mere conduit for the alleged infringing material. A federal district court rejected Verizon's claim and held that the DMCA offers liability protections to Internet service providers in exchange for their cooperation in copyright enforcement. The Court of Appeals reversed, however, agreeing with Verizon that it is impossible for an Internet service provider to take advantage of the limits on liability (e.g., the removal of infringing materials or the disabling of access to such materials) when the materials are not stored online. When infringing materials merely travel through the provider's space without storage, the provider has no way of identifying the material or the user and, therefore, cannot notify the user of the infringing conduct.

In the *Aimster Copyright Litigation* case, similar to the peer-to-peer file sharing case in *Napster*, the Court of Appeals for the Seventh Circuit upheld an injunction against Aimster, a file-sharing service that facilitates the transfer of files between users. Record companies and composers sought preliminary injunctions to shut down Aimster and argued that Aimster's operation constituted contributory and vicarious infringement. Instead of adopting an "actual knowledge of infringement" test as the Ninth Circuit did in *Napster*, the Seventh Circuit adopted an "economic balancing test:"

> [I]f the infringing uses are substantial, then to avoid liability as a contributory infringer, the provider of the service must show that it would have been disproportionately costly for him to eliminate or at least reduce substantially the infringing uses.[106]

The Seventh Circuit likened Aimster's response to the infringing uses to "willful blindness." Clearly, colleges and universities cannot afford this kind of visual acuity. In order to be eligible for the safe harbor limitations on liability afforded to Internet service providers and, in particular, educational institutions, colleges and universities must actively enforce policies that promote compliance with copyright laws.

## Patents

Inspired by the same constitutional clause that gives Congress the power to protect copyrights, patent law grants an inventor rights to exclude others from producing or using the inventor's discoveries, for a limited time, in furtherance of science and the useful arts. Under Title 35 of the United States Code, patents for "novel, useful, and nonobvious" inventions are granted for twenty years, measured from the date of application.[107] In an application for a patent, the applicant must provide a "specification" describing how the invention works and offer "claims" stating what is new, useful, and nonobvious (i.e., patentable) about the invention. Applications for patents are public documents.[108]

Unlike copyright law, which takes effect the moment an original work is fixed in a tangible medium of expression, there is no monopoly right in a patented invention until the United States Patent Office issues the patent. The patent office will search through past patents and all relevant literature to ascertain whether the claims are new, useful, and nonobvious. Patents are often granted to some, but not all, claims in an application. A potential patentee may submit an application more than once.

When multiple applications (including recently granted patents) make identical or nearly identical claims, the Patent Office will conduct an "interference proceeding" to determine which application first conceived and reduced the patent to practice. A successful applicant for a patent has the exclusive right to make, use, or sell the invention to the absolute exclusion of others for the twenty-year period of the patent.[109] These rights may be licensed or assigned to others. During the term of the patent, the patent owner has the right to determine who has the right to make, use, or sell the invention.[110] Such licenses may also be made on geographic bases. The law does not require the inventor to put the patent to use, although the exclusive rights act as incentives to make, use, and sell the patent for societal benefits. Exclusivity of rights is important and does not belong to the inventor until application is made. Putting the invention to use is called "working the patent." Allowing others to use it is called "compulsory licensing." It should be noted that patents cannot be renewed. At term expiration, the invention enters the public domain for others to make, use, or sell.

Infringement lawsuits may be filed for alleged unauthorized use of a patent. In such cases, the defendants may argue that the patent was unwarranted (e.g., failure to meet the novelty, utility, and/or nonobviousness requirements). The defendant may also argue that the patentee engaged in inequitable conduct. In addition, any person may ask the Patent Office to reexamine the patent, and any person may seek a declaratory judgment to determine the validity of the patent.

## Types of Inventions and Discoveries

Just as in copyright law, ideas are not patentable. In patent law, only the applications of those ideas are protected.[111] These applications come in the form of *products* and *processes*, both of which can be patented.[112] Products are physical entities—specifically, machines, manufactures, and compositions of matter. As long as the product fits into one or more of these three categories and meets the other requirements for patentability, it will be patented. Basically, a machine is an inventive thing that does something. A manufacture is a nonnatural human-made product. The most typical composition of matter is a new chemical compound. With these products, the components may be natural, but the composition is human-made.

Processes, contrary to products, are more intangible means to an end. For example, a chemical process that produces a compound through a series of steps may be patentable. Sometimes, the product that comes from the process will not be patented, while the process is. In other words, the patentability of the product is not relevant to the patentability of the process designed to produce it. Consider an experimental drug for the treatment of a disease. In one case, the drug itself may be patented. In another case, perhaps the process of producing the drug will be. Sometimes, both the process and the product will be patentable.

## Plant and Design Patents

The products and processes defined above are generally known as "utility" patents. There are two other types of patents, however, that are not dependent on utility. The first are plant patents.[113] Plant patentability requires novelty, distinctiveness, and nonobviousness. The right granted to a plant patentee is the exclusive right to reproduce the plant. Distinctiveness is measured by the characteristics that make that plant distinguishable from other preexisting plants. These characteristics include habit, health, soil, color, flavor, productivity, storability, odor, and form.[114] The second are design patents, obtained to protect a new, original, ornamental design for a manufactured article.[115] The three requirements for patentability of designs are novelty, ornamentality, and nonobviousness. The protection afforded a patentee of a design is protection against copying, very similar to the protections granted to copyrighted works.[116]

## Novelty, Utility, and Nonobviousness: Issues of Patents and Priority

Section 102 of the Patent Act defines the conditions for novelty of an invention. In layperson's terms, perhaps novelty can be thought of as belonging to the winner of a "race" to invention and patent. Certainly, there are simultaneous projects at colleges and universities around the world, where researchers are, for example, searching for cures for diseases. The processes and products that result from these projects are patentable, first, if they are novel. That is, the patent will belong to the winner of the race, the one who first brings the invention from conception to patent application and then to practice.

Within the novelty conditions are the concepts of *anticipation* and *statutory bar*. Anticipation, either domestic or foreign, refers to certain events that occur anytime prior to invention and, if they do occur, prohibit patentability. Statutory bar, on the other hand, refers to domestic or foreign events that occur more than twelve months prior to application for patent. Just like anticipation events, statutory bar events also prevent patentability. The following table outlines section 102 of the Act and the concepts of anticipation and statutory bar. The entries in the table are those that will *prevent* patentability (*See* Table 14-2).

## Table 14-2

|  | Anticipation Events  Will defeat an applicant's claim for patent if they occur at any time prior to invention | Statutory Bar Events  Will defeat an applicant's claim for patent if they occur more than 12 months prior to application |
|---|---|---|
| **Domestic** | Prior patent by anyone | Prior patent by anyone |
|  | Description in a printed publication | Description in a printed publication |
|  | Invention known or used by others | Public use or sale |
|  | Description in another's previously filed and eventually granted application | |
|  | Abandonment of the invention by the applicant him or herself | |
|  | Unabandoned, unsuppressed, and unconcealed invention by others | |
| **Foreign** | Prior patent by anyone | Prior patent by anyone |
|  | Description in a printed publication | Description in a printed publication |
|  | | Prior patent application by the applicant (if a patent is granted prior to domestic application) |

Note that the events listed in the table are limited by the "principle of substantial identity." In other words, to defeat an application for a patent, the prior knowledge, use, or other event must be substantially similar to the applicant's invention so as to qualify as a "disclosure" of the process or product. The test for "substantial identity" (substantial similarity) and "disclosure" is whether enough of the invention has already been disclosed so that a person skilled in the applicable art can duplicate the product or process. The one exception to this test is public use of the invention. Public use need not disclose the invention's secrets but only the benefits of the invention itself. Such public use need not be extensive.

Adding another wrinkle to this discussion is the requirement that the anticipation events raise not only substantial identity to the invention, but also realization of the anticipating events themselves. In other words, the anticipation must be so intentional or noticed that it can be duplicated. For example, if prior knowledge or use of an invention goes unnoticed, then it cannot be considered anticipatory to bar patentability upon later application. On the other hand, if a person is conscious of the existence of a process or a product, an anticipation has occurred, regardless of whether he or she has realized the novelty or utility. This turn of events may occur quite often in a university lab, where students discover new and useful products without realizing it. Imagine a case where a graduate student or postdoctoral student in one of the sciences creates or discovers a new, useful, and nonobvious composition of matter but assumes that the discovery has been made by much more experienced researchers in the past and that, as a new student, he or she would certainly not be "first in line" if a patent race were to start. Even so, realization of the product itself would be an anticipation event that may later bar a patent application by someone else, while chance discoveries without realization of their existence are not anticipation events.[117]

Some discussion of what it means for a process or product to be "described in a printed publication" is necessary here. The basic principle behind the statutory bar of a patent for information described in a printed publication is that such printed information may already be in the public domain (for patent purposes, not for copyright purposes), even against the claims of the true inventor. In other words, if the invention is described in a printed publication at anytime prior to *invention* or more than twelve months prior to a patent *application*, the patent application will be rejected. *In re Marshall W. Cronyn* provides an example.[118] In *Cronyn*, the Court of Appeals for the Federal Circuit held that senior theses written by undergraduates at Reed College as a requirement for their graduation did not constitute "printed publications" for patent purposes and, therefore, did not bar the application for patent more than one year after the thesis at issue was written.[119] In order for a publication to be considered "printed" for patent purposes, it must be "sufficiently accessible to the public interested in the art."[120] Dissemination and public accessibility are crucial to this determination. In *Cronyn*, the papers were catalogued, rather informally, in the college's library and in each student's department. This administrative set-up did not qualify as "accessibility."[121] Furthermore, an oral defense of a thesis in front of three faculty committee members is not sufficient for dissemination.[122]

In the race to patent an invention, priority claims are common. Patent law, at its core, promotes the progress of science and the useful arts and will grant patents to those who claim first and rightful invention to useful, novel, and nonobvious processes and products. The law will not reward slow movement in such matters, as a delay in application may be evidence of an inventor's attempt to extend the patent period and to delay the introduction of a useful product to the public. As a result, the law requires reasonable diligence on the part of an inventor.

But what about the case where the delay in application is not due to an attempt to extend the twenty-year exclusive rights but where the university or faculty member is merely attempting to strike the most lucrative financial deal in advance of application? Moreover, delays in patent application are sometimes due to faculty researcher workload with other projects. These issues were discussed in *Griffith v. Kanamaru*.[123] Griffith was a professor of biochemistry at Cornell University where he invented a compound useful in the treatment of diabetes. He conceived the invention in June 1981 and reduced it to practice in January 1984. Meanwhile, Kanamaru, a chemist employed at Takeda Chemical Industries, applied in November 1982 for a patent for the same invention. In response to Griffith's application for a patent, the Board of Patent Appeals and Interferences asked Griffith to show priority, e.g., reason for the delay in application.[124] Griffith cited two reasons. First, he was attempting to acquire external funding for the patent work. Second, he was waiting for a particular graduate student to enroll at Cornell.[125] The court rejected both arguments. In effect, holding onto a patent application until the best funding and/or the best graduate research assistants are available will rarely constitute reasonable diligence. "The reasonable diligence standard balances the interest in rewarding and encouraging invention with the public's interest in the earliest possible disclosure of innovation."[126] The court stated that Cornell University had "consciously chosen to assume the risk that priority in the invention might be lost to an outside inventor."[127]

The requirements for nonobviousness of subject matter are codified in section 103 of the Act. Nonobviousness requires that the differences between the current invention and the prior art be significant enough that they would not have been obvious to a person with ordinary skill in the art to which the subject matter pertains.[128]

## Ownership and Patentees' Rights

Under section 154 of the Patent Act, patentees have "the right to exclude others from making, using, offering for sale, or selling the invention throughout the United States or importing the invention into the United States, and, if the invention is a process, ... the right to exclude others from using, offering for sale or selling throughout the United States, or importing into the United States, products made by the process."[129] The grant of a patent is not the right to use the invention—the inventor already has that right—it is the right to exclude others from using it. Furthermore, the patentee is not obligated to put the invention to practice during the period of his or her monopoly.[130]

Upon the expiration of the twenty-year patent term, the patented article becomes public property. While royalties and other assignment contracts are popular between patentees and licensees, patentees are not permitted to extend the term of patent through the use of such agreements, as doing so would be against the public policy and the constitutional inspiration of patent law.[131] Commercial success cannot revive a patent monopoly.[132]

Under section 116, when two or more persons make an invention, they must apply for the patent jointly. Joint inventors are not required to work together physically or at the same time, nor must they make the same type or size contributions. Finally, each joint inventor need not have contributed to each claim on the application. If a joint inventor refuses to join in an application for a patent or cannot be reached after diligent effort, the remaining inventor(s) may attach that colleague's name on the application in his or her behalf. Similarly, if an inventor is either named or not named on an application as the result of an unintentional error, the Director of the United States Patent Office may amend the application as needed. Regarding the rights of joint owners of a patent, each joint owner "may make, use, offer for sale, or sell the patented invention within the United States, or import the patented invention into the United States, without the consent of and without accounting to the other owners."[133]

*University of Colorado v. American Cyanamid* provides useful information to college and university personnel involved in collaborative research work. Two medical school professors won a claim against American Cyanamid after another doctor in Cyanamid clandestinely obtained a confidential paper written by the professors and submitted the results in a patent application.[134] In the application, the doctor from Cyanamid claimed sole inventorship. In fact, the applicant was not one of the inventors at all. Per his request, the university professors had conducted research studies on one of the company's products. A federal district court held for the plaintiffs on a claim of unjust enrichment under state law. The court of appeals affirmed.[135]

## Policymaking and Institutional Ownership Rights

Patentees have the right, just as they would with any personal property, to assign property rights to other persons or entities, including the rights to make, sell, and use patented articles.[136] Assignment of rights is popular in colleges and universities as educational institutions draft and enforce intellectual property policies. These rights may be assigned or licensed in whole or in part.[137] For example, a university policy may require the taking of 50 percent of the net income from the invention of a faculty researcher,[138] or it may adopt a sliding scale where the university takes various percentages of the income, depending on the dollar amount.[139] Universities have to be clear in their policymaking, for the income that is derived from a patent does not emanate merely from its initial grant. There are marketing and licensing agreements and future research work with the invention (e.g., new tests, amendments, improvements, etc.). Similarly, faculty and student inventors must be aware of the policies. Even policies that grant percentage of "net income" may be limited if the full ownership of the patent remains with the university.[140]

Patent litigation in higher education often involves the relationships between faculty and student researchers and their institutions. What may seem like harmless and quietly effective patent policies could become loud and harsh when money and business (and ego, perhaps) take over. An important lesson to be learned here is that all faculty members (and student employees who engage in the production of intellectual property as part of their employment) sign on to their university's intellectual property policies when they sign their contracts. No special contract needs to be signed for the intellectual property policies to take effect.[141] Particularly instructive is the policy from West Virginia University (WVU), at issue in *University of West Virginia v. Vanvoorhies.*[142] Under the policy,

> [T]he University owns worldwide right, title and interest in any invention made at least in part by University personnel, or with substantial use of University resources, and unless otherwise agreed, this Policy applies to any invention conceived or first reduced to practice under terms of contracts, grants or other agreements.[143]

The WVU Policy defines "university personnel" as "all full-time and part-time members of the faculty and staff, and all other employees of the University including graduate and undergraduate students and fellows of the University." In *Vanvoorhies*, a WVU graduate student who became a post-doctorate instructor, also at WVU, refused to assign the rights to two inventions to the University. WVU sued and won. Similar breaches of contract claims occur when faculty members refuse to assign their rights under intellectual property policies,[144] or when the researchers feel they have been inadequately served by their universities.[145]

In a case involving alleged violations of university patent policy, Professor John B. Fenn filed suit against Yale University for conversion, theft, tortious interference with business relationships, and violation of Connecticut unfair trade laws.[146] Yale counter-claimed with an action for breach of contract. The lawsuit stemmed from an invention developed while Fenn was working at Yale.[147] Under Yale policy, all researchers were required to notify Yale first of any invention. Yale then works with the Research Corporation to carry out the patent and commercialization processes.[148] Unless otherwise agreed between the parties, Yale gets ownership of the inventions, the Research Corporation gets the titles to the patents, and the inventors get to share in the licensing royalties. Fenn had a long-standing disagreement with Yale's policies and made this fact known (as the percentage of royalties granted to professors decreased over the years with policy amendments). When Fenn developed his invention in mass spectrometry, he did not give the university first notice. Instead, he presented it in a paper at a national convention. Furthermore, Fenn discouraged Yale from pursuing the patent and significantly downplayed the commercial value of the invention. All the while, Fenn applied for and received the patent with the support of private companies with whom Fenn was to license the invention. A federal district court rejected Fenn's claims and found in favor of Yale on its breach of contract counterclaim.

Researchers and universities are not the only plaintiffs in higher education patent cases. In another case with disputed patent ownership, the Du Pont Company filed suit against a faculty researcher to enforce a contract it had with Washington State University (WSU), where the professor worked and helped to discover a gene important to fat metabolism.[149] Under WSU's patent policy, the university is the owner of patents developed by employees as a result of their employment. Although the professor notified both his home university and Du Pont of his discovery, he claimed that he was the rightful owner since the discovery occurred while he was working in a lab at another university. The court disagreed and found that the two central contracts at issue, the university policy and the license agreement between Washington State University and Du Pont, declared Du Pont the owner of the patent and licensing opportunities. As intelligent as higher education personnel are, there are many who are unfamiliar with the policies that affect their most outstanding creations and discoveries. This is not to say that colleges and universities do not have legitimate interests in their faculty members' creations. But it is to say that balances must be struck and education must be offered so that the parties are fully aware of their responsibilities.[150]

## Patent Infringement and Remedies

Patent infringement can be direct, indirect, or contributory. Anyone who, without permission, makes, uses, or sells the patented invention is a direct infringer of the patent.[151] Direct infringement can be committed innocently. If a person actively encourages another to infringe the patent, then he or she is an indirect infringer.[152] Contributory infringement occurs when a person sells or supplies a component of a patented product or an apparatus for use in practicing a patented process, knowing that the component constitutes a material part of the invention and/or is especially adapted for use in an infringement.[153] In most cases of direct or indirect infringement, there is no defense for good faith or ignorance of the patent. However, a patent owner is required to mark a product with a notice of patent or to provide actual notice of the patent to an infringer.[154]

There are only a few statutory defenses to infringement. In infringement cases, the patent and each of its claims independently are presumed to be valid. These presumptions are rebuttable, nonetheless, with evidence of invalidity (e.g., lack of novelty, utility, or nonobviousness). The defendant may also produce evidence of nonfringement, absence of liability, or unenforceability of the patent. The final statutory defense is a recent enactment. Under section 273, adopted in 1999, a defendant may argue that he or she, acting in good faith, actually reduced the subject matter of the patent to practice at least one year before the effective filing date of the patent at issue and commercially used the subject matter before the effective filing date.

Section 281 of the Act gives patentees the right to enforce intellectual property rights in a civil action. A court, for example, may grant an injunction to halt the infringement.[155] Furthermore, monetary damages in an amount adequate to compensate for the infringement may be awarded.[156] Damages must be in an amount at least as much as a reasonable royalty fee for the use made of the invention by the infringer. The court may hear expert testimony to determine damages and/or what the reasonable royalty would be and has the power to grant treble damages when it is shown that the plaintiff was damaged beyond the reasonable royalty rate.[157] Finally, a court may award attorneys fees in exceptional cases.[158]

## Trademarks

> In the fall of 1982, when the fancy of Georgia sports fans turned to thoughts of college football, Bill Laite Distributing Co., a Macon, Georgia wholesaler of novelty beers, began marketing "Battlin' Bulldog Beer." The beer was sold in red-and-black cans bearing the portrayal of an English bulldog wearing a red sweater emblazoned with a black "G." The Bulldog had bloodshot eyes, a football tucked under its right "arm," and a frothy beer stein in his left "hand."
>
> Laite hoped that the "Battlin' Bulldog" would pile up yardage and score big points in the always-competitive alcoholic beverage market. Unfortunately, however, the pug-faced pooch was thrown for a loss by the University of Georgia Athletic Association, ... which obtained preliminary and permanent injunctive relief in federal district court based on the likelihood of confusion between the "Battlin' Bulldog" and the "University of Georgia Bulldog."[159]

In a typical college trademark infringement case, the Court of Appeals for the Eleventh Circuit upheld the University of Georgia's injunctive relief with this vivid replay of the facts. Collegiate trademarking and licensing of goods and services is a booming business. Without trademark protection for its words, symbols, and slogans, this business would not be nearly as lucrative for higher education institutions. With such protection, this business, like any similar competitive arena, remains rather litigious.

Unlike patents and copyrights, there is no parallel constitutional provision referring to the promotion or protection of trademarks. The closest constitutional guideline is the commerce clause, which permits Congress to regulate interstate commerce. The legal protection of trademarks protects the public from confusion and protects the trademark owner from losing his/her market. Specifically, the intent of the current trademark act, the Lanham Act[160] is to make "actionable the deceptive and misleading use of marks" in commerce; "to protect persons engaged in such commerce against unfair competition; [and] to prevent fraud and deception in such commerce by the use of reproductions, copies, counterfeits, or colorable imitations of registered marks."[161]

While the commonplace term used is "trademark," the use of the word "mark," protected by the federal Lanham Act and individual state statutes, refers to trademarks, service marks, certification marks, and collective marks. A "trademark" includes "any word, name, symbol, or device, or any combination thereof used ... to identify and distinguish [a person's] goods ... from those manufactured or sold by others and to indicate the source of the goods."[162] Service marks are similar to trademarks but identify and distinguish services instead of goods. Certification marks allow an organization to indicate that goods or services meet certain quality standards or regional standards and exclude all others from making the same claim with the same or similar marks that might cause confusion. Finally, collective marks are trademarks or service marks used by groups to identify membership in those groups. A fine example of a collective mark in higher education is a university's alumni association.[163]

### Distinctiveness, Priority, and Trademark Registration

The primary requirement for trademark protection is distinctiveness—to serve the function of identifying the goods and avoiding confusion, deception, or mistake. Distinctiveness allows the trademark registrant to object to a later user of the same or similar mark. There is a significant exception though. The rule of "priority" that often favors the first user over others does not apply when the second use was established in good faith in a different geographical market. If a distant second user has no notice of the first mark and acts in good faith and there is no confusion or other deception, then the second user may prevail in an infringement claim.[164] Priority is codified in section 1052 of the Lanham Act. An applicant for a trademark will not obtain the rights if the use of the mark by the applicant is likely to cause confusion, mistake, or deceit with another existing mark. Actual evidence of confusion, mistake, or deceit is not required—only *likelihood.* In determining likelihood of confusion, the similarity of the marks, similarity of the goods and/or services, the area and manner of concurrent use of the competing marks, and wrongful intent are important factors.

Also significant to this discussion is the effect federal registration has on priority claims. Under section 1072 of the Act, the owner of a federally registered trademark can claim nationwide constructive notice. With this claim, everyone is presumed to have notice of the mark; in other words, there is no good faith defense in such circumstances. "If the mark at issue is federally registered and has become incontestable, the validity, legal protection, and ownership are proved."[165] In addition to the bar on registration for marks similar to those of others, there is also a bar against geographic marks,[166] immoral marks,[167] and surnames.[168] Of these three, the most applicable to this chapter is the bar on geographic marks. Geographic marks are typically the proper names for geographic entities, like nations, states, counties, cities, rivers, and lakes, and are often found in college and university names.

There are, generally, four types of marks: generic, descriptive, suggestive, and arbitrary or fanciful.[169] Suggestive and arbitrary marks are the easiest to register and protect because they are typically the most distinctive. For a higher education example, in *Board of Trustees of the University of Arkansas v. Razorback Sports and Physical Therapy Clinic*, the University of Arkansas filed suit against the Razorback Sports and Physical Therapy Clinic, alleging trademark infringement, unfair competition, and dilution of trademark.[170] In finding for the university, the court held, in part, that the term "Razorback" was not a geographic term. In fact, the court found the term "Razorback" to be "arbitrary" for trademark purposes (i.e., not directly descriptive of the goods and services provided), giving the term more strength as a trademark. According to the court, "the resultant identification of a geographic region with a collegiate mark never becomes so strong that it negates the primary identification of the mark with the University, at least not here in Arkansas."[171] Similar arguments can be made for colleges and collegiate mascots that bear the popular nickname of the state—for example, Ohio State Buckeyes, Wisconsin Badgers, and Nebraska Cornhuskers.[172]

Registration is easier for "arbitrary" words and pictures than it is for descriptive words and pictures; arbitrary marks can be more easily identified with the one good or service and, as a result, less confused with other goods and services bearing similar or identical marks. For a geographic mark and other descriptive marks to be registrable, it must be established that consumers associate the mark with a single source for the product.[173] Essentially, such a mark would have to acquire what the law terms "secondary meaning," where the public comes to associate the mark with the product synonymously or by "second nature." As one court stated:

> Secondary meaning converts a word originally incapable
> of serving as a mark into a full fledged trademark.... An
> arbitrary, fanciful, or otherwise distinctive word qualifies as
> a trademark immediately, because in the particular industry
> it has no primary meaning to overcome.[174]

Generally, for a trademark to withstand competition from an allegedly infringing mark, proof of secondary meaning is not required for arbitrary and fanciful marks but must be shown for descriptive marks.[175] Secondary meaning is typically shown through long exclusive use of a mark in the relevant market, size or public prominence of the institution, and success of the institution's promotional efforts. The decision in *President and Trustees of Colby College v. Colby College-New Hampshire* provides an example.[176] In *Colby College*, the court held that the defendant's name change from "Colby Junior College for Women" to "Colby College-New Hampshire" infringed the trademark held by Colby College, a four-year institution in Waterville, Maine, that had been conducting business under that name since 1899. Essentially, the vast majority of the public exclusively identified the name "Colby College" with the one in Maine and not the one in New Hampshire.[177] According to the court, "[t]here is sufficient secondary meaning as long as a significant quantity of the consuming public understand a name as referring exclusively to the appropriate party, for it is undesirable that such a quantity be deceived even if some, relatively small, number is not."[178]

Before moving to more formal discussions of unfair competition and trademark infringement, three additional factors for trademark registration are relevant here. For a mark to be registrable, it must actually be used to identify the goods or services. In other words, identification and distinctiveness must be the primary purposes for the mark. Sometimes, the "trade dress"—a device, name, or design that accompanies the goods—is also registrable, if it serves those primary purposes. In addition, a device that is solely functional or utilitarian cannot be registered as a mark. Goods having such a device could not be identified and distinguished from other goods performing that function because those other goods would have that same device. Finally, and nicely applicable to the identity (and sometimes distinctiveness) of colleges and universities, is color. Color alone will not normally earn trademark protection. Most often, the color will have to combine with some device or design for which color is an integral part in order to gain protection. [179] But if the design is not that complex and the colors are few, then trademark protection will be denied.[180]

## Trademark Infringement and Unfair Competition

Lanham Act claims generally fall into two categories. First is a claim for infringement of the plaintiff's service marks or trademarks.[181] There are three elements of a cause of action for infringement: (1) the mark is valid and legally protectable; (2) the mark is owned by the plaintiff; and (3) defendant's use of the mark to identify its goods or services is likely to cause confusion regarding the source or sponsorship of its goods and services.[182] Second is a claim for unfair competition.[183] The elements of a cause of action for unfair competition are identical to those for infringement, except that they apply to unregistered marks, which are protectable if they are found to be distinctive. Unfair competition claims may also take the form of claims for false advertising.[184]

"The touchstone of trademark infringement is likelihood of confusion."[185] Several factors are analyzed in a determination of likely confusion, and courts differ as to the number of factors and the specific wording of them. But the following list is representative and comprehensive:[186]

(1)  the degree of similarity between the owner's mark and the alleged infringer's mark (e.g., with respect to appearance, sound, connotation, and impression);

(2)  the strength of the owner's mark;

(3)  the price of the goods and other factors indicative of the care and attention expected of consumers when making a purchase;[187]

(4)  the length of time the defendant has used the alleged similar mark without evidence of actual confusion;

(5)  evidence of actual confusion;

(6)  intent, or lack thereof, of alleged infringer to pass off the trademark owner as the source or sponsor of the goods;[188]

(7)  the degree to which the products are in competition with one another (the similarity of "trade channels" and "competitive proximity");

(8)  the extent to which the targets of the parties' sales efforts are the same;

(9)  similarity of the goods or services in the minds of the public; and

(10)  variety of goods with which the mark is used.

All other things being equal, the more similar the marks, the more likely a finding of confusion. Likewise, the more distinctive a mark, the higher its "strength" and less likely a finding of confusion. Similarity of a mark can come from a variety of directions: physical design; sounds; psychological, commercial, or social connotations and significance; color scheme; or linguistic characteristics. When similar sounding marks are involved, for example, the inquiry is whether purchases are made under circumstances in which sound is more important than design, appearance, or spelling. This includes whether advertising is regularly done on radio and/or whether orders are typically offered by telephone.

Recall also that the law will provide trademark protection more often for a "fanciful or arbitrary" word or phrase (one that, in words alone, is rather distinctive) than it will for a word or phrase common to everyday language. In *Trustees of Columbia University v. Columbia/HCA Health-care Corporation*, for example, the court rejected Columbia University's infringement claim against a major health care and hospital system, in part because the defendant presented substantial evidence of "third-party use" of the name Columbia.[189] In other words, the word "Columbia" is used in connection with a variety of businesses, including but not limited to health care and education, and has been for years. Such evidence of third-party use will detract from the "strength" of the trademark and lean the case away from a finding of infringement. According to one court, "the use of collegiate marks by local businesses as part of their trade names is an old and venerable tradition."[190] But according to another, "[t]he strength of a mark is a measure of its tendency to identify the goods or services sold under the mark as emanating from a particular ... source."[191] Strength depends ultimately on the mark's distinctiveness or its "origin-indicating quality." In addition to the arbitrary nature of the mark and the evidence of third-party use, other indicia for strength of a mark include the presumptive validity of federal registrations; long-term use of the marks; extensive public exposure through advertising, promotion and unsolicited publicity; and the owner's actions to prevent infringement with cease and desist letters.[192]

Actual confusion, as a factor to weigh in a trademark infringement claim, is not required for a plaintiff's success.[193] However, it naturally does not hurt a claim.[194] Similarly, evidence of intentional infringement of a trademark is a near guarantee for injunction and/or damages. But, as Miller and Davis[195] wisely state, intentional infringement may not occur in an effort to take over the market of a trademark or service mark owner. An innocent infringer who is notified of a competing mark may continue to infringe, even with the notice, not to damage the investments of the mark's owner but rather to protect his/her own investments.

On the similarity of the markets, trade channels, and competitive proximity, if the plaintiff and the defendant actually do provide the same services and compete for the same customers, then the trademark owner deserves protection "so that it does not lose confused customers ... and so that people do not think they are receiving goods and services from the owner when they are, in fact, receiving them from the infringer."[196] Of particular importance today is the Internet as a trade channel. Seemingly different products and services from two different providers in vastly different geographic markets could still result in a finding of similar trade channels if the parties depend, at least in part, on the Internet for advertising and sales. In *Board of Regents of the University of Georgia v. Buzas Baseball, Inc.*, the court denied summary judgment motions and found a dispute of fact on whether the defendant's Salt Lake City minor league baseball mascot, "Buzzy," is confusingly similar to the Georgia Tech Yellow Jacket's mascot, "Buzz."[197]

Of course, similar marks (in sound, design, appearance, or impression) may not be infringing when the goods and/or services offered are not at all similar. The real test is whether the marks will confuse relevant consumers. Goods and services are considered similar if they serve the same purposes or fulfill the same needs. Additionally, what may be particularly important to the discussion of similarity and confusion of marks in higher education are not only the similarity or the marks or the goods themselves, but also the similarity of the markets for these goods. Despite differences in goods and services and their markets, consumers may tend to associate different goods if there is a public expectation that the goods came from the same source, say, a university.[198] But this is a balancing act. On one hand, the "related goods" doctrine should favor the owner of the mark if there is a likelihood that the owner's business will be harmed by the "relationship" it has with the infringing mark. On the other hand, the law does not usually tolerate such monopolies.

There are defenses available in trademark infringement cases. They come with significant challenges, however. Recall that formal registration of a trademark carries with it the presumption of validity, meaning that infringement cases begin in favor of the registrant.[199] Even with this presumption, though, the equitable doctrines of laches, estoppel, and unclean hands are applicable. Laches consists of two essential elements: (1) inexcusable delay in instituting the suit and (2) prejudice resulting to the defendant from such delay. In the noteworthy case, *University of Pittsburgh v. Champion Products*, the University of Pittsburgh filed suit against Champion Products for trademark infringement.[200] Champion had sold "Pitt" merchandise—clothing with university words, pictures, and slogans—for decades. For much of that time, Champion produced the merchandise and sold it in off campus locations. In 1980, however, at the height of Pitt's national football notoriety, the university realized its national market and registered its trade and service marks. Pitt then asked Champion to execute a licensing agreement; Champion refused. In 1981, Pitt filed suit. On the first element of the laches defense, the court held that Pitt's delay in filing the suit was not inexcusable. Until Pitt became a national power in athletics, Pitt was unaware that Champion's market for such merchandise went well beyond the Pittsburgh area. On the second element, the court found that Champion had not relied to its detriment on Pitt's delay and rejected the laches defense. According to the court, this was not a typical infringement case where both parties are competitors in similar markets selling similar goods and confusion is the issue. There was no real consumer confusion here. "With negligible exception, a consumer does not desire a 'Champion' T-shirt, he (or she) desires a 'Pitt' T-shirt. The entire impetus for the sale is the consumer's desire to identify with Pitt. ... From this point of view, then, it is Champion which seeks to profit from Pitt's investment."[201] Estoppel is related to laches in that it depends on the defendant's reliance on the plaintiff's implied or active acceptance of the infringing conduct.[202] The doctrine of unclean hands means that "he who comes into equity must come with clean hands"—the plaintiff must act fairly in order to enjoin the defendant's conduct. Importantly, implied license in-fact can defeat equitable defenses, where the parties' conduct is as though they had executed a license for the defendant to use the applicable marks. In *Villanova University v. Villanova Alumni Educational Foundation*, Villanova University and the Villanova Educational Foundation (later the Villanova Alumni Educational Foundation) parties conducted similar fundraising businesses for several years with a verbal agreement, later a written agreement, and with full knowledge of the parties' activities.[203] When negotiations on a new agreement stalled, the University delivered cease and desist letters and filed suit.

In addition, fair and collateral use defenses are available. Fair use permits the utilization of a mark for a purpose other than that which the mark is normally used. In *Villanova*, the defendant offered a fair use defense, that it was using the term "Villanova Alumni" to *describe* its group, not to *mark its trade*. The court held that the use was not merely to describe, but also to acquire and maintain attention. The court held that fair-use doctrine applies when the public is not deceived and the mark is used "to tell the truth."[204] Collateral use permits an entity to make use of a trademark as a component of a larger item or project, as long as the entity identifies the mark as protected by trademark. There is a caution, though. The entity making use of the mark must not give the impression the trademark's owner is the sponsor of the larger item or project.

The remedies available for trademark infringement include (1) injunctive relief, (2) an accounting for profits, (3) damages, (4) attorney's fees in "exceptional cases," and (5) costs.[205] Injunction is common in trademark infringement cases. But it is necessary to enjoin only illegitimate infringement and still permit legitimate competition. Accounting for profits allows a successful plaintiff to recover lost profits that resulted from the infringement. But the plaintiff need not show that the defendant's profits directly competed with the plaintiff's sales. This remedy supports the public interest in preventing unfair competition. Damages are in addition to the accounting for profits. Courts are permitted to award up to three times the amount of any demonstrated actual damages, pursuant to the statutory language, which states that damages must act as compensation for loss to the plaintiff and not as penalty to the defendant.

### Domain Names and Protection of Trademarks in Cyberspace

Protection of trademarks and service marks used by colleges and universities has recently moved into cyberspace. In 1999, Congress passed the Anti-Cybersquatting Consumer Protection Act (ACPA).[206] The ACPA amended the Lanham Act to protect registered "domain names"—"alphanumeric designation[s] which [are] registered with or assigned by any domain name registrar, domain name registry, or other domain name registration authority as part of an electronic address on the Internet."[207] Under the ACPA, any person who registers a domain name that is identical or substantially and confusingly similar to the name of another living person, without that person's consent, and with the specific intent to profit from such name, is liable in a civil action.[208] There is an exception for the person who registers the name as part of a copyrighted work protected under copyright law. In an action under the ACPA, a court may award injunctive relief, requiring the defendant to shut down the site or to transfer the domain name to the plaintiff. Attorneys' fees are also available.[209]

## Endnotes

1. U.S. CONST. art. I, § 8.
2. 17 U.S.C. §§ 101, *et seq.*
3. Bleistein v. Donaldson Lithographing Co., 188 U.S. 239 (1903); Gross v. Seligman, 212 F. 930 (2d Cir. 1914).
4. *See, e.g.,* Educ. Testing Serv. v. Katzman, 793 F.2d 533 (3d Cir. 1986).
5. Under 17 U.S.C. § 101, a "phonorecord" is a material object in which sounds (other than those accompanying an audiovisual work) are fixed and from which sounds can be perceived, reproduced, or communicated. Examples are LPs, cassettes, and compact discs.
6. 17 U.S.C. § 102.
7. 17 U.S.C. § 103.
8. 17 U.S.C. § 102(b). *See also* Mazer v. Stein, 347 U.S. 201, 217 (1954).
9. 17 U.S.C. § 117. *See also* Autoskill, Inc. v. Nat'l Educ. Support Sys., Inc., 994 F.2d 1476 (10th Cir.), cert. denied, 510 U.S. 916 (1993).
10. Applied Innovations, Inc. v. Regents of the Univ. of Minn., 786 F.2d 626 (8th Cir. 1989).
11. Raymond Nimmer, *Does Copyright Abridge the First Amendment Guarantees of Free Speech and Press?*, 17 U.C.L.A. L. REV. 1180, 1192-93 (1970).
12. 17 U.S.C. § 106. The Copyright Act examines the scope of particular exclusive rights according to the nature of the work: pictorial, graphic, and sculptural works (17 U.S.C. § 113); sound recordings (§ 114); distribution and performance of nondramatic musical works (§§ 115, 116); and noncommercial broadcasting (§ 118).
13. 17 U.S.C. § 201. *See also* the discussion below on ownership and duration of copyright.
14. 17 U.S.C. §§ 107-112, 117, 119.
15. 17 U.S.C. § 107.
16. College Entrance Examination Bd. v. Pataki, 889 F. Supp. 554, *modified on recons.,* 893 F. Supp. 152 (N.D.N.Y. 1995); Robinson v. Random House, Inc., 877 F. Supp. 830 (S.D.N.Y. 1995); Rubin v. Brooks/Cole Publ'g Co., 836 F. Supp. 909 (D. Mass. 1993); Ass'n of Am. Med. Colls. v. Mikaelian, 571 F. Supp. 144 (D. Pa. 1983).
17. 17 U.S.C. § 107.
18. 464 U.S. 417 (1984).
19. *Id.* at 425.
20. 471 U.S. 539 (1985).
21. *Id.* at 562.
22. 510 U.S. 569 (1994).

[23] Private uses are more often deemed fair uses than public uses are. *See, e.g.*, Sony Corp. of Am. v. Universal Studios, 464 U.S. 417 (1984) (use of VCRs to record television programs for home viewing is a fair use).

[24] *See, e.g.*, Henry Holt & Co. v. Liggett & Myers Tobacco Co. (1938) and Loew's Inc. v. Columbia Broad. Sys. (1955).

[25] 60 F.3d 913 (2d Cir. 1994).

[26] A & M Records, Inc., v. Napster, 239 F.3d 1004 (9th Cir. 2001).

[27] 571 F. Supp. 144 (D. Pa. 1983), *aff'd without op.*, 734 F.2d 3 (3d Cir. 1984).

[28] A national school tournament of academic games for students is a fair use of the games acquired from the plaintiff copyright holder. Allen v. Academic Games League of Am., 89 F.3d 614 (9th Cir. 1996).

[29] MacMillan v. King, 223 F. 862 (1914) (the court rejected the fair use defense from a teacher who copied substantial portions of an economics text for student use).

[30] Princeton Univ. Press v. Mich. Document Servs., Inc., 99 F.3d 1381 (6th Cir. 1996) and Basic Books, Inc. v. Kinko's Graphics Corp., 758 F. Supp. 1522 (S.D.N.Y. 1991).

[31] The district court judge in the *Kinko's* case, *supra* note 30, found a copyright violation but noted that the determination in such circumstances should remain case-by-case.

[32] Examples include form books and books of quotations. Copying is actually expected. *See, e.g.*, American Inst. of Architects v. Fenichel, 41 F. Supp. 146 (D.C. N.Y. 1941) (copying a form from a form book and delivering copies to six clients is a fair use).

[33] Eisenschiml v. Fawcett Publ'ns, Inc., 246 F.2d 598 (7th Cir. 1957) and Holdredge v. Knight Publ'g Corp., 214 F. Supp 921 (S.D. Cal. 1963).

[34] Rosemont Enters., Inc. v. Random House, Inc., 366 F.2d 303 (2d Cir. 1966), *cert. denied*, 385 U.S. 1009 (1967).

[35] 621 F.2d 57 (2d Cir. 1980).

[36] Salinger v. Random House, Inc., 811 F.2d 90 (2d Cir. 1987).

[37] Harper & Row, Publishers, Inc. v. Nation Enters., 471 U.S. 539 (1985).

[38] Lish v. Harper's Magazine Found., 807 F. Supp. 1090 (S.D.N.Y. 1993).

[39] Campbell v. Acuff-Rose Music, 510 U.S. 569 (1994).

[40] Consumers Union of U.S., Inc. v. Gen. Signal Corp., 724 F.2d 1044 (2d Cir. 1983), *cert. denied*, 469 U.S. 823 (1984).

[41] Maxtone-Graham v. Burtchaell, 803 F.2d 1253 (2d Cir. 1986), *cert. denied*, 481 U.S. 1059 (1987).

[42] Marcus v. Rowley, 695 F.2d 1171 (9th Cir. 1983)

[43] Salinger v. Random House, 811 F.2d 90 (2d Cir.), *cert. denied*, 484 U.S. 890 (1987).

[44] 506 F. Supp. 554 (D.D.C. 1981).

[45] Diamond v. Am.-Law Pub. Corp., 745 F.2d 142 (2d Cir. 1984).

[46] H.C. Wainwright & Co. v. Wall Street Transcript Corp., 558 F.2d 91 (2d Cir. 1977); Marcus v. Rowley, 695 F.2d 1171 (9th Cir. 1983); Harper & Row, Publishers, Inc. v. Nation Enters., 471 U.S. 539 (1987).

[47] Robertson v. Batten, Barton, Durstine, and Osborn, Inc., 146 F. Supp. 795 (D. Cal. 1956).

[48] *See, e.g.*, Campbell v. Acuff-Rose Music, 510 U.S. 569 (1994) and Fisher v. Dees, 794 F.2d 432 (9th Cir. 1986).

[49] Suntrust Bank v. Houghton Mifflin Co., 268 F.3d 1257 (11th Cir. 2001).

[50] 471 U.S. 539 (1985).

[51] Lack of monetary damages from defendant's use does not validate the fair use defense. Marcus v. Rowley, 695 F.2d 1171 (9th Cir. 1983).

[52] Campbell v. Acuff-Rose Music, 510 U.S. 569 (1994)

[53] In Acuff-Rose, the challenged parody was a piece of rap music with a different market from the source work, a classic rock ballad.

[54] New Era Publ'ns Int'l v. Carol Pub. Group, 904 F.2d 152 (2d Cir.); *stay denied*, 497 U.S. 1054, *cert. denied*, 498 U.S. 921 (1990) (critical biography of L. Ron Hubbard). *See also* Higgins v. Detroit Educ. TV Found., 4 F. Supp. 2d 701 (E.D. Mich. 1998)

(Use of short excerpts of plaintiff's music in anti-violence videos was fair and not damaging to plaintiff's market). *But see* Craft v. Kobler, 667 F. Supp. 2d 120 (S.D.N.Y. 1987) (Court held that defendant's use of quotations from earlier works was too extensive).

55  American Geophysical Union v. Texaco, Inc., 60 F.3d 913 (2d Cir. 1994) (Archiving is not a transformative use; copying deprives the publisher of revenue).

56  Encyclopaedia Britannica Ed. Corp. v. Crooks, 542 F. Supp. 1156 (W.D.N.Y. 1982).

57  Educational Testing Servs. v. Katzman, 793 F.2d 533 (3d Cir. 1986).

58  Princeton Univ. Press v. Mich. Document Servs., 99 F.3d 1381 (6th Cir. 1996), *cert. denied*, 117 S. Ct. 1336 (1997).

59  239 F.3d 1004 (9th Cir. 2001).

60  17 U.S.C. § 108.

61  The rights of reproduction and distribution under section 108 do not apply to a musical work; a pictorial, graphic, or sculptural work; or a motion picture or other audiovisual work other than an audiovisual work dealing with news.

62  420 U.S. 376 (1975).

63  17 U.S.C. § 110.

64  Mediated instructional activities are defined as "activities that use copyrighted materials … integral to the class experience, controlled by or under the actual supervision of the instructor and analogous to the type of performance and display that would take place in a live classroom."

65  Examples of protections universities can implement are passwords, PINs, and time-sensitive access.

66  The ownership of a copyright may be transferred in whole or in part, and may be bequeathed by will. Similarly, any of the exclusive rights comprised in a copyright may be transferred and owned separately.

67  490 U.S. 730, 751-752 (1989)

68  Of course, students and their works can be subjected to the *Reid* balancing test, as well, with much of the work completed by students as teaching, research, and administrative assistants also constituting works for hire.

69  847 F.2d 412 (7th Cir. 1988).

70  273 Cal. App. 2d 726, 78 Cal. Rptr. 542 (1969).

71  57 Wash. L. Rep. 286 (1929).

72  *See* Sunil Kulkarni, *All Professors Create Equally: Why Faculty Should Have Complete Control over the Intellectual Property Rights in their Creations*, 47 HASTINGS L. J. 221 (1995).

73  17 U.S.C. §§ 301-304.

74  Lolly Gasaway, *When U.S. Works Pass into the Public Domain, at* http://www.unc. edu/~unclng/public-d.htm. Per Gasaway, the chart may be freely duplicated or linked to for nonprofit purposes. No permission needed. Please include web address on all reproductions of chart so recipients know where to find any updates.

75  17 U.S.C. §§ 408, 409.

76  17 U.S.C. §§ 401, 402.

77  17 U.S.C. § 412.

78  17 U.S.C. § 501.

79  *See, e.g.,* Playboy Enters., Inc. v. Frena, 839 F. Supp. 1552 (M.D. Fla. 1993); Sega Enters., Ltd. v. Maphia, 857 F. Supp. 679 (N.D. Cal. 1994); and ALS Scan, Inc. v. RemarQ Cmtys., Inc., 239 F.3d 619 (4th Cir. 2001).

80  *See, e.g.,* A & M Records, Inc. v. Napster, Inc., 239 F.3d 1004 (9th Cir. 2001); *and In re* Aimster, 334 F.3d 643 (7th Cir. 2003).

81  *See, e.g., In re* Aimster, 334 F.3d 643 (7th Cir. 2003) and Lowry's Reports, Inc. v. Legg Mason, Inc., 271 F. Supp. 2d 737 (D. Md. 2003).

82  17 U.S.C. § 502.

83  17 U.S.C. § 503.

84 17 U.S.C. § 504.

85 Statutory damages must not be less than $750 or more that $30,000 with respect to the infringement of any one work. Courts also have the power to increase statutory damages in cases where the infringement was willful or to decrease the damages in cases of "innocent" infringement, where the infringer had no reason to believe that his/her action was infringing.

86 17 U.S.C. § 505.

87 17 U.S.C. § 106.

88 Computer programs and the hypertext used to create and maintain web sites are copyrightable publications.

89 *See, e.g.*, A & M Records, Inc. v. Napster, Inc., 239 F.3d 1004 (9th Cir. 2001), discussed above.

90 17 U.S.C. §§ 1201-1204.

91 17 U.S.C. § 512.

92 17 U.S.C. § 512(e).

93 17 U.S.C. § 1201(d)-(j).

94 17 U.S.C. §§ 1203-1204. Criminal liability exists, as well. But nonprofit libraries, archives, and educational institutions are exempt from criminal liability under the DMCA.

95 17 U.S.C. § 512.

96 Hendrickson v. Ebay, Inc., 165 F. Supp. 2d 1082 (C.D. Cal. 2001).

97 17 U.S.C. § 512(e).

98 Note that the Act is explicit with respect to its mention of *graduate* students instead of students in general. While undergraduate students may perform teaching and/or research functions as employees of a college or university, there is no mention of undergraduate students in the Act.

99 273 F.3d 429 (2d Cir. 2001).

100 *See also* United States v. Elcom Ltd., 203 F. Supp. 2d 1111 (N.D. Cal. 2002).

101 31 Cal. 4th 864, 878, 75 P.3d 1, 11 (2003).

102 Nos. 03-7015, 03-7053, 2003 U.S. App. LEXIS 25735 (D.C. Cir. Dec. 19, 2003).

103 239 F.3d 1004 (9th Cir. 2001).

104 334 F.3d 643 (7th Cir. 2003).

105 The alleged infringement occurred through peer-to-peer software (KaZaA).

106 334 F.3d at 653.

107 *See generally*, 35 U.S.C. §§ 1, *et seq.*

108 35 U.S.C. § 111.

109 35 U.S.C. § 154.

110 35 U.S.C. § 261.

111 Note that applications of ideas must meet the novelty, utility, and nonobviousness requirements of the Act. While the subjects of patents can be very technical and difficult to grasp, mere theoretical abstractions are not patentable.

112 There are some exceptions. To be patentable, an invention must be human-made: no naturally occurring substances are patentable. The products of them may be, however. In addition, printed matter is not patentable. The mere making or improving of a form does not warrant a patent. Finally, business methods are not patentable, no matter how "inventive" they may be.

113 35 U.S.C. § 161.

114 *See* ARTHUR R. MILLER AND MICHAEL H. DAVIS, INTELLECTUAL PROPERTY: PATENTS, TRADEMARKS, AND COPYRIGHT IN A NUTSHELL (1991).

115 35 U.S.C. § 171.

116 Unlike the twenty-year terms for other patents, the term for a design patent is 14 years. *See* 35 U.S.C. § 173.

117 *See* Standard Oil Co. (Ind.) v. Montedison, S.p.A., 664 F.2d 356 (3d Cir. 1981), as quoted in Miller and Davis, *supra* note 114, at 50-51, where the court held that junior

inventors were entitled to a claim for a crystalline form of polypropylene, despite "the inventors' failure to appreciate the product's crystallinity."

[118] 890 F.2d 1158 (Fed. Cir. 1989).

[119] Note that the professor/advisor to the student was the applicant for the patent. There was no discussion in the case about the potential ethical issues related to a faculty member applying for a patent on the basis of work produced by a student. Readers, however, are encouraged to consult university policies on the ethics of research and authorship. *See, e.g.*, *Ethical Standards of the American Educational Research Association*, EDUCATIONAL RESEARCHER (Oct. 1992), 23-26.

[120] 890 F.2d at 1160.

[121] *See also In re* Hall, 781 F.2d 897 (Fed. Cir. 1986) (dissertations were sufficiently and timely catalogued and shelved so as to be accessible).

[122] *See In re* Bayer, 568 F.2d 1357 (C.C.P.A. 1978). C.C.P.A. stands for the Court of Customs and Patent Appeals.

[123] 816 F.2d 624 (Fed. Cir. 1987).

[124] Pursuant to 35 U.S.C. § 135, priority questions go to the Board of Patent Appeals and Interferences for resolution. If a final decision from the Board is adverse to an applicant for a patent, then the decision shall constitute final refusal of the application. If the decision is adverse to a current patentee, then the decision shall constitute cancellation of the claims involved in the patent.

[125] The graduate student was not scheduled to enroll until the Fall of 1983.

[126] 816 F.2d at 626.

[127] *Id.* at 628.

[128] 35 U.S.C. § 103. To prevent a patent rejection on the basis of no nonobviousness, the law also requires certain biotechnological processes and their resultant compositions of matter to be patented either simultaneously in the same application or in separate applications with the same effective filing date.

[129] 35 U.S.C. § 135.

[130] Bement v. Nat'l Harrow Co., 186 U.S. 70 (1902).

[131] Brulotte v. Thys Co., 379 U.S. 29 (1964).

[132] H.D. Hudson Mfg. Co. v. Standard Oil Co., 60 F.2d 377 (8th Cir. 1932).

[133] 35 U.S.C. § 262.

[134] 342 F.3d 1298 (Fed. Cir. 2003).

[135] Note that unjust enrichment is not based in patent ownership or infringement, and is not preempted by patent law.

[136] 35 U.S.C. § 261.

[137] Zenith Radio Corp. v. Hazeltine Research, 395 U.S. 100 (1969).

[138] *See, e.g.*, Senkan v. Ill. Inst. of Tech., No. 93-2044, 1994 U.S. App. LEXIS 7201 (7th Cir., April 12, 1994).

[139] *See, e.g.,* Academic Charter for Bowling Green State University, § B-II.E(3) and (4), http://www.bgsu.edu/offices/facsenate/page471.html; and Policy on Patents and Copyrights for the Ohio State University, http://otl.osu.edu/documents/policy/Patent-CopyrightPolicy.pdf.

[140] *See, e.g.,* Senkan v. Ill. Inst. of Tech., No. 93-2044, 1994 U.S. App. LEXIS 7201 (7th Cir. April 12, 1994) (policy and practice of awarding the faculty inventor 50 percent of the invention's "net income" applied only to "patenting, marketing, licensing, protection or administering the invention," and not to future research grants that used the invention).

[141] *See, e.g.*, Chou v. The Univ. of Chi., 254 F.3d 1347 (Fed. Cir. 2001) (under Illinois law, a graduate student was obligated to assign her inventions to the university under the university's patent policy, even though no formal contract was signed requiring such assignment).

[142] 278 F.3d 1288 (Fed. Cir. 2002).

[143] *Id.* at 1292. Under the policy, 30 percent of the patent's net royalty income goes to the inventor.

[144] *See, e.g.,* Regents of the Univ. of N.M. v. Knight, 321 F.3d 1111 (Fed. Cir. 2003) (professors refused to assign ownership rights to the university for inventions resulting from cancer research; the university succeeded in a breach of contract claim against the professors).

[145] *See, e.g.,* Kucharczyk v. Regents of the Univ. of Cal., 48 F. Supp. 2d 964 (N.D. Cal. 1999) (professors filed unsuccessful breach of contract claim against their university to recover financial rewards of the patented medical device they developed. but the court held that licensing agreement between the university and a private corporation was not arbitrary and capricious).

[146] Fenn v. Yale Univ., 283 F. Supp. 2d 615 (D. Conn. 2003).

[147] The invention ultimately earned Fenn the 2002 Nobel Prize in Chemistry.

[148] It appears relatively common for universities to form affiliate companies to handle patenting, marketing, and licensing of patentable products and processes. *See also* ARCH Dev.Corp. v. Biomet, Inc., No. 02-C-9013, No. 03-C-2185, 2003 U.S. Dist. LEXIS 13118 (N.D. Ill. July 30, 2003) (ARCH is an affiliate of the University of Chicago).

[149] E.I. Du Pont de Nemours & Co. v. Okuley, 344 F.3d 578 (6th Cir. 2003).

[150] Inservices and workshops, perhaps at faculty orientations, are encouraged.

[151] 35 U.S.C. § 271(a).

[152] 35 U.S.C. § 271(b).

[153] 35 U.S.C. § 271(c).

[154] 35 U.S.C. § 287. The notice requirement has one important exception. The patent owner is not expected to provide notice on patented articles that have been reproduced by *other* infringers. As a result, the owner may recover damages even in cases where an infringement occurs through the use of an unmarked item.

[155] 35 U.S.C. § 283.

[156] 35 U.S.C. § 284. For a special provision on additional remedies for infringements of design patents, see 35 U.S.C. § 289.

[157] The court may also award reasonable interest and related costs.

[158] 35 U.S.C. § 285.

[159] University of Ga. Athletic Ass'n v. Laite, 756 F.2d 1535, 1536-1537 (11th Cir. 1985).

[160] 15 U.S.C. §§ 1051, *et seq.*

[161] 15 U.S.C. § 1127.

[162] *Id.*

[163] Villanova Univ. v. Villanova Alumni Educ. Found., 123 F. Supp. 2d 293 (E.D. Pa. 2000).

[164] *See* Trustees of Columbia Univ. v. Columbia/HCA Healthcare Corp., 964 F. Supp. 733 (S.D.N.Y. 1997) (Columbia Health Care had its primary place of business in Nashville, Tennessee, but had an operation in New York City, where it was alleged to infringe on the name of Columbia University).

[165] Villanova Univ., 123 F. Supp. 2d at 301-302.

[166] 15 U.S.C. § 1052(e).

[167] 15 U.S.C. § 1052(a).

[168] 15 U.S.C. § 1052(e).

[169] *See* Board of Regents of the Univ. Sys. of Ga. v. Buzas Baseball, Inc., 176 F. Supp. 2d 1338 (N.D. Ga. 2001).

[170] 873 F. Supp. 1280.

[171] *Id.* at 1287-1288.

[172] In *University of Arkansas*, the defendant offered an argument that the state was known as "The Razorback State," and, therefore, the term took on geographic significance. The plaintiffs' Internet search for verifying evidence revealed, however, that most "hits" referred to the University and its athletic teams.

[173] Miller and Davis, *supra* note 114, at 176.

[174] University of Ga. Athletic Ass'n v. Laite, 756 F.2d 1535, 1540-1541.

[175] *Id* at 1540.

[176] 508 F.2d 804 (1st Cir. 1975).

[177] The plaintiffs offered survey data to confirm this point.

[178] 508 F.2d at 807.

[179] *See, e.g.,* President and Fellows of Harvard Coll. v. Harvard Bioscience, Inc., 204 F. Supp. 2d 134 (D. Mass. 2002) (the defendant's use of its company name, Harvard Apparatus, is not infringing of the University's trademark, but its use of the same font and crimson color is).

[180] *See, e.g.,* Life Saver Corp. v. Curtiss Candy Co., 182 F.2d 4 (7th Cir. 1950).

[181] Section 32 of the Lanham Act, 15 U.S.C. § 1051.

[182] *See* Villanova Univ. v. Villanova Alumni Educ. Found., Inc., 123 F. Supp. 2d 293 (E.D. Pa. 2000).

[183] Section 43(a) of the Lanham Act, 15 U.S.C. § 1125.

[184] In a false advertising claim, if a plaintiff shows false statements and the likelihood of injury, then the plaintiff is entitled to injunctive relief. If the defendant has profited unfairly by these false statements, then the plaintiff may be entitled to damages as well as injunctive relief.

[185] Miller and Davis, *supra* note 114, at 255.

[186] Villanova Univ. v. Villanova Alumni Educ. Found., 123 F. Supp. 2d 293 (E.D. Pa. 2000). Note that fame or popularity of the plaintiff's mark is not enough for confusion. *See* University of Notre Dame v. Gourmet Food Imports Co., 703 F.2d 1372 (Fed. Cir. 1983) (the defendant's use of the mark "Notre Dame" did not infringe the marks owned by the well-known university).

[187] When dealing with a market where the competing goods are stocked close to each other, the marks are similar, and the purchaser spends less time deliberating over purchase (e.g., on an inexpensive item in a supermarket), courts are more likely to find confusion. For bigger ticket items where the consumer is a little more discriminating and deliberative, similar marks are less likely to result in confusion.

[188] For examples of intent to confuse, *see* University of Georgia Athletic Association v. Laite, 756 F.2d 1535 (11th Cir. 1985) and Board of Trs. of the Univ. of Ark. v. Professional Therapy Servs., 873 F. Supp. 1280 (W.D. Ark. 1995).

[189] 964 F. Supp. 733 (S.D.N.Y. 1997).

[190] Board of Trs. of the Univ. of Ark. v. Prof'l Therapy Servs., 873 F. Supp. 1280, 1289 (W.D. Ark. 1995).

[191] *Columbia Univ.*, 964 F. Supp. at 744 (internal citations omitted).

[192] *See* Board of Trs. of the Univ. of Ark. v. Prof'l Therapy Servs., 873 F. Supp. 1280 (W.D. Ark. 1995).

[193] *Id.* at 1291.

[194] *See* Villanova Univ. v. Villanova Alumni Educ. Found., 123 F. Supp. 2d 293 (E.D. Pa. 2000) (both the plaintiff and the defendant, operating under similar sounding names, raised money for student scholarships).

[195] Miller and Davis, *supra* note 114, at 269.

[196] *University of Arkansas*, 873 F. Supp. at 1290.

[197] 176 F. Supp. 2d 1338 (N.D. Ga. 2001).

[198] *See* Harvard Coll. v. Harvard Bioscience, Inc., 204 F. Supp. 2d 134 (D. Mass. 2002).

[199] 15 U.S.C. § 1057(b).

[200] 686 F.2d 1040 (3d Cir. 1982).

[201] *Id.* at 1047.

[202] *See* Board of Regents of the Univ. Sys. of Ga., 176 F. Supp. 1338 (N.D. Ga. 2001).

[203] 123 F. Supp. 293 (E.D. Pa. 2000).

[204] *Id.* at 304.

[205] 15 U.S.C. § 1117.

[206] *See* 15 U.S.C. § 1129.

[207] 15 U.S.C. § 1127.

[208] The profit referred to in the ACPA could be from the defendant holding the plaintiff's name "hostage" until selling it back to the plaintiff. *See, e.g.*, March Madness Athletic Ass'n v. Netfire, Inc., No. 3:00-CV-398-R, 2003 U.S. Dist. LEXIS 14941 (N.D. Tex. Aug. 28, 2003).

[209] For a discussion of domain name protection in higher education, see Note, *Harvard as a Model in Trademark and Domain Name Protection*, 29 RUTGERS COMPUTER & TECH. L. J. 475 (2003).

# 15 Business Management
## R. Craig Wood

## Introduction

Contemporary institutions of higher education are complex organizations with a multitude of tasks beyond the basic one of educating students. Institutions of higher education can differ greatly in the types of functions they perform, as they can have different missions and different educational purposes. While the business of colleges and universities is education, the business management of colleges and universities is a complex undertaking, often overlooked by both faculty and students. This chapter provides an overview of selected topics and issues that influence the business management of institutions of higher education.

Institutions of higher education operate under a myriad of constraints, rules, regulations, charters, statutes, and court decisions, all impacting the business management of the organization. These constraints vary, depending upon the classification of the institution. A state may have a variety of statutes, rules, and regulations applicable to public community colleges that are expressly inapplicable to four-year institutions. A state legislature may create state governing agencies with highly specific rules and regulations applicable to public colleges and universities and yet leave selected universities outside the control of those governing agencies.

A state's governance structure often yields a wide range of structural controls, and these structural controls influence the financial practices of institutions of higher education within that state. Public institutions of higher education may have different controls, financial and otherwise, compared to private institutions of higher education. Private institutions are incorporated within the state and governed by the provisions of their articles of incorporation.[1] Public institutions may also operate under a corporate charter, but most public institutions of higher education are created by statute or state constitutional mandate and are thus considered to be agents of the state.[2] While some states refer to higher education within the state constitution, and a few states grant constitutional autonomy to selected institutions of higher education,[3] it remains a state legislative responsibility to appropriate and account for the funds provided to public institutions.

As a general overview, institutions of higher learning may also be subject to a variety of rules and regulations of a local nature. Such rules and regulations include fire and safety codes, building codes, health codes, and a host of rules and regulations intended to protect public safety and welfare. Local governmental agencies generally possess this regulatory authority based on delegation of express powers by the state legislature. Private and public institutions may exist within the same local community but be regulated quite differently. For example, specific state statutes, rules, and regulations generally regulate public institutions through an administering agency, for example, a board of regents. A private institution would not be regulated by such rules and regulations but may fall under the regulations of the local government.

In some states, a public institution may be considered an agency of the State and thus immune from regulation by a local agency. Where immunity from local regulation is asserted, it must be clear that the public institution is engaged in an activity that is purely governmental or discretionary in nature and not in some way a proprietary function.[4] While the interpretation of what is a governmental function as opposed to a proprietary function will vary from state to state, an illustration of immunity from local building code regulation based on exercise of a discretionary function is provided in *Board of Regents v. City of Tempe*[5] where the court observed:

> The essential point is that the powers, duties, and responsi-
> bilities assigned and delegated to a state agency performing
> a governmental function must be exercised free of control
> and supervision by a municipality within whose corporate
> limits the state agency must act. The ultimate responsibility
> for higher education is reposed by our constitution in the
> state. The legislature has empowered the board of regents to
> fulfill that responsibility subject only to the supervision of
> the legislature and the governor. It is inconsistent with this
> manifest constitutional and legislative purpose to permit a
> municipality to exercise its own control over the board's
> performance of these functions. A central, unified agency,
> responsible to state officials rather than to the officials of
> each municipality in which a university or college is lo-
> cated, is essential to the efficient and orderly administration
> of a system of higher education responsive to the needs of
> all the people of the state.[6]

On the other hand, where an institution is engaged in an activity that may be judged as a proprietary function, local ordinances may control. In the illustrative case of *Board of Trustees v. City of Los Angeles*,[7] a state university leased certain facilities to a circus. The local municipality had ordinances regulating the operations of such entertainment activities.

The court supported the municipality and ruled against the university. The court distinguished between proprietary and discretionary functions, and then noted:

> The general statutory grant of authority to promulgate regulations for the governing of the state colleges and the general regulations promulgated pursuant to that authority contain no comprehensive state scheme for regulating the conduct of circuses or similar exhibitions with specific references to the safety, health, and sanitary problems attendant on such activities. Nor can the board point to any attempt by it to control the activities of its lessees for the purposes of protecting the public, the animals, or the neighboring community.

> In the absence of the enforcement of the city's ordinance, there would be a void in regulating circuses and similar exhibitions when those activities were conducted on university property, hereby creating a status for tenants of the university which would be preferential to tenants of other landowners. This preferential status, under the circumstances, serves no governmental purpose. The subject matter of the Los Angeles Municipal Code has not been preempted by the state.[8]

## Revenue Sources

Public institutions of higher education generally receive revenues from student tuition and fees, state aid or appropriations, sponsored research, endowment income, and auxiliary enterprises. Depending on mission and scope, private institutions are dependent on many of the same resources, although state appropriations are not as prominent a factor in operating revenues. Many states fund scholarships and loan programs that permit students to use the funding at either a public or private institution within the state. Several state legislatures provide direct grants to private institutions based on the number of students served by a private school who are residents of the state. Many institutions of higher education may enhance revenues by the sale of utilities, the sale of excess equipment, and a host of miscellaneous sources that vary from institution to institution. Many of these revenues are unique and may derive from such diverse sources as licensing agreements and patent royalties.

Because student tuition generally is a large portion of the revenue stream, litigation challenging an institution's discretionary authority to increase tuition can threaten a college or university's finances. Courts are reluctant to limit the authority of institutions to impose tuition increases and generally sustain the authority of institutions to increase tuition, provided there is an adequate basis in law for the institution's exercise of such authority. In 1998, students sued the City University of New York over tuition increases imposed on CUNY's community colleges. The lawsuit initially prevented CUNY from imposing tuition increases, but only until the City of New York met its funding obligation to CUNY. The appellate court ruled that CUNY was not an agency of the state for purposes of the students' claim for prevailing party attorneys fees and also reasoned that even if CUNY was regarded as an agency of the state, the students were not the prevailing parties under the statute in that CUNY prevailed on the main issue in the case: its ability to raise tuition.[9]

In some states, public institutions implementing tuition increases may be legally insulated from student suits. In 2004, students sued the University of Maryland System over a mid-year tuition increase that was predicated on substantial state government budget reductions instituted at the mid-point of the fiscal year.[10] Students, some of whom had already registered and paid the lower tuition rate in advance of the spring semester, sought to enjoin the increases, claiming violations of contract and consumer protection law. A state appeals court ruled that the Consumer Protection Act did not apply to the state, the state Board of Regents were an arm of the state protected by the sovereign immunity, and there was no evidence the higher education system had waived immunity.

Besides appropriations and tuition, charitable giving is also an important revenue source. A central concept supporting charitable giving is the concept of tax-exempt status, for without the incentive of lowering one's taxes, many benefactors would lose motivation to give. Nearly every institution receives gifts, pledges, and estates that are donated to the college or university for educational purposes. Assuming that the institution is legally qualified under tax law as a nonprofit institution, such gifts are generally tax deductible and may qualify for certain federal and state tax benefits.

Justice Marshall wrote in *McCulloch v. Maryland* in 1819, "the power to tax involves the power to destroy."[11] Generally, institutions of higher education are exempt from most forms of taxation because they are engaged in some public purpose such as education. Education and tax exemption have a concurrent history in which the courts have looked favorably on granting a variety of educational institutions some form of tax exemption.[12] This is particularly true for public institutions and, as a Wisconsin court stated in 1950, "When public property is involved, exemption is the rule and taxation is the exception"[13]

A landmark decision on tax exemptions for charitable giving to institutions of higher education was the 1983 case of *Bob Jones University v. United States*.[14] The principal question before the Court was whether the university, located in Greenville, South Carolina, qualified for tax-exempt status under the Internal Revenue Code. Supporting a national policy discouraging racial discrimination in education, the Internal Revenue

Service had denied the university tax-exempt status due to its practice of racial discrimination on the basis that "a [private] school not having a racially nondiscriminatory policy as to students is not 'charitable' within the common law concepts reflected in sections 170 and 501(c) (3) of the Code"[15]

The Court described Bob Jones University as a private corporation, operating a school with 5,000 students from kindergarten through college and graduate school. The university was dedicated to the teaching and propagation of fundamentalist Christian religious beliefs that included espousal of the view that the Bible forbids interracial dating and marriage. To effectuate this belief, African-Americans were completely excluded from attendance until 1971. From 1971 to May 1975, the University accepted no application from unmarried African-Americans but did accept applications from those already married to others of the same race. Beginning in 1975, the University permitted unmarried African-American students to enroll but a disciplinary rule prohibited interracial dating and marriage.

The Supreme Court had to balance the interests of a sincerely held religious belief, and the resultant noninterference with religious practice, with the public policy of nondiscrimination against minority racial groups. In a lengthy opinion delineating the relationship between charitable giving and the receipt of tax-exempt status, the judges emphasized the century-old case of *Perin v. Carey* and observed:

> [I]t has now become an established principle of American law, that courts of chancery will sustain and protect ... a gift ... to public charitable uses, *provided the same is consistent with local laws and public policy.*[16] (emphasis added by the Court)[17]

The Court went to great lengths to explain its denial of the university's claim. The majority examined the concept of charitable trusts over the years and noted the consistency of the courts, emphasizing that "the purpose of a charitable trust may not be illegal or violate established public policy."[18] The justices reinforced the concept that institutions of higher education that practice any form of racial discrimination for any reason should not receive tax exempt status:

> Few social or political issues in our history have been more vigorously debated and more extensively ventilated than the issue of racial discrimination, particularly in education. Given the stress and anguish of the history of efforts to escape from the shackles of the "separate but equal" doctrine of *Plessy v. Ferguson*, it cannot be said that educational institutions that, for whatever reasons, practice racial discrimination, are institutions exercising "beneficial and stabilizing influences in community life," or should be encouraged by having all taxpayers share in their support by way of special tax status.

There can thus be no question that the interpretation of §170 and §501 (c)(3) announced by the IRS in 1970 was correct. That it may be seen as belated does not undermine its soundness. It would be wholly incompatible with the concepts underlying tax exemption to grant the benefit of tax-exempt status to racially discriminatory educational entities, which "exer[t] a pervasive influence on the entire educational process." Whatever may be the rationale for such private schools' policies, and however sincere the rationale may be, racial discrimination in education is contrary to public policy.[19]

Generally, institutions of higher education accept gifts on behalf of the college in order to further the mission and goals of the organization. Although restrictions on the use of the gift may limit the discretion of the institution's agents in applying the funds generated from a gift to the financial needs of the institution, these gifts may contribute to the operating revenues of the institution. A gift is a transfer of something of value from one party to another without compensation. Thus, the donor who gives the gift will no longer have an interest or control of the gift. It now belongs to the new owner, who may do with the property as he or she wishes. A trust, on the other hand, is the transfer of an item having value, in which the person bestowing the trust will preserve some form of regulation over the item in question from the beneficial owner. While trusts take many forms, the most common in the higher education environment is that of a charitable trust.

An early dispute illustrates the nature of such a trust. In 1867 in *Jackson v. Phillips,* the court noted the distinct differences of a charitable trust and other forms of trusts. The court stated,

> The most important distinction between charities and other trusts is in the time of duration allowed and the degree of definiteness required. The law does not allow property to be inalienable, by means of a private trust, beyond the period prescribed by the rule against perpetuities, being a life or lives in being and twenty-one years afterwards; and if the persons to be benefited are uncertain and cannot be ascertained within that period, the gift will be adjudged void, and a resulting trust declared for the heirs at law or distributees. But a public or charitable trust may be perpetual in its duration, and may leave the mode of application and the selection of particular objects to be discretion of the trustees.[20]

When circumstances change, making the trust no longer operable, the trustees may petition the appropriate court to modify the purposes of the trust. Trustees of a trust are generally bound by a fiduciary duty to act in a manner that is consistent with the perceived desires of the original donors and the purpose of the trust. When the literal construction of the trust is no longer legal or practicable, the trustees may petition a court to invoke the doctrine of *cy pres*. [21] This doctrine provides for judicial interpretation and modification of the trust instrument so as to conform to the general intention of the testator while modifying the literal terms of the trust in order to avoid an illegal or impracticable result.

The University of Nebraska had sought to modify two charitable trusts that had been originally intended to provide loans to needy students. The University argued that the original trusts were designed for student loans and the availability of federal loan programs compromised the donor's intent to assist needy students because these students could obtain the federal loans at highly competitive rates. Seeking application of cy pres, the institution petitioned a state court to allow income generated from the trust to be given to students in the form of scholarships. The appellate court noted that the doctrine of cy pres is intended to apply when the purpose of the trust becomes illegal, impractical, or impossible to carry out. If this is established, then the court may direct the application of the trust to a charitable purpose that falls within the general charitable intent of the donor. The court upheld the trust and ruled against the university,[22] rejecting the application of cy pres because the university did not demonstrate that the purposes of the trust could not be realized. While students may be reluctant to arrange for the trust loans when the federal loans offer a more attractive interest rate, the court noted that the university had the authority to change the interest rate charged to students to make the trust's loans more desirable than the federal loans. Because the ultimate purpose of the trust had not been shown to be impossible, impractical, or illegal, the doctrine of cy pres was inapplicable.

## Construction Contracts

Controversies regarding bidding, awarding, and managing construction contracts have always been a highly litigious area within higher education law. As one legal authority has suggested,

> ... [C]ontroversies over construction bids and contracts continue to represent the largest number of property cases reported ... With few exceptions, these cases are routine disputes between colleges or universities and contractors over such issues as the return of bid bonds, recovery of additional costs for construction delays, payment for extra work, reimbursement for increased costs of building materials ... and recovery of damages for defective construction.[23]

Literally, hundreds of cases reflect conflicts between building contractors and higher education institutions at every phase of the contracting process. For example, one contractor sued regarding the rejection of the firm's construction bid with a community college in Ohio.[24] The community college had rejected the bid because the contractor failed to satisfy a minority business enterprise requirement included in a minority set-aside program adopted by the community college and required in the bid specifications. The community college asked the trial court to grant summary judgment based on qualified immunity. The court determined that if the community college sought to implement a race-conscious, affirmative-action plan, it must present evidence of an institutional history of past discriminatory practice in order to justify such a plan. Finding the stated purpose of the minority set-aside policy failed to mention past discrimination and appeared directed at societal discrimination rather than a previous history of institutional discrimination, the court rejected the qualified immunity defense, holding that the community college administrators knew or should have known that their actions in rejecting the firm's construction bid violated the construction company's equal protection rights.

Generally, cases involving suits between contractors and colleges and universities are contingent upon applicable state statutes, the actual bidding process, and the wording of the contract. A survey of reported cases includes issues related to the return of bid bonds,[25] recovery of additional costs,[26] payments for extra work,[27] and reimbursement for increased costs of building materials, as well as a host of additional issues.[28] Additionally, public institutions of higher education may be subject to prevailing wage statutes that apply to state agencies. Thus, the institution may have to pay wages on projects via contractors' services that are equal to the private sector. Generally prevailing wage laws apply to all public projects, and thus public institutions fall within the scope of these laws.[29]

## Goods and Services

Institutions of higher learning purchase a wide variety and large amount of goods and services every academic year. Applicable state statutes, contract law, and the uniform commercial code largely govern such purchases.

While a contract usually incorporates the basic elements of an offer, acceptance, compensation, and consideration, issues of performance and additional state statutory requirements may also be involved. State statutes on procurement codes, bid procedures, and qualified bidders govern purchasing by public institutions of higher learning, and each state is unique in terms of these statutes. Most states have highly specific statutory guidelines in terms of procedures, awards, method of payments, and manner of proof in terms of qualifications, workers compensation, and insurance. Similar to the area of construction contracts, this area generates numerous lawsuits involving institutions of higher education concerning disagreements over the elements of a contract and, when a public institution is involved, compliance with state statutes, particularly requirements and procedures for competitive bidding.

A food service provider, for example, successfully sued Texas Southern University for a variety of claims when the university failed to pay for contracted services. The appellate court ruled that the university waived any sovereign immunity status when the plaintiff provided evidence that the university ordered, accepted, utilized, and failed to pay for the contracted services. The court did note that the university was immune from suit on tort and constitutional issues but was subject to contract claims.[30]

In another example, Eastern Connecticut State University was successful in defending its actions regarding the bidding of a fire alarm system. The initial winning bid was disallowed due to a bid irregularity, and the university admitted the bid specifications needed to be refined and the project rebid. The next lowest bidder, who had met the terms of the initial bid, sued to compel the university to accept its bid under the initial bid specifications. The Supreme Court of Connecticut ruled on behalf of the university, stating that the losing bidder could show no statutory authority for its position. Thus, the university was free to start the entire project over in terms revising the bid specifications and awarding the contract.[31]

The selling of goods and services by institutions is generally an auxiliary activity that, depending upon applicable state statutes, may or may not be taxed. Generally, if the goods or services are provided by a nonprofit agency and purely educational in nature, then most jurisdictions allow tax-exempt status. Even if the college or university were to engage in activities in the nature of entertainment, e.g., football, these activities may not necessarily be taxable.[32]

## Private Sector Competition

Contemporary institutions of higher education offer a variety of auxiliary services ranging from housing and food service to travel agencies and beauty salons. In some cases, these services are contracted out to the private sector while the institution or its student government organization provides oversight. In another case, the institution might own and operate a hotel and conference center for its school of restaurant and hospitality management. Given the ever-expanding role of higher education institutions, the examples and instances of colleges and universities engaged in such activities are limitless. Additionally, many institutions sell the right to do business on campus to certain vendors. For example, it is not uncommon for one soft-drink distributor to have a license to operate soft-drink machines on campus. In most institutions, private, for-profit franchises lease spaces in order to do business. An example of this is the ever-growing popularity of food courts, in which restaurant chains lease space from the institution or make agreements with the institution to offer food services to students.

Many states have statutes that prohibit public institutions of higher education from selling goods and services that might compete with the private sector, although some state statutes may allow limited competition by particular exception. The exceptions may include educational programs and related activities, and it is not uncommon for the appropriate state board to review and authorize all such activities in order to minimize potential conflicts.

The authority for universities to engage in such operations depends upon whether constitutional and statutory provisions allow such operations. The question typically posed is "can the public college or university engage in a commercial enterprise, when the enterprise is reasonably incidental to or closely connected with a legitimate function of the state?" A case addressing this question is *Long v. Board of Trustees*[33] in which an Ohio appeals court upheld Ohio State University's decision to purchase the stock of a defunct private bookstore and operate the bookstore for students. The court noted that this service was 'reasonably incidental" to the university's mission. Another early and oft-cited case is *Batcheller v. Commonwealth ex re. Rector and Visitors of the University of Virginia*.[34] In this case, the issue was whether the university could own and operate an airport. The University argued that it had a program in aeronautical engineering and thus the airport was necessary to offer clinical experiences to the students. The permit issued by the State Corporation Commission gave permission to the university to operate an airport for civil airplanes involved in commercial aviation. Plaintiffs argued that the commission had no authority to issue the permit as the university had no authority to operate such an airport. The court quoted the commission in upholding the legal authority of the University of Virginia to operate the airport in question:

> The University in making application for the permit in question was not asking for the right to engage in commercial aviation, but only for the right to operate and conduct an airport for the landing and departure of civil aircraft engaged in commercial aviation, upon which their could be instruction in student flying so necessary and essential to its course in aeronautics ... [T]he University will be authorized by the permit to own and operate an airport upon which aircraft engaged in commercial aviation may land or take off, but his would not involve it in a purely commercial or industrial enterprise, but, as has been shown, in an enterprise necessary to and incidental to the full and complete instruction in the course in aeronautics which it has established.[35]

Competing with private, for-profit enterprises continues to be litigated in state forums. For example, a for-profit firm brought suit against Montana State University regarding the university's plan to rent and offer catering services to non-students.[36] The firm argued that the statutes that permitted such activities were an improper delegation of authority and violated the policy against utilizing taxes for non-public purposes. The Montana State Supreme Court upheld the statutory authority of the university, finding that the revenues from these activities were earmarked for capital outlay, which was clearly a public purpose.

Competition with the private sector can take many forms with unique circumstances. In one case, the University of Pennsylvania made known that it viewed a coin operated laundry and arcade that bordered its campus as a public nuisance. While it is axiomatic that a university can raise public health and safety concerns about the operation of a private, for-profit business adjacent to its campus, going beyond this right of petition may lead to a tort claim for interference with a private, for-profit firm's right to engage in a business activity. In this case, the question before the appellate court was whether the university had gone too far in its actions against the for-profit firm operating the businesses. The opinion of the court stated,

> [T]he crux of the plaintiffs' complaint is that the University went beyond merely complaining or petitioning the government; plaintiffs claim that defendants were integrally involved in not only initiating (or publicizing or vocalizing or rallying public support around) a complaint, by in, among other things, carrying out the Cease Operations order that L & I [License and Inspections] issued to plaintiffs' business … University police officers were present at the time the L & I representative executed the Cease Operations Order, and they directed patrons to leave because the businesses were being shut down. There is no petitioning element to this activity. As plaintiffs put it, "Here the University defendants went far beyond 'making their wishes known to the government.'" … The official presence of a University police officer at the posting and execution of the Cease Operations Order went beyond mere petitioning, and thus there is genuine issue of material fact as to whether the University's course of conduct as a whole went beyond First Amendment protected activity.[37]

Another area related to competition with the private sector is the authority of public institutions to exercise eminent domain. Public higher education institutions may have the statutory authority to acquire property by eminent domain for public purposes appropriate to their mission. A taking by eminent domain may involve a range of legal issues[38] including whether the purpose of the condemnation is necessary to achieve a public purpose or what constitutes a fair price in order to compensate the owner of the property. For example, the University of Minnesota was denied the right to take property by eminent domain when it failed to establish that the taking was necessary to realize its education purposes. The appeals court ruled against the taking by eminent domain because the university had failed to identify a specific purpose for the property in its master plan; had suggested several different, but mutually exclusive uses to which the property might be put; and had not developed a plan to deal with soil contamination on the site.[39]

## Property Management

It is not uncommon that individuals bequeath money or items of value to higher education institutions for future use. Often, such items of value are included as gifts in estates. These gifts are generally converted to trust funds in order to implement the purposes of the gift. A higher education institution may accept or turn down a gift, depending upon the nature of the gift and whether the gift is restricted or unrestricted. Assuming the college or university accepts a gift for a restricted purpose, a public institution may do so only if the gift meets a public or educational purpose.

The difficulty within this area is that once a institution accepts such a gift and implements the purposes of the gift, the purpose for which the gift was accepted may no longer be needed for the educational operations of the college or university in a more contemporary time. A case in point occurred in 1999 in which the heirs of a trust given to Yale University (as well as alumni donors and students) sued the university.[40] Yale University planned to demolish the divinity school quadrangle, which had been constructed with the trust fund. Connecticut's appellate court dismissed the suit, noting that the gift was an unrestricted gift and that the trust in question did not give control of the property to the trust. Further, the court ruled that the heir did not have standing to sue because the control was not in the name of the trust. The donors and the students also lacked standing in that they collectively and individually failed to allege an actual injury or have a legal interest in the dispute.

In a similar instance involving a challenge to a college's decision regarding property management, an individual sued a college for liquidating real property that was part of its campus. The appellate court ruled on behalf of the college, holding the plaintiff lacked standing since he was not a trustee, director, or officer of the college and that the college was engaged in actions that were reasonable and that promoted its educational interests by allowing for the payment for the sale of the property to be used to pay the college's debts.[41]

## Intellectual Property Management

While a complete discussion of intellectual property issues in the college and university environment can be found in chapter twelve, a range of issues involving intellectual property, patent and trademark protection, and licensure agreements relate to the business operations of colleges and universities. Generally, the intellectual property rights of faculty and the contractual rights of parties participating in patent and royalty contracts are detailed in individual agreements, institutional policies, or state rules and regulations. However, this does not necessarily mean that the institution can unilaterally change the terms of those contracts to which it had previously agreed.[42]

An ongoing issue in most research universities is the ownership of intellectual property. While intellectual property could be widely construed as lectures, textbooks, and other such activities, the most lucrative and visible application is research that may be patented and thus sold or licensed for large amounts of money.

In a recent example, Yeshiva University was successful in suing a former research assistant for the ownership rights in a cell line and antibodies related to the treatment of Alzheimer's disease. The appellate court upheld the trial court, noting that the university directed the work and its intended result, and thus the university was entitled to the ownership of the research.[43]

Another related area to intellectual property management is the management of royalty payments. An illustrative case occurred in 1999, when the Internal Revenue Service sought back-taxes from Oregon State University and the University of Oregon after the institutions conducted an affinity credit card program.[44] Both universities had received income of over one and a half million dollars each in exchange for allowing their names to be used on bank credit cards. The IRS position was that these moneys constituted business income. The tax court and the Ninth Circuit Court of Appeals rejected the IRS complaint and held that the funds generated from the credit card programs were royalties to the universities.

In an age where universities are dependent on funds from patents and royalties to augment operating revenues, new legal issues have evolved. The University of Minnesota sued a private business with which it had a licensing agreement over the amount of royalty due the university.[45] Columbia University prevailed on one element of a patent infringement claim in the area of genetic engineering when the federal district court ruled that federal courts had jurisdiction to determine the amount of royalties within the United States as well as beyond its borders.[46] Texas A & M University filed suit against a private company for patent infringement regarding a patent for treating highway guardrails. The private company defended by arguing the university failed to disclose a federal funding source that contributed to the development of the patent. While the court agreed that the university had a statutory duty to disclose the federal government's interest in the patent during the patent application process, it held that disclosure of the federal funding would not have caused a patent examiner to deny the patent. Therefore, the failure of the university to disclose the information did not affect the institution's patent, and the university's patent was enforceable against the private company.[47]

However, claims of a violation of licensing agreements may also be brought against the college or university. A federal trial court rejected the University of California's defense of Eleventh Amendment immunity when a firm sued the university over a patent marketing agreement. New Star Laser had sued the University over what it felt was a binding licensing and marketing agreement with the university, after the university had awarded the licensing agreement to another firm. The court reasoned that a receipt of a patent was evidence that the university had waived its immunity. [48]

A related area—one that has sparked great concern among universities over the years—is trademark infringement. Universities are concerned with the inappropriate uses of university names and symbols, i.e. athletic mascots usage, as well as the potential loss of revenue from such usage. Generally, if the university can show that such usage is without the permission of the university, is unlicensed, or is harmful to the image of the university, then courts will uphold trademark infringement claims by the university.[49]

## Land Use and Zoning

As indicated in chapter fifteen, business management in post-secondary institutions can be influenced by the decisions of local community zoning boards. Constraints on a college or university's strategic plan and the ability of an institution to be flexible in land and property use can create unanticipated financial costs. In terms of sovereignty, a state institution that is constitutionally chartered would have a superior position as opposed to local community colleges.[50]

There is a lengthy case history of private institutions seeking to overturn zoning regulations in the courts. These cases involve highly specific fact scenarios and reflect mixed results.[51] Several of the cases have challenged the constitutional authority of the local governmental agency to apply zoning ordinances to higher education institutions.[52] In some instances, an institution may have operated under special exceptions to local ordinances, and then, often due to a change in mission, clientele, or status, the special exception is challenged, and the zoning agency rescinds the special exception previously granted to the institution.[53] In other cases, the higher education institution may request variances regarding applicable zoning regulations. As one court explained:

> A variance is an exercise of the power of the governmental
> authority to grant relief, in a proper case, from the liberal ap-

plication of the terms of an ordinance. It is to be used where strict application of the ordinance would cause unnecessary and substantial hardship to the property holder peculiar to the property in question, without serving a warranted and corresponding benefit to the public interest.[54]

In some instances, there is a tension between a college and university and local planning agencies with regard to the use of institutionally main-tained or developed properties. Courts balance the authority of the local planning agencies against the interests of the institution in determining the applicability of local agency regulations. For example, an attempt by a local agency to restrict a private university's campus development was declared beyond the powers of the local agency in *President and Directors v. Board of Zoning Adjustment*.[55] This tension is also illustrated in *City of Marina v. Board of Trustees*[56] in which the local municipality attempted to have the Trustees of the California State University pay for the environmental impact of converting a closed military base into a new campus within the multi-campus system. The appeals court noted that the municipality was without legislative authority to direct the California State University system to pay the costs of the environmental impact and went on to emphasize the California State University system lacked authoriza-tion to pay those costs even if it desired to do so.

There is an abundance of case law in which individual or collective neighboring property owners have sued institutions of higher learning regarding property issues.[57] For example, in *Bidwell v. Zoning Board*,[58] local residents of a municipality challenged the local zoning board's decision to grant a change in a residential area to allow a private college to construct a library adjacent to its campus. When the validity of these changes are in question, the institution may be required to intervene in order to support the zoning board's decision and demonstrate that there was no abuse of discretion on the part of the board.

Any discussion of the applicability of land usage and zoning require-ments between institutions of higher learning and local agencies brings forth the fundamental issue of the applicability of statutes, rules, and regu-lations.[59] The case of *Rutgers, v. Piluso*[60] illustrates the use of a balancing test, where the interests of the local community are balanced against the interests of the state. In that case, the court observed,

> The rationale which runs through our cases and which we are convinced should furnish the true test of immunity in the first instance, albeit a somewhat nebulous one, is the legislative intent in this regard with respect to the particular agency or function involved. That intent, rarely specifi-cally expressed, is to be divined from a consideration of many factors, with a value judgment reached on an overall evaluation. All possible factors cannot be abstractly cata-

logued. The most obvious and common ones include the nature and scope of the instrumentality seeking immunity, the kind of function or land use involved, the extent of the public interest to be served thereby, the effect local land use regulation would have upon the enterprise concerned, and the impact upon legitimate local interests ... In some instances one factor will be more influential than another or may be so significant as to completely overshadow all others. No one factor, such as the granting or withholding of the power of eminent domain, is to be thought of as ritualistically required or controlling. And there will undoubtedly be cases, as there have been in the past, where the broader public interest is so important that immunity must be granted even thought the local interest may be great. The point is that there is no precise formula or set of criteria which will determine every case mechanically or automatically.[61]

The court went on to state,

With regard to a state university ... there can be little doubt, that, as an instrumentality of the state performing an essential governmental function for the benefit of all the people of the state, the legislature would not intend that its growth and development should be subject to restriction or control by local land use regulation. Indeed, such will generally be true in the case of all state functions and agencies.[62]

## Taxation

Public and private colleges and universities typically enjoy exemption from state and federal taxes because of the public purposes served by their educational mission. However, when these institutions become involved in enterprises that are unrelated to that primary mission, they may be vulnerable to taxation. By way of illustration, this section focuses upon exemption from property taxes imposed by state and local government, while chapter fifteen surveys the range of taxation issues that can arise between town and gown. For example, the Michigan Department of Treasury sued the University of Michigan in order to compel the university to charge sales taxes on activities ranging from photocopying in the library to food service and lodging for continuing education students, but a state appeals court ruled that the university did not have to charge sales taxes on these particular services.[63] In another case, the City of Chicago sued the University of Illinois Board of Trustees to force the Board "to collect parking, amusement, and telecommunications taxes and remit those funds to the City."[64] In a complex holding, the state appeals court ruled that the city did not have the statutory authority to collect amusement and parking taxes from the university, but state statute specifically allowed the city to require the board of trustees to collect and remit all municipal telecommunications taxes.

While it is generally the rule that public and private colleges do not pay property taxes on land and its improvements when these resources are being utilized for an educational purpose, the question often arises as to whether a given piece of property or facility on the property, meets the test for an educational purpose. These cases depend upon the exact wording of the controlling statutes, the charter of the institution, and a determination of how the property is actually utilized by the institution.[65]

In a case illustrating the complexity of land-use and taxation, a private, for-profit company challenged a determination that it must pay a privilege tax on buildings it constructed in a university research park. While the land itself was owned by the university and not subject to a property tax, the state imposed a privilege tax on the use of the property if the property were used in connection with a for-profit business. In determining whether the privilege tax applied, the state supreme court carefully scrutinized the statutory exemptions to the privilege tax and ruled that the tax was not applicable to the for-profit business because it paid rental fees to the university.[66]

State-owned institutions are usually exempt from paying *ad valorem* taxes; as such, property is expressly exempt under state statutes regarding property taxation. Private institutions of higher education that are chartered or statutorily authorized under state procedures generally enjoy tax-exempt status based on state statutory language exempting charitable, religious, and educational organizations from ad valorem taxes. This is assuming that these private institutions are genuinely educational, non-profit, eleemosynary organizations pursuant to state statutes. It is important to note, however, that college or university-related organizations may seek property tax exemptions for a variety of reasons. Generally, the activity must be educational in nature and be nonprofit in order to qualify for a tax exemption.[67]

Relying on the *Dartmouth* Doctrine,[68] the Indiana court of Appeals upheld that all property owned by Butler University was tax exempt. The University was founded in 1850 with a charter from the state that expressly exempted all property "held" by the university. While the state's Board of Tax Commissioners argued that the university had to use property for its educational function in order to receive tax-exempt status, the university argued the term "held" embraced all property whether or not it was used for strictly educational purposes. The state appeals court ruled on behalf of the university in that the charter was intended to embrace all property held by the institution whether it was used for educational purposes or not.[69]

Private institutions of higher education receive tax exemption generally because of the educational, religious, or charitable mission in which they engage. It is important to note that the institution, depending upon applicable state statutes, must be engaged in its educational, religious, or charitable mission in order to receive the exemption for each piece of property or activity. This generally includes college dormitories and related properties. Thus, the home of the president of an institution of higher education may be exempt from property tax if it is indeed utilized for the college's purposes and activities. However, the president's home could lose its tax-exempt status when state law varies or when the usage of the property varies from an education purpose.[70]

Institutions of higher learning engage in a variety of functions. Many of these functions are clearly educational in nature, and no legal question generally arises concerning taxes. However, when the institution engages in activities that are not clearly educational, the question of tax exemption may require judicial resolution. In *Southern Illinois University v. Booker,*[71] the issue was whether Southern Illinois University should receive tax-exempt status regarding married student housing operated by a foundation created by the university. The university chartered the foundation for the purposes of buying and selling property and maintaining property for the purposes specified by the trustees of the university. The university argued that the married student housing was property of the state and thus exempt. The county argued that the legal ownership was the foundation and not the university. The court upheld the university's position, finding that the university, not the foundation, controlled the property and enjoyed the benefits of the property. Noting that the foundation created by the university was a convenience in aid of long-term financing, the court emphasized the use and benefit derived from the property in holding that it was tax exempt.

> The property is used to house students of the university. The facilities are controlled, operated, and maintained by the university. From funds derived from the operation of the property, the university pays annual as rent the amount of the foundation's mortgage payments, as agent of the foundation, transmits the sum to the Federal National Mortgage Association. Furthermore, when the mortgage is eventually retired, the university will receive title to the improved property with no further payments whatsoever required as consideration for the transfer. The foundation holds but naked legal title to property plainly controlled and enjoyed by the university and hence the state.[72]

It is important to note that states treat the taxation of institutional assets in a variety of ways. Some states examine the actual usage of the property while others simply examine if the institution owns the property. In some instances a partial tax assessment is made depending upon its usage.[73] Judicial scrutiny of tax exemption often involves careful analysis of the history and intent of state statute law. For example, the North Carolina Supreme Court heard an appeal as to whether property owned by the University of North Carolina was tax exempt regardless of its usage. The cities of Chapel Hill and Carrboro attempted to place on the tax rolls several properties owned by the university, the most notably a historic inn owned and operated by the university. The state supreme court examined the Royal Proprietary Grant of 1665 in which the state was granted tax-exempt property and upheld the exemption of all university property, regardless of its usage.[74]

Student dormitories are with rare exceptions non-taxable.[75] Sorority and fraternity houses may or may not qualify for tax-exempt status.[76] The nature of the institution's property and how it is utilized has a major influence on the determination of the property's tax-exempt status. For example, in *Princeton University Press v. Borough of Princeton,*[77] a university press was denied an exemption as the court reasoned,

> There is no question that the petitioner has been organized exclusively for the mental and moral improvements of men, women, and children. The press's publication of outstanding scholarly works, which the trade houses would not be apt to publish because of insufficient financial returns, carries out not only the purposes for which it was organized but also performs a valuable public service. It cannot be likewise concluded, however, that the property is *exclusively used* for the mental and moral improvement of men, women, and children as required by the statute. A substantial portion of the press's activity consists of printing work taken in for the purpose of offsetting the losses incurred in the publication of scholarly books. Such printing, which includes work done for educational and nonprofit organizations other than Princeton University, is undertaken for the purpose of making a profit. Hence, in this sense the printing takes on the nature of a commercial enterprise and, therefore, it cannot be said that the property is *exclusively used* for the statutory purpose.[78]

However, despite a similar factual context, another court ruled on behalf of the university in *District of Columbia v. Catholic Education Press.*[79] The court stated,

> The Catholic Education Press does not stand alone. It is a publishing arm of the University. It is an integral part of it. It has no separate life except bare technical corporate existence. It is not a private independent corporation, but to all intents and purposes it is a facility of the university … If the Catholic University of America, in its own name, should engage in activities identical with those of its

subsidiary, the Catholic Education press, we suppose its right to exemption from taxation on the personal property used in such activities would not be questioned. We see no reason for denying the exemption to the university merely because it chooses to do the work through a separate non-profit corporation.[80]

As a general guide, courts consider a number of factors in granting higher education institutions and affiliated associations and enterprises tax-exempt status. First, the court will consider whether the educational institution owns the buildings and land associated with the enterprise. Second, there must be an absence of profit motive and no agent or employee receives a pecuniary benefit from the operation of the enterprise other than reasonable compensation for services. Third, the enterprise must be one that is reasonable and natural for an educational institution to operate or maintain. Finally, the court must determine that the use of the property is wholly in support of an educational purpose consistent with the mission of the higher education institution.[81]

# Endnotes

[1] The landmark case is Trustees of Dartmouth Coll. v. Woodward, 17 U.S. (4 Wheat) 518 (1819).

[2] *See e.g.*, Henn v. State Univ. of Iowa, 22 Iowa 185 (1867); Weary v. State Univ., 42 Iowa 335 (1876); Neil v. Ohio A & M Coll., 31 Ohio St. 15 (1876).

[3] *E.g.*, California, Michigan, and Minnesota.

[4] *See e.g.*, Board of Trs. v. City of L.A., 122 Cal. Rptr. 361 (Cal. Ct. App. 1975).

[5] 356 P.2d 399 (Ariz. 1960).

[6] *Id.* at 406-407.

[7] 122 Cal. Rptr. 361 (Cal. Ct. App. 1975).

[8] *Id.* at 365.

[9] Apollon v. Giuliani, 675 N.Y.S.2d 38 [127 [Educ. L. Rep. 985] (App. Div. 1998).

[10] Stern v. Bd. of Regents, 846 A.2d 996, [187 Educ. L. Rep. 632] (Md. 2004).

[11] 4 Wheat, 316, 4 L. Ed. 579 (1819).

[12] *See e.g.,* Lawrence Bus. Coll. v. Bussing, 231 P. 1039, (1925); Birmingham Bus. Coll. v. Whetstone, 82 So. 2d 539 (1955); Simpson v. Jones Bus. Coll., 118 So. 779 (Fla. 1960).

[13] State *ex rel.* Wis. Univ. Bldg. Corp. v. Breis, 44 N.W.2d 259 (1950).

[14] 461 U.S. 574.

[15] *Id.* at 579.

[16] Bob Jones at 588 (*quoting* Perin, 24 How. at 501).

[17] 24 How. at 501 (1861).

[18] *Id.* at 591.

[19] *Id.* at 595.

[20] Jackson v. Phillips, 14 Allen 539 (Mass. 1867).

[21] *See e.g., In re* Mary Holbrook Russell Mem'l. Scholarship Fund, 730 N.Y.S.2d 702 [157 Educ. L. Rep. 285] (N.Y. Sup. 2001).

[22] *In Re* R.H. Plummer Mem'l Loan Fund Trust, 661 N.w.2d 307 [176 Educ. L. Rep. 452] (Neb. 2003).

[23] Phillip Piele, *Property, in* THE YEARBOOK OF HIGHER EDUCATION LAW 23 (Parker Young ed. 1979).

[24] Buddie Contracting v. Cuyahoga Cmty. Coll., 31 F. Supp. 2d 584 [132 EDUC. L. REP. 117] (N.D. Ohio 1998).

[25] *See e.g.,* Balliet Brs. Const. v. Regents of Univ. of Cal. 145 Cal. Rptr. 498 (Ct. App. 1978).

[26] *See e.g.,* R & R. Const. Co. v. Junior Coll., 370 N.E.2d 599 (Ill. App. Ct. 1977).

[27] John Grace & Co. v. State Univ. Const. Fund, 390 N.Y.S.2d 243 (App. Div. 1976).

[28] *See, e.g.,* Christiansen Bros. v. State of Wash., 586 P.2d 840 (Wash. 1978); ABL Mgmt., Inc. v. Bd. of Supervisors of S. Univ., 773 So. 2d 131 [150 EDUC. L. REP. 295] (La. 2000).

[29] S. Goldblatt & R. C. Wood, *Financing Educ. Facility Construction: Prevailing Wage Litigation,* SCHOOL LAW UPDATE-1982, 269-293 (1983).

[30] Texas S. Univ. v. Araserve Campus Dining Serv., 981 S.W.2d 929 [131 EDUC. L. REP. 858] (Tex. Ct. App. 1998).

[31] Blesso Fire Sys. v. E. Conn. State Univ., 713 A.2d 1283 [128 EDUC. L. REP. 298] (Conn. 1998).

[32] *See e.g.* City of Boulder v. Regents of the Univ. of Colo., 501 P.2d 123 (Colo. 1972); City of Morgantown, v. W. Va. Bd. of Regents, 354 S.E.2d 616 [38 EDUC. L. REP. 827] (W. Va. 1987).

[33] 157 N.E. 395 (Ohio Ct. App. 1926).

[34] 10 S.E.2d 529 (Va. 1940).

[35] 10 S.E.2d at 535.

[36] Duck Inn v. Mont. State Univ., 949 P.2d 1179 [123 EDUC. L. REP. 351] (Mont. 1997).

[37] We, Inc. v. City of Phila. Dep't of Licenses and Inspections. 983 F. Supp. 637 [123 EDUC. L. REP. at 118-119] (E.D. Pa. 1997).

[38] *See e.g.,* Board of Regents v. Commanche Apts., 568 S.W.2d 449 (Tex. 1978); Lin v. Houston Cmty. Coll. Sys., 948 S.W.2d 328 [119 EDUC. L. REP. 1265] (Tex. Ct. App. 1997); Cook v. Cleveland State Univ. 122 S. Ct. 2648, (2001).

[39] Regents of Univ. of Minn. v. Chi. & N.W. Transp. Co. 552 N.W.2d 578 [112 EDUC. L. REP. 436] (Minn. Ct. App. 1996).

[40] Russell v. Yale Univ., 737 A.2d 941 [138 EDUC. L. REP. 441] (Conn. App. Ct. 1999).

[41] Friends World Coll. v. Nicklin, 671 N.Y.S.2d 489 [125 EDUC. L. REP. 782] (App. Div. 1998).

[42] *See e.g.*, Kucharczyk v. Regents of Univ. of Cal., 946 F. Supp. 1419 [114 EDUC. L. REP. 1118] (N.D. Cal. 1996); Shaw v. Regents of the Univ. of Cal., 67 Cal. Rptr. 2d 850 [121 EDUC. L. REP. 261] (Cal. Ct. App. 1997).

[43] Yeshiva Univ. v. Greenberg, 681 N.Y.S.2d 71 [131 EDUC. L. REP. 255] (App. Div. 1998).

[44] Oregon State Univ. Alumni Ass'n v. Comm'r. of Internal Revenue Serv., 193 F.3d 1098 [139 EDUC. L. REP. 90] (9th Cir. 1999).

[45] Regents v. Univ. of Minn. v. Glaxo Wellcome, Inc., 44 F. Supp. 2d 998 [135 Glaxo Wellcome, Inc. 85] (D. Minn. 1999).

[46] Trustees of Columbia Univ. v. Roche Diagnostics, 126 F. Supp. 2d 16 (Mass. 2000).

[47] Trinity Indus. Inc. v. Road Sys., Inc., 235 F. Supp. 2d 536, [173 EDUC. L. REP. 57] (E.D. Tex. 2002).

[48] New Star Laser v. Regents of Univ. of Cal., 63 F. Supp. 2d 1240 [139 EDUC. L. REP. 239] (E.D. Cal. 1999); *see also* Genentech v. Regents of Univ. of Cal. 939 F. Supp. 639 [113 EDUC. L. REP. 726] (S.D. Ind. 1996).

[49] *See, e.g.,* Villanova Univ. v. Villanova Alumni Educ. Found., 123 F. Supp. 2d 293 ([149 EDUC. L. REP. 513] E.D. Pa. 2000).

[50] *See, e.g.,* Appeal of Cmty. Coll. of Delaware County, 254 A.2d 641 (Pa. 1969); Regents of the Univ. of Cal. v. City of Santa Monica, 143 Cal. Rptr. 276 (Cal. Ct. App. 1978).

[51] *See e.g.,* Regents of Univ. of Cal. v. City of Santa Monica, 143 Cal. Rptr. 276 (Ct. App. 1978); Anderson v. Associated Professors of Loyola, 385 A.2d 1203 (Md. Ct. Spec. App. 1978); Northwestern Univ. City of Evanston, 370. N.E.2d 1073 (Ill. App. Ct. 1977).

[52] *See, e.g.,* Prentiss v. Am. Univ., 214 F.2d 282 (D.C. Cir. 1954); Northwestern Coll. v. City of Arden Hills, 281 N.W.2d 865 (Minn. 1979); Yanow v. Seven Oaks Park, 94 A.2D 482 (N.J. 1953); Long Island Univ. v. Tappan, 113 N.Y.S.2d 795 (N.Y. App. Div., 1952), *affirmed* 114 N.E.2d 432 (N.Y. 1953); Application of LaPorte, 152 N.Y.S.2d 916 (N.Y. App. Div. 1956), *affirmed,* 141 N.E.2d 917 (N.Y. 1957).

[53] *See e.g.,* Marjorie Webster Jr. Coll. v. Dist. of Columbia, 309 A.2d 314 (D.C. 1973); New York Inst. of Tech. v. LeBoutillier, 305 N.E.2d 754 (N.Y. 1973); Lafayette Coll. v. Zoning Hearing Bd., 588 A.2d 1323 [67 Educ. L. Rep. 203] (Pa. Commw. Ct. 1991).

[54] Arcadia Dev. Corp. v. Bloomington, 125 N.W.2d at 851 (Minn. 1964).

[55] 837 A.2d 58 [183 Educ. L. Rep. 887] (D.C. 2003).

[56] 135 Cal. Rptr. 2d 815 [177 Educ. L. Rep. 426] (Cal. App. 6 Dist. 2003).

[57] *See e.g.,* Pierce Jr. Coll. v. Schumaker, 333 A.2d 510 (Pa. Commw. Ct. 1975); Citizens Ass'n of Georgetown v. Dist. of Columbia, 365 A.2d 372 (D.C. 1976).

[58] 286 A.2d 471 (Pa. Commw. Ct. 1972).

[59] *See. e.g.,* State *ex rel.* County of Hamblen v. Knoxville Coll., 50 S.W.3d 93, (Tenn. Ct. App. June 7, 2002). In this instance, the college forfeited its right to claim exempt property tax status in that it did not appeal twice during applicable periods as allowed by statute.

[60] 286 A.2d 697 (N.J. 1972).

[61] *Id.* at 702-703.

[62] *Id.* at 703.

[63] University of Mich. Bd. of Regents v. Dep't of Treasury, 553 N.W.2d 349 [112 Educ. L. Rep. 1034] (Mich. Ct. App. 1996).

[64] Chicago v. Bd. of Trs. of Univ., 258 Ill. Dec. 253, 689 N.E.2d 125 (123 Educ. L. Rep. At 802) (Ill. App. Ct. 1997).

[65] *See e.g.,* City of Wash. v. Bd. of Assessment, 704 A.2d 120 [123 Educ. L. Rep. 245] (Pa. 1997); Case W. Reserve Univ. v. Tracy, 703 N.E.2d 1240 [131 Educ. L. Rep. 491] (Ohio 1999); Hays County Appraisal Dist. v. Southwest Tex. State Univ., 973 S.W.2d 419 [128 Educ. L. Rep. 922] (Tex. Ct. App. 1998).

[66] *See. e.g.,* County Bd. of Equalization of Salt Lake County v. Utah State Tax Comm'n, 927 P.2d 176 [114 Educ. L. Rep. 653] (Utah 1996).

[67] *See e.g.,* Illini Media Co. V. Dep't of Revenue, 216 Ill. 69 [109 Educ. L. Rep. 882] (Ill. App. Ct. 1996).

[68] Trustees of Dartmouth Coll. v. Woodward, 17 U.S. (4 Wheat) 518 (1819).

[69] Butler Univ. v. State Bd. of Tax Comm'rs, 408 N.E.2d 1286 (Ind. Ct. App. 1980).

[70] *See e.g.,* Appeal of the Univ. of Pittsburgh, 180 A.2d 760 (Pa. 1962); *In re* Albright Coll., 249 A.2d 833 (Pa. Super. Ct. 1968); Cook County Collector v. Nat'l Coll. of Educ., 354 N.E.2d 507; Bexar Appraisal v. Incarnate Word Coll., 824 S.W.2d 295 [73 Educ. L. Rep. 315] (Tex. Ct. App. 1992).

[71] 425 N.E.2d 465 (Ill. App. Ct. 1981).

[72] *Id.* at 471.

[73] *See e.g.,* Tusculum Coll. v. State Bd. of Equalization, 600 S.W.2d 739 (Tenn. Ct. App. 1980).

[74] *In re* University of N.C., 268 S.E.2d 472 (N.C. 1980).

[75] *See, e.g.,* Southern Ill. Univ. v. Booker, 425 N.E.2d 465 (Ill. App. Ct. 1981).

[76] *See e.g.,* Alford v. Emory Univ., 116 S.E.2d 596 (Ga. 1960); Johnson v. S. Greek Housing Corp., 307 S.E.2d 491 [13 Educ. L. Rep. 1154] (Ga. 1983); Cornell Univ. v. Bd. of Assessors, 260 N.Y.S. 2d 197 (N.Y. App. Div. 1965); Univ. of Rochester v. Wagner, 408 N.Y.S.2d 157 (N.Y. App. Div. 1978), *affirmed,* 392 N.E.2d 569 (N.Y. 1979). City of Memphis v. Alpha Beta Welfare Ass'n, 126 S W.2d 323 (Tenn. 1939).

[77] 172 A.2d at 420 (N.J. 1961).

[78] *Id.* at 424. *See also* City of Ann Arbor v. Univ. Cellar, 258 N.W.2d 1 (Mich. 1977) in which the affiliated corporation was found not to be tax-exempt.

[79] 199 F.2d 176 (D.C. Cir. 1952).

[80] *Id.* at 178-79.

[81] *See In re* Atlantic Coast Conference 434 S.E. 2d at 944 [85 EDUC. L. REP. 931] (N.C. Ct. App. 1993).

# 16 Athletics
John Decman

## Introduction

College athletics are big business. As a result, the numbers of lawsuits in this area continue to rise. Because athletic departments fall under the rules of the institutions in which they reside, many of the legal issues applicable to intercollegiate athletics are discussed in other chapters in this book. There are, however, issues that are unique to intercollegiate athletics. This chapter discusses selected legal issues involving intercollegiate athletics in higher education. In each of the sections of the chapter, key cases are presented to aid the reader in understanding the judicial reasoning applicable to these issues.

## Tort Liability in Athletics

Typically, athletes are thought to assume risks inherent in participating in athletics. Assumption of risk has often been asserted as a defense against a claim that an institution is liable in negligence for an injury to a student. For example, in *Schiffman v. Spring,*[1] a student on the women's varsity soccer team was injured when her foot became stuck in the mud while playing in a soccer match. She alleged that the athletic director and coach were negligent by electing to hold a soccer match on a field that was wet, slippery, and muddy. The university prevailed on a summary judgment motion after the judge concluded that the plaintiff was fully aware of the condition of the field before she voluntarily agreed to participate in the soccer match, thus establishing an assumption of risk. The institution established that plaintiff's injury was not the result of a breach of duty; rather, it was "a luckless accident arising from the vigorous voluntary participation in competitive inter-scholastic athletics."[2]

However, states have increasingly legislated a preference for the application of comparative negligence principles, a practice that allows the courts to discern levels of negligence among various parties and apportion damages among those deemed negligent. Under comparative negligence standards, a student-athlete's assumption of risk in an athletic activity may not be a complete bar to recovery when there is evidence that the institution or its agents were negligent.

Normally, an institution owes no duty to a student who sustains an injury unless a special duty to that student can be established. For example, in *Hanson v Kynast*,[3] the plaintiff was a team member of a visiting lacrosse team. Hanson sustained paralyzing injuries during a game between his team, Ohio State University, and Ashland University. Kynast, a player on the Ashland team, "body checked" an Ohio State player after he intercepted a pass and scored a goal. The plaintiff, Hanson, claimed Kynast was taunting the other player and feared for the safety of his teammate. He subsequently "bear hugged" Kynast, who in turn threw Hanson to the ground. Hanson sustained serious head trauma and paralyzing injury. Hanson then sought to hold Ashland University liable for his injuries, arguing that William Kynast was an agent of the university. Hanson also argued that Ashland University was negligent for untimely treatment resulting in further injury because the ambulance driver arriving on the scene could not gain entrance to the playing field due to an illegally parked car. Hanson underwent five hours of surgery to relieve brain swelling after he was transferred to the second of two hospitals. He also suffered a severe spinal cord injury and fractured vertebrae.

In responding to the claim, the Ohio Supreme Court noted that Kynast had voluntarily joined the team and purchased his own equipment. He was not on scholarship nor did he receive any compensation for his membership on the team. The court ruled that the relationship between Kynast and Ashland University was not based upon a principal-agent relationship. Consequently, the university could not be held liable for Kynast's actions. Regarding the claim for untimely treatment, the court accepted expert testimony indicating that the plaintiff's injuries were sustained upon initial impact and not due to the delay in treatment. Hansen lost his claim against the institution because he could not establish a special duty owed to him or that his injuries were a result of the institution's agents.

While an institution may not be liable for the actions of an intercollegiate athlete in the heat of competition, a special duty of care may be imposed on institutions to provide for reasonably safe conditions for intercollegiate athletes. The nature of this special duty was illustrated in *Kleinknecht v.Gettysburg College*,[4] when a student and member of a lacrosse team suffered cardiac arrest and died in an off-season practice. The student-athlete's parents claimed that the college's negligence was a legal cause of their son's death, as the college should have had the capacity to provide prompt treatment in the event a student suffered cardiac arrest at a practice or contest. The parents alleged that the college did not have a written plan to deal with medical emergencies, neglected to insure that coaches present at practices were certified in CPR, and did not have communication devices at the practice field. These measures, arguably, would have meant a faster response to their son's medical emergency. More rapid response, according to medical experts, might have prevented the student-athlete's death.

Initially, a federal district court in Pennsylvania rejected the claim of negligence brought by the athlete's family, however, the Third Circuit Court of Appeals reversed the lower court's decision. The appellate court reasoned that since Kleinknecht was participating in a scheduled athletic practice for an intercollegiate team sponsored by the college under the supervision of college employees, a special relationship existed between the college and the student sufficient to impose a duty of reasonable care on the college. Because Kleinknecht was recruited to play lacrosse and he was subject to control and supervision by the athletic program, the college owed him a duty of care.

Having determined that a special relationship existed, the court then reviewed the record to evaluate whether the incident was foreseeable and assess whether a duty of care was owed. The court determined that it was foreseeable that a member of the College's intercollegiate lacrosse team could suffer a serious injury during an athletic event and concluded the college owed a duty to the student to take precautions against the risks of injury. In making its determination, the federal court clearly intended to set limits on the class of students to which this decision would apply, suggesting that if the student had been participating in a fraternity football game, the institution might have owed no duty at all.[5]

Following *Kleinknecht*, other courts recognized a special duty relationship applicable to circumstances in which the institution may be said to exercise a greater degree of control over students engaged in intercollegiate sports. For example, in *Searles v. Trustees of St. Joseph's College,*[6] a court held that an institution may be liable for injuries to student-athletes in school-sponsored programs when college coaches or trainers are found to have breached a duty to exercise reasonable care for student-athlete safety. In this case, a member of a men's basketball team alleged that despite medical advice to the contrary, his college coach and an athletic trainer had insisted that the student continue to play basketball after several knee surgeries. Although the trial court granted summary judgment to the institution on the student's claims, the state appeals court reversed, holding that a duty of adequate supervision would arise from the level of control exercised by the coach and trainer over the athlete and finding that whether the duty was breached in this case was a question of fact for the jury's resolution.

The fact that an institution exercises a level of supervision and control over a student-athlete's training and participation in intercollegiate sports can create a duty of care to foresee potential risks. In *Moose v. Massachusetts Institute of Technology,*[7] a Massachusetts appeals court affirmed a jury verdict in favor of a student-athlete injured attempting a pole vault while under the supervision of his coach. The student sustained the injury when his heels hooked on the back edge of the landing pit and his head struck the unprotected surface on the track. Using a comparative negligence standard, the jury apportioned the fault proximately causing the injury between the institution and the student. On appeal, the state court emphasized there was sufficient evidence for the jury to find the risk of falling over the back of the padded landing pit was foreseeable and the coach's failure to evaluate the potential risk and take affirmative steps to reduce it was negligence. In a case with a similar result, *Trustees of Trinity College v. Ferris*,[8] a student-athlete participating in rowing practice was injured when his team's scull collided with a scull rowed by the women's team. The women's' scull was in the wrong lane at the time of the accident, violating a navigation rule. Following a jury verdict in favor of the student-athlete on the negligence claim, the defendants appealed, contending that the student had assumed the risk of the activity and pointing to the fact that the student had signed a release before participating in the practices. The state appeals court rejected this defense, ruling that the student athlete might have been aware of the general risks inherent in the sport, but a jury could find that he was not aware, and did not assume, the specific risk or harm associated with his injury.

Tort claims in sports don't always come from injuries on the field. In a slightly different situation, a collegiate baseball player sued Clemson University after receiving incorrect advice from a university counselor about transferring and eligibility. In *Hendricks v. Clemson University*,[9] the college advisor miscalculated the number of elective courses that the student-athlete could take. As a result, the student could not satisfy an NCAA rule that requires student-athletes to complete at least 50 percent of their course requirements toward their declared major to be eligible to compete as seniors. Because the student-athlete could not satisfy the rule, he was declared ineligible and could not play baseball, which happened to be the only reason he transferred to Clemson. He responded by suing Clemson for negligence, breach of fiduciary duty, and breach of contract.

The South Carolina Supreme Court ruled that Clemson owed the student no duty to give accurate advice concerning NCAA eligibility requirements. The court also refused to recognize a fiduciary relationship between an advisor and a student. Finally, because the student could not produce a written promise from Clemson to ensure his athletic eligibility, the court rejected his breach of contract claim.

In an analogous case, a high school student sued his high school and its insurer for a negligent mistake made by the high school counselor. In *Scott v. Savers Prop. & Cas. Ins Co.*,[10] the counselor indicated to the student that the high school's broadcast communication course was approved to fulfill one of the NCAA's core English requirements. The course was not approved, and as a result, the student was deemed ineligible for an athletic scholarship, a position that prompted the University of Alaska to withdraw its scholarship offer. The case made its way to the Wisconsin Supreme

Court, which, in part, agreed in sentiment with the plaintiff but was bound by *stare decisis* and further cited state statutes granting immunity to political subdivisions and officials for torts committed while performing their governmental function. The student's breach of contract claim failed as the court held that no contract existed between the student and his school. The school district had a statutory obligation to provide guidance counseling services, but that duty was not converted into a contract when the student asked for or used the guidance counselor's advice.

## Antitrust Law and the NCAA

The National Collegiate Athletic Association (NCAA) is a voluntary association, comprising approximately 1,200 member institutions, which administers intercollegiate athletic programs for the purpose of maintaining intercollegiate athletics as an integral part of a higher education institution's educational program. Section 1 of the Sherman Act[11] aims to promote and protect free-market competition by prohibiting restraint of interstate or foreign commerce. The regulatory activities of the NCAA are often scrutinized through the lens of the Sherman Act. In applying this and other antitrust laws to the NCAA, courts have held consistently that only "unreasonable" restraints of trade are prohibited.

One of the principal cases interpreting the application of the Sherman Act to the activities of the NCAA occurred in 1984, when the Supreme Court ruled in *NCAA v. Board of Regents*.[12] The controversy involved the NCAA's television contract with national broadcasters. The contract required the broadcasters to televise games featuring eighty-two different schools with the added requirement that no school could appear on television more than six times. It also prohibited member schools from selling television broadcast rights, "except in accordance with the plan." Thus, in effect, the NCAA's television contract constituted a limit on price and output. Two institutions in the NCAA, the University of Oklahoma and the University of Georgia, brought suit against the organization, alleging a Sherman Act violation.

On appeal from the Tenth Circuit, the NCAA contended that if its restrictions on television programming were not affirmed, fan interest in television games for top-ranked teams would adversely affect ticket sales for games that did not appear on television. The United States Supreme Court rejected this argument, finding that the regulation restricted, rather than enhanced, the place of college athletics. The Court held, after an evaluation of the competitive character of the NCAA television plan, that the plan constituted a restraint in the operation of a free market: a violation of the Sherman Act.

Acknowledging that the "great majority" of the NCAA's regulations heighten competition among colleges and universities, the Court emphasized that the NCAA failed to prove that procompetitive effects associated

424 / Chapter 16

with enhanced competition among members justified the regulations that might otherwise be regarded as restraints on trade. Regulations that promote a competitive balance among member institutions can be viewed as a procompetitive justification because the maintenance of equal competition will maximize consumer demand for the product. The "procompetitive" exception is a judicial acknowledgment that the NCAA, as the regulator of amateur collegiate athletic competition, is a unique entity in antitrust law and should be afforded latitude to realize that role.

In a case with similar marketing issues, promoters of men's basketball tournaments challenged the NCAA's Two-in-Four Rule limiting teams to two certified tournament events every four years as violative of the Sherman Act. NCAA Men's Division I basketball is divided into conferences; within each conference, the member schools individually play each other. Each school, however, makes its own schedule and may schedule several non-conference games. The NCAA sets the maximum number of games that each team may play per year. Throughout the year, there are various tournaments in which a school's team may participate, some of which are "certified" and some of which are not. Certified tournament events are multiple-game early season tournaments. Because of concerns that the more nationally prominent basketball programs would have disproportionate advantages, the NCAA adopted a proposal that increased the number of allowed games to twenty-eight per season for each team, provided that a team's participation in a certified event, regardless of how many games the team actually plays as part of that event, counts as one game toward the NCAA regular season maximum, and permitted each team to participate in a certified basketball event in one academic year, but no more than two certified basketball events every four years. While the NCAA defended the rule as an attempt to address competitive equity concerns among Division I institutions, the promoters saw the rule as an unreasonable restraint on trade. A federal district court agreed, permanently enjoining the NCAA from enforcing the rule.[13]

However, on appeal to the Sixth Circuit Court of Appeals, the lower court decision was reversed and remanded. In *Worldwide Basketball and Sports Tours, Inc. v. NCAA*,[14] the federal appeals court acknowledged that a rule of reason test applied but concluded that the district court's application of a "quick look" analysis was insufficient to conclude that the promoters met the burden of establishing that the NCAA rule "produced significant anticompetitive effects within the relevant product and geographic markets."[15] Placing a more stringent burden on the promoters to define the relevant market in which the anti-competitive effects of the policy can be evaluated, the appeals court reasoned the district court applied the wrong standard and held the promoters could not prevail on their claim that the Two-in-Four Rule violates the Sherman Act absent a more extensive proof of an anti-trust injury.

Other antitrust challenges to the NCAA's rules have involved student eligibility. One such case is *Jones v. NCAA*[16] in which a Canadian hockey player who had played for five years in "amateur" Canadian Hockey but received payments from his team was deemed ineligible by the NCAA. The player filed for an injunction, utilizing the Sherman Act, asking the court to prohibit the NCAA from declaring him ineligible to play and to restrain the NCAA and its Executive Director from imposing sanctions on Northeastern University for allowing him to play intercollegiate hockey. The player's counsel argued that the NCAA engaged in monopolizing behavior that injured the plaintiff in both business and property.

The court examined whether the Sherman Act applied to the NCAA in its function of setting eligibility standards for athletes and found that it did not. The court reasoned that the claim failed because the student was not a businessman and not truly a "competitor," as the competition in which the student sought to engage did not occur in a marketplace but as part of a university athletic program. In reaching this decision, the court referred to the purpose of the Sherman Act as governmental involvement to avoid control of the market by businesses that suppress competition. Because the NCAA, by setting eligibility guidelines, did not have an impact on business activities in which the plaintiff, a student, might participate, the Sherman Act did not apply.

In cases following the *Jones* decision, courts have continued to defer to the NCAA when student athlete eligibility rules are at issue. The deference given to the NCAA can be traced to well-established propositions. First, the NCAA has a goal of preserving amateur athletics and acts to retain "a clear line of demarcation between intercollegiate athletics and professional sports."[17] Second, the NCAA acts to create and enforce rules that have procompetitive effects designed to enhance the marketplace for intercollegiate athletics for all its member institutions. Third, the NCAA, through its competitions, seeks to maintain the integrity of the "student-athlete" concept. And fourth, the NCAA functions to maintain the competitive balance among institutions that participate in amateur athletics.

Despite the deference given to the NCAA on matters of eligibility, plaintiffs in student athletic eligibility cases regularly assert violations of the Sherman Antitrust Act as one of several arguments.[18] For this reason, eligibility litigation will remain linked to antitrust litigation. For example, *Tanaka v. University of Southern California*[19] evolved when a collegiate soccer player chose to transfer from one university to another, and the former university sought to enforce a regional conference rule requiring the student to lose some eligibility and sit out one year of competition at her new school. When the student brought a Sherman Act claim, the federal appeals court observed that three points must be successfully established for the claim to be actionable: (1) there must be a contract, combination, or conspiracy; (2) the agreement must have unreasonably restrained trade under a "rule of reason" test; and (3) the restraint must have affected interstate commerce. The court looked specifically at the "rule of reason" test and found that the student-athlete did not successfully demonstrate that the rule harmed competition more than it enhanced procompetitive effects. In failing to show that the eligibility restriction produced significant "anticompetitive effects" within the market, the student did not meet the initial burden to prove a Sherman Act violation.

In applying the Sherman Act to NCAA regulation, whether related to academic eligibility, restrictions on recruiting student-athletes,[20] or limiting annual compensation for certain classifications of college basketball coaches,[21] federal courts have consistently applied the "rule of reason" analysis. This rule provides a measure of insulation from anti-trust violations because it requires the court to look beyond the limitations of the regulation and assess whether any procompetitive benefits for the restrictions, such as increased efficiency or the creation of a new product, would outweigh the negative impact of the regulation.

## Athletic Scholarships and Related Services

Athletic scholarships are typically considered as contracts between the student and the institution. As a matter of routine, the institution pays the student's educational expenses while the student participates in a particular sport and maintains eligibility. In NCAA institutions, students sign a letter-of-intent while still in high school as a "promise" to attend a particular institution and participate in intercollegiate athletics. This document is generally treated as a contract between the institution and the student but must have some sort of financial aid offer to be binding on the parties.

In general, cases regarding scholarship contracts involve students who contest university action after a scholarship has been withdrawn or terminated when the student becomes ineligible for competition, fraudulently misrepresents academic or athletic credentials or eligibility, engages in misconduct or illegal behavior, or declines to participate in the particular sport.

A 1973 case in Tennessee, *Begley v. Corporation of Mercer University*,[22] occurred after a university withdrew its agreement to provide an athletic scholarship to a student who did not meet the NCAA minimum requirements. Apparently, an assistant coach at the university miscalculated the student's high school GPA, and the correct GPA was well below NCAA requirements. The court dismissed the suit, noting that the athlete was never able to meet the NCAA requirements and, thus, was never able to perform his part of the contract.

Another case occurred when a university opted to not renew the scholarships of two athletes as a result of serious misconduct. In *Conard v. University of Washington*,[23] the court found that the university action did not constitute a breach of contract as the scholarship language stipulated that it would be awarded annually and would be considered for renewal. It is important, however, that student athletes be afforded some due process in the form of notice and a hearing when scholarships are to be terminated or not renewed.

In a case that has been widely reported, Kevin Ross, a student at Creighton University, sued his school based on tort and a breach of contract theories.[24] Ross attended Creighton from 1978 until 1982. During that time, he maintained a D average and acquired ninety-six of the 128 credits needed to graduate. However, many of his earned credits were in courses such as marksmanship and theory of basketball and did not count toward a university degree. Ross alleged that he took these courses on the advice of Creighton's Athletic Department and that the department also employed a secretary to read his assignments and prepare and type his papers. He also asserted that Creighton failed to provide him with sufficient and competent tutoring, despite its promise to do so.

When he left Creighton, Ross had the overall language skills of a fourth grader and the reading skills of a seventh grader. Consequently, Mr. Ross enrolled, at Creighton's expense, for a year of remedial education at the Westside Preparatory School in Chicago. At Westside, Ross attended classes with grade school children. He later entered Roosevelt University in Chicago but withdrew because of a lack of funds.

His tort claims were summarily dismissed, but his breach of contract claim, originally dismissed by the trial court, was remanded by the appellate court for further findings of fact. The appellate court concluded that while the tort claims were speculative, Ross had a cognizable contract claim for breach of contract by the university. If his representations about the nature of the contract were proven, he could rely on the express and implied statements of the university and its agents as to the educational services that would be provided in exchange for his services as an intercollegiate athlete. Soon after the appellate decision, the parties settled out of court.

Negligent misrepresentation and fraud are often paired with breach of contract claims involving athletes. In one case, *Jackson v. Drake University*,[25] a former student-athlete contended that Drake failed to provide independent and adequate academic counseling and tutoring, failed to provide adequate study time, required the athlete to turn in plagiarized term papers, disregarded his progress (or lack thereof) toward an undergraduate degree, and urged him to register for easy classes. In making the claim for negligent misrepresentation, the student-athlete alleged that Drake supplied false information in the athletic recruiting process; he relied upon that false information, and the university failed to exercise reasonable care in communicating the information. In the fraud claim, he alleged that Drake knowingly made a material misrepresentation with the intent to induce him to enter into a contract (letter of intent), which he signed and, as a result of his reliance on the agreement, caused him damage. After a lengthy hearing, the court found that Jackson was able to proceed with his claims for negligent misrepresentation and fraud because Drake "did not exercise reasonable care in making the representations and had no intention of providing the support services it had promised."

In another case involving multiple legal claims, a collegiate baseball player, Michael Lesser, brought suit against a community college baseball program.[26] The former baseball player alleged fraud by silence, intentional misrepresentation, breach of contract, and several other claims. Among the baseball program practices were grooming standards (hair length and facial hair restrictions) and a fine system for being in violation of team rules (written and unwritten). Because the student was cut from the team, he did not receive exposure to college and professional scouts. Additionally, he did not receive personal coaching attention from the coaching staff, another representation made in the recruiting process. The court allowed the fraudulent misrepresentation claim, granting a trial on the merits of the athlete's assertion that he had relied on a false promise that participation in the baseball program would bring him positive attention from college and professional scouts.

## Discrimination on Basis of Disability

Athletes with disabilities have utilized the Americans with Disabilities Act (ADA)[27] and Section 504 of the Rehabilitation Act[28] to contest removal from intercollegiate athletic teams. Typically, the athletes have argued that participation in intercollegiate athletics is a "major life activity" and that by not allowing an athlete to participate, the university violates the ADA. A brief review of the ADA is essential to understand the connection between the ADA and athletic participation. Claims are typically brought against the NCAA, utilizing Title II of the ADA. This title prohibits discrimination in public accommodations based on a person's disability. The statute provides:

> No individual shall be discriminated against on the basis of disability in the full and equal enjoyment of the goods, services, facilities, privileges, advantages, or accommodations of any place of public accommodation by any person who owns, leases (or leases to), or operates a place of public accommodation.

Furthermore, the statute defines a disability as (a) a physical or mental impairment that substantially limits one or more of the major life activities of such individual; (b) a record of such an impairment; or (c) being regarded as having such an impairment. Discrimination then is a "denial of the opportunity of the individual or class to participate in or benefit from the goods, services, facilities, privileges, advantages, or accommodations of an entity."[29] In litigation against the NCAA, two areas of discrimination have commonly been alleged:

(i) the imposition or application of eligibility criteria that screen out or tend to screen out an individual with a disability or any class of individuals with disabilities from fully and equally enjoying any goods, services, facilities, privileges, advantages, or accommodations, unless such criteria can be shown to be necessary for the provision of the goods, services, facilities, privileges, advantages, or accommodations being offered;

(ii) a failure to make reasonable modifications in policies, practices, or procedures, when such modifications are necessary to afford such goods, services, facilities, privileges, advantages, or accommodations to individuals with disabilities, unless the entity can demonstrate that making such modifications would fundamentally alter the nature of such goods, services, facilities, privileges, advantages, or accommodations.

With regard to eligibility requirements, the plaintiff has the burden of showing the existence of a reasonable rule modification that would enable the plaintiff to participate in the specific activity. Once the plaintiff meets this requirement, the defendant must show that the modification would fundamentally alter the nature of the activity. The court then determines the issue of the reasonableness of any modifications.

In *PGA Tour, Inc. v. Martin (Martin II)*,[30] the Supreme Court emphasized that an evaluation of what constitutes a reasonable modification of rules for a disabled participant must focus on the individual. The Court noted that in individual cases, a rule peripheral to the nature of a certain program might be waived creating a fundamental alteration.[31] On the other hand, the Court recognized that a modification of rules for a disabled participant might constitute a "fundamental alteration" in two ways: (1) an alteration affecting an essential aspect of a defendant's policies or programs would be unacceptable even if applied to everyone equally; and (2) even a minor change might be unacceptable if it gave a disabled individual an advantage over others. In the *Martin* case, both the Ninth Circuit and the Supreme Court held that permitting Casey Martin to use a golf cart, despite the PGA Tour's rule requiring participants to walk, would not fundamentally alter the nature of the competition.[32] The courts pointed out that the nature of the competition in golf centers on making shots, which would not be affected by Martin's use of a cart. In the wake of the *Martin* case, courts have found that Title III of the ADA applies to the NCAA because of the extreme amount of control the association exercises over student-athletes' access to the playing field of competitive collegiate sports.

The factual complexity of disability law as applied to intercollegiate athletics is illustrated in *Bowers v. NCAA*.[33] The case involved the applicability of disability-based discrimination law to the practices of the NCAA's initial eligibility requirements that govern whether a student may participate in intercollegiate college athletics. Initially, the NCAA determined that Bowers took only three of thirteen required core courses in high school. This determination was based on the fact that Bowers had been enrolled in special education classes while in high school. The classes were found to be below "regular instructional level" and therefore did not qualify as substitutes for the required courses. Later, an NCAA subcommittee gave Bowers credit for more of the required courses, but the number was well short of the thirteen required courses that would have allowed him to be an academic qualifier.

Bowers' non-qualifier status negatively impacted his opportunity for a football scholarship. All of the efforts to recruit Bowers by the various defendant institutions, including Temple and Iowa, were contingent on the assumption that he would be an academic qualifier. Although he enrolled at Temple, Bowers did so as an ordinary student; he did not play football or receive an athletic scholarship. During his freshman year, Bowers sued the NCAA, two universities that stopped recruiting him once he was declared ineligible, and the ACT/Clearinghouse, claiming that the NCAA "core course" requirement violated the Rehabilitation Act and the Americans with Disabilities Act. Bowers sought an injunction allowing him to play four seasons of competition, damages in an amount exceeding one million dollars, a guarantee of four years of athletics scholarships, noninterference by the NCAA if he were to transfer to another institution, and an injunction prohibiting the NCAA from establishing a separate category for learning-disabled individuals. He contended that the NCAA discriminates against the learning disabled (a protected population) through initial eligibility requirements that dictate a student's participation in college athletics. Bowers sued under the Americans with Disabilities Act (ADA), section 504 of the Rehabilitation Act, and New Jersey anti-discrimination law.

The twists and turns of *Bowers* led to a number of federal court rulings and additional challenges. At one point, a reviewing court allowed the U.S. Department of Justice to file an amicus brief in support of the plaintiff, claiming the NCAA is subject to the ADA. The federal court found that the plaintiff had sufficiently pled that the NCAA operates a place of public accommodation and permitted discovery on the merits; that is, whether the NCAA's accommodations to plaintiff's handicap were reasonable. However, the court later granted an NCAA motion dismissing the claim against the NCAA under the ADA but allowed consideration of a claim for damages under the Rehabilitation Act, which required that the plaintiff show intentional discrimination. The court later ruled that the NCAA waiver process, one that permits students with learning disabilities to get core course credit for special education classes, is insufficient and does not constitute an appropriate accommodation.

Temple University then filed a third-party complaint against three other universities (Delaware State University, the University of Memphis, and the University of Massachusetts Amherst) who had discontinued recruiting Bowers after he was declared a non-qualifier.[34] The purpose of the suit was to seek contribution to help pay damages in the event that liability was found. In one of the nine separate decisions that have been made relating to this case, the Third Circuit Court of Appeals ruled that Temple University could not seek contribution from the other universities as these universities were not named in the original lawsuit. Shortly thereafter, Bowers passed away, and his mother was substituted as a party in the action.

Cases involving student-athletes with learning disabilities have been particularly prevalent in recent case law involving eligibility. One federal district court reasoned that the NCAA's certification of eligibility acts as an admission ticket to the playing field in that member institutions construct athletic facilities primarily for NCAA competition, and the NCAA governs those competitions and relies on use of the facilities. The court found that where more than one entity exercises control over access to a place of public accommodation, both entities, the institution, and the NCAA can be liable for discrimination prohibited by the ADA.[35] In another case, a federal district court adopted the view that a player declared academically ineligible to play intercollegiate football was protected by the ADA and that an NCAA waiver policy could be applied more than once without altering the purposes of the NCAA requirement or providing the athlete with an unfair advantage in competition.[36]

A few courts have addressed the specific issue of reasonable accommodations for learning-disabled student-athletes who cannot meet NCAA academic eligibility requirements. In *Cole v. Nat'l Collegiate Athletic Ass'n*,[37] a Georgia district court held that, "[a]bandoning the eligibility requirements altogether for ... any athlete is unreasonable as a matter of law and is not required by the ADA."[38] The plaintiff in *Cole* challenged the initial eligibility requirements for incoming student-athletes. Diagnosed with a learning disability, he earned a grade point average and SAT/ACT scores significantly below the minimum NCAA requirement. The court held that requiring the NCAA to grant a waiver of its academic eligibility requirements to a student-athlete whose scores fell so far below the rules' minimums would have exceeded reasonable modifications and, instead, would have undercut the academic eligibility standards and, consequently, compromised the educational purpose of the NCAA.

The Seventh Circuit addressed a different type of disability in 1996 when Nicholas Knapp sued Northwestern University for the right to play collegiate basketball.[39] While Knapp was a high school student, he suffered sudden cardiac death while playing basketball. He was resuscitated and a defibrillator was implanted in his body to restart his heart in case it stopped again. He was recruited by Northwestern University, which stated that it would honor his scholarship despite his medical condition. He was later found medically ineligible to play and, although he maintained his scholarship and his place on the team, he could not compete or practice. He filed suit against the university in federal district court alleging a violation of Section 504 of the Rehabilitation Act and requesting an injunction allowing him to play. The district court found that playing basketball was a major life activity for the student and granted the injunction. The university then appealed to the Seventh Circuit, which found that participating in intercollegiate athletics is not a major life activity. The court defined major life activities as basic life functions such as caring for one's self, walking, breathing, or speaking. According to the Seventh Circuit, performing a specific activity, such as playing basketball, is not within the scope of major life activities. The student's impairment did not prevent him from obtaining an adequate education and, therefore, did not limit his major life activity of learning. Furthermore, the court found that the student was not an "otherwise qualified individual" under the law because the student had not met all of the university's technical and physical requirements to participate in intercollegiate basketball.

A few cases have considered school team sports a major life activity in and of themselves. One such case is *Pahulu v. University of Kansas*.[40] Alani Pahulu, a University of Kansas student who was on a football scholarship, experienced an episode of transient quadriplegia during a scrimmage. The university's team physician examined Pahulu and discovered a congenitally narrow cervical canal. After consulting with a neurosurgeon associated with the university medical center, the team physician concluded that the student-athlete was at extremely high risk for subsequent and potentially permanent severe neurological injury including permanent quadriplegia. After reaching this conclusion, the team physician disqualified the plaintiff from participation in intercollegiate football.

Pahulu and his parents sought second opinions on the severity of his condition and on the prohibition against participating in intercollegiate football. The plaintiff saw three specialists, whose consensus was that the plaintiff could participate in intercollegiate football with no more risk of permanent paralysis than any other player. This information was shared with the team physician, and Pahulu offered to release and indemnify the defendants from liability should he be injured. Still, the team physician and consulting neurosurgeon, although acknowledging their decision was conservative, remained firm in barring the plaintiff from further intercollegiate football competition based upon their belief the plaintiff was at great risk for severe injury.

Pahulu testified that through playing football, he learned to be a team player and developed self-discipline. Additionally, he stated that his grades improved once he started playing football. His father testified to the educational and growth benefits Pahulu derived from participating in sports, particularly football. Additionally, his coach, Glen Mason, testified that athletics is an important component of learning.

Because of this testimony, the court found that for Pahulu, participation in intercollegiate football might be a major life activity, similar to learning. Still, the court found that the actions of the University of Kansas did not qualify as a substantial limitation on Pahulu's opportunity to learn. Pahulu continued on his scholarship and was given the opportunity to participate in the football program in a role other than one on the field.

## Sex Discrimination and Title IX

Title IX[41] was enacted as part of the Educational Amendments of 1972. The objectives of the statute are twofold: to avoid using federal resources in the support of discriminatory practices and to provide citizens effective protection against those practices. Title IX applies to both public and private institutions that receive federal aid and thus has significantly broader reach than the equal protection aspect of the Fourteenth Amendment, which applies only to public institutions. Title IX regulations mandate that institutions "provide equal athletic opportunity for members of both sexes."[42]

Measuring equality has become the major issue with regard to athletics. There are ten nonexclusive factors by which overall equality might be measured:

1.  whether the selection of sports and levels of competition effectively accommodate the interests and abilities of members of both sexes;
2.  the provision of equipment and supplies;
3.  scheduling of games and practice time;
4.  travel and per diem allowance;
5.  opportunity to receive coaching and academic tutoring;
6.  assignment and compensation of coaches and tutors;
7.  provision of locker rooms, practice, and competitive facilities;
8.  provision of medical and training facilities and services;
9.  provision of housing and dining facilities and services; and
10. publicity.[43]

Institutions must "provide reasonable opportunities for (scholarship) awards for members of each sex in proportion to the number of each sex participating in intercollegiate athletics."[44] Additionally, if the institution has separate teams for each sex, the institution may allocate athletic scholarships on the basis of sex to implement the separate teams, as long as the end result provides equal opportunity. The U.S. Department of Education provides financial assistance to educational programs and activities and is charged with the responsibility to direct and effectuate the provisions of Title IX. The ultimate sanction for non-compliance with Title IX would then be the termination of federal funding to the institution or the denial of future federal grants.

There have been three different categories of complaints regarding sex discrimination in intercollegiate athletics: first, that there is an unequal allocation of resources and, therefore, of opportunities for women to participate in women-only teams; second, that there is unequal treatment, such as salary disparities, in the administration of women's programs; and third, that female athletes, and sometimes male athletes, are denied access to sports that are selectively only offered to one sex by a school. While all three categories have involved litigation, the most controversial area, in part because of the potential cost of compliance, has been the unequal allocation of resources and opportunities for women to participate in women-only teams.

The leading case on the application of Title IX to this area of collegiate athletics is *Cohen v. Brown University.*[45] In this case, female members of Brown's volleyball and gymnastics teams brought suit under Title IX after the university eliminated their teams. Women comprised 48 percent of the school's student body but less than 37 percent of the athletes on campus. The university, because of financial constraints, cut four varsity programs, two men's programs, and two women's programs. While the cuts did not change the ratio of athletic opportunities, they did significantly reduce the budgeted funds for women's athletics. The plaintiffs brought suit alleging non-compliance in areas of both treatment and accommodation. Responding to plaintiffs' argument, the court imposed an injunction on Brown University for its failure to accommodate the interests of its female students. To be in compliance, a university must satisfy at least one of the three tests established in the Title IX Policy Interpretation:

1.  whether intercollegiate level participation opportunities for male and female students are provided in numbers substantially proportionate to the respective enrollments;

2.  where the members of one sex have been and are underrepresented among intercollegiate athletics, whether the institution can show a history and continuing practice of program expansion which is demonstrably responsive to the developing interest and abilities of the members of that sex; or

3.  where the members of one sex are underrepresented among intercollegiate athletes, and the institution cannot show a continuing practice of program expansion such as cited above, whether it can be demonstrated that the interests and abilities of the members of the sex have been fully and effectively accommodated by the present program.[46]

Plaintiffs have the burden of proving that the school has failed to meet the first prong. If successful, the burden then shifts to the defendants who bear the burden under the second and third prongs. In the *Brown* case, the court found that the university did not meet the first test. Because the athletic program was being constricted as opposed to expanded, the university failed to meet the second test as well. Finally, Brown was unable to meet the requirements of the third test, especially the "fully and effectively accommodated" portion. The court supported the district court's order to force Brown to maintain its women's varsity volleyball and gymnastics teams pending trial. The court then suggested that Brown would have to propose an athletic program in compliance with Title IX. By not pre-determining the specifics of the suggested program, the court sought not to be involved in the financial situation of the university. This ruling opened the door for universities to reduce opportunities for men's sports to the level available for women's sports in order to gain Title IX compliance.

The practice of reducing opportunities for men in athletics in order to gain compliance with Title IX requirements has led to claims of reverse discrimination. However, federal courts have overwhelmingly rejected this notion and have upheld remedial actions designed to ensure compliance with Title IX.[47] A representative case is *Kelley v. Board of Trustees, the University of Illinois*[48] in which the men's swim team challenged the decision to eliminate their team, claiming that the university discriminated against them on the basis of sex in violation of Title IX and the Equal Protection Clause of the Fourteenth Amendment. The Court of Appeals for the Seventh Circuit held that the institution's decision was not a violation of Title IX or the Equal Protection Clause, reasoning that the DOE regulations should be given considerable deference unless manifestly unreasonable or arbitrary. The court ruled that eliminating the men's team did not violate Title IX because the athletic opportunities for men were still more than substantially proportionate to the number of male students at the university.

In a challenge brought by several national associations representing men's athletic teams, *National Wrestling Coaches Association et al. v. United States Department of Education,*[49] the plaintiffs alleged that the Department of Education's interpretation and enforcement of Title IX led educational institutions to cut men's sports teams, artificially limit the number of participants on men's teams, and otherwise discriminate against men based on sex, thereby denying male athletes equal protection of the laws under the Fourteenth Amendment. The lawsuit sought a court order barring the use of all disparate-impact components of the Department's Policy Interpretation and Clarification until the Department promulgated new rules in the manner required by the Administrative Procedure Act. In dismissing the suit, the court gave considerable deference to the Department of Education in its interpretations and enforcement of Title IX language. Because of the importance of the protections offered by Title IX, the significant flexibility built into the enforcement standards, and the multiplicity of considerations beyond Title IX that influence educational institutions' athletic decision-making, the court rejected the standing of the national associations.

In response to the controversies surrounding compliance with Title IX in the area of athletics, in 2002 President George W. Bush delegated the responsibility of appointing a Commission on Opportunity in Athletics to review the current state of Title IX and the OCR Policy Interpretations to Secretary of Education Rod Paige. The Commission made twenty-three recommendations, though only fifteen of them were made unanimously. Secretary Paige ultimately rejected all of the proposed changes, and the DED issued a clarification statement, renewing support of Title IX as it currently stands.

## Race Discrimination in Athletics

Challenges that the NCAA engages in racial discrimination in its eligibility rules have been brought in two cases. The line of thinking behind these suits is that NCAA Proposition 16, an eligibility provision, has a disparate impact on African-Americans and therefore violates federal anti-discrimination law applicable to programs receiving federal financial assistance. A disparate impact case is based upon the idea that practices, adopted without a deliberately discriminatory motive, may in operation be equivalent to intentional discrimination because of the disparate impact of the presumably neutral policy on a protected minority. Proposition 16 was enacted by the NCAA in 1992 and essentially was a sliding scale system under which a high school student may use a higher GPA to offset a lower SAT or ACT score. Opponents of Proposition 16 argue that while the concept of a sliding scale is laudable, it does little to mitigate the impact of the inherent discrimination in standardized tests on minority populations.

Title VI prohibits discrimination on the grounds of race under any program or activity receiving federal financial assistance.[50] Initially, a federal district court concluded that the NCAA was a program or activity covered by Title VI because it is an "indirect recipient" of federal financial assistance through its relationship to member institutions.[51] The court held that Title VI covered the NCAA because the member schools of the organization receive federal funds and the NCAA has controlling authority over federally funded athletic programs.

However, in a later decision,[52] a federal appeals court overturned a ruling in favor of minority student-athletes who claimed that the National Collegiate Athletic Association discriminated against them by using SAT scores to determine freshman eligibility in Division I sports. The ruling in the appeals court never reached the issue of whether the use of SAT scores has a disparate impact on minority student athletes. Instead, the court found that the NCAA is not a "direct" recipient of federal funds and therefore cannot be sued under Title VI of the Civil Rights Act. With this decision, the remaining allegations became moot.

In *Pryor v. National Collegiate Athletic Association*,[53] the NCAA's Proposition 16 was again challenged. This time, the plaintiffs alleged intentional discrimination under Title VI and three additional claims. In addition to the Title VI claims, Title II of the Americans with Disabilities Act and Section 504 of the Rehabilitation Act were utilized to allege that the NCAA's eligibility requirements discriminate against learning-disabled athletes. Additionally, the plaintiffs alleged that Section 1981 of the Civil Rights Act forbids the discrimination inherent in Proposition 16 because the NCAA has denied African-American student-athletes the opportunity to make and perform contracts (letters of intent) since it limits their eligibility to attain athletic scholarships.

In 1999, the NCAA added a bylaw that granted learning-disabled student-athletes five years to use their four years of athletic eligibility. Nonqualifiers and partial qualifiers who are not learning disabled also are entitled to the opportunity. Because of the 1999 NCAA bylaw, the court found that the plaintiffs had no standing to sue under the ADA or the Rehabilitation Act. As partial qualifiers, the plaintiffs had five years to complete four years of eligibility, and therefore, the plaintiffs were not injured to the point where the court could offer a remedy.

Despite the plaintiffs' allegations of intentional discrimination, their Title VI claim was also found to be flawed. The claim cleared the first hurdle when the court found the NCAA to be an "indirect recipient" of federal funds, and thus subject to charges of intentional discrimination. Still, the plaintiffs were required to prove intentional discrimination. To do this, the plaintiffs argued that the NCAA used racial discrimination as a motivating factor in the development of the policy and was "deliberately indifferent" to the disparate impact of Proposition 16.

The appellate court found that the "deliberate indifference" argument had been rejected by the U.S. Supreme court in *Alexander v. Sandoval*[54] when the court ruled Title VI does not afford a remedy in such situations. Secondly, the context of racial discrimination as a motivating factor was further defined by the court, which ruled that the policy must have been created "because of" and not "in spite of" its adverse effects on a protected group. Stated another way, the policy must have been designed with the intended purpose of achieving a racially disparate impact. Proving this intent is far more difficult than identifying regulations and policies that incidentally create disparate impact. Finally, the court rejected the Section 1981 claim related to contracts because the plaintiffs neglected to fulfill their obligations under the National Letters of Intent, namely the obligations related to establishing eligibility.

## Drug Testing

Drug testing continues to be a focus of controversy in athletics, whether professional, amateur, or collegiate. Typically, legal issues are based on the Fourth Amendment's prohibition on illegal search and seizure and the

Fourteenth Amendment's due process clause. Various state laws guaranteeing civil rights and protecting individual privacy are also used. Most litigation refers to the "*Skinner* Standard," which emanated from *Skinner v. Railway Labor Executives Assn.*[55] In this case, the Supreme Court ruled that the validity of this type of search is subject to a reasonableness test that assesses the intrusion on the individual's Fourth Amendment rights against the promotion of legitimate governmental interests.[56]

The Colorado Supreme Court applied the *Skinner* standard in *Univ. of Colorado v. Derdeyn.*[57] As a condition to participation in intercollegiate athletics at the University of Colorado, all student-athletes were required to sign a form consenting to drug tests. The university began the program for multiple reasons: (1) to prepare its athletes for drug testing in NCAA sanctioned sporting events; (2) to protect the health of the athletes; (3) to promote a positive image of the university; and (4) to ensure fair athletic competition. Several student athletes challenged this program. Despite the university's argument regarding motive, the court found nothing to show that the university instituted its program in response to any actual drug abuse problem among its student athletes. There was no evidence that any person had ever been injured because of the use of drugs while practicing or playing a sport at the institution.

The Supreme Court of Colorado determined that the privacy interests of the students outweighed the governmental interests of the university and ruled the drug-testing program unconstitutional. An additional point from this case related to the consent form that the university required all student-athletes to sign. The court found that these "consents" were largely involuntary and invalidated them, reasoning that there is no voluntary consent when the failure of a student-athlete to consent will result in denial of a participation and loss of scholarship.

Despite the outcome in the *University of Colorado* case, the NCAA has required random drug testing of intercollegiate athletes participating in sanctioned tournaments and insisted upon consent to the policy through completing a signed release allowing random testing. Testing is implemented according to procedures that include collection and safekeeping of urine specimens that are checked for an extensive list of banned substances such as anabolic steroids and diuretics. A positive test result for any of the banned substances results in ineligibility for any further competition until the athlete obtains a negative test. Recognizing the serious side effects of many of the banned substances, the NCAA's main purpose for implementing random drug testing is to protect the health and safety of intercollegiate athletes. Because the NCAA is a private, voluntary, nonprofit organization, it has not been deemed a state actor for purposes of imposing its policies on member colleges and universities, and therefore the organization has evaded Fourth Amendment constraints because it is not engaged in state action.

In *Hill v. NCAA*,[58] Stanford University students sought injunctive relief against the NCAA's drug testing program, and the university intervened on behalf of the students. The trial court required the NCAA to show a compelling interest prior to taking away an individual privacy right and enjoined the drug-testing plan. However, the California Supreme Court reversed, noting that by participating in athletic activity that required physical examinations, intercollegiate athletes had a diminished expectation of privacy. The Court found athletes had advance notice of the testing and an opportunity to consent to the program and reasoned that disqualification from competition, the consequence of refusal to be tested, did not render consent involuntary, since the athletes had no legal right to participate in sports. Holding that the NCAA's program was reasonably calculated to safeguard the integrity of intercollegiate sports and protect the health and safety of students, the court upheld the testing program.

In Bally *v. Northeastern Univ.*,[59] a private university required its varsity athletes to sign an NCAA student-athlete statement, which included a drug-testing consent form. The university also required its athletes to sign a university drug testing consent form as a condition for participating in varsity athletics. The plaintiff initially signed all forms but later withdrew his consent by letter and refused to sign any NCAA forms. The university declared the plaintiff ineligible for varsity sports. After being declared ineligible, the plaintiff sued the university for violating the student's civil rights and won in a state trial court. However, upon appeal to the Massachusetts Supreme Court, the decision was reversed. According to the appeals court, to prove a case under the state civil rights act, the complaining party must prove that a right guaranteed by the Constitution or laws of the United States or the state had been interfered with by threats, intimidation, or coercion. The intent of the civil rights act, according to the court, was to provide a remedy for victims of racial harassment, not for voluntary participation in intercollegiate athletics. Because the student had not established the conditions necessary for relief under the act, the court reversed the trial court's decision.

Two recent decisions of the United States Supreme Court may strengthen the authority of institutions to require random drug testing of intercollegiate athletes. Ruling in *Vernonia School District v. Acton*,[60] the High Court upheld random drug testing of secondary school students who participated in interscholastic athletics because

- the school demonstrated a compelling interest that outweighed the students' reasonable expectations of privacy;
- impaired athletes presented a health and safety risk to themselves and other students engaged in the athletic activities;
- athletes had a limited expectation of privacy since participation meant dressing and showering together;
- the test was not overly intrusive of the students' privacy and was used only to test for drug use; and

- the school required the written consent of the athletes and parents before testing.

In a later decision, the United States Supreme Court upheld an Oklahoma school district's requirement that all middle and high school students participating in extracurricular activities consent to a drug-testing program. In *Board of Education of Independent School District No. 92 v. Earls,*[61] the Court examined a public school district's policy that required all students to submit to random testing when participating in extracurricular activities. The method of testing was by urinalysis, and results were not turned over to local police or used to discipline students. In reaching its decision, the Court majority reasoned that students who participate in extracurricular activities (including interscholastic athletics) voluntarily subject themselves to intrusions that lessen any expectation of privacy that might apply to the student body as a whole. The Court also noted that the character of the intrusion, urinalysis testing, was an insubstantial interference with privacy and the school district's interest was sufficient even if there was no evidence of a pervasive drug problem at the school or among students participating in extracurricular programs.

Returning to the analysis in the *Hill* decision, the court found that the NCAA's rules contained elements designed to accomplish its legal purpose, including (1) advance notice to athletes of testing procedures and written consent to testing; (2) random selection of athletes actually engaged in competition; (3) monitored collection of a sample of a selected athlete's urine in order to avoid substitution or contamination; and (4) chain of custody, limited disclosure, and other procedures designed to safeguard the confidentiality of the testing process and its outcome.[62]

In the absence of definitive court guidance regarding drug-testing programs, institutions are best served to address the following considerations:

1. Involve competent legal counsel at the earliest stages of policy development, specifically with regard to both federal and state privacy rights.

2. Articulate the rationale supporting the policy, particularly as it relates to the health and safety of athletes in intercollegiate competition.

3. Document past instances in which illegal drug use has occurred in athletic programs, particularly cases in which injuries may have resulted.

4. Detail the procedures to be used in implementing the program, including notice of testing; provisions for consent; selection of participants; protocols for obtaining, securing, and testing samples; and ramifications of positive tests.

5. Insure student confidentiality and testing accuracy to the maximum extent.[63]

## Pay for Play in Intercollegiate Athletics

Any sport's fan that has watched a college football game or the NCAA sanctioned post-season basketball tournament knows that college athletics is a corporate enterprise that involves millions of dollars in revenues. Critics of intercollegiate athletics cite the revenues that big-time athletic programs generate, the generous salaries paid to head coaches in the principal revenue-generating sports, and the perception that the athletes do not receive a share of the profits from the enterprise. While there are stipends for athletes related to tuition and fees, room and board, and related educational expenses, the NCAA has opposed compensation for collegiate athletes in an effort to preserve the status of amateur athletics in colleges and universities. From the NCAA perspective, compensation may alter the accepted view that collegiate athletes are students rather than employees of higher education institutions.

The argument for profit sharing through wage compensation to student-athletes is often referred to as "pay-for-play." Pay-for-play is predicated on the assumption that colleges and universities enjoy huge revenues from marketing their collegiate sports program and that the extraordinary profits that result from these revenues are not shared with the players who perform in the arena. As one illustration of this inequity, pay-for-play advocates insist that student athletes who contribute to an institution's success on the playing field are insufficiently protected if they sustain a debilitating or career-ending injury while playing their sport.[64]

One way to remedy the perceived inequity would be to recognize collegiate athletes as employees of their institutions in order to make workers' compensation available to them. Workers' compensation would allow an injured collegiate athlete to seek an award that would extend beyond his collegiate career. However, institutions and the NCAA fear that recognizing collegiate athletes as employees for workers' compensation purposes will reshape the mission of higher education institutions and lead to other employment demands for salaries, benefits, and collective bargaining.

Courts have generally denied worker's compensation benefits to intercollegiate athletes on the basis of a successful argument by institutions that their primary goal is to educate collegiate athletes and a corresponding recognition that a significant public policy change would result if workers' compensation laws were liberally interpreted to apply to these athletes. Although early decisions involving workers' compensation claims of collegiate athletes appeared to adopt a presumption that collegiate athletes had performed under some form of contract for hire, the more discrete issue to be resolved was whether this work was undertaken with a degree of freedom of action and choice that would characterize the athlete as an independent contractor.[65] If the athlete enjoyed sufficient independence from the employer's business and performed the specific work without control or direction from the employer, then the athlete could be considered an independent contractor, and the institution would be sheltered from liability for injuries suffered in the course of participation in athletics.

Two workers' compensation cases have formed the predicate for recognizing college athletes as employees of higher education institutions. In *University of Denver v. Nemeth*,[66] the Colorado Supreme Court determined that a full-time, enrolled student and football player was an employee who was injured in the course of his employment and was entitled to worker's compensation benefits. The collegiate athlete sustained neck and back injuries while engaged in spring football practice for the University of Denver. In addition to his participation on the football team, he was receiving fifty dollars a month from the university to care for the campus tennis courts, as well as free housing and meal deductions. It was established that these jobs were contingent on his enrollment as a student and his continued participation on the football team. The collegiate athlete brought suit contending he was an employee of the university and entitled to receive worker's compensation benefits. The University maintained that they were engaged solely in the field of education, that the injury did not arise out of or in the course of employment, and that the award would contravene public policy.

With no consideration for the possibility that the nature of the relationship might be other than one implicating an employment agreement, the Colorado court reflected its bias by noting that "higher education ... is a business, and a big one,"[67] and "[a] student employed by the University to discharge certain duties, not a part of his education program, is no different than the employee who is taking no course of instruction so far as the Workmen's Compensation Act is concerned."[68] The court emphasized that a work-related injury arises from the course of employment if it stems from the "nature, conditions, obligations or incidents of the employment; in other words, out of the employment looked at in any of its aspects."[69] Because the collegiate athlete's miscellaneous jobs were contingent on his participation in football, the court found that the athlete's injury arose during the course of his employment. The court held that an employer-employee relationship existed because his performance on the football field directly affected his compensation in the other jobs he performed on the campus.[70]

The value of *Nemeth* as a precedent was compromised by *State Compensation Insurance Fund v. Industrial Accident Commission*[71] in which the same Colorado court refused to grant benefits to the widow of a scholarship athlete killed during a football game. Despite finding that a contractual relationship existed between the plaintiff and the university and recognizing that worker's compensation rights arise out of employment contracts, the *State Fund* court held the injury did not arise in the course of employment, even under a "liberal construction" of the state worker's compensation laws.[72] The deceased student was employed by Fort Lewis A & M College to manage the student lounge and work on the college farm. In return, he was paid a student work-study wage in addition to his athletic scholarship. The court determined that the collegiate athlete's compensation was not in return for playing football and that, despite the parties' contractual relationship, the university received no direct benefit from the decedent's participation on the football team. Holding that no employment agreement existed, the court summarized its position by stating that it did not believe that the legislature intended the workers' compensation fund to be a "pension fund for all student athletes attending our state educational institutions."[73]

The analyses in *Nemeth* and *State Fund* are at variance because the two opinions took differing perspectives on the extent to which a collegiate athlete's participation in college athletics could be characterized by an employment agreement. While the athletes in these cases had contractual relationships with their respective universities, the *Nemeth* court adopted the presumption that the contract was predicated on an employment agreement. The *State Fund* decision tacitly rejected this presumption. The *State Fund* decision is consistent with a range of case law recognizing the nature of a contractual relationship between students and institutions that is not characterized by employment status.

In 1963, California fueled the argument for including collegiate athletes under state worker's compensation laws when the state supreme court decided *Van Horn v. Industrial Accident Commission.*[74] In *Van Horn,* the court awarded worker's compensation benefits to the family of a scholarship athlete who died when his plane crashed while returning from a football game. The court analyzed the collegiate athlete's relationship with the university by presuming that any person rendering service to another is either an employee or an independent contractor.[75] Relying on *Nemeth*, the court reasoned that the student received his scholarship for playing football and determined that the public policy behind workers' compensation involved a socially enforced bargain created for the benefit of employees and employers.[76] The opinion emphasized that not every collegiate athlete would be presumed to be an employee but adopted an initial bias that foreclosed consideration of the contract to educate, which constituted an alternative view of the relationship between the collegiate athlete and the institution.

Later cases have rejected the *Van Horn* and *Nemeth* rationales. For example, in *Rensing v. Indiana State University Board of Trustees,*[77] the Indiana Supreme Court denied workers' compensation benefits to a football player who sustained severe injuries while playing football. Adopting a viewpoint consistent with the concept of a contract to educate rather than to employ, the court found the scholarship was not remuneration; rather, it served as a benefit for the athlete's past ability as well as to enable him to pursue higher education. The Indiana Supreme Court based its decision primarily on the contractual element of intent and rejected the application of any test distinguishing the nature of an employment agreement. In reaching its conclusion, the court referenced NCAA regulations[78] that prohibit athletes from "taking pay" for their participation in a sport, and the fact that the Internal Revenue Service did not consider the scholarship income. The opinion emphasized, "scholarships are given to students in a wide range of artistic, academic, and athletic areas ... .Scholarship recipients are considered to be students seeking advanced educational opportunities and are not considered to be professional athletes, musicians, or artists employed by the university."[79]

Similarly, in *Coleman v. Western Michigan University*,[80] a state appeals court applied an "economic reality test" to determine if a collegiate athlete injured in spring training was an employee of the institution. The court found that the university did possess some means of control over the collegiate athlete, which would be consistent with status as an employee, but noted that it could not revoke the athlete's financial aid and emphasized that the institution's degree of control over academic activities was no greater than that for other students.[81] The court adopted the view that the scholarship did constitute "wages" within the meaning of the workers' compensation act but reasoned that the athlete's services were not performed as an integral part of the university's business.[82] Noting that the institution's representatives had repeatedly emphasized that the collegiate athlete was a student first and an athlete second, the state appeals court followed other precedents by acknowledging that the primary function of the university was to provide academic education, not manage a football program.[83]

More recently, in *Waldrep v. Texas Employers Insurance Association*,[84] another state appeals court applied an intent test to determine the status of a collegiate athlete who had been rendered quadriplegic as a result of an injury in a college football game. The former athlete sought a ruling that his status was that of an employee as a matter of law. The opinion stated, "[o]ne may receive a benefit from another in return for services and not become an employee."[85] Applying an intent test to the nature of the contractual relationship, the court reviewed materials published by the institution, the pre-enrollment letter of intent, and the financial aid agreement ensuring room, board, and tuition. Finding that the agreements did not constitute a contract for hire, the court reasoned that the intent of the parties was that the collegiate athlete would be considered an amateur and not a professional, a conclusion buttressed by the understanding that the contract was governed by NCAA rules.[86]

For pay-for-play advocates, the frustration occasioned by judicial rejection of workers' compensation benefits for collegiate athletes is compounded by judicial acceptance of the NCAA's position that collegiate athletes are not employees. Pay-for-play advocates emphasize the profitability of intercollegiate sports and demand equity in the form of profit sharing for collegiate athletes who perform on the playing field. This argument, however, fails to account for the many sports and athletic programs that do not generate enough revenue to meet expenses. Paying a salary to athletes in revenue-producing sports, such as football, would place an institution's athletic association in an awkward position with regard to the non-revenue-producing sports, whose athletes commit as much or more time to their sport.

More to the point, how would colleges and universities compensate student-athletes and still manage to comply within the federal guidelines legally mandated by Title IX? Because the provisions of Title IX governing college and university intercollegiate athletics would require equal opportunity for participation, treatment and benefits for all collegiate athletes, this mandate would overturn any proposed payment system that would compensate only those athletes in the major revenue-generating sports such as football and men's basketball. A pay-for-play requirement for all intercollegiate athletes would so burden institutional athletic budgets that existing support for non-revenue producing sports would be compromised. In this context, a broader mandate than "pay-for-play" already applies to gender equity in collegiate athletics.

## Endnotes

[1]   609 N.Y.S.2d 482 (App. Div. 1994).

[2]   *Id.* at 483-484. *See also* Rendine v. St. John's Univ., 735 N.Y.S.2d 173 (App. Div. 2001) for a case in which a cheerleader, injured when she fell while performing a stunt, was held to have assumed the risk of the activity because she was under no compulsion to perform the stunt and had been advised that no spotter was available.

[3]   494 N.E.2d 1091 (Ohio 1986), *on remand*, 526 N.E.2d 327 (Ohio. App. 1987).

[4]   989 F.2d 1360 (3d Cir. 1993).

[5]   *Id.* at 1368.

[6]   695 A.2d 1206 (Me. 1997).

[7]   683 N.E.2d 706 (Mass. App. 1997).

[8]   491 S.E.2d 909 (Ga. App. 1997).

[9]   578 S.E.2d 711(S.C. 2003).

[10]   663 N.W.2d 715 (Wis. 2003).

[11]   15 U.S.C. §§ 1-7 (2000).

[12]   468 U.S. 85 (1984).

[13]   Worldwide Basketball and Sports Tours, Inc. v. NCAA, 273 F. Supp. 2d 933, 954-55 (S.D. Ohio 2003).

[14]   388 F.3d 955 (6th Cir. 2004).

[15]   *Id.* at 959.

[16]   392 F. Supp. 295 (D. Mass. 1975).

[17]   Gaines v. NCAA, 746 F. Supp. 738, 744 (M.D. Tenn. 1990).

[18]   *See* Jones v. NCAA, 392 F. Supp. 295 (D. Mass. 1975) and Buckton v. NCAA, 366 F. Supp. 1152 (1973) in which hockey players challenged NCAA eligibility requirements on a variety of due process, equal protection, and anti-trust grounds.

[19]   252 F.3d 1059 (9th Cir. 2001).

[20]   Hairston v. Pac. Ten Conference, 101 F.3d 1315, 1319 (9th Cir. 1996).

[21]   Law v. Nat'l Collegiate Athletic Ass'n, 134 F.3d 1010, 1018-19 (10th Cir. 1998).

[22]   367 F. Supp. 908 (E.D. Tenn. 1973).

[23]   814 P.2d 1242 (Wash. Ct. App. 1991).

[24] Ross v. Creighton Univ., 957 F.2d 410 (7th Cir. 1992).

[25] 778 F. Supp. 1490 (S.D. Iowa 1991).

[26] Michael Lesser v. Neosho County Cmty. Coll. and Steve Murry, 741 F. Supp. 854 (D. Kan. 1990).

[27] The Americans with Disabilities Act of 1990, Pub. L. 101-336, 104 Stat. 327, 42 U.S.C. §12101 *et seq.*

[28] Section 504 of the Rehabilitation Act of 1973, 29 U.S.C. §794 (a) (1999).

[29] 42 U.S.C. §12182(b)(1)(A)(i)(1994).

[30] 532 U.S. 661, 121 S.Ct. 1879, 149 L. Ed. 2d 904 (2001).

[31] 121 S. Ct. at 1893.

[32] Martin I, 204 F.3d at 999; Martin II, 532 U.S. 661, 121 S. Ct. 1879, 149 L. Ed. 2d 904.

[33] 130 F. Supp. 2d 610 (D.N.J. 2001).

[34] 26 NDLR 201 (3d Cir. 2003).

[35] Ganden v. NCAA, 1996 U.S. Dist. LEXIS 17368, 1996 WL 680000 (N.D. Ill. 1996).

[36] Matthews v. Wash. State Univ., 179 F. Supp. 2d 1209 (E.D. Wash. 2001).

[37] 120 F. Supp. 2d 1060 (N.D. Ga. 2000).

[38] 120 F. Supp. 2d at 1071-72.

[39] Knapp v. N.W. Univ., *cert. denied*, 520 U.S. 1274 (1997).

[40] 897 F. Supp. 1387 (D. Kan. 1995).

[41] 20 U.S.C.A. §§ 1681-88.

[42] 34 C.F.R. § 106.41 (c).

[43] 34 C.F.R. § 106.41 (c)(1-10).

[44] 34 C.F.R. § 106.37 (c)(1).

[45] 991 F.2d 888 (1st Cir. 1993).

[46] 44 Fed. Reg. 71, 418.

[47] *See* Chalenor v. Univ. of N.D., 291 F.3d 1042 (8th Cir. 2002) (University did not violate Title IX by eliminating its men's wrestling program to comply with budget restrictions and avoid discriminating against women); Neal v. Bd. of Trs., 198 F.3d 763, 770 (9th Cir. 1999) (eliminating men's wrestling team did not violate Title IX); and Kelley v. Univ. of Ill., 35 F.3d 265, 270 (7th Cir. 1994) (eliminating men's swim team did not violate Title IX).

[48] 35 F.3d 265 (7th Cir. 1994)

[49] 263 F. Supp. 2d 82, (D.D.C. 2003), *affirmed*, 366 F.3d 930 (D.C. Cir 2004).

[50] 42 U.S.C. § 2000d.

[51] Cureton v. NCAA, 1997 U.S. Dist. LEXIS 15529, No. 97-131, 1997 WL 634376 (E.D. Pa. Oct. 9, 1997).

[52] Cureton v. NCAA, 198 F.3d 107 (3d Cir. 1999).

[53] 288 F.3d 548 (3d Cir. 2002).

[54] 121 S. Ct. 1511 (2001).

[55] 489 U.S. 602, 619 (1989).

[56] United States v. Montoya de Hernandez, 473 U.S. 531, 537 (1985).

[57] 863 P.2d 929 (Colo. 1993).

[58] 865 P.2d 633 (Cal. 1994).

[59] 532 N.E.2d 49 (Mass. 1989).

[60] Vernona Sch. Dist. v. Acton, 515 U.S. 646, 115 S. Ct. 2386 (1995).

[61] Board of Educ. of Indep. Sch. Dist. No. 92 v. Earls, 536 U.S. 822, 122 S. Ct. 2559 (2002).

[62] 865 P.2d 633 (Cal. 1994).

[63] *See Drug Testing Program. 2003-20004*, NCAA Publication. National Collegiate Athletic Association. Indianapolis, IN. Available at: *http://www.ncaa.org/library/ sports_sciences/drug_testing_program/2003-04/2003-04_drug_testing_program.pdf*

[64] While scholarship athletes are covered for athletics-related injuries during the term of their scholarship, they have no long-term benefits. The NCAA's catastrophic injury insurance plan is regarded as failing to cover the wide array of injuries that are preva-

lent in college athletics and the plan does not require a member college or university of the NCAA to subscribe to the plan or to any alternative insurance coverage. *See* Jason Gurdus, *Protection Off of the Playing Field: Student Athletes Should Be Considered University Employees for Purposes of Workers' Compensation*, 29 HOFSTRA L. REV. 907, 926 (Spring, 2001).

[65] *See* Van Horn v. Indus. Accident Comm'n., 219 Cal. App. 2d 457, 33 Cal. Rptr. 169 (1963) and University of Denver v. Nemeth, 257 P.2d 423 (Colo. 1953).

[66] 257 P.2d 423 (Colo. 1953).

[67] *Id.* at 425-426.

[68] *Id.* at 426.

[69] *Id.* at 426.

[70] *Id.* at 430.

[71] 314 P.2d 288 (Colo. 1957).

[72] *Id.* at 289.

[73] *Id.* at 290.

[74] 219 Cal. App. 2d 457, 33 Cal. Rptr. 169 (1963).

[75] *Id.* at 464.

[76] *Id.* at 465.

[77] 444 N.E.2d 1170 (Ind. 1983).

[78] *Id.* at 1173. The university had referenced the NCAA Constitution and bylaws in the financial aid agreements with the athlete and the court noted this incorporation by reference was a factor in determining the intent of the parties.

[79] *Id.*

[80] 336 N.W.2d 224 (Mich. App. 1983).

[81] *Id.* at 226.

[82] *Id.* at 227.

[83] *Id.* at 226-227.

[84] 21 S.W.3d 692 (Tex. App. 2000).

[85] *Id.* at 695.

[86] *Id.* at 700.

# 17 Town and Gown Issues
## David Dagley

## Introduction

The relationship between institutions of higher education and their surrounding communities is highly interactive, often symbiotic, sometimes favorable and at times unfavorable. Issues arise where the authority of one conflicts with the authority of the other. This chapter discusses some of the issues, sometimes called "town and gown" issues, which may arise between colleges and their communities.[1]

## Zoning

Postsecondary institutions are dynamic organizations. Increased student enrollments necessitate more residence halls, more parking spaces, and more classroom and office space. Facilities designed for one use may at some point need to be converted to another use. Changes in physical environment and use of facilities may implicate zoning laws.

Zoning laws are a manifestation of the police power of the state. "Police power" refers to the sovereign authority of a state to make rules for itself to promote order, safety, security, health, morals, and general welfare.[2] Land use planning and zoning law are created to allow a municipality to control the negative impacts of growth and development upon the community. Such laws can often pit the authority of the municipality against the authority of the college or university. While authority relationships underlie most zoning disputes, litigants in such actions can include a zoning board on behalf of a city, a city itself, an educational institution, a private entity affiliated with the educational institution, or a neighbor impacted by the land use. This section details court cases during the last twenty years in which zoning laws have affected postsecondary institutions.

The general rule is that, because public colleges and universities serve a state function, they may operate with limited interference from the local municipality. Four traditional legal tests supply alternative rationales for college and university immunity from local zoning laws: the Superior Sovereign Test, the Governmental Propriety Test, the Power of Eminent Domain Test, and the Statutory Guidance Test.[3] The Superior Sovereign Test exempts the state and its agencies (which includes public colleges and universities) from local zoning regulation because the state is in a superior position to the municipality in the governmental hierarchy. The Governmental Propriety Test exempts state property from local zoning when a governmental function is being performed but not when a proprietary function is being performed. Under the Power of Eminent Domain Test, a governmental body empowered to condemn is immune from local zoning laws when it acts to further its governmental function. The Statutory Guidance Test looks to the language in legislation to decide whether immunity exists or not.[4]

### Statutory Reference to Uses

In the last twenty years, the dominant rationale for immunity from zoning regulation for post-secondary institutions has been the Statutory Guidance Test. Courts commonly apply the facts of a situation to their own interpretation of statutes. A Massachusetts case illustrates the role of statutory language in sorting out relative authority between state-level entities and local governments.[5] Salem State College began construction of six, four-story dormitory buildings and one, single-story commons building. The city building inspector, who served as zoning administrator for the city, served a stop-work order on the general contractor and then filed a court action asking that the college be enjoined from continuing the work because the work was out of compliance with city zoning requirements. The trial court denied injunctive relief, and the appellate court affirmed. The question before the appeals court was whether a state statute gave primacy to the municipality. The provision permitted municipalities to subject religious and educational institutions to "reasonable regulations" concerning dimensional requirements and parking.[6] The court held that the city did not have primary authority and reinforced the rule that educational uses, as a state function, outrank city interests.

Statutory language under the Statutory Guidance Test often grants "educational uses" primacy over local zoning laws. In *Town of Islip v. Dowling College*,[7] a local New York community challenged the college's decision to provide catering services and driver's education for non-matriculated students. In holding that the challenged activities were permitted educational uses, the court described the distinctive position held by colleges and universities:

> Educational institutions enjoy special treatment with respect
> to residential zoning ordinances because these institutions
> presumptively serve the public's welfare and morals.
> Educational institutions are generally permitted to engage

in activities and locate on their property facilities for such social, recreational, athletic, and other accessory uses as are reasonably associated with their educational purposes.[8]

Another New York case involved a situation in which the city zoned to restrict the location of an educational institution within a historic residential district.[9] Although there is usually a presumption favoring educational uses, the ordinance was constructed to protect the historic district and disfavor other uses. The college could apply for a variance, which would require a showing of practical difficulties or unnecessary hardships. Because the college would be forced to meet a higher standard and because the ordinance failed to provide a means in which the college's educational use could be balanced against the public's interest in historic preservation, the court held that the ordinance served no end that substantially related to the police powers of the city and was, therefore, unconstitutional.

California zoning law differs from most states in that it allows community college boards, rather than a local zoning board, to exempt themselves from zoning regulations for property that is used for classroom uses.[10] The California exemption involves a narrower class of property—"classroom uses" rather than educational uses. In *People v. Rancho Santiago College*,[11] the college enacted a regulation declaring the use of a college parking lot for a swap meet on weekends as a classroom use. The college received approximately $5,700 per month in revenue from the operators of the swap meet. The court held that the swap meet was not a classroom use, reversed a lower court, and remanded with directions to enjoin the college from exempting the use.

What is an "educational use" is usually open to interpretation by the court. In *Varnado v. Southern University at New Orleans*,[12] a neighboring property owner sought an injunction to prohibit the university from converting two empty lots in a residential area to paved parking areas. The lots were not adjacent to other university property. In affirming the injunction, the appellate court held that this was not a situation in which the university was acting as an alter ego of the state, implying that the proposed use was not an educational use.

Wisconsin doesn't just protect educational uses; it also protects all governmental uses. In *Board of Regents of University of Wisconsin v. Dane County Board of Adjustment*,[13] the county board of adjustment (BOA) had ruled that a radio tower for a student-run radio station was not a governmental use. The university sought review by the circuit court, which reversed the BOA. The appellate court affirmed the lower court's decision that the radio tower was a governmental use and, therefore, was eligible for designation as a conditional use.

## Interpretation of Ordinances

Besides looking at state statutes, the language within city or county zoning ordinances is often examined to determine permissible educational uses. In *Capricorn Equity v. Town of Chapel Hill*,[14] plaintiff investors proposed to build duplexes to house graduate students. Each half of a duplex had approximately 3,000 square feet, with six bedrooms and three connecting bathrooms. The town manager denied building permits on grounds that the duplexes were rooming houses, as defined by the city's zoning law, and the town's board of adjustment agreed with the town manager. The Supreme Court of North Carolina looked to the language of the ordinance and observed that rooming houses denoted occupation by transient tenants, necessitating on-site property management. Reasoning that the duplexes were to be occupied for a longer term without an on-site manager, the court held for the investors.

Another situation in which interpretation of an ordinance was required occurred when the Borough of Glassboro, New Jersey, passed an ordinance permitting only those living in a family unit or the functional equivalent of a family unit to live in residential areas. The ordinance was designed to confine students to living in dormitories or in other zoning districts where apartments or townhomes were permitted.[15] However, the New Jersey Supreme Court thwarted the intent of the ordinance in holding that a group of ten, unrelated college students living in a rented house was a "family" within the definition of the restrictive zoning ordinance.

However, judicial rulings do not always favor the college or university. A Florida court determined that a private college for learning disabled students was not an "educational use" as defined by city ordinance.[16] The court's opinion detailed the negative impacts of the proposed college upon the residential areas of the town. In ruling that colleges were not schools under the ordinance, the court's interpretation protected the residential zones without confounding the general rule favoring educational uses.

Occasionally, city ordinances may conflict with each other, or a property may properly be classified under competing ordinances. When Oregon State University proposed to build a 156-room hotel and conference facility, the Land Use Board of Appeals (LUBA) for the City of Corvallis had to decide if the conference center should be classified as a civic use or a commercial use.[17] Although LUBA found that the conference center was indisputably a commercial use, it also determined the conference center to be "university services and facilities," a civic use. Petitioners challenged the decision on grounds that the uses were mutually exclusive. The Oregon Court of Appeals deferred to the local body under the standard established in *Clark v. Jackson County*.[18] The highly deferential standard under *Clark* is that the local interpretation cannot be overturned unless it is "clearly wrong," a standard in which no reasonable person could interpret the provision in the manner the local body did. Because one interpretation of city ordinances allowed for the conference center to be classified under both uses, the court upheld the LUBA classification.

In the District of Columbia, zoning regulations permit colleges and universities to locate in commercially zoned areas, but not residentially-zoned neighborhoods, as a matter of right.[19] In *Duke v. American University*,[20] plaintiff neighbors argued that the university had bargained away its right to locate its law school in an off-campus, commercially zoned setting. In negotiations, when neighborhood associations had indicated a preference that the law school be relocated downtown or to an off-campus location, the university had merely responded that an off-campus location was not a feasible alternative at the time and would not be considered. However, the fully integrated contract said nothing about such an agreement. Consequently, the appeals court affirmed the trial court's holding that the university had not promised to limit its options on where to locate its law school.

## Exemptions and Variances

In disputes involving higher education institutions and zoning, it may seem as though the scorecard tilts in favor of colleges. Educational institutions do not necessarily function without control from local zoning boards. Zoning regulations sometimes place location, height, or bulk restraints on a college or university's building program. In response, the institution might seek exemptions or variances to the regulation. An exemption grants to the building owner freedom from a general duty imposed by zoning law.[21] A variance grants to the owner permission to depart from the literal requirements of a zoning ordinance because of unique hardship arising from special circumstances regarding the owner's property.[22] While an exemption is aligned more with the concept of immunity, a variance is more in the nature of a waiver of the strict construction of a zoning law, arguably without sacrificing the spirit and purpose of the law.

Exemptions and variances played prominently in a court case in which condominium owners in neighboring buildings sued the Board of Zoning Adjustment (BZA) after it granted George Washington University (GWA) three special exceptions and two variances to build an addition to a medical school building.[23] The exceptions approved by the BZA included: 1) permitting the university to alter its campus plan; 2) permitting the university to exceed a statutory, floor-area ratio (FAR);[24] and 3) permitting the construction of a non-conforming roof structure. The variances approved by the BZA included 1) permitting the university to extend a non-conforming, floor-area ratio (FAR) into a building addition; and 2) permitting the university to have an open court area buffering its building with the neighboring condominium that was eight feet narrower than required. Exceptions granted by the zoning board were reviewed by determining if the exception was consistent with governing regulations and supported by substantial evidence. In contrast, variances required a showing that strict application of the regulation would create extraordinary and exceptional practical difficulties, that the non-conformity with regulations would not be detrimental to the public good, nor that the non-conformity would substantially impair the intent, purpose, and integrity of the existing zoning scheme.[25] The appellate court affirmed the zoning board's grant of all exemptions and variances.[26]

*Salve Regina College v. Zoning Board of Review of City of Newport*[27] found the college seeking a special exception (exemption) to convert a vacant carriage house into a dormitory. The zoning board denied the special exception, based largely upon the testimony of a neighbor. Although a lower court affirmed, the Rhode Island Supreme Court reversed, reasoning that because the neighbor was unqualified to testify as an expert witness on traffic patterns, the zoning board's denial of the college's application was an abuse of discretion. The court granted the college's request for a special exception.

Neighboring residents objected when a township zoning board granted a special exemption to allow a wholly owned subsidiary of St. Joseph's University to convert an apartment building into a dormitory.[28] The zoning ordinance provided for a special exemption for "educational institutions" in residential areas, and the neighbor plaintiffs argued that a dormitory was not an educational institution but instead was a "student home," which faced greater restrictions under zoning law. The state court noted that dormitories are not exclusively residential but are instead part of the overall educational experience.[29] Consequently, the court affirmed that the dormitory qualified for a special exemption as an educational institution.

## Spot Zoning

A somewhat unusual challenge to zoning decisions is that the classification creates spot zoning. Spot zoning is defined as "a singling out of one lot or a small area for different treatment from that accorded to similar surrounding land indistinguishable from it in character, for the economic benefit of the owner or to his economic detriment."[30] In *Sharp v. Zoning Hearing Board of Township of Radnor and Villanova University*,[31] a neighboring property owner appealed a board decision to rezone university property from residential to planned institutional district, in part on grounds that the board's decision constituted improper spot zoning. Because the property in question adjoined fourteen acres of university land that was zoned as institutional and contained dormitories, and was also across the street from the main campus, the court rejected the contention that spot zoning had occurred.

## Other Challenges

Some challenges by post-secondary institutions against local government zoning arise on procedural and fairness grounds. For example, when
a Rhode Island college expressed a desire to convert a hotel building into
a residence hall, the city responded with targeted ordinances designed
specifically to stop the college from using the building as a residence
hall. The state supreme court voided the ordinances because they did
not provide the college with sufficient notice under the governing state
statute.[32] Likewise, where Prince George's County, Maryland, created a
zoning classification of a "minidorm," defined as housing for unrelated
persons who are students, the court applied the rational basis test to hold
that classifying property on the basis of the occupation of inhabitants was
not rationally related to a legitimate governmental purpose.[33]

At times challenges arise from difficulty in ascertaining which body
has the power to make zoning decisions. In *Allegheny West Civil Council,
Inc., v. Zoning Hearing Board of Adjustment of City of Pittsburgh*,[34] a
community college sought approval to use an office building as a central
administrative office. Under the city's zoning ordinance, if a building was
part of an "educational institution," then the college was required to seek
approval by way of a conditional use application, acted upon by the city
council. However, if the building was not part of an "educational institution," then the conditional-use application was to go before the zoning
board of adjustment. Because the subject property was diagonally contigu-
ous with other college property, the college was required to approach the
city council to seek conditional-use approval.

In many instances, the roles of zoning boards and the role of the courts
are carefully circumscribed. Two cases illustrate this source of legal challenge. In *Lafayette College v. Zoning Hearing Board of City of Easton*,[35]
the zoning board denied the college's application for an exception to permit
the use of a single-family dwelling as housing for thirteen students. The
trial court changed the conditions for parking space requirements so that
it might grant a special exemption. The Pennsylvania Commonwealth
Court reversed, holding that the trial court exceeded its authority when it
added its own conditions and approved a plan that had not been submitted
by the college. The state court reasoned that in reviewing disputes over a
zoning board's decisions about granting exemptions, the court must return
the matter to the property owner and the zoning authority, rather than try
to fix the problem independently.

A second case turning on the role of the courts in zoning disputes was
*Town of Huntington v. Five Towns College*.[36] In this case, the Zoning Board
of Appeals denied a request by Five Towns College to build residence
halls as a permissible-use accessory to the college's educational function,
requiring instead that the college seek a special-use permit. The zoning
concern focused upon the size of the lot for the proposed residence halls,
which did not meet minimum size requirements. The trial court annulled

the zoning board's decision and granted the building permits. The appeals court reversed on grounds that the judiciary must defer to decisions of the zoning board of appeals, unless its decision is unreasonable or irrational. Two important factors should be underscored here. While the court was careful to balance the role of the courts with the role of the zoning board, the court's decision still provided an avenue of relief for the college. The college could still seek a special-use permit.

An unusual challenge arose from the likelihood that persons in local government also work at the local college or attend it as students. Zoning decisions might be challenged on grounds that decision makers are in a conflict of interest because of their dual roles. In *De Paolo v. Town of Ithaca*,[37] the Town Board amended zoning law to facilitate Cornell University's plan to implement a new cooling system for its campus buildings. Petitioners challenged the zoning change on grounds that four of the members of the town board either were employed at Cornell, a student at Cornell, or married to a retiree of Cornell. The court held that none of the four board members, in their university affiliation, had any direct involvement with the strategic plan of the university, so no conflict of interest existed.

Finally, the question of the proper standard of review was the source of one zoning challenge. A university sought a height variance to build an eighteen-story hotel and conference center on property zoned for only five stories. The property adjoined an old first-growth forest. The trial court ruled that substantial evidence was lacking to justify the grant of a variance. The Georgia Supreme Court ruled that the standard of review should have been an "any evidence standard," not a substantial evidence standard, and reversed the trial court.[38]

## Summary

In zoning disputes, the courts attempt to balance the needs of the post-secondary institution with the needs of the community, with a decided weighting in favor of the institution. In recent times, it is unusual for a court to invoke sovereignty of the state function of education as a rationale for denying the operation of a zoning ordinance. More likely, the rationale offered by the court will be based upon an interpretation of the wording of a statute or municipal ordinance. Particularly, many states offer, by statute, primacy for educational uses. There is a tendency to take an expansive view of what are permitted educational uses. Likewise, there is an attempt to interpret a city's own zoning ordinances in a manner that supports the balance in favor of the educational institution. Courts usually take a highly deferential view toward the decisions of administrative bodies like zoning commissions, but this is confounded by the tilt in favor of state educational use over the local community's ability to control the negative effects of development and change.

# Taxation

Conceptually, exemption from property tax closely follows exemption from zoning regulation. If a property is zoned for an educational use and is thus exempt from regulation by the local government, then the property is usually also exempt from taxation. The threshold question is whether the property is being used for an educational purpose, as articulated in state law.

## Educational Uses

Courts tend to take an expansive approach to what are considered educational uses under state law. For example, the National Collegiate Athletic Association (NCAA) created a corporation (National Collegiate Realty Corporation) to manage the property where it located its headquarters. The realty corporation challenged a decision by the Board of Tax Appeals that the headquarters was not tax-exempt as an "educational use" under Kansas law.[39] The Kansas Supreme Court acknowledged the role of the NCAA in assuring amateurism in intercollegiate sports and compared the NCAA with its Kansas State High School Activities Association, whose property was tax-exempt. The court held that NCAA's national headquarters was exempt from property taxes.[40]

In *Knox College v. Dept. of Revenue,*[41] the college appealed the lower court's decision to deny a property-tax exemption to properties owned by the college. The properties in question included buildings leased to national fraternities and an empty lot used by students for recreation purposes and surrounded by other exempt property. Illinois law provides an exemption for "all property of schools ... used by such schools exclusively for school purposes, not leased by such schools or otherwise used with a view to profit, including, but not limited to, student residence halls, dormitories and other housing facilities for students."[42] The state appellate court held that the property leased to fraternities qualified for the tax exemption. Likewise, the court found that open spaces, like the empty lot, serve as integral parts of college campuses and granted tax-exempt status for the empty lot.

A Wisconsin town appealed a court decision granting tax-exempt status for lakeside property owned by Indiana University.[43] From May to June each summer, the property was used for delivering a course in physical education. For the remainder of the summer, the property was leased to the alumni association and used for a summer camp. Wisconsin law provides tax exemption for property "owned and used exclusively by ... educational or benevolent associations."[44] The appeals court, noting the educational use of the physical education course and the integration of the alumni association with the operations of the university, held that the university property qualified for the tax exemption.

In a Georgia case,[45] where the Mechanical Trades Institute delivered an apprenticeship program in pipefitting and plumbing, the question before the court was whether the trade school was a "seminary of learning" as provided in Georgia's tax-exemption statute.[46] The court observed that throughout Georgia history, the term "seminary of learning" was used to describe any educational enterprise. The court ruled that the trade school program qualified for the tax exemption.

An interesting dispute arose out of a situation in which a college provided housing for some of its central service staff.[47] The college owned approximately fifty houses and rented eight of them to central service staff at a reduced rate. The county taxation board denied the college's tax-exempt status on the eight houses. In return for their availability on a twenty-four hour basis, staff members capable of performing maintenance, plumbing, electrical, and security work were given a 30 percent reduction in rent. The Pennsylvania Constitution grants exemption for "that portion of real property of such institution which is actually and regularly used for the purposes of the institution."[48] State law extends the exemption to "universities ... with the grounds thereto annexed and necessary for the occupancy and enjoyment of the same ... "[49] The Commonwealth court held that renting to staff members to answer emergency calls, even when occurring only a few times each year, was for the purposes of the institution and necessary for its occupancy.

Some state tax-exemption statutes are not as expansive as those discussed above. For example, Alabama's statute exempts, from ad valorem taxation, property that is used "exclusively for religious worship, for schools, or for purposes purely charitable."[50] The Auburn, Alabama, city industrial development board built a hotel and conference center on land owned by Auburn University and leased to the industrial board. The board in turn leased the facility to AU Hotel, a limited partnership. AU Hotel subleased the conference center back to Auburn University but contracted with a hotel management firm to operate the hotel. Because the hotel provided lodging for the general public and was thus not an exclusive educational use, the appellate court denied the partnership's request for tax-exempt status.[51]

Similarly, an appeals court interpreted the Texas tax-exemption statute to deny tax-exempt status for the college president's residence in *Bexar Appraisal District v. Incarnate Word College*.[52] Texas' property-tax code grants an exemption for school property "used exclusively for educational functions" and "reasonably necessary for the operation of the school."[53] The court held that the use of the building for the president's residence did not meet these statutory standards.

Occasionally, statutes must be harmonized to determine tax-exempt status. MiddleBury College had been granted a property known as the Snow Bowl, a park-like property held in trust by the college for the use and benefit of the public. The court was called upon to harmonize two statutes.

The first statute granted tax-exempt status to real estate "sequestered or used for public … uses."[54] The second statute withdrew tax-exempt status for property primarily used for recreation purposes.[55] Because the second statute limited the application of the first statute, the court held that the Snow Bowl property was not tax exempt.[56]

### Type of Property Interest

Universities and colleges must often pursue creative business arrangements to construct and operate buildings. For example, many university buildings are constructed using long-term lease agreements between the university and outside investors. In *Colleges of Seneca v. City of Geneva*,[57] a dormitory building and the land it was built on were the subjects of a tax-exemption dispute. The college leased the land to a developer for forty years and then entered into a master lease to build a dormitory on the land. During the master lease, the college controlled rental levels and selected students who could live in the dormitory. At the end of the lease, ownership reverted to the college. The lower courts provided a full exemption for the land but granted only a partial exemption for the building, proportionate to how much of the building was paid off. To retain tax exemption in lease agreements, a college must show that it has the incidences of ownership in the property. In this situation, the college argued successfully that it had all the incidents of ownership, emphasizing that the arrangement with the developer was analogous to financing the dormitory through a mortgage. The court agreed and granted tax-exempt status.

The University of Hartford leased an apartment building and used it for student housing. Approximately two-thirds of the apartments were rented to students. Elderly and disabled tenants rented the remaining apartments. The court stopped short of considering whether the usage was an educational use for tax-exempt status. Rather, the court determined that the university's leasehold was not the type of interest in the property that qualified for tax-exempt status.[58]

Illinois law provided exemptions for property owned by the state[59] and for property used exclusively for educational uses.[60] In a case addressing the property interest held by the university, where the building was owned by the university foundation, the university foundation argued that a building owned by the foundation and leased to the university as a conference center qualified for tax exemption under both statutory provisions.[61] Despite the close relationship between the foundation and the university, the court denied tax-exempt status on the basis of ownership. As it happened, the grantor of the property attached covenants and restrictions on the use of the property, with the possibility of a reverter to the grantor if the covenants and restrictions were not observed. Because the grantor retained substantial control over the property by limiting its use and maintaining a reversionary interest, the court held that the property was not owned by the state for tax-exemption purposes. The court further denied tax-exempt status on grounds of an exclusive educational use. In Illinois, qualification for exemption for educational use depends upon the use, not ownership.[62] Because the conference center was rented out to others with little connection to the university's educational function, the court denied tax-exempt status under the exclusive educational use provision.

In *Zach, Inc. v. Fulton County*,[63] Zach, a non-profit corporation created by a national fraternity, owned a fraternity house on land surrounded by Georgia Tech. An exemption on the property depended upon a showing of a sufficient nexus between the property and an educational function. However, in Georgia, it is usually essential for the property to be owned by the college. The court denied the exemption.

A contrasting case occurred after Georgia Southern College created a non-profit corporation, Southern Greek Housing Corporation (SGHC), to construct housing for fraternities and sororities on land owned by the corporation and surrounded on three sides by land owned by the college.[64] Georgia law exempts from property taxation "all buildings erected for and used as a college, incorporated academy, or other seminary of learning,"[65] provided that "such property is used exclusively for educational purposes."[66] Noting the nexus between the college and its foundation, as well as the educative function of fraternity and sorority housing and their connection to the life of the college, the court granted the tax exemption.

A final case addressing how the property interest in question leads to a determination of tax exemption occurred where professors at the University of California Irvine entered into a long-term lease with the university to build their homes on land owned by the university.[67] The professors challenged a ruling that the homes were not tax-exempt. The California Supreme Court held that the professors' leasehold was not property used exclusively for university purposes within the meaning of the state tax-exemption statute.[68]

## Proportional Exemptions

When university-owned properties have uses that are mixed, the dispute can be over whether the property is fully tax exempt or only partially exempt, proportional to the amount of use that is educational. Where the University of Pennsylvania leased a commercial building to a partnership consisting of two commercial partners and the university itself, the university argued for at least a partial exemption of taxes, proportionate to the university's interest in the property.[69] In the lease agreement, the university both paid rent to the partnership and received fair profits through the partnership. Emphasizing that Pennsylvania's tax-exemption statute grants exempt status for properties used for charitable purposes,[70] the court denied the university any tax exemptions in connection with the commercial building's lease or the ground it was on.

In *Hays County Appraisal District v. Southwest Texas State University*,[71] the university foundation purchased property known as the Fire Station Building and a nearby parking lot. 'The first floor of the building held offices and common areas, the second floor held a recording studio, and the third floor held men's and women's locker rooms. The parking lot was a block away. The foundation leased the property to the university in anticipation of beginning an academic program in sound recording. Because roughly 20 percent of the building and two-thirds of the parking lot were subleased to commercial interests, the lower court granted exemptions proportional to their use by the university. The appeals court rejected this view, holding that because the properties were owned by the university's private foundation, they were not public properties dedicated exclusively for public use under Texas law.

In another mixed-use dispute, DePaul University leased tennis courts and a clubhouse to a private tennis club.[72] Under the lease, the university used the facilities for physical education classes a set number of hours each day. DePaul University challenged a denial of a tax exemption for the property. In Illinois, to determine if the statutory requirement of exclusive educational use has been met in a property with more than one use, the inquiry involves a determination of whether the exempt purpose is primary and the non-exempt purpose is only incidental.[73] The appeals court affirmed the denial of the tax exemption because the property was used primarily for profit and not for school purposes.

Many universities fulfill their missions related to economic development through business incubator programs. Such a program was at the center of a tax-exemption dispute involving Case Western Reserve University.[74] The property in dispute included a university office building and adjacent parking garage. Tenants in the building included three, non-profit corporations and two, for-profit corporations. Two of the non-profit corporations were directly affiliated with the university. The court granted tax-exempt status for the space occupied by the university-affiliated corporations but denied such status for the space occupied by the other corporations and the parking garage.

Ohio law grants tax-exemption status when property is "used for the support of such institution."[75] This creates a broader exemption than that occurring in many states, which grant exemption for property that is used exclusively for educational purposes. A case involving the University of Cincinnati illustrates this attribute.[76] The State of Ohio held title to a building for the benefit of the university. The architecture school took up 88 percent of the building, but 12 percent was leased for commercial use as a laundry and convenience store. Because the rent from the commercial uses went into the university's general fund, the court held that all of the building qualified for the tax exemption.

Likewise, in *Board of Trustees of the Ohio State University v. Kinney*,[77] the disputed property was seventy-eight acres adjacent to the university airport. Much of the property was used as a control zone for the airport and for agricultural research. A house on a half-acre lot was leased to a private party, and the rentals were credited to the university's general operating fund. The bulk of the property was an educational use. Renting the house helped the university avoid the potential cost of demolition and the risks inherent in leaving university buildings vacant. Further, the rent on the house contributed to the support of the institution, which was consistent with the expanded exemption standard in Ohio. The court granted tax-exempt status for the entire property.

## Summary

Tax exemption follows closely the authority relationships between post-secondary institutions and local communities found in zoning regulation. However, interpretation of the wording of the tax-exemption statute is paramount in deciding which university properties receive tax-exempt status and which do not. The language of the exemption statute can be narrow (e.g., "exclusively educational use") or very broad (e.g., "for the support of the institution"). With the former type of language, the court is likely to be restrictive in recognizing university-owned property as tax-exempt so that for properties with a multitude of uses, some educational and some not, only a proportional share of the property maintains its tax-exempt status. With the latter type of language, even property with uses that are clearly proprietary and income producing may retain their tax-exempt status because the profits garnered by their use flow back to and benefit the university's educational function. In recent times, higher education administrators have employed creative financing and innovative business structures to build new facilities or breathe life into old ones. College and university administrators need to be careful in establishing such financing and business structures, which may end up losing tax-exempt status for all or a portion of the property involved.

## Community Access to University Property

Another source of dispute between higher education institutions and their surrounding communities is access by community members to university property, especially when those community members have no other connection to the institution. Colleges and universities are property owners, and as property owners, one might think that such institutions have considerable right to control access to their facilities. However, the extent to which institutions of higher education can exert control over their property is mitigated by the unique nature of higher education institutions and the unique role they play in the larger community. As the Colorado Supreme Court once observed:

Universities sponsor many functions outside those occurring within classrooms, and those activities provide educational benefit to students as well as outsiders.[78]

The extension of educational benefit to outsiders, or the decision by
institutional leaders to exclude outsiders from that benefit, implicates the
law of trespass. This section of this chapter reviews court cases in which
colleges and universities have attempted to exclude persons from their
campuses, invoking the law of trespass.

The law of trespass finds its roots in English common law, having
developed in the thirteenth century as a criminal offense against the King's
peace.[79] Trespass provided a remedy in the King's courts for forcible,
direct, and immediate injuries to persons or property for the kinds of
conduct that were likely to produce immediate retaliation. In that context,
trespass began as a criminal action, with damages awarded to the injured
party as an incidental award.

In the modern era, trespass is both a criminal claim and a civil tort
claim. However, higher education administrators typically attempt to
exclude others from campus by invoking criminal trespass statutes and
ordinances, rather than by initiating civil tort claims against the trespassers.
Criminal trespass law can be both general, which applies to all property
owners within the state, or specific to college campuses. Texas provides
an example of the former since its criminal trespass statute applies to a
person who enters or remains on the property of another without consent.[80]
An example of the latter can be found in California, which has a separate
criminal trespass law that protects college and university campuses from
incursions by outsiders.[81]

## Access to Public Versus Private Institutions

The body of case law on trespass in higher education institutional
settings demonstrates that the person charged with trespass will usually raise a constitutional defense, most often alleging violation of First
Amendment speech or assembly rights. Because a person charged with
the crime of trespass so often argues that the trespass statute, as written or
applied, violates a constitutional right, it would seem logical that public
colleges and universities would stand in a different place, compared to
private institutions, in their ability to control access to their facilities. One
might presume that public colleges and universities more often involve
state action and are thus subject to constitutional constraints, while private
universities are free to exert access controls unimpeded by constitutional
values. However, this presumption does not account for the application
of state constitutional rights that may apply with equal force of public
and private institutions.

In a case involving Princeton University, a private institution, the New
Jersey Supreme Court addressed whether a private university was subject

to state constitutional oversight.[82] The court took the position that the free speech rights vested in the state constitution provided broader protection for individual speech rights than the federal constitution. The court adopted a three-part test to decide when a state constitutional obligation attaches so that even a private property owner may be required to permit the reasonable exercise by individuals of their constitutional freedoms of speech and assembly. The test takes into account

1) the nature, purposes, and primary use of such private property, generally, in its "normal use;"

2) the extent and nature of the public's invitation to use that property; and

3) the purpose of the expressional activity undertaken upon such property in relation to both the private and public use of the property.[83]

Based upon this test, the New Jersey court held that Princeton University, even though it was a private institution, was subject to state constitutional oversight.

In contrast, a lower New Jersey court decided that another private institution was not subject to constitutional oversight. In *State v. Guice*, outsiders were charged with criminal trespass for distributing political literature on the campus of Stevens Institute of Technology, a private institution, after being asked to leave.[84] Using the test in *Schmid*, the court found that the private institute had not opened its campus to the public as Princeton University had done. Consequently, the defendants did not have a constitutional right to distribute materials, and their conviction stood.

## Rule-Making Concerning Access

In both public and private institutions of higher education, the ability to assert control over buildings, grounds, and facilities depends upon thoughtful decisions about the extent to which the campus is open to the public at large, where access is being provided or denied, and whether rule-making regarding access is reasonable. In the *Schmid* case, discussed previously, a non-student was convicted for criminal trespass for distributing pamphlets for a political party on the college campus. After deciding that Princeton University was subject to state constitutional control, the same as a public university, the court considered a second issue: whether the university's general regulations violated the pamphleteer's speech and assembly rights. Princeton University's regulations required that access by off-campus persons for the purpose of expression depended upon invitation and permission. They did not articulate standards for granting or withholding permission, nor did they address manner, place, or time restrictions that would provide information about when access could be obtained. Without reasonable regulations designed to notify off-campus visitors as well as to inform administrators charged with implementing the regulations, the court held that Princeton University had violated the pamphleteer's constitutional rights and overturned his conviction for trespass.[85]

Similarly, in *Reproductive Rights v. President of University of Massachusetts*, the absence of specific rule making proved fatal to the university's legal position.[86] In that case, university regulations were non-specific, requiring only the use of a written form for scheduling a room. Despite the form requirement, faculty had traditionally been allowed to schedule a room by verbal request. A student, on behalf of herself and a political action group, had solicited, through a faculty member, access to a classroom to be used for organizational meetings to plan a demonstration. After the group met once, two members of the board of trustees called the university president to protest the activists' use of the room. When the group convened a second time, the president sent a contingent of seventeen police officers to lock out the students. The activists then sued the university, alleging violation of the First Amendment and the state civil rights act. The appeals court held that the university had violated the group's speech and assembly rights because the policy on using campus facilities was vague, arbitrarily applied, and did not provide narrow, objective, and definite standards to assist administrators in determining who might have access to facilities.[87]

A better outcome, from the institution's perspective, came out of a situation involving Ohio University. That institution has a College Green, an open green space bounded on three sides by academic buildings and, on the fourth side, a public street. A gate separated the university property from the public street. By university regulation, students and non-students may pass out literature, engage in fundraising, and make public speeches at the gate and five other designated areas, after obtaining a permit. In *State v. Spingola*, a preacher who was not a student was arrested for criminal trespass after he refused to leave the university.[88] He had been preaching in an area by a monument on the College Green, which was not one of the six areas designated for public expression by the university. Ohio trespass law prohibits any person, without privilege to do so, from recklessly entering or remaining on the land or premises of another, when the person has been notified that his or her presence is unauthorized.[89] The preacher argued that he had a First Amendment right to preach at the monument because it was a public forum. The appeals court held that the monument area where the preacher had been speaking was not a public forum and affirmed his conviction. Critical to the outcome in this case was the university's well-articulated policy defining areas of the campus that constituted public forums and on where exactly access was provided and not provided.[90]

## Notice to Trespassers

Besides attention to rule making, college and university administrators must also consider means of providing notice. Notice is a critical factor in informing people when they stand to be prosecuted for trespass by marking territory that is off-limits, by using architectural features to delineate between open areas and closed areas, and by providing verbal or written notice of exclusion from an area. Ohio University, in the case above, provided notice, by regulation and by practice, that six campus areas were available for the exercise of speech and assembly rights. Another university in Ohio lost its case for lack of notice as to the areas of the campus that were subject to restrictions.

In *State v. McMechan*,[91] a student at Miami University was found building a fire in a park on the university campus at 1:22 a.m. A university police officer arrested him for criminal trespass. At trial, the student testified that he was a new student on campus, and he was unaware of any use restrictions, including that the park was closed at night. The university had posted signs at the front gate to the park listing restrictions for its use. The student had entered the park, in the dark, by a trail that did not have a posted sign. The trial court held that the student had a duty to go to the front gate and determine what any posted signs might say. The appellate court held that the university had failed to provide adequate notice on the use of the property. Rather than the student having a duty to ascertain the restrictions, the university had a duty to communicate restrictions on the use of a particular parcel of land or a particular building. Because it had only placed signs at the main entrance, the university had failed to provide adequate notice. An observation by the appeals court in that case is instructive:

> Adequate warnings of land or premises use restrictions can be communicated actually or constructively—that is, through the use of physical barriers such as barricades, barriers, fences and locks which actually limit or bar access, or by signs at the entrance to the land or premises which inform the use, i.e., act as constructive notice, of the restrictions which exist.[92]

A Texas case turned on the lack of architectural barriers to mark university property.[93] The University of Texas had a policy that prohibited the distribution of leaflets unless a student did the distribution and the leaflets had the name of the student or a student organization printed upon them. Political activists were forced to stop their distribution of leaflets outside a special-events center at the University of Texas. The activists sued the university, alleging violation of the First Amendment's protections of freedom of speech and assembly. The federal district court entered a declaratory judgment for the plaintiffs, ruling that the property where the leaflets were distributed was a public forum, and the university's outright ban on non-students handing out political leaflets in that area violated the activists' free speech rights.[94] The events center was framed on all four sides with sidewalks owned by the city. The areas around the sidewalks were landscaped and paved with crushed stones the same color as the sidewalk. On visual inspection, no signals were provided as to what was university property and what was city sidewalk. The appeals court agreed with the federal district court, holding that the entire area around the events center from its base to the curb was a public forum accessible to the protestors and not effectively restricted by the university.

Notice also implicates situations where the college or university administration elects to inform with an exclusionary letter. In *People v. Leonard*,[95] Leonard had been a student off and on at the State University of New York at Binghamton (SUNY-Binghamton) for ten years. For reasons not stated, the university president sent Leonard a "persona non grata" letter banishing him from all university property. When Leonard was later found at the pub in the university union building, he was arrested for trespass. At the time of his arrest, Leonard was not a student, but the university property, including the pub, was open to the public at large. The county court upheld his conviction, but the appeals court reversed. The appeals court held that the government had failed to demonstrate an essential element for criminal trespass in New York, a showing that the banishment letter had a legitimate basis, and, considering the nature and use of the property, its enforcement did not inhibit the defendant from engaging in protected conduct. The prosecutor for the state would surely have been assisted in showing this element of the crime, had the university held a hearing to discuss the matter and preserved a record of the hearing, before issuing the exclusionary letter.

A special warning about notice is pertinent to institutions of higher education. As organizations go, colleges and universities tend to be more loosely-coupled systems than for-profit organizations in society. Consequently, it is not unthinkable that one office in the university would be unaware of what another office is doing. An example of this situation can be found in *Bader v. State*,[96] in which the director of security for Texas A & M University gave a former student a written criminal trespass warning. The warning informed the former student that he would be arrested if he entered campus property without permission. The warning went on to say that the former student's exclusion would be nullified should he be readmitted as a student. The student had reapplied for admission in January and subsequently enrolled for summer school. There was no evidence that he had actually been accepted. A block on his re-admission was placed on his records ten days after summer school began. However, a state appeals court reasoned that because the registrar had enrolled him, his exclusion from campus had been nullified by the terms of the exclusion letter. Consequently, the court reversed the former student's trespass conviction.

## Administrative Hearings

A concept related to the duty to provide notice is the duty to provide administrative hearings related to exclusions. A federal district court in Maryland observed that an educational institution has the power to suspend students and teachers for proper reasons and has no less a right to exclude outsiders who engage in conduct that violates constitutional standards.[97] However, the court observed that Maryland's criminal trespass statute required a showing of three elements: that the trespasser had no lawful business on the campus; that the trespasser engaged in disruptive acts that violate state law; and that the trespasser returned to campus after being provided notice of exclusion. Consequently, the court held that the university could not deny access without providing an administrative hearing to prove the elements of lawful business and disruptive acts. In other words, the outsider's conviction for trespass, under Maryland law, required that the university hold a hearing to examine whether the outsider had lawful business on the campus and whether the outsider had engaged in disruptive acts.

Another Maryland case held that the university did not have a duty to hold an administrative hearing.[98] In this case, a photography instructor at another college was invited to exhibit his work at Towson State University for a three-week period, for a fee of $200. Two days before the exhibition was to commence, the instructor was given notice that the invitation was being withdrawn. The instructor showed up at the appointed time and attempted to hang his works. The supervisor of campus security told the instructor that he was denied the opportunity to display his works and that if he did not remove them, he would be held accountable under trespass law. The instructor left and returned fifteen minutes later. The security supervisor again told the instructor that he must remove his photographs, or he would be arrested within ten minutes. Ten minutes later, the instructor was arrested for trespass.

The instructor fought his conviction, arguing that he had a constitutional right to display the photographs, supported by the university's breach of contract. The court held that the university's breach of contract did not bestow upon the instructor a constitutional right to hold his exhibition. Nor did the Constitution require that the court approve of the instructor's violation of a valid criminal statute because the university authorities were wrong in breaching the contract. The photography instructor did not have a constitutional right to display his photographs when he was in violation of the trespass statute. Importantly, the court distinguished this situation from that in *Dunkel,* mentioned previously. In *Dunkel*, an administrative decision to send an exclusion letter required an administrative hearing prior to sending the letter. Here, according to the court, a decision to prosecute for a criminal act did not first require an administrative hearing on the exclusion because the due process attendant to a finding of criminality provided sufficient review.

The need to hold an administrative hearing prior to issuing an exclusion letter is reinforced in a Colorado case. In *Watson v. Board of Regents of University of Colorado*, the university president sent a letter to an applicant informing the applicant of his permanent exclusion from the university campus.[99] The applicant had been denied admission to the University of Colorado, based apparently on a prior felony conviction. The applicant applied again and was turned down a second time. The applicant then went with another person to the private home of a dean on the admissions committee. The next day, he returned to the dean's home with a group of persons. The dean felt intimidated and left town for two days. After this, the president wrote the exclusion letter. Subsequently, the applicant was found at the university center and was cited for trespass under a Boulder municipal ordinance. He then sued for injunctive and declaratory relief, alleging violations of his rights under the First and Fourteenth Amendment. The court held that, because the university opened its doors to the general public, it could not issue an exclusion order against the applicant without providing due process in the form of an administrative hearing.

## University Access and Commercial Speech

Two trespass cases involve the same corporation, American Future Systems, and that corporation's asserted right to engage in commercial speech on university property. Commercial speech is generally accorded less privilege than other types of speech, especially political speech, on university campuses.

In the first case, *American Future Systems, Inc. v. Pennsylvania State University*,[100] the university had a student handbook rule that prohibited commercial transactions in residence halls, except when an individual student invited a salesperson to his or her room for the purpose of transacting business with that student only. The student handbook did not prohibit businesses from advertising their products in student newspapers or on the student radio station, nor did it prohibit telemarketing to student rooms or solicitations through the mail. American Future Systems (AFS) was a company that sold house wares to students by way of a process that is popularly known as "Tupperware parties." AFS received invitations to residence halls by offering incentives to students they contacted randomly by telephone. The university offered to allow ASF to continue the parties, as long as ASF only made product presentations and did not consummate the sales of the products in those meetings. ASF was not willing to do this. After having several parties interrupted by university officials, AFS sought declaratory and injunctive relief against the university. A federal district court found in favor of the university, and AFS appealed. The Third Circuit Court of Appeal agreed with the university's argument, that the residence halls were nonpublic forums and that the university's restrictions were reasonable place and manner restrictions consistent with the educational purpose of the forums.

AFS appeared again in a New York case that made its way to the United States Supreme Court, *Board of Trustees of State University of New York v. Fox*.[101] At issue in this case was a State University of New York (SUNY) policy that stated:

> No authorization will be given to private commercial enterprises to operate on State University campuses or in facilities furnished by the University other than to provide for food, legal beverages, campus bookstore, vending, linen supply, laundry, dry cleaning, banking, barber and beautician services and cultural events.[102]

An AFS representative, who was invited to sell her products by a residence hall student, was charged with criminal trespass. The student filed suit, seeking injunctive relief and declaratory judgment that the resolution violated the student's First Amendment rights, and the company joined the student as a plaintiff. Although the district court initially granted a preliminary injunction,[103] it subsequently found for the university, on grounds that the university had not created a public forum for commercial speech and that the restrictions were reasonable in light of the residence hall's purpose.[104] The Court of Appeals for the Second Circuit reversed and remanded,[105] and the company withdrew. This left the student's First Amendment claim as the sole remaining issue. Applying a "least restrictive means" test (i.e., whether the resolution directly advanced the state's asserted interests and whether, if it did, it was the least-restrictive means to that end), the appellate court reversed and remanded. Under the least-restrictive means test, a university regulation of commercial speech would be unconstitutional unless the university could show that it had exhausted all other potential ways of regulating the commercial speech. On review, the Supreme Court rejected the application of a least-restrictive means test in the regulation of commercial speech in university residence halls, adopting, instead, a test requiring that the institution's regulation be "narrowly tailored" to achieve an important or substantial state interest. Under this test, the institution must demonstrate that the regulation of commercial speech is narrowly tailored in so far as it represents a reasonable and proportional fit between the regulation's ends and the means chosen to accomplish those ends. Given that the institution's regulation was intended to preserve student privacy and maintain the residence hall facilities as places in which students might live and study and provided that the institution insured that alternative forums for the exercise of commercial speech, such as lobby areas or other locations proximate to residence halls rooms were available, the institution's regulation of commercial speech met the narrow tailoring standard. Consequently, to control commercial speech on its property, a state university is given considerable leeway in deciding what manner of regulation may best be used, as long as it can show that it is narrowly tailored to achieve the desired objective.[106]

## Summary

The unique nature of colleges and universities make community access to the property owned by these institutions an important "town and gown" issue. Higher education institutions do more than offer courses and programs of study. They possess a special place in the life of their communities; by providing such activities as cultural, political, social, and athletic events; by having within their precincts such facilities as libraries and museums open for public use; and by having park-like settings that invite assembly and discourse. Institutions, both public and private, may face difficulty in using criminal trespass law as a means of controlling access to their facilities. To the extent that private colleges and universities open themselves to public access, they, like public institutions, may be subject to constitutional oversight under state law so that a trespasser may be able to assert free speech and association rights to access as a defense to a conviction for criminal trespass.

College and university administrators should review with legal counsel all aspects of institutional policy on access to the campus, including to what extent the campus is opened to the public at large, where access is generally provided or denied, and what rules apply to use of facilities. Those rules must articulate standards for granting or withholding permission and address reasonable time, place, and manner restrictions that inform the community about how and when access can be obtained.

Institutional administrators should also consider due process aspects of community access, particularly with respect to providing notice and administrative hearings. Notice may be actual or constructive. Actual notice may occur by giving a warning that someone is violating the law, or by providing an exclusion letter. Constructive notice may come from signage, barriers, or architectural features that serve to let outsiders know where they may be and may not be for particular purposes. An administrative hearing may not be necessary every time the institution wishes to use trespass law to exclude outsiders, but notice and an administrative hearing should certainly be provided before issuing an exclusion letter to a former student when student misconduct is involved.

Commercial speech on college and university property can be subject to reasonable restrictions, consistent with the educational purpose of the institution. Institutions need not show that they have exhausted all potential ways of controlling commercial speech; they need only adopt narrowly tailored regulations that are reasonable and proportional to their purpose.

## Environmental Protection

Environmental protection is the fourth "town and gown" issue that warrants discussion. Colleges and universities have a unique place in their communities; indeed, they are themselves often large and complex communities. By-products from nuclear research and medical waste from university hospitals must be gathered for disposal. Vehicles and equipment must be maintained, creating the need to dispose of parts, batteries, unused paint, and the like. Many campuses produce their own electricity and treat wastewater. The myriad activities occurring on a university campus can bring the institution under the control of federal and state environmental protection laws. Environmental protection laws can create significant problems beyond poor public relations for institutions. Fines, civil forfeitures, and criminal convictions face those who do not take seriously the potential liability arising from a failure to comply with environmental protection laws and regulations. Such laws are generally designed to control the activities of large industrial producers such as petrochemical companies; however, few exemptions are written into the laws, and colleges and universities, because of their expansive—and sometimes unusual—types of activities, find themselves and their leaders at risk.

## Clean Air Act

Colleges and universities come under the purview of the Clean Air Act[107] as a result of such activities as operating incinerators, heating plants, motor vehicles, and aircraft. The act was designed to reduce emissions of pollutants from a variety of sources, thus improving air quality. The act is administered by the federal Environmental Protection Agency, or a state agency if the state's environmental protection plan meets or exceeds federal requirements. Since its enactment, subsequent reauthorizations and regulations have set high standards in restricting air pollutants. Universities in large metropolitan areas that have failed to reach air quality goals face heavier burdens including, for example, requirements to purchase "greener" vehicles and increase the occupancy average of university-owned vehicles for work-related trips by certain percentages.

## Clean Water Act

Higher education institutions are subject to provisions of the Federal Water Pollution Control Act,[108] often called the Clean Water Act. Institutions that permit wastewater to be discharged directly into surface water are required to obtain a permit. The permit will usually limit what is permitted to be discharged. If the wastewater is discharged directly into a community's sewage treatment facility, a permit is not required, but the effluent may be under certain pretreatment standards. The act also regulates run-off to storm sewers, which is especially applicable to university agricultural programs that run feedlots. Likewise, construction sites may be subject to run-off requirements.

## Toxic Substances Control Act

The Toxic Substances Control Act of 1976[109] has provisions in two areas relevant to college and university facilities maintenance: disposal of polychlorinated biphenyls (PCB's) and limiting exposure to and disposal of asbestos materials. PCB's were commonly used in electrical equipment like capacitors and transformers. The act controls the inventory and disposal of electrical equipment containing PCB's. Fortunately, most institutions have minimized exposure under this act by using updated equipment that lack PCB's. The act also contains legislation concerning air emissions of asbestos during reconstruction or destruction of buildings containing asbestos.

## Radionucleotide Safety

Radionucleotides are commonly used in medical research, teaching, and treatment. The Atomic Energy Act[110] places university uses of radionucleotides under the supervision of the Nuclear Regulatory Commission (NRC). An important provision makes the institution subject to civil forfeitures. The NRC is permitted to recover the cost of license and inspection fees from universities for radionucleotides used in medical applications but not for educational (research and teaching) applications. The Low-level Radioactive Waste Policy Amendment Act of 1985 covers issues concerning disposal of radionucleotides.[111]

## Hazardous Waste Management

The Resource Conservation and Recovery Act of 1976 (RCRA)[112] covers solid wastes that have any one of four characteristics: toxicity; ignitability; reactivity; or corrosivity. Solid wastes under the act include compressed gases, liquids, and semi-solids, not just solids. Because of its activities, an institution might qualify for oversight under the act as a generator of solid waste; as a transporter of solid waste; or as a facility that treats, stores, or disposes of solid waste. Civil fines under the act of up to $25,000, and criminal fines of $50,000 can be assessed against persons in a position of responsibility. The institution may be subject to a maximum fine of $1 million. The Comprehensive Environmental Response, Compensation and Liability Act (CERCLA),[113] often called the Superfund, imposes liability for institutions, including universities, for finding and cleaning up abandoned or uncontrolled hazardous waste sites. The Environmental Protection Agency, or a state agency, administers the Superfund and notifies potentially responsible parties of their liability for cleanup costs. An institution may have strict liability, meaning that even though it was legal to dispose of waste in a particular way in prior years, the existence of current hazardous waste is sufficient to trigger the application of CERCLA.

## Summary

Environmental protection laws and regulations provide special challenges concerning the relationship between a higher education institution and its community. Because of the expansive and unusual types of activities in which many research universities are involved, universities and their leaders are particularly vulnerable to fines, civil forfeitures, and criminal convictions from both the federal and state levels if they fail to comply with the array of environmental protection laws governing emissions, water treatment, toxic substances, radionucleotides, and hazardous waste.

# Conclusions

Because of their unique character, institutions of higher education occupy an important place in society and interact repeatedly with the communities in which they are located. These interactions produce a multitude of "town and gown" issues. Without spotlighting them as such, previous chapters of this book address various "town and gown" issues. For example, an institution's governance structure is an expression of its relationship with the larger community. As a corporate body, a college or university can contract or sue and be sued and, thereby, interact with its community. As an employer, a higher education institution provides employment for a community and helps build the community by bringing skills and talent into the community. This chapter addresses four "town and gown" issues: zoning, tax exemption, community access, and environmental protection.

Zoning regulation represents an attempt to balance the educational needs of the post-secondary institution with the community's need to control negative effects of development and change. Historically, the statewide educational function was viewed as sovereign over a local community's zoning needs. In recent years, courts have rationalized this balance in favor of the educational institution by invoking an expansive interpretation of statutes or ordinances that provide exemptions or variances favoring educational uses.

Conceptually, tax exemption closely follows zoning exemption. Each state has adopted statutory tax exemptions for educational uses, with some states providing only narrow exemptions and other states providing very broad exemptions. In states with narrow exemptions, the court will look at the property usage and determine whether or not the usage comes within the statute. Consequently, properties may not be educational, as interpreted by the court, even though monies collected through the usage flow to an educational use. In such situations, the courts may permit tax exemptions, proportional to the amount of the building being used for an educational purpose. In states with broad exemptions, property usage may be considered educational, even though its only connection to education is the revenue produced for the overall benefit of the institution.

Community access to university property is a "town and gown" issue in which the educational institution invokes criminal trespass statutes to control access by outsiders to its facilities, buildings, and grounds. Criminal defendants characteristically invoke a First Amendment right to speech or assembly as a defense to a trespass charge. Private institutions, as well as public institutions, may be subject to constitutional review if the private institution has, by policy or practice, opened itself up to the community. The ability of a higher education institution, whether public or private, to control access to its facilities by outsiders depends greatly upon the rules developed by institutional officials and the law of the jurisdiction where the institution is situated. These rules must spell out standards for access and provide manner, place, and time restrictions that inform the community about campus access. Further, institutions must provide notice to potential trespassers by giving verbal or written notice, by signs and barriers, and by using architectural design to signal what areas are open forums and what areas are closed to the public.

The final "town and gown" issue discussed in this chapter is environmental protection. Conformity to state and federal environmental protection laws are paramount concerns for higher education institutions and their leaders because of the potential for creating hazards and subjecting the institution to criminal and civil liability. Research universities, in particular, engage in a host of activities that place them and their leaders at risk of fines, civil forfeitures, and criminal convictions for failure to comply with the provisions of these laws.

Town and gown issues focus upon the interdependent relationship between the college and university and its surrounding community. Compliance with the law applicable to the many facets of that relationship is an essential aspect of being a good neighbor and a valued contributor to the life of the community in which the institution finds its home.

## Endnotes

[1] Each of these topics is touched upon briefly in other chapters, in the context appropriate for that chapter. This chapter attempts to capture current trends, based upon case law or statutory changes within the last two decades.

[2] BLACK'S LAW DICTIONARY (6th ed.) West's Publishing Co., St. Paul, Minn., p. 1156.

[3] Macon-Bibb County Planning and Zoning Comm'n v. Bibb County Sch. Dist., 474 S.E.2d 70, 71 [111 EDUC. L. REP. 1382, 1383] (Ga. App. 1996).

[4] Macon Ass'n v. Macon-Bibb County Planning and Zoning Comm'n, 314 S.E.2d 218, 222 (1984).

[5] Inspector of Bldgs. of Salem v. Salem State Coll., 546 N.E.2d 388 (Mass. App. 1989).

[6] G.L. Mass. c. 40A §3. Many states have tipped the balance back in favor of municipalities, granting them the authority to exercise control over the state entity in limited situations. This is an example of such a statute.

[7] 712 N.Y.S.2d 160 [146 EDUC. L. REP. 839] (N.Y.A.D. 2000).

[8] 712 N.Y.S.2d 160, 161 [146 EDUC. L. REP. 839, 840].

9   Trustees of Union Coll. v. Members of Schenectady City Council, 667 N.Y.S.2d 978 [123 Educ. L. Rep. 1247] (N.Y. App. 1997).

10  West's Ann. Cal. Gov. Code § 53094.

11  277 Cal. Rptr. 69 [64 Educ. L. Rep. 857] (Cal. App. 1990).

12  621 So.2d 176 [84 Educ. L. Rep. 868] (La. App. 1993).

13  618 N.W.2d 537 [148 Educ. L. Rep. 478] (Wis. App. 2000).

14  431 S.E.2d 183 [83 Educ. L. Rep. 1161] (N.C. 1993).

15  Borough of Glassboro v. Vallorosi, 568 A.2d 888 [58 Educ. L. Rep. 668] (N.J. 1990).

16  DeSisto Coll., Inc. v. Town of Howey-in-the-Hills, 706 F. Supp. 1479 [52 Educ. L. Rep. 520] (M.D. Fla. 1989).

17  Schwerdt v. City of Corvallis, 987 P.2d 1243 [139 Educ. L. Rep. 673] (Or. App. 1999).

18  836 P.2d 710 (Or. 1992).

19  *See* Spring Valley Wesley Heights Citizen's Ass'n v. Dist. of Columbia Bd. of Zoning Adjustment, 644 A.2d 434, 435 (D.C. 1994).

20  675 A.2d 26 [109 Educ. L. Rep. 275] (D.C. App. 1996).

21  Blacks Law Dictionary, 570 (6th ed. 1991).

22  Black's Law Dictionary, 1553 (6th ed. 1991).

23  Draude v. Bd. of Zoning Adjustment, 582 A.2d 949 [64 Educ. L. Rep. 818] (Draude II) (D.C. App. 1990).

24  A building's floor area ratio (FAR) is determined by dividing the gross floor area of the building by the gross area of the lot on which the building is built.

25  *See* D.C. Code 5-424(g)(3) (1988).

26  The court noted that the building addition had been constructed while the matter was before the court. The court further offered that, had it ruled oppositely, it would not have hesitated to order the university to make modifications to the addition or even tear it down. Fortunately, the court did not call upon itself to test its own resolve. 582 A.2d at 951 [64 Educ. L. Rep. At 820].

27  594 A.2d 878 [69 Educ. L. Rep. 477] (R.I. 1991).

28  Greaton Props., Inc. v. Lower Merion Township, 796 A.2d 1038 [164 Educ. L. Rep. 809] (Pa. Cmwlth. 2002).

29  The view that dormitories have broader educational uses than just housing has been shared by several jurisdictions. *See, e.g.*, Connecticut v. Laurel Creast Acad., 198 A.2d 229 (Conn. 1963); Schueller v. Bd. of Adjustment of City of Dubuque, 95 N.W.2d 731 (Iowa 1959); Western Theological Seminary v. City of Evanston, 156 N.E. 778 (Ill. 1927).

30  Milac Appeal, 418 Pa. 207, 210, 210 A.2d 275, 277 (1965).

31  628 A.2d 1223 [84 Educ. L. Rep. 1069] (Pa. Cmwlth. 1993).

32  Johnson & Wales Coll. v. DiPrete, 448 A.2d 1271 (R.I. 1982).

33  Kirsch v. Prince George's County, 626 A.2d 372 [83 Educ. L. Rep. 1037] (Md. 1993).

34  628 A.2d 122, [84 Educ. L. Rep. 1069] (Pa. Cmwlth. 1993).

35  588 A.2d 1323 [67 Educ. L. Rep. 203] (Pa. Cmwlth. 1991).

36  740 N.Y.S.2d 107 [163 Educ. L. Rep. 936] (N.Y.A.D. 2002).

37  694 N.Y.S.2d 235 [137 Educ. L. Rep. 343] (N.Y.A.D. 1999).

38  Emory Univ. v. Levitas, 401 S.E.2d 691 [66 Educ. L. Rep. 475] (Ga. 1991).

39  K.S.A. 1983 Supp. 79-201.

40  National Collegiate Realty v. Bd. of County Comm'rs, 690 P.2d 1366 [21 Educ. L. Rep. 713] (Kan. 1984).

41  523 N.E.2d 1314 [47 Educ. L. Rep. 277] (Ill. App. 1988).

42  Section 19.1, Revenue Act of 1939 (Ill. Rev. Stat. 1985, ch. 120, par. 500.1).

43  Trustees of Ind. Univ. v. Town of Rhine, 488 N.W.2d 128 [77 Educ. L. Rep. [470] (Wis. App. 1992).

44  Sec. 70.11(4), Wis. Stats.

45  J.A.T.T. Title Holding Corp. v. Roberts, 371 S.E.2d 861 [49 Educ. L. Rep. 449] (Ga. 1988).

46 OCGA § 48-5-41(a)(6).

47 *In re* Swarthmore Coll., 645 A.2d 470 [93 EDUC. L. REP. 834] (Pa. Cmwlth. 1994).

48 PENN. CONST. art. VIII, sec. 2.

49 72 P.S. § 5020-204.

50 CODE OF ALABAMA § 40-9-1(1) (1975).

51 AU Hotel, Ltd. v. Eagerton, 689 So.2d 859 [117 EDUC. L. REP. 383] (Ala. Civ. App. 1996).

52 824 S.W.2d 295 [73 EDUC. L. REP. 315] (Tex. App. 1992).

53 TEX. TAX CODE ANN. §11.21(a) (Vernon 1982).

54 32 V.S.A. § 3802(4).

55 32 V.S.A. § 3232(7).

56 President and Fellows of Middlebury Coll. v. Town of Hancock, 514 A.2d 1061 [35 EDUC. L. REP. 202] (Vt. 1986).

57 709 N.Y.S.2d 493 [145 EDUC. L. REP. 1103] (N.Y. App. 2000).

58 University of Hartford v. City of Hartford, 477 A.2d 1023 [18 EDUC. L. REP. 637] (Conn. App. 1984).

59 ILL. REV. STAT. 1987, ch. 120, par. 500.5.

60 ILL. REV. STAT. 1987, ch. 120, par. 500.1.

61 Northern Ill. Found. v. Sweet, 603 N.E.2d 84 [78 EDUC. L. REP. 930] (Ill. App. 1992).

62 *See*, Childrens Dev. Ctr., Inc. v. Olson, 288 N.E.2d 388 (Ill. 1972).

63 520 S.E.2d 899 [139 EDUC. L. REP. 703] (Ga. 1999).

64 Johnson v. S. Greek Housing Corp., 307 S.E.2d 491 [13 EDUC. L. REP. 1154] (Ga. 1983).

65 OCGA § 48-5-41(a)(6).

66 OCGA § 48-5-41(c).

67 Connolly v. County of Orange, 824 P.2d 663 [72 EDUC. L. REP. 1089] (Cal. 1992).

68 West's ANN. CAL. REV. & T. CODE § 270 *et seq.*

69 Trustees of Univ. of Pa. v. Bd. of Revision, 649 A.2d 154 [95 EDUC. L. REP. 306] (Pa. Cmwlth. 1994).

70 72 P.S. § 5020-204.

71 973 S.W.2d 419 [128 EDUC. L. REP. 922] (Tex. App. 1998).

72 DePaul Univ. v. Rosewell, 531 N.E.2d 884 [50 EDUC. L. REP. 1104] (Ill. App. 1988).

73 Illinois Inst. of Tech. v. Skinner, 273 N.E.2d 371 (Ill. 1979).

74 Case W. Res. Univ. v. Tracy, 703 N.E.2d 1240 [131 EDUC. L. REP. 491] (Ohio 1999).

75 R.C. Ohio 3345.17.

76 State for Use of Univ. of Cincinnati v. Limbach, 553 N.E.2d 1056, 60 EDUC. L. REP. [178] (Ohio 1990).

77 449 N.E.2d 1282 [11 EDUC. L. REP. 988] (Ohio 1983).

78 Boulder v. Regents, 501 P.2d 123 (Colo. 1972).

79 W. PAGE KEETON, ET AL, PROSSER AND KEATON ON THE LAW OF TORTS 29 (5th ed. 1984).

80 TEX. PENAL CODE ANN. §30.05 (Vernon 1989).

81 CAL. PENAL CODE § 626.4.

82 State v. Schmid, 423 A.2d 615 (N.J. 1980).

83 423 A.2d 615, 630.

84 621 A.2d 553 [81 EDUC. L. REP. 883] (N.J. Super. 1993).

85 State v. Schmid, 423 A.2d 615 (N.J. 1980).

86 699 N.E.2d 829 (Mass. App. 1998).

87 699 N.E.2d 829, 839.

88 736 N.E.2d 48 [147 EDUC. L. REP. 283] (Ohio App. 1999).

89 R.C. Ohio 2911.21(A)(3).

90 The court also rejected the preacher's argument that the failure of officials to arrest students who were mocking and heckling him was evidence of viewpoint discrimination. 736 N.E.2d 48, 54.

[91] 549 N.E.2d 211 [58 EDUC. L. REP. 266] (Ohio App. 1988).

[92] 549 N.E.2d 211, 213 [48 EDUC. L. REP. 266, 268] (Ohio App. 1988).

[93] Brister v. Faulkner, 214 F.3d 675 (5th Cir. 2000).

[94] However, the court also held that the plaintiffs had suffered no constitutional injury because their activities had impeded access to the events center. 214 F.3d 675, 678.

[95] 477 N.Y.S.2d 111 (N.Y. App. 1984).

[96] 777 S.W.2d 178 (Tex. App. 1989).

[97] Dunkel v. Elkins, 325 F. Supp. 1235 (D. Md. 1971).

[98] Kirstel v. State, 13 Md. App. 482, 284 A.2d 12 (Md. App. 1972).

[99] 512 P.2d 1162 (Colo. 1973).

[100] 618 F.2d 252 (3d Cir. 1980).

[101] 492 U.S. 469, 106 L. Ed. 2d 388, 109 S. Ct. 3028 (1989).

[102] SUNY Resolution 66-156 (1979).

[103] American Future Sys., Inc. v. State Univ. of N.Y. Coll. at Cortland, 565 F. Supp. 754 (N.D.N.Y. 1983).

[104] 649 F. Supp. 1393 (1986).

[105] 841 F.2d 1207 (1988).

[106] 109 S. Ct. 3028, 3035.

[107] Clean Air Act of 1955, 42 U.S.C. § 7401 *et seq.* 40 C.F.R. 50 *et seq.*

[108] Federal Water Pollution Control Act, 33 U.S.C. § 1251 *et seq.*

[109] 15 U.S.C. § 2605 *et seq.*

[110] 42 U.S.C. § 2134 *et seq.*

[111] 42 U.S.C. § 2021b *et seq.*

[112] 42 U.S.C. § 6901 *et seq.*

[113] 42 U.S.C. § 9601 *et seq.*

# Index

# D